Malaya

The British Documents on
the End of Empire Project
gratefully acknowledges
the generous assistance of
the Leverhulme Trust.

BRITISH DOCUMENTS ON THE END OF EMPIRE

General Editor S R Ashton
Project Chairman D A Low

Series B Volume 3

Malaya

Editor
A J STOCKWELL

Part I
THE MALAYAN UNION EXPERIMENT
1942–1948

Published for the Institute of Commonwealth Studies
in the University of London

LONDON : HMSO

ISBN 0 11 290540 4

British Library Cataloguing in Publication Data

A CIP catalogue record for this book
is available from the British Library

Write to PC11C, Standing Order Service, HMSO Books, PO Box 276,
LONDON SW8 5DT quoting classification reference 040 30 017 to
order future volumes from the British Documents on the End of
Empire project.

Published by HMSO and available from:

HMSO Publications Centre
(Mail, fax and telephone orders only)
PO Box 276, London SW8 5DT
Telephone orders 0171 873 9090
General enquiries 0171 873 0011
(queuing system in operation for both numbers)
Fax orders 0171 873 8200

HMSO Bookshops
49 High Holborn, London WC1V 6HB
(counter service only)
0171 873 0011   Fax 0171 831 1326
68–69 Bull Street, Birmingham, B4 6AD
0121 236 9696   Fax 0121 236 9699
33 Wine Street, Bristol BS1 2BQ
0117 9264306   Fax 0117 9294515
9–21 Princess Street, Manchester M60 8AS
0161 834 7201   Fax 0161 833 0634
16 Arthur Street, Belfast BT1 4GD
01232 238451   Fax 01232 235401
71 Lothian Road, Edinburgh EH3 9AZ
0131 228 4181   Fax 0131 229 2734
The HMSO Oriel Bookshop
The Friary, Cardiff CF1 4AA
01222 395548   Fax 01222 384347

HMSO's Accredited Agents
(see Yellow Pages)

and through good booksellers

Printed in the United Kingdom by HMSO
Dd299901   C7   7/95

Contents

Foreword

The main purpose of the British Documents on the End of Empire Project (BDEEP) is to publish documents from British official archives on the ending of colonial and associated rule and on the context in which this took place. In 1945, aside from the countries of present-day India, Pakistan, Bangladesh and Burma, Britain had over fifty formal dependencies; by the end of 1965 the total had been almost halved and by 1985 only a handful remained. The ending of Britain's position in these formal dependencies was paralleled by changes in relations with states in an informal empire. The end of empire in the period at least since 1945 involved a change also in the empire as something that was more than the sum of its parts and as such formed an integral part of Britain's domestic affairs and international relations. In publishing official British documents on the end of empire this project is, to a degree, the successor to the two earlier series of published documents concerning the end of British rule in India and Burma which were edited by Professors Mansergh and Tinker respectively.[1] The successful completion of *The transfer of power* and *The struggle for independence*, both of which were based on British records, emphasised the need for similar published collections of documents important to the history of the final stages of Britain's association with other dependencies in Africa, the Middle East, the Caribbean, South-East Asia and the Pacific. In their absence, scholars both from sovereign independent states which emerged from colonial rule, as well as from Britain itself, lack an important tool for understanding and teaching their respective histories. But BDEEP is also set in the much wider context of the efforts made by successive British governments to locate Britain's position in an international order. Here the empire, both in its formal and informal senses, is viewed as an instrument of the domestic, foreign and defence policies of successive British governments. The project is therefore concerned with the ending of colonial rule in individual territories as seen from the British side at one level, and the broader political, economic and strategic considerations involved in that at another.

BDEEP is a sequel, not only to the India and Burma series but also to the still earlier series of published Foreign Office documents which continues as Documents on British Policy Overseas (DBPO). The contemporary volumes in DBPO appear in two parallel series covering the years 1945 to 1955. In certain respects the documents published in the BDEEP volumes will complement those published in DBPO. On issues where there is, or is likely to be, direct overlap, BDEEP will not provide detailed coverage. The most notable examples concern the post-Second World War international settlements in the Far East and the Pacific, and the immediate events of the Suez crisis of 1956.

---

[1] Nicholas Mansergh et al, eds, *Constitutional relations between Britain and India: the transfer of power 1942–47*, 12 vols, (London, 1970–1983); Hugh Tinker, ed, *Constitutional relations between Britain and Burma: the struggle for independence 1944–1948*, 2 vols, (London, 1983–1984).

Despite the similarities, however, BDEEP differs in significant ways from its predecessors in terms both of presentation and content. The project is of greater magnitude than that undertaken by Professor Mansergh for India. Four major differences can be identified. First, the ending of colonial rule within a dependent empire took place over a much longer period of time, extending into the final years of the twentieth century, while having its roots in the Second World War and before. Secondly, the empire consisted of a large number of territories, varying in area, population, wealth and in many other ways, each with its own individual problems, but often with their futures linked to those of neighbouring territories and the growing complexity surrounding the colonial empire. Thirdly, while for India the documentary record for certain matters of high policy could be encapsulated within a relatively straightforward 'country' study, in the case of the colonial empire the documentary record is more diffuse because of the plethora of territories and their scattered location. Finally, the documents relating to the ending of colonial rule are not conveniently located within one leading department of state but rather are to be found in several of them. As the purpose of the project is to publish documents relating to the end of empire from the extensive range and quantity of official British records, private collections and other categories of non-official material are not regarded as principal documentary sources. In BDEEP, selections from non-official material will be used only in exceptional cases to fill gaps where they exist in the available official record.

In recognition of these differences, and also of the fact that the end of empire involves consideration of a range of issues which operated at a much wider level than that normally associated with the ending of colonial rule in a single country, BDEEP is structured in two main series along with a third support series. Series A represents the general volumes in which, for successive British governments, documents relating to the empire as a whole will be published. Series B represents the country or territory volumes and provides territorial studies of how, from a British government perspective, former colonies and dependencies achieved their independence, and countries which were part of an informal empire regained their autonomy. In addition to the two main documentary series, a third series – series C – will be published in the form of handbooks to the records of the former colonial empire which are deposited at the Public Record Office (PRO). The handbooks will be published in two volumes as an integral part of BDEEP and also as PRO guides to the records. They will enable scholars and others wishing to follow the record of the ending of colonial rule and empire to pursue their inquiries beyond the published record provided by the general studies in series A and the country studies in series B. Volume One of the handbooks, a revised and updated version of *The records of the Colonial and Dominions Offices* (by R B Pugh) which was first published in 1964, is entitled *Records of the Colonial Office, Dominions Office, Commonwealth Relations Office and Commonwealth Office*. It covers over two hundred years of activity down to 1968 when the Commonwealth Office merged with the Foreign Office to form the Foreign and Commonwealth Office. Volume Two, entitled *Cabinet, Foreign Office, Treasury and other records*, focuses more specifically on twentieth-century departmental records and also includes references to the records of inter-departmental committees, commissions of inquiry and international organisations. These two volumes have been prepared under the direction and supervision of Dr Anne Thurston, honorary research fellow at the Institute of Commonwealth Studies in the

University of London.

The criteria which have been used in selecting documents for inclusion in individual volumes will be explained in the introductions written by the specialist editors. These introductions are more substantial and contextual than those in previous series. Each volume will also list the PRO sources which have been searched. However, it may be helpful to outline the more general guiding principles which have been employed. BDEEP editors pursue several lines of inquiry. There is first the end of empire in a broad high policy sense, in which the empire is viewed in terms of Britain's position as a world power, and of the inter-relationship between what derives from this position and developments within the colonial dependencies. Here Britain's relations with the dependencies of the empire are set in the wider context of Britain's relations with the United States, with Europe, and with the Commonwealth and United Nations. The central themes are the political constraints, both domestic and international, to which British governments were subject, the economic requirements of the sterling area, the geopolitical and strategic questions associated with priorities in foreign policy and in defence planning, and the interaction between these various constraints and concerns and the imperatives imposed by developments in colonial territories. Secondly, there is investigation into colonial policy in its strict sense. Here the emphasis is on those areas which were specifically – but not exclusively – the concern of the leading department. In the period before the administrative amalgamations of the 1960s,[2] the leading department of the British government for most of the dependencies was the Colonial Office; for a minority it was either the Dominions Office and its successor, the Commonwealth Relations Office, or the Foreign Office. Colonial policy included questions of economic and social development, questions of governmental institutions and constitutional structures, and administrative questions concerning the future of the civil and public services and of the defence forces in a period of transition from European to indigenous control. Finally there is inquiry into the development of political and social forces within colonies, the response to these and the transfer of governmental authority and of legal sovereignty from Britain to its colonial dependencies as these processes were understood and interpreted by the British government. Here it should be emphasised that the purpose of BDEEP is not to document the history of colony politics or nationalist movements in any particular territory. Given the purpose of the project and the nature of much of the source material, the place of colony politics in BDEEP is conditioned by the extent to which an awareness of local political situations played an overt part in influencing major policy decisions made in Britain.

Although in varying degrees and from different perspectives, elements of these various lines of inquiry appear in both the general and the country series. The aim in both is to concentrate on the British record by selecting documents which illustrate those policy issues which were deemed important by ministers and officials at the time. General volumes do not normally treat in any detail of matters which will be fully documented in the country volumes, but some especially significant documents do appear in both series. The process of selection involves an inevitable degree of

---

[2] The Colonial Office merged with the Commonwealth Relations Office in 1966 to form the Commonwealth Office. The Commonwealth Office merged with the Foreign Office in 1968 to form the Foreign and Commonwealth Office.

sifting and subtraction. Issues which in retrospect appear to be of lesser significance or to be ephemeral have been omitted. The main example concerns the extensive quantity of material devoted to appointments and terms of service – salaries, gradings, allowances, pension rights and compensation – within the colonial and related services. It is equally important to stress certain negative aspects of the official documentary record. Officials in London were sometimes not in a position to address potentially significant issues because the information was not available. Much in this respect depended on the extent of the documentation sent to London by the different colonial administrations. Once the stage of internal self-government had been reached, or where there was a dyarchy, the flow of detailed local information to London began to diminish.

Selection policy has been influenced by one further factor, namely access to the records at the PRO. Unlike the India and Burma series and DBPO, BDEEP is not an official project. In practice this means that while editors have privileged access (in the form of research facilities and requisitioning procedures) to the records at the PRO, they do not have unrestricted access. For files which at the time a volume is in preparation are either subject to extended closures beyond the statutory thirty years, or retained in the originating department under section 3(4) of the Public Records Act of 1958, editors are subject to the same restrictions as all other researchers. Where necessary, volume editors will provide details of potentially significant files or individual documents of which they are aware and which they have not been able to consult.

A thematic arrangement of the documents has been adopted for the general volumes in series A. The country volumes in series B follow a chronological arrangement; in this respect they adopt the same approach as was used in the India and Burma series. For each volume in both series A and B a summary list of the documents included is provided. The headings to BDEEP documents, which have been editorially standardised, present the essential information. Together with the sequence number, the file reference (in the form of the PRO call-up number and any internal pagination or numeration) and the date of the document appear on the first line.[3] The second and subsequent lines record the subject of the document, the type of document (letter, memorandum, telegram etc), the originator (person or persons, committee, department) and the recipient (if any). In headings, a subject entry in single quotation marks denotes the title of a document as it appears in the original. An entry in square brackets denotes a subject indicator devised by the editor. This latter device has been employed in cases where no title is given in the original or where the original title is too unwieldy to reproduce in its entirety. Security classifications and, in the case of telegrams, times of despatch and receipt, have generally been omitted as confusing and needlessly complicating, and are retained only where they are necessary to a full understanding. In the headings to documents and the summary lists, ministers are identified by the name of the office-holder, not the title of the office (ie, Mr Lyttelton, not secretary of state for the colonies).[4] In the same contexts, officials are identified by their initials and surname. In general

---

[3] The PRO call-up number precedes the comma in the references cited. In the case of documents from FO 371, the major Foreign Office political class, the internal numeration refers to the jacket number of the file.

[4] This is an editorial convention, following DBPO practice. Very few memoranda issued in their name were actually written by ministers themselves, but normally drafted by officials.

volumes in series A, ambassadors, governors, high commissioners and other embassy or high commission staff are given in the form 'Sir E Baring (Kenya)'. Footnotes to documents appearing below the rule are editorial; those above the rule, or where no rule is printed, are part of the original document. Each part of a volume provides a select list of which principal offices were held by whom, with a separate series of biographical notes (at the end) for major figures who appear in the documents. Minor figures are identified in editorial footnotes on the occasion of first appearance. Link-notes, written by the volume editor and indented in square brackets between the heading and the beginning of a document, are sometimes used to explain the context of a document. Technical detail or extraneous material has been extracted from a number of documents. In such cases omission dots have been inserted in the text and the document is identified in the heading as an extract. Occasional omission dots have also been used to excise purely mechanical chain-of-command executive instructions, and some redundant internal referencing has been removed, though much of it remains in place, for the benefit of researchers. No substantive material relating to policy-making has been excised from the documents. In general the aim has been to reproduce documents in their entirety. The footnote reference 'not printed' has been used only in cases where a specified enclosure or an annex to a document has not been included. Unless a specific cross-reference or note of explanation is provided, however, it can be assumed that other documents referred to in the text of the documents included have not been reproduced. Each part of a volume has a list of abbreviations occurring in it. A consolidated index for the whole volume appears at the end of each part.

One radical innovation, compared with previous Foreign Office or India and Burma series, is that BDEEP will reproduce many more minutes by ministers and officials.

All government documents are reproduced and quoted by permission of the Controller of HMSO. All references and dates are given in the form recommended in PRO guidelines.

$$* \quad * \quad * \quad *$$

BDEEP has received assistance and support from many quarters. The project was first discussed at a one-day workshop attended by over thirty interested scholars which, supported by a small grant from the Smuts Memorial Fund, was held at Churchill College, Cambridge, in May 1985. At that stage the obstacles looked daunting. It seemed unlikely that public money would be made available along the lines provided for the India and Burma projects. The complexities of the task looked substantial, partly because there was more financial and economic data with which to deal, still more because there were so many more territories to cover. It was not at all clear, moreover, who could take institutional responsibility for the project as the India Office Records had for the earlier ones; and in view of the escalating price of the successive India and Burma volumes, it seemed unlikely that publication in book form would be feasible; for some while a choice was being discussed between microfilm, microfiche and facsimile.

A small group nevertheless undertook to explore matters further, and in a quite remarkable way found itself able to make substantial progress. The British Academy adopted BDEEP as one of its major projects, and thus provided critical support. The Institute of Commonwealth Studies served as a crucial institutional anchor in taking responsibility for the project. The Institute also made office space available, and negotiated an administrative nexus within the University of London. Dr Anne Thurston put at the disposal of the project her unique knowledge of the relevant archival sources; while the keeper of the Public Records undertook to provide all the support that he could. It then proved possible to appoint Professor Michael Crowder as project director on a part-time basis, and he approached the Leverhulme Trust, who made a munificent grant which was to make the whole project viable. Almost all those approached to be volume editors accepted and, after consultation with a number of publishers, Her Majesty's Stationery Office undertook to publish the project in book form. There can be few projects that after so faltering a start found itself quite so blessed.

Formally launched in 1987, BDEEP has been based since its inception at the Institute of Commonwealth Studies. The work of the project is supervised by a Project Committee chaired by Professor Anthony Low, Smuts professor of the history of the British Commonwealth in the University of Cambridge. Professor Michael Crowder became general editor while holding a visiting professorship in the University of London and a part-time position at Amherst College, Massachusetts. Following his untimely death in 1988, Professor Crowder was replaced as general editor by Professor David Murray, pro vice-chancellor and professor of government at the Open University. Mrs Anita Burdett was appointed as project secretary and research assistant. She was succeeded in September 1989 by Dr Ashton who had previously worked with Professors Mansergh and Tinker during the final stages of the India and Burma series. Dr Ashton replaced Professor Murray as project director and general editor in 1993. When BDEEP was launched in 1987, eight volumes in series A and B were approved by the Project Committee and specialist scholars were commissioned to research and select documents for inclusion in each. Collectively, these eight volumes (three general and five country)[5] represent the first stage of the project which begins with an introductory general volume covering the years between 1925 and 1945 but which concentrates on the period from the Second World War to 1957 when Ghana and Malaya became independent.[6]

It is fitting that the present general editor should begin his acknowledgements with an appreciation of the contributions made by his predecessors. The late Professor Crowder supervised the launch of the project and planned the volumes included in stage one. The volumes already published bear lasting testimony to his resolve and dedication during the project's formative phase. Professor Murray played a no less crucial role in establishing a secure financial base for the project and in negotiating contracts with the volume editors and HMSO. His invaluable advice and expertise during the early stages of editing are acknowledged with particular gratitude.

---

[5] Series A general volumes: vol 1 *Colonial policy and practice 1924–1945*; vol 2 *The Labour government and the end of empire 1945–1951* (published 1992); vol 3 *The Conservative government and the end of empire 1951–1957* (published 1994).

Series B country volumes: vol 1 *Ghana* (published 1992); vol 2 *Sri Lanka*; vol 3 *Malaya* (published 1995); vol 4 *Egypt and the defence of the Middle East*; vol 5 *Sudan*.

[6] Plans are currently in preparation to commission new research for a second stage covering the period 1957–1964.

The project benefited from an initial pump-priming grant from the British Academy. Thanks are due to the secretary and Board of the Academy for this grant and for the decision of the British Academy to adopt BDEEP as one of its major projects. The principal funding for the project has been provided by the Leverhulme Trust and the volumes are a tribute to the support provided by the Trustees. A major debt of gratitude is owed to the Trustees. In addition to their generous grant to cover the costs of the first stage, the Trustees agreed to a subsequent request to extend the duration of the grant, and also provided a supplementary grant which enabled the project to secure Dr Ashton's appointment.

Members of the Project Committee, who meet annually at the Institute of Commonwealth Studies, have provided valuable advice and much needed encouragement. Professor Low, chairman of the Committee, has made a singular contribution, initiating the first exploratory meeting at Cambridge in 1985 and presiding over subsequent developments in his customary constructive but unobtrusive manner.[7] In addition to the annual meeting of the Project Committee, the project holds an annual seminar to discuss issues arising from the research of the volume editors. Valuable comments have been received from academic colleagues attending the seminars by invitation. The director and staff of the Institute of Commonwealth Studies have provided administrative support and the congenial surroundings within which the general editor works. The editors of volumes in Stage One have profited considerably from the researches undertaken by Dr Anne Thurston and her assistants during the preparation of the records handbooks. Although BDEEP is not an official project, the general editor wishes to acknowledge the support and co-operation received from the Historical Section of the Cabinet Office and the Records Department of the Foreign and Commonwealth Office. He wishes also to record his appreciation of the spirit of friendly co-operation emanating from the editors of DBPO. Dr Ronald Hyam, editor of the volume in series A on *The Labour government and the end of empire 1945–1951*, played an important role in the compilation of the house-style adopted by BDEEP and his contribution is acknowledged with gratitude. Thanks also are due to HMSO for assuming publishing responsibility and for their expert advice on matters of design and production. Last, but by no means least, the contribution of the keeper of the records and the staff, both curatorial and administrative, at the PRO must be emphasised. Without the facilities and privileges afforded to BDEEP editors at Kew, the project would not be viable.

S R Ashton
Institute of Commonwealth Studies
November 1994

---

[7] Professor Low retired in November 1994 and has been succeeded as chairman of the Project Committee by Professor Andrew Porter, Rhodes Professor of Imperial History in the University of London.

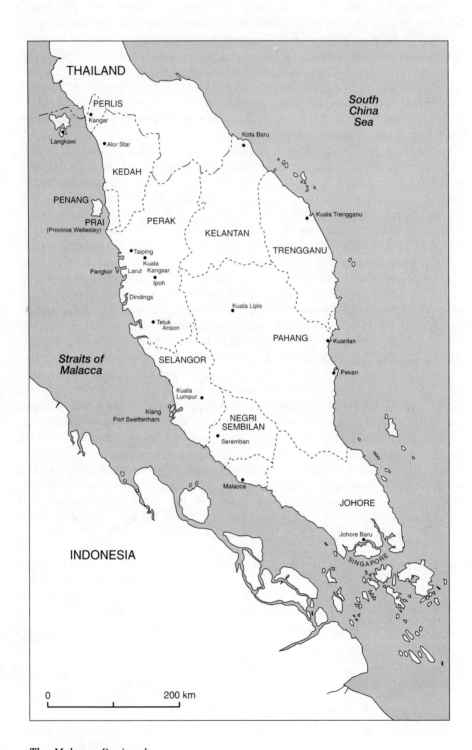

The Malayan Peninsula

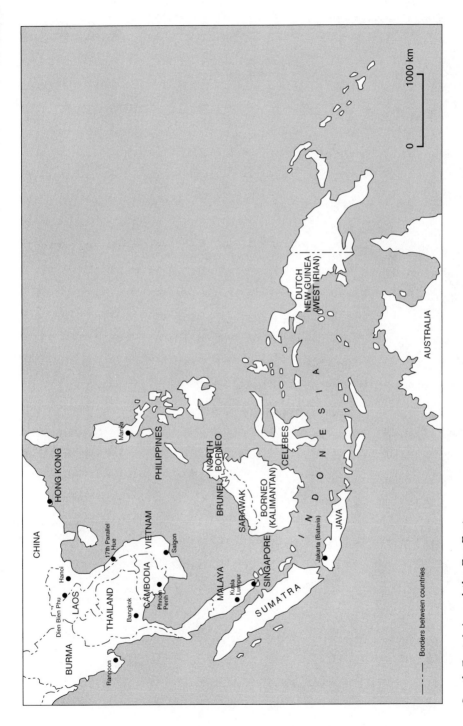

South-East Asia and the Far East

Malaya

Schedule of Contents: Parts I–III

Abbreviations: Part I

ADC	aide de camp
AJA	Anti-Japanese Army
AJUF	Anti-Japanese United Front
ALFSEA	Allied Land Forces South-East Asia
AMCJA	All Malayan Council of Joint Action
API	Angktan Pemuda Insaf (youth movement for justice)
BBCAU	British Borneo Civil Affairs Unit
BDEEP	British Documents on the End of Empire Project
BMA	British Military Administration
BNB	British North Borneo
BSA	British South Africa Company
CA	civil affairs
CAB	Cabinet
CAU	civil affairs unit
CCAO(M)	chief civil affairs officer (Malaya)
CIGS	chief of the imperial general staff
C-in-C	commander-in-chief
CMG	Companion of the Order of St Michael and St George
CO	Colonial Office
Col	colonial/colonel
Con	Conservative Party (MP)
COSSEA	Chiefs of Staff South-East Asia
DCCAO	deputy chief civil affairs officer
Dept	Department
DQMG	deputy quarter master general
DSO	Companion of the Distinguished Service Order
ECAFE	Economic Commission for Asia and the Far East

FMS	Federated Malay States
FO	Foreign Office
FTU	Federation of Trade Unions
GCMG	Knight Grand Cross of the Order of St Michael and St George
GLU	General Labour Union
GOC	general officer commanding
gov	governor
gov-gen	governor-general
HH	His Highness
HM	His Majesty
HMG	His Majesty's Government
H of C Debs	House of Commons Debates
H of L Debs	House of Lords Debates
HQ	headquarters
IEFC	International Emergency Food Council
INA	Indian National Army
IPR	Institute of Pacific Relations
IRD	International Relations Department (CO)
ISUM	intelligence summary
KBE	Knight Commander Order of the British Empire
KC	King's Counsel
KCB	Knight Commander of the Bath
KMT	Kuomintang
Lab	Labour Party (MP)
Lieut	lieutenant
Lt-Col	lieutenant-colonel
MCA	Malayan Chinese Association
MCP	Malayan Communist Party
MCS	Malayan Civil Service
memo	memorandum
MNP	Malay Nationalist Party
M of I	Ministry of Information

MP	Malayan Planning/member of parliament
MPAJA	Malayan Peoples' Anti-Japanese Army
MPAJU	Malayan Peoples' Anti-Japanese Union
MPU	Malayan Planning Unit
MU	Malayan Union
Nat	Nationalist (MP)
OF	Overseas Finance (Division, Treasury)
O-in-C	Order-in-Council
OSS	Office of Strategic Services (USA)
PMCJA	Pan-Malayan Council of Joint Action
PMFTU	Pan-Malayan Federation of Trades Unions
PMMC	Pan-Malayan Malay Congress
PRO	Public Record Office
PUTERA	Pusat Tenaga Raayat (lit. centre of people's strength: Malay movement for justice)
RGA	Rubber Growers' Association
SACSEA	Supreme Allied Command(er) South-East Asia
SCAO	senior civil affairs officer
SEA	South-East Asia Command
SEACOS	South-East Asia Chiefs of Staff
SEALF	South-East Asia Land Forces
sec	secretary
S of S	secretary of state
SS	Straits Settlements
tel	telegram
TU	trade union
UFMS	Unfederated Malay States
UK	United Kingdom
UMNO	United Malays National Organisation
UN(O)	United Nations (Organisation)
US(A)	United States (of America)

Principal Holders of Offices 1942–1948: Part I

UNITED KINGDOM

1. *Ministers*

(a) *Wartime coalition (10 May 1940 – 23 May 1945) and Conservative caretaker government (23 May – 26 July 1945): prime minister Mr W L S Churchill*

S of S colonies	Viscount Cranborne (23 Feb 1942) Mr O F G Stanley (24 Nov 1942)
S of S foreign affairs	Mr R A Eden (22 Dec 1940)
S of S dominions	Mr C R Attlee (Lab) (19 Feb 1942)[1] Viscount Cranborne (24 Sept 1943)
S of S India & Burma	Mr L S Amery (13 May 1940)
S of S war	Sir J Grigg (Nat) (22 Feb 1942)

(b) *War Cabinet Committee on Malaya and Borneo*

The Committee sat between Mar and Dec 1944. Lord president of the Council (Mr Attlee, chairman), S of S colonies, S of S dominions, S of S India and Burma, S of S war, attorney-general (Sir D Somervell), parliamentary under-secretary of state, FO (Mr G H Hall (Lab)).

(c) *Labour government (from 26 July 1945): prime minister Mr C R Attlee*[2]

S of S colonies	Mr G H Hall (3 Aug 1945) Mr A Creech Jones (4 Oct 1946)
Parliamentary under-secretary of state for colonies (junior minister)	Mr A Creech Jones (4 Aug 1945) Mr I B Thomas (4 Oct 1946) Mr D R Rees-Williams (7 Oct 1947)

[1] Attlee was also deputy prime minister, 1942–1945, and lord president of the Council, Sept 1943 – July 1945.
[2] Details to Feb 1948, the concluding date for part I of this volume. In part I of this volume, ministers outside the CO in the Labour government are identified where necessary in editorial link notes and footnotes to the documents.

2. Civil servants

Colonial Office

Permanent under-secretary of state	Sir George Gater (1942–1947) Sir Thomas Lloyd (1947–1956)
Deputy under-secretary of state	Sir William Battershill (1942–1945) Sir Arthur Dawe (1945–1947) Sir Sydney Caine (1947–1948) ⎫ Sir Charles Jeffries (1947–1956) ⎬ joint

Assistant under-secretary of state,
  with superintending responsibility
  for Eastern Department
	G E J Gent (1942–1946)
	T I K Lloyd (1946–1947)
	G F Seel (1947–1948)

Assistant secretary, head of Eastern Department	J J Paskin (1942–1947) H T Bourdillon (1947–1948)

SOUTH-EAST ASIA

(a) *Supreme Allied Command, South-East Asia*

Supreme Allied Commander	Admiral Lord Louis Mountbatten (1943–1946)
Chief political adviser to SACSEA	M E Dening (1943–1946)

(b) *British territories in South-East Asia*

Governor-general	Mr M J MacDonald (1946–1948)
Commissioner-general	Mr M J MacDonald (1948–1955)
Special commissioner	Baron Killearn (1946–1948)

MALAYA

(a) *British Military Administration Malaya (Oct 1945 – Mar 1946)*

Chief civil affairs officer	Maj-gen H R Hone

Deputy chief civil affairs officer,
  Mainland (Malay Peninsula)
  Division[3]
	Brig H C Willan (1945)
	Brig A T Newboult (1945–1946)

---

[3] The BMA Malaya was divided into two divisions, the other being the Settlement of Singapore, the deputy chief civil affairs officer for which was Brig P A B McKerron.

(b) *Malayan Union (Apr 1946 – Jan 1948)*

Governor	Sir Edward Gent
Chief secretary	A T Newboult

(c) *Federation of Malaya (from 1 Feb 1948)*

High commissioner	Sir Edward Gent
Chief secretary	A T Newboult

(d) *Rulers of Malay States*[4]

Johore	HH Ibrahim (1873–1959) Accession 7 Sept 1895
Pahang	HH Abu Bakar (1904–1974) Accession 23 June 1932
Negri Sembilan	HH Abdul Rahman (1895–1959) Accession 3 Aug 1933
Selangor	HH Alam Shah (1898–1960) Accession 4 Apr 1938
Perak	HH Abdul Aziz (1886–1948) Accession 1938
Kedah	HH Badlishah (1894–1958) Accession 15 May 1943 (position confirmed by British in 1945)
Perlis	HH Syed Putra (b 1920) Accession 4 Dec 1945
Kelantan	HH Ibrahim (1897–1960) Accession 21 June 1944 (position confirmed by British in 1945)
Trengganu	HH Ismail (b 1907) Accession 16 Dec 1945

---

[4] Rulers are listed in order of seniority, not with their full titles but with the name by which they are normally referred to.

SINGAPORE (from Apr 1946)

Governor   Sir Franklin Gimson

Colonial secretary   P A B McKerron

Chronological Table of Principal Events:
Parts I–III

1942

Feb	General Percival surrenders to General Yamashita in Singapore (15 Feb)
Feb	Lord Cranborne appointed S of S for colonies
Nov	Oliver Stanley appointed S of S for colonies

1943

July	Malayan Planning Unit established
Aug	Mountbatten appointed SACSEA

1944

Jan	Cabinet Committee on Malaya and Borneo set up (6 Jan)
May	Rangoon falls to 14th Army; draft directive for Malaya approved by War Cabinet (31 May)

1945

May	Allied defeat of Germany
July	General election in Britain; Labour Party victory under Clement Attlee
Aug	George Hall appointed S of S for colonies
Aug	Japanese surrender (15 Aug)
Sept	British Military Administration set up in Malaya
Oct	Malayan Union announced in parliament (10 Oct)
Oct–Dec	Sir Harold MacMichael's mission to the Malay rulers

1946

Jan	White Paper on Malayan Union published (22 Jan)
Mar	Pan-Malayan Malay Congress meets in Kuala Lumpur (1–4 Mar)
Apr	Sir Edward Gent sworn in as gov of Malayan Union (1 Apr)
May	UMNO formed (11–12 May); Malcolm MacDonald sworn in as gov-gen of Malaya, Singapore and British Borneo (21 May)
Aug–Nov	Constitutional discussions of Anglo–Malay Working Committee
Oct	Arthur Creech Jones appointed S of S for colonies
Dec	Constitutional proposals for Malayan federation approved by Cabinet (5 Dec) and published (24 Dec); Council of Joint Action formed; Consultative Committee (under Cheeseman) appointed

1947

July	White Paper on Federation of Malaya published (21 July)
Aug	India and Pakistan become independent (14–15 Aug)
Oct	Malaya-wide 'hartal' held (20 Oct)

1948

Jan	Burma becomes independent (4 Jan)
Feb	Federation of Malaya inaugurated with Gent as high commissioner (1 Feb); MacDonald appointed commissioner-general of SE Asia; Ceylon becomes independent (4 Feb); communist coup in Czechoslovakia; US Congress approves Marshall aid proposals; rioting in Accra, Gold Coast (28 Feb)
May	Britain withdraws from Palestine
June	State of Emergency declared (16–18 June); Gent recalled for consultations (29 June)
July	Gent killed in air crash (4 July); MCP proscribed (19 July)
Oct	Sir Henry Gurney sworn in as high commissioner
Oct–Nov	Dato Onn visits London for talks

1949

Jan	Communities Liaison Committee formed
Feb	MCA launched
Apr	NATO set up; Attlee makes parliamentary statement of British intentions in Malaya (13 Apr)
Sept	Stafford Cripps announces devaluation of the pound from US$4.03 to US$2.80 (18 Sept)
Oct	Chinese communists proclaim People's Republic in Peking

1950

Jan	Britain recognises communist China; Colombo Plan proposed
Feb	General election in Britain; Labour Party returned with narrow majority; James Griffiths appointed S of S for colonies
Apr	Cabinet Malaya Committee appointed; Gurney proposes member system
May	General Briggs draws up Briggs Plan
June	James Griffiths and John Strachey visit Malaya; Korean war breaks out
Nov	China enters Korean war

1951

Feb	General election in Gold Coast; Nkrumah released from prison and becomes leader of government business
Feb–Mar	London meetings to consider slow progress of counter-insurgency
Apr	Member system inaugurated with Dato Onn as member for home affairs
Aug	Tunku Abdul Rahman replaces Dato Onn as leader of UMNO
Sept	IMP launched by Dato Onn (16 Sept)

Oct   Assassination of Gurney (6 Oct); Conservative victory under Winston Churchill in general election; Oliver Lyttelton appointed S of S for colonies

Dec   Lyttelton visits Malaya; first municipal elections held in Georgetown (Penang); Libya becomes independent

1952

Jan   Alliance of UMNO and MCA formed in Selangor to fight municipal elections in Kuala Lumpur

Feb   Sir Gerald Templer sworn in as high commissioner; Alliance wins Kuala Lumpur elections; legislation passed enlarging federal citizenship

Mar   Nkrumah becomes prime minister of the Gold Coast

Oct   State of emergency declared in Kenya

1953

Feb   Anglo–Egyptian agreement on self-government and self-determination for the Sudan sets target date for independence of Sudan

Apr   Malayan 'National Conference' meets for first time

Aug   Alliance's 'National Convention' meets for first time

Sept   Templer declares part of Malacca a 'white area'; Templer appoints Ismail bin Dato Abdul Rahman and H S Lee members of the Executive Council

Oct   Cheddi Jagan and his Progressive Party (elected Apr 1953) dismissed and constitution suspended in British Guiana

1954

Feb   Federal elections committee publishes its report

May   Dien Bien Phu falls to Vietminh; Alliance delegation comes to London to meet Lyttelton; Alliance launches boycott of government

May–July Geneva conference on Korea and Indochina

June   Sir Donald MacGillivray sworn in as high commissioner; general election in Gold Coast and an all African Cabinet appointed

July   Alan Lennox-Boyd appointed S of S for colonies

Sept   Britain signs Manila Treaty setting up SEATO

Oct   MIC starts negotiations to join the Alliance

1955

Apr   Sir Anthony Eden replaces Churchill as prime minister in UK

May   Warsaw Pact signed by USSR and seven East European states; Conservatives increase their majority in the general election in the UK

June   MCP makes first 'peace offer'

July   Alliance landslide victory in first federal elections (27 July)

Aug   Tunku Abdul Rahman becomes chief minister; Lennox-Boyd visits Malaya

Sept   Alliance government announces amnesty and MCP proposes talks with Alliance leaders

Nov   State of emergency declared in Cyprus

Dec   Tunku Abdul Rahman meets Chin Peng at Baling talks (28–29 Dec)

1956

Jan   Sudan becomes independent (1 Jan)
Jan–Feb   Federation of Malaya constitutional conference in London; date of independence set for 'August, 1957, if possible'
June–Oct   Reid commission visits Malaya
July   Nasser nationalises Suez canal (26 July)
Sept   Date of Gold Coast independence set for 6 Mar 1957
Oct–Nov   Suez crisis
Dec–Jan   Alliance leaders visit London to discuss defence and financial arrangements

1957

Jan   Harold Macmillan replaces Eden as prime minister in UK
Mar   Gold Coast becomes independent as Ghana (6 Mar)
Mar–May   Working committee in Malaya reviews Reid report
May   Federation of Malaya constitutional talks in London
Apr   British defence White Paper ends national service in 1960 but sustains British presence east of Suez
Aug   Federation of Malaya becomes independent (31 Aug)

Introduction

Editors of *BDEEP*'s 'country volumes' were set the task of presenting 'the key documents which illustrate how various British governments arrived at their decision to grant self-government and ultimately independence to their former dependencies when they did and in the form they did'.[1] This collection is the outcome of the exercise with respect to end of empire in Malaya. Many years of research have gone into its production and the first object of this introduction is to describe the records from which the documents have been chosen and to discuss the editorial problems encountered, together with the criteria employed and the judgments formed, in making the final selection. The second purpose is to situate the documents in the context of government policy by considering official thinking and the ways in which decisions were reached and presented. Thirdly, in an historical account of the last phase of British rule in Malaya, events are narrated and arranged so as to identify turning-points and a coherent periodisation. While it is accepted that the documents should stand with minimum support in the form of editorial interpolation and interpretation, during the course of this introduction we shall consider the extent to which the collection sheds light on the questions raised in the editor's terms of reference.

Documents and their selection
BDEEP editors did not embark on their journey with a free hand and full room for manoeuvre. On the contrary, given that history is not what happened but what historians think happened, *BDEEP* editors are as much the prisoners of their sources and children of their own time as are other scholars. Of the factors affecting the selection, probably the most significant was the decision taken at the outset of the project to confine the collection to government papers held at the Public Record Office, Kew. Given the focus of the project upon British policy, this decision made sense; it also made the operation more manageable. On the other hand, it threw up a number of editorial problems and it also determined the perspective of the final collection. Before discussing these issues of editorial policy and practice, however, we should consider the nature of the record from which the documents have been chosen.

The first feature of the sources is their vastness and complexity. The sheer quantity of material on individual colonial territories during the 1940s and 1950s, which is not only spread across a number of documentary classes emanating from the Colonial Office but also involves a range of other Whitehall departments, means that there is no easily distinguishable cache of papers on transfer of power. Whereas India and Burma were covered almost entirely (though not exclusively) from the archives of the India and Burma Offices and the files of the Cabinet Committee on India and Burma, a similarly stark identification and demarcation of papers is not possible in the case of the territories of the colonial empire. Despite the fact that PRO class lists and call-up numbers differ from those originally employed in the registries of Whitehall, it is not possible to find one's way round the archives without some knowledge of the administrative machinery that created them, and we shall briefly survey the organisation of the Colonial Office and its position in government.

Until the Second World War, the Colonial Office was largely organised on a territorial basis. The Eastern Department, which dealt *inter alia* with the affairs of British Malaya, was one of four geographical sections dating from the early nineteenth century. Since then these sections had grown, multiplied and had been reorganised in conformity with the expansion of colonial responsibilities. The last reform to take place before our period gets underway was in 1932 when the Eastern Department took charge of the following territories: Hong Kong, Straits Settlements, Malay States, Mauritius, Seychelles and Ceylon. In addition it supervised British relations with Sarawak and North Borneo. In 1949 the Eastern Department was renamed the South-East Asian Department and its remit included the Federation of Malaya, Singapore, Sarawak, North Borneo, Brunei and the colonial aspects of the office of the commissioner-general in South-East Asia. In 1954 its title changed to Far Eastern Department and its portfolio once more included Hong Kong.

The arrangement of CO records was shaped by alterations in office management. For the pre-war period metropolitan papers on British policy towards Malaya are more or less embraced within two PRO file series generated by the Eastern Department: CO 273 (Straits Settlements Original Correspondence) and CO 717 (Federated Malay States Original Correspondence). For the years covered by this volume, however, it is not possible to restrict examination to these two runs of papers. Although CO 273 continues until 1946 and CO 717 until 1951, other territorial classes bulk larger and their existence is a reflection of developments in official attitudes as well as office organisation. CO 825 (Eastern) is a regional class for South-East Asia as a whole, as distinct from a more narrowly defined territorial category; it contains most of the Colonial Office papers on wartime planning for post-war Malaya. Another major series is CO 537; beginning as 'General Supplementary' this took on a new lease of life in 1944 when it became the depository for the files of the CO secret registry. CO 537 has turned out to be a crucial source for the immediate post-war period for Malaya as it is for other CO dependencies.

Between 1935 and 1951 files were registered with standard numbers to facilitate cross-referencing and the pursuit of issues over time. Thus, for example, 50823 for 1945 on 'Policy – Malaya' was continued at 50823 for 1946. These original file numbers or internal references (which are not reproduced in the *BDEEP* collection) are not the same as the PRO call-up numbers. What is more, cognate files are not always held in the same PRO class but often straddle a number of them: for example the file, containing memoranda submitted by the Malay rulers to Sir Harold MacMichael during his mission to acquire their agreement to new treaties in 1945, was originally registered as 50823/7/3 for 1945–46 and now bears the PRO call-up mark of CO 273/675/18, whereas the immediately following and complementary files (50823/7/4 and 50823/7/5) are to be found at CO 537/1540 and CO 537/1541 respectively. In 1951 the various regional and territorial series were amalgamated in a single South-East Asia category (CO 1022), in which individual files include papers for the three-year stretch of 1951–1953. Another reordering of the records occurred in 1954 with the formation of the Far Eastern Department, whose papers (CO 1030) were similarly filed (and subsequently released according to the 'thirty year rule') in three-year batches, viz 1954–1956 and 1957–1959.

One way into British policy-making might be by examining the exchanges between secretary of state and governor, but it should be noted that none of the changes in filing systems and record keeping during this period brought together in sequence and within a single class the complete run of correspondence between the secretary of state for the colonies and the high commissioner of Malaya. The despatches, telegrams and letters that passed between them – and this is the case for other colonial territories too – crop up instead at appropriate places interspersed throughout the relevant territorial files and sometimes, depending on the topic in question, are to be found in 'subject' classes as distinct from 'geographical' runs.

Although the main lines of the story can be most easily and comprehensively traced through the papers of the 'geographical' sections of the Colonial Office, the editor of a country volume has not been able to confine inquiry to country or geographical classes but has been obliged, in addition, to examine series ranging over a number of 'subject' sections. These increased from the 1930s and particularly during the Second World War as the Colonial Office became more and more involved in economic and welfare planning common to the empire as a whole, and as officials tended to consider the affairs of individual territories in the wider context of regions such as West Africa (CO 554), East Africa (CO 822), Africa (CO 847), and, as has been already mentioned, South-East Asia (CO 825). Notable subject series including Malayan material are: economic (CO 852), defence (CO 968), personnel (CO 850 and CO 877), and the private office of the secretary of state (CO 967).

Furthermore, the study of colonial policy necessitates examination of government archives other than those of the Colonial Office. Since the parameters within which colonial policy was devised were often laid down by non-CO personnel and in arenas outside the Colonial Office – in, say, Cabinet, the Treasury and the Foreign Office, or by the Chiefs of Staff or by the Bank of England – and since the details and implementation of that policy were worked out by the Colonial Office in conjunction with other Whitehall departments by means of inter-departmental correspondence, working parties and committees, the *BDEEP* editor has been obliged to trawl the records of the Foreign Office, Treasury, Cabinet (and its committees) and so on. Thus, in addition to the conclusions and memoranda of the full Cabinet (CAB 65 and CAB 66 for the war years and CAB 128 and CAB 129 for the post-war period), papers of Cabinet committees covering various aspects of South-East Asian policy have been consulted in the following series: CAB 21, CAB 98, CAB 104, CAB 130, CAB 134, etc. Of the departmental files (other than those of the CO), extensive use has been made of the unwieldy FO 371 series (with respect to British policy towards South-East Asia), T 220 (the Treasury's imperial and foreign division, particularly on the subject of Treasury assistance to Malaya during the Emergency), WO 203 (in connection with the British Military Administration and South-East Asia Command in 1945–46) and DEFE 4 and DEFE 7 (the chiefs of staff papers on the Anglo–Malayan defence negotiations in 1956–1957). Although prime ministerial interventions in Malayan affairs were infrequent, appropriate PREM files are valuable sources because they often contain, for the prime minister's easy edification, copies of the major high-policy papers on the subject in question.

Not only do the documents in this collection range across the spectrum of government departments, they also vary in type from the scribbled minute to the printed memorandum. In reproducing the documents every effort has been made to present each item as faithfully as possible to its original, but *BDEEP*'s printed format may yet mask some of the differences between them, differences which can be gauged, for example, in terms of origin and objective, of author and audience, of the mood in which they were written and the amount of time taken to compose them. A few, like Gurney's offer of resignation (235), are in manuscript and intended for one pair of eyes only, while one or two – perhaps MacDonald's assessment of great power relations in the Far East following the Geneva Conference (336) is one of these – were composed with a view to the wider sweep of history. Again, while not personal in tone, some were intended to be read by a small coterie of CO officials, while others were printed for wider circulation within Whitehall. Some, like the telegrams between Malaya and London at the height of the Malayan Union crisis (82, 83, 86–89, 92, 96, 97) or at dramatic moments leading up to and during the emergency (147, 148, 151, 152, 154–157, 246, 247, 350, 371, 373–375, 377, 378) or, again, at the time of the Alliance boycott in 1954 (327, 328, 333, 334) were composed in haste and occasionally became garbled in transmission. Others, such as Cabinet memoranda (21, 31, 76, 153, 257, 356, 356) are the smoothly honed products of a lengthy process of drafting and revision by several hands. Documents also varied in authority according to the rank of the authors; some were written by relatively junior senior civil servants (to adapt George Orwell on class to categories within Whitehall's hierarchy), while others bore the signature of the secretary of state.

The PRO contains, therefore, a veritable embarrassment of riches, but, vast though its holdings are, it has its lacunae and limitations which have inevitably contributed to the shape of this collection. We should note, first of all, that losses and the destruction of documents 'under statute' have made inroads into the historical record at Kew. Survival of material even from the recent past can be haphazard and capricious, as is revealed in dicussions that took place in 1958–1959 about the disposal of the archives of the governor-general in South-East Asia. Hard-pressed for office space, A M MacKintosh of the commissioner-general's secretariat, asked the Colonial Office to reconsider an earlier decision not to house its papers in London. CO officials had previously stated the orthodoxy that the records should remain the property of dependent (or formerly dependent) territories, but they now relented on the ground that, despite his title, the governor-general had never enjoyed executive responsibility in any British dependency. In elaborating the case for retrieving the files from Singapore, John Hennings developed a less legalistic line and one that had implications for the preservation of records on decolonisation. He wrote:

> I can't see that we can justify any reluctance over this, when on other papers we are exhorting the Governor to withdraw a mass of material from Singapore records which we don't want Ministers under the new [self-governing] constitution to see, and either burn it or hand it over to the UK Commission [successor to the commission-general]. We did the same in Kuala Lumpur before independence, and recently received from Singapore a mass of records of the old Chinese secretariat there.[2]

32 boxes of papers were consequently despatched to Britain, but when the first consignment of 14 boxes arrived, D Gregory discovered large gaps in the archive. His report betrays, however, not so much a concern that the record was seriously incomplete but more an irritation that his time should have been wasted in dealing with such scraps.

These files were weeded in 1956 and I find that in a great number of cases all that remains are either file covers or, as in a few instances, covers plus minute sheets. I am at a loss to understand why Singapore took the trouble to forward so much rubbish (of a total of some 567 files listed . . . only 124 remained after destroying the file covers etc). In a further 19 cases I have destroyed the files as the contents contain only minor correspondence or corres. [sic] with the C.O. The 14 boxes have now been reduced – as Singapore could well have done – to a total of 8 boxes.[3]

These CO minutes have been quoted at some length since they provide a rare glimpse into the vagaries that can beset even the most systematic arrangements for preserving the official record. This exchange might also shed light on the absence at the PRO of a series of files devoted specifically to the governor-general (subsequently the commissioner-general) in South-East Asia, who played a major part in the formulation of regional policy with respect to foreign, colonial and defence matters. Communications with Malcolm MacDonald and Robert Scott (and with their deputies) are, like those with individual governors and the high commissioner, distributed across the runs of files in territorial series.

Another area where the record seems to be uneven is the correspondence between Templer and Lyttelton. Telegrams to and from King's House and the Colonial Office are frequent and abundant but letters and despatches between the high commissioner and secretary of state are in shorter supply. The reason for this may be that Templer left his deputy to draft the formal despatches on many issues relating to political and constitutional developments, and, indeed, there is a regular flow of correspondence between MacGillivray and senior civil servants in the CO, and particularly with Sir John Martin. Perhaps also the speed of developments in the post-war period and the ease of communications through telegram and personal visits reduced the time and the need for the measured correspondence that was a feature of pre-war days, and resulted in near-redundancy for the gubernatorial despatch. Nonetheless, we do know that Templer maintained a routine and demi-official correspondence with Lyttelton. Copies of these letters were used by his biographer and are deposited in the Templer Papers at the National Army Museum.[4] The originals, therefore, should be at the PRO but they may lie in files which still remain closed to public examination.

As regards inaccessible material, it should be remembered that *BDEEP*, not being an official project, is bound by the rules that apply to the public, notably the 'thirty year rule' regulating access to government papers. In general terms this means that files relating to the British period in Malaya are open, with the exception of those that are embargoed for 50 or 75 or even 100 years and those that have been retained under section 3(4) of the 1958 Public Records Act. The term 'retained' means that the originating department or its successor (in our case this usually means the Foreign and Commonwealth Office) has decided against transferring material to the PRO, but government departments regularly review the classification of papers which have been withheld for longer than thirty years. Although restricted access has affected the research for this volume, it has not presented an insuperable obstacle to the presentation of the continuities and changes of policy-making and decision-taking. From time to time, however, policy files do slip out of reach behind the thickets of 50-year, 75-year or 'retained' restrictions. Examples of closed files which probably have a significant bearing on contemporary official thinking are the following: CO 967/81 and CO 967/83 on the recall of Gent and the appointment of Gurney; CO 967/50 containing minutes from the secretary of state to the prime minister in 1950; CAB 130/118, GEN 538/3 being a letter by R H Scott probably written in 1956 and containing an assessment of Britain's role in South-East Asia; and CAB 129/79, CP(56)12 for January 1956, being Lennox-Boyd's Cabinet memorandum on policy at the forthcoming constitutional conference.

Occasionally it happens that papers which are unobtainable in one quarter crop up in another. For example, internal evidence, including a reference by Sir Charles Arden-Clarke (governor of the Gold Coast) to Gurney's despatch of 30 May 1949 about the federal government's response to the communist insurrection, would suggest that this important document should be held somewhere in the group of files between CO 537/6403 and CO 537/6406, all of which remain closed.[5] This might have been an occasion to resort to the printed version, which had been made available from a Malaysian source, had not a copy been unexpectedly discovered in the file entitled 'Federation of Malaya: implications of possible imposition of martial law' (CO 537/4773) (189). Again, although the Cabinet memorandum CP(49)207 (on UK policy in South-East Asia and the Far East, October 1949) is withheld from CAB 129/37/1, a version is to be found in the collection of ministerial briefs at CO 967/84 (196), while a version of Lennox-Boyd's paper on the forthcoming Malayan constitutional talks (January 1956), referred to in the previous paragraph, is available amongst the papers of the Cabinet Committee on Colonial Policy (CAB 134/1202, CA(56)3) and has been printed in this volume (394).

In addition to gaps in the record arising from destruction or retention of papers, the PRO perspective has moulded the shape of this volume. Since documents have been deliberately chosen to reveal the thinking of the British government and since they have been selected from the metropolitan archives, we should anticipate and attempt to answer criticism from those who may be tempted to dismiss the volume on the grounds that it presents Malayan affairs largely from the point of view of the government in London, and that, in so doing, it exaggerates the part played by British decisions in ending the empire. Victor Purcell once scathingly referred to CO attitudes as 'the Wimbledon view of Malaya', and Harry Miller, a journalist with *The Straits Times* during the emergency, voiced the local viewpoint when he asserted that 'Whitehall had no conception of the problem, nor any idea of the growing dangers'.[6] Although the enormous and complex archive of central government does not comprehensively embrace the imperial periphery, nonetheless communications from Malaya bulk large in this collection, a major feature of which is the constant interchange of views and information between Kuala Lumpur, Singapore and London.

It should be noted, however, that the Malayan papers found in PRO holdings (and, therefore, in this volume) differ in kind from the metropolitan record. Whereas we can trace the evolution of official thinking and continuing policy discussions in London through internal departmental minutes, memoranda and reports, the views of the Malayan authorities on any matter are confined to the papers which reached London and these tend to be the final assessment made by the high commissioner plus documentation in support of the locally preferred option. What we have from the Malayan government are largely documents generated at the highest level of the local administration, in, for example, the offices of the high commissioner, commissioner-general, chief secretary or director of operations. Those Malayan documents which reached Whitehall from other levels of local administration or from outside official circles altogether, did so because they were selected by the most senior colonial servants on the spot. Differences of opinion, say between the commissioner-general and the high commissioner appear only when one or other felt the need to seek London's arbitration.

Furthermore, Malayans themselves are presented here through British eyes. The activities of nationalist politicians, their inter-relations and the extent of their support are recorded by British observers. UMNO and the campaign against the Malayan Union, the Malayan Communist Party and the outbreak of armed violence, the Alliance and the electoral landslide – these developments are documented here but in records compiled by British officials. When Dato Onn or Tunku Abdul Rahman visited London, a civil servant made notes of the meetings that took place with officials and ministers; only rarely do we hear Malayan leaders at first hand in, say, a brief letter forwarded to London by the high commissioner (114) or in an exchange of correspondence with the secretary of state (313, 314, 319, 321, 365, 369). By focusing on ministers and mandarins cocooned in Church House, this collection of documents, it might be claimed, deflects attention from nationalism and popular movements to the safe havens of offices and committee rooms, where cultivated minds constructed patterns from the puzzles of human affairs on the fragile assumption that 'quiet calm deliberation disentangles every knot'.[7] Thus it may tempt the reader to accept not only that government decisions always mattered but also that what mattered was invariably committed to paper, which was clearly not always the case, even in the highly literate environment of Whitehall, owing to the increasing pace of events and widespread use of the telephone. In responding to such criticisms we would say in this introduction, which is not a substitute for scrutinising the documents themselves, that no documentary collection can or should ever claim to be definitively comprehensive. This volume, being the product of years of intense research and rigorous selection, is reasonably representative of the vast and wide-ranging official documentation on the end of British rule in Malaya and fairly reflects the circumstances and considerations which the archive reveals as having influenced the making of policy and decisions at this time.

So far we have discussed the extent, complexity, accessibility and perspective of PRO material, and we have noted the constraints that it has placed upon selection and ways in which the record has fashioned this volume. The shape of the collection has also been affected by editorial judgment and one of the most significant of these was the decision taken at the start of the project to fix the size of *BDEEP* volumes. Consequently, the editor of a country volume has had the remit to present within a preordained number of pages a continuous record of decision-making culminating in the achievement of independence by the territory concerned. The limitations of space, however, are demonstrably so tight as to make this more difficult for Malaya than it was for India and even for Burma. Mansergh's *Transfer of Power* series on India was not limited at the outset to a specific number of volumes. Tinker, by contrast, was restricted to two volumes totalling approximately 1,800 pages.[8] He admitted to encountering difficulties arising from this limitation. Even so, Burma's page allowance was more than that allocated to *BDEEP Malaya*, although the period covered in the former (1942 – January 1948) is less than half the length of the Malayan story (1942 – August 1957). Pressure of more documents upon less space has forced the editor into hard decisions about what to put in and what to leave out. Just as in other forms of scholarship documents rarely speak for themselves but frequently become the dummies of ventriloqual historians, so in enterprises of this kind the key documents did not select themselves but were judged by the editor for their historical significance. In the process of sifting material, some were more eye-catching than others for the light they shed on events and on policy but it is accepted that the final selection is unlikely to be to everyone's taste.

In this trek through the record, the route taken by the editor has been influenced by his perception of the goal, his interpretation of his task and the glosses he has placed upon 'end of empire' and 'British policy'. The very title of the project perhaps suggests agreement on definitions that does not yet exist amongst historians, while the terms of reference presume a similar consensus about what precisely was being transferred by the British or seized by the Malayans: was it power or authority or sovereignty or merely status? Another implication here is that the thrust of 'policy' was towards ending the empire, whereas much of it was demonstrably directed towards the maintenance of empire, to the achievement of a 'new imperialism' or 'a second occupation' immediately after the Second World War, and, as time went on, to the conversion of 'formal empire' into 'informal empire' or the pursuit of what has been variously called 'neo-colonialism', 'damage limitation' and the 'management of decline'. The very term 'policy' is itself open to interpretation. Is it a guide to action or the justification for inertia? Is it strategy devised in the anticipation of events or rationalisation drawn up in reaction to them? Is it confined to general statements or must it include detailed schemes and the techniques essential to their execution? Is it the reflection of party ideology or rather the expression of state interests? Is it the pursuit of national needs or retreat before nationalist pressures? Is policy pronounced in public or contrived behind closed doors? Is it what ministers instruct their civil servants to carry out or what the latter advise the former to approve? The editor's position on each of these issues clearly has a bearing on the way he handles the sources.

Policy and policymaking
Public statements claiming that 'the central purpose of British colonial policy is simple'[9] were often pitched in terms so general as to encourage rather than snuff out speculation. In themselves such pronouncements amounted to little more than reiterations of, and variations upon, Stanley's 1943 theme: 'we are pledged to guide Colonial people along the road to self-government within the framework of the British Empire'.[10] Moreover, these delphic utterances had a political rather than an administrative intent; they were, after all, primarily designed to please as many different groups as possible, to parade fresh goals without reneging on existing commitments, to win new friends while nurturing vested interests, to take the heat out of cross-party conflict or to accommodate intra-party differences, to satisfy conservatives that the empire remained at least half-full and at the same time convince progressives that it had become half-empty. When, in April 1949, Attlee declared Britain's ultimate goal to be Malayan self-government, his object was to revive business confidence by promising that there would not be a premature withdrawal;[11] when, in December 1951, Lyttelton sought to restore British morale by stressing the need for law and order in Malaya, government assured liberals that this did not mark an abandonment of goals but merely a realistic assessment of immediate priorities.[12]

The authoritative statements made by ministers in parliament or included in Command Papers were certainly logged by civil servants (they had, after all, drafted them in the first place) and subsequently used as navigational aids when discussion was in danger of foundering upon details, technicalities and contradictions. But, like their political masters, administrators fought shy of precise public commitments. It was Templer, a high commissioner who had not been schooled in colonial traditions, who startled officials with brusque demands for instructions on the policy he was to carry out (286). In doing so Templer was perhaps the exception proving the rule that civil servants were prone to seek refuge in jungles of jargon and swamps of semantics rather than give hostages to fortune by defining sovereignty and self-government or issuing timetables for constitutional change. Forthright declarations of policy from London were generally held to be counterproductive. For example, in November 1947 Trafford Smith felt that J S Bennett's memorandum on 'The future of Cyprus in relation to the withdrawal from Palestine' tended 'to speculate far beyond what is legitimate for us in the Colonial Office' and he went on to warn colleagues of the dangers of considering 'policy from the outside as a whole with an analytical "Latin" point of view' or of attempting 'to shape it on a procrustean bed of logic and coherence'.[13] On another occasion the Colonial Office legal adviser recommended the advantages of obfuscation. 'I think we can, and should, avoid saying anything which would imply an answer to this problem', he wrote with respect to the vexed question of the sovereignty of the Malay rulers.[14]

Indeed, just as in the hey-day of colonial rule, Pope's aphorism – 'For forms of government let fools contest, what e'er is best administered is best' – had struck a chord with those who administered the empire, so in the era of decolonisation ministers and officials perceived prudence in constitutional imprecision. 'May there not be wisdom in not laying down any general Constitutional rules?', asked Sir Gilbert Laithwaite in February 1953 with reference to Commonwealth membership, and he went on to refer to the 'infinite trouble' that had arisen over the previous thirty years from terms such as 'Dominion status', 'full Dominion status', 'the Whitehall form of Dominion status', 'independence' and 'full self-government'.[15] On 1 December 1955 'independence' became a taboo word by order of the Cabinet which laid down that as a general rule its use was to be discontinued in all references to colonial constitutional development in order to avoid a climate of secession and disintegration, and that the alternative 'full self-government' was to be preferred.[16] It would appear, therefore, that 'policy' was open to interpretation at the time and that its identification has since become a matter for historical judgment.

We decided early on that the original security classification of a document (that is to say whether it was rated 'top secret', 'secret', 'confidential' and so on) was an unreliable guide to a document's historical significance. Secrets have an ephemeral quality and some of the high security ratings were amended and down-graded as time passed; for example, many intelligence reports on Malayan political developments, which were assigned high security ratings at the time, reflected current perceptions of immediate dangers and exhibited the anxieties of a particular group of intelligence officers whose business was to unearth threats to which, rightly or wrongly, policymakers may not have given much attention anyway. Moreover, it is often the case that these reports contain little more than that which was appearing in the press and which has long since been in the public domain. For these reasons little heed was paid to the original security grade in the process of selection and we decided to dispense with security ratings in the presentation of documents here. We have, nonetheless, included several intelligence reports in this collection to indicate the atmosphere in which decisions were taken, to illustrate contemporary assessments of political problems and security issues, and also to provide the reportage of events necessary to the narrative content of this collection (72, 90, 94, 162).

A document's 'importance' has to be assessed, therefore, by reference to benchmarks other than security classification, for example those indicating British interests, Malayan demands and the changing nature of Anglo–Malayan relations. In sifting through documents which (to take examples of each of these areas) dealt with the dollar-earnings of Malaya or her place in the Cold War, with rural development or federal elections, with the member system or negotiations for an Anglo–Malayan defence treaty, each item was considered in the context of four overlapping circles of policymaking.

The first of these was 'colonial policy' and took into account issues which ran in parallel and bore comparison with developments in other colonial dependencies. Examples of such issues are local government, elections and member or ministerial systems, policing and the localisation (or 'Malayanisation') of administration, development programmes and welfare measures. General parallels were sometimes drawn by officials as by the press with Britain's withdrawal from India and particularly Palestine whence personnel, notably Gurney and W N Gray, were transferred to Malayan service after May 1948. Since the Gold Coast was jumping its fences just ahead of Malaya, the West African experience was kept in mind and sometimes explicitly cited, as with respect to responsibility for internal security, and East African models were also referred to in the construction of the member system or closer association (sometimes referred to as union) with Singapore. Given the transfer of officials from territory to territory and the extent of consultation between the CO territorial departments with the General and Legal Departments frequently acting as brokers, there was a shared experience on the problems of local government, elections, citizenship and nationality, and ready-made formulae were held up against the Malayan body-politic to see whether a certain amount of tailoring might bring about a match.

On the other hand, an enduring article of faith subscribed to in the Colonial Office and Colonial Service alike, was that, as Cranborne pointed out to the Chinese ambassador in October 1942 (10), general theories of government and models of administration were of limited value because the conditions of each dependency were *sui generis*. The second circle, therefore, concerned issues which were peculiar to Malaya or, while consonant with developments elsewhere, were applied in a manner appropriate to Malayan circumstances, and included all aspects of Malayan communalism and politics. With respect to both these circles, the CO territorial classes are the leading sources, revealing Malayan developments through communications from Kuala Lumpur and British reactions and proposals. One Malayan issue which is a theme in this collection is the very identity of Malaya. A term of art encompassing the Straits Settlements, Federated Malay States and Unfederated Malay States before the war, from 1942 onwards 'Malaya' was applied sometimes to the peninsula together with Singapore and sometimes to the peninsula without Singapore. The meaning of this geographical expression fluctuated with the British commitment to create a 'Dominion of South-East Asia' embracing the peninsula and Singapore and, ultimately, the Borneo dependencies as well. Malaya should certainly be examined from the perspective of South-East Asia and regional issues form the third of our circles of policymaking. In this context the documents reveal Malaya (with Singapore) as the fulcrum of British power in South-East Asia and the Far East, as a country standing in the front line in the containment of world communism and as a platform from which to project British influence into emergent Asia. Malayan affairs cannot, therefore, be treated in isolation from Britain's relations with the independent Asian states or with her dealings with other Powers, especially the USA, in South-East Asia and the Far East, nor can they be adequately comprehended without reference to Foreign Office and Defence papers.

This brings us to the final circle, that of 'imperial policy'. Here Malaya is considered in relation to British domestic and global interests, and its significance is assessed as, on the one hand, a British asset earning dollars, supplying vital commodities and providing a link in the chain of imperial defence, and, on the other hand, as a liability consuming taxpayers' money, draining limited military resources and straining Commonwealth relations. To explore these issues thoroughly one must supplement CO material with the papers of other Whitehall departments and the Cabinet.

Most documents in this collection were written both to inform and to persuade, although they do not achieve both objects in equal measure. In doing the first, a document contributes to the narrative of events; in performing the second it assists in the illumination of policy. The more persuasive its case, the more effective a document was likely to be in shaping the course of decision-making at the time and of beguiling subsequent historians. The clarity of Cabinet memoranda, scarcely dimmed by the passage of years, is evidence of the care that was taken over their composition. But there were occasions when compelling arguments went unheeded, as happened when Sydney Caine put the economic argument against the separation of Singapore from the Malayan Union (19). Negative thinking may be a characteristic commonly associated with the bureaucratic mind, but obstructionism stood little chance of stopping a scheme once it had gathered sufficient momentum; alternatively, if a civil servant was felt to be leaping far ahead of his colleagues or if he was wanting in 'bottom', his views may not have commanded the attention they otherwise deserved. Those coming to the record thirty years on must be on the look out for prophetic yet ineffectual papers, and should be ever circumspect lest a document be given a prominence out of proportion with its influence on contemporary policy.

In making this selection particular account has been taken of the readability as well as the content and authorship of a document. Readability is by no means a frivolous consideration. A barely legible minute, except, of course, one in the minister's hand, was not likely to gain much notice at the time, and poorly composed, semi-coherent pieces, which are dense with minutiae and clouded by allusion and obscure references, would need to have strongly redeeming features to merit consideration for inclusion here. Stylish items have obvious attractions and ministerial intercessions, whose quips and barbs can have the effect of lightening the tone and switching the direction of discussions, are particularly tempting. Briefs prepared for the information of ministers can be similarly arresting, not so much because they advanced debate at the time – this was generally not the function of a brief – but because they provided coherent summaries of developments to date, clarifying issues and identifying contemporary priorities.

Another strong candidate for inclusion on grounds of readability was the principal's minute. It should be explained that assistant principal was the point where entrants (who were generally graduates from Oxford or Cambridge) joined the administrative grade (the 'heaven-born') of the Home Civil Service, and that principal was a senior civil servant, usually in his early thirties and looking forward to promotion to at least assistant secretary. It was customary for the appropriate principal in the department to offer the first comment on communications coming in from the 'man on the spot' or from another department in Whitehall. Likewise, it was usual for the principal to compose the early drafts of plans being contemplated in the section. It was, for example, Monson's memorandum on 'Plans for the constitutional reconstruction in Far East' which became the foundation document for the Malayan Union scheme (12), and it was Bourdillon who summarised the reports of Malay reactions to the Malayan Union White Paper (73). Such papers did not, however, amount to decisions, nor do they necessarily indicate that the principal was himself seizing the initiative with respect to policy. On the contrary, it was rare for principals to take decisions on anything other than routine matters, and the departmental papers which they drafted were likely to have been roughed out on the basis of what the author understood to have been current office thinking. Again, we should not be deluded into measuring the authority of an official according to the number of words in his submissions, since it generally happened that the higher a matter rose in the government hierarchy the more succinct the comments became. These reservations aside, however, the historical value of the principal's contributions lies in his lucid and comprehensive exposition of the problem in hand, identifying the issues, relating them to existing policy and suggesting alternative responses. Since the principal did not make policy but set out the stall for his masters to pick over the possibilities, this would appear the appropriate moment for us to turn from the question of policy to the manner in which it was made.

In addition to its content, another yardstick by which to judge the significance of a document is the significance of its author. Ranking in the government hierarchy is certainly a helpful guide to discovering those who took the initiative, who commanded attention during discussions and who took decisions in the end, although status alone is not an infallible index of a person's importance to Malayan policymaking. It might be instructive, therefore, to identify the procedures and personalities involved in the formulation of policy.

Within the Colonial Office, as we have already noted, the geographical department that had prime responsibility for Malayan affairs was the Eastern Department and its successors. It consisted of a small team of no more than half a dozen senior civil servants including an assistant secretary as head of department. The head of department reported to an assistant under-secretary, who supervised a number of departments, and he in turn was answerable to the permanent under-secretary or his deputy. During the period covered by this volume the departmental heads were G E J Gent (1939–1942), J J Paskin (1942–1947), H T Bourdillon (1947–1948), J D Higham (1948–1953), A M MacKintosh (1953–1956) and J B Johnston (1956–1957). Its supervising assistant under-secretaries were Gent (1942–1946), T I K Lloyd (1946–1947), G F Seel (1947–1948), Paskin (1948–1954), J M Martin (1954–1956) and E Melville (1956–1957). The principal on the Malayan desk usually got first sight of in-coming correspondence, composed the first departmental reactions to Malayan developments and minuted meetings that took place in the CO. It was his superiors (assistant secretary and upwards) who decided which matters warranted consultation with other Whitehall departments and who communicated directly with the high commissioner and chief secretary in Kuala Lumpur, and with the commissioner-general based first in Johore Bahru and later in Singapore (about whose organisation more is said below). Amongst these Gent and Martin stand out. Gent, who had accompanied the parliamentary under-secretary of state (Ormsby-Gore) on his visit to Malaya, Ceylon and Java in 1928, was the principal architect of the Malayan Union and later its governor. Martin, who had been seconded to the MCS in 1931–1934, performed a major role in setting up the Lancaster House constitutional conference of January–February 1956.

Many routine issues were dealt with entirely within the Eastern Department but few of the items selected here fall in this category. Contentious matters were at some stage referred up to the supervising assistant under-secretary or through him to the permanent under-secretary (PUS), and maybe to a minister. Sir George Gater was PUS during the Malayan Union experiment (1942–1947) and Sir Thomas Lloyd (PUS, 1947–1956) was head during the worst of the emergency and the major constitutional advances. Despite his experience as a Malayan civil servant between 1921 and 1937, Sir John Macpherson, who succeeded Lloyd as PUS in 1956 had little part to play in the last days of British rule in Malaya.

The ministerial team consisted of the secretary of state, the parliamentary under-secretary of state and, from January 1948 onwards, the minister of state. Oliver Lyttelton (secretary of state, 1951–1954) had been involved in the Malayan tin industry before the war while David Rees-Williams (parliamentary under-secretary, 1947–1950) had been a lawyer in Penang during the early 1930s and maintained close links with Tunku Abdul Rahman in the 1950s. Civil servants disturbed the secretary of state with Malayan matters only when burning matters arose principally in connection with government finance, internal security, notable political developments and constitutional changes. Although rank obviously carried authority when policy was shaped, as a rule little congruence obtains between the status of decision-makers and the contributions they made to the written record of decision-making. Indeed, the higher an issue rose in government the more cryptic written comments became, and, whenever major decisions were taken at higher levels, they tended to rest on the cogent yet comprehensive expositions of alternative courses of action submitted from below. Nonetheless, ministers were involved at key moments: the approaches to Cabinet with respect to the Malayan Union policy; the conduct of the emergency; the appointments of Gurney and Templer as high commissioner and the reorganisation of Malayan administration in 1951–1952; the conduct of constitutional talks in 1955–1957. The secretary of state also met leading Malayan personalities in London (Dato Onn, Tunku Abdul Rahman, the Sultan of Johore), and, in contrast with the pre-war period, visited Malaya, Griffiths going out in 1950, Lyttelton in 1951 and Lennox-Boyd in 1955.

Colonial policy-making in London did not, however, invariably remain the preserve of the secretary of state for the colonies and his officials. Since the Colonial Office hovered in the middle order of the Whitehall league and since the prime minister, chancellor of the Exchequer, foreign secretary, minister of defence and other ministers (acting either separately as masters of departments or collectively in Cabinet) not infrequently took an interest in Malayan affairs, the locus of policy-making sometimes shifted outside the CO to inter-departmental committees of officials or ministers. Moreover, it should be remembered that at all times Malayan policy was devised within guidelines set by the Treasury as regards sterling, by the

Foreign Office with respect to international relations in South-East Asia, and by the Ministry of Defence in connection with Britain's military capabilities in the Far East. Might it not be the case, therefore, that the papers of the prime minister, of senior ministers and of the Cabinet as a whole are more fruitful sources of Malayan policy than series of files generated by the Colonial Office? The answer, of course, very largely depends on the subject that was under review at any given time.

As regards prime ministerial involvement in Malayan affairs, Attlee was kept informed about the growing crisis over the Malayan Union in the spring and early summer of 1946 (80, 93) and also about the conduct of the emergency (185, 230, 238), agreeing to the appointment of General Briggs as director of operations and to Shinwell's request for a Cabinet Committee on Malaya in March 1950 (206, 207, 209, 210) and chairing crisis meetings in connection with the slow progress of the Briggs Plan in the following February and March (232–234). His own minutes, written in blunt crayon, were terse and generally unrevealing directions to action. Churchill was concerned about Malaya in his capacity as minister of defence as well as prime minister in the first months of the Conservative government from October 1951 to the appointment of Templer in January 1952. He considered the problem in swashbuckling style, scribbling brief but nonetheless grandiloquent minutes, exchanging telegrams with Oliver Lyttelton in mid-Atlantic when he was bound for New York on board the *Queen Mary*, and summoning Templer to Ottawa for appraisal over dinner (259–263). The directive to Templer was sent to Churchill for final approval on 1 February (268), and he was also consulted about the appointment of MacGillivray as his successor (308). As foreign secretary, Eden took a somewhat petulant interest in Malaya as part of the wider problem of regional security (338–340), and, on becoming prime minister in April 1955, he was kept informed about insurgency, communist entryism and political changes both in Malaya and elsewhere in South-East Asia by Lennox-Boyd (351, 353) and Sir Robert Scott, who, under the revised terms of his appointment as commissioner-general, communicated directly with 10 Downing Street (374, 375). Chairing the Cabinet Colonial Policy Committee, Eden was particularly anxious to block the communists' resumption of legitimate politics (380). By the time Macmillan became premier in January 1957, all was over bar some shouting about the final form of the independence constitution, financial arrangements, the defence agreement and internal security after the end of British rule. Macmillan steered Malaya's application for Commonwealth membership through the Commonwealth Prime Ministers' Meeting (457, 458) and approved the final touches to the defence agreement (462). Macmillan also penned some memorable asides on the trivia of transfer of power, such as: presents for the Malayan people (455); the composition of the British delegation to the independence celebrations and whether the wives of British dignitaries attending these festivities should do so at taxpayers' expense; his radio broadcast to Malaya (463) and his message of greeting to Tunku Abdul Rahman (467).

Every minister jealously guarded his prerogatives and on the whole respected those of his colleagues; as Eden wrote to the secretary of state for war, Antony Head, 'I shall not comment upon your estimate of educated opinion in Malaya as this is a matter for the Colonial Secretary' (340). There were occasions, however, when ministers felt that Malaya was too important a matter to be left to the secretary of state for the colonies and made it their business to be sure he minded his business. Defence was clearly one such issue. Wartime planning for reoccupation and emergency operations necessitated close liaison between Colonial, Foreign and War Offices. After the fall of Malaya in 1942, the Colonial Office and Foreign Office approached the question of reoccupation from markedly different angles, the Foreign Office being more inclined, at least initially, to contemplate the abandonment of claims to lost colonies in deference to American opinion (4–9). When the South-East Asia Command was established in April 1943, Dening was seconded from the Foreign Office as political adviser to Mountbatten and thereafter the FO strove to ensure the co-ordination of British policies in the region (39–42, 81). It was this concern which eventually led to the appointment of regional authorities in the shape of the special commissioner (1946–1948) (71, 118, 119) whose functions were merged with those of the governor-general (1946–1948) to become the UK commissioner-general in South-East Asia in 1948. Between 1950 and 1953, and at a critical time in Malayan affairs, Robert Scott was instrumental in fashioning the FO view on Malaya. Respected for his vast experience of East and South-East Asia and occupying the positions of assistant under-secretary with responsibility for the Far East and chairman of the inter-departmental Far East (Official) Committee, Scott did not conceal his doubts about certain aspects of colonial policy. He attacked the CO tendency to blame Malayan unrest on non-Malayan forces, notably the supposed interference of communist China, and he expressed concern about the conduct and organisation of civil administration, not least the workings of the office of commissioner-general in South-East Asia (249).

The co-ordination of colonial and military interests during the war and its immediate aftermath was effected firstly through the Malayan Planning Unit, which was led by Major-General Hone formerly of the Colonial Legal Service (16) and which, after a year in London, was attached to the headquarters of Mountbatten's South-East Asia Command (23, 26–30). On the Japanese surrender, liaison continued via the British Military Administration in Malaya (44, 45, 53, 62, 70). When stalemate appeared to have been reached during the emergency, Shinwell (minister of defence) and Strachey (secretary of state for war) grew increasingly impatient with the civil authorities which, in their eyes, were ineffective in the pursuit of counter-insurgency operations (226, 230). Indeed, the plan whereby Templer combined the functions of high commissioner and director of operations had its origins in anxieties which long predated the assassination of Gurney and the visit of Lyttelton to Malaya.

The Treasury became involved in Malayan affairs firstly in connection with its post-war economic rehabilitation and subsequent development plans (32–35, 37, 38, 201). The Treasury, of course, appreciated the extent of British economic interests in South-East Asia (421, 440) and especially the dollar-earning capacity of Malayan commodities (214) and were sympathetic, though not over-generous in their response, to requests from the Malayan government for assistance in financing emergency operations (200, 223–225, 228, 229, 302, 305, 306). As Malaya advanced towards 'full self-government', the Treasury was consulted over the financial implications of constitutional change (396, 403, 441).

Colonial policy towards Malaya was clearly entwined with Britain's foreign, defence and economic policies in South-East Asia and the Far East, and co-ordination was facilitated in London via a number of official and ministerial committees of Cabinet. The highest level was, of course, the full Cabinet itself. There is not space enough to incorporate in this collection every Cabinet paper relevant to

Malaya, and, indeed, not all of them are central to an understanding of British decision-making as regards end of empire. Matters that reached full Cabinet fall into a number of categories which can be detailed as follows. First of all Cabinet considered proposals involving significant changes of policy, either departing from a previously agreed line or making a marked advance upon a position already approved by Cabinet, for example: the Malayan Union plan and its subsequent abandonment in the face of Malay protests (20, 25, 48, 56, 69); plans for constitutional advance following the federal elections (356–358); and the line to be taken at the 1956 Lancaster House conference (400, 404–406). Secretaries of state were, on the whole, prepared to seek Cabinet endorsement of a policy; it reassured the hesitant and protected them from criticism. Secondly, issues over which there was inter-departmental disagreement might well reach Cabinet; one of these was the question of Britain's recognition of communist China in 1949–1950 (on which the FO and CO had distinctly different views) and its implications for Britain's position in Malaya (197). Thirdly, questions relating to the security of Malaya and, indeed, the progress of counter-insurgency operations were discussed, notably the declaration of the emergency and the proscription of the Malayan Communist Party (158–160), contingency plans for the defence of Malaya in the event of the fall of Thailand to communists, authorisation of the use of a new tear gas, and the Baling Talks between Tunku Abdul Rahman and Chin Peng at the end of 1955 (379). The visits to Malaya of Griffiths and Strachey (June 1950) and Lyttelton (December 1951) were made primarily in connection with emergency operations, and each minister reported to Cabinet on his return (219–221, 257). Fourthly, matters which had potential for repercussions at home or abroad but which were not in themselves central to Malayan policymaking might reach Cabinet: one of these was the politically embarrassing incident of the publication in *The Daily Worker* of a photograph showing a Royal Marine holding the severed head of communist insurgent.[17] Another was the proposal to exchange Lee Meng, who had been sentenced to death for being in possession of a hand grenade, for Edgar Sanders who had been held in Hungary as an alleged spy.[18] Neither of these issues is documented in this collection. Finally, Malaya would come up in connection with the wider problems of sterling balances, the Colombo Plan, British policy in the Far East and South-East Asia, imperial defence and colonial security, and colonial policy and the future of the Commonwealth.

In constitutional terms the most important forum where policy was discussed and shaped was parliament yet its debates hover in the wings of this collection. The reason for this is not because ministers and civil servants took little account of the legislature or held the democratic process in disdain – this was patently not the case as is revealed in the official papers preparing parliamentary questions and parliamen-tary statements (notably that made by Attlee on 13 April 1949)[19] – but because its proceedings passed immediately into the public domain through the columns of *Hansard* and, given the pressure upon space, it has been decided not to include material which has long been readily accessible there or in the form of Command Papers. Out of sight should not be out of mind, however, and we need to remember the parliamentary dimension to government policymaking during end of empire in Malaya. Although there was, as has already been noted, a fundamental bipartisanship on imperial and colonial policies for much of this period, ministers were not above adding lustre to their own conduct by ridiculing the record of their opponents, and they always kept their guard up to parry thrusts from their shadows across the floor of the House or from those amongst their own backbenchers who were sufficiently independent-minded to be critical or were engaged in lobbying on behalf of a particular cause. Stanley Awbery, sometimes Tom Driberg and, of course, Fenner Brockway were vigilant on the Labour side while Leonard Gammans ('the honourable member for Malaya') and Walter Fletcher were the watchdogs of the right. In the House of Lords, Elibank and Marchwood were particularly vocal during the Malayan Union dispute. Although Malayan affairs took up comparatively little parliamentary time, at a few key points debates in Westminster turned the course of Whitehall planning. One of these was the Commons debate on the Malayan Union proposals, which took place on 8 March 1946 and led to a government concession on the citizenship scheme (80).[20]

So far we have considered policymaking in London, but what about the Malayan imput? In considering this question we need to deal in turn with the government of Malaya, its position in the region and, thirdly, the relations between metropolitan and local authorities. With regard to the first of these dimensions, as has been already noted, the PRO documents provide a sketchy record of its workings. For an understanding of the context in which policy was formulated certain features of the Malayan Union and Federation constitutions should be noted. Although intended to unite the peninsula and provide strong central government for the first time, the Malayan Union scheme was hamstrung from the moment it was announced by political protest and, as a result, was never fully implemented. Its replacement, the Federation of Malaya, retained many of the features of the Union, but it represented a major concession to Malay vested interests with the result that administration from 1948 onwards was uneasily shared between state governments, which lay in the hands of Malay chief ministers (the *mentri mentri besar* or *mentris besar*) and their staff, and the British-dominated central government. Malay mistrust of centralism and British frustration with state obstructionism thwarted efficiency and, in addition, aggravated the schisms between the administration, police and military during the emergency. It was largely in order to correct these faults in the federal structure that Gurney pressed ahead with his proposal for a member system, whereby leading Malayans held portfolios in the Federal Executive Council (212, 237), and Briggs planned a chain of war executive committees linking districts, states and the centre of operations (216).

In Kuala Lumpur itself, the federal secretariat threatened to succumb to increasing pressures and burdens caused by political change, economic development and internal security in the post-war period. The key official, managing the business of the Federal Executive and Legislative Councils and liaising with heads of federal departments and British advisers in the states, was the chief secretary. The strain of this job took its toll of Newboult, who was chief secretary of the Malayan Union and Federation from 1946 to 1950 and acting high commissioner in the three months between Gent's death and Gurney's installation, while his successor, del Tufo, was handicapped by the paralysis that gripped Malayan government on the assassination of Gurney. The office was, however, placed on a far more effective footing by Watherston, who came in as chief secretary as part of Lyttelton's reforms in 1952 and remained in that post until independence. Indeed, the changes of 1952 broke the deadlock in government in major ways: Templer acquired unprecedented powers, combining the offices of high commissioner and director of operations; MacGillivray, in the new post of deputy high commissioner, had special responsibility for political and constitutional matters; and General Sir Robert Lockhart was appointed deputy director of operations. The power which Templer commanded locally was matched, as we shall discuss further below, by the trust placed in him by the secretary of state, something which neither Gent nor Gurney had enjoyed to the same degree.

Britain's avowed and ultimate intention after the Second World War was to create a 'Dominion of Southeast Asia', and consequently Malayan affairs were supervised regionally by the governor-general (1946–1948) and later by the colonial branch of the office of the commissioner-general. A measure of the importance placed on the need for the liaison between departments and co-ordination of policies in South-East Asia, even though they were not always able to achieve it, is Britain's concern with regional organisations. Beginning in 1941 with the short-lived and ill-fated appointment of Duff Cooper as minister in Singapore, British 'supremos' appeared in succession and with differing functions and powers. Mountbatten as supreme allied commander South-East Asia (1943–1946) was charged with military objectives and the reoccupation of Dutch and French colonial territories as well as British possessions. For two years following the end of military administration, Lord Killearn, as special commissioner, and Malcolm MacDonald, as governor-general, acted on behalf of the Foreign Office and Colonial Office respectively. In 1948 their functions were amalgamated in a single office; Killearn retired and MacDonald stayed on as commissioner-general in South-East Asia, a position which he occupied for seven years until he was replaced by Sir Robert Scott in 1955. The commissioner-general had a supervisory rather than an executive role in the fields of colonial and foreign affairs (with respect to which he was answerable to the appropriate secretaries of state) and he also chaired the British Defence Co-ordinating Committee, Far East.

MacDonald dealt with South-East Asian governors both individually, as problems arose in different dependencies, and in concert, when long-term issues such as closer association were discussed. Although he was not responsible for Malaya's internal affairs, he became involved in its government and politics, particularly during the 1946–1952 period, and his views carried immense authority locally and commanded the respect of the Colonial Office and of ministers. In mid-1946, for example, MacDonald endorsed Gent's doubts about the Malayan Union's feasibility and he convinced London of the wisdom of entering into negotiations with Malay leaders for its replacement (92, 96). Thereafter, however, his relations with Gent deteriorated: MacDonald increasingly expressed unease about Gent's approach to Britain's friends and enemies, arguing that the high commissioner needlessly antagonised Dato Onn and UMNO but was insufficiently vigorous in meeting the communist threat. The commissioner-general was instrumental in persuading London to recall Gent, although his recommendations regarding his successor were not accepted by Creech Jones (151, 152, 154, 156, 157, 164–166). Nevertheless, despite his initial reservations about the appointment of Gurney, MacDonald worked well with him and admired his pursuit of co-operation between communal leaders and closer association between the federation and Singapore. As Malayan government was scrutinised by so many departments in addition to the Colonial Office, one senses that Gurney resented the fact that he was not given a chance to defend his corner but that it was MacDonald who was consulted at the highest level. Certainly Gurney made his exclusion from Downing Street talks in March 1951 a resigning matter (235, 236).

MacDonald fruitlessly advised against the appointment of a soldier after Gurney's assassination (250) and, with the arrival of Templer, he became less prominent in Malayan affairs. The commissioner-general's functions in Malayan defence were reduced and Whitehall came to value the office more and more for the role it played in British foreign rather than colonial policy in the region (324, 335, 338, 348).

Turning to the relationship between metropolitan and local authorities, we should note that the history of colonial administration is peppered with disputes between secretaries of state and governors. While it was usual for the secretary of state to choose the menu and the governor to prepare the dishes, the former did not shrink from interfering below stairs and occasionally caused consternation in the kitchen and the cook to flounce out; nor was it unknown for a governor to get above himself and try to dictate his own terms. They approached the task from complementary but different angles, of course, for whereas the secretary of state had the dual function of presenting British requirements to Malaya and Malayan needs to Cabinet, so the high commissioner was both the agent of British policy and the defender of Malayan interests. Precise instructions or even general guidelines issued from on high were not always easily implemented on the spot; at every twist and turn of events London clung to its good intentions while deferring to the high commissioner with respect to the timing and manner of their implementation. Successive secretaries of state accepted, for example, that 'the initiative for a closer association of Malaya and Singapore must come from the two territories and there should be no question of imposing unification from Whitehall'.[21] There were moments, however, when good intentions seemed to be inadequate to the situation: London was seen to eat humble pie over the Malayan Union, and four years later at the nadir of Britain's fortunes in the emergency, the main doubt related 'not to our intentions in Malaya, but to our physical capacity for carrying them out'.[22]

Opportunities for spanning the gulf between London and Kuala Lumpur increased with improved contact between the metropole and periphery after 1945. No serving secretary of state for the colonies had visited Malaya during the seventy-year history of Britain's relations with the Malay states between 1874 and 1942. In the post-war period, by contrast, James Griffiths went out in June 1950 (218–222), Oliver Lyttelton in December 1951 (248, 252–257), and Lennox-Boyd in August–September 1955 (359, 363, 365–370, 372). MacDonald, Templer and MacGillivray, for their part, regularly flew to London for consultations (232–234, 283, 286, 299, 300, 307, 402, 450). Contacts between London and Kuala Lumpur increased after 1945 at other levels, too: Bourdillon assisted MacMichael in his mission in 1945; Paskin accompanied Lyttelton to Malaya in 1951; and Higham was seconded to the Singapore government between 1953 and 1957. In addition, experts were invited out from Britain to examine policing, housing, local government, trade unions, and so on.[23] What turned out to be the most rickety bridge crossing the London-local divide was the appointment of Gent as governor of the Malayan Union and later high commissioner of the Federation. Because he had spent the previous quarter-century in the Colonial Office, he never settled into his new role and, like his contemporary Gerald Greasy in the Gold Coast, Gent failed either to win the confidence of local leaders or retain that of the British.

Both Gent and his successor, Gurney, were career officers and team players, they knew their place and were prepared to be overruled, as, indeed, they occasionally were not only by the commissioner-general but also by the Colonial Office. As

MacDonald's colonial role faded from early 1952, however, so the importance of the high commissioner rose. Having been head-hunted for a new job, Templer was far better placed *vis à vis* both the commissioner-general and the Colonial Office, and, like Mountbatten in India, enjoyed greater powers and trust than had his predecessors. Scrupulous in seeking instructions before he embarked on his two-year stint as high commissioner and director of operations, Templer was unfettered by precedent and revelled in the unorthodox when it came to carrying them out. 'In short, he dominated the scene', Lyttelton later recalled, and '[i]n a few months I had almost dismissed Malaya from its place in my mind amongst the danger spots. My role had become simple: it was to back him up and support him'.[24]

In MacGillivray the high commission reverted to an orthodox colonial servant with twenty-five years' experience of overseas administration. Like Templer, however, though for different reasons, MacGillivray was strongly placed in relation to the Colonial Office. His importance lay not so much in his local power as in his local knowledge and influence. Gurney's member or quasi-ministerial system had marked a shift in the seat of decision-making and by the time MacGillivray became high commissioner more and more of the decisions for Malaya's government and economic development were being taken in Kuala Lumpur rather than London. From August 1955, following the first federal elections, the high commissioner was obliged to work in co-operation with a Malay chief minister in a relationship not unlike that binding Arden-Clarke with Nkrumah in the Gold Coast. Pointing the way across the quicksands of Malayan politics, he tutored the Colonial Office in the art of the possible.

This survey of policymaking indicates that the roles and relative importance of the London and local authorities changed over time. During their wartime exile from Malaya, planners in London were not only given the opportunity, but were also forced by circumstances, to seize the initiative, with the result that the British returned in the autumn of 1945 with a blueprint for post-war rehabilitation and eventual progress towards self-government. During the next five and a half years the centre of decision-taking oscillated between London and Kuala Lumpur as Malayan conditions – the aftermath of war, the Malayan Union crisis and the communist insurrection – affected the pace of political development, altered the course of metropolitan plans, provoked local initiatives and required continuous consultation between metropole and periphery. From early 1952 the locus of policymaking switched to Malaya in response, firstly, to the commanding presence of the high commissioner and, secondly and more importantly in the end, the Malayanisation of government. That said, however, a feature of the last phase of British rule was the constant exchange of views between London and Kuala Lumpur illustrated by the two-way flow of high-level personnel between the two capitals. Moreover, it should be noted that the principles upon which the details of transfer of power were subsequently worked out were agreed at a conference in London (January – February 1956) over which the secretary of state presided and about which the Cabinet was kept informed (400–406), while the final arrangements for independence were approved in May 1957 at a conference chaired by Lennox-Boyd and again held in London (450).

Events and the chronology of the three parts
The documents in this collection have been chosen from a wide range of Whitehall

departments and also represent a variety of types, including telegrams and despatch-es, manuscript minutes and printed memoranda. During the course of selection their value has been assessed according to their readability, authorship and content, and especially with a view to the light they shed on policy and policymaking. In making these judgments, we have borne in mind how British policy was shaped by different personalities, at a number of levels of government and with respect to various dimensions ranging from the specifically Malayan to the generally imperial. It has already been suggested in this introduction, however, that a collection which focuses solely upon British decision-taking runs the risk of exaggerating the grip which the official mind exerted over developments to the neglect of the unexpected, the irrational and events outside British control. For this reason a deliberate effort has been made to document unsettling incidents which disturbed rather than assisted the fluency of policymaking.

Drama abounds in the Malayan story: the fall of Singapore on 15 February 1942; the turbulent interregnum between the Japanese surrender and the establishment of the British Military Administration in August–September 1945; the Malay campaign against the Malayan Union in 1946; the outbreak of insurrection and the declaration of the emergency and subsequent recall and death of Gent in June–July 1948; the assassination of Gurney in October 1951; the non-co-operation campaign mounted by the Alliance in May–July 1954; the talks between Tunku Abdul Rahman and Chin Peng at Baling in December 1955; and so on. It can happen, of course, that some occurrences are inadequately documented at the Public Record Office, perhaps because London remained in the dark about what was going on 7,000 miles away or because the import of cataclysmic happenings, about which civil servants might first have been informed by the press rather than through official channels, took time to sink in and elicit a considered reaction on paper. In so far as it is possible to document crises, the editor has tried to strike a balance between items demonstrat-ing continuity and those showing change, between the development of policy over a number of years and the shocks which interrupted it. Whereas concentration upon the evolution of official thinking could result in a documentary collection with few contours, a preoccupation with crises and turning-points would tempt us to regard these as exciting ports of call in an otherwise featureless voyage and warranting many more snapshots than the miles of intervening sea.

And so we come to the question of periodisation and the chronological arrange-ment of the collection. Not only has this volume been subject to the nature of the sources and the editor's assessment of them, it has also been moulded by the artifice of presentation. Thus, although the editor has not been obliged to collate the documents under thematic heads, he has yet applied his judgment, and some may think a degree of arbitrariness, with regard to the periodisation of the narrative and the identification of breaks in its flow.

The volume starts on 15 February 1942 with the conquest of British Malaya by the Japanese and ends on 31 August 1957, the day when the Federation of Malaya achieved formal independence from Britain. The end date needs no justification but the starting-point calls for comment. It is generally held that the fall of Malaya marked the beginning of the end of British imperialism in South-East Asia, if not elsewhere. Indeed, the military disaster provoked wide-ranging criticism of Britain's conduct as an imperial power. This sea-change is not easily spotted in the official documents which tend to deal in the ebb and flow of the daily round rather than turns in the tide in the affairs of men. The record does reveal, however, a shift in public opinion on colonial issues and a reappraisal in official attitudes to Britain's future role in Malaya; it gradually sank in that there was no returning to the *status quo ante bellum* (1, 2). 1942 is the clearest turning-point in the history of British Malaya: before that date policy was based on the belief in indefinite rule; afterwards the premise became that of eventual self-government.

The years between 1942 and 1957 are presented in three parts. This sectionalisation suits the preordained format of the volume. Each part also represents a more or less coherent period. The first, called 'The Malayan Union experiment', covers the following episodes: wartime planning for the restoration of colonial control; the Allied reoccupation of Malaya and the British Military Administration (September 1945 – March 1946); the return to civil rule on 1 April 1946 in the shape of the radical but short-lived Malayan Union; the formation of the United Malays National Organisation and the Malay campaign against the new constitution; and the negotiations which led to its replacement by the Federation of Malaya. It ends with the inauguration of the Federation in February 1948. Part II covers the communist insurrection to the establishment of the first 'white area' in early September 1953. During these years successive high commissioners in Malaya (Gent, Gurney and Templer) and successive governments in Britain sought ways of successfully combating armed violence and latent communal conflict. The third part, called 'The Alliance route to independence', gets underway in September 1953 when Templer invited two Alliance leaders onto his Executive Council. In 1953–1955 preparations were made for state and federal elections which culminated in the Alliance landslide victory in July 1955. With the appointment of Tunku Abdul Rahman as chief minister, political and constitutional developments moved at an increasingly breathless pace and were marked by the Tunku's talks with Chin Peng at the end of 1955, the Lancaster House Conference in January–February 1956, the Constitutional Commission chaired by Lord Reid, and the final arrangements relating to continuing Anglo–Malayan relations with respect to defence, finance and Commonwealth membership. Each part is itself subdivided into a number of chapters also on chronological lines.[25]

* * * *

I *The Malayan Union experiment 1942–1948*

Acquired as East India Company bases, Penang (1786), Singapore (1819) and Malacca (1824) were known as the Straits Settlements from 1826 and together became a single Crown Colony in 1867. Singapore in particular was increasingly valued as a commercial centre and a strategic base. Between 1874 and 1914 further British expansion led to the appointment of residents and advisers to the courts of the Malay rulers of each of nine Protected States on the peninsula, four of which formed the Federated Malay States (FMS) in 1896. According to treaties and engagements concluded at various times with the rulers, the British recognised the sovereignty of the sultans, the autonomy of their states and the special position of their people as 'princes of the soil'. The extraction of tin from circa 1850 and the cultivation of rubber from the 1890s, added to the revenues and profitability of these dependencies and also led to the emergence of a 'plural society' where the communal differences between Malays and immigrants from China and India were reinforced by their economic functions and the places assigned to them in Malayan society. As British administration expanded and the economy developed, so the power of Malays and their position in 'modern Malaya' receded. Yet the principles underlying the British presence remained the same and became ingrained through reiteration. The high commissioner, Sir Hugh Clifford, declared in 1927 that the Malay states 'were, they are, and they must remain – unless our duties, our obligations and our engagements to the Rajas, the Chiefs and to the people of these countries are to be wholly ignored or forgotten – *Malay* States'.[26]

In the interwar period, however, officials were struck by the inadequacies of the system of government for fulfilling British obligations to Malays and accommodating the growing proportion of non-Malays who had settled permanently in the country, quite apart from the fact that territorial fragmentation stood in the way of administrative and economic efficiency. Various attempts were made, notably by Sir Lawrence Guillemard (governor and high commissioner, 1920–1927) and Sir Cecil Clementi (governor and high commissioner, 1930–1934), to decentralise the FMS with a view to placing all Malay states on a uniform footing preparatory to the ultimate recentralisation of British Malaya. Such experiments foundered on vested interests, not least the suspicions of the sovereign rulers, with the result that a number of officials, such as G E J Gent, head of the CO's Eastern Department, became impatient with the 'barren policy' which, by simply respecting 'the traditional apprehensions of the Malay Sultans', prevented their Malay subjects from standing 'on their own feet', ignored 'the undoubted interests' of other races and obstructed 'a right and orderly relationship between the different Empire territories in the East'.[27]

During the night of 7–8 December 1941 Japanese forces attacked Pearl Harbor, Malaya, the Philippines and Hong Kong. The US Pacific Fleet was crippled, half the American air force in the Far East was destroyed at Clark airfield and British naval power in Asia was wiped out when HMS *Repulse* and HMS *Prince of Wales* were sunk off the Pahang coast on 10 December. Having achieved supremacy in the air and at sea, Japan pushed into the territories of colonial South-East Asia on several fronts. In Malaya, British and Commonwealth troops failed to halt the advance through the peninsula; Kuala Lumpur was captured on 11 January, and on 31 January the British withdrew to Singapore destroying the causeway between Johore Bahru as they retreated. They held out until 15 February 1942 when General Percival surrendered to General Yamashita.

Although the British government did not hold an official or public enquiry into the loss of Singapore, debate over the reasons for Britain's defeat started immediately after the loss of Malaya and has been going on ever since.[28] Inadequate resources to defend a two-hemisphere empire, failure to reinforce the naval presence and provide air-cover, the costly demands of other military fronts nearer home, British under-estimation of Japanese fighting skills, fifth column activities, lack of preparation for a land attack launched from the north, poor leadership, inter-service disputes, complacency in the civil service and the administrative disunity of British possessions – all these factors have been cited singly or together in various post-mortems on the military debacle and shaped the attitudes of men planning for the restoration of British rule (1, 11).

The effects of defeat were keenly felt and plainly seen. 130,000 British and

Commonwealth troops were lost as either casualties or prisoners of war, Britain surrendered a supposedly impregnable naval base and valuable dependencies, and the rest of the eastern empire was exposed to attack as the Japanese advanced south to the Coral Sea and east to the gates of India itself. As well as being materially damaging, the military disasters of 1941–1942 profoundly humiliated Britain in Asian eyes. Moreover, her self-esteem suffered another blow when it became clear that world war had eroded Britain's imperial capacities to such an extent that the restoration of lost territories would depend upon assistance from the USA whose president and people were in no mood to save England's Asian colonies.

Anglo–American differences affected joint-operations in the field and also joint-planning for post-war South-East Asia. For a time it was feared by some ministers as well as the CO's Eastern Department that the Foreign Office might succumb to American anti-imperialism, accept the case for international supervision of European colonies in the region and sacrifice British territorial claims in the Far East and South-East Asia for the greater good of the wartime alliance (4–9). Cranborne, for one, put up stout resistance on this point and the Colonial Office boldly set out the arguments favouring the post-war restitution of former dependencies, but it turned out that the hostility of the US towards the British empire diminished as the war went on and as Americans themselves assumed an imperial role in Asia and the Pacific.

Almost as soon as they had lost their South-East Asian empire, Colonial Office officials accepted that a new deal was required for the region (2). They were encouraged in this belief in part by the wartime opportunity of correcting pre-war problems, in part by the demands of war itself and in part by their assessment of Britain's post-war interests in the area. Although, in contrast to the significance of the Netherlands East Indies to Holland and Indochina to France, Britain's South-East Asian dependencies were on the fringes of an imperial system which centred upon India, their actual and perceived value grew with the prospect of the loss of India, Britain's need for dollars and the great power rivalry in the region. Specific preparations for post-war Malaya were initiated by a request for guidance on long-term policy from those preoccupied with the invasion, reoccupation and military administration of South-East Asian territories. Unlike Burma, whose governor in exile at Simla presided over planning for a return to British rule, the Colonial Office in London directed arrangements for post-war Malaya and Borneo, principally because so few British officials from these territories had escaped Japanese detention. By the summer of 1943 a Malayan Planning Unit (MPU) had been set up (there was a separate unit for British Borneo) (3, 10, 12–16). With Major-General Hone at its head, the MPU was composed of colonial officials holding military rank. It was attached to the Directorate of Civil Affairs in the War Office but it followed long-term policies simultaneously being devised in the CO. The result was a fresh departure designed to consolidate the administration of British territories, facilitate their economic development and eventually transform the 'plural societies' of the 'Malaysian' region into a self-governing nation. The assumption of direct rule was planned for each British dependency (including Sarawak and North Borneo which had hitherto been under the jurisdiction of the Brooke family and a Chartered Company respectively) and the new post of governor-general would be established to supervise and co-ordinate British colonial policies throughout the region.

Whereas planning for post-war Burma rested on principles enshrined in the 1937 constitution, wartime thinking in Malaya encouraged a radical departure. The resulting Malayan Union scheme amounted to new imperialism in two senses: it envisaged unprecedented direct rule in the short term and it committed Britain to Malayan self-determination in the long term. Because it intended to break with the past, the CO took pains to consult other Whitehall departments and, in conjunction with the War Office, to seek Cabinet authority for the new course (17, 18, 20). In the spring of 1944 the Cabinet Committee on Malaya and Borneo, which was chaired by Attlee, scrutinised and endorsed the proposals (21, 22, 24, 25). The full Cabinet accepted the CO's contention that the 'restoration of the pre-war constitutional and administrative system will be undesirable in the intersts of efficiency and security and of our declared purpose of promoting self-government in Colonial territories', and on 31 May 1944 approved the new principles which would underwrite subsequent military planning and long-term colonial policy.

The Malayan Union had three novel features: first, a peninsular union (including the nine Malay states, Penang and Malacca but not Singapore) with a strong central government; second, a common citizenship scheme for all who regarded Malaya as home; and, third, fresh treaties whereby the Crown would acquire from the Malay rulers full power in their states. From the end of May 1944 the detailed directives were worked out both for the military administration, which would be set up after liberation, and for the civil government which would succeed it. Because they departed from the traditions and ideology that had determined British policy in Malaya since the late 1870s and because they anticipated opposition from vested interests and 'old Malayan' hands, the Colonial Office insisted that the Malayan Union be planned in secret (23, 26–31, 36). Despite its progressive thrust which, as Mountbatten pointed out, would have appealed to emergent Asia and sugared the pill of imperial restoration, the outlines of the scheme were not announced until October 1945 and even then another three months were to pass before its details were published (56, 69). Not only was policy kept under wraps but it was also drawn up in ignorance of current circumstances in Malaya. Up to a point planners were correct in assuming that the Japanese invasion, occupation and eventual defeat vitiated those conditions which had been fundamental to the viability of the old-style colonial regimes, and that British over-rule would be necessary for the rehabilitation of the country. But if the infrastructure had been damaged, the economic equilibrium upset and the administrative fabric eroded by war, then social and political relations had also become more volatile, and, apart from the links which Force 136 (or Special Operations Executive, Far East) established with the communist-dominated resistance force (Malayan Peoples' Anti-Japanese Army, MPAJA), the British remained largely in ignorance of these developments until their return.

Meanwhile on the field of battle, the appointment of Mountbatten as supreme allied commander South-East Asia (SACSEA) in August 1943 had breathed new life into this theatre. Although plan 'Culverin' for the reconquest of Sumatra in 1944 was not proceeded with owing to Anglo-American disagreements, Slim's 14th Army withstood Japanese offensives at Imphal and Kohima in March–June 1944, and then advanced to retake Rangoon early in May 1945. South-East Asia Command (SEAC), whose headquarters had moved from New Delhi to Kandy in April 1944, now set about preparing operation 'Zipper', the seaborne invasion of Malaya which was to be assisted from within the peninsula by Force 136. The war came to an end, however, before 'Zipper' was mounted. Air-raids upon Japan from November 1944 onwards reached a crescendo in the massive offensive on Tokyo and other cities in May–August 1945. On 6 August the first atomic bomb was dropped upon Hiroshima and this was followed by the second on 9 August on Nagasaki, and on 15 August the Emperor announced his surrender.

It had been decided at the Potsdam Conference in July 1945 to divide the responsibilities for the military administration of Japan's empire between American, British and Chinese commands. According to these arrangements the Philippines, Korea and Japan itself fell to the US, which also assisted Chiang Kai-shek in China, while the British-led SEAC assumed charge of 'colonial' South-East Asia (apart from North Vietnam which was to be occupied by Chinese troops as far south as the sixteenth parallel). Thus, on Hirohito's surrender, SEAC's frontier was extended to embrace Thailand, southern Indochina and the greater part of Indonesia as well as Burma, Malaya and Sumatra, and Mountbatten's headquarters were transferred from Kandy to Singapore. SEAC's remit was to accept the Japanese surrender and repatriate Japanese personnel, to evacuate allied prisoners of war and others in detention, to maintain law and order, and, finally, to prepare for the restoration of colonial rule.

The problems facing Europeans in South-East Asia after 15 August 1945 were enormous (81). The restoration of colonial rule would be impossible without the deployment of men, materials and military power on a scale far larger than Europeans had ever found the need to wield before, yet their homelands were bled white, their old possessions were broken-backed and their problems provided nationalists with opportunities to assert themselves, particularly in Indonesia and Vietnam. The assumption by SEAC of sole responsibility for the reoccupation of 'colonial South-East Asia', therefore, saddled Britain with heavy burdens and obligations some of which she would be hard-pressed to fulfil. SEAC's resources were inadequate to its tasks. The Americans were not willing to make substantial contributions to it and Britain was already stretched by military commitments in Europe, the Middle East and India. Loss of initiative in India meant that Britain could no longer freely deploy Indian troops in patrolling imperial territories elsewhere in the world. Moreover, the Labour government was under domestic pressure to demobilise Britain's conscript army as soon as possible, and was facing bankruptcy and 'starvation corner' at a time when it was committed to a programme of massive expenditure on social welfare.

Nonetheless, while it would be misleading to underrate their difficulties, we should not underestimate the determination of the British, Dutch and French to restore their colonial power. On the contrary, in the immediate post-war period the region experienced a 'new imperialism' or, to borrow a concept from African historiography, a 'second colonial occupation'.[29] This was particularly the case in Malaya where the British were eager to reorganise the government and rehabilitate the economy in order to be in a position once more to tap its dollar-earning commodities. Indeed, Malaya is sometimes cited as the exception to the rule that in South-East Asia colonialism died in 1942 and nationalism came of age in 1945, but even in Malaya the British faced a post-war imperial crisis since the collapse of the old colonial system under the Japanese led to near anarchy in August–September 1945, and, as is discussed below, Britain's pursuit of new policies provoked Malay opposition in the first half of 1946.

Despite the contemporary reports of joyous welcomes accorded to the returning

Allies, SEAC's reoccupation of the region was something of a shabby scramble. From the outset SEAC was wrong-footed by the unexpected swiftness of the war's end. Its troops were deprived of the chance to redeem their military reputation in the eyes of locals by force of arms; its administrators were called upon to set up military governments over the whole region immediately instead of step by step (43–46). An understandable lack of preparedness largely accounted for that anarchic hiatus between the Japanese surrender and the Allied return. The landings at Morib on the Selangor coast (operation Zipper for the reoccupation of the Malayan peninsula) could easily have turned into a military debacle had SEAC met with resistance, and when British troops eventually arrived in Java they encountered armed opposition and lawlessness on a large scale.

SEAC's position did not improve significantly after headquarters and a framework of military administration had been established in each territory. Throughout the region food shortages, worthless currency, political uncertainty and administrative collapse meant that SEAC found few foot-holds from which to assert itself over profiteering and banditry, vigilantes and kangaroo courts, communal conflict and competing bids for power of various nationalist groups. The army of occupation was unable, therefore, to confine itself to military administration *tout court*; it became increasingly involved in local politics, in say Java and Cochin-China, and in international difficulties with, for example, the Dutch and French (81). It was a relief when in March 1946 General Gracey handed over to the French in Indochina and when the last British troops withdrew from Indonesia by the end of November 1946.

As regards British South-East Asia, Singapore resumed its role as the seat of British military power – it was in Singapore where Mountbatten received the Japanese surrender on 12 September (54) – and it resumed its position as the centre for the diffusion of Britain's political, economic and cultural influence throughout the region (58, 71). Territory by territory, military administrations were set up in British Malaya and British Borneo (44); Major-General Hone was the chief civil affairs officer for Malaya and his deputies, Brigadiers Willan and McKerron established their headquarters in Kuala Lumpur and Singapore respectively. The tasks of the BMA were to assume political control, repair the rudiments of an infrastructure for the provision of essentials and prepare for the return of civil government (61). Presented as 'liberation', the period of British Military Administration was in fact tarnished by administrative cack-handedness on a scale to cause grievous damage to both Anglo–Malayan relations and relations between Malayan communities (65).[30] It was a tense and confused few months punctuated by outbreaks of Sino–Malay fighting and enveloped in uncertainty with respect to the intentions of either the British or the communists.

The communist-dominated MPAJA had come out of the jungle to establish control in villages and some towns, and to put collaborators on trial. The BMA were at first obliged to collaborate with the MPAJA while making plans for their disarmament and supersession (43, 46). Just as he was identified with liberal colonialism in Burma, so with regard to Malaya, Mountbatten was anxious that the British should command the moral high ground by giving full publicity to the progressive aspects of the Malayan Union scheme which appeared to meet the eight-point programme of the Malayan Communist Party on every count (47, 51, 52). Advance publicity was embargoed, however, until the foundations of the Malayan Union had been laid, chief amongst which were the new treaties to be signed by the rulers and HMG's special representative, Sir Harold MacMichael (53).

From the moment MacMichael was provisionally appointed for this task after his return from Palestine and Trans-Jordan in 1944, he was anxious to know how far he could go in making it clear to the sultans that they would have no option but to sign the new treaties. The CO consulted the India Office which advised against strongarm tactics and MacMichael's terms of reference with respect to the resort to coercion remained unresolved until the eve of his departure from London in September 1945 when he was authorised to check the credentials of the rulers and to telegraph to the secretary of state for the colonies (through SEAC) the names of any deemed unworthy of the throne and the credentials of any he recommended in their place (50, 55, 56).[31] Preparatory to the arrival of Sir Harold MacMichael, Willan visited the Malay rulers in turn (8–29 September), deposing the Japanese placemen in Selangor, Trengganu and Perlis, gauging the loyalty of newcomers elsewhere and examining the records of the others (57). On 10 October MacMichael disembarked at Port Swettenham and, starting with Ibrahim of Johore, by the end of the year he had concluded new agreements whereby Their Highnesses effectively surrendered to the Crown that sovereignty enabling the imposition of the Union constitution by Order-in-Council (59, 60, 64, 66). The MacMichael mission was intended to be the harbinger of an efficient and democratic Malaya; in fact, it became a symbol of misplaced good intentions and, worse, arbitrary imperialism. A newcomer to Malaya, MacMichael obeyed his instructions to a fault: he delivered the new agreements but in such an overbearing manner as to unite the rulers in opposition to the British and as unlikely figureheads of unprecedented protest on the part of the mass of Malays who feared for their future in a Malaya dominated by non-Malays. At a stroke, the mission alienated Britain's traditional collaborators, yet the new policy (which was not fully revealed until the White Paper was published on 22 January 1946)[32] singularly failed to attract support from the non-Malays it was supposed to benefit. Consultation was brushed aside in the headlong rush to get the new structure in place (67, 68).

In the pursuit of constructive colonialism, the Malayan Union amounted to direct and centralised British rule, although it was also intended to pave the way for an eventually self-governing Malayan nation. Because this constitution was a radical departure from pre-war principles, it had always been held that the key to the success of the Malayan Union lay in secret planning and swift implementation. In fact, it was these very methods as much as the content of the policy that provoked the anger of 'old Malayans' in Britain, cast the Labour government in the role of reactionaries and aroused Malay protest culminating in the convention of the Pan-Malayan Malay Congress on 1 March (72–75, 78, 79). In Britain opponents of the scheme mounted an impressive parliamentary and extra-parliamentary campaign. Businessmen had little time for political progressivism (63) and retired Malayan civil servants objected to the wholesale abnegation of past principles and practices. They wrote to the press and lobbied MPs, such as Leonard Gammans in the Commons and Elibank and Marchwood in the Lords. Led by Sir George Maxwell, a former chief secretary of the FMS, a proconsular delegation including two former high commissioners, Sir Cecil Clementi and Sir Frank Swettenham, confronted the secretary of state at a meeting in the CO on 26 February, but they came away empty-handed. On 8 March in the House of Commons, letters from aggrieved sultans were read out and Arthur Creech Jones (who was standing in for George Hall) was forced into a significant concession with respect to the citizenship scheme, promising to consult Malayan opinion before proceeding further with it (80). As we have seen, the CO had expected a certain amount of hostility from these quarters, but what took everyone, including the 'old Malayans', by surprise was the extent and vigour of protest coming from the so-called 'quiescent' Malays. Of course, the Malayan Union policy and the MacMichael mission did not by themselves create Malay nationalism. Its origins can be traced to the previous century[33] and it is clear that the disruption of 1941–1945 had so sharpened political consciousness and aspirations that the Malay community and their leaders were ready to assert their claims to be 'princes of the soil'. The Malayan Union, however, provided a target upon which hitherto diffuse activities could be focused. Nonetheless, the Colonial Office was not yet shaken from its chosen course. Cabinet had endorsed the policy (69, 76) and Gent prepared to leave London for his installation as governor of the Malayan Union when the military bowed out to the civil government on 1 April 1946.

For long regarded as figureheads, the Malay rulers played a pivotal role in the mounting crisis over the Malayan Union. The constitution hinged on the new agreements, and the rulers' individual and initial doubts about the legitimacy of these treaties grew into vigorous repudiation in a spate of telegrams to London and the United Nations. Even Ibrahim of Johore, who had signed so promptly before departing for London, questioned the legality of the treaty when he was informed of a conspiracy of Johore Malays to dethrone him on the ground that he had contravened the state constitution and betrayed Malay rights. For their subjects (*raayat*), the sovereignty of the rulers was a bastion against non-Malays; expressions of fervent loyalty to what progressives took to be unlovable autocrats may have seemed out of keeping with the age of nationalism, democracy and the common man (84), but it was explicable by reference, not merely to Malay atavism, but also to their very real fear that, once sovereignty was wrested from the rulers, Malays would have no defence against an eventual Chinese take-over through the gaping portals of Malayan Union citizenship (77).

On 1 April 1946 the Malay rulers, who had gathered in Kuala Lumpur to attend Gent's installation, were persuaded by Dato Onn bin Jaafar, the president of the Pan Malayan Malay Congress, to boycott the ceremony and, instead, to acknowledge the support of a crowd demonstrating in support of sultans' sovereignty and against British imperialism (82, 83). It was a highly charged moment. Never before had rulers acted in concert, nor had they aroused such displays of popular support. Aware of revolutionaries toppling royal houses in parts of Indonesia, the rulers were unnerved; so, too, were some British officials who appreciated that Malay collaboration had traditionally underpinned the British position in the peninsula (85).

Meanwhile the Pan-Malayan Malay Congress of some forty associations formalised its objectives and organisation, even though it would, for several years to come, still retain its loose and disparate character. Meeting in Johore Bahru on 11–13 May the Congress converted itself into the United Malays National Organisation (UMNO) with Dato Onn as president and the Dato Panglima Bukit Gantang as secretary-general (90). Committed to the immediate defeat of the Malayan Union and the long-term improvement of the Malay position in the country, UMNO was from the outset a communal party whose leaders insisted that Malaya was not yet ready (*belum layak*) for independence. Led by Malays with government experience and run like a government department, UMNO did not pose a fundamental challenge to the continued British presence, but only to specific British policies, and the authorities swiftly recognised that an accommodation should be reached with this new party.[34] Indeed, they turned a blind eye to the involvement of Malay government servants in its activities and MacDonald, for one, was soon advocating conciliation of UMNO, which he saw as a genuine nationalist movement whose co-operation it would be in British interests to cultivate (92, 96).

The first indication the CO received that Gent was wavering in his support for the Union came in early May (86, 88). Anxious lest the governor should cave in to protests, George Hall reaffirmed fundamental principles and briefed Malcolm MacDonald, governor-general designate, on the government's commitment to the Union constitution, to common citizenship and to the treaties (91). In London the secretary of state and his officials could not contemplate ditching a scheme that had consumed much of the Eastern Department's time since 1943 and had received Cabinet authorisation at several junctures during its construction. Moreover, they believed that the policy was in the best interests of both Britain and Malaya, despite the opposition it had aroused in parliament and the press. Within days of his arrival in Malaya, however, MacDonald was supporting Gent's call for compromise, and by the end of May the secretary of state had been persuaded to countenance exploratory talks with Malay leaders (92, 93). So began a process of constitutional negotiations in which an Anglo–Malay twelve-man working party, reporting at intervals to plenary sessions of officials, rulers and UMNO leaders, drafted an alternative constitution. In the Anglo–Malay discussions both sides gave ground; the British used their 'fundamental principles' as bargaining counters, the secretary of state clinging to the MacMichael treaties until he was sure that the Malay side had agreed to a strong central government (albeit in federal form) and a common (though more restrictive) citizenship (97, 99–106). The proposals were brought to London towards the end of November, discussed by the Cabinet's Colonial Affairs Committee on 2 December and approved three days later by the Cabinet subject to the resolution of a few points to be referred back to Kuala Lumpur and consultations with non-Malays (107–110). On Christmas Eve the *Constitutional Proposals* were published[35] and a consultative committee was appointed.

The reasons for the British volte-face are open to debate. At first sight, it would appear that unprecedented direct rule met and was overturned by unprecedented Malay resistance. But further exploration of the documents suggests that it was not so much direct confrontation with the Malays as the wider repercussions of their campaign that convinced firstly the colonial government and then the Colonial Office that conciliation was essential. On 11 May Gent reported 'that almost universal Malay political opinion here gives no basis for expecting effective operation of consitution' on the basis of the Orders-in-Council, that the strength and depth of Malay feeling had surprised all and that there were worrying signs of Malay non-co-operation 'in practical ways, such as police rank and file resignations' though these were 'on very small scale at present'. The governor then drew attention to the assessments of his security advisers who, given the 'growing scale of Malay non-co-operation', apprehended that 'substantial Indonesian elements in West coast states may develop acts of violence against non-Malay communities'. Gent emphasised that it was generally agreed 'that Malay leaders will not come to accept "Union" and the situation will deteriorate with consequent frustration in every essential object of unity and political progress' (88). In a subsequent telegram despatched on the same day, Gent also drew attention to the problem of the Malayan Communist Party which exploits 'opportunities at any time to disturb the peace' in order to overthrow British government in Malaya through the methods of 'intimidation, violence and extortion'. One of the MCP's weapons, continued Gent, was 'infiltration into any Malay Indonesian groups or organisations', hence the importance of ensuring 'that Malay opinion is sufficiently met' (89).

MacDonald deployed similar arguments, though from a wider, regional perspective and, given his quasi-ministerial status, with more telling effect:

> If we can get agreement now, we can retain full trust in British leadership in this region which is the main base of the British position in the Far East. If we do not, we shall begin to lose acceptance of our leadership by local peoples and process of our being at each stage bit behind local political opinions (such as has been so unfortunate in the history of the Indian problem) will start. We must, of course, keep in mind that there are powerful political groupings in Asia which are ready to exploit any weakening of our position i.e. Indian nationalists and Imperialism, Chinese Imperialism and especially Pan Malayan Movement led by Indonesians. (92)

Towards the end of June MacDonald remained adamant that the priority lay in appeasing Malay opposition. 'Malay opinion is roused as never before.' While he recognised that 'it is highly desirable that Malays become politically conscious so as to prepare themselves to play appropriate part in developing self Governing insitutions', he stressed that 'it will be extremely unfortunate if this awakened political consciousness and interest gets rail-roaded into extremist and anti-British channels'. Compromise would restore Malay confidence in the British and ensure their co-operation but refusal to meet Malay objections would sweep Malay nationalism 'into Indonesian anti-European currents' and the 'opposition and bitterness which has led to such damaging situations elsewhere' (96).

The documents reproduced here suggest two conclusions: the first is that arguments based upon security assessments proved decisive in changing the course of policy, and the second is that the British already perceived the uses of their adversary, UMNO. Concern lest non-co-operation should permeate and corrode the fabric of government – it had, for example, already resulted in Malay resignations from the police force – together with fear of the unruliness that might flourish as a consequence caused the British to think again. In deciding to appease UMNO and the rulers they were not surrendering to violence or conceding to enemies; rather they were anxious to regain their assistance in anticipation of the possibility of violence arising from other quarters. Their particular dread was that an essentially conservative movement might be hijacked by militant Malays eager to provide Indonesian activists (and possibly Chinese communists too) with the opportunity of destabilising the regime at a time of bloody communalism (94). Now it is possible that intelligence reports may have derived from an exaggerated assessment of the threat to Malaya posed by Indonesian nationalist and revolutionary groups of one kind or another; certainly, by January 1948 MacDonald no longer regarded the Indonesian republican movement to be a grave danger to Malayan security (137). Nonetheless, at this time both governor and governor-general took very seriously signals of political extremism and subversion (116).

The outline for a federation having been agreed between British officials and Malay leaders and approved by Cabinet, on the constitutional front 1947 saw, not merely detailed drafting, but more especially further consultations (111). The Consultative

Committee, chaired by H R Cheeseman (director of education), sounded the opinions of leaders of non-Malay communities and others who had not been represented in the earlier discussions. This committee reported to the governor at the end of March and its recommendations were discussed first by the Anglo–Malay Working Committee in April and finally by a plenary session of representatives of the Malayan Union government, the rulers and UMNO. On 11 May, Gent forwarded the agreed scheme to the Colonial Office (123, 124), and, after further exchanges between London and Malaya (126, 127), Creech Jones submitted them to Cabinet (128). Cabinet approved the revised constitutional proposals on 3 July, and on 21 July a parliamentary paper announced a federation substantially the same as that outlined in the Anglo–Malay *Constitutional Proposals for Malaya* which had been published in the previous December.[36] It had been hoped to inaugurate the Federation on 1 January 1948 but more fine tuning was required to the elaborate written constitutions for the federation and the states, and there was a late hitch over British control of defence and external affairs. At last on 21 January the Federation of Malaya Agreement, which contained the written constitution for the federation, was signed by the governor and the rulers and inaugurated on 1 February (136, 138).

It was a long-drawn out and increasingly irritable process. In December 1946 the Pan-Malayan Council of Joint Action was formed by non-Malay groups and Malay radicals who had withdrawn from UMNO to protest against the Anglo–Malay concordat, and it later split on communal lines into the All-Malaya Council of Joint Action and PUTERA (Pusat Tenaga Raayat, centre of people's strength). Acting in tandem they boycotted the Cheeseman committee and produced *The People's Constitutional Proposals for Malaya*.[37] Published in English, Malay and Chinese, this pamphlet advocated a common nationality and democratic self-government. When ignored, the coalition resolved on 17 August to mount a *hartal* (or peaceful stoppage of work) and this took place on 20 October. MacDonald was more sympathetic to the Chinese demands for a constitutional review than was Gent, whose priority was now to restore good relations with Malay leaders as soon as possible by pushing ahead with a federal constitution (131–134).

At the same time, the UMNO leadership fretted at the delay in replacing the Union constitution and grew suspicious that the British might succumb to Chinese demands or revert to the Malayan Union. Dato Onn's reputation as a political leader in large measure rested on his resistance to the scheme: the longer negotiations dragged on, the greater the risk to UMNO integrity; once the negotiations were complete, however, there would be a danger of his stock declining. Thus it was that in his communications with British officials and in speeches to his own supporters, Dato Onn embroidered the theme of British perfidy which the Malayan Union epitomised (114, 135). Although MacDonald accepted Onn's nationalist credentials from the start and continued to believe in them long after they had waned, Gent's relations with the charismatic though mercurial leader of UMNO were never better than correct, principally because Onn continued to mistrust Gent as the original architect of the Malayan Union who yet remained committed to restoring some of its features.

Indeed, although the replacement of the Union by Federation was seen at the time, and has been interpreted since, as a defeat for British policymakers because it restored sovereignty to the Malay rulers, reinforced the position of the Malay traditional elite in state government and subordinated non-Malay political pretensions to those of the Malay community, it is clear from the documents that the British never lost sight of the principles and objectives of Malayan Union policy, either during the constitutional talks or after the Federation was inaugurated. Strong central government, multi-racial citizenship and closer association with Singapore leading to the emergence of a 'British Dominion in South-East Asia' were aims that distinguished postwar from prewar policy and survived the Malayan Union crisis (98, 112, 115, 121). When they appeased the Malays over the Malayan Union, the British government changed tack instead of altering course. They adopted a more circuitous route towards the goals of strong government for the peninsula and common citizenship for all peoples, goals which continued to guide British policy for the next decade. If British intentions were not in doubt, however, their capacity for carrying them out had been affected by the marginalisation of the Chinese and the elevation of Malays in the government of the country. The powers and functions of the Federation were now divided between the Malays, who assumed control of state governments, and the British, who were dominant at the centre. This was an arrangement that obstructed the promised advance to elections, alienated the Chinese and, from mid-June 1948, hampered the authorities' approach to insurrection.

II The Communist insurrection 1948–1953

Following the murders of three European planters and their Chinese assistants in Sungei Siput on 16 June 1948, Gent declared a state of emergency in Perak and parts of Johore which he extended to the whole peninsula two days later (148). Criticism of his handling of the crisis, however, led to his recall but he was killed in an air crash as his plane approached London on 4 July. A fortnight later the Cabinet decided to proscribe the Malayan Communist Party (160) and a month after that the Cabinet Defence Committee agreed on military reinforcements for Malaya (161). So began an armed struggle which lasted beyond the achievement of independence in August 1957 and even beyond August 1960, when the emergency was officially called off. It was not until 2 December 1989 that the communist leader, Chin Peng, formally laid down his arms in separate agreements with Malaysian and Thai authorities.[38]

Since the declaration of emergency, questions have been raised and discussed relating to the origins, nature and outcome of this conflict in Malaya.[39] Was it communist insurrection or nationalist rising? Was it war or civil disturbance? Did it hasten or retard the pace of decolonisation and in what ways did it affect the manner of British withdrawal? With respect to the origins of the upheaval, historical enquiry has focused, firstly, on the relative significance of local and international factors in determining the course of events, and, secondly, the extent to which either the Malayan communists or the British authorities were prepared for the outbreak of armed violence. Some have argued in favour of a conjuncture of Malayan developments and those elsewhere in the communist world and have emphasised the importance of the Cominform's switch from the 'united front' to Zhdanov's 'two camp' doctrine in bringing cold war in Asia. According to this last interpretation, the call to action, which was voiced at conferences in Calcutta early in February 1948, signalled the launch later that year of uprisings by the Burma Communist Party, the Indonesian Communist Party, the Hukbalahap in the Philippines and the MCP, while the Vietminh were given new heart. Others, by contrast, have concluded that Malayan circumstances were the principal determinants of the MCP's decision to take to the jungle and resort to violence. Amongst these have been cited changes in MCP leadership, when Lai Tek was replaced by Chin Peng as secretary-general, and the socially dislocating effects of post-war colonialism, in particular the high prices and low wages suffered by labourers and squatters, which prepared a fertile field for insurrection. Some commentators have suggested that the outbreak was neither premeditated nor the culmination of exact planning on the part of the MCP, and they have drawn attention to the almost accidental manner in which the Sungei Siput murders committed the MCP to 'armed struggle', tipped the scales against British toleration of the party and triggered a twelve-year emergency.

Whether the British authorities caused or in any way contributed to the outbreak, or, conversely, whether they could have prevented or prepared for it, are also questions that continue to divide historians of the emergency and on which the available documents unfortunately shed little new light. It has been suggested, for instance, that the regime deliberately provoked violence in order to identify and isolate communist activists and coerce and subdue fellow travellers. An alternative view is that armed violence was the result, less of a colonial conspiracy and more of a successful counter-revolutionary strategy to block 'entryism' in trade unions and political parties.[40] Some of these explanations presuppose a degree of knowledge which the authorities did not possess, for the documents reveal that accurate intelligence, which was to prove a key to the eventual success of counter-insurgency, was not available to the high commissioner. Gent was furnished with neither sufficiently precise warnings as to MCP intentions nor information which could be relied upon as the basis for appropriate action. Thus, although the US State Department was given to understand by the American consul that Gent was recalled because of 'his failure to take action on intelligence reports reaching him',[41] on 13 July 1948 the British Cabinet concluded that the Malayan disturbances necessitated a comprehensive review of colonial police 'with a view particularly to improving their intelligence work' (158).[42]

We should note, however, that the causes of Malayan violence, the reasons for declaring an emergency and the decision to proscribe the MCP a month later had their own dynamics, as may be noted from chronological discrepancies between them. Violence did not simply erupt in June 1948; it had been a constant factor in post-war Malaya, sometimes waxing and sometimes waning but never disappearing altogether. Since labour unrest and 'brutal outrages' had been reported regularly for well over a year (122, 125, 129, 130), why did the federal government choose mid-June for a declaration? Indeed, there was little prospect of massive support from a united nationalist movement (139, 140) and in late May 1948 officials in the Colonial Office believed that Malaya was, if anything, more stable than it had been for some time (146). A number of equally plausible explanations come to mind for the timing of the emergency: that it was, for example, the culmination of steadily growing unrest and frustration; that it was provoked by changes in the nature and scale of violence; that it indicated a British reappraisal of a festering problem; or, as in the review of the Malayan Union policy two years before, that it occurred because concern over Malayan unrest was heightened by other anxieties. One interpretation resembles Corfield's explanation for the delay in declaring an emergency in Kenya in 1952,[43] namely: the post-war Malayan regime, being intrinsically progressive and sensitive to liberal opinion at home and internationally, was naturally unwilling to infringe civil liberties and resort to coercive measures until alternative courses had been explored and exhausted. Similarly, but more pragmatically, it might be held that Gent was loth to introduce draconian measures which would have had the effect of driving subversives underground, out of sight and beyond reach.

The high commissioner has usually been presented as weak and vacillating at this time, lacking a grasp of the problem, suggesting few ideas for its solution and having little stomach for tough action. The particularly shocking murders at Sungei Siput were the last straw for his critics. Gent, losing popularity within the administration, criticised by the military, hounded by the British business community (149, 150) and abandoned by his superiors, was a desperate man driven to desperate measures and in the end he clutched at the declaration as at straw. And yet there was little consensus amongst his critics about the nature of Malayan violence. The security services failed to penetrate the MCP, identify their plans and anticipate the crisis (162). MPs, even ministers, also disagreed in their assessments, and it would appear that Gent, who had lacked credibility as high commissioner since the Malayan Union debacle, was finally sacrificed by his masters as a scapegoat for their own confusion and as a gesture to restore confidence in government (151–157). It is perhaps significant that Gent had lost the backing of Malcolm MacDonald at least a month before he declared the emergency (for it was agreed to re-post him during talks which the commissioner-general had in London in May), and that MacDonald seemed to be as much dismayed by the way Gent had antagonised Dato Onn, the leader of UMNO, as he was by his handling of Malayan communists (144, 164).

When the crisis was debated in Parliament on 8 July some MPs pointed out connections between Malayan unrest, the advent of Cold War and the spread of subversion to British colonies.[44] From the outset the Labour government, keen to preserve its progressive credentials, scotched any suggestion that the Malayan problem was connected with Asian nationalism. Creech Jones maintained:

> Malaya, after all, is the only colonial area in South-East Asia where no genuinely anti-European movement has emerged since the war. . . . I would say emphatically, particularly in view of the vilification of Britain – the wilful lies in regard to the Malayan situation which have been put across from Moscow – that we have not here at all the emergence of a nationalist movement which Britain is engaged in putting down. This is not a movement of the people in Malaya. It is the conduct of gangsters who are out to destroy the very foundations of human society – orderly life.

On this point there was cross-party agreement, with Gammans (Conservative MP for Hornsey) asserting that 'this is not a nationalistic uprising in any sense of the word'. Beyond that, however, opinions differed: gangsters, bandits and criminals in the eyes of some, the perpetrators of violence were seen by others as agents of international and revolutionary communism. Oliver Stanley claimed that the outrages were part of 'a widespread and long concocted plot to overthrow government in Malaya'. Gammans identified the source of the problem to be 'primarily a terrorist organisa- tion, Moscow-inspired, Communist in origin' and he pressed ministers to admit, 'considering that Mr. Malcolm MacDonald has said it', that '[t]his is part of a worldwide attack against Great Britain, of which another part is going on in Berlin at this moment'. Walter Fletcher, by contrast, insisted that '[w]hat we are seeing now is not due to the Communists, although they are a large element in the situation and will certainly use it to their own purposes' but 'we are throwing dust in our own eyes to use the word "Communist" '. He urged the government not to 'deceive themselves by saying this is Communism; it is not. This is lawlessness due to a disrespect of the law which is not being sufficiently firmly or effectively administered, and the cause of that I place fairly and squarely on the shoulders of the Government'. During this debate ministers were unwilling publicly to shift the blame for Malayan unrest upon Moscow and world communism. Moreover, while there was a temptation to play up the evils of terrorism in order to legitimise British counter-measures, they also recognised the need to play down the extent of violence in order to repair confidence in the colonial government. Rees-Williams, for example, suggested that Malayan violence was a revival of the gangsterism with which he had been familiar in pre-war Penang.

By late June both Gent and MacDonald were convinced that communists were behind the violence but the Colonial Office and Cabinet remained sceptical. On 13 July Cabinet concluded that whatever the origins of unrest, '[t]here was little doubt that the situation in Malaya had been exploited by Communists, and similar attempts to foment disorder must be expected in other parts of the Colonial Empire' (158). But it refrained from banning the MCP and it was not until 19 July, a month after the start of the emergency and a fortnight after the death of Gent, that the Cabinet decided to outlaw the party (159, 160). This delay does not indicate that the Labour government was soft on communism; on the contrary, the foreign secretary, Ernest Bevin, was in the vanguard of the Cold War in 1948. Ministers held back, we would suggest, possibly because they feared that extension of the Cold War to Malaya might dilute efforts being made to contain communism in western Europe and the Middle East, probably because they did not wish emerging states of Asia (notably newly independent India) to identify Britain with intolerance and authoritarianism, partly because they lacked watertight evidence that the MCP was indeed the perpetrator of violence and certainly because they were reluctant to drive the communists underground. Notwithstanding the coincidence, if not conjuncture, of Malayan violence and Cold War and notwithstanding the Labour government's belief that colonies would fall prey to worldwide subversion, what eventually persuaded the Cabinet to follow MacDonald's advice was not so much wider international consid-erations but rather the specific predicament of the colonial government in Malaya. Although ministers did not welcome his recommendation, they were in the end willing to accept it both because they trusted the commissioner-general's judgment and because they hoped that the smack of firm government would go a long way to restoring confidence in the Malayan regime. Nearly two years later, in May 1950, a captured MCP pamphlet, which was entitled *Present day situation and duties* and had been produced in June 1949, satisfied at least some members of the Cabinet Malaya Committee that the Malayan troubles had been fomented by the MCP rather than bandits (215). By the time the Labour government gave way to the Conserva-tives, it had become axiomatic that Britain was confronted by 'communist terrorism in Malaya' and that the 'enemy is the Malayan Communist Party, which is almost exclusively Chinese'.[45]

The declaration of the emergency in mid-June and the proscription of the MCP a month later by no means initiated masterful government in Malaya. On the contrary, this episode suggested the inadequacy of the colonial regime in a number of areas – policing, economic development, labour relations and constitutional engineering. Although the first set of emergency regulations (they were considerably reinforced later) empowered the authorities to impose the death penalty for unlawful possession of arms, to detain any persons, to search persons and premises without warrant and to occupy properties, many regarded them as too little and too late. Moreover, there was continuing confusion in the official mind about the nature of the problem and the identity of the enemy. Furthermore, the longer it lasted and the more it cost, the emergency increasingly threatened to make the British position untenable and jeopardised their plans for Malaya: it saddled Britain with a war it could ill afford; it damaged the Malayan economy; and it arrested advance towards devolution of power. However, although the declaration of emergency had the immediate effect of putting constitutional concessions on ice, it marked neither the abandonment nor a significant turning-point in Britain's long-term Malayan policy. Alongside, albeit subordinate to, the conduct of counter-insurgency operations, the British doggedly and unspectacularly pursued those Malayan Union goals of regional consolidation and nation-building (141, 143). Of course, the restitution of law and order was now their principal priority, yet in this area the next three and half years were punctuated by false dawns and dashed hopes.

After Gent's death, MacDonald, who seemed to waver in his assessment of the gravity of the security problem, suggested that the inauguration of the next high commissioner be delayed until law and order had been restored (166). As it was, despite an interregnum of three months, when Gurney arrived in October the disorders were still the government's top priority. Cold War and the government's commitment to contain communism, imperial prestige and memories of the 1941–1942 disaster, Britain's economic needs and its interests in the region (196, 198, 201), all meant that there could be no thought of withdrawing under pressure. The Chiefs of Staff supplied military reinforcements and the Treasury accepted the need to provide financial assistance for emergency operations (175, 200).

Until the end of 1949, Gurney's period as high commissioner was marked by diagnoses of the problem, recommendations for its solution and optimism that success was round the corner. Gurney's first despatches on what became known as 'the Chinese problem' largely developed out of his briefing before leaving London. Already the authorities were aware not only of the need to enlist Chinese support but of their own ignorance of the Chinese community (163). Lamenting the lack of Chinese commitment to Malaya (which had, after all, been a reason why the Malayan Union had failed to win popular endorsement), Gurney identified two objectives: the first was to deprive the communists of assistance from squatters and the other was to encourage the formation of a Malayan Chinese Association (168–172, 176, 179). Gurney insisted, and the military accepted, that counter-insurgency was first and foremost a matter for a multi-racial police force (188, 189, 199). Even at this stage in the emergency, therefore, the immediate problems of law and order were being examined in the context of nation-building, and, although not yet enunciated in so many words, 'winning the hearts and minds' of the Malayan people was already regarded as an essential ingredient of counter-insurgency.

What exactly longer-term policy was and just how it was to be achieved were, nonetheless, vexed issues. However committed they remained to the nostrums of the Malayan Union, if they were going to win the support of all communities in Malaya and, at the same time, reassure businessmen and allies in the region, the authorities needed to do something other than try to re-activate that burnt-out model (174). That the Malayan Union wounds proved slow to heal was revealed during Onn's visit to London towards the end of the year (173). That Gurney required the crutch of a firm ministerial statement of intent was shown in what the CO regarded as his unprofessional complaint to the deputy leader of the opposition (177, 181, 183–186) – a complaint which, together with others, contributed to Attlee's balanced assurance to Parliament on 13 April 1949 that, while it was Britain's policy to lead Malaya to self-government within the Commonwealth, there would be no premature withdrawal from responsibilities.

Meanwhile, initiatives were launched in Malaya to build bridges across a number of communal, geographical and constitutional divides. MacDonald persuaded community leaders to form the Communities Liaison Committee in order to foster multi-racialism in a number of practical ways related to the extension of citizenship to non-Malays and the improvement of the Malays' economic position (192, 195); the prospect of closer association between British dependencies and particularly between Malaya and Singapore was cautiously explored; and on 31 December 1949 Gurney proposed a member system, whereby leading local members of the Federal Legislative Council might be appointed members of the Executive Council with responsibility for certain federal departments (205). At the end of the year, despite anxieties about the repercussions of British recognition of communist China (197, 202), the Malayan authorities were hopeful, though not complacent, concerning their measured approach to communism and communalism.

Although Gurney's plans for a member system came to fruition in 1951 (212, 217, 237), optimism with regard to the central issue of internal security was eroded during 1950–1951 by operational disorganisation and the lack of lasting success against terrorism. Following the British general election of February 1950, which returned a Labour government but with a drastically reduced parliamentary majority, Emanuel Shinwell was appointed minister of defence. His prime responsibility was the direction and co-ordination of the armed services according to policy devised by the Defence Committee of the Cabinet, and, turning to Malaya, Shinwell proposed the appointment of General Briggs as director of operations and, in addition, a Cabinet Committee on Malaya (206, 207, 209, 210).

By the end of May, Briggs had presented his plan to resettle squatters in New Villages and erect a chain of War Executive Committees for the co-ordination of activities across the various services and throughout the Federation (216). Early in June, and before there had been time to implement the Briggs Plan let alone allow it to take effect, James Griffiths (secretary of state for the colonies) and John Strachey (secretary of state for war) visited Malaya. They were informed by MacDonald that the pace of constitutional change would have to accelerate if Britain were to retain both the initiative in Malaya and influence in the region beyond, though it is clear that the Labour government still maintained that the ending of the emergency was a prerequisite for significant constitutional concessions (218–221). Dreams of political progress were yet overshadowed by operational nightmares, and the outbreak of the Korean War in June 1950 aggravated problems: on the one hand, the galloping defence budget stretched resources that might otherwise have been available for the Federation (223–225, 228, 229); on the other hand, Malaya, being a front-line state in the Cold War, appeared threatened not only by subversion from within but also by invasion from the north (231).

On 11 December 1950, the day Attlee returned from talks with Truman about the Korean War, he received a letter from Strachey, in which the secretary of state for war demanded radical changes in personnel and the structure of administration in

South-East Asia (230). Service chiefs had for some time been urging the appointment of a supremo who would have overriding powers in the direction of affairs at
least in Malaya, if not in the wider area. The Foreign Office also doubted whether the
current regional arrangements adequately safeguarded British interests in South-
East Asia and the Far East. One ground for anxiety lay with the high commissioner,
who appeared hamstrung by the federal constitution and disputes between administrators, policemen and soldiers; another was the commissioner-general whose
temperament and responsibilities were more appropriate to a conciliator than a
director of contentious men. Malayan problems were back on the prime minister's
agenda and MacDonald and Sir John Harding (commander-in-chief, Far East Land
Forces) were called to London in February for three meetings at 10 Downing Street
(232–234).

Gurney, who had a reputation for touchiness, boiled over in frustration when he
heard from MacDonald that Malaya had been discussed at the highest level but in the
absence of its high commissioner. His letter of resignation, which was courteously
declined by Griffiths, reveals his mounting despair (235, 236). Malaya was getting on
top of Gurney, just as it had got on top of Gent. Not only had operations reached
deadlock, but Malayan politics were hopelessly entangled. Dato Onn, possibly in
response to suggestions from both MacDonald and Gurney to convert UMNO into a
multi-racial party, was unable to shake its communal orientation, and left the
movement he had founded to inaugurate (with Tan Cheng Lock, amongst others) the
non-communal Independence of Malaya Party in September 1951 (240, 241, 244).
Gurney was not deluded by the celebrations accompanying the launch of the IMP:
Onn without UMNO might be a broken reed and UMNO without Onn could be a
rudderless ship. Anyway, the high commissioner was by this time despairing of a
genuine commitment on the part of the Chinese to a multi-racial Malaya. Gurney's
so-called 'political will', known to have been written two days before his death, is a
bitterly pessimistic document, and the meetings which the acting high commissioner held with Malay and Chinese leaders after Gurney's assassination confirmed that
communal antagonism was as ingrained as it had ever been (245, 247).

The murder of Gurney on 6 October 1951 (246) marked the lowest point in British
morale in Malaya. It occurred at the start of the general election campaign in Britain
and to the Conservatives, who won with a slender majority, it was symptomatic of
Labour drift. Their supporters, and particularly business interests, expected a more
obviously determined approach from Churchill's colonial secretary (251) and Oliver
Lyttelton did, indeed, identify Malaya as his first task (248, 252, 253). Having visited
the country in December, he recommended a major overhaul of government and the
appointment of General Templer as Malayan supremo (254–260). Like General de
Lattre de Tassigny in Indochina,[46] Templer was put in charge of both military
matters and civil administration. Like de Lattre, he might appeal to American
opinion which was reported favourably disposed to strong action in Malaya as part
of what was seen to be a general war against communist aggression. Again like de
Lattre, Templer had an immediately electrifying impact upon the military campaign.
In contrast to the French experience, however, the arrival of the new supremo in
Kuala Lumpur coincided with a lasting improvement in British fortunes, and
Lyttelton later presented the advent of Templer in the manner it has generally come
to be regarded, that is as the turning-point in both military operations and
nation-building.[47]

Clearly personalities played their parts in the ebb and flow of the Malayan emergency and the eventual failure of the communists' armed struggle, but this familiar assessment makes too much of the impact of Gurney's death upon Britain's approach to Malayan problems. One does not need to swallow Disraeli's dictum that 'assassination has never changed the history of the world' to recognise many areas of continuity between the policies of Labour and the Conservatives and between the regimes of Gurney and Templer. Although Lyttelton's statement to the Malayan press insisting that the priority lay with the restoration of law and order caused something of a furore (254, 255), it was held not to have breached the bipartisan pledge 'to guide Colonial people along the road to self-government within the framework of the British Empire'. Lyttelton himself publicly reiterated the broad principles of Labour's colonial policy.[48] We also know from the official papers that the appointment of a Malayan supremo had been in the air for a year before the advent of the Conservatives; it originated neither with the new secretary of state nor, indeed, with Montgomery, for all the field marshal's huffing and puffing (258, 260). Moreover, although MacDonald was overruled when he advised against the appointment of a soldier on the grounds that it would alienate local opinion (250), Templer functioned as a civil (not a military) high commissioner who was directed to assist the peoples of Malaya to achieve self-government (268). Continuity is further demonstrated by the Gurney legacy: Templer inherited both the Briggs Plan for the resettlement of Chinese squatters and a number of political and constitutional initiatives, notably the quasi-ministerial member system and proposals to enlarge federal citizenship. Indeed, the events bracketed by the death of Gurney and advent of Templer did not deflect the British from their pursuit of those Malayan Union objectives of a strong central government and a multi-racial nation. If anything, violence reinforced the pattern of British policy, placing a premium on effective direction from the top, reinforcing Anglo–Malay collaboration and focusing effort on winning Chinese co-operation in counter-insurgency and their active participation in legitimate Malayan politics.

Quite as significant for the outcome of the emergency as the British reorganisation of government in 1951–1952 was the more-or-less simultaneous review undertaken by the MCP of its strategy, about which the authorities later learned from captured documents.[49] Despite the prize of Gurney's death, which, like the Sungei Siput murders in June 1948, seems to have occurred by chance rather than in fulfilment of a directive, communist leaders were deeply perturbed by the failure of terrorism to wreck the economy and administration or suborn the majority of the population. Consequently, the MCP's central committee decided in October to abandon indiscriminate violence, though not all violence, and to mount a political campaign in order to build up their popular base. But just as the launch of the armed struggle in 1948 may have been criticised in certain radical quarters on the ground that its timing had been premature, so the decision to temper terrorism may have struck some cadres as odd when violence appeared to have been secretly vindicated by the assassination of the high commissioner.

If the aims of British policy were not in doubt (268, 292, 293), the timing, manner and very chances of their achievement were by no means certain. Templer went about his task with a will, however: government was reorganised and monitored at every level (269, 291); the police force was reformed under Colonel Arthur Young, commissioner of police in the City of London;[50] the intelligence and information services were overhauled; and the direction of military operations was tightened up. His methods, like the collective punishment imposed upon Tanjong Malim, were often high-handed and provoked questions in parliament and liberal fury (as in his particularly vitriolic quarrel with Victor Purcell), but Lyttelton stood by him (272, 285, 309). 'To the *New Statesman* I shall never be liberal', Lyttelton once commented, 'but that fact will not keep me awake at night or when reading the journal.'[51] More to the point, Templer brought about results and by September 1953 he was confident enough to relax the emergency regulations in the first 'white area' of Malacca (303). Not that he believed the war was won; on the contrary, mopping-up was to demand prolonged and costly campaigning. It was complicated, too, by the precariousness of regional dominoes and by the Malayan Communist Party's renewed interest in 'entryism' and political subversion (284, 301, 311). The latter placed a premium on the authorities' bid to win the 'hearts and minds' of the people and to involve all communities in the running of the country.

'Hearts and minds' had several dimensions: the Malayanisation of the administration (287) and the federal armed forces (281); economic and especially rural development (273–275, 278, 282, 289); social provision, particularly education; elections to representative institutions (270, 277, 280, 283, 290, 298, 307, 310, 312); and the extension of executive responsibilities to Malayan members (294, 304). The Korean war boom in commodity prices temporarily alleviated the Federation's financial problems and assisted in paying for 'hearts and minds' programmes, but in the second half of 1953 fiscal difficulties returned and once again the Colonial Office went cap in hand to the Treasury on Malaya's behalf (302, 305, 306).

The Federal Agreement of 1948 had looked forward to the introduction of elections at some unspecified date in the future.[52] The rudimentary state of party political development together with the emergency had dampened enthusiasm for democratic experiments but in December 1951 the first municipal elections were held in Georgetown (Penang) and were followed by elections in Kuala Lumpur in February. In his first speech to the Legislative Council in March, Templer publicly committed the government to further advance along the road of local elections (270) and his deputy, MacGillivray, shouldered the responsibility for overseeing these developments (280). 'Nation-building' involved the cultivation of multi-racial as well as popular politics, and a British precondition for the transfer of power was the emergence of a responsibly-led and democratically-endorsed multi-racial party of government. In the run-up to the Kuala Lumpur elections the local branches of UMNO and the MCA formed an alliance effectively to scotch the challenge of Dato Onn's IMP. This *ad hoc* arrangement proved to be a significant portent, and in March 1953 the central leadership of both parties formalised their Alliance (the Malayan Indian Congress joining in 1954). But, since UMNO and the MCA strenuously retained their communal identities, objectives and constituencies, the Alliance in its early days struck the British as fundamentally flawed. They had little confidence in either Tunku Abdul Rahman or Tan Cheng Lock, and, casting around for a platform for a genuinely multi-racial movement, Templer and MacDonald held secret talks with a number of Malay notables in the hope of using them either to oust the Tunku from the UMNO presidency or to set up an alternative to the UMNO–MCA Alliance (244, 295, 296, 297). Herein lay the beginnings of the National Conference, which was composed largely of *mentris besar* (state chief ministers) and other conservatives, and also of Dato Onn's Party Negara which succeeded the ill-fated IMP and, unlike the latter, appealed to Malay communalism.

The pursuit of closer relations with Singapore was another postwar goal which acquired a new urgency under Templer. The high commissioner was anxious to amalgamate the administrations of peninsula and island for the sake of internal security and external defence (286, 288, 300). Closer association was, as we have seen, an issue which MacDonald particularly took to heart (276) and, while he was by this time effectively on the margins of much other Malayan business, in June 1953 Lyttelton authorised the commissioner-general to set up the Joint Co-ordination Committee to examine ways of bringing about closer association.

During Templer's first year the authorities did not feel under pressure to make constitutional concessions (277). On the contrary, they remained doubtful about the abilities of Malayan politicians and the capacities of their parties to respond to electoral opportunities. They nonetheless pressed ahead with preparations for elections in the hope that, in so doing, they would encourage the democratic process to take root and national leaders to flower. In 1952 the British saw themselves as determining the pace of constitutional advance and, during his visit to London at the end of the year, Templer outlined a tentative time-table which placed 'the earliest possible date for self-government at 1960' (283). As Templer rolled back the insurrection, so in 1953 the Alliance began to press for self-government, producing a blue-print for a federal constitution with a legislative council of which the majority of members would be elected (297). Alliance leaders also embarked upon a campaign to persuade the British to hold federal elections in 1954. The authorities were still eager to train Asian politicians to assume government responsibilities (294) and a noticeable note of anxiety now crept into the exchanges between Kuala Lumpur and London lest the political initiative should slip from British hands. It was in order to prevent this happening that, on 1 May, Templer recommended an early announcement of a working party to examine the question of federal elections, and later in the month MacGillivray and Hogan (attorney-general and chairman designate of the working party) were planning its proceedings with CO officials (298). In July 1953 the high commissioner formally appointed a Legislative Council committee to examine the issue of federal elections. Meanwhile, the Alliance's 'National Convention' and the 'National Conference' of Dato Onn and the *mentris besar* squared up to each other; both Dato Onn and Tunku Abdul Rahman were members of the elections committee but Onn's supporters, favouring a measured march to independence, outnumbered the Alliance representatives who demanded a sixty per cent popularly elected council and elections in 1954.

III   *The Alliance route to independence 1953–1957*

At the end of September 1953 Templer appointed to the Executive Council Dr Ismail and Colonel H S Lee as member for lands, mines and communications and member for railways and ports respectively. This move marked a new appreciation on the part of the British of the political significance of the Alliance. The two Malayans reluctantly agreed to serve, since they did not wish to appear compromised by the colonial regime, and they placed political conditions upon their co-operation; for example, they made it clear that they represented UMNO and the MCA, and that they would resign if general elections were not held by the end of 1954.[53]

The report produced in February 1954 by the Federal Elections Committee contained two Malayan viewpoints: the majority report of 'National Conference' members favoured an official majority and elections at a 'proper' date; the minority report of the Alliance, however, proposed a three-fifths elected majority (or 60 seats) and laid down November 1954 as the date for elections.[54] A compromise was worked out in two meetings which MacGillivray had with the rulers (whose approval was required before the federal constitution could be amended), whereby elections would be held in 1955 and 52 seats (a bare majority) would be filled by elected representatives.

For the Alliance this provision of elected seats was inadequate, and in April a delegation flew to London to lobby Lyttelton (313–321). It was largely due to the intercession of Lord Ogmore (formerly Rees-Williams) that the Tunku and his colleagues secured a meeting with the secretary of state on 14 May (315, 316). That Malaya was to proceed at one bound from a fully-nominated Legislative Council to one that would have a majority of elected members was unprecedented and, since he regarded the advance as both generous and stretching the limits of expediency, Lyttelton was not able to accede to the Alliance's demand for a larger proportion of elected members. The Alliance leaders were now under pressure to court danger; with radical elements in UMNO led by Abdul Aziz bin Ishak and Sardon Jubir baying for success, the Tunku, for one, could not risk being labelled a 'colonial stooge', as Sir Dato Onn bin Jaafar was being called, and, with Gandhian non-co-operation and Ghanaian 'positive action' very much in their minds, on their return from London the Alliance leaders launched a nation-wide boycott of the federal elections and public service (322, 323, 325).[55]

MacGillivray was installed as high commissioner on 1 June 1954 at an unpropitious moment in Anglo–Malayan relations. Eager to avoid confrontation of Malayan Union proportions, he presented the dispute as one between Malayans (329–332). MacGillivray was at the same time anxious to reach an accommodation with the Alliance (328, 329). Neither side wished to lose face but a way out of the deadlock was negotiated on board HMS *Alert* on 2 July (333, 334). The successful formula was a variation of the proposal emanating from a group of Labour MPs that, once the results of a general election were known, the high commissioner should consult with the leader of the party commanding majority support in the new council before filling the nominated seats. On 7 July, following the exchange of letters summarising the *Alert* agreement (334), the Alliance called off its boycott and, in the words of a *Straits Times* journalist, there opened a period of 'friendly and cordial discussions' between Tunku Abdul Rahman and Sir Donald MacGillivray.[56]

The Alliance boycott took place against the backdrop of end of empire in French Indochina. Between mid-March and early May the Vietminh besieged General de Castries at Dien Bien Phu, and at the Geneva Conference (May–July) a settlement was devised for the temporary partition of Vietnam along the 17th parallel. There is no firm evidence that British actions in Malaya at this time were directly affected by what was going on in Indochina or that the authorities were scrambling to do a deal with the Alliance lest the Malayan communists were spurred into action by the successes of the Vietminh, but that there is some connection between regional developments and British approaches to Malayan issues is revealed in the documents. For example, throughout these months ministers referred to Britain's Malayan commitments as a reason for not participating in any international military strike against the Vietminh,[57] and they also scrutinised Malaya for any signs of a reinvigoration of insurgency or a recrudescence of administrative ineptitude. Taking stock of colonial responsibilities and military operations in the context of the Geneva agreements and the subsequent formation of the South-East Asia Treaty Organisation,[58] provided an opportunity for a reaffirmation of UK aims and policy in Malaya as well as a reappraisal of the role of the commissioner-general in the region (335–343, 348) and the likelihood of his bringing about the union of the Federation and Singapore in the foreseeable future (346, 349).

Meanwhile, as guerrilla fighters surrendered in increasing numbers and as the federal elections drew closer, the Malayan Communist Party further shifted its attention to entryism and infiltration and made a bid to re-enter legitimate politics. Their penetration of Chinese schools was giving the Federation particular cause for concern (342, 345, 347, 355, 364). Then, in June 1955, the British authorities in Malaya were startled by an MCP peace offer. Their first priority was to verify its authenticity; their second was to decide how far to proceed with it. After rapid consultations between Kuala Lumpur and London, the government agreed to reject the MCP initiative. The British saw it as a poisoned chalice, not an olive branch. They were on their guard against falling into the trap of giving the communists a share in the political settlement or providing them with a stage upon which they might replay the 'united front' strategy of 1945–1947 (350–353). Although, the importance of tying the allegiance of Malayans to Malaya was a reason for accelerating the localisation of public services (344, 354) and for expanding the areas of self-government, the British were adamant that power should be transferred to 'safe nationalists' and when 'conditions were right'. It was with this end in mind that, even before the first federal elections had been held, their results assessed and the new councils put into operation, the Colonial Office was making preparations for further constitutional concessions and Cabinet was being briefed accordingly (356–358). At this stage, however, the prerequisite for full self-government was the restoration of law and order and the end of the emergency.

From the start of the emergency it had been axiomatic that Malaya was too valuable to fall into enemy hands. While this remained central to British thinking, official perceptions of Malaya's value to Britain may have been changing during the period. In the late 1940s Malayan rubber, and to a lesser extent its tin, had been major dollar-earners. HMG continued to insist on the importance of retaining Malaya within the sterling area, but, from 1955, however, one senses that the significance of natural rubber declined as Britain began to compete with the USA in the manufacture of synthetic rubber. On the other hand, while alterations in Malaya's economic importance may have reduced British reluctance to relax direct control over the country, its continued strategic significance following the Geneva settlement and the creation of SEATO seems to have hardened the resolve of those who wished to retain control over the Federation, not least the defence planners and Robert Scott, MacDonald's successor as commissioner-general.

In order that the credibility of politicians and their parties should be tested and that the authority of the new Legislative Council enhanced, the British took pains to ensure a large turn-out on polling-day, 27 July, and were gratified when approximately one million of an electorate of 1,280,000 voted. Although they expected the Alliance to win a majority, the authorities were surprised by the size of a landslide in which the Alliance polled about 80 per cent of the votes cast and won 51 of the 52 electable seats. The six other parties fielding candidates collapsed completely, including Dato Onn's Party Negara. The single opposition member was returned from the Pan-Malayan Islamic Party. The Alliance had clearly established their nationalist credentials and, since fifteen MCA candidates were returned by a predominantly Malay electorate, they also claimed to have demonstrated their multi-racialism. Good organisation together with the slogan of 'Independence within Four Years' had secured them a popular following (360–362).

While encouraged by the full turn-out, convincing result and the degree of racial co-operation within the Alliance, the British were under no illusion that the election guaranteed the future harmony of intra-Malayan and Anglo–Malayan relations. First of all, although the Malays accounted for just less than half the total population of the federation, they comprised 84 per cent of the electorate because many of the adult non-Malays were not yet federal citizens or, if they were, had failed to register on the electoral roll. The Chinese, for example, amounted to 37 per cent of the population but only 11.2 per cent of the electorate. In effect, the first federal election was a triumph for Tunku Abdul Rahman's UMNO over Dato Onn's Party Negara, Dr Burhanuddin's PMIP and Ahmad Boestamam's secular radicalism in the contest for Malay (as distinct from Malayan) support. Secondly, officials felt that the landslide might lead to tension between the Alliance and the British or between branches of the Alliance, particularly in the event of Alliance leaders attempting 'to jump their fences too fast' or falling out with each other over the spoils of victory. On balance, however, the British authorities in Malaya looked forward to 'responsible and co-operative' conduct from Alliance members and ministers.

Following the announcement of the election results, MacGillivray and the Tunku had a series of meetings to discuss nominations to reserved seats (according to their agreement on board HMS *Alert* the previous year) and the appointment of ministers. The Tunku insisted on, and the high commissioner did not object to, the title of chief minister, and, after some haggling with colleagues, the Tunku produced a slate of nine other names for his government (360). The new Federal Executive Council, consisting of ten Alliance ministers and five British officials (high commissioner, chief secretary, attorney general, minister for economic affairs and secretary for defence) was inaugurated on 9 August. Now that Malaya enjoyed a large measure of internal self-government, the stage was set for a visit from the secretary of state to discuss further constitutional advance and future relations between the Federation and Britain with respect to the external defence, internal security and finance of the country (359, 365–370).

Lennox-Boyd established a good rapport with the Tunku and was generally encouraged by his visit (372), but, with preparations in swing for a full-scale constitutional conference in London, best-laid plans threatened to come unstuck. First of all, the ever-fragile relations between princes and politicians showed signs of crumbling with the approach of independence, and Sultan Ibrahim attempted to retain his British adviser in order to safeguard Johore from Alliance pretensions (388, 435). Secondly, pressed by radicals from within UMNO, the Tunku raised the stakes to demand immediate transfer of power in matters of internal security, the achievement of full independence by August 1957 and the appointment of an independent (possibly Commonwealth) commission to draft the independence constitution (384, 387, 390, 392). Thirdly, and most alarmingly, the Tunku was eager to respond to a second peace initiative from the communists and to meet Chin Peng in order to discuss surrender terms (371, 373–382, 385, 386, 391). The first development threatened Malay solidarity, the second jeopardised relations between the British and Alliance and, the British feared, the third endangered the very future of the country.

The prospect of peace talks with the MCP revived those fears of communist entryism which the British had expressed in May–June 1955. Once again the authorities were on their guard against a return by the MCP from the underground of terrorism to the open arena of national politics. The timing of the communists' second initiative, however, made it far more menacing than the first, since Tunku Abdul Rahman was now chief minister and preparing to lead the Malayan delegation at the forthcoming constitutional talks in London. The authorities did not for one moment believe that the Tunku was a fellow-traveller but they recognised that, because the continuing emergency stood in the way of advance to independence, the Tunku would be tempted to respond to the radical demands of his own supporters by seeking a short-cut and negotiating the end of the emergency in peace talks with the communists. Constitutionally and in practical terms, of course, the British were still responsible for internal security and counter-insurgency operations, but to stand in the Tunku's way now that he was leader of a popularly elected government would be to court massive opposition in Malaya. The second peace initiative and the British response to it were a pivotal moment in the events leading to Malayan independence and the documents reveal how the episode shaped both the timing and manner of end of empire. One way of reining in the Tunku, MacGillivray suggested, might be to assure the chief minister that the British would no longer insist on the end of the emergency preceding the achievement of independence (378). Eden and Lennox-Boyd at first felt that such a message, by reversing Britain's commitment to 'law and order first', would be a sign of weakness. Towards the end of November, and at a time when the British were anxious to remove in advance as many potential hazards to the London talks as they could anticipate, the Cabinet Colonial Policy Committee authorised the high commissioner to announce publicly that the continuation of war would not stand in the way of advance to full self-government (380). The talks went ahead in the Kedah village of Baling at the end of December 1955. The Tunku was accompanied by Tan Cheng Lock and David Marshall (chief minister of Singapore) and had previously been instructed on communist negotiating techniques.[59] Tunku Abdul Rahman refused to discuss surrender terms; he simply insisted on surrender (391). For Chin Peng it proved an abortive attempt to re-enter open politics as leader of a lawful party; for the Tunku it completed his transfiguration from agitator to statesman.

The Tunku's firm handling of Chin Peng, together with the popular mandate he had won at the federal elections, persuaded the British to advance rapidly to *merdeka* (independence) and, if need be, to compromise their principle of multi-racialism in order to satisfy the politically dominant Malays. Indeed, when in January 1956 the Malayan delegation arrived in London for constitutional talks, Sir John Martin welcomed them with the promise of independence 'on a golden platter'.[60] It would appear, therefore, that the pace of decolonisation quickened and the nature of the successor state was modified in 1955–1957 as a result of both the improved security situation and also the growing reliability of the Alliance. There are, indeed, strong grounds for concluding that the Tunku got what he wanted at Lancaster House because he was trusted by the British as a conservative force and as an anglophile who would keep Malaya in the Commonwealth and the sterling area.

There is, on the other hand, compelling documentary evidence indicating that the

Tunku got what he wanted because the British feared what he might do if he were thwarted at the conference. Before the talks got underway, the Alliance was publicly committed to achieving independence by 31 August 1957. Moreover, Chin Peng's undertaking (made at Baling) to end hostilities 'as soon as the elected Government of the Federation obtain complete control of internal security and local armed forces'[61] put pressure on the Tunku to wrest responsibility for these matters as soon as he could. For two reasons therefore – to take the wind out of the sails of the MCP and to demonstrate his nationalist credentials – the Tunku could not afford defeat on either issue. The Alliance was also on record as demanding an independent, as opposed to a British, commission to draft the independence constitution. Were the talks to break down on any of these matters, but particularly over the issues of the date and responsibility for internal security, and were the Tunku to return to Malaya empty-handed, it was believed he might turn his back on a negotiated settlement and adopt the stance of a radical nationalist, possibly re-opening discussions with Chin Peng or probably launching a non-co-operation campaign. British officials in Kuala Lumpur and London convinced the secretary of state, and in turn he persuaded the Cabinet, that nothing should be done to antagonise the Alliance at the conference (387, 389, 390, 394, 399, 400). So it was that, in order to avoid a confrontation which might precipitate the wholesale resignation of Alliance ministers, the British government decided to depart from precedent set in the case of the Gold Coast and transfer control over internal security in advance of the achievement of 'full self-government'. The government also accepted the Malayan demands for independence by August 1957 and the appointment of a commission of Commonwealth jurists to draft the independence constitution (401, 404–406).[62]

The British side had gone into the conference fully aware 'from past experience and from the very nature of things alike' that in matters of constitutional change no line could be held for long, but they had expected, nonetheless, that the 'stage of full self-government would not be reached before 1959' (394, 399, 400). Moreover, their public protestations notwithstanding, Alliance leaders were reported to acknowledge in private that the target date of 31 August 1957 was not feasible. Both sides covered themselves against future accusations of insincerity, therefore, by resorting to the following form of words: 'self-government and independence within the Commonwealth should be proclaimed by August, 1957, if possible'.[63] However hedged about with qualifications, this date, once stated, became the target to which both sides worked. The mass of business to complete before that day included the following: drawing up the independence constitution and defining citizenship and nationality; negotiating the defence agreement; working out financial provisions; settling the peculiar problems of Penang and Malacca; reaching a decision on the question of appeals to the Judicial Committee of the Privy Council; reaching terms for expatriates, pushing ahead with Malayanisation and establishing the public services commission; selecting Malaya's head of state and designating Malayan governors for Penang and Malacca; submitting an application for Commonwealth membership; and preparing for independence celebrations. The pace of business was breathtaking. Nor was it without controversy, tension and dispute.

The constitutional commission was appointed jointly by the Queen and Malay rulers, and it reported to them. Chaired by Lord Reid and composed of nominees from the UK (Sir Ivor Jennings), Australia (Sir William McKell), India (Mr B Malik), and Pakistan (Mr Justice Abdul Hamid), it was charged to make recommendations for a federal constitution for Malaya as a parliamentary democracy with the following features: firstly, a strong central government; secondly, safeguards for the position and prestige of the rulers as constitutional monarchs of their respective States; thirdly, a head of state for the Federation to be chosen from among the rulers and to be called the Yang di-Pertuan Besar (later Yang di-Pertuan Agong); fourthly, a common nationality for the whole Federation; and, fifthly, guarantees for 'the special position of the Malays and the legitimate interests of other communities'. They took evidence in Malaya between late June and October; and they repaired to Rome to write up the Report which was published in February 1957 (423–430, 438, 439, 442, 443).[64]

The commission had to strike a number of balances between establishing a strong central government and guaranteeing state autonomy, between safeguards for the rulers and the provision of democratic institutions, between the special position of Malays and the interests of all. Particular tension built up over the question of nationality and citizenship even before the Reid Commission had arrived in the Federation (409, 411, 412), and, although of the 131 memoranda received in Malaya the commissioners inevitably followed that of the Alliance as closely as possible (426, 427, 429), the Alliance parties fell out with each other when the commission's report was published. Members of the commission themselves also disagreed on some issues and Mr Justice Abdul Hamid in the end could not be dissuaded from submitting a minority report (439). Its proceedings seemed to have been marred, and at times jeopardised, by insensitive chairmanship as well as the arrogant behaviour of Lord and Lady Reid (443).

Discussions on defence matters, including the role of British troops in Malaya after independence (413, 422, 437, 461, 464–466) and Britain's use of Malayan bases for regional security, revolved round negotiations for the Anglo–Malayan Defence Agreement. A working party, chaired by Sir Robert Scott (commissioner-general), composed of a British delegation (led by Sir Harold Parker, permanent secretary at the Ministry of Defence) and a Malayan delegation (with the Tunku at its head) and attended by observers from Australia and New Zealand, met in Kuala Lumpur between 16 April and 5 June 1956 (402, 407, 408, 410, 414, 417). Similarly, Lennox-Boyd later discussed the draft agreement with Commonwealth representatives in London (431, 432). Although broad agreement was reached on the need for such a treaty, the Alliance side was understandably fastidious about the implications of British bases for Malaya's sovereignty, and, in particular, the duration of the agreement and the terms of clause 6 setting out the conditions in which the two countries would come to each other's assistance. Although they sensed a neutralistic streak in Malayan attitudes – and, indeed, Malaya would stay clear of SEATO membership – the British did not doubt the Tunku's anglophilia which the Suez crisis did nothing to shake (433, 434). The location of talks shifted to London in mid-December when all but minor points were settled (441). The treaty was finalised before independence but, since it was to be an international agreement between sovereign states, it was not signed until 12 October 1957 (462).[65]

Another issue that was settled in the second round of talks in London (December 1956 – January 1957) was the extent of Britain's financial assistance to Malaya. Starting from the premise that 'political independence connoted financial self-sufficiency', the British argued that 'it would be incompatible with this doctrine for the United Kingdom to grant exchequer assistance towards the development programme of an independent country'. Nonetheless, in addition to the unspent balances remaining from allocations for the expansion of Malaya's armed forces and for colonial development and welfare, the British government agreed to give assistance towards the cost of the emergency (besides, of course, paying for the UK forces engaged in those operations) since it 'was a part of the struggle against Communism in which the whole of the free world was engaged' (440). The amount fell short of the sum desired by the Alliance, but the Colonial Office felt it was a generous grant, maintaining that the 'reason why Malayan requests were not met in full was not, as Tunku ingenuously said in Dublin, because "Britain is broke", but because Federation could not prove the need for more'.[66]

The final substantive issue to settle was Malaya's membership of the Commonwealth. Since 1951, when Dr D F Malan, prime minister of South Africa, had insisted that the admission of an independent territory to Commonwealth membership required the assent of existing members, British governments had been on their guard against South African attempts to sabotage the emergence of a multi-racial Commonwealth. In 1953 the Cabinet began to address the possibility of the Gold Coast's future membership and the following year discussed, but rejected, the creation of a two-tiered association of old (or 'first class') and new (or 'second class') members.[67] When J G Strijdom replaced Malan in November 1954, the attitude of the South African government hardened and the British expected trouble as the Gold Coast approached the goal of 'independence within the Commonwealth'. Since Strijdom accepted Ghana as a member with some reluctance,[68] CO and CRO officials anticipated his obduracy when Malayan membership came up for consideration. Although they conceded that Malayan membership was likely to be less provocative than that of Ghana, they took no chances and prepared careful arguments in anticipation of any objections Strijdom might raise (444, 445, 447). In the event, South Africa did not impede Malaya's advance to 'independence within the Commonwealth' to which all heads of government gave their assent at the Commonwealth prime ministers' meeting in July (457, 458).

Whereas, between 1945 and 1948 Dato Onn had repeatedly declared that Malays were *belum layak* (not yet ready) for independence, from 1954 onwards Tunku Abdul Rahman eagerly demanded *merdeka*. He did so for a number of reasons: one was the improving security position which permitted the revival of politics; another was the fact that he was under pressure from radicals within his own party to seek an early date for independence; a third was the need felt by UMNO members to win control of the country before the Chinese managed to add political strength to their existing economic dominance; a fourth was the example set by Ghana; and a fifth was the fact the British appeared willing to make concessions.

Indeed, the close collaboration between the British and Alliance and the contiguity of their essential interests, which are revealed by the documentary record, may suggest a number of conclusions about the reasons for, and the manner and timing of, the end of formal British rule in Malaya: that, for example, it was a stratagem to beat the communists or that it was the pursuit of imperialism by other means. Certainly, as Malaya slid down the slipway to be launched with éclat as an independent state within the Commonwealth, the air reverberated with congratulatory messages (467). As much by judgment as by luck, it seemed, a peaceful and mutually beneficial transfer of power was taking place, with Britain deftly shedding an empire to assume a new role in South-East Asia (421), while Malaya continued to provide her with essential raw materials, dollars for the sterling area, a base for regional defence and 'a symbol for British influence in the area' (454).

Yet, it would have been imprudent to declare the ship unsinkable. The Chinese were anxious about their future in a Malay-dominated state (451, 452), and in the British camp there was a last minute panic that their troops might be called in to keep the races apart on independence day (461, 464–466). Moreover, although the Tunku was at present 'firmly in the saddle', a medium-term forecast prepared in the office of the commissioner-general reckoned that, after the euphoria generated by *merdeka* (independence) had subsided, the problems of communism, communalism and economic development would crowd in on Britain's friends in Malaya. 'Time is thus not on the side of the Tunku' (454). Furthermore, what the record also reveals is that the Malayan Alliance was neither a British creature nor a British stooge. Initially the authorities mistrusted this marriage of convenience and placed little faith in its leaders. They feared it would institutionalise communalism and divide the country on Palestinian lines. Hoping instead for the emergence of a genuinely multi-racial movement, they were taken aback by the size of the Alliance's electoral majority in 1955. As independence approached they were not altogether confident about the future of Malaya under an Alliance regime.

Indeed, what the documents also show is that the British did not have it all their own way in the run-up to independence. Not only did the crisis over the Malayan Union and the outbreak of the communist insurrection knock them off course, but also the Alliance moved them further and faster than they would otherwise have gone in the period from 1954. At key moments the British and Alliance disagreed and the former made significant concessions to the latter over, for example, the following: the composition of the Federal Council, the response to the communists' peace initiative, the timing of independence, local responsibility for internal security, the appointment of the constitutional commission and the provisions of the defence agreement. Most significantly, Malaya became independent before three oft-stated preconditions were in place: firstly, the war against communist insurgents was not over; secondly, a genuine multi-racial movement and sense of nationhood had yet to be created; and, thirdly, fusion with Singapore and Britain's Borneo territories remained to be accomplished.

It is conceivable that the British might have stood their ground and slowed up Malaya's advance to independence. That they chose not to was, one can surmise from the documentary record, due to their pragmatic appreciation of the possible. Since 1945 it had been declared British policy to withdraw from Malaya sooner or later. By the mid-1950s it was clear that this moment would come sooner rather than later. Time was running out on colonial empires in South-East Asia. After July 1954 the British were, to all intents and purposes, the last European colonial power left in the region, and, after the federal elections a year later, the Alliance emerged as their obvious successor in Malaya. From this point onwards the British recognised the Alliance as their best bet. 'Any possible alternative to the present Alliance Government at present in sight would certainly be less well disposed to the United Kingdom' (454). Moreover, as they demonstrated by their willingness to meet Alliance demands at the London conference in January–February 1956, the British realised that any attempt to retard the pace of political change would only undermine the Alliance's credentials and encourage challenges to its leadership. In many respects the British were simply lucky in Malaya. At any rate by 1957 they had managed to lay the spectre of chaos and shabby scuttle that had dogged them since the humiliating retreat and defeat of 1941–1942. In contrast to their experiences in Burma and Palestine, it appeared that formal empire came to an end in Malaya with British interests, even their honour, intact. Not everyone, however, shared this bland assessment of end of empire in Malaya. Some felt that it took little account of the yet unfinished business of nation-building, while others, including the British prime minister himself, knew in their hearts that it amounted to putting a brave face on the management of British decline. Pleased though he professed to be with the final outcome, it is clear from his refusal to make a radio and television broadcast on the BBC to welcome the birth of independent Malaya that Macmillan was reluctant to 'celebrate what many people may think to be a weakening of the United Kingdom' (463).

*　　*　　*　　*

During the preparation of this volume I have incurred debts to many institutions and people. I wish to acknowledge constant assistance received from the staff of the Public Record Office, Kew, the generous support of Royal Holloway, University of London, and the stimulating guidance offered by members of the seminar on the Recent History of South East Asia, SOAS, and by fellow editors of BDEEP. I am particularly grateful to the following: Stephen Ashton, Barry Bloomfield, Anita Burdett, Joseph Fernando, John Gullick, Robert Holland, Ronald Hyam, Anthony Low, Albert Lau, David Murray, James Pullé, Andrew Porter, Anthony Short, Ralph Smith, Simon Smith, Anne Thurston and Nicholas White. Finally, I must thank Jane, Tom and Amy for their unflagging encouragement and patience.

A J Stockwell

Notes to Introduction

1   Letter of invitation to editor from Professor Michael Crowder, 25 June 1987.

2   CO 1030/691, minute by J Hennings, 22 Jan 1959.

3   *Ibid*, minute by D Gregory, 25 Sept 1959.

4   John Cloake, *Templer tiger of Malaya: the life of Field Marshal Sir Gerald Templer* (London, 1985).

5   See BDEEP series B, vol 1, Richard Rathbone, ed, *Ghana*, part I, Appendix, 'Draft report on disturbances in the Gold Coast, 1950'.

6   Harry Miller, *Menace in Malaya* (London, 1954) p 137.

7   Macmillan pinned this quotation from *The Gondoliers* on the door of the private secretaries' room at 10 Downing Street. Alistair Horne, *Macmillan 1957–1986* (London, 1989) p 13.

8   Nicholas Mansergh et al, eds, *Constitutional relations between Britain and India: the transfer of power 1942–7*: 12 vols (London, 1970–1983) and Hugh Tinker, ed, *Constitutional relations between Britain and Burma: the struggle for independence, 1944–1948*: 2 vols (London, 1983–1984).

9   *The Colonial Empire (1947–48)*, Cmd 7433 (HMSO, 1948) para 3.

10   Oliver Stanley, *H of C Debs*, vol 391, 13 July 1943, col 48.

11   *H of C Debs*, vol 463, 13 Apr 1949, col 2185; see also Attlee, *H of C Debs*, vol 473, 28 March 1950, cols 180–181.

12   CO 1022/81; *H of C Debs*, vol 494, 6 Dec 1951, cols 2617–2618; Lord Chandos (Oliver Lyttelton), *The memoirs of Lord Chandos* (London, 1962) p 364.

13   BDEEP series A, vol 2, R Hyam, ed, *The Labour government and the end of empire 1945–1951*, part III, 235.

14   CO 717/148/51534/3/1945–1946, minute by K Roberts-Wray, 11 Apr 1946.

15   CAB 134/1203, CA(O)(56)6, 6 Feb 1953, cited in A N Porter and A J Stockwell, *British imperial policy and decolonization, 1938–64* vol II *1951–64* (London, 1989) p 72.

16   CAB 128/29, CM 44(55)5, 1 Dec 1955, reproduced in BDEEP series A, vol 3, D Goldsworthy, ed, *The Conservative government and the end of empire 1951–1957*, part II, 197. As regards the application of this 'general rule' to South-East Asian territories, see CO 1030/98, GEN 174/203/01.

17   CAB 128/24, CC 47(52)3, 29 Apr 1952 and CC 49(52)2, 6 May 1952; CAB 129/51, C (52)142, 2 May 1952. See also CO 1022/45.

18   CAB 128/26/1, CC 4(53)7, 22 Jan 1953; CAB 129/59, C(53)52, C(53)75, C(53)96, C(53)98, Feb–Mar 1953. See also CO 1022/3–6.

19   For papers leading up to the prime minister's statement, see PREM 8/1406/1 & CO 537/4751.

20   *H of C Debs*, vol 420, 8 Mar 1946, cols 639–667, 701–706, 711–729.

21   CO 1022/61, J D Higham to J J Paskin, 20 Jan 1953.

22   R H Scott, Cabinet Far East Official Committee, 8 Jan 1952, CAB 134/897, FE 1(O)(52).

23   For example, on trade unions S S Awbery & F W Dalley, *Labour and Trade Union Organization in the Federation of Malaya and Singapore* (Kuala Lumpur, 1948); on police *Report of the Police Mission to Malaya* (Kuala Lumpur, 1950); on local government Harold Bedale, *Establishment Organisation and Supervision of Local Authorities in the Federation of Malaya* (Kuala Lumpur, 1953).

24   Chandos, *op cit*, p 382.

25   For published works on British policy and Malayan politics during this period, see the select bibliography in part three of this volume.

26   Sir Hugh Clifford, speech to the Federal Council, 16 Nov 1927, in J de V Allen, A J Stockwell and L R Wright, eds, *A collection of treaties and other documents affecting the states of Malaysia 1761–1963* vol II (London, Rome, New York, 1981) p 79.

27   CO 273/667/1, G E J Gent, 23 Sept 1941.

28   The following is a selection from the mass of published material on the failure of British naval strategy and the fall of Singapore 1942: W. David McIntyre, *The rise and fall of the Singapore naval base, 1919–1942* (London, 1979); James Neidpath, *The Singapore naval base and the defence of Britain's eastern empire, 1919–1941* (Oxford, 1981); Malcolm Murfett, *Fool-proof relations: the search for Anglo–American naval co-operation during the Chamberlain years, 1937–40* (Singapore, 1984); Arthur J Mardar, *Old friends, new enemies: the Royal Navy and the Imperial Japanese Navy, strategic illusions, 1936–41* (Oxford, 1981); Louis Allen, *Singapore 1941–1942* (London, 1977).

29   D A Low and J Lonsdale, 'Introduction: towards the new order, 1945–63', in D A Low & Alison Smith, eds, *History of East Africa*, vol II (Oxford, 1976) pp 12–16.

30   When drafts of the official history of the BMA were being checked in 1953, both Templer and Sir John Nicoll (governor, Singapore, 1952–1955) advised against publication lest it revive memories of an unsavoury period and sour current relations with local communities. Lloyd passed the request to Brook (Cabinet secretary) who replied that, since publication could not occur before the end of 1954, political objections might be less compelling by the time it appeared in print. In fact it came out even later than that: F S V Donnison, *British military administration in the Far East, 1943–46* (London, 1956). See 1022/468.

31   S R Ashton, 'The India Office and the Malayan Union: the problem of the Indian princes and its possible relevance for policy towards the Malay rulers, 1943–1946' in R B Smith and A J Stockwell, eds, *British policy and the transfer of power in Asia: documentary perspectives* (London, 1988) pp 136–138.

32   *Malayan Union and Singapore: Statement of Policy on Future Constitution*, Cmd 6724 (1945–46) contained a full description of policy and was published on 22 Jan 1946.

33   See, for example, W R Roff, *The origins of Malay nationalism* (New Haven & London, 1967).

34   The most comprehensive source for the early years of the party is the extensive collection of UMNO papers held at the Arkib Negara Malaysia (Malaysian National Archives).

35   *Constitutional Proposals for Malaya: Report of the Working Committee appointed by a Conference of His Excellency the Governor of the Malayan Union, Their Highnesses the Rulers of the Malay States and Representatives of the United Malays National Organisation, 19 December 1946* (Kuala Lumpur, 1946).

36   *Federation of Malaya: Summary of Revised Constitutional Proposals*, Cmd. 7171 (1947).

37   PUTERA and AMCJA, *The People's Constitutional Proposals for Malaya* (Kuala Lumpur, 1947).

38   *Far Eastern Economic Review*, 7 Dec 1989.

39   The emergency has an extensive bibliography. Contemporary analyses and first-hand accounts by participants and journalists include the following: Noel Barber, *The war of the running dogs: how Malaya defeated the communist guerrillas, 1948–60* (London, 1971); Richard Clutterbuck, *The long, long war: counterinsurgency in Malaya and Vietnam* (New York, 1966) and *Conflict and violence in Singapore and Malaysia 1945–1983* (Boulder, Colorado, 1985); Gene Z. Hanrahan, *The Communist Struggle in Malaya* (New York, 1954 & Kuala Lumpur, 1971); Harry Miller, *Menace in Malaya* (London, 1954); Edgar O'Balance, *Malaya; the communist insurgent war, 1948–60* (London, 1966); Lucian Pye, *Guerrilla communism in Malaya: its social and political meaning* (Princeton, 1956); J B Perry Robinson, *Transformation in Malaya* (London, 1956); Robert Thompson, *Defeating communist insurgency: experiences from Malaya and Vietnam* (London, 1966). Barber and Miller were journalists, Clutterbuck served in the army in Malaya and Singapore (1956–1958 and 1966–1968) and Thompson, who joined the MCS in 1938 and was a Chindit during the Burma campaign, stayed on in Malaya after independence as permanent secretary for defence, 1959–1961. For more recent analyses by historians and students of warfare, see the select bibliography in part three of this volume.

40   See M R Stenson, *Repression and revolt: the origins of the 1948 communist insurrection in Malaya and Singapore* (Ohio, 1969) and *Industrial conflict in Malaya: prelude to the communist revolt of 1948* (London, 1970).

41   State Department memorandum from Reed to Butterworth, 9 July 1948, National Archives, Washington DC, General Records of the Department of State, RG 59:846E.00/7-948.

42   See Anthony Short, *The communist insurrection in Malaya* (London, 1975) pp 77–90, Richard Stubbs, *Hearts and minds in guerrilla warfare: the Malayan emergency 1948–1960* (Singapore, 1989) pp 67–69, and the retrospective view of one CO official, R L Baxter, 8 Feb 1955, CO 1030/16.

43   F D Corfield concluded that the Kenyan government had been 'inhibited from taking action by a feeling that it would encounter the opposition of world opinion', *Historical Survey of the Origins and Growth of Mau Mau, May 1960*, Cmnd 1030, p 284. Likewise, the *Straits Times* journalist, Harry Miller, later recalled that had Gent 'acted too soon without evidence he would have been branded locally and throughout the world as an "imperialist" ogre'. *Menace in Malaya*, p 77.

44   *H of C Debs*, vol 453, 8 July 1948, cols 601–605, 610–611, 623–629, 698–700.

45   *Colonial Territories (1950–51)*, Cmd 8243 (May 1951) p 12.

46   General de Lattre de Tassigny arrived in Vietnam in Dec 1950 but died in early 1952; he was made a Marshal of France posthumously.

47   See Chandos, *Memoirs*, Miller, *Menace*, and Cloake, *Templer*.

48   On 7 Nov 1951 Lyttelton proposed to the prime minister a parliamentary statement on continuity in colonial policy which was designed to be particularly reassuring in West Africa. He made it a week later. See BDEEP series A, vol 3, D Goldsworthy, ed, *op cit*, part II, 173 & 174 and CO 537/6696.

49   See CO 1022/187.

50   Colonel Arthur Young (1907–1979) was commissioner, City of London Police, 1951–1971; he visited the Gold Coast to make recommendations on police re-organisation in 1951; served as commissioner of police in Malaya, 1952–1953, and Kenya, 1954; and was seconded as chief constable, Royal Ulster Constabulary, 1969–1970.

51   CO 1022/298, minute by Lyttelton, Sept 1952.

52   The agreement stated: '. . . whereas it is the desire of His Majesty and Their Highnesses that progress should be made towards eventual self-government and, as a first step to that end, His Majesty and Their Highnesses have agreed that, as soon as circumstances and local conditions will permit, legislation should be introduced for the election of members to the several legislatures to be established pursuant to this Agreement.' Allen, Stockwell and Wright, eds, *Treaties*, II, p 101.

53   Both Ismail bin Dato Abdul Rahman and Lee Hau Shik resigned from the Executive Council when the Alliance launched its boycott in May 1954.

54   Federation of Malaya, *Report of the Committee Appointed to Examine the Question of Elections to the Federal Legislative Council* (Kuala Lumpur, 1954).

55   For an account from the point of view of Tunku Abdul Rahman see Tunku Abdul Rahman Putra, *Looking Back* (Kuala Lumpur, 1977) pp 17–22 and Harry Miller, *Prince and premier* (London, 1959) pp 134–55.

56   Miller, *Prince and premier*, p 161; see also Tunku Abdul Rahman, *Looking back*, pp 23–30.

57   For example, CAB 129/68, C(54)155, 27 Apr 1954, record of two emergency meetings of ministers at 10 Downing Street, 25 Apr 1954, to consider US proposal for Anglo–American military intervention in Indo–China, reproduced in BDEEP series A, vol 3, D Goldsworthy, ed, *op cit*, part I, 61.

58   The Manila Treaty (or South-East Asia Collective Defence Treaty) was signed on 8 Sept 1954 by Australia, France, New Zealand, Pakistan, the Philippines, Thailand, the UK and the USA. It set up the South-East Asia Treaty Organisation (SEATO) with a Council and Secretariat in Bangkok. The Council met for the first time in Feb 1955.

59   For preparations for the talks, see CO 1030/27; for transcripts and reports of the talks held on 28–29 Dec 1955, see CO 1030/29–31; see also Tunku Abdul Rahman, *Looking back*, pp 5–13.

60   William Shaw, *Tun Razak: his life and times* (Kuala Lumpur, 1976) p 106; see also Miller, *Prince and premier*, p 197.

61   CO 1030/29.

62   See Great Britain, *Report by the Federation of Malaya Constitutional Conference*, Cmd 9174 (1956).

63   *Ibid*, para 75.

64   *Report of the Federation of Malaya Constitutional Commission 1957*, Colonial No 330 (1957).

65   *British and Foreign State Papers 1957–58*, vol 163, pp 49–53, also reprinted in Allen, Stockwell and Wright, eds, *Treaties*, II, pp 264–268.

66   CO 1030/683, telegram from CO to high commissioner, 16 Jan 1957.

67   BDEEP series A, vol 3, D Goldsworthy, ed, *op cit*, part II, 178–180, 186–188, 192, 193, 195, and BDEEP series B, vol 1, Richard Rathbone, *op cit*, part II, 139–144.

68   BDEEP series B, vol 1, Richard Rathbone, *op cit*, part II, 166, 229 & 234.

Summary of Documents: Part I

Chapter 1
Wartime planning, Mar 1942 – Aug 1945

Chapter 2
British Military Administration, Aug 1945 – Mar 1946

Chapter 3

Constitutional conflict: from Malayan Union to Federation, Apr 1946–Feb 1948

1   CO 875/14/9   18 Mar 1942

[Criticisms of colonial policy in the light of the Malayan campaign]: memorandum by N J B Sabine[1]

The time has come when it seems opportune to record briefly the origin and scope of the criticisms of Colonial policy which have arisen since the campaign in Malaya started: to examine the weight and validity of some of the less irresponsible and ill-informed of these criticisms: to attempt an appraisement of the effect they have had on public opinion: and to try to state (for what it is worth) the estimate of the character and achievements of our Colonial policy which has recently been made by public opinion; and what action seems to be expected by the public—or such sections of the public who have views to register or to express—from those charged with the responsibility for the conduct of Colonial affairs.

2. It will be agreed, I think, that these matters fall within my province as Public Relations Officer. I propose, however, in this note to go somewhat beyond that, and to put forward one or two suggestions, based on my experience both inside this office and outside it, which I hope may be considered. I am conscious that some or all of them may appear to be far-fetched and perhaps extravagant. I have tried to keep them practical, and I hope that, if it is thought that the leisure which I have enjoyed for the last few days—with its unusual opportunity for detached reflection—has proved altogether too stimulating, judgment will be tempered with indulgence. I hope also that the proposals will not be regarded in any way as sops to public opinion or window dressing. Nothing could be farther from my intentions.

3. *Public opinion on colonial policy*
I have a deep rooted belief that the creation of an interested, well-informed public opinion is vitally necessary to the successful solution of our Colonial problems. That is not to say that the public will ever lead the way: there will not be—and it would be much too much to expect—the necessary detailed and practical knowledge or the necessary freedom from other preoccupations. But I do believe that in attacking the problem, the Secretary of State and his officers—in England and overseas—would be greatly fortified in their task by understanding, sympathy, criticism of the right kind, and encouragement, all of which, I am convinced, the people of this country, with their unique qualities of humanity and common sense, could offer. I believe that now is the time to ask for it, and I will deal with this aspect later in this note.

4. *Recent publicity policy*
The first publicity measures with which I was concerned in the office were those taken when the White Paper on the new Colonial Development and Welfare Policy was published in February 1940. For this event, a somewhat complicated directive was prepared, which, on paper and with some necessary modifications, has served since as a model and a guide. This directive laid emphasis on the fact that it was both worthy of notice and of praise that in the midst of war we could take this practical and forward step to meet our Colonial responsibilities: but any charge of complacency was anticipated by a saving clause to the effect that we were only at the beginning of the problem, and that much remained to be done etc. A reference to the loyalty and support of the Colonial peoples, the financial soundness of the exchequer which

---

[1] Public relations officer, CO.

could support such a burden (a guarantee of "ultimate and inevitable victory however long and hard the road") and a somewhat (it must be confessed) smug comparison of our policy with some of the more revealing passages in "Mein Kampf " completed the picture.

5. The loyalty and support of the Colonial peoples had not then been tested so cruelly as they have been since, and "business as usual" had hardly begun to be discredited. So the press (and the public) were good enough to follow the directive almost as it stood: and there was in the press for a day or two a considerable and unwonted flood of material about Colonial affairs which subsided as quickly as it had arisen. In terms of inches of space in the press the campaign had been an unqualified success, and there is no doubt that, in spite of its short life, it did spread abroad the idea that we had embarked upon a new, progressive Colonial policy.

6. Since that time, however, the pace of the war has progressively quickened; its character has changed, the threat has come nearer and clearer, and our reactions too have changed accordingly. In practice, therefore, we have in our publicity policy concentrated on two aspects: the generous support which the Colonies have shown for the war effort in so many ways: and, complementary to that, what we have been able to do for them. There was nothing false or artificial about this treatment; although it did not and could not purport to give the whole of a very complicated picture. But it can be claimed, I think, that a good deal of it got across. Bitter complaints are often made—and with good reason—that children in schools think that Nairobi is in South Africa, describe Canada as a Colony, and have never heard of Uganda. But I fancy that a good many people in this country, of all ages and classes, know that Colonies have bought Spitfires and mobile canteens: and a fair number also know that we have bought Jamaica's bananas, and that we encourage trade unions in Colonies by appointing professional trades unionists from this country to posts abroad.

7. So it may be said that until the last month or so it was generally accepted that the Colonies were loyal and happy under our rule and helping us to the limit of their resources: that our policy was enlightened, humane, and reasonably progressive: and that our Colonial Service was, in the best traditions of our Services, worthy of approval and even pride. There was—rightly and justly—least questioning of the last assertion. On the first two, awkward questions about Bustamente and Uriah Butler, labour conditions in British Guiana, and strikes on the Copper Belt struck from time to time an occasional unharmonious note; and Fabians and others sometimes referred to the "Colour Bar" and suggested that the provision for Colonial Development should be £50 million a year instead of £5 million. But by and large these were merely ripples in the pool: there was little real public interest and therefore no widespread public curiosity. In such circumstances came the Malayan disaster.

8. *Malaya*

It must be said that everything possible—and it was a great deal—had been done to ensure that if Malaya went seriously wrong the press and the public should be raised to a pitch of record fury. Everyone had an ill-defined and ill-informed contempt for the Japanese as a fighting force, based on the long drawn out, still unresolved conflict with China, and no one could believe that she would go to war with America, ourselves, the Netherlands, and possibly Russia. They had been told of the defences of Singapore (described quite inaccurately as an impregnable fortress); and during the month of tension before December, they had been lulled into a sense of security by talk of reinforcements of men and equipment pouring into Singapore. No doubt there was good reason for all this but it is not easy to explain.

9. It did not get any easier, as with every day that passed, it was evident that things in Malaya were going very badly wrong. Added to that, public irritation was continuously and progressively aggravated by the complacencies of military spokesmen, difficulties of censorship, reports of internal quarrels and inefficiency—everything, in fact—that could have been devised by the most malignant fate, as the tragedy ran its course, true to its early form, from Khota Bahru to Fort Canning.

10. It is not always easy to foresee the reaction of the British people to any given event but it is always safe to say that they will react positively and energetically to adversity. It had proved the case during the days of Dunkirk, when nearly everybody could find some opportunity for strenuous service—in civil defence, in the factory, in the Home Guard: and it proved the case now—but with this difference, that there was very little anyone could do about it. So the energy found its outlet in furious, and not too well balanced or well informed criticism. The first target was in the C.-in-C. Far East:[2] then it appeared that not only had he been been relieved of his command, but that this step had in fact been taken before the campaign started. With a certain feeling of baffled rage, the press and the public looked for another scapegoat: and at this convenient juncture the Editor of the "Straits Times", a newspaper in Singapore, saw fit to make a violent attack on the alleged deficiencies of the Malayan Civil Service. This was telegraphed home and, since any attack on any Civil Service is a popular and well tried gambit, it was taken up: not very violently, however, and not with any great confidence, except by some of the more disreputable Sunday papers. It is pleasant to record that many papers kept clear of it, and that at least one not only took a strong line against ill-informed criticism, but even telegraphed in full at its own expense the text of an article and an excellent leader to the press in Malaya, Ceylon and parts of the West Indies.

11. In quite a short time the campaign had subsided, and the Malayan campaign fell once more into perspective as a first class military disaster.

12. During the earlier part of the controversy "The Times", apart from one or two casual and acid references to rubber planters, had kept aloof from it. But on February 18 it published an article from a correspondent in Batavia which analysed the causes of the fall of Malaya.[3] The article was written as all "Times" articles are, in a sober and moderate style and was accurate in certain, though not all, particulars. In general it ascribed the fall of Malaya to military factors but it contained one very significant phrase. It described the Government of Malaya as "having no roots in the life of the people of the country."

13. The effect of this article in this country and abroad was immediate and striking. By the use of this significant—and to many—damning phrase, it called into question the whole spirit and basis of our Colonial policy in a way that the previous, more personal and more limited attacks could never have done. It could not be countered by showing that in Malaya we were advisers, not rulers, or by questioning

---

[2] Air Chief Marshal Sir H R M Brooke-Popham, governor of Kenya, 1937–1939, had come out of retirement to be commander-in-chief, Far East, 1940–1941.
[3] None of the press articles cited in this memorandum has been printed here. *The Times* correspondent covering the Malayan campaign was Ian Morrison, author of *Malayan postscript* (London, Faber, 1942).

our moral right to invite peaceful Malays to fling themselves unarmed in front of the Japanese tanks to stem for a few minutes the advance on Singapore. It did in fact contain the substance of a reasoned and fundamental criticism which was instinctively recognised, appreciated and given weight, by public opinion.

It was of course taken up in the House of Commons, and several members read out extracts from the article. In his reply, the Lord Privy Seal in referring to these comments confined himself to a bare statement that there was a new Colonial Secretary and that he would no doubt review Colonial policy and administration.

14. The position has thus been created in which it is widely recognised that while our Colonial policy, reflecting as it does the virtues and defects of our whole political system, has achieved much that is good, a revision and review of our existing principles and administration is urgently called for. There has been a good deal of comment in the press and elsewhere but naturally enough, nothing tangible or definite has emerged. I would, however, invite particular attention to the articles attached to this note: (i) an article in the "Economist" of March 7 and (ii) two articles[4] by Miss Margery Perham in "The Times" of March 13 and 14, and a "Times" leader of the latter date. All these articles, while they contain statements and implications which can be seriously challenged, are written with considerable knowledge and care and contain constructive ideas: they are in effect, however (and are probably intended to be) designed to stimulate questioning rather than to supply any of the answers. And we are left with the situation I have described: in which recognition is given to our approach to the problem and to our considerable achievements, but in which has emerged an ill-defined feeling of malaise and a vague demand for urgent and dynamic remedial action. Is any such action called for? If so, what is it to be[?]

15. *Some general considerations*

It would be neither fitting nor profitable if I were to attempt in this note to generalize about the principles underlying our Colonial policy: but before putting forward certain specific suggestions I should like to refer briefly to two aspects of our administration which have in fact been in my mind for some time.

16. The first concerns the administration by the Colonial Office of the Colonial policy formulated by Parliament. On this, with the greatest diffidence, I would make the following comment: that a wholly disproportionate amount of time, thought and energy appears to me to be devoted to matters of routine as compared with that given to wider, fundamental issues ultimately affecting the personal wellbeing and happiness of millions of people. Thus, the annual estimates of Colony X, an application for funds for a hospital, proposals for new taxation, proposals to promote various officers will be examined with the greatest care. I do not for a moment put forward the suggestion that this is not essential (although I believe some of the matters which are the subject of decisions in the Colonial Office might be better left for decision locally): but I cannot help seeing at the same time that bigger questions, such as: Why is Colony X, with its accounts in good order, its constitution and public services working efficiently, in reality a most unhappy little state with no real harmony between Governors and governed, are not even asked, let alone answered. I am fully aware of the difficulty of raising these general questions and aware of the argument that they are matters for the Governor. One explanation may be that the

---

[4] Later reprinted in Margery Perham, *Colonial sequence, 1930–1949* (London, Methuen, 1967).

lack of statesmanship and vision which has characterised the conduct, on the highest plane, of our affairs for a good many years now has resulted in an imperfect and unrealistic definition of policies and principles, which makes it fruitless and of no avail to raise questions which, in the absence of a completely worked out policy, cannot in the nature of things be answered. I know that in certain spheres e.g. the economic sphere, the sphere of social services, the sphere of education, and in connexion with the organization of the Colonial Service, a great deal of wide and bold planning has been done and beneficial action has been taken. But even so, I cannot resist the conclusion, and I feel it my duty to state it, that for whatever reason it may be, routine matters receive an amount of attention disproportionate to that given to the consideration of larger issues.

17. The second concerns the basis of our relations with what we call "the Colonial people." There is in this country very little indication of any realization that the British Empire is very largely a coloured Empire and that this applies particularly to the Colonial Empire. The colour question has never been squarely faced by the public of this country, with all its implications for the future: and the result is the kind of question which is crystallised in the following passage from the second of Miss Perham's articles in "The Times".

> "Many an officer works and overworks with the utmost devotion for the group in his charge, while in their clubs and in European residential quarters, he and his wife may live wholly insulated from the real life of the people and the country. Why are the stimulating and friendly relations possible in this country between ourselves and coloured visitors and students almost wholly barred in some of our colonies? Is the answer, which has to do with official and racial prestige, sufficient to justify this numbing of personal relationships? No impossible alternative need be presented. Differences of race, colour, language and customs are barriers; backwardness is a dividing fact. But there is a level of education and of potential common interests upon which we are held back only by our prejudices from co-operation and friendship. Yet, without these, imperial rule cannot change into the working partnership which the coming age demands."

The attitude characterised in the passage is, I think, fairly general in the Colonies. It may be right or wrong; it is certainly in existing circumstances inevitable because it has its roots and origin in the attitude of the public in this country. The truth is that the public here has not been in fact educated into regarding coloured people as fellow human beings and potential fellow citizens in the fullest sense. I am aware that a great deal of careful thought has been given to this subject and that any process of eduction must be a long one. But although the establishment of a Welfare Department was a considerable advance, the subject has not been fully ventilated in public; and I consider that it is so closely bound up with fundamental issues in our Colonial policy that it should be brought more formally and explicitly to the notice of the public as an urgent, pressing and delicate problem, than it has been hitherto.

18. *Some suggestions*

Arising out of the matters discussed in this note, I would submit the following suggestions.

(1) That the question of making some pronouncement defining our Colonial

policy should be considered as a matter or urgency. At the present time, the position is perhaps necessarily not altogether clear. The stock definition of our Colonial policy which I state, subject to correction, is something on the following lines, "By means of education in its widest sense, to raise the standard of life of the Colonial people and to develop their resources so that in due course they may take an ever increasing share in the ordering of their own affairs." It may not be possible to go beyond a statement on these lines, but yet this statement leaves a number of questions and implications unanswered. It is at the same time sometimes assumed and stated in public, though not with any official backing, that we have promised full self-government to Colonies. This again begs all kinds of questions. The effect of a satisfactory pronouncement, if it could be produced, would be two-fold; it would produce useful and, I hope, fruitful discussion in this country; and it would, I am sure, have a good effect in many of the Colonies. It would be necessary, of course, to consult Governors on the terms of the pronouncement.

(2) I have referred above to an impression which I have, which may be right or wrong, that there is in general not enough time in the office to think about really fundamental issues. It has occurred to me that it might be possible to devise machinery in the form of a small working committee composed of a nucleus of members of the office with power to co-opt from time to time other persons outside the office who are interested and knowledgeable about Colonial affairs. I will not burden this note with any further suggestions about the composition of this committee, but I merely say that I would visualise a body which would in some sense correspond with the Hailey Committee,[5] except that it would be dealing with current problems instead of the problems of the future in so far as these can be separated. It would add greatly to the usefulness of this committee if individual members of it could at times find it possible to make short visits to Colonies which were the subject of any particular enquiry. It would be necessary to take Governors with us on this proposal also.

(3) The third proposal I would make arises from the experience I had recently of hearing a two day debate in the House of Commons at which Colonial questions were discussed with a lamentable lack of knowledge and appreciation of the issues which lay behind them. I wondered whether it would be possible for the Parliamentary Under Secretary to sound a few members of all parties and try to get them interested in Colonial matters. This would be quite informal and there would be no suggestion of creating a small caucus to defend the Colonial Office in the House of Commons. That would have to be made clear.

(4) I would recommend that immediate consideration be given to the publication of some statement about the colour question. Something has already been said by the late Secretary of State on this subject, but it has not been fully ventilated. I would visualise a short straightforward statement of our views on this important matter together with urgent action, in consultation with other Departments concerned, to try to remove some of the disabilities under which Colonial people at present find themselves in this country. I am fully aware of the difficulties attendant on both these courses of action but one thing can be done immediately as ground work and that is to keep up and expand as much as possible the practice

---

[5] The Colonial Research Committee, chaired by Lord Hailey, 1943–1948.

started by Mr. Hall when he was Under secretary here, of inviting Colonial visitors to this country and residents in this country to the Colonial Office as frequently as may be practicable.

(5) The last proposal is one which I find some difficulty in putting forward, since it concerns my own sphere. I am very far from satisfied with the progress that has been made to date both in projecting to people in the Colonies certain aspects of life in this country and in projecting the problem of the Colonies to the people of this country. I am aware that arrangements are in train to improve the position but there are one or two other matters which I should like to raise at a convenient opportunity.

19. I have tried to show in this minute that the members of the public are expecting some kind of reaction from the office to the recent comments and criticisms. I have tried to indicate for consideration some of the steps which might be taken, but it is clear to me that some action must be taken, whether it is positive, i.e. certain changes, or whether it is negative, i.e. a full statement about what is being done already, and the reasons why it is impracticable or unnecessary to make any change. The question of the publicity measures to be taken in either case is one which must, I think, wait until some decision has been reached.

20. There is only one further point which I should like to put. That is that while some of the measures I have advocated may seem to be a little remote from the war I feel strongly that if at least some of them could be taken and put across to the public together with some further statement of the problems involved in a robust and realistic way, and with an indication that we knew what we were doing, the result would be bracing and beneficial to the general war effort rather than the reverse.

2 CO 825/35/4, f 253   2 Apr 1942

'Question of the restoration of government in Malaya, Hong Kong, etc': minutes of the CO Committee on Post-war Problems (CPWP 35(42)2)

Mr. Jeffries[1] said that the Eastern Department assumed that these places would be re-occupied by military reconquest. In the first instance administration would be undertaken by the military, and persons were being designated to advise the military on civilian administration in that stage. The final reconstitution of civil government would raise many very complicated questions which would be the concern of several departments of the Colonial Office. It was accepted that the arrangements existing before the Japanese occupation would not be restored. We have to envisage a new deal. It was agreed that the Committee need not at present concern itself with this matter, but might assume that the Secretary of State would set up a special committee to deal with the subject, as was done in the case of Somaliland. If later a stage arrives at which the Committee on Post-war Problems can help, the subject will then or [?be] brought up.

---

[1] C J Jeffries, assistant under-secretary of state, CO, 1939–1947; joint deputy under-secretary of state, 1947–1956.

3   CO 825/35/4, no 15   12 June 1942

'Record of a discussion which the S of S had with Dr Van Mook,[1] Dutch
colonial minister at the Colonial Office on the 12th June': minute by
Lord Cranborne on post-war colonial restoration. *Minute* By G E J
Gent

M. Van Mook came to see me this morning. He told me that he had a particular point
which he wished to put to me, speaking not as a representative of his Government,
but personally. It related to the future of the Netherlands East Indies and its relation
to Holland. He felt that the present relationship could not be recreated after the war,
and he, and I gathered some of his colleagues, had in mind the possibility of some
kind of federation. There would be a Netherlands Government and a Government of
the Netherlands East Indies, which would have an equal status, and above them,
responsible for defence and foreign policy and matters of general interest, an
Imperial Government. He was anxious, if his Government agreed, to make some
announcement to this effect at an early date, for several reasons. First, he wanted to
give to the people of the Netherlands East Indies some attractive alternative to the
propaganda which was being daily pumped into them by the Japanese. And secondly,
he wanted to counter the vigorous propaganda which was going on in the United
States and in China to the effect that recent events had shown the Dutch—and the
British—not only to have been Imperialists but bungling Imperialists at that, whose
day was now over. He evidently thought that, taking a long view, the danger from the
United States and China was far greater than that from Japan. They would come to
the Peace Conference claiming to have won the war in the Pacific, and would demand
a say in the post-war set up over the whole of that area. He wanted to forestall their
interference, so far as the Netherlands East Indies were concerned. But he did not
want to cause embarrassment to Great Britain. He therefore came to ask, had we yet
formulated our post-war policy for Malaya?

I told him that, while we were of course considering all these matters, we had not
yet come to definite conclusions. Indeed, to do so pending a settlement of the
problem of security in the Pacific seemed to me to be difficult. To announce a
detailed programme of constitutional reform in our territories there seemed to me to
be premature pending a settlement with the Chinese and the Americans as to how
the status quo was to be maintained after the war. Moreover, he would know that our
position in Malaya was complicated by the fact that it rested in part on agreements
with local rulers, who were now unhappily in enemy hands. It would be difficult, if
not impossible, to make any announcement as to the future of their states except
after consultation with them. In general, of course, our colonial policy had always
aimed at gradually increasing the association of colonial peoples with the Government of their countries. I assumed that we should continue that policy in the future.
But whether the time had come for a general announcement to that effect I was not
so sure. At any rate, I would think over what he had said, and have a further talk with
him later.

---

[1] Dr H J van Mook was minister for colonies in the Dutch government in exile and lt-governor of the
provisional and post-war government of the Netherlands East Indies, 1942–1948.

Minute on 3

This is a most interesting expression of Dutch views and the Dutch apprehensions at (A)[2] are I think shared by many of us. I have had some conversations in recent days with Sir John Brenan[3] of the Foreign Office who is concerned with the prospective Pacific Relations Conference in the U.S.A.[4] and the need for formulating at least an outline of British post war policy in the Far East for the guidance of the British delegates at the Conference. Mr. Ashley Clarke, Head of the Far East Department of the Foreign Office has recently come back from America, where he has been impressed by the volume and nature of certain vocal American criticism of British Colonial Administration in the Far East. He has written a long, and in Sir John Brenan's view, interesting memorandum on his visit, and it is being printed and a copy of it will in due course come to us.[5]

But what seems to be lacking in the F.O. is any sign of robust reaction to American largely uninformed criticism on this matter such as the practical line the Dutch take in the Secretary of State's note about Mr. Van Moek [sic]. There is a kind of defeatism in the Foreign Office Far Eastern outlook which is not a new phenomenon. They suffer from what to my mind is a quite fatal lack of belief and confidence themselves in our position in the Colonies, and they seem to be fascinated by the belief that H.M.G. must be subservient to the supposed American policy of preventing the restoration of British sovereignty in Malaya, Hong Kong, and possibly Burma too. There are various side currents which tend to encourage the Foreign Office in their inclination to abase themselves before "American" opinion right or wrong e.g. the possibility of American forces themselves being in the position of liberators of Malaya and Hong Kong when the time comes: and also the predominant part which it is likely that American relief and reconstructive organizations will play in the Far Eastern sector. It is certain that the Foreign Office need stimulating in order that their phobia in these urgent practical questions of the formulation of post war policy in the Far East, including the restoration of British Authority in Malaya and Hong Kong, may be removed. I told Sir John Brenan, when I saw him yesterday, that it seems to me that it may be necessary for the Colonial Office to start the ball rolling by convening an interdepartmental meeting if it was impossible for the Foreign Office (whose function it ought to be) to do so, since any plans we make in the Colonial Office must envisage our restoration in Malaya and Hong Kong whatever changes might *thereafter* result from negotiations with China or other of our present allies.

G.E.J.G.
17.6.42

---

[2] ie the first paragraph of Cranborne's minute.

[3] Consul-general, Shanghai, 1929–1937; adviser on Chinese affairs at the FO since 1937.

[4] In fact the conference of the Institute of Pacific Relations was held at Mont Tremblant, Quebec, in Dec 1942.

[5] Gent commented on Ashley Clarke's report in his minute of 29 June, see 4.

4   CO 825/35/4, f 8   29 June 1942

[Post-war colonial restoration and US anti-imperialism]: minute by G E J Gent on forthcoming talks at the FO

[On the afternoon of 17 June, Cranborne and Eden spoke about the desirability of initiating discussions between the CO and FO on future policy towards Malaya and Hong Kong.]

I have arranged with Mr. MacDougall[1] that we shall have a talk with Mr. Ashley Clarke at the Foreign Office tomorrow evening. Mr. Ashley Clarke tells me that he is under instruction from Mr. Law[2] to compile a set of questions on policy of the sort which will contain all the chief points of criticism, particularly, with which he met in the United States, and also his ideas of the answers to them. He was proposing to do this first before having any consultation with the Colonial Office, but at my suggestion he agreed that it might be a good thing for us to have a talk first.

His report to Mr. Eden of June 11th on his visit to the United States shows him to have been very receptive of the contemporary tendency in the United States State Department, and the unofficial circles in America which correspond to our Chatham House,[3] to ascribe our military failure so far in the war against Japan to some inherent faults of "Imperialism" and selfish exploitation of the territories and peoples concerned. He credits "public opinion" in America with a feeling that it would feel itself cheated if the status quo in Hong Kong, Malaya, Burma, India, and the Netherlands East Indies were restored as a result of our victory in this war.

He touches upon the question of the United States access to the raw materials of Malaya and the Netherlands East Indies, and no doubt that is an economic interest of the United States which is responsible for a good deal of hopeful thinking in New York and Washington.

I think we should all agree with the conclusions he reaches in paragraphs 21 and 22, *viz.* that we should make more extensive and whole-hearted arrangements to make known in the United States the facts about our war effort and the facts about our efforts in our Far Eastern territories to promote the interests of the local people and the production of commodities to which the whole world had access. But there is a tendency throughout Mr. Ashley Clarke's report to put the whole problem and its answer in the terms of current American expressions of criticism and the policy by which we should be governed in order to secure American consent in a post-war settlement. He makes it clear that American opinion attaches importance to China as an equal Power with themselves (and presumably ourselves) in the future organisation in the Far East, but it seems that His Majesty's Government is to have regard to Chinese views only as reflected indirectly through America.

While it is, of course, politically necessary to take into account serious American opinion, we should not necessarily allow our policy to be formulated for us by that opinion. On the contrary, we should ourselves formulate it in direct relation to what

---

[1] D M MacDougall of the Hong Kong Civil Service was attached to the CO in 1942 and then to the embassy in Washington, 1942–1943.

[2] Richard Law, parliamentary under-secretary of state, FO, 1941–1943; minister of state, FO, 1943–1945.

[3] ie Royal Institute of International Affairs.

we ourselves believe to be in the best interests of China and ourselves, and what we believe would secure future friendly relations with China. When, on that basis, the framework of our policy is completed, we could then let the Americans know the lines on which we were working, and possibly make some minor adjustments to meet any needs of Anglo-United States collaboration after the war. Certainly in such matters as freedom of access to the raw materials of Malaya, or freedom of the port of Hong Kong, the Americans can have no serious grumble at our record, nor need they be apprehensive of our post-war policy.

Further, the future of Malaya and Hong Kong, and of course Burma, should be a matter primarily for consultation and decision by this country and the Dominions; even if Canada were specially responsive to American opinion that need not necessarily be so in the case of Australia and India. Mr. Ashley Clarke presents in his paragraph 18 a reported distinction between the breaking up of the British Commonwealth and the breaking up of the Colonial Empire. That is possibly a snare which the Foreign Office may be in particular danger of falling into, and it would be very desirable to make it clear at the first opportunity that the disposal of the Colonial Empire, particularly of the territories of such Empire importance as those in the Far East, could not be contemplated for a moment except in the fullest agreement with the Dominions and India.

As a quite provisional policy or programme it might be well for the Colonial Office view to be somewhat on the following lines.

1. We envisage the restoration of our sovereignty in both Hong Kong and the Straits Settlements and of our former Treaty relations with the Malay States.

2. As a matter of policy we should at some convenient moment (possibly when we make an approach to China in the matter of extra-territoriality) let the Chinese Government know that this is our intention, but that we should hope to discuss with them the lines of a closer liaison in both Colonies with Chinese Government representatives—possibly in Hong Kong taking the form of an Anglo-Chinese Council which would have a special influence in ocean and coastal trade with China through the port of Hong Kong. This would be an immediate post-war arrangement, and thereafter we could at leisure discuss and negotiate with the Chinese Government some longer term policy (even possibly involving the transfer of the sovereignty of Hong Kong to China).

3. When the chief structure of a policy on these lines had been thought out and settled, we should then bring into consultation, and hope to obtain the collaboration of, both the United States and the Dutch, but as regards British policy in respect of the British territories concerned, it should primarily be our own and not an American policy, and one in which our relations are direct with the Chinese, and not one in which we follow American guidance and permit ourselves to be unduly influenced by current American pressure, which is partly at least based on American business interests which are customarily hostile to us in the Far East.

4. A most important point underlying all our policy as affecting China and the Chinese shd. be that the Chinese must be able to see for themselves that British policy (a new, progressive, and generous policy towards China) is not one which is dictated by America, but is formulated by ourselves, and particularly that in any concessions which we make to China they shall be concessions freely given to China by ourselves, and not under American pressure.

5   CO 825/35/4, f 10   1 July 1942
[Postwar colonial restoration and US anti-imperialism]: minute by
G E J Gent on talks at the FO

Mr. MacDougall and I had a talk yesterday evening with Mr. Ashley Clarke, head of the Far Eastern Department of the Foreign Office, and Mr. Denning [sic][1], a member of the same Department, and Mr. Nevile Butler, who is head of the American Dept. The immediate need for the formulation of a basis of our policy in the Far East has arisen, Mr. Ashley Clarke explained, on account of the impending Pacific Relations Conference in the United States,[2] and the desirability of giving the British unofficial delegates to that Conference the necessary guidance.

I explained that our provisional feelings in the Colonial Office regarding the future of Hong Kong and Malaya were generally as set out in my minute of 29.6.,[3] and it was agreed by the Foreign Office representatives that it was an important point that we should not allow the Chinese to get the impression that our policy was dictated under pressure from the United States, and particularly that in any arrangements we contemplate for giving the Chinese in the future some more influential position in Hong Kong, we should so play our cards that the Chinese would not be left with the impression that for any such concessions it was the Americans to whom they were indebted and not ourselves.

Mr. MacDougall said that official Chinese Government opinion was that Hong Kong was British, and it was not for the Chinese to take the initiative in proposing any other status for the Colony when the Japanese had cleared out. Unofficially, however, in Chungking, there was plenty of speculation as to the future of Hong Kong and an irredentist attitude towards it. In the course of the discussion the following points were made on the Foreign Office side:—

(1) If Hong Kong were recovered from the Japanese by Chinese land forces and American sea forces, our claim for the restoration of British sovereignty might be a little difficult to sustain.

(2) If we were hoping that after the war international peace in the Far East should be maintained by the collective action of the United Nations, we might not feel that we had a very strong case for claiming that we should resume British sovereignty and administration in Hong Kong and the Straits Settlements.

(3) The Chinese, following their usual subtle course, are quite likely to incite American "anti-Imperialist" criticisms of the British position in Hong Kong and the Straits Settlements in order that we shall be intimidated into surrendering Hong Kong to China.

The Foreign Office attitude as expressed by Mr. Ashley Clarke at the end of the meeting was that "we must be prepared to give up non-essentials in order to maintain the really important things", and that he did not think that Hong Kong or even Malaya must necessarily be regarded as an essential. I said that I could see his point if it were simply a matter of pieces in the game of international politics, but that our attitude towards British territories—fully-going communities and concerns at the moment when our military weakness cut them off from us—must be a rather

---

[1] ie M E Dening.   [2] See 3, note 4.   [3] See 4.

different one, and that our policy must be based on what we believed to be right
rather than solely on what would be the best moves from the point of view of foreign
politics.

The Far East Department, Foreign Office, are now commissioned to supply Mr.
Law with their provisional notes and suggestions on H.M.G.'s Far Eastern policy, and
they have promised that we shall have a copy. At the same time they ask that we will
put down corresponding notes from our point of view on the matter of the future of
Hong Kong, Malaya, and Borneo, and let them have a copy so that both can be
considered by the Ministers.

This we are getting on with.[4]

---

[4] See 6.

6   CO 825/35/4, f 227   [July 1942]
'Note on future policy in the Far East': memorandum by G E J Gent
and D M MacDougall   [Extract]
Minute by Lord Cranborne

General points

1. Recognition of China as an equal Power in our conduct towards her.
2. Recognition of British rights and obligations in British and Protected Territories.
3. Recognition of Dominions' (particularly Australia and Canada) and India's
right to full consultation and association with the United Kingdom in any
modification of 2.
4. Recognition of the interest of the United Nations (particularly the United
States of America, China and Netherlands) in the post war order, and reconstruction,
and in the preservation of peace in the Far East.
5. Recognition of the economic and other declarations in the Atlantic Charter.

Particular points—Hong Kong, Malaya, Borneo[1]
. . .

7. *Malaya.* The Malay Peninsula comprises (1) the British territories of the
Straits Settlements, and (2) nine Malay States. In the Malay States the British
position is dependent on Treaties and Agreements with each of the Malay Rulers, who
are constitutionally independent Sovereigns. Owing to the development by foreign
capital (British, Chinese, American, etc.) of the valuable natural resources of the
States, it has fallen to the British to develop the local administrative systems and to
ensure law and order.

(a) *Straits Settlements.* The present majority of the population consists of
immigrant Chinese who come to Malaya to engage in business and professions, and
who maintain their links with China. The port of Singapore has flourished as a free
port visited by ships of all the nations engaged in Far Eastern trade. Its strategic and

---

[1] Only the section on Malaya is printed here.

commercial importance is obvious, and if the life and trade of the Malayan archipelago, as well as the ocean trade of the East, is to be promoted, the port of Singapore must be maintained under reliable and efficient control. The Netherlands, China, Australia, and India, besides the United Kingdom and other Powers, have all a direct interest in the services of Singapore as a port and mart, and the source of the raw materials of the Peninsula. Free access to these materials and to the services of the Port must be assured as the basis of British policy.

We should be agreeable, if that were favoured by the United Nations (including India), to the establishment of a Commission to control the port of Singapore which would comprise representatives of all the principal countries interested in the services of the Port. The British sovereignty of the Straits Settlements would remain unaffected.

(b) *Malay States.* Our policy has been to maintain the sovereignty of the Malay Rulers, and to make it continually more real in those States where it had tended to become overlaid by our own direct Administration under the pressure of economic development (e.g. the decentralisation policy in the Federated Malay States). Our declared policy has also been to promote the well being and efficiency of the Malay peoples and their educational fitness to fill the official Services in their own territories.

The continual and legitimate fear of the Malays has been that they would be swamped by the more efficient and numerous Chinese and to a lesser extent the Indians. Chinese immigration has been controlled for this reason and limited to the economic capacity of the tin and rubber industries.

These policies are in the interests of the people of the country and should be maintained for their paramount advantage. But in order to show our own good faith it might be considered whether, on our resumption of authority in Malaya, we should not propose that the Malay Rulers be invited to negotiate with ourselves and the United Nations new Treaties which would in form be multilateral agreements to which each Ruler and each of the United Nations would be parties and contain clauses

(1) declaratory of the above principles,
(2) assuring most favoured nation treatment to all non-Malays in the matters of access to raw materials, tariffs and residence,
(3) accepting resident British Officers in each Malay State to advise the Malay Administrations (Great Britain being the Power with whom they are accustomed to deal in practice and the Power with the modern experience and resources most needed to ensure the practical purposes of the economic clauses in the Treaty).
(4) Providing for periodical meetings of the Treaty Signatories to review developments and to agree upon any new proposals. . . .

Minute on 6

I have read Mr. Gent's and Mr. MacDougall's note on Far Eastern Policy, and should like to have a discussion on it. It contains most interesting and far reaching proposals. But I must confess I do not feel altogether happy about them. They involve considerable concessions by us, without any *quid pro quo* by the other Pacific Powers. This will only be regarded by China and the United States as a confession of failure on our part, without any reflection on them, whereas it is in fact the United States who have above all brought about the present situation in the Far East by their refusal to shoulder their responsibilities and co-operate with other nations in restraining Japan in the years before this war. Moreover, were we to accept such a post-war settlement as this in respect of our Far Eastern territories, it would be difficult, if not impossible, for the Dutch to refuse to do the same, and they would certainly, from what Dr. Van Mook said to me,[2] regard us as having let them down, if not actually betrayed them.

It seems to me that what we have first to decide is where, if anywhere, we have failed. Is it in the administration of our territories or merely in their defence? It may well be said that our administration has not been perfect, that it was too rigid, that it did not show itself capable of adapting itself to the conditions of war, that it was too much concerned with material improvements and too little inspired by a high spiritual outlook, and so on. But, taken by and large, our record of administration is not one of which we need be ashamed. We created Singapore and Hong Kong, two of the greatest ports in the Pacific, out of nothing. We made of Malaya one of the richest and most vital producing areas of the world. We brought to her peoples law and order, happiness and prosperity. These are no mean achievements. Where we did fail was in giving them protection from Japan, and this criticism may equally be levelled against the Dutch and the Americans. I suggest that, in considering the future of the Far East, it is on this defence aspect that the Allied Powers—and the Institute of Pacific Relations—should concentrate. The Allied Pacific nations must aim at building up in the Pacific an effective system of mutual defence. This will no doubt involve considerable concessions by all concerned. There may have to be international ports, where all members of the peace system will have equal rights. As a consequence, those ports may well have to be managed, both as to their defence and administration, by international bodies. We should, I feel, be prepared to agree to Singapore and Hong Kong coming under such a regime. But it must be on a basis of reciprocity. Concessions which we make at Singapore and Hong Kong, the Americans should also make at Manila and Honolulu, the Dutch in their ports, and the Chinese at certain selected places.

Hong Kong, no doubt, is in a slightly different category from Malaya and our other Pacific territories. It forms almost part of the mainland of China. It may be that we may have to agree to a resumption of Chinese sovereignty there. But this should surely form part of the general deal, and be conceded in return for facilities given to us and other Pacific nations in treaty ports in China. I agree strongly with Sir G Gater that we should not decide now to lower our flag there after the war. To put it on no higher plane, that would be to surrender one of our main bargaining counters before the negotiation begins.

Nor do I much like the idea of multilateral agreements between the local Rulers in Malaya and the United Nations. The Malayan States will never be strong enough to stand on their own feet in the modern world. They must come in to some great power's sphere of influence. If they have treaties with several nations, they will only play off one against another and become a source of friction. We are the obvious people to keep an eye on them. It may well be, of course, that the Chinese and Americans, and possibly the Australians, will want some international cartel to

---

[2] See 3.

control and supervise the production of Malayan rubber and tin, and that we may think it wise to agree to this. But we should, I feel, maintain political control of these areas.

In conclusion, I think it is most important that we should not allow ourselves to be manoeuvred into the position of having been alone responsible for what has happened in the Far East. In fact, I feel that the responsibility of the United States is far heavier than ours. If they had been willing to collaborate with the League of Nations in the early days of the China incident, all that has happened since might, and probably would, have been averted. In fact, they hung back not only till it was too late to save the situation, but until they were actually attacked. By all means, let us shoulder our share of the blame. But do not let us shoulder theirs too.

C.
14.7.42

7   CO 825/35/4, no 46   20 Aug 1942
'British post-war policy in the Far East': minute by G E J Gent of a meeting between Lord Cranborne and Mr Law on 19 Aug

The Secretary of State had a visit from Mr. Law, Parliamentary Under-Secretary, Foreign Office, and two Foreign Office officials, yesterday, in which Sir G. Gater and I took part. Mr. Law is very shortly going to America and he felt that he should as far as possible equip himself with ideas to cope with the current American criticism of our Colonial administration and their vague ideas about a post-war organisation in the Far East.

The discussion covered a good deal of ground, and the following points were made:—

(1) Convincing answers to American criticisms require a conviction in England that our record was, in general, a good and progressive one, and a conviction that the Empire was not a thing to be ashamed of, and that the British people had a useful mission to continue in the Colonies; in short, that we must first show confidence in ourselves before we could expect to remove the lack of confidence in us which others are expressing. This is a matter for propaganda to be organised by the Ministry of Information in association with the Colonial Office.

(2) That Colonial peoples were not possessions to be bartered round the peace table but that we had continuing obligations which we must be prepared to fulfil. Our record in the Eastern Colonies was a good one. Our only principal failure being our failure to defend them against Japan.

(3) Similar failures took place by the Americans in the Philippines, by the Dutch in the Netherlands East Indies, by France in Indo-China—and not only by the colonial powers, but also by independent states like Siam. Having regard to our operational commitments against Germany and Italy at the time of the Japanese assault the major blame for the failure of the United Nations to resist the enemy in the Pacific could not be said to lie at our doors.

The Secretary of State referred to the memorandum and letter which he was on the point of sending to the Secretary for Foreign Affairs and which contains specific, though provisional, proposals for our policy in respect of British territories in the Far East. /

It was agreed that Hong Kong was a special case, and that any matter about our sovereignty there was primarily one for negotiation between ourselves and China. The memorandum explained that the maintenance of British sovereignty was not indispensable to us in Hong Kong, and that we should be prepared, at a suitable time, to discuss the whole position with China, not even excepting the question of sovereignty. As regards Malaya, the memorandum set out the political make-up of the Peninsula and our treaty obligations to the rulers of the nine Malay States. Reference was made to a telegram received in the Foreign Office which purported to represent the personal views of President Roosevelt, in which he appeared to assume that it was impossible for the British to return to their old position in Malaya. It was thought likely that the President, like other distinguished Americans, had only a very vague understanding of the Malayan position, and we certainly should not concede the assumption that the restoration of our sovereign position in the Colony and our Protecting position in the Malay States was impossible. It was a matter for ourselves to decide what, if any, new grouping or constitutional arrangements in Malaya (and possibly in Borneo too) would best suit new conditions.

The Secretary of State's conclusions were on the following lines:—

(1) That a propaganda campaign in this country was needed to convince ourselves that we had no need to be ashamed of our record in Colonial administration, and that we had continuing obligations towards our territories in the East which we should not only be resolute in carrying on but which also we were well fitted to carry on from our experience and qualities.

(2) This should be the basis of our attitude towards American and other foreign critics, and we should studiously avoid standing in a white sheet over an alleged failure in the East in Colonial administration or in a progressive policy towards the local peoples.

Our only substantial failure was the failure to protect our territories, which was a matter not lying at our doors alone, but one which was shared, possibly to a major extent, by other sovereign powers in the Far East and particularly by the Americans.

(3) Post-war conditions after the victory of the United Nations would call first and foremost for association in achieving security to prevent another disastrous armed conflict, and this association in security should be the basis and essential justification of the United Nations' policy in the Far East and of any contributions—political or economic—which we and others would be able to make.

(4) With this basis of mutual defence obligations we should contemplate the institution of some sort of regional council of the United Nations concerned with the Pacific area.

(5) The British Government as the authority in Malaya, the Dutch in the Netherlands Indies, and similarly the effective authorities in the Philippines, and those in other territories of the Pacific area constituting the United Nations would be in constitutional and administrative control in their own several territories.

(6) Hong Kong was a subject for special consideration, and, as explained above, was a territory in which the maintenance of our sovereignty need not in the new

conditions be regarded as a cardinal point of British policy. If there were advantages to us as well as general advantages in a post-war settlement, its sovereignty should revert to China. We must, however, be ourselves the judges of our action *vis-à-vis* China in respect of Hong Kong, and we should avoid being placed in a position of acting, or appearing to act, under the pressure of American criticism in any discussions we had on the matter with the Chinese Government.

(7) The British delegates at the International Pacific Relations Conference were looking to H.M.G. for some guidance on questions of British policy in the Far East, and it was, therefore, desirable for the interested Departments here to get together to advise Ministers on the policy to be adopted. Lord Hailey, as leader of the British delegation, could be confidentially informed of H.M.G.'s policy on particular points.

(8) Our publicity line should be that the British, Dutch, Americans, etc. have remarkably fine records of progressive and enlightened administration in their Eastern territories—we *all* fell down over the question of defence, and that is the primary matter to be remedied. We can all contribute to the establishment of greater strength and cohesion to prevent another successful aggression, and in common with our allies we shall be ready to play our part.

8   CO 825/35/4, no 52   [Aug 1942]
'A post-war settlement in the Far East: need for a definite policy': joint CO-FO memorandum   [Extract]

At latest when victory has been won and probably before that we shall be called upon to declare our aims in the Pacific area (including Australasia and the Far East generally). But we cannot leave the working out of those aims until then and there are in fact several reasons why it is becoming increasingly urgent to undertake this task now.

2. The first of these reasons is the widespread and constant speculation on the subject in the United States which has been stimulated by speeches by the Vice-President,[1] Mr. Hull,[2] Mr. Sumner Welles,[3] and other high officials of the Administration. These utterances, although (perhaps fortunately) lacking in precise proposals have abounded in general statements concerning the post-war world the effect of which may be to make opinion crystallise in forms which we should not desire. Another is the fact that in December next an unofficial international conference is being held in the United States to discuss the problems of the Pacific area. At this conference one of the subjects which will arouse most interest will be the future of the territories of South-East Asia and it will be necessary for the British delegation (representing Chatham House) to express their views.

Forthcoming I.P.R. conferences
3. The Conference presents a danger and an opportunity. The danger is that if not adequately prepared and enabled to strike out on a positive line of their own the

---

[1] Henry A Wallace, vice president of the USA, 1941–1945. [2] Cordell Hull, US secretary of state, 1933–1944.
[3] Sumner Welles, US under-secretary of state, 1937–1941.

British delegation will be forced on to the defensive by American and Chinese attacks on the right of Great Britain to maintain her position in the Far East. That we should be put by our allies in such a situation (even unofficially) in time of war may be highly deplorable, but it is an eventuality which must be faced. The trend of the speeches and press speculation in the United States referred to above may be summed up in Mr. Welles' phrase "the age of imperialism is dead" and in the observation of the well-known writer on Far Eastern affairs, Mr. W.H. Chamberlain, that "It would be futile and stupid to pledge great numbers of American lives for such an objective as the integral restoration of British and Dutch imperial rule". These utterances give an idea of the line which is likely to be taken by some members at least of the American and indeed Chinese delegations and it can only be met effectively by showing not only the benefits which have been conferred by British rule in the past but by indicating, however summarily, that British participation in the management of the affairs of Asia is essential to its stability and welfare in the future and the lines on which we shall contribute to these objects.

4.   In this respect the Conference offers an opportunity. British policy in the Far East, notably towards China, and the British genius for colonial administration have lately fallen into disrepute on account largely of the military and naval weakness which permitted our humiliation in China (e.g. at Tientsin) and (after the outbreak of war with Japan) of our military and naval disasters at Hong Kong, in Malaya and in Burma. The unexpected magnitude of these latter have blotted out not only our long record of positive and beneficent achievement in the Far East but even the extent to which British naval and military preponderance prior to the Washington treaties of 1922 was responsible for the stability and peace of Australasia as a whole: although there are signs of an increasing realisation in America that the débâcle at Pearl Harbour was largely responsible for our disasters and that the ordeal under which we failed was one to which we ought not to have been exposed. The Conference offers the opportunity to make known to a wide public our record, which is an outstanding one. No one will deny that the creation of the British Commonwealth of Nations is a political achievement of the first order: our record of achievement in the Colonies is less well-known.

Need for a campaign of education

5.   But this is not enough. Our territories in the Far East and the work we have done there entitle us to a leading part in the post-war settlement in the Far East but we cannot convince others of this unless we can put forward with conviction constructive ideas for the future. At present there is in this country not only no unanimity as to our objectives in the Far East, even among those who are actively studying these problems, but there is a great degree of ignorance and a serious atrophy of our power to "think imperially". An essential basis for establishing our leadership depends therefore on promoting new awareness at home of the problems involved and on arousing the nation to a sense of having a mission to continue and fulfil in the world at large, particularly in our colonial Empire. However true it may be that this Empire grew almost unconsciously out of our instinct to trade with the world and to give our trade the protection of our flag, we had at least during the 19th century a sense of responsibility for furthering the interests of those parts of the world over which we had established our control. That sense of responsibility has not altogether been lost but it is no longer nation-wide and it has lost its purposefulness.

This is what we have to regain, since this is what gave us a preponderating voice in the counsels of nations. Once we have convinced ourselves afresh of our civilising mission in the world and of our determination and ability to rule in pursuance of that mission we should have little difficulty in convincing others.

6. It is not the purpose of this paper to examine how this campaign should be launched and sustained: but one way is clearly for Ministers to cover some of the ground in their speeches in this country. It is not necessary that we should here and now make detailed public proposals: but it is necessary that we should know our own minds and be able to indicate in public the general principles on which we propose to work.

General principles of a post-war settlement

7. To work out a detailed policy at the present stage is impossible. That will necessarily be conditioned by the future course of the war and the state of affairs prevailing at the end of the war. The suggestions as to the future of particular territories made below are to be regarded as the barest outlines and highly tentative. We may however postulate that on the victorious conclusion of the war against Japan the reconstruction plans of the United Nations will be based on:—

(a) the general interest which all would have in keeping Japan within bounds and assuring the collective defence of the whole area;

(b) the economic and commercial interest which all would have in access to raw materials, markets and ocean ports and in opportunities for investment and development;

(c) conformity with the general principles of the Atlantic Charter where applicable and of Article VII of the Anglo-American Mutual Aid Agreement.

8. Accordingly our own plans should fall demonstrably within these limits. It should in particular be noted that any policy for which we require the support of the United States Government and therefore of American public opinion should if possible be based on broad principles. The key to obtaining American support may also be found in our attitude towards China. An orderly and unified China is in any case a necessary requirement for the maintenance of stability in the Far East and, up to a point, a guarantee against the resurgence of a menacing Japan. Commercially too we have everything to gain by earning China's goodwill. If we can show the Americans that we are dealing liberally with their friend China, we may hope to find it easier to enlist American support in applying to China the implications of Mr. Welles's dictum that "the age of imperialism is dead" if and when Chinese aspirations go beyond what is legitimate and in directions dangerous or inconvenient to ourselves. In formulating our plans for the future therefore there must throughout be a double process, namely, first that of laying down what we consider to be desirable and practicable, and secondly the translation of such plans into terms of principles acceptable to all.

9. The first and in many ways the most crucial problem for us is our future relationship to our Far Eastern territories. A number of different possibilities are being canvassed at the present time. At one end of the scale is the notion that these territories should be "liberated" on the model of the undertakings given by the United States to the Philippines: at the other is the notion that they should return to British sovereignty on exactly the same basis as before. In considering the feasibility

or desirability of either of these courses or of any lying in between, it is well to consider what is essential to us and to the populations of the territories themselves in terms of defence, economic development and administration.

Essential British requirements

10. From the economic point of view, the things which it is essential for us to preserve in our colonies are precisely those things which are mentioned in (b) in paragraph 7 above, namely access to raw materials, markets for our manufactures, access to ocean ports and opportunities for investment and development. From the defence point of view it is essential that we should not find ourselves again in the position which we have been in during the last decade, namely of being responsible for the defence of vast territories with totally inadequate forces and no certainty of outside help. It is therefore necessary that there should be a system of collective defence in which we shall participate but in which above all we should be able to count on the United States also participating. From the administrative point of view it is essential that we should resume the fullest measure of internal responsibility and that we should not be called upon to share such responsibility with one or more outside Powers (i.e. no condominiums). Subject to these essential requirements, it should be possible for us to offer to cooperate with other similarly placed Powers by adjusting the resumption of our sovereign rights in the British territories in the Far East so far as may be necessary to meet the requirements of collective defence and economic development, and indeed to treat our administration of those territories as a trusteeship in the interests of their populations. It may be supposed that some form of United Nations Council for the Pacific would be established to which those countries responsible for dependent territories would be answerable. It would of course be understood that our acceptance of any obligations of this nature would be dependent on the acceptance of similar obligations on the part of the other Powers concerned.

International supervisory councils

11. In considering the nature and degree of such an international supervision it cannot be too strongly emphasised that a primary objective must be the encouragement of the maximum cooperation of the United States in post-war arrangements in the Far East. The danger for the peace of that area and of the world is indeed likely to arise less from an excessive interference in the affairs of other nations on the part of the United States than from a reversion by the latter to isolationism, leaving the same problem for the United Nations as the United States left for the Allies in 1919. This, even more than the material contribution to victory in the Pacific which the United States are likely to make, is the compelling reason for taking due account in our plans of American thought on this subject.

12. We are not yet informed as to the exact lines of American official thought and it will probably be well, before committing ourselves in public, to probe this matter. But we have good indications that United States Administrations, whether Democrat or Republican, will favour a general world responsibility for the maintenance of peace on the part of the four Powers, the United States, Great Britain, Russia and China, acting in some sense with the sanction of the United Nations as a whole. The implications of any such Four-Power plan are being examined in another paper but we may probably take it for granted that any arrangements made for the future

settlement of the Far East will include some such Council as suggested in paragraph 10, on which these Powers will be represented. It is possible that in particular parts of the world the form and membership of the Council will vary and it may be expedient in the Far East, for example, for certain purposes to co-opt representatives of Australia and New Zealand and of the Netherlands. The extent of the powers of the Council would doubtless also vary in relation to different territories.

13.   While the foregoing is as yet indefinite, it must serve as a rough and ready background for the examination of our future relations with the various territories of the Far East which we may now proceed to do in greater detail. . . .[4]

Malaya, North Borneo and other British territories in the South Seas

25.   These will perhaps provide the most contentious issues at the eventual peace conference. While we may readily assume that our resumption of control is the obvious and only reasonable arrangement, it is desirable to examine the grounds on which our right to it can be presented to other governments and to public opinion (including certain sections of public opinion in this country). In particular what is the bearing on this problem of the third article of the Atlantic Charter?[+]

26.   It is proposed here only to suggest in very general outline how this problem might be approached, *viz.*

(a) it is our intention to foster self-government in accordance with the spirit of Article 3 of the Atlantic Charter but it is evident that the attainment of complete self-government involves a degree of responsibility to which some peoples have not yet attained.

(b) it is our intention to promote and accelerate the processes by which the inhabitants of such territories under our charge attain to this degree of responsibility.

(c) we have long-standing obligations by treaty and otherwise towards the inhabitants of these territories which it is our intention to discharge;

(d) in accordance with article 6 of the Atlantic Charter* we are bound to assure freedom from fear and freedom from want to those territories which are not in a position to provide them for themselves;

(e) freedom from fear should be provided by a system of collective defence in which we are ready to bear our full share;

(f) the most rapid and the surest way of achieving freedom from want is to leave the task to those who have successfully carried it out in the past and who have in addition long experience of local administrative problems;

(g) meantime, while resuming full administrative responsibility (it is better to

[+] Third, they respect the right of all peoples to choose the form of government under which they will live; and they wish to see sovereign rights and self-government restored to those who have been forcibly deprived of them. (N.B. Although the U.S. have expressly admitted the applicability of the Atlantic Charter to the Far East, we have not.)

* Sixth, after the final destruction of Nazi tyranny, they hope to see established a peace which will afford to all nations the means of dwelling in safety within their own boundaries, and which will afford assurance that all the men in all the lands may live out their lives in freedom from fear and want.

---

[4] Paras 14–24 on China omitted.

avoid the word "sovereignty") for these territories, we are ready to co-operate with the other Powers concerned in the creation of a regional council of the Pacific, or for any particular areas bordering on the Pacific, on which the principal United Nations would collaborate in measures for the advantage of all. In other words, all the Powers exercising administrative responsibility within any given area should declare their willingness to treat their administration as a trusteeship, under the supervision of a suitable international body in respect of certain matters to be defined.

27.   It is suggested that these principles should form the basis for the resumption of control over other territories by the Dominions (the mandated territories), the United States (the Philippines), China (Formosa) and (with modifications) for the assumption of control over new territory on the part e.g. of the United States (over the Japanese mandated islands).

28.   It should be noted that a system of collective defence may render necessary special measures of cooperation at certain strategic points, e.g. the Kra Isthmus, Singapore, Corregidor, Chilung (Formosa). This will be especially so if an "international police force" is created as proposed by Mr. Sumner Welles. From our own point of view such special measures are desirable in that these strategic points will form a concrete and perpetual reminder of the joint responsibility of all the Powers concerned in the preservation of peace and stability in the whole area. It may reasonably be held that such security measures do not constitute a derogation from the Atlantic Charter, since they do not amount to "aggrandisement, territorial or other".

Malaya

29.   The Malay Peninsula comprises (1) the British territories of the Straits Settlements, and (2) nine Malay States. In the Malay States the British position is dependent on treaties and agreements with each of the Malay Rulers, who are constitutionally independent Sovereigns. Owing to the development by foreign capital (British, Chinese, Americans, etc.) of the valuable natural resources of the States, it has fallen to the British to develop the local administrative systems, to build up the social services, and to ensure law and order.

30.   (a) *Straits Settlements*. The present majority of the population consists of immigrant Chinese who come to Malaya to engage in business and professions, and who maintain their links with China. The port of Singapore has flourished as a free port visited by ships of all the nations engaged in Far Eastern trade. Its strategic and commercial importance is obvious, and if the life and trade of the Malayan archipelago, as well as the ocean trade of the East, is to be promoted, the port of Singapore must be maintained under reliable and efficient control. The Netherlands, China, Australia and India, besides the United Kingdom and other Powers, have all a direct interest in the services of Singapore as a port and mart, and the source of the raw materials of the Peninsula. Free access to these materials and to the services of the Port must be assured as the basis of British policy. But the same must be true of the products and ports in the territories of other powers in the Far East. Concessions which we make must not be unilateral.

31.   (b) *Malay States*. Our policy has been to maintain the sovereignty of the Malay Rulers, and to make it continually more real in those States where it had

tended to become overlaid by our own direct Administration under the pressure of economic development (e.g. the decentralisation policy in the Federated Malay States). Our declared policy has also been to promote the well being and efficiency of the Malay peoples and their educational fitness to fill the official Services in their own territories. The continual and legitimate fear of the Malaya [Malays] has been that they would be swamped by the more efficient and numerous Chinese and to a lesser extent the Indians. Chinese immigration has been controlled for this reason and limited to the economic capacity of the tin and rubber industries. These policies are in the interests of the people of the country and should be maintained for their paramount advantage.

32.   It may be necessary after the war to take steps to achieve some form of closer union of the Malay States (probably not only with each other but involving the Straits Settlements also) with a view to ensuring a common policy in matters of concern to Malaya generally, and indeed to other countries which have interests in Malaya. It is probable that the views of the State authorities in such negotiations will be coloured by their recent experience and that they will attach particular importance to reassurances about defence. It may therefore be that while the Treaties would be concluded as between Great Britain and the Malay States the defence provisions would necessarily fit into the more general plan of the United Nations for mutual support in the Pacific.

33.   This conception of British policy for Malaya would form part of a wider scheme in the Pacific area arranged by the United Nations in co-operation, and sealed by a United Nations mutual engagement for defence and for economic development as suggested earlier in this paper.

Borneo

34.   The territories under British protection in Borneo comprise: (1) the State of Sarawak under the sovereignty of Rajah Brooke[5] and under an Agreement with His Majesty's Government which places the responsibility for foreign relations and defence upon the shoulders of His Majesty's Government; (2) the State of Brunei under the sovereignty of a Malay Sultan who is in similar Treaty relations with His Majesty's Government as the Malay States in the Peninsula; (3) the State of North Borneo which is administered by a Chartered Company in London as an independent State under His Majesty's protection.

35.   Of these three territories Sarawak and Brunei would continue to be independent States under His Majesty's protection by treaty but if some form of Malayan Union were developed it would be appropriate that Brunei at least and possibly Sarawak also should be associated with that Union.

36.   In North Borneo the continued sovereignty of a Chartered Company would not be impressive as a desirable and modern form of authority. Although the Chartered Company differs from other examples in that it does not itself engage in trade but confines itself to its functions of administration, it nevertheless has the outward form of a commercial concern with shareholders, occasional distribution of dividends etc., and cannot be regarded as having the resources, experience, or international authority to exercise sovereign functions over a backward people. Under the plan of reconstruction in the Pacific, therefore, an opportunity will arise

---

[5] Charles Vyner Brooke had succeeded his father, Charles, as third rajah in 1917.

for proposing the direct assumption by the British Government of administrative responsibility for North Borneo, and that the Company's Charter be extinguished on suitable terms. If that course were adopted, the State of North Borneo might also be associated with the Malayan Union since its communications are largely with Singapore and its administrative problems and needs are similar to those of the less developed States in the Malay Peninsula.

37. A Malayan Union which includes the States in North Borneo might need a different name but would be a substantial block of territories with Singapore as its natural centre of trade and communications and would possess a potential strength which would offer promise of economic and political development. . . .[6]

---

[6] The memorandum next turned to other territories such as the Japanese mandated islands.

9 CO 825/35/4, no 53   11 Sept 1942

[Post-war settlement in the Far East]: minute by G E J Gent of a meeting of ministers on 10 Sept to discuss the joint CO-FO memorandum[1]

Mr. Attlee said that the memorandum was based on the idea that the Far East was to be treated as a separate problem from that of Colonial territories in other parts of the world, but could there not in general be said to be a single Colonial problem having much the same general characteristics everywhere?

Mr. Eden said that the special feature of the Far East was that, besides the British, there was a group of the leading countries in the United Nations which was intimately concerned with the territories in the Far East, the United States, China, Holland and to some extent Russia; whereas they had no such interest, for instance, in Africa.

Mr. Amery said that he was not happy about the proposal in the memorandum that we should give up Hong Kong. In his view we should approach the whole subject from the standpoint that we are giving up nothing, and particularly he stressed the overriding importance of strategic considerations; if it were proposed that we should give up any territory we should first be quite sure that it would not be a strategic loss to us, but what we might give up would be counter-balanced by gaining something of no less strategic value.

Mr. Eden stressed that our aim was to secure collective defence in the Far East and particularly to ensure that the United States committed themselves to play their part in a United Nations defence system. His idea was that each country would be responsible for maintaining the defence of their own territories but would share in a general collective undertaking and in reciprocal facilities for each other's forces in the bases etc. in the several territories.

He said that there were three objects before us: (1) Guidance for the British

---

[1] See 8. The meeting was attended by Attlee (DO), Cranborne (CO), Eden (FO), Amery (India Office) and officials from their respective departments.

Delegation at the Pacific Relations Conference. (2) The education of opinion here and in America. (3) The question of Mr. Cordell Hull's suggestion for a joint Anglo-U.S. declaration about the future of Colonial territories as a kind of appendix to the Atlantic Charter.

Mr. Amery repeated his warning as to the importance of judging the future requirements of our policy in the Far East according to the dictates of strategy. What the future value of Hong Kong might be could not at present be accurately judged. Possibly its cession to China might be considered in exchange for such a place as Hainan on the ground that the latter would be more useful to us from the strategic point of view.

Lord Cranborne explained that there was nothing in the memorandum to commit the British Government to surrendering any British territories, and especially it envisaged that any settlement between the United Nations should not be merely one-sided as far as we were concerned, but that all would contribute to the general advantage.

Mr. Attlee explained that there was an important political aspect about all this, and that in the view of the Labour Party the British electorate would not be content to go on bearing a financial burden in respect of Colonies for which the advantage mainly accrued to a capitalist group. The maintenance of national sovereignty over Colonies required the maintenance of national armaments; and in respect both of armaments and sovereignty over backward peoples the political views which he shared were in favour of the substitution of an international system of responsibility and control. National sovereignty and national armaments had shown poor results and would inevitably lead to renewed war in due course. A new conception of international collaboration and responsibility and a pooling of the burden, including the financial burden, of armaments was required.

Lord Cranborne said that he did not accept that our record in the Colonies, and particularly in Malaya and Hong Kong, was a poor one. Not only we but also the Dutch in the Netherlands East Indies and the Americans in the Philippines had rendered great service, and effectively established great reforms in our respective territories to the great advantage of the native peoples. We have all fallen down in one respect, namely, defence, and as far as the British were concerned we might be said to have less blame for this than the Americans *vis à vis* Japanese aggression.

Mr. Eden said that our principal object must be to establish a system in the Pacific region in which the United States will not only consent to participate but will be definitely anxious to participate. Clearly the mere restoration of the *status quo* with all concerned clinging rigidly to their pre-war rights and policies would not attract the Americans to incur any obligations for the future defence of such an arrangement. There must be an agreed system of administration, standards, responsibilities, and mutual obligations which would be sealed by a willingness of all concerned to contract to defend, and it would be important from our point of view that the Dominion Governments should be at every stage at one with us in formulating British policy in this region.

Lord Cranborne explained that his idea of the Pacific Regional Council proposed in the paper was that it should comprise representatives of the great Pacific powers and the Dominions. The Council would be responsible for stipulating a certain set of principles to which the local governments would conform. But the sovereign authority in each territory would rest with the power or country concerned and not with an international body. The chief difference which he saw in the new Regional Council as compared with the former Mandates Commission of the League of Nations was that the new Council would comprise a body of experts with colonial experience—and experience of the region—whereas the Mandates Commission's influence was compromised by the fact that it was often composed of representatives of Norway, Poland, Venezuela, etc. who had no such experience.

Mr. Attlee asked what would be the sanction for the Regional Council's authority, and *Mr. Amery* expressed the view that while the only ultimate sanction in international affairs was war, it would be in this case the interest of all the powers concerned in the region to secure compliance with the standards and obligations which all had agreed to regard as the basis of co-operation and peace in the Pacific. He thought that some special international system might well be established in the economic field and *Lord Cranborne* agreed that the special needs of America in particular for the rubber and tin of the region might be usefully met by a special economic control.

Mr. Attlee represented his preference for an international system of administration and said that it was not sufficient to condemn such a system by pointing to the inefficiency of the international system at Tangier or the Condominium in the New Hebrides. In neither of those cases was there an obvious effort to promote efficiency. But something on a much larger scale deriving from an intention to collaborate to mutual advantage and the achievement of results is worth examination. It would not necessarily mean that the local executive in any territory would be a polyglot mixture of officials but the international authority would need to be the sovereign authority with the power of laying down standards and regulations and to carry out inspection in any way and matters thought necessary.

Mr. Amery felt that this would be incompatible with Parliamentary responsibility – in so far as a Minister in H.M.G. would be involved in an international council to be established with sovereign authority responsible to no one but itself.

Mr. Eden said that he felt there were only two courses possible and there was no middle way. (1) We must either be responsible for the administration of our territories and have the ultimate power of Government or (2) sovereign authority must lie elsewhere and H.M.G.'s responsibility to Parliament for the local administration would disappear. There were obviously high matters of policy to be settled by H.M.G. before further progress could be made on this memorandum and he suggested, and *Mr. Attlee and the other Ministers* agreed, that further discussion of British Far Eastern policy and of the memorandum must be deferred for the present.

10 CO 825/35/4, no 61 1 Oct 1942

'Record of conversation between the secretary of state and the Chinese ambassador at the Colonial Office on Wednesday, 30 September, 1942': minute by Lord Cranborne

I had a visit yesterday afternoon from the Chinese Ambassador.

He told me that he was shortly returning to his own country for a visit and when he arrived there he would be bound to be asked what was the view of the British with regard to the future of their Colonial Empire. He wondered whether I could give him any information about our post-war colonial policy.

I asked the Ambassador whether he had in mind a policy for the Far East or for the Colonial Empire generally.

He said that he would be glad of information about both.

I then told him that so far as the Colonial Empire generally was concerned he had asked me a difficult question. The one thing which had impressed itself most upon my mind during the six months that I had been in the Colonial Office was that it was almost impossible to lay down a cut and dried policy applicable to all colonies alike. I was in charge of the administration of no less than 50 territories, and in all of them conditions were to some extent different from those that obtained in the others. For instance, how could it be said that one could lay down exactly the same policy for Malta and Nyasaland, or for Bermuda, which had enjoyed a Constitution of its own for over 200 years. My experience led me to believe that the conditions in each colony must be considered individually, and that any attempt to standardize policy would be bound to lead to disaster. At the same time, it would be true to say that there were certain general principles which we accepted for the administration of backward peoples. We had long believed in what was known as the doctrine of trusteeship, that is to say, the training of backward peoples with a view to their ultimately taking over the government of their countries. To that principle we adhered. I should, however, make it clear that in some parts of the world it was bound to be a very long term policy, and we had lately tried to speed it up by bringing in to our own administration outstanding representatives of the indigenous peoples. We had made a start in West Africa, and had achieved a measure of success. This development, as he knew, had been given the name of 'partnership', and no doubt this process of bringing in the local population into British administration would be continued and extended. I would not, however, like him to form the impression that an extension of partnership would lead in the near future to anything like dominion status for the more backward areas. Dominion status, to my mind, meant something very special. It indicated that a particular territory was now an adult nation responsible for its foreign policy and defence. This was clearly not true of the more backward parts of the British Empire at the present time, and would probably not be so for some considerable period.

The Ambassador then turned to the question of the Far East, and asked what were my views about this. I said that the principles which I had tried to define regarding our future policy towards the Colonial Empire as a whole clearly applied equally to our territories in the Far East. In the case of Malaya the population was evidently more advanced than in Africa, and there the policy could no doubt be speeded up more rapidly after the war. I did not accept the view which had been propounded in some quarters that the actual administration of our Far Eastern dependencies had been defective in the past. No doubt there had been faults, but on the whole the period during which we had had control of them had been one of steady development and increased prosperity. Where there had undoubtedly been a gap had been in the matter of defence. It was there that we had fallen down, but this applied equally to the Dutch and the Americans. He would remember the years before the war and how we had hoped that it would be possible for the United States to play a full part in maintaining peace in the Pacific. But unfortunately at that time it had been politically impossible for them. It seemed to me—and here I explained that I was speaking merely for myself—that it would be essential after the war that there should be some scheme of mutual defence agreed between the Pacific powers. Only so should we avoid a repetition of the present disasters. I hoped very much that in such a defence scheme China would find it possible to play a part. To this the Ambassador appeared to assent. I also said that it seemed to me possible that it would be to the advantage of the powers concerned that there should be some international consultative body which could meet frequently and discuss questions of mutual interest to the member powers.

The Ambassador said that he was glad to know the kind of direction in which our minds were moving in this country. It would be most helpful to him when he got to Chungking.[1]

---

[1] Chungking was the capital of Chiang Kai-shek's Nationalist regime.

11   CO 877/25/7/27265/7, no 1   4 Dec 1942
[Lessons from Hong Kong and Malaya]: report by Sir W Battershill,[1] G E J Gent and W L Rolleston[2]

Introduction

1. Our terms of reference:— "To consider and report what lessons, from the point of view of Colonial administration in wartime, can be drawn from the experience of Hong Kong and Malaya".

For the sake of brevity we use the word "Colony" to cover all forms of Colonial dependency and the word "military" to cover all fighting services.

2. We would emphasise first that owing to the differences which exist between the various Colonies some of our conclusions are stated in general terms and can only be applied with considerable variations from Colony to Colony. And secondly that the evidence and data on which we have based our conclusions are very incomplete. Our conclusions must be read in the light of this fact.

Relations with the fighting services

3. There is evidence that relations between the civil government and the military could have been improved, though however good the administrative arrangements may be to ensure this end, everything must in the last resort depend very largely on the personalities of the men at the top.

4. In Malaya, apart from the complications of the civil machine owing to the existence as separate entities of the Straits Settlements, the Federated Malay States and the Unfederated Malay States, there existed military, naval and air force commanders for Malaya, and also Commanders-in-Chief commanding areas larger

---

[1] Sir William Battershill, deputy under-secretary of state, CO, 1942–1945, and governor of Tanganyika, 1945–1949.
[2] W L Rolleston, Royal Engineers, 1925–1946, and colonial service, Singapore and North Borneo, 1947–1950.

than Malaya but having their headquarters inside the territory.* In addition there were representatives of various other branches of the Home Government, e.g. the Ministry of Economic Warfare, the Ministry of War Transport and the intelligence services. Each of these many organisations corresponded separately with their own headquarters in this country. As a result of these complications in the administrative machine there was, at all levels, too often uncertainty and delay in reaching decisions.

5. In Hong Kong there was a simpler administrative machine and a less complicated hierarchy among the fighting services. In fact there was no evidence of discord in the direction of the Colony's defence.

6. Some of the difficulty of the position in Malaya seems to have been recognised before the invasion took place and no doubt this was one of the reasons for Mr. Duff Cooper's journey to the Far East.[3] But it seems that his few weeks' tenure of office did not remedy all the defects and on General Wavell's appointment as Commander-in-Chief he left Malaya some weeks before its fall. Difficulties of a comparable order have been recognised in the Middle East and West Africa, and partly with the object of meeting them a Minister of State has been appointed to the Middle East and a Resident Minister to West Africa. In Ceylon, Admiral Layton has been given a position of special authority.

7. The first lesson we draw is that there should in wartime be some authority on the spot with the necessary power of direction in a time of crisis to resolve at once any differences between the civil and military. There seem to us three possible ways of achieving this. First a Regional Authority such as a Minister of State or Resident Minister, who even if not actually in a Colony would be near enough to it to have first-hand knowledge of its problems and personalities. Secondly the Ceylon model under which there is in the Colony itself not only a Governor and a General-Officer-Commanding but a Commander-in-Chief with a co-ordinating authority. Thirdly an arrangement could be made for either the Governor or the Senior Military Officer to have authority over the other, either at all times or preferably in time of military crisis only.

Value of regional authority

8. We believe that the Ceylon arrangement is working very well in that Colony but we doubt whether it would be suitable for general application to other Colonies. We are however much impressed with the value in war-time of a Regional Authority, properly established before a crisis arrives. From a civilian standpoint his value can be stated briefly as follows:—

(a) He can take a wide view of the needs and requirements, strategic, political and economic, of his whole area.

(b) He can secure co-ordination of policy between the civil administrations and the military.

* Though General Wavell's headquarters as Commander-in-Chief, South West Pacific, were outside Malaya.

[3] In Aug 1941 Alfred Duff Cooper, chancellor of the Duchy of Lancaster, left for the Far East to examine the co-ordination between various British authorities in the region. After Pearl Harbour he was appointed resident minister in Singapore. See 39, note 4.

(c) He will be in a position to smooth out any local difficulties between the civil and military which arise from time to time and in a crisis will be able to take immediate decisions on the spot with all the authority that goes with Cabinet rank.

(d) He can correlate the work of the representatives of the various branches of the Home Government mentioned in paragraph 4 above, many of whom are of comparatively junior rank, and assist them by the weight of his authority.

(e) By personal visits to Colonies within his area he can help to dispel that sense of isolation, as to the existence of which we have evidence, and can ensure from his knowledge of local personalities that the administration is carrying out its task efficiently and is imbued with the proper war-time mentality.

9. We consider the value of a Regional Authority to be the prime lesson to be drawn from the fall of Malaya. There may be special political or other conditions which would prevent a Regional Authority in other parts of the Colonial Empire from having the same value, but we recommend that the possibility of their appointment as an emergency measure of war-time organisation should be carefully considered. The three regions which suggest themselves are East Africa (in which we would include Mauritius and Seychelles), the Western Pacific and West Indies. Clearly a decision on so important a matter should not be left till the moment of crisis has arrived.

10. There may come a time when even the authority of a Regional Authority is too distant. If for instance Mauritius and the Seychelles were invaded or closely threatened, a Resident Minister for East Africa would be little better able than his colleagues in London to ensure unity of effort between civil and military in those Colonies. We think therefore that there should be for every Colony, whether or not it forms part of the sphere of action of a Regional Authority, administrative arrange- ments whereby in time of imminent military crisis some one individual actually in the Colony or very close to it becomes supreme.[+] Who that person should be would require consideration in each case. Where there was a Regional Authority it would be for him to decide when the situation was such that he could no longer exercise his power and when therefore the local man should take over. If the military commander became the supreme authority, the civil government should continue as long as possible under his general direction.

11. We certainly do *not* advocate that the present arrangements between the Governor and the military commander should be altered except at a time of real military crisis such as invasion or an imminent threat of it. But we do think it should be quite clear what is to happen in such a crisis and that all arrangements should be worked out beforehand.

A war council

12. Harmonious working of all the branches of the public services civil and

---

[+] A complication arises where the Colony forms only part of the command of the General Officer Commanding and yet is close to his headquarters—as in Kenya, Uganda and Tanganyika. In this case it may be preferable not to have a supreme authority actually in each Colony but to have one authority (either civil or military) for the three. In Mauritius or the Seychelles, however, which are also in the East Africa Command but geographically remote for the G.O.C.'s headquarters, a single authority in each island seems desirable.

military, will not necessarily be ensured solely by the existence either of a single authority in each Colony or of a Regional Authority for some larger area. There must be the most careful arrangements for collaboration at all levels.

13. We have evidence as to the value of war councils as a factor in co-operative working of all branches of the civil and military machines. The Minister of State at Cairo has a war council consisting of the Governors of the territories within his sphere, the British Ambassadors and the Chiefs of the fighting services, and we are aware of the existence in various colonies of similar councils consisting of the Governors and representatives of the military and civil administration. Meetings of these Councils not only serve to expedite decisions and to cut down paper work, but also afford a common meeting ground for the exchange of information and the frank expression of views. They have no legal status and need none. We recommend that, where these do not exist, Governors should be asked to consider whether it would not be advisable to include them in the administrative machinery.

14. A lesson to be learnt from Malaya is the desirability of recording at the actual meeting of the Council clear-cut decisions, beyond the possibility of misunderstanding, on which action can be taken immediately.

Liaison officers

15. It seems to us very desirable that there should be some regular day to day liaison between the Governor and the Secretariat on the one hand and the military on the other. We think that all Governors should normally have a military officer on their personal staffs. In Colonies with small military establishments an officer of the ordinary rank of an A.D.C. may suffice. In other Colonies Governors might find it useful to have a more senior officer attached to them who might be known as "Military Secretary". Such an officer while living at Government House as a member of the Governor's personal staff could maintain contact between Secretariat and the military and could generally assist the Governor in keeping the closest day to day contact with them.

16. There are considerable advantages in the headquarters of the various services being close to one another. In Malaya the various headquarters were for various reasons many miles apart. This made close liaison more difficult.

Liaison arrangements in districts

17. In all potentially "front-line Colonies" arrangements for co-operation between various services must be as carefully made in the districts as they are at the capital. There were plenty of complaints from Malaya of poor co-operation between civil and military in the districts, for instance in Penang. A large part of the trouble seems to have been due to the receipt of different orders from the respective headquarters. If co-operation at the centre is good, the likelihood of difficulty in the districts will be minimised.

18. We have suggested that in each territory there should at a time of crisis be one supreme authority. We do not see how similar provision could be made district by district. Very often military and civil boundaries will not coincide, troops may be moved suddenly from the district, new troops may come in, and so forth. Accordingly, we must rely on good personal relations and on each side receiving similar orders from the centre to avoid difficulties. If active operations are proceeding, the district commissioner must without question comply immediately

with the requirements of the military. It would be convenient at such times for the district commissioner to be attached to local military headquarters. Events in Malaya made it abundantly clear that it was of great value to the local officer commanding to have on his staff and constantly available to him during active operations an experienced civilian official speaking the local language and knowing the local customs as well as the lay-out of the civil administration.

19   It might be possible to have in some districts a projection of the war council and this might do much to solve local problems and to educate both civil and military in the difficulties and point of view of the other. In any case the district commissioner should regard it as part of his duty to take the initiative in establishing close liaison with the military authorities.

20.   During active operations a district may be cut off entirely from the centre of government, and it has been suggested to us that in such circumstances the district commissioner may require extra powers to enable him to carry on the administration. We suggest that all "front-line Colonies" should be invited to consider this point.

Social contracts [contacts] with the fighting services
21.   We have so far been concerned only with administrative arrangements at the centre of government and in districts for co-operation between the civil and military authorities. But good relations cannot be attained merely by administrative order or official procedure. Friendly social contact is also important, and this should not be only of the impersonal or "institutional" variety. Civil officials should go out of their way to get to know members of the fighting services socially.

Organization of manpower
22.   One of the clearest lessons of the Malayan campaign is the importance in a period of crisis of utilizing to the best advantage all the available manpower, official and unofficial. In Malaya most Europeans and some responsible Asiatics, in both cases official and unofficial, had been trained for employment in the Volunteer Force. Some attempt was made to ensure that those whose work would be of importance in war-time were not taken to serve in the Force, but in the event it proved that not nearly enough exceptions had been made and that those who served in the Force were too often employed on unimportant jobs as ordinary rank and file. Many would have been doing more valuable work in their civil jobs, while others would have been of greater value in the military as guides, interpreters and advisers (of which they stood in great need) than as ordinary volunteers. There was thus a serious waste of manpower. We suggest that all "front-line" Colonial governments should keep their manpower arrangements in constant review with particular reference to those enrolled in combatant forces.

23.   It is important that special care should be taken in the organization of labour on essential services of all kinds. Everywhere in Malaya labour melted away as soon as heavy bombing developed. After the bombing of Penang practically all the labour employed in the town disappeared, while during the last few weeks only 1,000 men could be found to work for the military in Singapore when many thousands were needed. Shortage of labour was undoubtedly a major difficulty during the last weeks in Malaya.

24.   It is not possible to lay down any hard and fast rules for the treatment of

labour so as to ensure that it does not disappear under the stress of operations. Each Colony will have to consider the problem for itself. But generous provision for the dependants of labourers who suffer through enemy action, adequate shelter accommodation at their places of employment, and the provision of canteens and other welfare services are factors which have a considerable bearing on the staunchness of labour under war conditions. It goes without saying that where any trade unions exist those responsible for organizing essential labour should work in close touch with the trade union leaders.

Financial latitude

25. The civil Governments in Malaya undoubtedly had an advantage over the military authorities in that they had a wider financial latitude. They were able to finance urgent defence works without reference either to the Legislature or the Secretary of State, while the military authorities had in certain matters to refer to London. For instance when it was difficult to obtain labour the Governments were able to pay whatever wages seemed to them to be necessary but the military had to refer home. As uniformity between civil and military was obviously desirable, there was delay in a matter on which the decision was urgent.

26. We recommend that this question of financial latitude should be brought to the notice of the military authorities. We recommend also that other Colonial Governments should be given, either by the Secretary of State or the Legislature, a latitude similar to that enjoyed by the Governments of Malaya. In Ceylon the government have obtained from the Legislature a block grant for defence purposes. It might be useful for other governments to do this too.

Maintenance and distribution of essential supplies

27. Special emergency plans should be ready for the maintenance and distribution of essential supplies. The food distribution scheme in Malaya "was well worked out but relied too much on the maintenance of normal civil supply channels and ignored the risks of shops being shut". After the Penang raid all the shops shut and most of the municipal employees disappeared. In Colombo the shops shut after their big raid.

28. It is, of course, of the greatest importance that Colonies should be kept au fait with the latest developments in Air Raid Precautions technique and should have sufficient equipment and staff for that purpose. We understand that satisfactory arrangements exist to ensure that these requirements are met and that no recommendation on our part is necessary.

Information and propaganda

29. The Government of Malaya and high military officers there were at great pains to magnify in public estimation the preparations for defence and the impregnability of Malaya. Their primary object was to deceive the Japanese, though whether they succeeded is not apparent. What is however clear is that they deceived many members of the Government service. The policy may have been necessitated by the weakness of our defences, but the effect of it on our own people indicates sufficiently clearly the dangers of misleading propaganda.

30. There is no doubt that it is most important to provide means for the rapid dissemination of accurate news throughout the country during active operations. It

may not be possible to produce newspapers or to distribute them. They should be supplemented by wireless broadcasts and by the use of loud speakers at pre-arranged points or, as was done in Hong Kong, on mobile vans. Care must, however, be taken against assembling large crowds where there is a danger of sudden air attack.

Evacuation

31. The Governments of both Malaya and Hong Kong have come in for much criticism in the matter of their evacuation policies and, particularly in Malaya, their methods of handling the problem.

32. There are at least two distinct sets of circumstances in which evacuation of civilians has to be considered: first, the complete evacuation beforehand of "useless mouths" from potential war areas, and secondly the withdrawal of civilians from actual zones of operations. In both cases, we consider that policies must be governed strictly by defence considerations. For that reason in Hong Kong the evacuation of the majority of British women and children was carried out more than a year before the actual event of war with Japan. It was based on the difficulty of the supply in siege conditions of the kinds of food necessary for Europeans. There was very bitter local criticism alleging that British families alone were separated by their women and children being forced to leave the Colony whereas others were left undisturbed.

33. The other set of circumstances in which an evacuation policy has to be framed relates to withdrawal from actual zones of operations. In Hong Kong the military defence scheme provided for a withdrawal of the garrison to the island to prepare for a siege which might last for many months with a consequent food problem as a major concern on the island. It was, therefore, a vital defence interest to prevent a numerous Chinese population moving on to the island when the troops withdrew from the mainland. In the event, this policy was carried out, and was naturally strongly criticised by the Chinese.

34. In Malaya it was the policy of the War Council that British men should be progressively withdrawn for further useful service as the troops withdrew down the Peninsula. It was also the policy that British women and children, having regard to their particular exposure to the risk of atrocities at the hands of the Japanese forces, should also be removed. In the case of the men, the defence considerations were in our view correctly given a decisive influence, and in regard to the women and children we have no criticisms to offer. As far as possible opportunities of evacuation were also offered to Asiatics and, if a larger proportion of Europeans than Asiatics were in fact evacuated, one of the reasons was that the Asiatics either definitely preferred to stay or so continually changed their minds at the last moment that they repeatedly missed the boat.

35. It is to be recognised that the withdrawal of British officials, District Officers and others, led to the particularly damaging criticism that at the moment of danger our administration deserted the people, and it is widely suggested that this feeling will continue to be strongly held and will add to our difficulties when we reoccupy the country.

36. We repeat our view that considerations of national prestige or of the personal feelings of administrative officers or managers of estates, creditable as they are, should not override the defence advantage if the latter is best served by the withdrawal of the British manpower possessing local experience of the teritory and the people. This may be of the greatest possible value in the counter-advance of our

forces and the re-establishment of our position in districts temporarily occupied by the enemy. It might be that instead of their being withdrawn some British civilians could best serve the defence by being entrusted with special post-occupational tasks of a para-military nature. We have seen suggestions that the hinterland of Malaya would have offered suitable opportunities for such work. But that is a decision to be taken in accordance with the military plan of operations.

37.   The essential point is that there should in no territory be any uncertainty as to the authority who is to give the orders in matters of evacuation of civilians, and that those orders should be given in the clearest and most definite form and detail in good time for them to reach all concerned. We have no doubt from our study of Malayan experiences that the orders, in circumstances of actual invasion at any rate, should emanate from the military.

38.   The policy which suits one Colony may be inapplicable or wrong in another, and we suggest that the present instructions should be reviewed in order to ensure that in all Colonies the paramount defence needs, as they develop, are primarily and fully served.

The administrative machine
39.   Many criticisms have been made of the Malayan Civil Service. It is said that before the invasion they carried on much as in peace-time, that much of their work was not connected with the war effort, and that the administrative machine failed to adjust itself to the critical conditions of the last few weeks.

40.   It is our business to draw lessons for the future, not to apportion blame for the past. But we think it right to say that much of this criticism seems to us misguided. In an enemy attack no amount of efficiency on the part of the civil administration can make up for military weakness. As regards the type of work done before the invasion, it is not always realized that the civil administration must continue to handle the great majority of its normal work e.g. revenue, posts, lands, schools, health services or that the production of foodstuffs or raw materials may itself be of great value to the war. As regards events during the invasion, the cataclysm was so abrupt and so contrary to what everyone had been led to expect from the publicly expressed views of high military and civil authorities that it must have been exceedingly difficult for the administration to adjust itself to it; much as it must have been very difficult for the civil administration in France to adjust itself to events in the last days before the capitulation of their country. It was indeed difficult enough to adjust oneself in this country; and it is permissible to doubt whether from an administrative point of view at any rate that adjustment has yet been satisfactorily completed.

41.   Yet this difficulty of adjustment emphasizes how important it is that Colonial civil servants, especially those in posts of authority, should be men with what we may call a "war-time mentality". By that phrase we mean an alertness of mind to a new situation, a sense of grim realism, and unhesitating recognition of the new values. We mean also a readiness to see a change of tempo and method in administration, a disappearance of peace-time checks on the possibility of mistakes, and a general rending of all red tape. It is impossible to expect an automatic over-night change to this new mentality. Even in England exhortation, propaganda, and numberless instructions have been needed and are constantly being repeated by Ministers, by the press and by the radio. How much more are such methods needed to spur on a civil

service depleted in numbers, working for years under a very heavy strain in a bad climate, mostly separated from their families with considerably reduced comforts and few opportunities for leave!

42.   Apparent slowness in the Colonies to respond to new conditions was no doubt partly due to an absence of direction from on top. While the main effort to secure a change must come from Governors and senior officials in the Colonies, Whitehall itself must give a lead. A clear-cut instruction from the Colonial Office in the early days of the war could have done much to assist in inculcating the proper spirit of the times. We think that such an instruction, very carefully framed, might still have a distinct value.

43.   In addition we think it important that there should be continuous personal contact between Colonial Office officials and officials in the Colonies. In peace-time there was such contact, partly by means of visits by senior officials from this office to the Colonies, though in our opinion there was not enough of this, but chiefly by contacts made with Governors and others coming to this country on leave. Since the war both these contacts have to a large degree disappeared. They are, however, certainly no less important now than in peace-time. We feel strongly, therefore, that every opportunity should be taken to send senior officials of the Colonial Office, who are themselves engaged in the current stress of war problems in London, to visit the Colonies on which the war is making the heaviest demands. We think that the Colonial Office should not be hesitant in asking for air passages for this purpose and should not regard the obvious difficulty of sparing staff from this office as an effective reason against regular visits.

44.   It has been suggested to us that the Colonial Office and Colonial Govern-ments are not nearly drastic enough in getting rid of officials who have passed their maximum ability or who are no longer capable of standing up to the stresses and strains of war-time administration. We appreciate that it may be difficult to make now a fundamental change of policy to meet a temporary and abnormal situation. But whether or not any such fundamental change need be involved, we have been made keenly aware how important it is that no difficulties should prevent the displacement of individuals among the higher personnel in the Colonies, if this is necessary to secure war-time efficiency and a war-time tempo in the machine. Whether or not the officers displaced can be usefully employed in other appoint-ments elsewhere in the Service or must be placed on pension (if only temporarily) would, no doubt, be considered in each case. But nothing should be allowed to prevent their removal if they are not up to the exacting standards of key appointments in war-time conditions.

45.   A certain number of officials have been kept on after they have reached the retiring age and a certain number of Governors after their normal tour of duty has expired. In some cases the extension has been made for a year or more. We feel certain that it is a mistake to make any promises as to the length of time such officers will be retained in the Service. Their services should be retained on short notice so that they can be retired at say one month's notice if required. We suggest that instructions be issued on these lines.

46.   If the quality of freshness of mind and energy in execution is to be maintained, a periodical holiday or change of occupation and environment is essential for Colonial officials. The difficulties are formidable but we believe they could be overcome. We understand that this question is at the moment under

consideration in the Colonial Office. We are glad of this, as we are sure that action is urgently required.

47. If officers are to take leave, that will only make the greater the need for extra staff. Nor have we only to think of the present. Great demands will be made of the Colonial service in the immediate post-war period and we must be ready for all developments, including the reconstitution of the administrations in the Far East. We understand that an attempt is being made at present to recall to the Colonial services as many as possible of those who have been lent to the fighting services. We would only say that it seems doubtful whether this will provide sufficient staff, even if the Director of Recruitment continues to be as successful in the future as he has been in the past in maintaining a reasonable flow of recruits to most of the Colonial services. We suggest that the question should be considered whether it might not be advisable to offer short service conditions with a promise of a gratuity at the end to men who might hesitate here and now to decide to spend the whole of their future careers in the Colonial service.

48. We think that it should be possible to simplify some of the administrative machinery in some Colonies, that a general devolution of authority to a lower level than at present should be insisted upon and that the risk of mistakes being made should be accepted. Suggestions to this end on the lines of the Prime Minister's instructions (which could be quoted with advantage) should be made to all Governors. When staff is short and overworked, every legitimate form of delegation and simplification is desirable.

49. We are glad to note that the question of increasing the power of Colonial Governors to authorise additional expenditure has already been taken up. We feel that this is a matter on which considerably greater latitude might well be given with considerable advantage.

General political questions

50. One criticism which has been levied [? levelled] against the civil administration both in Malaya and Hong Kong may be briefly summed up, in the words of an article in the Times, as the "lack of larger purpose".[4] This, says the article, "was the flaw in our Far Eastern Empire beside which other criticisms are trivial. . . . At the level of practical attainment and routine administration the Colonies were indeed successful. . . . The populations were free, prosperous and reasonably happy. Yet something was missing from both Government and governed which prevented the fusion of the community into a living whole. . . . Without a common aim, able officers who should have been thinking in terms of high policy devoted more and more time to organizing the incidentals of local administration."

51. Another observer writes: "The weak point was that the Government were alien to the whole of the population save to the small minority of Europeans. There was not and could not be any patriotic feeling."

52. We take it that the ideas underlying these criticisms are as follows: first that the local Governments were too much concerned with day to day administration, secondly that there was no clear policy on ultimate objectives, thirdly that the administration was alien to the people, and fourthly that, partly for the last two reasons, there was an absence of what Lord Hailey calls "that sentiment of common

---

[4] cf 1.

purpose between the administration and the people which is so essential to all progressive government".

53. We think that there may well be lessons to be learnt from these criticisms. As regards the first, it is a general criticism of all civil servants that they tend to become immersed in detail; it is true of civil servants in the Colonial Office and it is no doubt equally true of those in the Colonies. We can propound no easy remedy for this failing, but it is very desirable that all senior civil servants here and in the Colonies should have the time and the machinery for thinking ahead. Time can be secured only by the devolution of responsibility and increased staff. The machinery must vary from Colony to Colony. Possibly something comparable to the machinery of the Joint Planning Staff might be useful both here and in certain Colonies or regions—though colonial questions are not susceptible to the same treatment as strategic plans.

54. As regards the criticism that there was no clear policy on ultimate objectives, that is a criticism which has been levied [? levelled] against most Colonial Governments and even against successive Secretaries of State for the last twenty years or more. The degree to which one ought to try to lay down in advance a course of evolution which must be largely affected by external events, is limited. Nevertheless it may be that the fresh and increased attention, which is being given to Colonial questions now and will no doubt continue to be given to them throughout the post-war settlement, may produce some clearer definition than there has been in the past. There is no comment that we can usefully make in this report.

55. As regards allegations that in Malaya and Hong Kong the Government was alien to the people and that there was no sentiment of common purpose, there were special difficulties in both countries. In Malaya a large proportion of the population was not of the Malay race or for the most part even born or domiciled in Malaya. Consequently there were many divided loyalties. Much had been done in Malaya to bring Malays and other Asiatics of the country into the government services and, if in the Straits Settlements there was constitutionally no direct association of the people with the government, in the Malay States the traditional government of the Sultans remained and its structure was, as a matter of policy, continually being strengthened. Actually we doubt whether any closer association of the people in the government or any greater sentiment of common purpose would have appreciably altered the course of events in either Malaya or Hong Kong: unarmed civilians, however patriotic, cannot do much to check the invasions of modern armies supported by naval and air superiority. But, even if from that point of view there is no particular lesson to be learnt from events in Hong Kong and Malaya, it undoubtedly remains an important objective of Colonial policy generally, in peace as in war, that the people of the Colonies should be associated in the government and that everything possible should be done to foster the sentiment of common purpose.

In concluding our Report we wish to record our appreciation of the services rendered to us by our Secretary, Mr. Eastwood.

12 CO 825/35/6, no 2 20 Mar 1943

'Plans for constitutional reconstruction in Far East': memorandum by W B L Monson

[Towards the end of 1942 Cabinet decided that immediately after their reoccupation military administrations would be set up in Burma, Malaya and Borneo. In Feb 1943 weekly inter-departmental meetings got underway between the CO and the WO in preparation for the Malayan Planning Unit which was formally established in July under Major-General H R Hone. In order to provide military planners with guidance on future policy, Gent, Paskin and Monson discussed the question of constitutional changes with Sir K Poyser, the CO's legal adviser. Document 12 was a revised version of Monson's first draft of 5 Mar which emerged from the meeting with Poyser the previous day. Gent next sought the opinion of an 'outsider', Lord Hailey, who had effectively defended Britain's colonial record at the Pacific Relations Conference and who in his response drew attention to the particularly sensitive issue of the sovereignty of the Malay rulers (see 13). Fortified with Hailey's support, Oliver Stanley approved the framework for the new policy at a meeting on 13 May (see 14). The revised memorandum on 'Constitutional reconstruction in the Far East: Malaya, North Borneo and Sarawak' (see 15) would form the basis of the later directive on Malayan planning.]

(N.B. These notes are intended to set out the main lines of policy to be followed in constitutional reconstruction of British or British protected territories in the Far East, now in Japanese hands. They do not, of course, cover all implications of the programme envisaged in each of the territories concerned.)

I. *General aim*

1. The object will be to secure closer co-operation and control of policy throughout the territories concerned in Malaya and Borneo at the least, and possibly also Hong Kong.

2. Before the Japanese invasion such co-ordination, as was possible locally, was due to the exercise by the Governor of the Straits Settlements of the additional functions of High Commissioner for the Malay States and British Agent for Borneo (including Sarawak).

3. It is suggested that any future plans should envisage the appointment of a supreme British regional authority without direct governmental functions within any of the units concerned but with direct control over all the chief officers of the several administrations.

4. In this memorandum this officer is for convenience referred to as the Governor-General

II. *Territories in Borneo*

(A) *North Borneo*

(a) Pre-occupation status was that of a Protected State, administered by a sovereign Chartered Company with Headquarters in London. His Majesty's Government possessed certain limited powers over the operations of the Chartered Company by virtue of the terms of its Charter and of the agreement placing the State under His Majesty's protection.

(b) It is agreed that the continuance of Chartered Company rule would be an anachronism, and that the first step is to reach an agreement whereby the Chartered Company would relinquish its administrative rights in the territory.

Provided due provision is made for the interests of the Company's shareholders and staff, this should not be difficult to secure.

(B) There remains the question of the future status of the territory: here there appear to be three courses open:—

(i) The transfer of the State to the rule of a native ruler, as in a Malay State. There is no obvious choice as the territory was not, previous to Company rule, a political entity, and the various native stocks have no traditional ruling house to whom they would naturally look for leadership. The Company's rights are derived from the transfer of more or less shadowy rights over the area possessed by the Sultanates of Sula [Sulu] and of Brunei. The former house has been deposed by the United States authorities in the Philippines, and the latter has shown no qualities which would justify an extension of its territories. This course can, therefore, be ruled out.

(ii) Annexation by the Crown as a Colony. This would on political grounds probably be regarded as nearly as anachronistic as the continuance of Chartered Company rule.

The United Kingdom authorities (especially the Home Office) have also generally objections to the admission of inhabitants of backward non-European areas to the full rights of British subjects at law.

(iii) The establishment of the State as a British Protectorate. This is probably the best solution.

There is a precedent in the procedure adopted in Northern Rhodesia after the "buying-out" of the British South Africa Company's administrative rights there.

The chief officer of the administration would be a Governor, assisted by Executive and Legislative Councils. (A basis of this framework already exists in the State).

III. *Labuan*

1. This is already British territory, as being part of the Colony of the Straits Settlements.

2. If proposals for North Borneo go through as suggested above, it should most conveniently be included in North Borneo for administrative purposes. (The union in one administrative entity of a Colony and Protectorate is frequently found elsewhere in the Colonial Empire, e.g. Nigeria, Gold Coast, Kenya, etc).

IV. *Brunei*

This is at present a Malay State (Unfederated). The present constitutional position is governed by a Treaty with the Sultan on the usual Malay State lines (i.e. for the appointment of a British Adviser whose advice must be taken on all matters not affecting Malay religion and custom). This position is satisfactory.

V. *Sarawak*

1. A Protected State ruled by a Rajah of the Brooke family.

2. Relations with His Majesty's Government rested on:—

(i) an agreement of 1888 giving His Majesty's Government control of foreign relations and a right to decide any "question" arising about the succession, but no right to intervene in the internal administration.

(ii)   an agreement of 1941 (never implemented owing to the outbreak of war) for the appointment of a British representative whose advice would have to be accepted in matters relating to foreign relations and defence, but who would be available for advice and consultation on other matters.

3.   It is probably safe to accept the premise that the inhabitants of Sarawak would not revolt against a restoration of Brooke rule. On that basis we should aim at the conclusion of a Treaty on the usual Malay State lines.

4.   The present Rajah may not wish to accept these conditions or indeed himself to resume actual leadership in the State at all. If any question arises of buying out his rights, it should be remembered that he may be said to have only a life-interest in the succession, and that the heir in the male line of descent (his brother and successively his nephew) have a right to be considered.

VI. *General*

1.   The arrangements envisaged above would secure uniform British administrative control of the territories in northern Borneo through the subordination of the Governor of North Borneo and the British Residents in Brunei and Sarawak to the Governor-General (see Section I). This would be strengthened by the institution of common senior Civil Services for Malaya and the Borneo territories.

2.   It may be thought attractive to increase this by linking the three Borneo territories in a federation as between themselves or in a larger Malayan federation that may be envisaged.

3.   In practice it is, however, doubtful whether any closer form of constitutional union would be justified in the present stage of their development. They have little direct inter-communication and trade between each other and they are racially disunited.

VII. *The Malay Peninsula*

(A) *Singapore*

It is suggested that in any constitutional re-arrangement of the present political system a special status should be given to the island of Singapore on the following grounds:—

(i)   it has a special position as an entrepôt and distributing centre for all the United Nations territories in South East Asia. Its "free port" policy should, therefore be preserved;

(ii)   it will have a similar special importance to the United Nations as a naval base;

(iii)   its wealth gave it a preponderance in pre-war Malaya which was resented by other political units in the Peninsula and so created a barrier to closer union since the latter feared that, in any closer union, their interests would be subordinated to the rather special different interests of Singapore;

(iv)   the problems of government in Singapore which is so much urbanised are in important respects different from those in the rest of the Peninsula.

It is, therefore, suggested that the Island should be excluded from any federation and/or customs union that may be established in the rest of the Peninsula.

Local government could be based in the organisation of the Municipality of Singapore, but the Island should also be the headquarters of the Governor-General.

Such central administration as is necessary in respect of Christmas Island and the Cocos-Keeling Islands could also be carried on from Singapore and the Islands would remain part of the Settlement: but past practice of normally excluding them from the operation of legislation applicable to the Straits Settlements should be continued.

VIII. *Remaining territories in the Malay Peninsula*

It is assumed that the present separate identities of the Malay States under their Rulers will be preserved.

It is suggested that all States in the Peninsula (whether in the present Federation or not) together with the Settlements of Penang and Malacca (which are British territory) should be linked in a new Federation with its capital at Kuala Lumpur, which would be the headquarters of a High Commissioner who would be subordinate to the Governor-General. The internal government of the Settlements of Penang and Malacca would be in the hands of Residents acting with municipal councils. It is not envisaged, however, that the Province Wellesley portion of the present Settlement of Penang should be retroceded to or divided between the States of Kedah or Perak.

One important consideration should be borne in mind in framing the constitution of the Federation. So far, His Majesty has not possessed "even a scintilla of jurisdiction" in the Malay States. This has been difficult administratively since it has not been possible to take legislative action here e.g. to extend the Emergency Powers (Defence) Act to the States, or to establish the status of Chinese born in a Malay State as British protected persons. The latter point is of political importance since the Malay Rulers have never been ready to recognise Chinese, however long established in their States, as being nationals of those States. It is desirable, even at this stage, that the formal status of 'British protected persons' should be given to those Chinese who are domiciled in the Malay States. Whether they must retain Chinese nationality is a matter dependent on Chinese law.

One solution for this particular problem may be found in the conditions existing on re-occupation of Malaya by British troops. It is contemplated that this will be followed by the establishment of a military administration in which jurisdiction will be assumed by the G.O.C. by Proclamation deriving its authority from the usages of war. A fortiori His Majesty will have acquired jurisdiction in the course of that process and the problem will be to determine how that jurisdiction can be made to survive the termination of the G.O.C.'s authority.

It is suggested that this question and the whole problem of closer union generally should be made the subject of investigation by a Commission of Enquiry to be sent out during the period of military administration.

In addition to the points mentioned above, the following considerations also come to mind:—

(i) *Financial.* The Straits Settlements and Federated Malay States Governments have issued loans secured on their revenues. It is important that the standing of these loans, particularly the sterling loans of the Federated Malay States Government should not be lowered or the terms of issue disregarded. The question of the arrangements for the servicing of these loans and for their ultimate conversion would require careful consideration.

(ii) In any new Federation, care should be taken to leave with the central authority the residual powers of legislation over matters not specified in the convention establishing the respective powers of central and state etc. authorities.

(iii) It is envisaged at present that the legislature of the new Federation should be constituted at any rate in part by some form of election of representatives by the State and Settlement legislatures.

It is also suggested that the State Rulers should form a quasi-Chamber of Princes with a special position of interest in relation to legislation affecting their princely status and Muslim law and custom. As a matter of form the High Commissioner would preside and would himself represent His Majesty in respect of the Colony.

IX. *Hong Kong*

It is to be anticipated that a strong move will be made by the Chinese to secure the rendition of Hong Kong (both Colony proper and New Territories), and it would be as well to reckon on the probability of the New Territories being restored to China before the end of the present 99 years' lease (which runs from 1898), or on China being admitted to joint jurisdiction in this area.

On commercial grounds, however, there is a strong case for preserving some portion of British territory at Hong Kong to allow China merchants to take advantage of e.g. the facilities for registering British ships and of a secure currency as a backing to their trade. For this purpose the maintenance of Hong Kong Island and the tip of the Kowloon Peninsula already in the Colony proper might be sufficient, but such a territory would hardly warrant the appointment of a full-rank Governor, rather than a Chief Administrator or Commissioner. In any case the head of the Government of Hong Kong should be closely connected with (even perhaps subordinate to the direction of) the Ambassador in China. Alternatively he might be under the control of the Governor-General at Singapore.

13　CO 825/35/6, no 3A　　　　　　　　　　　　　　19 Apr 1943
[Constitutional reconstruction]: memorandum by Lord Hailey[1] on the CO proposals

I recognize that the proposals contained in the Memorandum[2] below are in the main directed to finding an answer to the question which the military authorities must ask when they set about the reconquest of these areas. They will, of course, ask what they are to indicate to their "political staff" as the arrangements which the U.K. Government contemplates for the future constitutional or administrative make-up of these territories.

It is necessary that we should be ready with this answer, and I do not wish to suggest that we must attempt at this stage to look too far forward into the future. But we must realize that others than the British military authorities will in time ask us this question. Recovery of these territories may possibly be a joint Anglo-American

---

[1] Lord Hailey (1872–1969); entered the Indian Civil Service, 1895; governor of the Punjab, 1924–1928, and United Provinces, 1928–1930, 1931–1934; director, African Research Survey, 1935–1938; member, Permanent Mandates Commission of the League of Nations, 1935–1939; chairman, Colonial Research Committee, 1943–1948.
[2] See 12.

operation, and unwelcome as it may be to us to contemplate that America may seek to have a voice in deciding on their future, nothing could prevent American opinion from expressing itself freely on the subject. Adverse expressions of American opinion might not necessarily impair our co-operation in military operations, but they would strengthen the hands of our own domestic critics if they thought that our policy was not sufficiently "forward looking". Critics will not fail to search in the record of our previous administration of these areas for reasons why the inhabitants did not seem to support us in our campaign against the Japanese, or why—as may happen—they do not give active assistance to our forces when we begin the campaign for ousting the Japanese. The reasons which our critics discover may be the wrong ones. But it will be troublesome if we have at the same time to correct false impressions about the past, and encounter difficulty in justifying our plans for the future.

The administrative dispositions to which we look forward are largely a matter for the Colonial Office. Outside opinion will attach chief importance to our answer to the question—What are your plans for the future political status of these areas? On what terms do you propose to readmit private European enterprise to these territories? My point in referring to these questions now is that in framing our statement to the military authorities, we should not commit ourselves to anything inconsistent with what we may have to contemplate when we consider the answer to be given to these two questions.

Turning now to the Memorandum, I agree that a post of Governor General, with Singapore as his headquarters, should be created for the control of these areas. It will be one step forward in the process of grouping the colonies under control of "intermediate authorities" which many have advocated. But it does not seem to me adequate to say that the Governor General must be "without direct governmental functions". This leaves him, so to speak, *in vacuo*. It is necessary that we should from the first have some conception of his relations firstly, with the Secretary of State, and secondly, with the officers in charge of the administrations included in his Governor generalship.

The Secretary of State must retain his responsibility to Parliament. That would not, however, prevent his devolving on the Governor General a considerable number of functions now discharged by the Colonial Office. In the case of India this was effected in the first instance by measures of financial decontrol. In this case the Governor General might have authority to dispose of all financial matters (other than those affecting the pay of services recruited by the Secretary of State, or certain similar matters) up to a certain amount. The convenience of this arrangement lies in the fact that, as time proceeds, the amount can be progressively increased. He might, again, be the final authority for sanctioning local budgets, save where they involve tariff questions or where a budget is seriously unbalanced. He would dispose of contracts or concessions, up to a figure to be fixed. He would dispose of petitions from Government employees, other than those recruited by the Secretary of State, and would also dispose of petitions from the public subject to periodic report to the Colonial Office on action taken by him, or reference on important matters of policy. I give these as illustrations—there is some material for filling out the list in a Memorandum I wrote for the Colonial Office regarding the executive relations of the Secretary of State to colonial governments.

As regards the relations of the Governor General to the authorities in charge of areas under his control, he would not himself be a source of legislation. This would only be possible if the areas were grouped in some form of federation, with a federal council, and I agree with the Memorandum (VI (3)) in holding it premature to contemplate this. But nevertheless he could (subject to the orders of the Secretary of State) control legislation, so long as any legislative authority—e.g. the Malayan Council—had an official majority, or alternatively, so long as the Governors or similar authorities had "reserved" powers. When self-governing institutions are introduced, this point would have to be reconsidered. Legislation is, however, at this stage a less important factor than executive supervision. The Governor General would be ineffective as an agency for initiating or directing schemes of economic or social development unless he had his own staff of advisers. Each of the areas—or at all events the largest—would have its own departmental services under their departmental heads. But India in the pre-1935 period again offers a useful precedent here. There were at different times attached to the Governor General in Council certain officers, known as Inspectors General of Irrigation and Forests, the Health Commissioner and Educational Adviser. They had no executive control over the provincial Departments, but they rendered advice to the Governor General on policy, and their technical advice was also valued by the Provincial Governments themselves. They spent a great part of their time touring in the Provinces.

Coming now to the detailed proposals in II and the following sections of the Memorandum, there is one preliminary observation. It would be well to be clear as to the juridical situation created by the temporary loss of sovereignty over these areas. I do not suggest that the juridical position is decisive as to any obligations we may decide to recognize, for this depends also on moral and political considerations; but we should be more at ease in applying these considerations if we knew the juridical position. Moreover, others may raise the point. It is the fact that agreements, contracts or commitments into which we have entered are 'frustrated' by the loss of control over these territories? If so, are they to be regarded as terminated, or only held in suspense pending recovery of the territories? I attach a paper[3] given me by Mr. Gent, with whom I raised some of these questions in the course of discussion. I do not think that it supplies a final answer to these questions. I propose, however, to assume for the purpose of this note, that any agreements made by us remain in suspense. Whatever the juridical position, it may well be that this is the attitude we should take, on political grounds.

As regards North Borneo, there has already been a general agreement (in which the representative of the Company has apparently joined) that the Company has outlived its use as an agency for administration. In any case, public opinion would not support the restoration of the territory to Chartered Company rule. The Chartered Company had sovereign rights in North Borneo, acquired by agreement or purchase from the indigenous rulers. Our charter did not, therefore, create those rights; it only recognized them, and in return for the promise of protection, the Company agreed to certain limitations on their exercise. The assets held by the Company were acquired by the use of their own capital and by the exercise of their revenue raising powers. Our reconquest of North Borneo would put us in a position to allow the Company to renew its sovereign powers, but I doubt if there is anything in our Agreement which would compel us to do so, unless indeed it is felt that the

---

[3] Not printed.

promise of "protection" implies this. On the other hand, we should probably decide, as a matter of policy and of equity, that we ought to compensate the Company for the loss of the sovereign rights taken over by us; we should of course be obliged in any case to compensate it for any standing assets which we acquired, as these are private property. It is to be hoped that we shall acquire *all* rights and property from the Company and shall avoid the precedent by which we left mineral rights to the B.S.A. in the Rhodesias, with very embarrassing results. (I have given in a separate note some figures about the capital of the Company and the dividends paid by it. It has not proved to be very profitable to the shareholders.)

As regards the choice of form under which we should assume jurisdiction (annexation as Colony or establishment as a Protectorate) I differ from what is said in II.B.(ii) regarding annexation. If it is meant that annexation is an anachromism [sic] because we are bound to refrain from "territorial aggrandisement", this argument does not really apply. In the eyes of the rest of the world, North Borneo is already British territory. We should have no difficulties on that score. Coming, however, to the forms under which jurisdiction may be exercised, it is the form of a Protectorate which is really an anachromism [sic], not that of a Colony. When so much has been said about the Empire or Commonwealth ideal, it seems strange that we should hesitate to admit the inhabitants of a dependency to the status of "British subjects". (The legal differences in status have been examined in a Memorandum prepared for the Post-war Committee.) The issue is, however, a general one, affecting many important dependencies, and until it has been settled I agree with the conclusion in II.B.(iii) that North Borneo should be treated as a Protectorate. This will involve the extension of the Foreign Jurisdiction Act[4] to it.

As to Labuan (III) I agree.

In regard to Brunei (IV) please see what is said below about the Malay States.

Sarawak (V) is another of the constitutional oddities which are included within the orbit of the British Empire. Public opinion is likely to feel that we should either dissociate ourselves entirely from Sarawak, or should exercise full jurisdiction over it. We now extend "protection" to it, but have no control over its internal administration. If it is undeveloped—as it most certainly is—or badly ruled—as it might at any time become—we have to stand the discredit.

Our reconquest of Sarawak would (as in the case of North Borneo) put us in a position to allow the Raja to resume his sovereignty, under our protection. I suggest, however, that the proper course is to declare Sarawak a Protectorate, and to extend the Foreign Jurisdiction Act to it, so that we shall have complete legislative and executive authority in the area. By virtue of that authority, we could then assign to the Raja such position as we considered fit. He might in this case suitably be given a position analogous to that of the Sultan of Zanzibar.

I agree with the suggestion about Singapore (VII). The strongest argument for its treatment as a separate entity lies in the great predominance of Chinese in the population.

The treatment of the rest of Malaya is our most difficult problem. There is on the

---

[4] The Foreign Jurisdiction Acts of 1890 and 1913 empowered the Crown to exercise jurisdiction within a foreign country as if it had acquired that jurisdiction by conquest or the cession of territory. Theoretically interpreted as jurisdiction over British subjects alone, in practice the Act was brought to bear upon indigenous peoples as well.

one hand, the obligation of honour to replace the Sultans in the position which our Treaties have assigned to them; there is, on the other hand, the need to take account of our announced policy of promoting self-government in the Colonies. It is obvious that there are many advantages in the existing system, which is practically one of direct official rule, under the facade of "advice" to Malayan rulers. It pays respect to the declarations made—as for instance by the Parliamentary Under-Secretary of State in 1925[5]—that the maintenance of the authority and prestige of the Rulers must always be a cardinal point in British policy. It affords the Malay population a guarantee against political submergence by Chinese and Indian immigrants—now amounting to 56.5 per cent. of the total Asiatic population. That it is convenient to the official administration is clear from the almost passionate devotion with which some of them support it. Moreover—and this is a substantial fact—it has enabled us in the last half century to make an advance in the improvement of economic and social conditions which, in a considerable part of the country at least, has been almost dramatic in its character.

But we shall be obliged to face two questions, first, whether the system is capable of being adjusted to the promotion of self-governing institutions, and secondly, whether it will enable a suitable status to be given to those Chinese and Indian immigrants who may acquire a permanent interest in the country. Is it intended, for instance, that self-government shall take the form of a progressive relaxation of official control over the Sultans and their councils? That might be termed self-government; but unless we retained authority to prescribe and regulate their functions, it would mean something like autocratic rule in the hands of the Sultans and their Malay advisers. Such rights as the immigrant population might acquire would only be obtained on sufferance, nor would there be any guarantee for any co-ordinated policy in economic and social matters throughout Malaya as a whole. But would the retention of a really effective measure of control in our own hands be compatible with the principle of self-government?

I suggest that there is one essential requirement. We must obtain undisputed rights of jurisdiction throughout this area, and this can be achieved only by its treatment as a Protectorate, and the extension to it of the Foreign Jurisdiction Act. I do not suppose that any lawyer would question that we have obtained that "scintilla" of jurisdiction which would justify this. In this regard, usage is as solid a source of authority as treaty. We shall thus make it impossible to raise those questions of "ultimate jurisdiction", of possible "concurrent authority" and the like which have proved so embarrassing to us in Basutoland and elsewhere, and which some officials are inadvisedly attempting to revive in Northern Nigeria. We should then be in a position (a) to define the exact scope of the authority of the Sultans and their councils, (b) to give such status as we consider reasonable to the immigrant population and (c) to introduce a uniform system of rule throughout Malaya.

What would be the effect of such a measure on our treaties with the Sultans? The general tenour of Privy Council judgements points to the conclusion that where the

---

[5] W G A Ormsby-Gore, under-secretary of state for the colonies 1924–29. Hailey may have been referring to Ormsby-Gore's report of 1928 in which he stated: 'Our position in every State rests on solemn treaty obligations. . . . We have neither the right nor the desire to vary this system of government or to alter the type of constitution or administration that now obtains.' W G A Ormsby-Gore, *Report on His Visit to Malaya, Ceylon and Java* (Cmd. 3235, December 1928) p 17.

Foreign Jurisdiction Act has been applied, no previous treaty has any force, in the sense that it cannot be quoted against the Government in any municipal court. But this would not cancel the moral obligation to respect it. If we take as an example the Treaty with the Chiefs of Perak in 1874, it provided that the Sultan would accept a British Resident, whose advice had to be taken on all matters except those relating to Malay custom and Mohammedan religion; all revenues were to be collected and appointments made in the name of the Sultan, but the collection of revenues and the control and general administration of the country would be regulated by the advice of the Resident. The agreements which formed the basis of the constitution of the Federated States do not seem to have modified this basic position to any significant extent.[6]

It is advisable to see how far any constitutional development which we may envisage for the future would conflict with a Treaty of this type. I put forward the following mainly by way of illustration; many variants are of course possible. The functions of the Sultans and their own Councillors would be confined to the field of matters relating to Muslim law or custom. The financial position of the Sultans would be safeguarded by giving them a civil list, which would include the possession of family lands. Each State would have a Legislative Council, of which the composition would be laid down by the Governor, and of which membership would in the first place be obtained by his nomination. It would have a defined sphere of local legislation only, including "local" taxation. It is a question whether the Sultan should or should not be given the honorary position of President. The main legislation, including civil and criminal law, taxation (other than local) would be conducted by a Malayan Assembly which would be directly representative of the Legislative Councils, together with representatives nominated personally by the Sultans. On the executive side, all orders would be expressed as those of the Governor, following the usual practice where the Crown has sole jurisdiction. Such a constitution would provide the basis on which self-government could ultimately be built up. Representation would in time have to take some other form than nomination, though I do not mean to suggest that election on the ordinary lines (save perhaps in townships) would be the sole alternative.

In form, a constitution of this type would involve some invasion of the position given to the Sultans by Treaty. But the position actually established by usage is unreal, even in relation to the terms of the Treaties. Are all duties, for instance, really collected in the name of the Sultan? What is the real value of making appointments in the name of the Sultan? Actually, the greater part of the administration is carried out, in the Federated States at all events, by officers of departments acting under direct orders of the Governor. Sooner or later, we shall have to face squarely the question whether we are to allow the facade of Sultan-rule to persist, with all the difficulties which it presents to the attainment of any form of self-government, or to build up a constitution on the basis of realities. There are doubtless many who might feel that a well-conducted official régime might be the best for these territories; but it is not the ideal which we have professed to the rest of the world.

I come to the second question to which I have referred above—the terms on which we are to allow the resumption of private enterprise in these areas. I raise it partly

[6] Hailey is referring to articles 6 and 10 of the Perak Treaty of 20 Jan 1874 and the Federal Treaty of July 1895.

because a great deal has been said on the subject in various quarters, and partly because it is bound, in the natural course of things, to force itself on our notice at an early stage in the "reconstruction" period. There can be no question of the past benefits to Malaya from the operations of private enterprise. But two questions have now to be faced. First, whether the revenues of the country have actually had a due share of the profits made by private capital? Secondly, whether production such as that of rubber should in the future remain so largely in the hands of companies, or whether "peasant" production (under suitable regulation) should not take an increasing share in it. The answer to both questions may be simple; but it would be a mistake to allow the present economic system to be re-established without first giving some consideration to them.

The questions arising out of the future position of Hong Kong are of a very different nature to those of Malaya. The constitutional issue is relatively unimportant. There seem to be three questions to consider. How far do we need on our own behalf or that of the United Nations to retain possession of Hong Kong for strategic purposes? How far is it essential in the interests of international trade that it should be maintained as a free port? How far in either of these two cases would it be possible to meet the claims of China—which have received considerable support elsewhere— by recognizing Chinese sovereignty subject to conditions which would give us effective control? We cannot usefully consider the questions of the form under which control is to be exercised, until we know the attitude of the United Kingdom Government on these questions.

14   CO 825/35/6, no 4   14 May 1943
'Constitutional reconstruction in the Far East': CO conclusions of a departmental discussion on 13 May

I. *Singapore:* proposals in para. VII (a) of the Eastern Department's memorandum of 20.3.43[1] are acceptable.

II. *Remaining territories in Malay Peninsula*
It was agreed that a restoration of the 1941 arrangements was impossible on the grounds of

    (a) proper and efficient administration & security of the territories
    (b) our declared intention of promoting self-government in the Colonial Empire.

In particular it was important to avoid the dilemma towards which pre-war arrangements were developing, *viz.* that the logical alternative to the system of direct official rule behind a facade of Sultan rule was its replacement by a system of autocratic rule by the Sultans and their Malay advisers.

But at the other extreme it was important to secure that self-government did not rest on a numerical counting of heads which would mean the swamping of the

---

[1] See 12.

permanently resident communities (especially the Malays) by immigrants without a lasting interest in the country.

The steps to be taken to achieve our policy should be:—

(1) the extension to the area of the Foreign Jurisdiction Act.
) the negotiations of a new treaty which would establish

(a) a central body representing both the States and the residue of British territory, outside Singapore, and in which would be vested any residual authority not specifically delegated to State Governments.
(b) that within this framework, the Sultans should preserve their existing social and religious position and the State Governments be vested with the exercise of such administrative functions as might from time to time be allotted to them by the central authority.

The declaration of our purpose in carrying through the policy (the implementation of which would have to be studied on the spot) would be that Malay interests must be recognised as paramount in carrying through such a scheme but that other communities with permanent interests in the country must be given their due opportunity to share in an advance towards self-government.

III. *Sarawak.* This State should be declared a Protectorate and the Foreign Jurisdiction Act should be extended to it. The position of the Rajah under this new status will be a matter for future consideration and negotiation.

IV. *North Borneo.* Steps should be taken immediately to acquire for His Majesty's Government the sovereign rights in this territory possessed by the B.N.B. (Chartered) Company.

15 CO 825/35/6, no 5   18 May 1943

'Constitutional reconstruction in the Far East: Malaya, North Borneo and Sarawak': revised memorandum by G E J Gent   [Extract]

Malaya

1. A full restoration of the pre-war constitutional and administrative system will be undesirable in the interests of efficiency and security and of our declared purpose of promoting self-government in Colonial territories. The first of these interests requires a closer union of the territories comprising the relatively small area of the Malay Peninsula: and the second requires that self-government should not merely develop towards a system of autocratic rule by the Malay Sultans but should provide for a growing participation in the Government by the people of all the domiciled communities in Malaya, subject to a special recognition of the need to preserve the political, economic and social rights of the Malay race.

2. On the re-occupation of Malaya direct authority would be exercised by the Military Commander and the old position in which H.M. had no jurisdiction in the Malay States would thus disappear, and it would be possible to legislate for the

territory under the Foreign Jurisdiction Act. This jurisdiction should be preserved when the Military Administration gives way to a permanent civil administration.

3. The port and Island of Singapore had distinctive characteristics in the Malayan picture and should be treated as a special "free port" area in which self-government would develop by municipal methods and which would be a district administered separately from the rest of Malaya.

4. For the rest of the peninsula including the British Settlements of Penang and Malacca a constitution should be devised which would provide for a single united authority representing the States and the Settlements but resting on the ultimate authority of British power and jurisdiction under the Foreign Jurisdiction Act. The present treaties with the Malay rulers which are at present to be regarded as still operative, though for practical purposes in suspension owing to the enemy's occupation of the country, should be revised to accord with the new position and especially with H.M.'s new power of jurisdiction.

Subject to the overriding authority of this central constitutional power the several States and Settlements would have local institutions empowered to deal with such local affairs as may be devolved upon them by the central authority. These local bodies would be constituted so as to be representative of the principal communities and interests in the State or Settlement concerned.

The Malay rulers would retain their customary position of eminence in such social, religious etc. respects as accord with Moslem ideas. The elaboration of this general policy should be left for examination by a commission which would be appointed to consider the problems as soon as hostilities ceased and local conditions permitted. . . .[1]

---

[1] The sections on North Borneo and Sarawak are not printed here.

16 CO 825/35/6, no 14   28 July 1943

'Post-war constitutional arrangements for the mainland of Malaya': memorandum by Major-General H R Hone

[Hone was released from his duties as adviser, Political Branch GHQ Middle East, to be head of the Malayan Planning Unit. A senior member of the Colonial Legal Service, Hone had no previous experience of Malayan affairs and drafted this memorandum less than a month after he had taken charge of the MPU. Since it significantly directed planning away from federation and towards union, it may well have reflected the thinking of other members of the MPU, notably Brigadier H C Willan. The CO Eastern Department endorsed the notion of 'Malayan Union' and at the end of Aug submitted to the secretary of state two papers on future policy in respect of Malaya and North Borneo (see 17). Stanley recommended further inter-departmental consultations before taking the matter to Cabinet. The CO memoranda met with 'a fairly good reception' within Whitehall (see 18) although Sydney Caine objected strongly on economic grounds to the separation of Singapore from the peninsula (see 19).]

Arising out of recent discussions in the Colonial Office there are two matters which I should like to ventilate further, firstly to clarify my own mind, and secondly, in order that some covering memorandum to the Colonial Office policy paper may be prepared for the information of the Cabinet, in order that H.M.G. may appreciate the present proposals represent a change in policy, and that we, for our part, may be satisfied that the Cabinet is prepared to stand by its decisions, even though there may be an outcry from certain quarters.

New treaties with the Sultans

I have reflected further on the question of the proposed new treaties by which the Sultans will cede jurisdiction to H.M. in all States both Federated and un-federated. It is argued by Lieut. Colonel McKerron[1] that the change proposed is merely a legal one, but that in practice there is in fact no change. He points out that the present situation is that though in law the Rulers are independent, they have bound themselves by treaty to accept the advice in all matters of the British Resident (in the case of the Federated States) and the British Adviser (in the case of the un-federated States). Thus, if any law is to be passed or any action is to be taken, uniformity is achieved through the advice device and the Sultans have in fact no power at all. Further, in Federated States the Rulers have only these theoretical powers when the Federal Government (which means the Governor) is willing to delegate any particular subject to a State Government.

Though Lieut. Colonel McKerron's argument is attractive, I do not think that it is likely to carry any weight with the Sultans themselves when asked to sign on the dotted line: our real purpose in negotiating this change is not really connected with the day to day government of the country. It is based, I suggest, solely with the question of the future constitutional arrangements. If we get this concession of jurisdiction, we can set up a new constitution by an Order in Counsil [sic], whether the Sultans like it or not. If we do not get this jurisdiction for H.M., any change in constitution will require the negotiation of fresh treaties with all the Rulers in all the states; one recalcitrant Ruler could ruin the whole plan. In any case I think that Lieut. Colonel McKerron's argument is unsound, for there is only one sphere in which that Sultans have *not* bound themselves to act upon the advice of the British Advisers and Residents, *viz.*, the negotiation of new treaties with Great Britain.

It is for consideration, how far I should come out into the open when negotiating the new treaties with the Sultans. Am I to say frankly that this is a step towards setting up a new constitution? If I do, I must be in a position to tell the Sultans roughly what the new constitution is to be and what part they themselves may expect to play in it. I must have good arguments in favour of such a new constitution and, if possible, I must be able to give something in exchange for what I am taking away. If, in the case of Johore, I could promise a piece of Malacca, and, in the case of Kedah, I could promise Province Wellesley, I should have bartering cards of great value. Is the Cabinet likely to provide me with these weapons? And what about a bit of Siam for Kelantan and Perlis?

Failing these inducements, the best line of approaching the Sultans may be something like this:—

> "The British public are perturbed about Malaya. They consider that the loss of
> the dependency was partly due to the break-down of the administrative

---

[1] P A B McKerron, MCS since 1920, was a member of the Malayan Planning Unit. Under the British Military Administration he was deputy chief civil affairs officer, Singapore, and on the return of civil government he became colonial secretary, Singapore, 1946–1950.

arrangements in a time of great stress which they consider was due to the number of small units into which the administration of the Peninsula was divided. They are determined that the errors of the past shall not be repeated and that a more cohesive Government must be established. A great deal of British money will be required to rehabilitate the trade and social services of Malaya and to ensure its proper economic organisation to meet the difficulties of the post-war problems. Unless this proposed change in administrative arrangements is agreed to, the British public will not be prepared to vote the large sums of money which Malaya requires, and, therefore, it is essential that the Treaty changes that the British Government proposes should be accepted."

But I doubt if I ought to take a line of this sort without Cabinet approval.

For nearly a century our policy in Malaya has pivoted on the recognition of the independent local status of the Rulers, and there can be no doubt that the new treaties, if negotiated, will destroy their independence. No further treaties will ever again be necessary. I regard it as most important that the Cabinet should be fully aware of this reversal of policy which is fundamental in its importance. It is also necessary for me to know whether H.M.G. is prepared to go so far as to remove from office any Sultan who refuses to sign away his independence.

Federation or Union

The Colonial Office policy paper envisages a strong central government for the whole of Malaya Peninsula which will delegate in its discretion certain subjects to the State Councils for legislation. This proposition seems to indicate that the future constitutional policy in Malaya is to be developed on the lines of a Federation including in the future, the five States which have not hitherto joined the existing Federation.

The Federation of the four States which was effected in 1895 and developed by the Agreements of 1909 and 1927, gradually resulted in a situation which seriously threatened the submergence of the identity of the States. There was in fact a marked tendency towards "amalgamation" as opposed to "Federation"; in addition, it was suggested that the term "Federation" as applied to the form of union created by the treaties was a misnomer.

As a result of General Wilson's report of 1933,[2] it was decided by H.M.G. to take steps to reverse the tendency of amalgamation among the four States and to endeavour to establish a truer form of Federation by a process of decentralisation of powers to the Rulers and their State Councils. General Wilson reported that "there is a strong case on political grounds for giving the Rulers of the Federated Malaya [sic] States control of their own domestic affairs". To this end he advised putting the following Departments under State Control as soon as possible:—

a. Agriculture
b. Co-operative Societies
c. Education
d. Electricity
e. Forestry
f. Medical
g. Mining
h. Public Works
i. Veterinary

---

[2] Brigadier-General Sir Samuel Wilson, *Report on His Visit to Malaya 1932* (Cmd 4276, March 1933).

General Wilson advised further that as soon as possible financial responsibility for the domestic services of the States, should be vested in the Rulers in Council, the object being to make the State Governments increasingly independent as regards their State services. This envisaged the ultimate transfer of certain sources of Federal Revenue to the States, coupled with the right to impose State taxation so as to put the States in a position to meet all their expenditure without subvention from central resources.

I think it is important that the Cabinet should decide whether the policy recommended by General Wilson is to be persisted in after the military administration or not. It seems to me that the policy of decentralisation will inevitably lead to greater and further demands by the States for the control of additional subjects until we reach the position when the Federal Government will be shorn of all its authority except for external matters such as international trade treaties and agreements, customs and defence. It must be remembered that I think it necessary, if the personal position and prestige of the Rulers are to be maintained, to give them during the period of military government certain local powers. This is decentralising and, once started, we shall be committed to that course and General Wilson's report will be continually urged upon us as being the approved policy of H.M.G. in Malaya. If, in the post war period, General Wilson's policy is to be followed, there is no more to be said, but, if not, I must know what the new policy is and see that I do not give more power to the Sultans than they are likely to have in the post-military period.

The issue which is really to be placed before the Cabinet is whether H.M.G's future policy is to be based on a conception of the Federation or the ultimate union of the native States of Malaya.

One can see at once that from the point of view of administrative economy and convenience, there can be no question but that we should establish a single Protectorate over the whole of the mainland of the Malaya Peninsula, and set up a single government for it. This would indeed be to abolish the Sultans and the Cabinet must say whether this is our ultimate aim or not.

Experience in history proves the difficulties which assail small independent nations, and the lesson is that wherever possible small countries should unite with others of like race and traditions, or where union is impracticable, Federation at least should be attempted in order that the congregation of these small countries may stand together in line with the larger powers.

So far as my limited knowledge of Malaya goes, it would seem that the existence of ten different entities in the Peninsula is due to historical accident. The native inhabitants of all the States are predominantly of the same race, characteristics and tradition—all having common interests. If they had been left to themselves, the probability is that strong Sultans who [sic] would have emerged in certain areas, and they would have extended their influence to adjoining territories till the Malaya Peninsula might have been divided between two or three powerful potentates. Indeed, at some point of time, one supreme Sultan might have emerged; this development might have been all to the good, but with our present policy no such development can ever take place.

We have repeatedly stated that the principal aim of British Colonial policy is to train the peoples of the territories under our control to take an increasing part in the government of their own countries, so that in process of time they may ultimately stand as independent units of the British Commonwealth of Nations. Though the day upon which this result will be achieved in Malaya must be far distant, I assume that no-one suggests that this is not the ultimate policy which H.M.G. is applying to Malaya.

We have therefore, to consider whether the policy of Federation is one best designed to bring Malaya to the ultimate goal of all our Colonial possessions. On the one hand, it may be fairly argued that experience in State Control must be given to the Malaya [sic] Rulers and their people in order to fit them for wider responsibility in the future. On the other hand, the policy of decentralisation which strengthens the State Governments, can only result in emphasizing the individuality of the State Governments, thus making the ultimate union more and more impossible. It may, in fact, be true to say that in following the policy of decentralisation H.M.G. is leading the States down a road which can never lead to ultimate independence, but rather pledges them indefinitely to the protection and tutelage of a strong outside Power.

The question is then, are we aiming at ultimate union or Federation?

Common sense urges union of the States but, as indicated above, this could only be achieved by the elimination of the Sultans one by one until, by the progressive fusion of States, we were left with one State and one Sultan. I doubt if this is practical politics, but one cannot refrain from flirting with the idea. As each existing Sultan dies, could we put across a fusion with the neighbouring State[?] I suspect not. Alternatively could we form a Board of Sultans who jointly, would exercise jurisdiction over all the States[?] This august body might be a sort of second chamber presided over by the Governor-General whilst the legislative council would be presided over by the Governor of the Malayan Protectorate. All the Sultans could sign each law which would have currency throughout all the States. The law, however, would of necessity be in rather more general terms than we are at present accustomed to. Many of the Sections would, (I hope) give power to the various States to promulgate regulations which though framed on the same general lines would give latitude to deal with special local problems in differing ways according to local needs. Such a system of Government would not be Federal but would of course be union and the finance control would be centralised completely. That each State got its fair share of available revenue, would be insured by the budget. I see that in an earlier paper emanating from the Colonial Office, it was suggested that if a Council of Sultans were set up as a second chamber, that body would have no control over money bills. I doubt if this would work in the system suggested above; in any case I think Sultans are entitled to have some say, though not, of course, a final say in the allocation of the money between the various States. At present it is true that they have no such function.

If however, we are not aiming at unity, we must state what the object in view is, for the Sultans will certainly want to know. As indicated above, failing a union of the States, the next best aim is Federation. This means that the step we have in view is not the creation of a Malaya Protectorate but a Federation of Malay States covering the whole peninsula. We must try, therefore, to devise a constitution which is a true Federation and not something which is betwixt and between that and union or amalgamation. It seems to me that this is where we come up against a serious practical difficulty. The Sultans will want to know what subjects are to be dealt with by the Federal Government. I have not had time to study the constitutions of the other Dominions in which a system of Federal Government exists, but in those constitutions we may find a guide to help us. But I do know that in the Dominions, the Federal form of Government which now exists has been built up on a firm foundation. Generally, the process has been that the States forming the Federation have previously existed as such with a full measure of independent Government and the new Federal Government has grown out of that established order. The States themselves have surrendered [sic] certain rights and powers which have then been vested in the Federal Government to cover all those subjects of peculiar local interest.

In Malaya we are faced with the practical difficulty that all subjects are really of common interest and there is none of purely local interest. An examination of the present laws of the Federation and of the several States will show that in practically every subject for which the Federation has not legislated, almost identical laws have been passed in every State, whilst in the Unfederated States nearly all the Federal laws have, in addition, been adopted as State laws, in similar terms. In these circumstances it is very difficult to see how a true Federal system of Government for the whole of the Malaya Peninsula can be justified. It all boils down to the fact that any constitution based on the Federation idea [is] born only of the desire to retain the office of Sultan in each. In fact, the policy is based on sentiment instead of common sense, but, be it emphasised, sentiment of the highest character, *viz* the honouring of treaties and Britain's declared word.

17   CO 825/35/6, f 150 & no 22   30 Aug – 2 Sept 1943
[Future policy in Malaya and Borneo]: minutes by G E J Gent and Sir G Gater on the preparation of Cabinet memoranda

Sir G Gater
I am sorry at a time when he is pressed with the business of his W[est] A[frica] tour to have to put forward for submission to the Secretary of State, as a matter for direction to myself and the Eastern Department, the attached two memoranda[1] dealing with future policy in respect of Malaya and North Borneo.

These memoranda are the result of prolonged discussion and consideration in this Department, and, in the case of Malaya, with General Hone and the Malayan Civil Affairs unit at the War Office.

In the case of Malaya, the general policy advocated is the constitution of a Malayan Union, comprising the States and Settlements in the peninsula, less Singapore, which we propose should become a distinct political unit with a Governor of its own. This will be represented—by those concerned to do so—as a reversal of the pre-war policy of emphasising the individuality and sovereignty of the Malay States. But in his earlier discussions, in which Lord Hailey joined,[2] the Secretary of State was himself sympathetic to the idea of some closer union of the present 9 or 10 separate Governments in Malaya, both for defence and economic and general administrative strength. The policy of a union cannot be expected to be favoured by the individual rulers unless they themselves may come to share the view that unity is strength. It would be a false hope that the rulers' long-standing fears of submersion of the Malays by the Chinese and Indian immigrant communities will have been allayed as the

---

[1] Not printed.   [2] See 13.

result of their war experiences. On the contrary, it is not unlikely that the Japanese will have given particular position and powers to the leading Indian and Chinese quislings who have no doubt placed themselves at the Japanese disposal during the occupation of Malaya.

Borneo. The proposal in the memorandum as regards the territories in Borneo is that the British Government should assume direct responsibility for the Chartered Company's State of North Borneo, and that the island of Labuan, which lies off the North Borneo shore, should thereafter be attached politically to North Borneo. Brunei and Sarawak will be affected by our proposals to the extent that their rulers shall be required to transfer to H.M. such jurisdiction as is necessary for legislation for those territories under the Foreign Jurisdiction Act. In Sarawak there will be a Resident British Officer with similar powers to those possessed by the British Residents in the Malay States.

Over all this group of territories in Malaya and Borneo will be, if our proposals are accepted, a Governor-General with his headquarters at Singapore.

The second memorandum relates to North Borneo and its present administration by the Chartered Company. We propose that negotiations should be opened with the Chartered Company as soon as convenient, with a view to the transfer to the British Government of the present sovereignty and administrative authority possessed and exercised by the Chartered Company in London. This proposal has been very semi-officially discussed with the Treasury, and their main response is that any negotiations now with the Chartered Company should reserve for future decision, when the condition of the territory is ascertainable, the question of monetary compensation. We think that this is not impossible and that there is a good deal of spade work to be done with the Court of Directors, in the first place to determine the precise extent of the functions and properties which a British Administration would have to take over in the State.

In the case of both these memoranda, what we need is the Secretary of State's general blessing on the policies proposed and his approval of our proceeding to discuss with the Departments concerned on an official basis and at the official level, the final forms of memoranda to be prepared for the Secretary of State on his return to present to the War Cabinet.

G.E.J.G.
30.8.43

Mr Gent

I spoke to the Secretary of State yesterday in reference to the memoranda dealing with future policy in respect of Malaya and North Borneo. I explained to him that these memoranda were based upon the decisions reached in the conferences with him on these two subjects. The Secretary of State agreed that we could proceed with discussions with the Departments concerned on the official level with a view to preparing memoranda for the consideration of the Secretary of State on his return. The Secretary of State also agreed that an approach might be made to the North Borneo Company in regard to the handing over of responsibility for the Territory from the Chartered Company to H.M.G.

The Secretary of State said that the presentation of the memoranda to the War Cabinet would need careful consideration. In his judgment it was of great importance to indicate with some care the reasons why these matters must be considered *now*. Otherwise the War Cabinet might take the line, as they did in the case of Burma, that consideration is premature and that the future policy of these territories can be considered at a later date. The Secretary of State felt that it could be shown that it was vital to the immediate framing of plans in connection with the reoccupation of Malaya and Borneo for the future policy to be determined now.

The Secretary of State also said that the actual date of presentation to the War Cabinet would have to be considered on his return in the light of the war situation at that time.

G.H.G.
2.9.43

18 CO 825/35/6, f 29   18 Nov 1943
[Future policy in Malaya and Borneo]: minute by W B L Monson on Whitehall reactions to draft Cabinet memoranda

[Although Monson commented that CO policy had had 'a fairly good reception from all the Departments whom we consulted', it should be noted that both the FO and WO drew attention to the likelihood of opposition to the scheme. Sir Frederick Bovenschen, joint permanent under-secretary at the War Office, accepted that the proposals made 'common sense' but recommended caution in their implementation: 'You are, in fact, asking the Sultans to give away a large measure of their sovereignty, which I understand for many years past we have always boasted that we would maintain. I assume, nevertheless, that in discussing his Paper in the Cabinet, your Secretary of State will take the opportunity of impressing upon his colleagues the gravity of the decision which they are about to take, and indicate the form of public outcry which may be expected from certain sections of opinion in the country, unless some steps are taken to explain fully the reasons for the policy, and to educate the various political parties to accept it as a wise and proper course' (Bovenschen to Gater, 17 Nov 1943, CO 825/35/6).]

Our two Cabinet Memoranda on future constitutional policy in South East Asia and on the buying out of the British North Borneo (Chartered) Company have had a fairly good reception from all the Departments whom we consulted.

The North Borneo memorandum has in fact met general acceptance (and strongly expressed approval from the Foreign Office). The Treasury only have expressed some doubts as to whether there is a basis for financial discussions at the moment, but we have, I think, substantially met their points in our wording of the memorandum.

We have not had the War Office views yet, but we understand that they will take the form of (a) approval of our intention to administer Singapore separately from the mainland as fortuitously fitting in with their own plans for Military Administration. They anticipate that they would be able to hand the mainland territory over to the Civil Administration at an early date after reoccupation, but that Singapore would have to remain under Military Administration probably until the conclusion of the war against Japan; and (b) we understand that the War Office are going to say that the Military authorities cannot be expected to accept responsibility for the negotiation of fresh treaties with the Rulers as envisaged in our memorandum, and that therefore some civil mission will have to enter Malaya immediately after reoccupation to negotiate the necessary instruments with the Rulers in the name of H.M.G.

The Air Ministry have suggested that the Governor-General's duties should include that of centralizing R.A.F. requirements in the area. The Admiralty have made the same point in that they welcome the appointment on defence grounds. Our memorandum was (in paragraph 9 which deals with the functions of the Governor-General) silent on his duties as regards defence, and I have added a sentence to that paragraph to cover the omission.

The Admiralty make two further suggestions, to wit that the Governor-General should be made directly responsible for the administration of Singapore and of the areas in Johore immediately adjacent which would be in the defence system of the naval base. I am quite sure that it would be wrong to vest the Governor-General with direct governmental responsibility in Singapore Island, since he would inevitably become associated with the special economic interests of the Island, and any partition of Johore State would inevitably wreck our chances of creating the closer cooperation on the mainland to which we look.

The Admiralty have also suggested that we should submit our memorandum to the Post Hostilities Planning Committee. We have in fact sent copies of it personally to Rear Admiral Bellairs, the Secretary of the Committee, so that he is aware of our plans. It will no doubt be considered in due course whether we should make a formal reference of the paper to the Committee.

The Dominions Office have said that when the matter has been considered on the ministerial level, they would wish at some time to refer the question to the Dominions and suggest that the meeting of the Dominion Prime Ministers envisaged for next year might serve as a suitable opportunity. They have drawn particular attention to the interest of Australia in this matter. They have also expressed a dislike of the proposed title of Governor-General. We are not in our memorandum irretrievably committed to its use, which is explicitly stated to be used for convenience only. At the same time I regard it as a natural title, and it is, of course, the title normally borne by the chief Dutch and French officials in South East Asia.

The Foreign Office, in their letter at (47), concern themselves particularly with the presentation of our proposals to public opinion in the world at large. To meet their point [that] it is not clear how the strengthening of direct British rule and diminishing the powers of native rulers leads to self-government, I have added some sentences to paragraph 10 of the memorandum.

They also suggest that we should be more specific about our plans for developing the Malayan Union into an independent selfgoverning unit. I confess that I find it difficult to see how we can go beyond a general assertion of policy at the present moment and that there is no alternative to working out on the spot after reoccupation a detailed application of this policy in the light of the circumstances which exist at that time. We are, of course, without direct information as to the real extent to which the Japanese have taken the local populations into the administration of Malaya, and there is no guarantee that such information as we have at present will represent the conditions which will exist on our reoccupation. (ie We know that they have been associating representatives of the different communities in "Advisory" councils with their administration, and have made the Sultans Vice-Presidents (under a Japanese Governor) of the Advisory Council in each State. They would be running true to form if, when we get nearer Malaya, they gave a "phoney" grant of independence, as they have done in Burma and the Philippines.)

We are at the moment, at the request of the War Office, preparing a number of directives on longterm policy in different departments in Malaya. These inevitably hang on the memorandum in this file, and accordingly it would be convenient if a decision could be reached as soon as possible on our two memoranda.

19   CO 825/35/6, no 50   30 Nov – 1 Dec 1943
[Future links between Malaya and Singapore]: minutes by S Caine and G E J Gent

Mr. Gent
The discussion yesterday afternoon about the future constitutional position of Singapore took me a little by surprise, as I had not had any opportunity of seeing the documents until five minutes before the meeting. A few hours' further reflection has, however, only confirmed the opinions I expressed at the meeting.

I am concerned primarily with the economic position.[1] As I said at the meeting, I think that the clash between the interests of the mercantile community of Singapore and the producers of the mainland is very much over-emphasised. Fundamentally their interests are very largely identical. They depend on one another, and it would be just as foolish to suppose that Singapore could exist without the mainland community behind it as to suppose that the tin and rubber producers of the mainland could make profits if they had no merchants to market their produce for them. What we ought to do is to encourage the idea that they need each other and must co-operate with each other, and not to encourage what I regard as an entirely mischievous idea that their interests are distinct and necessarily opposed.

It is of course inevitable that on particular issues from time to time the immediate interests of Singapore will be different from those of some of the mainland territories or even all the mainland territories together; but the same is true of any other individual section of the mainland. It would, for instance, benefit the rice-producing areas at the expense of say the Kinta Valley if a heavy tariff were put on imported rice, or it would benefit Port Swettenham at the expense of both Penang and Singapore as well as the producing areas if railway rates were so framed as to discriminate in favour of Port Swettenham. These are all, however, divergences of interest which are bound to appear in any human society, and the logical conclusion of an approach to politics on the basis of divergence of interest is the abolition of all government whatsoever, so that each individual can be its own political unit. It is far more likely that the differences will be amicably settled within the framework of a single Government than if they have to be thrashed out at a high plane between independent Governments.

I suppose that the apparent clash of interests appears most clearly in relation to the Customs Union. Here, I would not dispute that it is probable that a rather different customs regime would suit Singapore taken by itself from that which would suit the mainland taken by itself. There are, on the other hand, certain advantages, both administrative and from the point of view of convenience of traders, in the Customs Union itself with its consequence of the abolition of barriers between

---

[1] Sydney Caine was currently financial adviser to the secretary of state.

Singapore and the mainland. If we were considering a Customs Union alone, I should not dispute the conclusion reached in Sir Cecil Clementi's[2] time that the balance of advantage was against the Customs Union. It was, however, only a balance of advantage, and since I believe there would be other advantages in a union between Singapore and the mainland extending to a much wider range of matters than the customs regime, I should say that such disadvantage as a Customs Union taken by itself might possess was now substantially outweighed by the other advantages.

In saying this, I am assuming that it would be possible to make adequate arrangements for free port facilities in Singapore to give reasonable assistance to the entrepot trade originating in Indonesia. I see no reason why that should be an insoluble problem.

I need not dilate here on the other advantages which I should believe to arise from a union of Singapore with the mainland. Briefly, they are: the encouragement to the formation of a Malayan national consciousness, much greater administrative convenience, avoidance of cultural fissure and, though here I speak with much greater hesitation, defence considerations.

S.C.
30.11.43

Mr. Caine
This is an issue which, as I am sure you know, has for years been debated in Malaya—on a host of practical issues.

Our first and foremost object is to secure a unification of the Malay States. That must be the essential basis for any larger union. It is the general view of those with real experience that this will be assisted by the non-inclusion of Singapore at any rate at the first stage. That in itself is a very important and almost an overriding argument.

On defence grounds the separate treatment of Singapore has been strongly approved by the Admiralty. (The suggestion that the defence of Singapore was shown to depend on resistance on the mainland is, I think you will agree, a quite superficial one. Singapore is worth defending as a naval base. Its loss to us was due to our loss of sea power.)

Singapore is a city, in the main, of Chinese immigrants. If its chief function as an international seaport and mart are [sic] maintained it will continue, as far as one can estimate, to have that character, and its contribution to Malayan national conscious-ness will be less than nil. Administrative convenience can be met in essentials by the methods we are proposing for particular branches of administration.

We have made, in subsequent discussion with Colonel McKerron, some alteration of the memoranda which I will send to you as soon as it is copied.

G.E.J.G.
1.12.43

Mr. Gent
These minutes will no doubt be recorded on the relevant Eastern Dept. file. My primary object is to place on record my view that the economic grounds for political

---

[2] Sir Cecil Clementi, governor of the Straits Settlements and high commissioner of the Malay States, 1929–1934.

separation between Singapore and the mainland are quite inadequate, and such economic disadvantages as there may be could well be [?ignored] if there are any other advantages to be gained by fusion. Whether there are such other advantages is strictly outside my sphere, but I should like to make one or two further points.

(a) On the borderline between economics and politics there are a number of matters in which identical legislation and a common administrative structure would be distinctly advantageous, and even minor divergences might be dangerous, e.g. Company and Banking Law, income tax administration. I believe the necessary uniformity would be more easily attained under a single Government than under two.

(b) As regards local opinion, I observed that the views of General Hone's advisers were four to one against any present decision in favour of separation. I was much struck by Colonel McKerron's plea that we should not prejudge a matter in which local opinion could only be ascertained after, and in the light of experience of, the Japanese occupation.

(c) It may well be that there is virtually no prospect of a Malayan national consciousness ever developing at all, but I find it very difficult to visualise its developing if the metropolis of the peninsula—a city as large in relation to the country as a whole as London is in relation to the United Kingdom—is cut off from the rest.

(d) Is it not an easy step from the proposition "Because Singapore is nearly all Chinese in race, it cannot be part of Malaya" to the proposition "Because Singapore is nearly all Chinese in race, it ought to be part of China"? I have always myself believed that Malaya's comparative freedom from communal disorders has been the result of a broadly non-discriminatory policy as between the different races. I believe that we have everything to gain by blurring and not by sharpening the distinctions between one race and another in the peninsula.

S.C.
1.12.43

20   CAB 66/45, WP(44)3   3 Jan 1944
'Directive on constitutional policy in Malaya and Borneo': joint War Cabinet memorandum by Mr Stanley and Sir J Grigg

[In early Dec the CO's Eastern Department submitted a draft Cabinet paper to Stanley who, reluctant to risk a Cabinet rebuff over such radical proposals, preferred a joint application with Grigg (secretary of state for war) for a Cabinet committee. On 6 Jan 1944 the War Cabinet agreed to the appointment of the Committee on Malaya and Borneo, consisting of the lord president (Attlee, chairman), the secretaries of state for the Dominions (Cranborne), India (Amery), the Colonies (Stanley), War (Grigg), the attorney general (Sir D Somervell), and the parliamentary under-secretary at the Foreign Office (George Hall) (see CAB 65/41, WM 2(44)3, 6 Jan 1944). Although Stanley completed papers on Malayan policy on 14 and 15 Jan (see 21 and 22) the committee postponed meeting until 22 Mar and did not report back to Cabinet until May (see 24 and 25).]

1.   As our colleagues are aware, steps were taken some time ago to commence the planning of the Administration of Malaya and Borneo, after reoccupation. This

planning is being conducted under the War Office in close association with the Colonial Office and has made considerable progress. A Chief Civil Affairs Officer for Malaya has already been selected, and under him the nucleus of the future Malayan Administration during military period is in the course of assembly in this country. A similar nucleus Administration for all the territories concerned in Borneo is also being collected here.

2. The detailed planning work on which these bodies are engaged must be governed by the general intentions of His Majesty's Government for the future, since it is important that, if possible, nothing should be said or done at the beginning of the reoccupation period which is incompatible with the long-term policy which we intend to adopt. This work of detailed planning has now reached the stage at which the planners find themselves in need of authoritative guidance on the broad issues of long-term policy, and in our view it is now necessary that a preliminary decision should be taken as to the future constitutional and administrative systems for the territories concerned. There is, of course, no necessity for any public announcement at this juncture.

3. There are many problems, some of considerable complexity, to be faced in determining the future system. For example there are—

(a) the position of our Treaties with the Malay rulers who, though subject to extensive political control, are yet in the position of sovereign princes;
(b) the positions of the territories in Borneo which comprise Labuan, a British Colony, Brunei, whose position is similar to a Malay State, Sarawak under the sovereignty of a European Rajah and North Borneo under a Chartered Company;
(c) the participation of the important Chinese and Indian communities in the local government institutions of the country, in view of the attitude of the Malay rulers to Asiatics who are not of Malay race or Mohammedan religion.

It is clear that problems of this magnitude will raise great political and legal difficulties and our decisions upon them will attract widespread attention both in this country and in the United States.

4. For that reason it would, we think, be most helpful if a Cabinet Committee could consider the full proposals which we are prepared to put before them, and, in the light of those full proposals, recommend to the Cabinet a directive upon which the planning authorities could base their work.

21   CAB 98/41, CMB(44)3   14 Jan 1944
'Future constitutional policy for British colonial territories in South-East Asia': memorandum by Mr Stanley for War Cabinet Committee on Malaya and Borneo

1. The policy which should be adopted as regards the political organisation of British and British-protected territories in South-East Asia after the termination of the present Japanese occupation has been under consideration in the Colonial Office. The administration of the territories immediately after the expulsion of the Japanese will, of course, be a matter for the military authorities and plans are already under

consideration on this basis. In particular a Chief Civil Affairs Officer for Malaya has already been selected, and under him the nucleus of the future Malayan military administration is in course of assembly at the War Office. A similar nucleus administration to cover all British-protected territories in Borneo is also in process of assembly.

2. The planning must, however, be from the outset conditioned by the arrangements which His Majesty's Government decide upon as regards future constitutional and administrative systems. The time has come for such general decisions to be taken. It is further important that, in so far as those decisions may represent a change from past policy, the military authorities should be satisfied that any steps which they take in conformity with those arrangements will be supported by His Majesty's Government in the face of possible opposition from any quarter. For reasons set out below it is also necessary to consider future plans for Malaya with some reference to those for British territories in Borneo. Proposals for the area as a whole are therefore included in this memorandum.

3. The territories concerned comprise the Colony of the Straits Settlements (Singapore, Penang and Malacca in Malaya, Labuan off the north coast of Borneo, and Christmas Island and the Cocos-Keeling Islands to the South of Java); the Federated Malay States of Perak, Selangor, Negri Sembilan and Pahang in the Malay Peninsula; the Unfederated States of Johore, Kedah, Kelantan, Trengganu and Perlis in the Malay Peninsula and Brunei in Borneo; and the States of North Borneo and Sarawak in Borneo. (It is not necessary in this memorandum to refer to the future position of Hong Kong.)

4. The Malay Peninsula, as organised under British control, consists, as explained, of a British Colony and of nine Malay States under their Malay Rulers, four of them being joined in a Federation. Until the seventies of [the] last century it was the policy to restrict British control to the three Settlements comprising the Colony and to discourage penetration into the Malay States. These States were at that time essentially reverine communities, each under their own ruler and isolated to a large extent by mountains and jungle. Even by 1870, however, the States were subject to disturbances occasioned by bands of pirates and by the impact on Malay society of traders and miners from the outside world, particularly Chinese. The resulting anarchy led to requests from the Rulers of the four States, which were later included in the Federation, for assistance in administration from the British Government. This assistance was embodied in Treaties providing for the appointment in each State of a British officer whose advice was to be asked and acted upon in all questions other than those concerning Malay religion and custom. Similar treaties were concluded at later dates with the other five States outside the Federation. In the Federated States these officers were styled British Residents, in the others British Advisers. It is, however, important to realise that from the legal point of view these Treaties involved no derogation from the position of the Rulers as sovereign princes, nor did they confer any jurisdiction on His Majesty in the Malay States.

5. The introduction of this system in the 1870s was followed by a rapid development of the resources of the States concerned (mainly by immigrant capital and labour), which resulted in the breakdown of their previous physical isolation. It was natural that this process should have led to proposals for administrative machinery for closer union and in fact the States of Perak, Selangor, Negri Sembilan and Penang [Pahang] did agree in 1895 to the formation of a Federation.

Paradoxically enough the existence of the Federation proved an obstacle to further unification of the Peninsula. For the rapidity of the country's material development had outstripped the advancement in education and administrative capacity of the Malays, and the British Residents found themselves compelled in fact to take over more or less direct control of the administrative system in the Federated States. As a result there emerged a highly centralised bureaucracy based on the Federal capital, and the Rulers of the States outside the Federation fought shy of the loss of power which they felt they would suffer in the administration of their States by joining the Federation. In the cases of Kedah and Perlis the British Agreements of 1923 and 1930 respectively include, in fact, a Clause by which His Majesty's Government have undertaken not to merge or combine these States with other States, or (in the case of Kedah) the Straits Settlements, without the written consent of the Ruler in Council. The attitude of the Malay Rulers was also coloured by the fact that in the main the penetration of Malay communities by immigrant races had gone further in the Federated than in the Unfederated States.

A further obstacle to the unification of the Peninsula lay in the divergence of economic interest between Singapore, which as a great entrepot was essentially mercantile in character, and the mainland of the peninsula which was mainly producing for export and which feared that in any closer union its interests would be sacrificed to those of Singapore.

6. Some attempt was made in the period between the two wars to meet the grievances of the Rulers of the Federated States by the policy of decentralisation, i.e., by the gradual transfer of many governmental functions from the Federal to the State Governments. It is important to realise however that this policy was regarded as an essential preliminary step for the achievement of a longer term policy, *viz.*, the promotion of closer co-operation between the constituent parts of Malaya *as a whole*, by removing the deterrent which the existing Federation constituted against the closer association of the Unfederated States.

7. Such administrative co-ordination as existed throughout the territories under discussion both in the Malay Peninsula and Borneo up to the date of Japanese occupation was achieved by the exercise by the Governor of the Straits Settlements of the additional functions of High Commissioner for the Malay States and British Agent for Borneo. As Governor of the Straits Settlements he was in direct charge of the Colony's administration: on matters pertaining to the Federated Malay States, as High Commissioner, he controlled the Federal Government through the Federal Secretary at Kuala Lumpur and the State Governments through the four British Residents; on the business of the Unfederated States, again, as the High Commissioner, he controlled the State Governments through the British Advisers in each State. Finally as British Agent for Borneo he was the channel of communication between His Majesty's Government and the Governments of Sarawak and North Borneo, but apart from the emergency appointment in 1940 of a Defence Liaison Officer for Sarawak he had no direct representative in either territory.

8. In the novel conditions which will exist in our return to Malaya there will be an opportunity to achieve closer co-operation between the constituent parts of the territory as a whole without going through the lengthy process which the sponsors of the decentralisation policy had to envisage.

Experience has shown that the interests of efficiency and security require closer integration of both the legislative and administrative arrangements in Malaya. United action in the past required separate action by ten Governments, a process which, without taking into account the opportunities it presented for local disagreement and the development of differences, did not conduce to speedy administration. On a longer view, too, the pre-war system does not seem capable of adjustment to the promotion of broad-based governing institutions in accordance with our proclaimed purpose in Colonial policy. There are important non-Malay Asiatic communities in the country which have substantially contributed to its development and have acquired permanent interests therein. But the Malay Rulers have always set their faces against any proposals to recognise as their subjects any persons not of Malay race or Mohammedan religion. The relaxation in due course of British official control over the Rulers would therefore, on the basis of the pre-war constitutional system, not be likely to provide the other communities with adequate prospects of participation in the government of the country.

9.   It is advisable that the function of co-ordination and direction should not be entrusted to an officer already burdened by detailed administrative responsibilities in any particular territory of the group. The appointment is therefore envisaged of a high British Authority (for convenience styled here a "Governor-General") for the whole area, *viz.* Malaya and British Borneo, without any direct administrative functions within any of the territories concerned, but with direct supervisory control over the chief officers of all those territories. This officer would have his own secretariat and a staff of expert advisers to assist him in supervising the political, economic, and social development of the territories and he could also be concerned with the representation of the interests of His Majesty's Government in the United Kingdom in any regional Council which may eventually be set up by the United Nations in that area. He would in any event have particular duties in securing due co-ordination on the civil side of all measures relating to the defence of the area. The headquarters of the Governor-General could conveniently be placed at Singapore, which is the natural centre of communications with all the British territories concerned and with neighbouring foreign administrations.

Malaya

10.   Within Malaya considerations of dynastic pride and local particularism militate against the emergence within any foreseeable future of a union of the existing Malay States under a native Ruler; nor, for reasons explained above, would the emergence of a united Malay monarchy for the whole province be acceptable to other non-Malay communities with substantial interests in the country. The British Crown alone provides the common link of loyalty which will draw the separate communities together and promote a sense of common interest and the development of common institutions. It is therefore necessary that, as a first step, the old situation in which His Majesty has no jurisdiction in the Malay States should be remedied. The legal view is that our present Treaties with the Malay Rulers are at present to be regarded as still operative (though for practical purposes in suspension owing to enemy occupation of the territory). A fresh treaty, therefore, with each Ruler should be concluded as soon as possible after reoccupation under which such jurisdiction would be ceded to His Majesty as would enable him to legislate for the States under the Foreign Jurisdiction Act, notwithstanding, in the case of Kedah and Perlis, the Clauses mentioned in paragraph 5 above. Thereafter it will be possible to proceed to create a new constitution for Malaya by Order-in-Council under statutory powers.

This will involve fresh legislation in the United Kingdom Parliament in respect of the Straits Settlements.

11. Our constitutional scheme should be designed, first and foremost, to provide for a union of all the Malay States and the settlements of Penang and Malacca. A central authority representing these States and Settlements should be created, and at its head there should be a Governor with an Executive and Legislative Council. The seat of Government of this Malayan Union would be conveniently at or near Kuala Lumpur, the capital of the present limited Federation. Subject to the new central authority, the several States and Settlements would be empowered to deal with such local affairs as may be devolved upon them by the central authority. These local authorities would be so constituted as to be representative of the principal communities and interests in the State or Settlement concerned.

12. It is desirable that the Island of Singapore should not be included in the present conception of the Malayan Union. Its inclusion might adversely affect the Malay attitude towards the proposals for the Union of the States, which is the first and foremost object of our policy and the necessary basis for any more extensive Union. The basis for a separate organisation for the Island of Singapore already existed in the Municipality of Singapore, but the appointment of a separate Governor or Lieutenant-Govrenor for the Settlement will be desirable. There will, of course, be many matters of administration, e.g., Posts and Telegraphs, on which the closest collaboration will be required between the authorities at Singapore and the rest of the Peninsula, but these can be the subject of particular agreements. Nevertheless, it should be made clear that His Majesty's Government has no desire to preclude or prejudice in any way the fusion of the two Administrations in a wider Union at any time should they both agree that such a course were desirable.

13. Separate consideration is required for the extra-peninsular portions of the Straits Settlements not mentioned above, i.e., Labuan, Christmas Island and the Cocos-Keeling Islands. Labuan can most conveniently be considered in connection with the British-protected territories in Borneo. The remote Christmas Island and the Cocos-Keeling group hardly raise any questions of constitutional principle. Their sole links with other Malayan territories are with Singapore and they should for administrative purposes be subject to the direct authority of the Governor of Singapore.

14. It is recognised that this programme will require the sacrifice by the State Rulers of some part of the authority and jurisdiction hitherto exercised by them. The interests of Malaya as a whole clearly require such a sacrifice. But there is no intention that the Rulers should lose their personal position as the natural leaders of their Malay people within their State territories. Indeed, the association of their territories in the Union will give the Rulers an opportunity to play their part in a wider sphere of affairs, for it is intended to devise means to associate the Rulers personally with the machinery of the central authority, possibly as an advisory body to the Governor in respect of Malay and Mohammedan affairs. In any event, our past obligations will require that the elaboration of the new constitutional arrangements should have regard to the political, economic and social interests of the Malay race.

15. The complete details of the application of this policy and in particular the detailed measures to be designed for the creation of self-governing institutions can only be worked out on the spot after reoccupation in the light of the prevailing conditions. It is, however, necessary that a general directive on future policy should

be issued for the guidance of the officers concerned with planning for the period of the military administration. The draft of a directive for this purpose in respect of Malaya is submitted as a separate paper (CMB (44) 4).[1]

Borneo

16. To turn now to the territories concerned in northern Borneo, these comprise:—

(a) The State of North Borneo, administered as an independent State under British protection by the British Borneo (Chartered) Company, in which all rights of sovereignty are vested. The State is by agreement under His Majesty's protection and its foreign relations are subject to the control of His Majesty's Government;
(b) The island of Labuan, a detached part of the Colony of the Straits Settlements, lying off the Western shore of the State of North Borneo;
(c) the State of Brunei, a Malay State, subject to the terms of a Treaty on the general lines of those concluded with the States in the Malay Peninsula; and
(d) The State of Sarawak, a Protected State under the sovereignty of Rajah Brooke. This State, like North Borneo, is under His Majesty's protection, but His Majesty's Government has no right to intervene in the internal administration.

17. The primary object of our policy in regard to these territories should be to see that, for the future, their machinery of government is of such a character as will conduce to their social and political development in conformity with our general Colonial policy.

18. So far as the State of North Borneo is concerned, this will involve the removal of the limitations inherent in a system of government by a Chartered Company. This matter is the subject of a separate memorandum (CMB (44) 5), and all that need be said here is that, on the transfer of the Chartered Company's constitutional authority in the territory to His Majesty, the union of North Borneo with Labuan under a single Governor with a local Executive and Legislative Council is envisaged.

19. As regards Brunei, His Majesty possesses (but does not exercise) a certain limited jurisdiction in the State. It is now desired that the Sultan of Brunei (like the Rulers in Malaya) should be invited to cede such jurisdiction to His Majesty as will enable him to legislate for the State under the Foreign Jurisdiction Act to the fullest extent.

20. As regards Sarawak, however, it is most desirable that His Majesty's Government should be placed in a position to exercise effective control over the administration. To this end it is proposed that the Rajah (like the Malay Sultans) should be invited to cede such jurisdiction to His Majesty as will enable him to legislate for the State under the Foreign Jurisdiction Act.

21. The territories in Borneo under discussion are still comparatively un-developed, and they have few racial or other affinities. At this stage the basis for closer union hardly exists, but community of policy can be assured by the subordination of the Governor of North Borneo and Labuan, and of the resident British Advisers in Brunei and Sarawak to the authority and direction of the Governor-General at Singapore.

---

[1] See 22.

22.   The draft of a directive on future policy in respect of the four territories in Borneo for the guidance of the officers concerned with planning for the period of the Military Administration is submitted in a separate paper (CMB (44) 6).

22   CAB 98/41, CMB(44)4   15 Jan 1944
'Draft of a directive on policy in Malaya': memorandum by Mr Stanley for War Cabinet Committee on Malaya and Borneo

1.   The restoration of the pre-war constitutional and administrative system will be undesirable in the interests of efficiency and security and of our declared purpose of promoting self-government in Colonial territories. The first of these interests requires a closer union of the territories comprising the relatively small area of the Malay Peninsula; and the second requires that self-government should not merely develop towards a system of autocratic rule by the Malay Rulers but should provide for a growing participation in the Government by the people of all the communities in Malaya, subject to a special recognition of the political, economic and social interests of the Malay race.

2.   On general grounds, and more particularly in order that His Majesty's Government may be in a better position to ensure the development of the country on the lines indicated above, it is necessary that the old position in which His Majesty had no jurisdiction in the Malay States should be remedied and that it should be possible to legislate for those States under the Foreign Jurisdiction Act. Immediately on the reoccupation of Malaya, direct authority will be exercised by the Military Commander, who will carry with him sufficient authority to enable him to exercise such direct powers and control over the territory as will be necessary during the period of military administration. This military authority will, however, not enable His Majesty to legislate for the Malay States under the Foreign Jurisdiction Act, and moreover, the jurisdiction of the Military Commander will not persist when the military administration gives way to a permanent civil administration.

It is considered that the proper way to achieve our purpose will be to make fresh treaties with the Sultans under which such jurisdiction would be ceded to His Majesty as would enable him to legislate for the States under the Foreign Jurisdiction Act. A fresh Treaty with each Sultan should for this single purpose be concluded on behalf of His Majesty at the earliest opportunity on reoccupation.

3.   The acquisition of this jurisdiction by His Majesty will enable an Order-in-Council to be made to provide for the future central and local government of the country. This jurisdiction will render unnecessary any further dependence on Treaties with Rulers in any future revision of the constitutional arrangements.

4.   The new constitutional arrangements for Malaya should provide for the special treatment of the port and Island of Singapore in the early stages at any rate in view of its distinctive characteristics in the Malayan picture.

5.   The rest of the peninsula including the British Settlements of Penang and Malacca should be constituted a Malayan Union. For the Malayan Union a constitution should be devised which would provide for a single united authority representing the States and the Settlements, subject to the jurisdiction of His Majesty under

the statutory powers. At the head of the Union Government would be a Governor with an Executive and a Legislative Council. The seat of this Government would conveniently be in or near Kuala Lumpur.

6. The co-ordination and direction of the policies of Government in the Malayan Union and Singapore will be secured by the appointment of a "Governor-General" at Singapore, with the power of control over the local Authorities in Malaya and Borneo.

7. Co-operation in all adminstrative matters requisite between Singapore and the Union will be ensured by particular agreements for joint consultation and action.

8. It will be no part of the policy of His Majesty's Government that the Malay Rulers should lose their personal dignities in their State territories. Indeed it will be the intention that, by the association of their territories in the Union, the Rulers will have opportunities to take part in wider activities than hitherto for the general advantage of the country as a whole, and may thereby enhance their sphere of influence and prestige in Malaya.

23   CO 825/42/3, no 7   4 Feb 1944
[Publicity for postwar policy]: letter from Admiral Mountbatten to Major-General H R Hone

[At the time of Mountbatten's correspondence with London about giving publicity to the progressive aspects of the new Malayan policy (see also 26–30) the military tide was turning in favour of South-East Asia Command. Between Feb and July General Slim's 14th Army repulsed the Japanese at Arakan and Imphal-Kohima, and forced them into retreat. On 15 Apr Mountbatten transferred his headquarters from India to Kandy.]

I am writing this letter, as I promised I would, to embody the points I made in the paper I sent you on January 27th and to add a few thoughts on how those points can be presented to public opinion (both at home and in America and elsewhere) and to the people of Malaya themselves.

When we re-occupy Malaya we shall have a golden opportunity, if we choose to take it, to put the place on a firmer and more rational footing than was the case before; and I am convinced that the way the military administration kicks off will make the whole difference to the prospect of our introducing a reasonable constitution in the future.

To begin with, I feel very strongly that the whole of Malaya (that is the Unfederated and Federated Malay States as well as the Straits Settlements) should become one unified administration under some such name as "Union of Malaya".

I consider that we should introduce some means by which the more educated classes can elect representatives to an Advisory Council, which would advise the C.C.A.O. during the military administration. This body would subsequently form a sound basis for a Legislative Council under a Civil Government.

I am not in favour of reinstating the Sultans even as constitutional rulers, and certainly not as autocratic rulers. The Japanese have kept them in position and it is inconceivable that most of them have not been actively collaborating with the Japanese, even though the more clever ones, like Jehore [sic], may when the time comes embarass [sic] us by turning round and siding actively with the victorious British armies. In any case, their prestige cannot fail to have been seriously impaired by the Japanese occupation.

But we must be careful not to abolish the Sultans ruthlessly. I understand that they are regarded as the religious leaders in their states and this aspect of the matter we should of course in no way interfere with. I think that they should form a "Chamber of Princes", who would act as an Upper House to the Advisory Council. In this way, we should not only respect the religious feelings of the Malayans, but we should have during the military administration the benefit of the experience of the Sultans.

A point which would require very careful consideration is what should be done with this "Chamber of Princes" when the military administration is transformed into a Civil Government. Personally, I think it would be the greatest mistake to give back to the Sultans any form of hereditary right, either to legislate or even to implement legislation in their States. Those who had proved themselves thoroughly competent and worthy might be appointed as Prime Minister of their own State; but in backward States, or in States where the loyalty of the Sultan had been called in question, a separate Prime Minister should be appointed, chosen from the elected members representing that State.

In other words, the Prime Minister of each State should come either from the Upper or the Lower House, according to his suitability.

Our intentions will have to be put over, of course, to our own people, to the world at large and to the Malayans, by the Press and by broadcasting, etc. I believe it would help enormously in the vital and difficult task of making our troops out here understand the necessity of continuing the war out here after the defeat of Germany, if it were clear to them that we have a constructive plan which their victory will enable us to put into operation: there has been so much written and said about the mismanagement of Malaya that I do not believe it is enough to let them think they are fighting to restore the status quo.

In the same way, public opinion in America and in the democracies in general, has been sharply critical of our handling of this part of the world.

I do not think we need fear the reactions of the democratic peoples to a move which is designed to unify the present very loose agglomeration of administrations in Malaya. This move seems to me progressive, in the sound sense of the word and is a "rationalisation" which I feel could only be condemned on feudal or romantic grounds. It would have been a different matter to undertake this tidying up in peacetime, but there has been a clean break with the past, in the form of foreign occupation and it should be fairly easy to accomplish quite painlessly, merely by omitting to restore what was neither necessary nor beneficial in a previous set-up.

I feel that we must take a firm lead now. Events in North Africa and in Italy have shown that it is essential to choose from the first the line which one will inevitably have to follow, so that one can lead public opinion, in fact, instead of having to modify one's plans, which one will then appear to be abandoning under the pressure of public criticism.

Since the invasion, no part of the world had come in for so much criticism as Malaya has and condemnation of the pre-invasion state of affairs has come from many angles. But, although I realise that any action we take will be closely watched by the many people who are waiting for a chance to criticise, I do not think these critics will condemn innovations if these are reasonably progressive and tend to tidy up what had degenerated into a most unsatisfactory situation. Our waiting critics, I think, are far more likely to suspect that we have not the vision or the will to prevent a return to the bad old days.

Criticism from the Left will, I think, chiefly concern itself with the economic and financial aspects of the re-occupation. A great deal has been said about rubber, etc., and I imagine that the constitutional status of the Sultans will seem comparatively unimportant to those who are gunning for the vested interest, particularly as any modification in their hereditary and autocratic powers will seem a step in the right direction to those who are suspecting us of wanting to put the clock back.

Criticism from the Right will perhaps be forthcoming from the "traditional" point of view; but such opinions sound very feudal nowadays and many people who hold them are shy of stating them. From the more realistic and constructive point of view, I do not see why there should be more criticism: we are depriving the Sultans neither of their possessions nor of their revenues: and we are actually giving them, if they choose to use it, a chance of constituting themselves into a powerful, united body which can defend their interests far more satisfactorily than in the piecemal [sic] fashion of the past. As regards British capital investment, I cannot believe that in the more closely knit post-war world of cartels and large-scale enterprises, it will not be of advantage to deal with a unified peninsula, rather than by a method of treaties more suitable to the days of Clive.

As regards the people of Malaya themselves, it is of course hard to gauge what effect the Japanese occupation may have had on their attitude to us and to their rulers. But it has been widely suggested that the apathy with which the Malay watched us being turned out by the Japanese was chiefly due to our not having sufficiently interested ourselves in securing his co-operation. If it is true that the Malay regarded us largely as people who came to make money there, and who returned to England when they had made enough, any extension of our interest in his government will be a good thing: and he will no longer feel that we are prepared to let his autocratic Sultans have a free hand so long as they do not impede our rights to the wealth of his country. Our new attitude can be presented to him as a form of "paternalism" and at all events he can be made to feel that he can no longer justly accuse us of a purely mercenary neglect and indifference towards him.

You may use this letter as representing my considered views.

24 CAB 98/41, CMB(44)1 22 Mar 1944
[Future policy]: minutes of the War Cabinet Committee on Malaya and Borneo[1]

The Committee had before them a Memorandum on the future constitutional policy

---

[1] The following were present at this first meeting of the committee: Mr Attlee (chairman, lord president), Mr Amery (India Office), Mr Stanley (CO), Sir J Grigg (War), Sir D Somervell (attorney-general), Mr Emrys-Evans (parliamentary under-secretary of state, DO), H Ashley Clarke (FO), G E J Gent (CO) and Sir G Laithwaite (War Cabinet Office). E H T Wiltshire and W B L Monson served as secretaries.

for British colonial territories in South East Asia (C.M.B. (44) 3);[2] draft of a Directive on policy in Malaya (C.M.B. (44) 4);[3] a Memorandum on the acquisition of administrative rights of the British North Borneo (Chartered) Company (C.M.B. (44) 5)[4] and a draft Directive on policy in Borneo (C.M.B. (44) 6).[5]

1. Draft directive for Malaya

The Secretary of State for the Colonies said that the object of the draft directive for Malaya was to set out minimum conditions within which planning in relation to re-occupation should proceed, and to guide the military authorities while they were administering the country. No question arose of drafting a detailed constitution or of giving publicity to the policy proposed in the directives.

The main purposes of the policy put forward (paragraph 8 of C.M.B. (44) 3) were:—

(a) To secure a greater unity in administration than had existed prior to the Japanese invasion by creating a Government at the centre with power to enforce its decisions while allowing latitude in local affairs to territorial sub-divisions.

(b) To revise the treaties in such a way that while the social and religious position of the Rulers was unimpaired, the object at (a) should be achieved and the Rulers prevented from denying rights of citizenship to non-Malay elements in the community.

The Secretary of State for India endorsed the draft Directive. He welcomed the proposal for growing participation in Government by all communities, while recognising the force of the special reservation regarding the rights of the Malay race in the last sentence of paragraph 1. He saw no awkward precedent either in relation to Burma or the Indian States.

The Committee then discussed the extent to which the proposed Directive committed His Majesty's Government to supporting the rulers even though their subjects might oppose the maintenance of their rule.

The Lord President of the Council felt that there was no evidence as to the present conduct of the Rulers or attitude of the people themselves, and the draft did not indicate an alternative course of action. The Directive was, however, mandatory, and the expression of an intention to re-negotiate treaties with the rulers might commit us to reinstate them whatever we or the people might wish.

The Secretary of State for the Colonies said that there was no evidence from Malaya which suggested that the sentiments of the Malays towards the institution of the Sultanate had changed. The fact that certain rulers might be found to have been quislings, was not an argument against the institution and it should be remembered that actions which seemed democratic and progressive in the West might be very differently interpreted in the East.

The Secretary of State for War said that the Military Commander must know what form of civil administration was intended. To this extent a directive was indispensable. He would not oppose amendments which took account of the contingency that the people did not want the ruler back.

The Attorney General explained that the treaties were still valid; if the purposes set

---

[2] See 21.   [3] See 22.   [4 & 5] Not printed.

out by the Secretary of State for the Colonies were to be achieved the only alternative to re-negotiation was annexation.

| After a full discussion it was agreed that the Directive should be so qualified 'X' as to take account of the contingency mentioned by the Lord President of the | Council.

Further points which were raised in discussion were as follows:—

(a) *The Secretary of State for War* emphasised that if difficulty with rulers was apprehended, the right must be reserved to the Military Commander to advise the Secretary of State for the Colonies to delay an approach until the situation was ripe for it to be made, in the light of current military situation.

(b) *The Committee* agreed with the statement of the Secretary of State for War that the area under discussion lay within the military sphere of His Majesty's Government and not that of the United States Government.

(c) *Mr. Ashley Clarke* considered (i) that even a slight dimunition [sic] of the powers of the rulers would have to be carefully presented: and (ii) that it would be wise to bear in mind that Malaya might have to be fitted into a regional system, in the constitution of which other countries, particularly China would have a say. He recongnised [sic] of course that such a system would not give them the right to interfere in Malaya's internal affairs. *The Lord President of the Council* endorsed the view at (i) above.

Mr. Emrys Evans said that the Dominions, particularly Australia and New Zealand, would expect to be informed of our policy at the forthcoming Prime Ministers' Conference.

The Committee:—

(i) Took note of C.M.B. (44) 3 and 4 and were in general agreement with the policy set out in the latter, and

(ii) Invited the Secretary of State for the Colonies to cause the draft directive to be amended in the sense of 'X' above, and to be circulated for the information of the Committee.

2. Draft directive for Borneo

The Secretary of State for the Colonies, in introducing C.M.B. (44) 5 and 6, referred to the difficulties of communication and diversity of population in the four territories which made a closer form of association than that now proposed impracticable. He did not anticipate that either the Rajah of Sarawak or the Sultan of Brunei would raise any difficulties over the cession of jurisdiction to His Majesty.

| *The Secretary of State for War* referred to the division of military responsibility between the Americans and ourselves in the area. If a directive were issued to the Military Commander it would have under present arrangements to be transmitted via the Combined Chiefs of Staff to an American Commander. For this reason the directive under consideration should be restricted to the use of our 'Y' own planning authorities. A separate directive should be prepared in due course for transmission to an American Commander in which he thought it would be desirable to omit references to negotiations with the British North Borneo (Chartered) Company and the Rajah of Sarawak in case such an extention [sic] of His Majesty's Government's direct influence in this area would be unwelcome to an American Commander.

The Secretary of State for the Colonies emphasised that in any discussions with the Americans we had a safeguard in Article 6 of the Charter of the Combined Civil Affairs Committee.

The Committee:—

(i)   took note of C.M.B. (44) 5 and 6 and were in general agreement with the policy set out in them.

(ii)   Endorsed the observations of the Secretary of State for War set out at 'Y' above, and invited the Secretary of State for the Colonies to take action accordingly.

25   CAB 66/50, WP(44)258   18 May 1944
'Policy in regard to Malaya and Borneo': War Cabinet memorandum by Mr Attlee. *Appendices*: I 'Draft directive on policy in Malaya' and II 'Draft directive on policy—Borneo'

[On 31 May 1944 the War Cabinet considered WP(44)258 and authorised the secretary of state for the colonies to do the following: firstly, to issue the directives at Appendices I and II to those responsible for planning civil administration in Malaya and Borneo; secondly, to open confidential discussions with the directors of the British North Borneo Company about the transfer of North Borneo to Crown control; and, thirdly, to open confidential discussions with the Rajah of Sarawak with a view to the preparation of a new agreement (see CAB 65/42, WM 70(44)3).]

We were appointed by the War Cabinet at its meeting on the 6th January (W.M. (44) 2nd Conclusions) to consider the question of the constitutional policies to be followed in Malaya and in the British territories in Borneo on their liberation, and to recommend a directive on which the authorities responsible for planning the Civil Administration of these territories after liberation can work.

The composition of the Committee was as follows:—

> The Lord President of the Council (*Chairman*).
> The Secretary of State for Dominion Affairs.
> The Secretary of State for India.
> The Secretary of State for the Colonies.
> The Secretary of State for War.
> The Attorney-General.
> The Parliamentary Under-Secretary of State for Foreign Affairs.

2.   *Malaya.*—A directive on the probable lines of future policy is indispensable for those who have the duty of planning the Civil Affairs policies and as a basis for the directive to be issued in due course on these matters to the Supreme Allied Commander, S.E.A.C.; and, on the understanding that no publicity is given to the policies contained therein, we are in agreement on the terms of the directive for this purpose, which form Appendix I to this report.

3.   *Borneo.*—The four British territories concerned (North Borneo, Sarawak, Labuan and Brunei) are at present in a United States sphere of command, the S.W. Pacific. His Majesty's Government are entitled, under the terms of the Charter of the

Combined Civil Affairs Committee, to provide the American Commander with directives on Civil Affairs policies in these British territories, and a directive on Civil Affairs will need to be framed at the appropriate time for issue to him. But it is not our function to examine the form in which any such directive for that purpose will need to be framed. We have concerned ourselves only with a directive on which the British planning staff should work. For this limited purpose we have agreed upon a directive in the terms of Appendix II to this report.

4. It will be noted that the Borneo directive proposes the acquisition by His Majesty's Government from the British North Borneo (Chartered) Company of its sovereign and administrative rights in North Borneo. We are of opinion that confidential discussion for this purpose should be opened with the Court of Directors of the Chartered Company, though we recognise that in the present uncertain position as to the value of the Chartered Company's assets in the Far East it would be premature to reach any agreement on the financial terms on which such a settlement could be reached.

5. In the case of the Borneo directive, as in that of the Malayan, there is no question of any publicity being given to the policies beyond the confidential discussions which will be involved with the Chartered Company and the Rajah of Sarawak.

6. To sum up, we accordingly recommend, with the proviso that no publicity for these policies is involved, that the Secretary of State for the Colonies be authorised—

(a) To issue the directive at Appendix I to the authorities responsible for planning for the Civil Administration of Malaya on liberation;
(b) To issue the directive at Appendix II to the British officials at present planning for Civil Administration in British Borneo after liberation;
(c) To open confidential discussions with the Court of Directors of the British North Borneo (Chartered) Company with a view to coming to an understanding (without at this stage any financial commitment) as to the conditions on which the administration of North Borneo would be transferred from the Company's responsibility and control to that of His Majesty's Goverment; and
(d) To open confidential discussions with the Rajah of Sarawak, who is at present residing in this country, with a view to the preparation of a new Agreement on the lines proposed in paragraph 3 (c) of Appendix II attached.

Appendix I to 25

1. The restoration of the pre-war constitutional and administrative system will be undesirable in the interests of efficiency and security and of our declared purpose of promoting self-government in Colonial territories. The first of these interests requires a closer union of the territories comprising the relatively small area of the Malay Peninsula; and the second requires that self-government should not merely develop towards a system of autocratic rule by the Malay Rulers but should provide for a growing participation in the Government by the people of all the communities in Malaya, subject to a special recognition of the political, economic and social interests of the Malay race.

2. On general grounds, and more particularly in order that His Majesty's Government may be in a better position to ensure the development of the country on

the lines indicated above, it is necessary that the old position in which His Majesty had no jurisdiction in the Malay States should be remedied and that it should be possible to legislate for those States under the Foreign Jurisdiction Act. Immediately on the reoccupation of Malaya, direct authority will be exercised by the Military Commander, who will carry with him sufficient authority to enable him to exercise such direct powers and control over the territory as will be necessary during the period of military administration. This military authority will, however, not enable His Majesty to legislate for the Malay States under the Foreign Jurisdiction Act and, moreover, the jurisdiction of the Military Commander will not persist when the military administration gives way to a permanent civil administration.

3. In considering the proper way to achieve these objects, it is necessary, on the one hand, to make certain basic assumptions and, on the other hand, to be prepared to meet a situation when the liberation of Malaya has been effected, on which those assumptions may be found to be wrong or incomplete and in consequence the prepared plans may have to be varied. The future position and status of the Malay Rulers in particular cannot finally be judged before liberation when it will be possible to assess not only their individual records but also and especially the attitude of the people of Malaya to the advantages or otherwise of maintaining the Sultanates as institutions in the several States. For the present we have no reason for any other assumption than that the Sultanates as an institution will continue to enjoy the loyalty and traditional respect of the Malays.

4. On that assumption, it is considered that the proper way to achieve our purpose will be to make fresh treaties with the Rulers under which such jurisdiction would be ceded to His Majesty as would enable him to legislate for the States under the Foreign Jurisdiction Act. A fresh Treaty with each Ruler should for this single purpose be concluded on behalf of His Majesty as soon as feasible after reoccupation. The actual signatory of such Treaties on behalf of His Majesty would appropriately be the G.O.C., but the negotiations would be carried on under instructions from the Secretary of State for the Colonies by Civil Affairs Officers or special representatives of His Majesty's Government, subject always to be proviso that the actual time for opening negotiations with the Rulers must be governed by Military exigencies and left to the discretion of the Military Commander.

5. The acquisition of this Jurisdiction by His Majesty will enable an Order-in-Council to be made to provide for the future central and local government of the country. This jurisdiction will render unnecessary any further dependence on Treaties with Rulers in any future revision of the constitutional arrangements.

6. The new constitutional arrangements for Malaya should provide for the special treatment of the port and Island of Singapore, in the early stages at any rate, in view of its distinctive characteristics in the Malayan picture.

7. The rest of the peninsula, including the British Settlements of Penang and Malacca, should be constituted a Malayan Union. For the Malayan Union a constitution should be devised which would provide for a single united authority representing the States and the Settlements, subject to the jurisdiction of His Majesty under statutory powers. At the head of the Union Government would be a Governor with an Executive and a Legislative Council. The seat of this Government would conveniently be in or near Kuala Lumpur.

8. The co-ordination and direction of the policies of Government in the Malayan Union and Singapore will be secured by the appointment of a "Governor-General" at

Singapore, with the power of control over the local Authorities in Malaya and Borneo.

9. Co-operation in all administrative matters requisite between Singapore and the Union will be ensured by particular agreements for joint consultation and action.

10. On the assumption explained in paragraph 3 it will be no part of the policy of His Majesty's Government that the Malay Rulers should lose their personal position in their State territories. Indeed, it will be the intention, that, by the association of their territories in the Union, the Rulers will have opportunities to take part in wider activities than hitherto for the general advantage of the country as a whole, and may thereby enhance their sphere of influence and prestige in Malaya.

Appendix II to 25

1. The restoration of the pre-war constitutional and administrative systems in the four territories will be undesirable in the interests of security and of our declared purpose of promoting social, economic and political progress in Colonial territories. These purposes require:—

(a) The direct assumption by His Majesty's Government of responsibility for administration in North Borneo.
(b) The integration of Labuan with North Borneo.
(c) The cession to His Majesty of full jurisdiction in Brunei and Sarawak.

The purpose of political progress requires also that self-government in Brunei and Sarawak should not merely develop towards systems of autocratic rule but should provide for a growing participation in the Government by people of all communities in each territory.

2. On general grounds, and more particularly in order that His Majesty's Government may be in a better position to ensure the development of the country on the lines indicated above, it is necessary that the old position in which His Majesty had not full jurisdiction in these territories, with the exception of Labuan, should be remedied and that it should be possible to legislate for them all by Order-in-Council. Immediately on the reoccupation of these territories, direct authority will be exercised by the Military Commander, who will carry with him sufficient authority to enable him to exercise such direct powers and control over the territories as will be necessary during the period of military administration. This military authority, even if it fell to be exercised by a British Commander, would, however, not enable His Majesty to legislate for the three States, North Borneo, Brunei and Sarawak, by Order-in-Council, and, in any case, the jurisdiction of the Military Commander would not persist when the military administration gave way to a permanent civil administration.

3. It is considered that the most effective way to achieve our purposes will be:—

(a) To acquire from the British North Borneo (Chartered) Company the sovereign and administrative rights which they possess and have hitherto exercised; and thereafter to provide for the future government of the territory on its liberation by an Administration under the direct authority of His Majesty's Government.
(b) To incorporate the present Settlement of Labuan in the New Administration for North Borneo.

(c) To conclude new treaties with the Sultan of Brunei and the Rajah of Sarawak at the earliest opportunity which will accord to His Majesty such jurisdiction in their States as will enable His Majesty to legislate for these territories under the Foreign Jurisdiction Act to the fullest extent. In the case of Sarawak, the new treaty should also secure the acceptance by the Rajah of a resident British Adviser whose advice must be sought and acted upon in all substantial matters of policy and administration. (The present treaty with Brunei already provides for a resident British Adviser.)

3. The territories in Borneo are still comparatively undeveloped and they have few racial or other affinities. At this stage, therefore, the basis for closer union between them hardly exists. Community of policy and of administrative action can, however, be assured from the outset under the direction of the Governor-General at Singapore, whose appointment is recommended and the promotion of closer union should be a continuing matter of our policy.

26   CO 825/42/3, no 21   13 June 1944
[Future policy in Malaya]: letter from Mr Stanley to Admiral Mountbatten

Cranborne has passed on to me your letter of the 19th March about the future constitution of Malaya. I had actually already been shown by Hone on his return from India your letter to him of the 4th February[1] on the same subject, but I have held up my reply as your letter reached me at a juncture in which proposals on this very subject were under consideration by the War Cabinet. These have now concluded and I have been authorized to issue a Directive on our Policy in Malaya for the confidential guidance of Civil Affairs planners.[2] A copy of this will reach you officially through Service channels but I enclose another for convenience of reference.

Let me say at the outset that I thoroughly share your conviction that the way the military administration kicks off will make the whole difference to the smooth development of a new constitution in future, and that as I am responsible for our future policy I was, if I may say so, very glad to see the realistic and co-operative spirit with which you have approached the delicate issues involved in setting up a military administration in Malaya. Moreover I was glad to see that your ideas on policy were by and large on similar lines to those on which our minds had been working at this end during our consideration of the "directive" enclosed.

There are however one or two factors in the existing and prospective situation of Malaya which do not seem to me and my advisers fully accounted for in your letter to Hone.

In the first place your analysis of the position in Malaya does not seem to me to bring out fully the complicated situation introduced by the presence in the country of a plural society. You will realise that the presence in substantial numbers in Malaya of Chinese and Indians makes the future constitutional development a matter

---

[1] See 23.   [2] See 25, Appendix I.

of some delicacy, particularly as these communities are likely to demand a more intimate place in the constitutional set up in the future than they have been given in the Malay States in the past, while at the same time the great economic power which they have already secured has led to antagonism between themselves and the Malays. We must be prepared to face a risk of sectional antagonisms showing themselves more definitely in the settlement of a new constitution.

As regards the Malays themselves, I am not sure from paragraph 16 of your letter to Hone whether you intended to give the impression that the average Malay resented us in the past because we were prepared to allow their autocratic Sultans to have a free hand. It is, of course, a fact that the autocratic powers of the Malay Rulers were most considerably curbed under our "advice" and direction to the undoubted benefit and the manifest security of the average Malay.

As regards your suggestions for the future, I notice that you propose a completely unified administration for the whole of Malaya. We here have felt that if we are to secure a greater degree of unification which is clearly essential for the wellbeing and security of the country but which must to some degree depend on the consent of the Malays, we may have to exclude Singapore from any such union, at any rate in the early stages, because of the predominantly Chinese element in its population. I should have thought too, that such an exclusion would be likely to be desirable in view of the special reservation of military control which you may think it necessary to maintain in the case of Singapore for a prolonged period as a defence base.

I also note that you suggest that the military administration should set up an *elected* advisory council to form the foundations of a legislative council and civil government. My feeling is that the introduction of a principle of election during the military period would certainly be a matter of considerable administrative difficulty and would very likely prejudice the implementing of plans for the post military period. For instance, the introduction of any system of an elected council would mean decisions on the basis and extent of a franchise and that would stir the main apprehensions of Malays, Chinese, and other communities.

As regards the Sultans, I notice that you recognise that because of their peculiar status in Islamic society they cannot be ruthlessly deposed and that you suggest they might be created an Upper House of the advisory council to be set up in the military period. If we are to put through schemes for a closer unification of the country, the necessary political measures will inevitably have an effect on the relations between the Sultans and any British authority. We have derived our powers in the States from Treaties and Agreements with the Malay Rulers. The conception behind our Directive is that we must obtain from the Rulers similarly by fresh Treaties the further jurisdiction we shall need. If in fact the circumstances on liberation in any of the States, e.g. "quisling" conduct by the Ruler or a clear feeling amongst the people themselves, point to the desirability of our not according recognition to the ruling personage, our course of procedure in any such State to achieve our purpose there will have to take account of the local factors. But whatever the procedure suitable in any State I would personally regard it as a vital part of our plans for the future that the Sultans should derive *from a central Malayan authority* any temporal authority which they are to exercise in the post war arrangement, and that they should not be given any grounds for believing that they will have derived authority in the constitution—apart from their personal prestige and dignity—either by reason of delegation from *any* external British authority or by reason of their own royal status.

Finally, I note that it is your view that our new policy, if adopted, should be put over to the public here and abroad by the press and by broadcasting. Our feeling here is that we should go extremely easy on any publicity for our future plans at present, partly because our knowledge of developments particularly in the sentiment of the people of Malaya under Japanese occupation is so scanty, and partly because I feel that publicity in Malaya itself might be a double edged weapon. With the presence in the country of rival communities who have so far developed no strong common sense of nationality, it seems to me that there is a risk that a statement of our intentions might well provide the enemy in present circumstances with an opportunity to play off one community against another and to weaken their desire for our return.

Now that the general basis of our policy has been approved by the War Cabinet, the resulting constitutional and administrative problems are being elaborated here with all the expert assistance available to the Colonial Office, and we shall continue, as now, to keep in close touch with the War Office and with Hone.

27   CO 825/42/3, no 25   29 July 1944

[Directive on policy in Malaya]: letter (reply) from Admiral Mountbatten to Mr Stanley

Thank you for your Top Secret and Personal letter to me dated 13 June[1] enclosing an advance copy of the Directive on Policy in Malaya.

I welcome the prospect which this affords of a single Malayan Union embracing all the States and Settlements of the peninsula, and of constitutional progress directed towards the development of democratic self-government.

These are great points and I am not entirely convinced by the arguments which have decided you to keep them under a bushel. I should like to have seen them blazoned to the World.

I also like the proposal in paragraph 8 of the Directive for regional co-ordination under a Governor-General at Singapore, which is a development I hope we may see repeated in other parts of the Colonial Empire.

In some respects, however, the Directive is less far reaching than I had hoped and in two particulars leaves me with a feeling of uneasiness. I do appreciate the complications which we must expect to find on our return to Malaya, brought out in your letter, and it is considerations of just this kind which make me feel we should cultivate a new mind in our approach to them.

Paragraph 3 of the Directive, which cautions against undue rigidity of intention, is my excuse for putting forward views which doubtless have already been considered but which I am sure in the changing situation we shall meet with will be found deserving of further attention.

My first cause of uneasiness is in the proposal that as soon as feasible after the reoccupation we should set about negotiating fresh treaties with the Malay Rulers. I should have doubted the wisdom of that in any case but when I read that the avowed object of these treaties is the acquisition by His Majesty of new powers not hitherto enjoyed by him I feel sure that the procedure proposed is psychologically question-

---

[1] See 26.

able. That acquisition of such powers is fundamental to continued constitutional progress is obvious, but I do feel we lay ourselves open to a charge of hypocrisy if in the first flush of our success, and with overwhelming force at our disposal, we invite the rulers in effect to sign or resign.

I know that is a distorted view of what is proposed but I am sure it is how it will be represented. It will be said we used our force to extract cessions which would not otherwise have been granted, and what I should like to see done as an act of deliberate policy may, I fear, come to be represented by our detractors as a legislatic [legalistic] sham.

Let me put my objection in this way. What happens if a Ruler, otherwise unexceptionable, declines to conclude a new treaty on the desired lines? Do we have to find a successor who will? Or do we have to forego our aims?

What the constitutional solution should be it is beyond my province to suggest but I am in entire agreement with the statement in your letter that you personally regard it as a vital part of our plans for the future that the Sultans should derive *from a central Malayan authority* any temporal authority which they are to exercise and that they should be given no grounds for believing they have derived authority from any other source. I do not find this altogether compatible with the necessity for "opening negotiations" with them (para. 4 of the Directive) and I must admit I am not very happy at the prospect of my Commanders or my Civil Affairs Officers becoming embroiled during the military period in negotiations about the status of the Rulers, or their powers, or their futures.

My second point refers to the sentence in paragraph 1 of the Directive which reads that participation in the Government by all the communities in Malaya is to be promoted, *subject to a special recognition of the political, economic and social interests of the Malay race.* I cannot help feeling that in the long run nothing could perhaps do more to perpetuate sectional antagonisms, to the risk of which you pointedly refer in your letter, than the giving of special recognition to one race.

I feel our objects should be to break down racial sectionalism in every way open to us, politically, economically and socially, and to endeavour to substitute for it the idea of Malayan citizenship.

I incline to agree that I was premature in suggesting that the military administration should set up an *elected* Advisory Council and on further consideration I feel our efforts should be directed towards promoting responsible democratic institutions at the bottom by beginning with the village and the ward. In such modest beginnings, as it seems to me, may lie the key not only to future self-government but to the difficulties inherent in a plural society.

If we can make a start in this way by getting people, whether Malays, Chinese or Indians, to combine together to deal as citizens (and not as racial communities) with the local problems of their village or ward we may hope that one day they will come to look at the wider problems of Malaya in the same light, and that at least Malayan-born and Malayan-domiciled Chinese will begin to identify themselves with Malaya instead of seeking political guidance and interference from China. If any such result is to be obtained increased recognition of the Chinese, and perhaps their increased employment in Government services, would seem necessary and although I am aware that the question bristles with difficulties I do feel that the sentence in the directive to which I have referred may add to them by conducing to the sectional point of view.

As regards the suggestion that publicity should not at present be given to our intentions, for fear of misrepresentation by the enemy, I deplore the idea that one should be deterred by such a consideration from making one's position perfectly plain to the whole world. I can think of no pronouncement one could make that could not be misrepresented by the enemy: that is his job, and is a permanent factor in his political warfare against us. What is far more damaging, and has done us an infinity of harm elsewhere, is that we can often be represented as afraid to admit what our designs really are. It is this which seems to me the greatest present we can make to enemy propaganda.

I must apologise for having sent my last letter to Cranborne, but in a mental lapse I thought he was still Secretary of State for the Colonies, otherwise of course I would have addressed my letter direct to you.

28   CO 825/42/3, no 27   21 Aug 1944
[Directive on policy in Malaya]: letter (reply) from Mr Stanley to Admiral Mountbatten

I am hastening to reply to your letter of the 29th July,[1] which I have read with the greatest interest. Thank you very much for this frank and stimulating expression of your views.

As I see it, there are three main points on which you are not fully satisfied about our present policy. The first point is the proposal to negotiate, immediately on the liberation of Malaya, fresh treaties with the Sultans in order to provide us with the jurisdiction we need. I have taken careful note of what you say, but I do not see that we have any alternative. We are advised that the treaty position and the constitutional rights of the State Governments are in abeyance only for the period of operational needs and military Government. It will therefore be too late if we do not obtain our fresh powers during the period of military Government. We need our new constitutional arrangements, which I am glad to see you entirely favour, to succeed immediately upon the termination of military Government. Any recalcitrant Sultan is likely to be far more of a problem and far more recalcitrant if allowed to regain his previous sovereign position before the change is made. The British relations with the Malay States rest *solely* upon our treaties. The only alternative course for securing jurisdiction is annexation.

I should add that it is our intention that the negotiations with the Sultans should be carried out by a special mission on behalf of the Secretary of State for the Colonies. Your military staff would thus not be directly embroiled.

Your second point of disagreement is on the proposals to safeguard the special position of the Malay race. The Malays are by general consent not at present capable of competing on equal terms, economically and educationally, with the "immigrant races"—Chinese and Indian. From the beginning of our relations with the States we have pursued in the Malay States the policy of taking positive measures to prevent the submergence of Malays in the public services and in the ownership of land by the

[1] See 27.

more energetic, competent, and resourceful Chinese. The most damaging criticism of our new policy will be precisely on these grounds, since we are endeavouring to admit non-Malay communities to a political equality with the Malays in the State territories. We shall make certain of estranging the Malays unless we can assure them of measures not only in the political and social field, which will prevent such "equality" inevitably resulting in their submergence, but also in such matters as the reservation of Malay lands, which otherwise will certainly pass into the hands of the ubiquitous Indian money-lender. Even Tan Cheng Lock, a leading Chinese of Malacca, admits this himself to a large extent.

Thirdly you have a good deal to say about the arousing of communal antagonism. On this point too I think we have a satisfactory answer. For a long time at any rate, we must expect that the natural China and the India ties of the Chinese and Indian domiciled communities will tend to be stimulated by the nationalist politics of those two countries. Our pre-war experience offered hardly a sign of any conception amongst the three peoples that they were *Malayans*. Our plan is to proceed both from the top and the bottom in fostering the growth of such a conception—*viz.* by a single representative legislature at the top and at the same time the institution of local bodies which will not be purely Malay but more broadly based and representative of the people of the country. The social basis of Malayan society for some time to come cannot be expected to be other than communal, seeing that inter-marriage is virtually non-existent, and religion, language and domestic customs must be potent factors in maintaining the present distinctions.

Finally I note, and to a large extent agree, with what you say about publicity. I believe however that Gater, in your recent talk with him, explained more fully our point of view on this matter. He gives me to understand that you are not in any immediate hurry in that respect provided that His Majesty's Government's policy is ventilated in good time before military operations to liberate Malaya are undertaken.

29 CO 825/42/3, no 28   6 Sept 1944
[Directives on policy]: letter (reply) from Admiral Mountbatten to Mr Stanley

Thank you very much for your letter of 21st August,[1] which has interested me enormously.

I feel that we are substantially in agreement: certainly in what we would wish to see emerging as the post-war Malayan state, and to a great extent, I think, in the means by which this can be achieved. I am sure you share my wish to see the country politically unified and racially united, since these are indispensable prerequisites to the building of a free and happy country there.

I fully appreciate that the social basis of Malayan society cannot for some time to come be other than communal, and that the fostering in the three peoples of Malaya of the conception that they are in fact Malayans, will be an uphill business. But I feel sure that you are on the right track in aiming at reducing, and eventually

---

[1] See 28.

eliminating, these barriers by a single representative legislature at the top, accompanied by the institution of broadly based and representative local bodies.

Since I wrote to you, I have received from the War Office copies of the Directives on Chinese policy, and on the Creation of Malayan Union Citizenship.[2] It is essential that the Chinese and Indian elements should be legally assimilated, and should be made to feel committed, to local responsibility, instead of being merely a group of exploiters, or a source of cheap labour. While we are on the subject of citizenship, what is H.M.G.'s attitude to the responsibilities of the domiciled British community? Presumably we shall be equally debarred from local activities without statutory residence or formal naturalisation. Will you let me know about this[?]

I am sorry to see from your letter that the Malays should by general consent be found incapable of competing on equal terms, "economically and educationally", with the Chinese and Indians. I have no reason to suppose that this opinion is not fully borne out; but it seems to me that indigenous peoples sometimes appear lazy and unambitious, largely because they are unwilling to compete with lower standards of living and wage conditions established by immigrants, who are without roots in the country, and cannot afford to turn down a standard of wages which those who have homes and relations on the spot are not forced to sink to. I do not suggest that the Malayan is at the mercy of cheap coolie labour imported from China; but it is so easy to give a dog a bad name that one is inclined to fear that an opinion of the natives' qualities may become an *idée fixe*, which will militate against a proper appreciation of their potentialities under improved conditions. But in any case I feel that your proposals, to which I have made allusion above, should go a long way to mitigate this difficulty, if it actually exists.

It is the question of the Sultans that I am still not quite happy about. I quite appreciate that their legal position may present a problem; and if the treaty position and the constitutional rights of the State Governments are in abeyance only for the period of operational needs and Military Government, it certainly looks as though we should have to obtain our fresh powers during the period of my administration. But I still feel that it is most unfortunate that negotiations of this character should be entered into as an immediate consequence of our arrival in the country with overwhelming force at our disposal. Even though I whole-heartedly approve the use to which we intend to put these powers, and understand our necessity to have them in good time, it seems to me that our manner of obtaining them cannot fail to create a bad impression in Malaya, and anywhere else where we may expect hostile criticism. I feel, therefore, that we must not only have our answers ready if accused in press or parliament of using Military force to get a tighter grip on Malaya, but that we should forestall criticism by propaganda which the M. of I. should start to put out as soon as we have got Malaya back.

I am glad to see that it is your intention that these negotiations shall be carried out by a special mission, and that I and my Military Staff will thus not be directly embroiled, but the British as a nation will still be involved. I am not clear as to the extent to which it is proposed that the Sultans should be utilised, and entrusted with a measure of authority, for the purpose of carrying out the Military Government under my orders.

---

[2] Copies of the long-term directives including those on the 'Creation of Malayan Union citizenship' and 'Chinese policy' are at WO 203/5642, no 68/16/45.

The last thing I should wish to do would be to prejudice in any way the future intentions of H.M.G. by any action during the military period. At the same time, it is clear that the military period will be used for gaining experience of the problems of the future, and for generally moulding the administration on the right lines; and it is likely that this will entail a system of trial and error. Since, presumably, everything which is found to be desirable, and which works, will be carried over and incorporated in the Civil administration, whatever is found to be mistaken or harmful will remain associated in the minds of the Malayans with the period of Military administration. The only way I can see of ensuring that this shall not redound to the discredit or unpopularity of the armed forces of the Crown, is that H.M.G. should announce their policy, unequivocally, so that these trials (and possibly errors) can be judged against that background.

But the need for H.M.G. to announce their policy is a matter of urgency, in my opinion, for a much weightier reason. I am relieved to see, in the last paragraph of your letter, that H.M.G's policy is to be ventilated in good time before military operations to liberate Malaya are undertaken. Alas, this is coupled with your statement, that Gater has given you to understand that I am not in any immediate hurry in that respect.

Since my discussions with the Chiefs of Staff in London, this is no longer the case. I understand that the general view is that the Japanese war may be over by the end of 1945, and if I am given the resources, S.E.A.C. will certainly be back in Malaya before that. There is therefore now no more time to lose. I consider that the time to announce our policy, and to give it full publicity, is NOW, and that there is no time to be lost, if I am not to be asked to undertake a campaign against a part of the world which should have been prepared by suitable Political Warfare, but where on the contrary we will have again missed the bus.[3]

I hope I can rely on your help in this matter. The political aspect of such an announcement is not a matter with which I feel I need concern myself; but the example of what the helpful attitude of the local populations in Italy and France has meant to our fighting forces makes me apprehensive at the thought that we may be neglecting to procure for ourselves a weapon which may not be as potent as in the European countries occupied by the Nazis, but which it seems to me that it would be folly to underestimate. Putting it at its very lowest, if we can expect but little help and sympathy from the Malayan populations (which I personally do not believe) we should at the very least be able to ensure their benevolent neutrality in our invasion of the country.

I would be very grateful, if you are of my opinion, if you would use your influence to see that something is done about this very vital matter before it is too late.

---

[3] This paragraph has been boldly marked by the recipient with a large cross in the margin of the original. Mountbatten was looking forward to an invasion of Malaya from the sea; he did not, of course, know of the existence of the atomic bomb until he attended the Potsdam Conference in July 1945.

30   CO 825/42/3, no 30   17 Oct 1944
[Implementation of future policy in Malaya]: letter (reply) from Mr Stanley to Admiral Mountbatten

I am sure that you will forgive me for having taken a little time before sending you my ideas on the points made in your letter to me of 6th September.[1] We necessarily have to take a view of future arrangements and policies in Malaya in circumstances in which there is obscurity on some important factors in the situation. Nevertheless there are factors of at least equal importance which we may rely upon as constant, such as the communal division of the population and, on the other hand, the essential unity of the social and economic questions of the country as a whole.

We can also expect to find a continued reluctance of the Malay Rulers to concede political equality to the Chinese and Indian inhabitants in any of the States. Your main uneasiness is that we should have to appear to choose the moment of our military strength to present our policies for the Rulers' acceptance. The question how far that position will be resented by public opinion in Malaya or elsewhere, is likely to be influenced by the local experiences of the Rulers' conduct and influence during the period of Japanese occupation; for instance, whether they have shown themselves, or have been able to show themselves, defenders of the people, and if so, whether of the Malay people only or of the Chinese and Indians in the States as well.

But in any case we are, I am convinced, right in taking a long term view that the prospect of self-government in any real sense in Malaya must depend on the achievement of some constitutional unity in the Peninsula, and as it is our avowed policy that self-government is an important aim in Colonial territories, we should rightly be criticised if we fail to take this opportunity of achieving the basis of a unity which must then develop itself with our further assistance in the years to come. We shall have, I do not doubt, to exercise pressure on the Rulers or some of them in order to achieve the cohesion we believe to be in the general interest, if Malaya is to be capable in the future of standing on its own feet as a territory of substantial importance though of relatively small area. If in the last resort any recalcitrant Malay Ruler has to be coerced, I do not myself think that we should defer the process, or indeed could do so, until after the military administration had come to an end.

I very heartily agree with you that the public presentation of our policies must play an important part in the smooth achievement of what we believe to be right, and I welcome the support which I know you will give me in ensuring that this is done in good time. As soon as I can see the way to making any general disclosure of policies in our territories in the Far East I shall write to you about it.

I have concentrated on the main question in your letter as I am sure it is the one of prime importance. You did, however, mention in your fourth paragraph the position of the British community. I don't think this will be a difficulty as British subjects will not suffer any discrimination as compared with Malayan Union Citizens, according to the plans which we are working out.

---

[1] See 29.

31   CAB 66/60, WP(44)762   22 Dec 1944
'Constitutional Policy in Malaya': War Cabinet memorandum by Mr Attlee

[Mountbatten's demand that the new policy be widely publicised led Stanley to raise the issue with the Cabinet Committee on Malaya and Borneo chaired by Attlee. The committee accepted Stanley's recommendation that SACSEA should be furnished with a broad and brief statement for 'background use of restricted circles', but Cabinet, discussing WP(44)762 on 9 Jan 1945, found it an unsatisfactory compromise. Since Stanley was by then in the USA, any decision on publicity was put off for another six months (see 36 and also CO 825/43/15 and CAB 65/49, WM 3(45)2, 9 Jan 1945).]

On the 31st May, 1944, the War Cabinet approved a directive on policy in Malaya to the authorities responsible for planning for the Civil Administration of Malaya on liberation. The War Cabinet's approval was subject to the understanding that no publicity should be given to the policies contained therein.

2.   Since the date on which the War Cabinet reached their decision, the Colonial Office and War Office have been moving forward with the necessary plans for the administration of these territories on the basis then authorised. These plans have, of course, been disclosed only to those directly concerned in them, but the increasing disadvantages of this secrecy have been urged with great weight from various quarters. The Secretary of State for the Colonies has been in correspondence with the Supreme Allied Commander, South-East Asia, who has strongly represented to him the importance of making known our future plans in general to the peoples whom those plans will affect. Admiral Mountbatten holds that the proper reception of our future policy in Malaya depends upon its being fully explained beforehand, and that the time is now ripe to do this.[1]

3.   In advancing this point of view, the Supreme Allied Commander is thinking not only of long-term considerations, but also of the creation of a favourable atmosphere for the setting up of a military administration for which he will be responsible. Moreover, those responsible for present operations of a special character within his Command have made the same case for their own reasons. So much so that the organisation in question has had to be given certain general guidance on the subject for the use of its agents. It has also been necessary to give similar guidance to the organisation engaged in similar operations in Borneo.

4.   Then again, the authorities engaged in Political Warfare and in the enlightment of the public both in this country and in the United States of America have strongly pressed their need for a new Malayan directive which will be based on a forward policy and will reflect that policy.

5.   The Secretary of State for the Colonies is not yet convinced that the time has come for our plans to be divulged in full, since this would involve committing ourselves to every feature of those plans, at a time when many relevant facts are by force of circumstances unknown to us. Nevertheless, he attaches great weight to the Supreme Allied Commander's views, and believes that the essential needs of Admiral Mountbatten and others could be met for the present by the distribution to selected circles of a broad statement of the fundamental problems in Malaya which bear

---

[1] See 26–30.

directly upon the political, administrative and economic future of the country. At the same time there would be distributed, not for publication, but in confidence purely for the background use of restricted circles which can guide and influence thought and discussion of the subject, a brief statement actually setting out the main features of our proposed policy. Drafts of these statements and proposals as to their distribution are enclosed at Annexes I and II.[2]

6. The Ministerial Committee on Malaya and Borneo have considered and concur in the Colonial Secretary's proposals and in the draft statements, which I submit for the covering approval of the War Cabinet.

---

[2] Not printed.

32 T 220/52   29 Mar 1945
[Malaya reconstruction finance]: letter from S Caine to Lord Keynes

[Colonial planners came under immense financial pressure in 1945 as, on the one hand, they sought to earmark funds for the rehabilitation and development of colonies while, on the other hand, they faced demands from those eager to channel colonial resources into domestic reconstruction. Keynes, for example, in his capacity as financial adviser at the Treasury, suggested that large amounts of colonial sterling balances should be appropriated in order to reduce Britain's own problems. CO officials, not least Caine, recognised that such a policy would hamper post-war reconstruction of war-damaged dependencies, jeopardise schemes for development and welfare, and, consequently, create political unrest in the colonies. The debate was conducted at a number of levels; documents 32–35, 37 & 38 relate specifically to Malayan matters. See also CAB 66/65, WP(45)301, note by the chancellor of the Exchequer enclosing 'Overseas financial policy in stage III' by J M Keynes, 3 Apr 1945.]

Eady[1] mentioned incidentally in the course of conversation yesterday that you have expressed considerable scepticism about the estimate of probable expenditure in our Far Eastern Colonies of £200 millions, which I had mentioned in my letter to Eady of 15th March on the general subject of Colonies' claims on sterling. When I included the figure in that letter, it was certainly a wild guess, but we have just had some rather carefully worked out estimates from the Malayan Planning Unit, which help to give a rather more precise idea of the position, and you may be interested to have them.

The Malayan Planning Unit's figures have been compiled largely as a guide to the calls which may be made on Government finances, including the United Kingdom Exchequer, and I have therefore had to add to them such estimates as we have of probable expenditure from private funds on capital reconstruction. The principal items are as follows:—

Reconstruction and repair of "public utilities",
i.e. Government owned railways, electricity, water,
telecommunications, roads, etc.   £37,150,000

---

[1] Sir W Eady was chairman of the Board of Customs and Excise, 1941–1942.

Administrative expenditure during first two years in excess of local revenue (including upwards of £20 millions for outstanding claims in respect to arrears of salary, pension, etc.)	£24,000,000
Relief supplies during initial emergency period . . .	£22,825,000
Rehabilitation of industry:—	
(1) Tin mines	£26,000,000
(2) Rubber estates (largely renewal of stocks of estate supplies and work of capital character in re-clearing overgrown estates)	£12,000,000
(3) Other industries . . .	£5,000,000
Total:	£126,975,000

These figures are for Malaya alone. We have also to consider Hong Kong, Borneo and the Pacific Islands, which are certainly smaller but would still require quite respectable sums. My guess of £200 millions may be a little on the high side but not, I think, wildly inaccurate if one is thinking, as one must in this kind of juggling, in figures accurate to the nearest hundred million.

33 T 220/52   19 Apr 1945
'Malaya reconstruction finance': memorandum by A J D Winnifrith[1]

(1) We have at last got the promised Colonial Office memorandum. This shows the following broad picture:

	1st 2 years		*Next 5 years*
	£m.		£m.
Capital Expenditure	36		20
Budget Deficits	6		5
	42		25
		67	
Assets available		32	
Prospective Deficit		£35m.	

(2) My first comment is that this shows the picture at its worst. Capital expenditure may very well not reach these figures, because Malaya will not be able to get the manufacturing capacity. Even more doubtful is the gloomy view taken of revenue prospects. It is assumed that, even on the austerity basis, the budget will not balance till after the fourth year. Obviously a lot hangs on the prosperity of rubber and tin, but given reasonable world markets one would hope for a far better revenue outlook than now is envisaged.

(3) *Analysis of the programme*

The problem in Malaya seems to be widely different from that in Burma. In Burma

---

[1] A John D Winnifrith, a Treasury official since 1934, rose to permanent under-secretary in the Ministry of Agriculture, Fisheries and Food, 1959–1967.

the cost of reconstruction is very largely made up of the restoration of private industries, with somewhat smaller expenditure on public utilities. Capital replacement on Government Services accounted for a large part of the original programme but is reduced to quite small proportions in the revised austerity proramme. Outstanding liabilities were put at £8 millions and the budget deficit at £7.5 millions for each of the first two years.

In Malaya, on the other hand, private industry is expected to look after itself. There is no scheme as in Burma for Government controlled projects and capital expenditure is practically confined to Government owned public utilities, particularly Railways, which account for half of the total. The other main item is outstanding liabilities mainly on account of arrear of salaries and pensions which are put at a capitalised figure of £18 millions. Finally, there is the estimated budget deficit over the first two years which is put at £6 millions. Finance for private industry is virtually negligible at £0.170 million. The total of £42 millions is made up as follows:

	£m.
1. Capital finance for public utilities	17.9
2. Outstanding commitments capitalised	18.0
3. Capital Finance for private industry	0.1
4. Budget Deficits	6.0
	42.0

(4) *Public utilities*
The appendix to the Colonial Office memorandum shows how the £17.9 millions is spread among the main public utilities. The railways account for nearly half the total. The appendix also shows the percentage of restoration up to pre-war standards to be aimed at in the first two years. It will be observed that over the 7 year programme the aim is to achieve 100% restoration. My comment on this part of the programme is that the percentage of restoration proposed for the first two years is not unreasonable and that in a prosperous place like Malaya it is equally not unreasonable to aim at 100% restoration over 7 years. Merely as a matter of estimating, however, I doubt very much whether they will be able to spend the full amount of £17.9 millions over two years. Capacity, especially for railway equipment, is going to be very short and they will be lucky if they get half of what they want.

(5) *Outstanding commitments*
These are estimated at somewhere between £16 millions and £20 millions. Clearly there can be no question of Malaya repudiating her legal liabilities, but with a total of 54,000 claimants it would be very surprising if all claims were actually presented. Certainly some of them would not be presented at once. I should have thought that the actual cash required over the first two years might be considerably less than the full liability.

(6) *Capital finance for private industry*
This is a very small part of the programme, and I have no particular comments on it, except that Malaya will have to take good care to secure her title to the assets so as to be in a position to recover her expenditure as far as possible.

(7) *Budget deficits*
These are put at £6 millions over a period of two years. I have asked the Colonial Office what standard of Government services they aim at providing, and their answer is that the standard will be well below that of 1940. A good test is the number of

European employees, and it is estimated that they will not have more than half the 1940 strength in the first years.

(8) The foregoing liabilities do not give the full picture. In addition to the expenditure listed in paragraph 3, there will be expenditure estimated at £29,825,000 on Relief Supplies. The whole of this expenditure, however, is recoverable. The basis of procurement is the Young estimates, and I think we need not question the standard of provision since I understand that the Young Committee[2] did not allow for anything particularly lavish. Furthermore, I think it is a reasonably sound expectation that the expense will, in fact, be recovered.

(9) *Dollar expenditure* Of the total programme, only some £5,650,000 is expected to be spent in dollars. This is a far lower proportion than for Burma.

(10) *Other U.K. liabilities*
To complete the picture of U.K. liabilities, a note should be taken of two further items:—

(a) The cost of military administration during the military period. This might be put at £2 [sic].
(b) The fact that Malaya is not under the present plan continuing her contribution to Imperial Defence. This, before the war amounted to £   .[3]

(11) *Malaya's ability to pay for the above programme*
The memorandum states that Malaya holds free assets to a value of some £32 millions. In addition, she has lent this country £2 millions as a war loan. O.F. will no doubt be able to comment on the question whether she has other assets not disclosed which could be realised. Finally, nothing is said in the Colonial Office memorandum about Malaya's ability to raise reconstruction loans on her own account. Her public debt position seems eminently satisfactory since for this very rich community it only amounts to £20 millions which will be extinguished by 1970. It seems to me that she should be able without any difficulty to raise substantial loans on her own account.

(12) *Questions for decision*
The following questions require a decision:

(a) How far should Malaya finance her reconstruction expenditure herself?
(b) Is her reconstruction programme reasonable or should it be pruned?
(c) What degree of Treasury control over her programme is required?

(13) *How far can Malaya finance her programme herself?*
The assets which Malaya has immediately available amount to £32 millions. O.F. will no doubt say whether there is any objection to her realising these assets forthwith. Subject to there being no objection on this account, I should have thought that Malaya should exhaust these assets in the first place. Her immediate requirements are her capital expenditure of £18 millions starting now and going on for two years,

---

[2] Arthur Stewart Young MP was commissioner of the Treasury in 1942.
[3] This figure is left blank in the original. In 1939–1940 the Malay rulers of the Federated Malay States supported the British government's war effort with gifts totalling nearly £1.5 million. The Unfederated Malay States also made large financial contributions; for example, in 1940 the Sultan of Johore donated £250,000 and provided an interest-free loan of £100,000; in 1941 he made a further gift of £500,000 in 1941. See CO 717/139, no 51888/1939, CO 717/143, nos 51888/1940, 51888/3/1940 and 51888/15/1940, CO 717/147, no 51888/15/1941.

and her Relief Supplies programme also extending over a period amounting to some £30 millions. This makes a total capital commitment of some £48 millions. If one discounts this total to allow for:—

(a) inevitable failure to secure the full amount of the programme
(b) the spreading over of the payments into the 2nd or 3rd year, it might well be that only some £30 millions would be required in the next twelve months. By that time civil Government may have been restored in Malaya. Malayan Government would then be faced with outstanding liabilities under their capital programme, liabilities in respect of salaries and pensions and prospective budget deficits, but at that stage could set about raising the reconstruction loan.

(14) We have already approached the Colonial Office on the question of the method by which any financial assistance to Malaya should be provided. The Colonial Office reply is given in Mr. Mayle's letter of 16th February. It will be seen that he asks for any financial assistance to be made as an advance on the understanding that at a later stage it should be decided how much of the advances should be converted into grants, and what terms of repayment should be arranged for any residue to be regarded as loan.

(15) I do not think we can be content with such a solution. If the above appreciation is anywhere near the mark Malaya will be able to meet all that can be spent for the next twelve months out of her own resources. Until those resources are exhausted there can be no question of any assistance from the U.K. Exchequer. Furthermore, the Colonial Office should be told now that having regard to our difficulties in regard to overseas finance we shall expect Malaya as far as possible to finance her own requirements. She should not hesitate to raise reconstruction loans. Nothing is said in the memorandum about taxation policy, though the Colonial Office told me that the plan is to raise as much taxation as possible and to go on with the wartime device of income tax. At this stage I think we should say that we expect Malaya to raise all the revenue she can consistently with encouraging the return of prosperity to the country.

(15) [sic] *Is the present programme reasonable?*
I see no reason to suppose that the present programme is extravagant, and bearing in mind that we are asking Malaya to finance her own expenditure and remembering that she, unlike Burma, is a community with good economic prospects, I do not see that we should have any ground for insisting on an austerity programme.

(16) *What degree of Treasury control is required?*
If my suggestion about Malaya finding her own expenditure is agreed, I think the Treasury control should be very lightly exercised, and we should confine our action to getting information from time to time about the progress of expenditure from the standpoint that if, despite all efforts, Malaya cannot find all the finance herself, the U.K. Exchequer may have to come to her aid with a loan.

34   T 220/52   23 Apr 1945

[Malaya reconstruction finance]: letter (reply) from Lord Keynes to S Caine

My attention has been so much engaged in the last month in other directions that it is only now I have got down to answering your letter of March 29th[1] about probable expenditure on relief and reconstruction in our Far Eastern Colonies.

I find from your letter that your figure covers a much more comprehensive field than I had in mind. It is, in fact, the grand total of all public and private expenditure from the beginning to the end. I can well believe that your figure is not much on the high side to cover all this, including what is desirable as well as what is essential. But some of it might never happen and a good deal of it might have, inevitably, to be spread over a longish period.

However that may be, I agree that it is your comprehensive figure which is relevant to our balance of trade problem. For, except in so far as we can get outside assistance, the cost will fall on our balance of trade whether the money comes from the existing sterling balances of the Colonies in question, or from a British grant, or from a British credit.

What is your present idea of the sources of finance? Malaya and Hong Kong sterling balances are very substantial, some £130 million. How far do you contemplate drawing on these? Have any decisions been reached about the source or sources of compensation, if any, *e.g.* for the tin and rubber concerns?

Have you given any thought to collecting an Imperial, British Commonwealth pool from which to draw contributions?

It would be very helpful to me, in connection with Stage III plans,[2] to know rather more clearly than I do at present how all this stands.

---

[1] See 32.   [2] ie plans for the period after the defeat of Japan.

35   T 220/52   28 Apr 1945

[Malaya reconstruction finance]: letter (reply) from S Caine to Lord Keynes

Thank you for your letter of the 3rd [sic] April[1] about probable expenditure on relief and reconstruction in the Far Eastern Colonies. There has been a good deal of departmental correspondence about the sources from which the various items of probable expenditure ought to be met, and perhaps I ought to preface anything I say with the qualification that it is without prejudice to any argument the Colonial Office may have with the Treasury on the subject either in particular cases or generally.

Obviously the three main sources of funds are the holdings of the Far Eastern Governments themselves, grants or loans from the United Kingdom Exchequer, and private funds including both private assets recorded in your figures as belonging to residents in the Far Eastern Colonies and other funds which business concerns interested in those Colonies can command or borrow in this country.

---

[1] See 34.

I have myself always assumed that at one stage or another the Far Eastern Colonial Governments will have to put in pretty well all their liquid assets. The recorded sterling balances held on Government account for Malaya and Hong Kong as at 30th September 1944 total £96,500,000. Of these, £49,200,000 consisted of currency funds. Maybe some part of those currency funds will ultimately be found to be in excess of prudent reserve requirements, but we cannot at present regard any part of them as definitely available for non-currency purposes, particularly as there are all sorts of potential but at present unascertainable currency liabilities, e.g., in respect of forced issues of banknotes in Hong Kong. Actual liquid funds amounted to £19,000,000 held in Malaya, and other invested funds including loans to H.M.G. amounted to £28,300,000. Some part of these invested funds may be available, but to some extent at least they consist of sinking funds or other earmarked funds not available for general use. It would perhaps, therefore, be taking an optimistic view if we put down £40,000,000 as the possible contribution of the Far Eastern Governments themselves towards the total.

The United Kingdom Exchequer is no doubt as usual likely to be called upon to fill in the residual gap, so that we should look next at the private funds which may be available. Our understanding is that the re-equipment and rehabilitation of the rubber industry is likely to be dealt with by the rubber companies themselves without calling on Government financial assistance, but most of the tin companies appear likely to ask for help, and some at least of the smaller industries in Malaya will need help also. In Hong Kong, there is good reason to hope that the Hong Kong and Shanghai Bank, which has substantial sterling holdings and is very deeply interested in the re-establishment of Hong Kong trade, will be prepared to finance a number of the enterprises, e.g., docks, electricity undertakings, etc., without asking for advances or guarantees from Government. I should expect also that there would be a good deal of other miscellaneous private financing by trading concerns either from their own reserves or from privately arranged bank advances. It is extremely difficult to put any total to this kind of private financing, and if I had to guess, it would be within the wide limits of £20 to £40 millions.

It looks, therefore, as if the third partner, i.e. the Exchequer, will have to find the lion's share if finance is required on the scale indicated in my letter of the 29th March.[2] Whether any such financing should be by way of grant or by way of credit is one of the issues lying between the Colonial Office and the Treasury. No doubt much of it, particularly any part which is attributable to the costs of rehabilitation of private businesses, would be on a loan basis, and the Treasury are at present insistent that any money found by the Exchequer should be treated as a repayable advance, at any rate in the first instance, until we can see the whole situation more clearly and decide whether the territories need assistance by way of grant.

I am afraid we have not given very much serious consideration to the possibility of an Imperial or Commonwealth pool into which other parts of the Commonwealth besides the United Kingdom would pay contributions. The idea did receive a little thought indirectly when we were recently discussing arrangements for the winding up of Commodity War Risk Insurance funds in other Colonies where such schemes had been in existence under U.K. Government guarantee, but we felt in that small instance that it would not be practicable to ask the Colonial territories concerned to

---

[2] See 32.

make any contribution out of the surpluses on such schemes towards possible costs of war damage compensation in the Far East. If, however, it were thought that the wealthier members of the Commonwealth, i.e. the Dominions, would be willing to contribute, we should certainly see no financial objection, particularly if it rendered more likely the payment of satisfactory war damage compensation to the people who have suffered in the Far East. I should say, however, that it is possible that the political side of the Colonial Office might be a little suspicious of any such arrangement if it implied any recognition of political control over the Far Eastern Colonies by other members of the Commonwealth.

36   CO 825/43/16, WP(45)287   7 May 1945
'Constitutional policy in Malaya': Cabinet memorandum by Mr Stanley. *Annex* 'Draft statement of fundamental problems in Malaya'

[This memorandum picks up the inconclusive War Cabinet discussion on 9 January (see 31). On 8 May Churchill declared the war in Europe finally at an end and on 23 May formally resigned. He was then invited by the King to form what was to be a caretaker government until the general election, which was settled for 5 July. The Caretaker Cabinet considered Stanley's memorandum on 15 June and agreed that the statement in the Annex should be distributed to the official agencies listed in paragraph 4 of the memorandum (see CAB 65/53, CM 8(45)8).]

I invite the attention of my colleagues to Paper No. W.P.(44)762, of the 22nd December, 1944, which was a Memorandum by the Chairman of the Committee on Malaya and Borneo, dealing with future Constitutional Policy in Malaya.[1]

2. The Memorandum contained proposals for a measure of publicity about our political plans for Malaya. The War Cabinet considered these proposals on the 9th January, and it was then felt that the proposals either went too far or not far enough. On the one hand, they did not offer the advantage which would result in publicity for a settled policy on which we were prepared to stand. On the other hand, they provided for a distribution of information wide enough to create a risk of leakage, and to entail embarrassing questions. Largely in view of these doubts, the War Cabinet did not reach a decision on the matter, but preferred to await my return from the United States.

3. Since my return, I have carefully considered these criticisms. I feel that we should not contemplate, for the time being, a *greater* measure of publicity than that previously proposed, since we should thereby commit ourselves further than I consider necessary to a new and important line of policy which we may possibly wish to modify later on, at any rate as regards some of its details. I am still impressed, however, both by the need to prepare and influence general opinion both here and in the East amongst circles whose good will and understanding are important for us to secure, as well as the need to provide material for a progressive scheme of political warfare.

4. In order to meet these needs I now propose a somewhat modified course of action which should, I think, for the present achieve the essential objectives of my

---

[1] See 31.

earlier proposals. I propose that only the broad statement of the chief problems in Malaya (in the terms recommended by the Ministers' Committee) should be issued (see Annex). Its distribution would be confined to the following *official* Agencies, *viz.*: all United Kingdom Government Departments and Representatives in Great Britain and abroad who are concerned with policy in Malaya, including S.E.A.C., United Kingdom High Commissioners in the Dominions, Political Warfare Missions and Ministry of Information Representatives, Colonial Governors and Diplomatic posts in the East.

One of the purposes for which these agencies could use the statement would, of course, be to guide unofficial thought on the problems involved and direct public attention and discussion towards a political and social development of Malaya along the fresh and progressive lines of consolidation and unity which our provisional policy envisages.

5. In due course we shall need to be more explicit, but when that time comes our course will have been aided, if my present proposal is approved.

Annex to 38

Malaya, though a geographical unity, is not in fact a single country, in the sense in which Great Britain or France are single countries. Malaya forms neither a racial nor a constitutional entity, and an appreciation of this fact is essential to any understanding of the problems we shall meet on our return.

2. The Malay Peninsula, as organised under British control, consists of a British Colony (the Straits Settlements, the most important of which are Singapore, Penang and Malacca) and of nine Malay States, four of which are joined in a Federation. Until about 1870 the nine States remained entirely separate and entirely independent— they were largely isolated by mountains and jungle—and British control was confined to the Colony. From then on, disturbances caused by pirates and by foreign (mainly Chinese) infiltration caused the several Malay Rulers, separately and at different times, to seek British protection. To this day the whole British position in the Malay States rests upon Agreements concluded with the individual Rulers— agreements which in substance and interpretation provide for British advice (to be acted upon in all matters other than Malay religion and custom), but which leave the Rulers, from the legal point of view, as sovereign princes.

3. The spread of British influence has brought co-ordination in many things, but the separate entity of the States remains none the less a reality. The Malays cherish a definite loyalty towards their Rulers, and this feeling conflicts with the development of any allegiance towards a larger unit than the State. There is no widespread conception amongst the Malays that they are "Malayans," with common duties and problems; and this is the first problem which must be faced in Malaya, if the country is to advance towards nationhood and self-government within the British Commonwealth.

4. The second problem is that of race. The extraordinary economic development which has accompanied the spread of British influence, and the extensive introduction of capital and enterprise from China and India has led to a situation in which the non-Malay population in Malaya now outnumbers the Malays, though the majority of the former still regard their original lands rather than Malaya as their real home. The

resultant problem presents special obstacles to the development of a sense of common citizenship in Malaya. On the one hand, the relations of the British Government with the Malay States are based on a recognition of the right of the Malay peoples to a secure position in their lands and in their educational and other facilities for progress. On the other hand the enterprise and capacity of the non-Malay peoples of the country, provided they be accompanied by a sense of civic responsibility, assert a claim that should exercise a due share in the moulding of Malaya's future.

5. Mention has been made above of economic development. It must not be thought that racial or parochial factors have been allowed to hinder all progress. Far from it. The economic, social and educational record of Malaya under British control is unsurpassed in the Far East. In these fields the work of great research organisations, such as the Rubber Research Institute and the Medical Research Institute, is recognised throughout the East. Along with the task of guiding Malaya towards her political destiny, the duty of restoring these and other valuable institutions and adapting them to future conditions and needs will clearly rest upon the Government and industry. The economy of Malaya has in the past been founded on the two great industries of rubber and tin. The importance of these natural resources must be re-established, and also a healthy broadening of the basis of Malayan economic life will be a pressing need.

6. The condition of the country and the temper of the people which we shall find on the eviction of the enemy after his prolonged period of occupation remain to be ascertained. But it is not too early to think and plan in terms of a forward policy in the country for the promotion of a growing cohesion and sense of political unity. If any of the features mentioned in this note are found to be obstacles to such a development, and if liberation is to be comprehensive and not merely related to the eviction of enemy forces, measures will need to be considered and concerted with all concerned to liberate the new Malaya from old barriers and prejudices, and it will be important that those who have the responsibility for the lines on which the new Malaya is built shall also be vested with the power to overcome any reactionary interests.

37   T 220/52   18 May 1945

[Malaya reconstruction finance]: minute by Lord Keynes to A J D Winnifrith

(1) I return my correspondence with Caine to be added to your files.[1]

(2) I find myself in full agreement with your memorandum of April 19th[2] and your general line.

(3) I note down a few random points which have occurred to me in looking through these papers.

(i)   I see no discussion of the currency problem. Presumably the inhabitants will have quite a quantity of Japanese military notes (or something of the kind)

---

[1] See 32, 34–35   [2] See 33.

in their pockets. Is the intention to declare these valueless or to accept them at some prescribed rate?

(ii) The decision here partly affects the question whether the currency reserves, which amount to £m35, do not provide an additional source of funds. The strict Treasury principle is, I know, that all the Currency Boards keep 100 per cent reserves in sterling against the outstanding note issue, and in fact the reserves often amount to more than 100 per cent. In other words, no fiduciary issue is allowed to the Colonies whatever. I am increasingly doubtful whether this is a position which can be sustained. Is it in fact reasonable that a Colony should be required to invest in U.K. the whole of the equivalent of their currency issues? I cannot see why. At any rate, the reconstruction of war damage would seem to me to be a good excuse for a breach in the principle, even if it is retained generally. I suggest, therefore, as a mild beginning that (say) one-third of the currency reserves might be covered by local Malayan Treasury Bills instead of British Treasury Bills. This would release a further £m10. From the balance of trade point of view, this comes to exactly the same thing as a British grant. But, at long last, it will turn out much more prudent from our point of view, if I am right in thinking that we cannot permanently sustain the present principle of pinching for our own purposes the whole of the currency reserves. If some liability has to be accepted in respect of locally-held Japanese notes, this would also constitute a charge that might properly be met by creating a fiduciary issue. Even so, however, there might be about £m10 left, which could reasonably be taken for reconstruction purposes. I suggest that this line of thought deserves serious consideration.

(iii) Railway reconstruction, which is I see a large item, inevitably and properly runs into improvements. Indeed, it would be only sensible that a fairly important element of improvement should be included in the programme of reconstruction. This is a further reason why it would be proper to cover the expense with a Malayan loan.

(iv) I agree that, from the very start, any sums required should be in the shape of loans borrowed on her own credit or, at any rate, in her own name, covered with our guarantee, if this is unavoidable. You show beyond doubt that Malaya is well able to carry even an important increase in the burden of debt.

(v) Do not overlook that Malaya might be quite a proper candidate for borrowing from the projected International Bank for Reconstruction.[3] This would have the advantage of saving our balance of trade, since they would obtain dollars from this source. We could, at least, aim at covering dollar expenditure by such a loan. But I should go a little further than this and put in at an early stage for a loan of (say) $m50 from this source.

(4) I note that the question of war damage compensation, is still very much in the air. But you are assuming that our liability under this head will be, at worst, fairly small. I agree with this policy, but feel that it will be very difficult to hold to. How far is the position appreciated and accepted by the principal companies concerned? If the pressure for assistance becomes strong, the first line of defence would be to advance

---

[3] The International Bank for Reconstruction and Development, known as the World Bank, was set up, with the International Monetary Fund, by the United Nations Monetary and Financial Conference at Bretton Woods in July 1944. The Articles of Agreement of the Bank came into force in December 1945.

loans on easy terms rather than grant outright compensation. One way or another, I should expect that it will be necessary eventually to make some addition to the estimates beyond what is made already on this heading.

38 T 220/52   [June 1945]
'Malaya Reconstruction Programme': minute by A J D Winnifrith to A F B fforde[1]

My letter and enclosed memorandum of 31st May gave the Colonial Office our views about U.K. responsibility and the degree of Treasury control over the programme. I told the Colonial Office (rightly I hope) that if they wanted to dispute our general point that U.K. assistance could only be provided as a last resort and then only by way of loan, they should take the matter up at a Ministerial level. News so far is that they are in a high state of indignation and are working themselves up into the required state of frenzy before seeking to get the support of their Secretary of State.

I hope that we shall be able to maintain our attitude, and if it transpires that Malaya can finance this programme without U.K. support, then I suggest we can be rather more forthcoming on the degree of Treasury control. If, on the other hand, we have to provide even limited assistance, the case for proper Treasury control is undoubted. Until we know what the position on this matter will be, we cannot get any further on the question of control. But I am sending you this note not only to report on the general Colonial Office attitude, but also so that you may have time to think about the matter of control.

The programme falls into three main categories.

(a) Consumer goods which are bought for resale and in regard to which the intention is to operate without any final charge to Government funds, sales recouping the whole of the costs.

(b) Capital equipment which for the most part will be ordered on Government account for the Government-owned public utilities, etc. such as the railways. Here, of course, the charge will be to the Government, whether local or U.K. according to the final decision.

(c) Budget deficits and accumulated obligations like arrears of pay and pension, which again is a final charge to Government.

The Colonial Office have taken up a complete non possumus attitude in regard to the production of detailed information such as we are getting from Burma. They say:—

(a) The programme is in any case not under the control of the Colonial Office, but of the Planning Unit of the territory concerned. (This Planning Unit is a body of men at present disguised in Military uniform who will form the Civil Affairs staff during the Military occupation, but who will thereafter assume their pre-war occupation of being local Civil Servants). The Planning Units are already in the Far

---

[1] A F B fforde was posted from his legal practice to be deputy director general at the Ministry of Supply in 1940; he rose to under-secretary in 1943 and served as under-secretary at the Treasury, 1944–45. After the war he was headmaster of Rugby School, 1948–57, and chairman of the BBC, 1957–64.

East, so that any information we required would have to come from them. In any case they are not organised on the comprehensive Government of Burma scale and would not be able to produce the detailed information for which we have been asking.

(b) In any case, the Treasury demand is in bad taste because the whole of the programme now in contemplation is based on the Ministry of Production's Survey, known as the Brett Report. The Treasury were represented by Mr. Copleston[2] when the Brett Report was being considered and we ought no to go back on it.

As regards the consumer goods which are to be sold at cost, these were drawn up on the basis of the Young Enquiry and although we have had full details of the Burma programme, the information sent gave us no useful basis of criticism, and I should be quite content if we got no detail from the Colonial Office. For the rest of the programme I do not think we can accept the Colonial Office attitude. If the position is that there is no one in the future Malayan Government with a grasp of the financial programme comparable to that of Mr. Waight[3] for the larger and more complex Burma programme, then it is time that such an appointment was made. And answering the Treasury questions will be a very useful piece of education for the holder of the new appointment.

As regards the sanctity of the Brett programme, this was drawn up without any regard to financial considerations, in fact the recommendations were made in terms of quantities and not of cash. Furthermore, Brett himself recognised that his recommendation was made in the absence of up-to-date knowledge of what equipment might be found undestroyed. He therefore recommended that orders should only be placed for what was immediately required, and that the full programme should not be put in hand until information about actual conditions was available.

The Brett items total some £17 million, of which £11 million are on account of immediate needs, and the Colonial Office would be content for authority to proceed with the £11 million alone for the present. This is something, but they are not apparently in a position to tell us how the £11 million is made up.

I suggest that subject to any further thoughts when we know whether or not Malaya is willing to finance the whole programme, we should tell the Colonial Office that whilst we are willing to waive the production of any further information about the consumer goods programme, we must ask for details, under heads, of the £11 million programme now in hand, and for arrangements to be made for us to be supplied with similar detailed information for any further orders to be placed in the future beyond these limits. Equally we shall expect information about the Budget Deficit and other liabilities consequent upon the restoration of civil Government. If the Colonial Office say that this cannot be done with the present staff, then we should press for the appointment of a Financial Adviser and any necessary staff working under him capable of producing such information.

---

[2] E R Copleston joined the Inland Revenue in 1932 and moved to the Treasury in 1942.
[3] L Waight was financial adviser to the governor of Burma from 1944.

39 CO 273/677/3, no 5   26 June 1945
'Political co-ordination in South-East Asia': memorandum by M E Dening

[While the CO had been planning the closer association of British dependencies in South-East Asia through the office of a regional governor general, the FO, urged by M E Dening (political adviser to Mountbatten since September 1943) contemplated the creation of a regional organization within the framework of SEAC.]

The increasing importance which political and economic questions are assuming in the war against Japan make[s] it desirable to review the circumstances in which a Political Adviser was appointed to the Supreme Commander, South East Asia, in September, 1943, and to consider whether any change is desirable.

2. When this appointment was made, it was not clear how the functions of a Political Adviser would develop, and his terms of reference (copy attached)[1] were, in consequence, somewhat restricted, and related in the main only to his advisory capacity. Nor did the Political Adviser have any brief to act in matters concerning other Government departments such as the Burma Office and the Colonial Office.

3. The office of Political Adviser has now been in existence for some eighteen months. In practice the Adviser tends to be regarded and treated as a senior Staff Officer of the Supreme Commander, though unlike Service Staff Officers he has independent cypher communication with the Foreign Office, to which he reports direct.

4. It is questionable whether this situation, whereby the Political Adviser virtually serves two masters, should be allowed to continue, for while on the one hand a Staff Officer to the Supreme Commander should be solely responsible to him, there is on the other hand a need for the Foreign Office to have in South East Asia a representative who is responsible to the Secretary of State.

5. But the matter does not end there, for it has been found that in practice questions frequently arise which, though of concern to the Foreign Office, are sometimes of primary concern to other Government Departments (e.g. the Burma Office and the Colonial Office). Though the Government of Burma has established a practice whereby a senior civil servant visits the Supreme Allied Headquarters from time to time, questions of importance frequently arise when he is not there, with the result that decisions are sometimes reached without the prior consultation which is essential if political pitfalls are to be avoided. In the case of Burma there is at any rate the advantage of a civil government in being (even though inconveniently situated),[2] but in the case of Malaya there is no similar situation, with the result that the nearest consultative authority is the Colonial Office in London. But no direct channel of communication exists with that authority.

6. One of the results of the present position is that political questions tend to be referred to the Chiefs of Staff who are then under the necessity of referring them to the political departments concerned in London. An added burden is thus imposed at the one end on the military staff of the Supreme Commander and at the other on the machinery of the Chiefs of Staff organisation without in any way obviating the

---

[1] Not printed.   [2] It did not return to Burma until Oct 1945.

necessity of consultation with the political departments. As the tempo of military operations increases, this burden is likely to become increasingly irksome, while on the other hand the complexity and urgency of political and economic problems will grow progressively greater as territory after territory is liberated until the final problem of dealing with Japan herself has to be faced.

7. There is another disadvantage in dealing with political matters through the official Chiefs of Staff channel, and that is that the Headquarters of the Supreme Command in South East Asia is an allied organisation and that the official SEACOS and COSSEA series of telegrams is known to and seen by American officers. Where British and American opinion does not necessarily coincide, or where it is known to differ on political questions, it is an embarrassment to an allied staff to have to deal with them, and they should more properly be handled through a political channel. The Supreme Commander is an allied commander who has, at any rate in theory, a dual allegiance to the Governments of Great Britain and the United States, and he should not be put into the position of having to take sides in any question where the policies of these two Governments may be at variance, as for example in relation to colonial territories.

8. It would seem from the above that from the point of view of the chain of responsibility, of greater efficiency and of procedure some change should to made in the political representation as it is now established in the headquarters of the South East Asia Command.

9. Two alternatives suggest themselves. The first is that the Political Adviser should be established outside the headquarters though in the closest possible relationship with the Supreme Commander and his Staff, that he should be given authority to advise the Supreme Commander on all political and economic questions, irrespective of the departments in London which they concern, and that he should be authorised to report direct to London and to refer such matters as require reference. In this event the Political Adviser would have to have an increased staff to cope with his enlarged responsibilities and it might be necessary to attach additional officers with the requisite experience to deal with matters affecting British territories, economic and financial questions and possibly also public relations. In view of the conditions prevailing in South East Asia it would still be necessary for the military command to be responsible for accommodation, transport, rations, security etc.

10. If the above alternative is decided upon, it would seem necessary to issue directives to both the Supreme Commander and the Political Adviser which would regularize their position in relation to one another and define their responsibilities.

11. The other alternative would be to follow the practice adopted in other theatres and to appoint a Minister of State for South East Asia. This is not a new idea, and it was discussed by the Foreign Office and India Office in 1943 when the South East Asia Command was about to be set up. But as the headquarters of the Command were at first to be set up in New Delhi, the India Office held that it was not constitutionally possible to appoint a Minister of State with authority over matters in India. In the event the Vicerory was given an extra-statutory capacity to deal with matters of administration affecting other than Indian interests, and Sir Archibald Rowlands was appointed, with a staff, as Adviser to the Viceroy on War Administration.

12. With the removal of the Supreme Allied Command to Ceylon, this arrange-

ment, which at no time had satisfied the political requirements of the situation external to India, fell into comparative disuse. It is not the purpose of this paper to discuss whether it should be maintained, but there is clearly an urgent need for a new arrangement which will safeguard our political and economic position throughout the Far East.

13.   In 1943 no territory occupied by the enemy in South East Asia had yet been recovered. To-day the greater portion of Burma is in our hands and within the next year the recovery of further regions may be expected which will present problems affecting not only our political position and economy within the Empire, but also our relations with America, China, France, the Netherlands and Siam. In these questions the Dominions in general, and Australia and New Zealand in particular, are likely to display a strong interest. Finally Japan will have to be dealt with, and this will be a matter in which all areas of the British Commonwealth will be vitally interested as well as all the allied Powers including Russia.

14.   Before this war British territories east of Suez tended to be governed largely on parochial lines. Thus India, Ceylon, Burma and Malaya were all chiefly concerned with their own internal problems. They were largely unfamiliar with each other's problems, and still less with the problems of the non-British territories in the Far East (i.e. the Netherlands East Indies, Siam, Indo-China, the Philippines, China and Japan). That such a state of affairs was both strategically and politically undesirable was proved by subsequent events when Japan delivered her attack. To-day there is a danger that, with the preoccupations of reconstruction and rehabilitation and the major political problems affecting the internal structure of India, Burma, Ceylon and Malaya, we shall drift once more into the same position as we were before the outbreak of hostilities.

15.   While it is yet early to determine our post-war requirements in the Far East, there does seem to be an imperative need at the present and at any rate for the period until conditions are stabilised, for the appointment of a central authority who can report direct to the Cabinet and whose task would be to coordinate the views and the needs of all the British territories involved and to relate these with developments in other non-British territories as the war develops against Japan.

16.   The solution of this problem would appear to be the appointment of a Minister of State, on the precedent of the Middle East and the Mediterranean,[3] with a staff of civil servants competent to advise him on the numerous problems with which he is likely to be confronted and adequately representing the various interests involved.

17.   A Minister of State, if appointed, would take over the functions of the Political Adviser as set out earlier in this memorandum, and his relationship with the Supreme Command would presumably be defined in his directive and in a similar directive to the Supreme Commander.

18.   It should be noted that the United States Government have not, up to the present, though fit to appoint a Political Adviser to the Supreme Allied Command in South East Asia, though there has been nothing to prevent their doing so as far as the Government of the United Kingdom is concerned. It would probably be desirable to notify the United States, as a matter of courtesy and to avoid misunderstanding, of

---

[3] Oliver Lyttelton, minister of state in Cairo, 1941–1942; Harold Macmillan, minister resident in N W Africa, 1942–1945.

any decision to alter the existing status of the Political Adviser to the Supreme Allied Commander, or to appoint a Minister of State who would absorb his functions.

19. In considering the question of the appointment of a Minister of State, reference is invited to the report of Mr. Duff Cooper as a result of his mission to the Far East in 1941 (W.P. (41) 286 of 29th October 1941).[4]

---

[4]'British administration in the Far East', WP(41)286, 29 Oct 1941, is at CAB 66/120. Duff Cooper, chancellor of the Duchy of Lancaster, 1941–1943, was sent to Singapore in Aug 1941 to examine co-ordination between the various civil and military authorities in the region. His report recommended the appointment of a commissioner-general for the Far East based at Singapore and supported by a War Cabinet and War Council. On the Japanese attack in Dec he himself was appointed resident minister in Singapore and was authorised to form a War Cabinet, but the arrival of General Wavell as supreme commander of the SW Pacific made his job redundant and he returned to Britain in Feb.

40   CO 273/677/3, no 5   2 Aug 1945
[Political co-ordination in SE Asia]: letter from Sir O Sargent[1] to Sir G Gater

We had, before the change of Government,[2] been giving some thought to the machinery, both within the Foreign Office and interdepartmentally, for dealing with Far Eastern questions in the political and economic spheres. The Far Eastern Committee had been reconstituted under the chairmanship of the Minister of State, steps were being taken to form a small political planning staff for the purpose of preparing papers for the Far Eastern Committee, and the Overseas Reconstruction Committee had agreed to the extension of the work of the Economic and Industrial Planning Staff to questions affecting ex-enemy countries in the Far East. Within the Foreign Office the work of the Far Eastern Department has been somewhat re-organised.

The Far Eastern Committee will no doubt have to be freshly re-constituted. Meanwhile a further important question is that of political liaison with the military commands in the Far East and the connected, if wider, question of political co-ordination in South-East Asia. Dening, Political Adviser to the Supreme Allied Commander, was recently in this country and, after consultation with various members of the Foreign Office, prepared a memorandum[3] on this subject. I enclose a copy, but as it has not yet been seen by my Secretary of State I would ask you to regard it as a purely personal and unofficial basis for discussion.

As you will see, Dening suggests that the time has come to make a change in the form of the political representation as it is now established in the Headquarters of the South-East Asia Command, and he expresses the opinion that the present arrangement, whereby the Political Adviser virtually serves two masters and has no brief to act in matters concerning any Government Departments other than the Foreign Office, is one which involves several disadvantages on both the civil and military side. Dening puts forward alternative suggestions for improving the position, namely:—

---

[1] Deputy under-secretary of state, FO; permanent under-secretary of state, 1946–1949.
[2] Attlee became prime minister on 26 July and appointed Philip Noel-Baker minister of state at the Foreign Office under Bevin. Noel-Baker was promoted to secretary of state for air in Oct 1946.
[3] See 39.

(a) to detach the office of Political Adviser from Admiral Mountbatten's staff, to make the Political Adviser responsible to London and to give him additional staff to enable him to advise the Supreme Commander not merely on questions of foreign affairs, as at present, but on political, financial and economic matters regardless of the Department in London which they concern, i.e., affecting British as well as foreign territories.

(b) to appoint a Minister of State for South-East Asia.

These suggestions are not mutually exclusive and acceptance of the first might possibly be the initial step towards the creation at a later date of a wider political organisation under a Minister of State. In our view the detachment of the Political Adviser from Admiral Mountbatten's staff is *prima facie* in itself a sound measure which need not involve any alteration in the present physical arrangements in S.E.A.C. but would merely mean altering the responsibility of the Political Adviser.

We are doubtful whether it would be helpful now to appoint anyone with such wide powers and responsibilities as those contemplated by Mr. Duff Cooper in his report from Singapore of the 29th October, 1941,[4] to which Dening refers in the final paragraph of his memorandum. But we think it would be most desirable to have in S.E.A.C. some political authority of high standing to undertake the local centralisation and co-ordination of matters affecting more than one Department of His Majesty's Government, and at the same time to relieve the Supreme Commander of a great deal of non-military work with which he should not be burdened. The best solution might be to appoint at an appropriate moment, perhaps immediately after the re-capture of Singapore, a Minister of State who would undertake clearly defined responsibilities in a prescribed area. This proposal would need to be considered in the light of possible changes in command boundaries, but there seems no reason why a Minister of State should not function in regard to the extended area of S.E.A.C. which is at present under consideration.

We are now considering the preparation of a Paper for the Cabinet on the whole question for submission to the Secretary of State but before proceeding further we should like to know whether you are in general agreement with our views. We should also be grateful for any observations you may care to offer on Dening's memorandum generally.

Meanwhile, if you should wish Dening, in his present capacity and in addition to his functions under his present directive, to hold a watching brief for the Colonial Office in Kandy,[5] we should be glad to discuss with you how this can best be arranged and how it would work in practice.

I am writing similarly to Machtig, Monteath, Bovenschen, Markham and Street.[6]

---

[4] See 39, note 4.   [5] ie headquarters of SEAC.
[6] Sir Eric Machtig, permanent under-secretary for the Dominions (Commonwealth relations), 1940–1948; Sir David Monteath, under-secretary for India and Burma, 1941–1947; Sir Federick Bovenschen, joint permanent under-secretary of state for war, 1942–1945; Sir Henry Markham, permanent under-secretary at the Admiralty, 1940–1946; and Sir Arthur Street, permanent under-secretary for air, 1939–1945.

41   CO 273/677/3, ff 13–14   7 Aug 1945

[Political co-ordination in SE Asia]: minute by G E J Gent on the FO proposals[1]

We have had much evidence ourselves both from Mr. Dening (at present Political Adviser to Admiral Mountbatten) and from Air Marshal Joubert (one of Admiral Mountbatten's Deputy Chiefs of Staff with the portfolio of "Civil Affairs") that the arrangements in S.E. Asia Command for ensuring full regard for political considerations badly needed strengthening. Both the above mentioned officers are on Admiral Mountbatten's staff and have not sufficient independence to ensure that the Supreme Allied Commander does not take decisions on political matters until they have, if of sufficient importance, been referred to H.M.G.

In the memorandum which he now submits, Mr. Dening advocates the detachment of the Political Adviser from the Supreme Allied Commander's staff and giving him an independent responsibility to London; or, alternatively, the appointment of a Minister of State for South East Asia.

Sir O. Sargent considers that these are not necessarily alternatives, and we should agree with him in the sense that a decision to proceed with the first would not necessarily rule out later proceeding with the second; if, however, a Minister of State were now appointed with a political responsibility to H.M.G. in London, there would in fact seem to be no place for a distinct Political Adviser responsible to London.

Sir O. Sargent considers that prima facie the detachment of the Political Adviser from Admiral Mountbatten's staff is in itself a sound measure and one which need not involve any alteration in the present physical arrangements in S.E. Asia Command but would merely re-align the Political Adviser's responsibilities.

We agree with this view.

Sir O. Sargent goes on to doubt whether it would be helpful now to appoint anyone with such wide powers and responsibilities as those recommended by Mr. Duff Cooper in his report of 29th October, 1941. In that report Mr. Duff Cooper (who had then for some months been exploring the situation in the Far East and had not taken up his later appointment as Resident Minister) turned down the conception of a Resident Minister in the Far East and advocated instead the appointment of an *official* with the title of "Commissioner-General". The sort of man he had in mind would be "a former Ambassador or some exceptionally distinguished civil servant". His prime function would be to keep the War Cabinet furnished with a complete picture of the whole situation in the Far East and he would report direct to, and receive instructions from, the various Ministers whose Departments were represented at that time in the Far East on matters concerning them. Sir O. Sargent does not, however, refer to the fact that Mr. Duff Cooper's recommendation was expressly for an official and not a Minister, and he goes on to suggest that the best solution might be to appoint at an appropriate time (possibly after the recapture of Singapore) a Minister of State with clearly defined responsibilities in a prescribed region— possibly the area of S.E.A.C.

The experience of Mr. Duff Cooper as Resident Minister in Malaya was an unhappy one and unless it is certain that it can already be foreseen that there will be

---

[1] See 39 & 40.

overriding need for a Minister of State to be reappointed in the Far East, the decision would, I believe, be received with apprehension and criticism.

We have ourselves in mind, under the plans provisionally approved by the War Cabinet, the appontment of a "Governor-General" with direct powers over the British authorities in Malaya, Singapore, North Borneo and Sarawak. Primarily he would need to be a first-rate and highly experienced administrator to direct the various fields of reconstruction, including local foreign relations of those territories.

I should be inclined to suggest that the first and only step necessary now is the appointment of a Political Adviser in S.E. Asia Command, who is of greater weight and experience than Mr. Dening and is responsible directly to London. Whether it will be desirable to make any fresh decision in the future, e.g. after the recapture of Singapore, so long as S.E. Asia Command exists, had much better be left to be considered in the light of needs and events. Quite possibly there may be no appropriate place for a Resident Minister and, equally possibly, there may be need for a detached Political Adviser to continue with the "Governor-General" at Singapore after the S.E. Asia Command has ceased to exist as an allied military command.

42   CO 273/677/3, no 6   13 Aug 1945
[Political co-ordination in SE Asia]: letter (reply) from Sir G Gater to Sir O Sargent

Many thanks for your letter of 2nd August (F 3944/149/G)[1] which I have now had an opportunity of discussing with my Secretary of State. In the current situation in the Far East no doubt your own views and those of Dening will be recast but you may like to know our present reaction to the question of reforming the arrangement for giving political advice to Admiral Mountbatten.

We feel that the first and only step necessary at the moment, is the appointment of a Political Adviser in S.E. Asia Command, who should be an experienced person of acknowledged calibre and who would be responsible directly to London. This responsibility could be exercised to the Foreign Office as regards your sphere and through the Foreign Office to ourselves and other Departments as far as our respective spheres are concerned.

Whether it would be desirable to make any fresh decision in the future, for instance, after SACSEA is established in Singapore and so long as S.E.A.C. exists, should be left to be considered in the light of needs and events. Quite possibly after S.E.A.C. has ceased to exist as an allied military command and when civil government is re-established in Malaya, we may see an appropriate place for a Political Adviser to be appointed to the staff of the proposed Governor-General, in view of the relations which the Governor-General may be expected to have in practice with neighbouring foreign territories.[2]

---

[1] See 40.

[2] On 15 Aug Emperor Hirohito surrendered. Discussion of regional co-ordination is resumed at document 58.

43   WO 203/5642, no 7/16/45   13 Aug 1945

'Directive to AJUF on conclusion of the armistice': signal from B A C Sweet-Escott[1]

[The Far Eastern branch of Special Operations Executive grew out of GSI(K)—part of the intelligence staff at GHQ India—and in Mar 1944 took the name of Force 136 under the command of Colonel Colin MacKenzie. On 23 May the previous year a reconnaissance party led by Lt Col John Davis arrived by submarine on the Perak coast. Further landings took place until Sept 1943 while a Malay group, led by Captain (later General Tan Sri) Ibrahim bin Ismail, was brought by Catalina flying-boat to an island off Kota Bahru. On 1 Jan 1944 Davis, Captain Richard Broome, Major Lim Bo Seng of the KMT and Major (later Lt Col) F Spencer Chapman, who had stayed behind Japanese lines since the fall of Singapore in 1942, met Lai Tek and Chin Peng who between them represented the Chinese-dominated MCP, MPAJU and MPAJA. At this meeting it was agreed that, in return for arms, money, training and supplies, the resistance forces would accept British orders during the war and in the subsequent period of military occupation. Political matters were not touched upon. News of the agreement did not reach SEAC until a year later and its terms were confirmed on 17 Mar 1945 at a second meeting between Force 136 and MCP representatives. Thereafter arms, supplies and men were parachuted in from SEAC HQ in Ceylon. What control Force 136 asserted over the MPAJA declined rapidly as the delay between the Japanese surrender and the arrival of British troops lengthened, see 46 and 47. SEAC forces landed in Penang on 3 Sept and Singapore on 5 Sept but it was not until 12 Sept that Brigadier Willan set up the headquarters of the Malayan British Military Administration in Kuala Lumpur.]

Object

1. To prevent seizure of power in MALAYA by A.J.U.F. and to avoid unnecessary bloodshed before the arrival of regular forces.

Information

2. No regular forces will reach MALAYA for at least 14 days.

3. There are, however, 80 Allied officers liaising with A.J.U.F. and communicating with CEYLON through about 40 W/T set[s].

4. A.J.U.F. is a body of some 3,000 guerillas, mostly Chinese Communists, and containing elements desirous of preventing a permanent return of British rule. All are, however, violently anti-Japanese, and have agreed to accept SACSEA's orders with the object of throwing the Japanese out of MALAYA. They are located mainly in the hills and more than 2,000 arms have been sent to them since May.

Considerations

5. Experience has shown, particularly in GREECE, that resistance movements must be given clear instructions what to do when their country is liberated. If they receive NO such instructions they will inevitably cause trouble, and may well attempt to seize power in the principal towns.

6. At the same time, A.J.U.F. have been very nearly our only friends during the occupation. We are under an obligation to them, and do NOT wish to give them the impression that we are ready to drop them now that we NO longer have any use for them.

---

[1] B A C Sweet-Escott (1907–1981) served with Special Operations Executive in Western Europe, the Balkans, Middle East, and South-East Asia; from Jan to Dec 1945 he was chief of staff to Force 136 and acting commander during the absence of Colonel MacKenzie.

Courses open

7. To do nothing pending the arrival of regular forces. This runs the risk of leading to the results described in 5 above.

8. To tell A.J.U.F. to co-operate with the Japanese in the administration of the country, pending the arrival of Allied troops. This would NOT be understood, and would certainly NOT be accepted, for the reasons in 4 above.

9. To instruct the Allied Liaison Officers:—

(i)   to prevent contact between A.J.U.F. and the Japanese.

(ii) to keep A.J.U.F. in the country districts where there are no Japanese.

(iii) to give A.J.U.F. the task of keeping order generally in such districts.

Recommendations

10. It is recommended that the course in 9 above be adopted. A draft telegram in this sense to the Allied Liaison Officers is attached at Appendix A.[2]

---

[2] Not printed.

44   WO 203/5642, no 14/16/45   15 Aug 1945
'A proclamation to establish a military administration': British Military Administration, Malaya, proclamation no 1 issued by Admiral Mountbatten

[This document is also reproduced in F S V Donnison, *British Military Administration in the Far East, 1943–46* (London, 1956) Appendix 3, pp 450–51.]

Whereas by reason of military necessity and for the prevention and suppression of disorder and the maintenance of public safety it is necessary to place the territories of the Settlements of Singapore, Penang and Malacca, all islands and places forming part thereof and all British waters adjacent thereto, and the Malay States of Perak, Selangor, Negri Sembilan, Pahang, Johore, Kedah, Kelantan, Trengganu and Perlis, all islands forming part of such States and the territorial waters thereof (hereinafter called Malaya) under military administration:

Now, therefore, I, Admiral Lord Louis Mountbatten, Knight Grand Cross of the Royal Victorian Order, Knight Commander of the Most Honourable Order of the Bath, Companion of the Distinguished Service Order, Personal Aide de Camp to His Majesty the King, Honorary Lieutenant-General and Air Marshal, Supreme Allied Commander South East Asia, *hereby proclaim as follows:*

Establishment of a military administration

1. A Military Administration to be called the British Military Administration is hereby established throughout such areas of Malaya as are at any given time under the control of Forces under my command and shall continue only so long as I consider it to be required by military necessity.

Assumption of powers and jurisdiction

2. I hereby assume for myself and my successors full judicial, legislative, executive and administrative powers and responsibilities and conclusive jurisdiction

persons and property throughout such areas of Malaya as are at any given time under the control of the Forces under my command.

Delegation

3. Subject always to any orders and directions which I may issue from time to time, I delegate to the General Officer Commanding Military Forces, Malaya, all the powers, responsibilities and jurisdiction assumed by me, and such General Officer Commanding is authorised to delegate such powers, responsibilities and jurisdiction as he may deem necessary to any Officer under his command and to empower such officer further to delegate any of such powers, responsibilities and jurisdiction.

Orders to be obeyed

4. All persons will obey promptly all orders given by me or under my authority and must refrain from all acts which impede the Forces under my command or are helpful to the enemy, from all acts of violence, and from any act calculated to disturb public order in any way.

Existing laws to be respected

5. (i) Subject to the provisions of any Proclamation of the British Military Administration and in so far as military exigencies permit:

(a) all laws and customs existing immediately prior to the Japanese occupation will be respected:—
Provided that such of the existing laws as the Chief Civil Affairs Officer considers it is practicable from time to time to administer during the period of military administration will be administered;

(b) all rights and properties will be respected:—
Provided that rights and properties acquired during the Japanese occupation may be subject to investigation and to such action as justice requires.

(ii) With regard to paragraph (a) of sub-section (i), the inhabitants of the said territories are advised to consult the nearest Civil Affairs Officer if in doubt as to whether any existing law is being administered.

Suspension of courts

6. All Courts and tribunals, other than military courts established under my authority, are hereby suspended and deprived of all authority and jurisdiction until authorized by me to re-open.

Revocation of Japanese military administration proclamations

7. It is hereby declared that all Proclamations and legislative enactments of whatever kind issued by or under the authority of the Japanese Military Administration shall cease to have any effect.

Short title

8. This Proclamation may be cited as the Military Administration Proclamation.

Signed at Kandy, this fifteenth day of August, 1945.

(*Signed*) LOUIS MOUNTBATTEN
Supreme Allied Commander, South East Asia.

45   WO 203/5642, no 66/16/45   17 Aug 1945

'Directive on civil affairs for Malaya to the supreme allied commander, South East Asia Command': directive from Mr Lawson[1] to Admiral Mountbatten

1. Upon the liberation of Malaya or within such territories thereof or adjacent thereto as are under the control of your forces you will set up a military administration for the government of the civil population of the territory. To this end you will assume for yourself by Proclamation such powers as are necessary for the administration of the liberated territories, and will also arrange for the delegation of such powers to the Military Commander designated by you, as General Officer Commanding, Military Forces, Malaya. You will likewise suspend the powers and jurisdiction of all existing courts and tribunals and in their place set up military courts which will derive their authority from your proclamation and deal with all offences committed by the civil population. Such courts will administer the laws in force in Malaya prior to the Japanese occupation modified or supplemented by proclamation as may be necessary for the security of the liberating forces and the maintenance of order.

2. In order to enable you (or the Military Commander designated by you for the purpose) to carry on the Military Administration, a Chief Civil Affairs Officer, Malaya (C.C.A.O.(M)) has been appointed. He will on your behalf and subject to your general directions (or those of the Military Commander) administer the civil population of the liberated territories during the operational phase in the name of the Military Commander, and subsequently in his own name. For all purposes in connection with military administration, the Military Commander referred to above will be formally designated "General Officer Commanding, Military Forces, Malaya". He will at no time assume the title of Military Governor.

3. The C.C.A.O.(M) will be provided with a staff of military officers augmented, as may be necessary, by civilians and subordinate military and civil staffs. In so far as is possible, personnel for this staff will be made available by the Colonial Office from officials of the former Government of Malaya, who know the country, the language and the people.

4. During the currency of the military period, military consideration will be paramount. The duties of the military administration (as *distinct* from those of C.C.A.O.(M) referred to in para 5 below) will be two fold. *Firstly*, in those territories under military administration C.C.A.O.(M) and the Civil Affairs Officers under his direction will administer the civil population in such a way as to meet the requirements of local Military Commanders and to further the general well being of the territory. To this end, they will restore law and order among the civil population, distribute essential supplies and advise and act on behalf of the local Commanders in their dealings with the civil population. *Secondly*, C.C.A.O.(M) will (as soon as military exigencies permit) take the necessary steps to establish as far as possible the essential framework of administration within the liberated territories as territory is uncovered, and lay the foundations of stable future government.

5. The liberation of Malaya necessitates the immediate resumption of H.M.G's

---

[1] John James Lawson, secretary of state for war, 3 Aug–Oct 1946; created 1st Lord Lawson 1950.

responsibility to the peoples of Malaya for their protection and good government. This will, in addition to those measures indicated under para 4 above, call for energetic administrative action and involve a number of activities of government which have no military significance and for which the War Office has no responsibility to Parliament; these matters will be the responsibility of the Colonial Office. It has been decided, therefore, that C.C.A.O.(M) will have a dual responsibility which he will discharge in accordance with the decisions and directions of His Majesty's Government as recorded in the memorandum on this subject which has been communicated to you separately.

6. In furtherance of your function under para. 4 you will during the period of Military Administration be responsible, subject to operational requirements, for the provision of supplies for the needs of the civil population, and for local industries and agriculture to a level necessary to prevent disease and unrest and to secure the maximum assistance for the progressive restoration of the territory. In addition you should render such assistance as is feasible to enable those natural resources of the territory as are urgently required to meet the general world shortage to be obtained. Sufficient supplies will be demanded for 6 months for the whole of Malaya. In addition you will demand additional supplies in the form of Inducement Goods for military labour employed directly for military purposes should you consider it necessary to do so to ensure proper supplies of labour. Other necessary supplies for the civil population of the liberated territory during the period of Military Administration may be procured by the Colonial Office and for those you will provide such transportation and other facilities within your Command as may be possible in the circumstances of the case. All supplies for the civil needs of the territory for the periods following the 6 months military provisions are being procured through civil channels as a Colonial Office responsibility and for those, also, you will provide such transportation and other facilities within your Command as may be possible.

7. It is the policy of His Majesty's Government that the Administration of the territories in question should be transferred to the responsibility of the Colonial Office as soon as possible as and in so far as conditions are such as to enable the latter to function. It will be for you to recommend when and in what areas such transfer can take place without embarrassment to military needs bearing in mind that so far as the Malayan mainland areas are concerned (excluding Singapore) it is likely to be impracticable for the Colonial Office to take over responsibility until the whole of that area can be so transferred. Subject to military exigencies, the Government of the civil population during the period of Military Administration in Malaya will be carried on in the various administrative spheres in accordance with long-term policy which the Colonial Office has in mind to pursue when it resumes responsibility for the civil administration of the territory. In order that you may be aware of this policy, and be in a position to pursue it so far as circumstances and military considerations permit, you will be supplied from time to time with long-term policy directives framed by the Secretary of State for the Colonies and transmitted to you through the War Office.

8. If, in your judgement, a departure from these or any subsequent instructions is required for urgent and over-riding military reasons, you have discretion to authorise action accordingly and you will submit a report on the matter as soon as possible.

46   WO 203/5642, no 1/16/45   19 Aug 1945
'Force 136 Policy—Malaya': signal from B A C Sweet-Escott

1. The following message has been recieved from Lt. Col. J.L.H. DAVIS,[1] D.S.O., who is head of Force 136 mission with MPAJA in MALAYA.

"Your recent telegrams are disturbing. Following must of course be obvious to you. Controlled AJUF are soldiers under command of SACSEA. They expect and await specific orders and not vague directives. I am satisified they will obey such orders provided they are reasonable. Orders for them to remain half starved in the hills while the Allies leisurely take over the administration from the Japs will not be reasonable. Some arrangement must be made with the Japs for controlled AJUF to emerge during the interim period though they need not interfere with the Japs admin. AJUF must be given full share in the honours of victory. Controlled AJUF should now be limited to those already armed by us plus other armed men who will accept our control. They must be fully equipped rationed and used by us at the earliest opportunity until time for disbandment. Good treatment of controlled AJUF will have an excellent effect on uncontrolled AJUF many of whom may later be absorbed. Do your utmost to preserve and strengthen central control otherwise discipline will collapse. The alternative to all this is chaos and anarchy which may take decades to eradicate. The matter is very urgent. There is serious risk of a disastrous anticlimax."

2. The telegrams referred to in the first paragraph of this message include the following:—

"Victory is now at hand and your contribution has been important and is appreciated.

Allied Troops will shortly arrive but meanwhile to avoid clashes and unnecessary bloodshed you and those under you should avoid all towns and other districts where Japanese are present."

---

[1] J L H Davis, entered Federated Malay States police, 1930; served in Force 136 rising to rank of lt colonel; transferred to colonial administrative service in Malaya 1947; see 43, note.

47   WO 203/5642, no 12/16/45   24 Aug 1945
[Publicity for Malayan policy]: signal from C MacKenzie[1]

The inevitable delay between the cease fire and the re-occupation of MALAYA is rapidly increasing the difficulties with which we shall be faced in connection with the A.J.U.F.

2. It must be borne in mind that the A.J.U.F. is

(a) Almost entirely composed of domiciled Chinese whose status as citizens has

---

[1] Colin Hercules MacKenzie, lost a leg at Passchendaele, 1917; served in SEAC, 1941–1945, and was commander of Force 136; British Economic Mission to Greece, 1946; see also 43, note.

been inferior to that of the Malays in various important respects, and

(b) Contains within its ranks Communists who have undoubtedly widened their influence considerably during the last 3 years. The Communist Party was treated before the war as an illegal association and as such was subject to the attention of the police.

3. The new Colonial Office policy almost entirely removes these two grievances. It is understood that the paper containing the policy of the future government for MALAYA is now again before the Cabinet.

4. It is more earnestly urged that the SUPREME ALLIED COMMANDER should be requested to send a further signal stressing the importance of an immediate authorisation to disclose the relevant details of the policy now.

5. Every hour increases the danger of some occurrence which may place the A.J.U.F. irretrievably in the wrong and subsequently lead to the embitterment of relations after the necessary counter-action has been taken by the British.

6. Moreover, any further delay in disclosing essential details of this policy will expose us to an increasingly serious risk of it appearing that the policy has only been extorted from us by fear of further A.J.U.F. activity which might be detrimental to order and good government.

7. The best chance we have of avoiding these problems is to strengthen the hands of the Liaison Officers now with A.J.U.F. One of the best ways of doing this is to be able to authorise them to inform the members of A.J.U.F. of the Government's new policy.

8. It is understood that one reason given for the delay in announcing the policy is that it is necessary first to inform the Sultans that the new policy will involve some loss in their powers etc. If, as we suppose, it is not a question of negotiating with the Sultans but simply of informing them for the sake of courtesy of the incidental effect on their position we urge that the information it is desired to pass to the Sultans be set out in a fixed form and communicated to the appropriate Force 136 officers who could quickly arrange for the communication to reach the various Sultans.

9. We again urge the increasing and serious dangers of further delay.

48   CAB 129/1, CP(45)133   29 Aug 1945
'Policy in regard to Malaya and Borneo': Cabinet memorandum by Mr Hall

[The sudden end to the war in Asia forced the pace of planning in the CO. On 13 Aug Bourdillon was instructed to prepare a draft Cabinet paper in which Hall would seek the final approval of his colleagues for the policy provisionally approved in May 1944 (see 25). A revised draft was discussed in the CO on 22 Aug at a meeting attended by Hall, Creech Jones, Gater, Gent, Duncan, Paskin, and Bourdillon. Hall wrote to Attlee on 27 Aug and the prime minister instructed the secretary of state to put the matter before Cabinet (see 50; also CO 825/42/2 and PREM 8/459).]

At their meeting on the 31st May, 1944, the War Cabinet gave provisional approval to certain proposals regarding the future policy of His Majesty's Government in Malaya and Borneo. These proposals had been formulated by a Ministerial Committee appointed for the purpose, and the Committee's report was circulated to the War

Cabinet on the 18th May, 1944, under the number W.P.(44)258.[1] A copy of the report forms the Annex to this paper.

2. As regards Malaya, the Committee expressed the view that the restoration of the pre-war constitutional and administrative system would be undesirable in the interests of efficiency and security, and of our declared purpose of promoting self-government in Colonial territories. The Committee went on to point out that His Majesty has at present no jurisdiction in the Malay States, and that his relations with the States rest upon treaties with the individual Rulers, under which the Rulers remain nominally independent, though bound to accept British advice on all matters except Mohammedan religion and Malay custom. As a necessary preliminary to all further changes in Malaya, the Committee recommended that fresh Treaties should be made with each of the Rulers, under which such jurisdiction would be ceded to His Majesty as would enable him to legislate for the States under the Foreign Jurisdiction Act. Thereafter an Order-in-Council would be made which would provide for the future central and local government of the country. There would be established a Malayan Union with a central legislature; a Malayan Union Citizenship would also be created, which would not be confined to the Malays, but would be open to persons of whatever race, who may have been born in the country or who have genuinely adopted Malaya as their home. Thus the existing racial and parochial barriers would be broken down.

3. The Committee went on to recommend that the British Settlements of Penang and Malacca (at present part of the Colony of the Straits Settlements) should be incorporated in the Malayan Union, but that Singapore should for the time being (and without prejudice to the possibility of later amalgamation with the Malayan Union) be administered as a separate Colony under a separate Governor. Finally, the Committee envisaged that there should be appointed a "Governor-General," who would reside at Singapore and who would have the power of control not only over the Governor of the Malayan Union and the Governor of Singapore, but also over British Representatives in Borneo.

4. War Cabinet approval for these proposals was only given provisionally and for planning purposes. Plans have now been proceeding on this basis for over a year, and Sir Harold MacMichael, until recently High Commissioner for Palestine, has been provisionally selected as the special Representative of His Majesty's Government who will go out to Malaya to conclude the new Treaties with the Malay Rulers. Sir Harold has already paid a preliminary visit to India and S.E.A.C., and has thoroughly acquainted himself with the whole subject.

5. It has been strongly represented to me by Admiral Mountbatten that a proper reception of His Majesty's Government's policy in Malaya and elsewhere depends upon its timely publication in advance. I find much force in Admiral Mountbatten's arguments, but I am not in a position to make any recommendation as to publication or policy so long as the proposed policy has merely received the *provisional* approval of the Cabinet, and that only for the confidential guidance of planners.

6. I am aware that we cannot fully gauge the temper of the people in Malaya until our return has been actually effected, and that a final decision on all the details of our future policy is therefore not yet possible. I am convinced, however, that the initial step of negotiating new Treaties with the Malay Rulers must be taken as soon as

---

[1] See 25.

possible, and that any delay on this cardinal point, particularly if it were to involve a return to the state of affairs existing before the Japanese occupation of Malaya, might result in the loss of a unique opportunity for setting the territory on the road to political progress.

7. Accordingly I now seek the definite confirmation by my colleagues of the policy outlined above, and approval for Sir Harold MacMichael's appointment. I consider it essential that he should depart for the Far East in the very near future. If the policy is now confirmed, I shall make a separate recommendation as soon as possible regarding the question of publicity.

8. As regards Borneo, the Ministerial Committee, as in the case of Malaya, reached the conclusion that the restoration of the pre-war constitutional and administrative system in the four territories involved would be undesirable in the interests of security, and of our declared purpose of promoting social, economic and political progress in Colonial territories. The territories in question are the State of *North Borneo*, at present (as regards its internal affairs) under the independent administration of the British North Borneo (Chartered) Company, the small Island of *Labuan*, at present administered as one of the Straits Settlements, the State of *Brunei*, which is ruled by a Malay Sultan on the same lines as the nine States in the Malay Peninsula, and *Sarawak*, which (as regards its internal affairs) is under the control of an independent white Rajah of British nationality (Sir Vyner Brooke). The Committee recommended the direct assumption by His Majesty's Government of responsibility for administration in North Borneo, the integration of Labuan with North Borneo and the cession to His Majesty of full jurisdiction in Brunei and Sarawak. In the case of Sarawak, the Committee recommended that the new Treaty providing for this cession of jurisdiction should also secure the acceptance by the Rajah of a Resident British Adviser, whose advice must be sought and acted upon in all substantial matters of policy and administration. (The present Treaty with Brunei already provides for a Resident British Adviser).

9. In approving the above recommendations of the Committee, the War Cabinet authorised my predecessor to open confidential negotiations with the British North Borneo (Chartered) Company for the transfer of their sovereign and administrative rights over North Borneo to His Majesty's Government. No financial commitment, however, was to be entered into without further authorisation. The War Cabinet also authorised my predecessor to open confidential discussions with the Rajah of Sarawak.

10. Discussions with the North Borneo Company have in fact been proceeding since that date, but I am not at present asking for a Cabinet decision, since I am awaiting from the Company's Representatives an expression of their view on the terms upon which a settlement by arbitration might be based.

11. As regards Sarawak, the Rajah has shown considerable reluctance to enter into any discussions with His Majesty's Government with a view to concluding a fresh Agreement. After many delays, he represented that, owing to the impossibility of consulting his people, he was not in a position to enter into a new engagement. My predecessor agreed, therefore, that discussions should be for the purpose of coming to an understanding on the terms of a new Agreement which, when the time came, the Rajah would be prepared to recommend for acceptance and which would be implemented in accordance with the appropriate procedure of the Sarawak Government. The Rajah, however, was still hesitant and by October last progress had only

reached the point of securing his consent to consider a note of His Majesty's Government's proposals.

12. In November, however, the Rajah decided to reinstate his nephew, Mr. Anthony Brooke, as Rajah Muda (a step which can be taken to mean that he must be regarded as heir-presumptive), and suggested that he should take part in the proposed discussions, which eventually began in March.

13. The Rajah Muda and the two other members of the Sarawak Commission nominated by the Rajah to represent him have shown themselves opposed to the proposals which have been made to them on the basis of the decision of the War Cabinet and, since the fourth meeting, which was held on the 10th May, a state of stalemate has existed, while the Sarawak Government consult their legal adviser on His Majesty's Government's definition of the international position of Sarawak. My predecessor, therefore, wrote to the Rajah in July requesting that active consideration should be given to the measures which were necessary on the Sarawak side for the resumption of discussions. The Rajah replied that the Rajah Muda was now administering the Government and that in accordance with the terms of the Sarawak Constitution, Colonel Stanley's letter had been passed to him for action. Nothing further has been heard from the Sawarak side.

14. The Rajah Muda and members of the Sarawak Government have from time to time expressed the wish that Civil Government in Sarawak should be restored as soon as possible, and that the Rajah Muda, as a member of the Brooke family administering the Government, should be allowed to return to the country during the period of military administration.

15. I propose that I should now be authorised to tell the Rajah that the relations with His Majesty's Government are governed by the Agreements of 1888 and 1941, and that so long as he remains Rajah His Majesty's Government cannot recognise any claim on his part to devolve his powers and prerogatives as Rajah on to an "Officer Administering the Government" or any other person. In this connection it is to be observed that Section 18(ii) of the Order of 1941 (providing for the future government of Sarawak) which enacts that "In the event of the Rajah having occasion to leave the State or to be temporarily absent from the seat of Government the Rajah in Council may appoint an officer to administer the Government and such officer shall forthwith assume all the powers and prerogatives of the Rajah (subject to the provisions of this Order)"—has local application only, and does not apply to the present position where the Rajah is in this country and capable of negotiating with His Majesty's Government.

16. I should further propose to say that His Majesty's Government look to the Rajah to ensure that an agreement satisfactory to His Majesty's Government is reached within a period of two months and that, failing the conclusion of such an agreement within that time, it will be necessary for His Majesty's Government to consider what course they must take to ensure that they are in a position and have the necessary authority in the internal as well as the external policies of the Sarawak administration to carry out the responsibility for the territory which they bear to the British Parliament and in the international field. I should like to have authority to add that there can be no question of the Rajah or his Government being permitted to return to Sarawak until such arrangements as are satisfactory to His Majesty's Government have been made.

17. The proposed future changes in the status of Labuan and Brunei are of

comparatively minor importance, and need, I think, present no difficulties. I should, nevertheless, be grateful if my colleagues could now give their final approval to the proposals as regards these territories which were considered by the War Cabinet on the 31st May last year.

18. To sum up, I request the approval of my colleagues for the following measures:—

(a) the definite confirmation of the policy as regards Malaya which is described in paragraphs 2 and 3 above; the first step towards the implementation of this policy being the definitive appointment of Sir Harold MacMichael and his visit to Malaya to conclude new treaties with the Rulers of the several States;
(b) a communication to the Rajah of Sarawak in the sense indicated in paragraphs 15 and 16 above;
(c) the proposed changes in the administration of Labuan and in the matter of His Majesty's jurisdiction in Brunei.

49   T 220/52, IF 23/01   31 Aug 1945
[Economic adviser for Malaya]: letter from Sir G Gater to Sir H Wilson Smith[1]

From the early days of our planning for the post-liberation administration of Malaya, we have had very prominently in mind the importance of securing first-class advice on the economic problems which are certain to beset that administration. The physical rehabilitation of the rubber and tin industries and the proper re-establishment of Malayan production of those and other commodities in world markets will themselves raise problems of considerable difficulty, and inevitably they will be complicated by the difficulties of short supply of food and other consumer goods, with all the consequential problems of price control, anti-inflation measures, etc. We have therefore felt that the administration ought to have at its command an Economic Adviser of really first-class ability and of considerable experience in the task of economic administration. We have thought it wise to refrain from making any stop-gap appointment of a second-rate man, but so far we have not been successful in finding a man of the quality we want, who would be willing to take the appointment.

We have given careful consideration to the possibility of getting somebody from the business world, which, in itself, might have advantages, as the holder of such an appointment would have many dealings with the business interests connected with tin and rubber. After various enquiries in connection both with this post and others of a similar character, we have, however, come to the conclusion that we are very unlikely to get a man of the quality required because this appointment is necessarily only temporary, and men of ability and energy in the business world are at present looking primarily to the establishment of permanent positions and would not be tempted into a temporary overseas post at this rather crucial stage in the reversion to peacetime business unless we were to offer some absurdly high salary. We have therefore come round to the view that we ought to try and secure the services of

---

[1] Sir Henry Wilson Smith, under secretary at the Treasury, 1942–1946; permanent secretary at Ministry of Defence, 1947–1948; additional second secretary at the Treasury, 1948–1951.

either a permanent civil servant or possibly a man from the academic world who has been in Government employ during the war, since a man of that kind, having a definite job to come back to, would not be deterred in the same way by the temporary character of the Malayan post.

Major-General Hone, Chief Civil Affairs Officer in the military administration of Malaya, has pressed very strongly for an early appointment. He himself contemplates that the appointment should be for a period of five years, and suggests a salary of anything from £3,000 to £5,000 on the assumption that we should try and get a man from the commercial world. We are not ourselves convinced that an appointment for so long a period in the first place would be necessary, and if a permanent civil servant were appointed, we need hardly go so high in salary.

We hope that we may secure the goodwill and the active assistance of the Treasury in filling this post in the manner I have suggested above. I am sure that it will be agreed that the re-establishment of the principal Malayan industries on a really sound basis is of very great importance not merely to the territory itself but to the Empire as a whole. As you know, Malaya was before the war probably the most prosperous part of the Colonial Empire and, what is no doubt more important at the present, was among the most important dollar earners in the sterling block. We believe that Malaya can be restored to that position, but to do so will require good management. As the Treasury are well aware, the reconstruction of Malaya is likely to make quite heavy calls on British resources, both Government and private, and here again it is reasonable to hope that good management in the economic field could reduce those calls and do a good deal to ensure that any money spent was wisely used. I think, therefore, that we are justified in suggesting that the post in question has a high Imperial importance and ought to be ranked pretty high in priority among analogous posts in the whole sphere with which the United Kingdom is concerned.

If you agree in principle that it would be justifiable to make some sacrifice in order to fill this post and to spare a really good man from the ranks of Government Service in this country, you will no doubt expect us to make some definite suggestion. I would suggest that the possibility might be considered that Archer of the Ministry of Supply, who, according to my information, has either terminated or is about to terminate his connection with the Ministry of Supply Mission in Washington, might be spared and might be willing to undertake this job. We should be grateful for your advice on that, and if Archer would not be available, to have any alternative suggestion which you feel able to make.[2]

---

[2] Since G Archer was unavailable, C J Pyke, principal assistant secretary in the Ministry of Supply since 1942, was later seconded to be economic adviser to the government of Malaya. He arrived in Kuala Lumpur towards the end of 1946, see 105. In 1949 he was appointed head of the Finance and Economics Department, Foreign Office Administration of African Territories.

50   CAB 128/1, CM 27(45)3   3 Sept 1945
'Malaya and Borneo': Cabinet conclusions authorising the MacMichael mission

The Cabinet had before them a memorandum by the Secretary of State for the Colonies (C.P. (45) 133)[1] submitting proposals regarding the future policy of His Majesty's Government in Malaya and Borneo.

The Secretary of State for the Colonies recalled that, at their meeting on the 31st May, 1944 (W.M. (44) 70th Conclusions, Minute 3), the War Cabinet had provisionally approved for planning purposes proposals for the establishment of a Malayan Union with a central legislature. For this purpose it would be necessary to make fresh treaties with the rulers of the Malay States and it was now proposed that Sir Harold MacMichael should go to Malaya in order to conclude these treaties.

With regard to Borneo, it had been proposed that His Majesty's Government should assume direct responsibility for the administration of North Borneo, which had hitherto been independently administered by the British North Borneo (Chartered) Company; that the island of Labuan should be integrated with North Borneo, and that full jurisdiction in Brunei and Sarawak should be ceded to His Majesty by their rulers. In the case of Sarawak it was recommended that the new treaty should secure the acceptance by the Rajah of a Resident British Adviser. Negotiations with the British North Borneo (Chartered) Company were proceeding satisfactorily and no difficulties seemed likely to arise with regard to Labuan and Brunei. The Rajah of Sarawak had shown great reluctance to enter into discussions, and the Secretary of State for the Colonies felt that he should now be authorised to tell him that, unless an agreement satisfactory to His Majesty's Government could be reached within a period of two months, His Majesty's Government must consider what course they must take to ensure that they were in a position to have the necessary authority in the internal as well as the external policies of the Sarawak administration to carry out the responsibility for the territory which they bore to the British Parliament and in the international field. He would also desire to inform the Rajah that neither he nor his Government would be permitted to return to Sarawak until arrangements satisfactory to His Majesty's Government had been made.

In discussion there was general approval for the proposal that Sir Harold MacMichael should now take up the question of negotiating new treaties with the Malay rulers. With regard to the position in Sarawak, the question was raised whether it would not be desirable to take this opportunity to bring to an end the rule of the Rajah of Sarawak, subject to the payment of compensation on an equitable basis. In any event it was felt that, during the period of military occupation, we should have no hestitation in sending observers into Sarawak.

The Chancellor of the Exchequer[2] said that he hoped that the Treasury would be kept in close touch with the negotiations both with regard to Malaya and with regard to Borneo. He understood that the negotiations carried out by Sir Harold MacMichael would be purely political, but he thought that consideration should also be given to pooling the financial resources of the Malay States.[3]

---

[1] See 48.   [2] Dr H J N Dalton, chancellor of the Exchequer, 1945–1947.
[3] A Treasury minute on the colonial secretary's memorandum contained the following comment: 'There is

The Cabinet:—

(1) Confirmed the policy as regards Malaya set out in paragraphs 2 and 3 of C.P. (45) 133 and authorised the appointment of Sir Harold MacMichael and his visit to Malaya to conclude new treaties with the rulers of the several States.

(2) Approved the proposed changes in the administration of Labuan and in the matter of His Majesty's Government's jurisdiction in Brunei.

(3) Invited the Secretary of State for the Colonies to consider, in the light of the Agreements of 1880 and 1941, whether it would not be possible to bring to an end the rule of the Rajah of Sarawak.

---

clearly a lot to be said for this proposal, which should secure a more efficient and progressive Government in this part of the world, but Treasury points arise in the following respects: (1) The Colonial Office have frozen the Treasury out of their preliminary discussions, and whether as a result of this or not, no mention has been made hitherto of the financial complications. Malaya is faced with a big and expensive Reconstruction programme. There is little doubt that the accumulated financial resources of Malaya as a whole will be able to meet a large part, if not the whole of the bill, but if Malaya is to be treated as a whole, arrangements will have to be made to ensure that the existing resources of the several units in the country are pooled. Sir Harold MacMichael's negotiations seem to be confined to the political aspects. At some stage the financial aspect will have to be included. . . .' Further points raised in this minute concerned Borneo, see T 220/52.

---

51 WO 203/5642   3 Sept 1945

[Publicity for British policy and the aims of the Malayan Communist Party]: inward telegrams nos 433 and 434 from M E Dening to FO

[Returning to the theme of publicity (see 23, 26–31, 36 and 47), Dening argued that the matter was made the more pressing by the political manifesto of the MCP.]

Telegram 433

When I was in London recently I discussed with GENT the question of publicity for British policy about MALAYA in connection with the plans for operation ZIPPER.[1]

2. With the surrender of Japan the situation has entirely changed. Our forces will be replacing the Japanese and our administration will be taking the place of the Japanese sponsored administration within a very much shorter space of time than was at that time contemplated. Furthermore the politically minded elements of the population have had notice of our return and time to prepare plans for our reception. At the same time the population have been given only the most general and non-commital outline of the policy that H.M.G. proposes to follow.

3. It has now been reported that a declaration was signed by the Central Executive of the Communist Party in MALAYA on 25th August giving eight aims of the party. Text is contained in my immediately following telegram.[2] The sentiments expressed in this manifesto are irreproachable.

4. It will be seen that the Communist Party have rather stolen our thunder and that we have lost that element of surprise for our own progressive policy which would politically have been so valuable. Much of the programme could be subscribed

---

[1] Operation Zipper was the code-name for the military reoccupation of Malaya.

[2] Telegram 434, immediately following 433, is reproduced here as an integral part of document 51.

to by H.M.G. with very little amendment. The population is of course not yet ready for a full electoral system but our policy does envisage a larger measure of participation in the government by the people. The reference to "freedom of societies" reflects the anxiety of the Chinese as to whether the societies to which they belong will be declared illegal. A decision has already been taken on this point and it would be to our advantage to make this clear at once.

5. It is not of course suggested that any sort of "reply" should be made to this declaration, but the very reasonableness of it makes it all the more important that the speediest and fullest practicable publicity should be given to our own plans lest uncertainty and distrust should lead the resistance movements (the great majority of whose numbers are Communists) to adopt an attitude towards the return of British Administration from which it might be difficult for them to withdraw and which might unnecessarily complicate our post-war tasks in MALAYA.

6. It is the view of the Supreme Commander, which is shared by General HONE, that an early announcement of H.M.G's policy, even in the most general terms, is necessary if we are not to create for ourselves a very difficult situation upon re-entry into MALAYA.

7. Please pass to Colonial Office.

Telegram 434

Following is text referred to in my immediately preceding telegram. Begins:—
Aims of Communist Party in Malaya.

1. To support the United Nations of RUSSIA, CHINA, BRITAIN and AMERICA and new organisation for world security.

2. To establish a democratic government in MALAYA with the electorate drawn from all races of each State and the anti-Japanese Army.

3. To abolish Fascism and Japanese political structure laws in MALAYA.

4. To enforce freedom of speech, publications and societies, and obtain legal status for anti-Japanese Army.

5. To reform the educational system and improve the social conditions of the people.

6. To improve living conditions, develop industry, commerce and agriculture, provide relief for unemployment and poor, increase wages to standard minimum and establish eight hour working day.

7. To punish traitors, corrupt officials, hoarders and profiteers, and stabilise prices.

8. To ensure good treatment for the members of the anti-Japanese Army and provide compensation for the families of those who died for the Allied cause.

52   CO 273/675/7   6 Sept 1945

[Publicity for Malayan policy]: minute by H T Bourdillon

[Following Cabinet authorization of Malayan policy (see 48 and 50), officials turned to issues consequent upon it, amongst which was the question of how much publicity could be given to MacMichael's mission whose purpose was highly sensitive and whose success in obtaining fresh agreements with the Malay rulers depended upon an element of surprise.]

I have attached as No. 4 a copy of the Secretary of State's recent Cabinet paper about future policy in regard to Malaya and Borneo.[1] The steps proposed in the paper (with a "rider" as regards Sarawak) were approved by the Cabinet on Monday September the 3rd,[2] and my minute on 55104/45 above sets out the various consequential steps which are now necessary.

2.   One of the matters which now requires further consideration, as a question of immediate urgency, is the problem of publicity for the approved policy in so far as it concerns Malaya. In paragraph 7 of No. 4, the Secretary of State foreshadowed further action by himself on this point, and the question has now become particularly urgent in view of developments on the files attached beneath.

3.   The most important of these files for our immediate purposes is 50926/45, which deals with the handling of resistance movements in Malaya. The Secretary of State is already aware that Admiral Mountbatten has long pressed for a measure of publicity for our proposed Malayan policy, on the grounds that his power to utilise resistance forces in Malaya would thereby be greatly increased.[3] The history of his representations is set out at length in my minute of 9/8/45 on 50926/45. With the termination of hostilities in the Far East, the *operational* significance of this matter has of course ceased to exist, but it has taken on a new and very important *political* significance. In this connection, I would draw attention to the telegrams from Mr. Dening at 31 and 32 on 50926/45.[4] These telegrams show the extreme relevance of our future Malayan policy to the aims and aspirations of the most influential[5] body of Chinese in Malaya, and the great advantages which we will secure in dealing with that body if our policy can be made known to them. We cannot of course send an immediate affirmative reply to Mr. Dening's telegrams without considering the whole question from a broader angle, but we can show him that we appreciate the value of what he has told us, at the same time finding out from him in greater detail the exact points in our policy which in his view require stressing. I submit drafts on 50926/45.

4.   So much for that particular aspect of the matter. In considering publicity for our Malayan policy as a whole, we must first see what progress has already been made. The last page of the enclosure to No. 4 on 55140/52/45 shows that we have in fact authorised those conducting political warfare in the Far East to go a long way in the right direction. We know that the Political Warfare authorities made good use of this material, but authority to use it has of course been confined to them. The other

---

[1] See 48.   [2] See 50.
[3] See 23, 26–31 and 36.   [4] See 51.
[5] In a manuscript annotation, Bourdillon inserted square brackets around the word 'influential' and added the words 'politically difficult'.

important file in this connection is 55104/15/45. I would draw attention to the second enclosure to No. 22 on that file, which is a statement of fundamental problems in Malaya together with a general indication (in the last paragraph) of the direction in which a solution must be found.[6] With Cabinet approval, this statement has been issued to a wide range of official recipients at home and overseas, but these recipients have been told to be very guarded in their use of it pending a further move by the Secretary of State.

5. The question now is, how much further can the Secretary of State go at this juncture towards meeting the genuine and pressing demand for publicity, without endangering the policy itself? Clearly, he cannot go the whole way. That is to say, he cannot make a public statement here and now, giving the details of our aims and the steps by which we hope to achieve them. This would be impossible if only because it would forewarn the Sultans of the purposes of Sir Harold MacMichael's mission,[7] which would thus lose that element of surprise which may be essential to its success. On the other hand, it seems equally clear that the situation calls for something a good deal more definite than has been done hitherto. I submit opposite a very rough draft,[8] which might be used as the basis for any form of announcement by the Secretary of State (or under his authority) in the near future. The draft is entirely taken from the two documents which have already been approved—that is, the Political Warfare material and the "Statement of Problems", but I wonder if these two documents do not in fact, between them, give us everything we want.

6. If the Secretary of State would be willing to make or to authorise an early statement on these lines, it remains to be decided whether or not he should first seek Cabinet approval. When the War Cabinet gave provisional approval to our Malayan policy on the 31st May 1944, they imposed a condition that the plan should not be published without further reference to them. On the other hand, our affairs have moved a long way since then, and the draft statement involves little or no material which has not already been approved (for limited purposes). If the question of publicity could be entirely dissociated from all other aspects of our Malayan policy, I should be inclined to suggest that further Cabinet sanction is not necessary; but we had an interesting discussion with Sir Harold MacMichael last night, at which the implications of publicity were considered, and I think these implications alter the picture. Sir Harold, ever since he was first provisionally appointed for this task, has been very anxious to know how far he can go in making it clear to individual Sultans that H.M.G. intends to bring the policy into effect, notwithstanding possible resistance by any or all of them. Sir Harold feels that unless he has firm backing from H.M.G. on this point, the whole purpose of his mission will be undermined. Naturally, it is to be hoped that the necessity for "a show of force" will not arise, and that the Sultans will be persuaded to agree freely to their new status. But this cannot

---

[6] See 36, Annex.

[7] When MacMichael's term as high commissioner of Palestine and Trans-Jordan ended in the autumn of 1944, Gater invited him to prepare for a mission to negotiate fresh treaties with the Malay rulers as soon as possible after the British reoccupation of Malaya. In May and June 1945 MacMichael paid preliminary visits to Kandy, Calcutta and New Delhi. Accompanied by Bourdillon, he flew from London to Colombo on 27 Sept and on 7 Oct boarded HMS *Royalist* for Port Swettenham where he disembarked on 11 Oct, a few hours after the secretary of state announced in Parliament the government's intention to introduce constitutional changes in Malaya.

[8] Not printed.

be taken for granted, and Sir Harold points out that unless he has a clear mandate to make it plain, the last resort, that the policy must in any case prevail, resistance on the part of one Sultan may ruin the whole programme. In that event, the last state will be worse than the first, since nothing would be more damaging for H.M.G. than to embark on the new policy and then withdraw in the face of opposition.

7. The exact measures which H.M.G. might have to adopt in order to enforce their policy in the face of opposition by one or more Sultans would seem to be as follows:

(a) The rejection of individual Sultans in favour of other claimants who would be ready to co-operate. Elaborate steps have already been taken to warn the Military Authorities, on entering Malaya, not to recognise the Sultan or pretending Sultan in any State as Ruler of that State, pending Sir Harold MacMichael's arrival. This makes it possible for recognition of any Sultan to depend upon that Sultan's willingness to co-operate in H.M.G's policy.

(b) Simple annexation of the whole territory.

The latter course is open to numerous and obvious disadvantages. As stated above, it is to be hoped that even the former course will not in fact be necessary, but Sir Harold MacMichael insists that the success of his mission may depend upon the authority to make it clear to any Sultan who may prove recalcitrant, that the policy will go through, whatever the obstacles.

8. The connection of all this with *publication* of the new policy is easy to see. The use of a statement on the lines of the draft which I have prepared (see in particular paragraph 6 of the draft) would in fact commit H.M.G. to the implementation of their policy. Once we have said openly "each of the races forming the population of Malaya must have all the full opportunity of helping to build the country's future, and reaping the benefits of their efforts, provided they in fact regard Malaya as an object of loyalty", we are irrevocably committed to the policy. Such a commitment is of course exactly what Sir Harold MacMichael requires, but it does seem to require a further reference to the Cabinet. The fact that the Secretary of State, in paragraph 5 of No. 4 hereon, has already foreshadowed further recommendation on the matter of publicity, gives us the opportunity which is needed, and I submit opposite, as a second draft,[9] a draft Cabinet paper which the Secretary of State might circulate in the very near future. As shown, the draft statement referred to earlier in this minute, as amended in pencil, would be attached as an annex to the draft Cabinet paper.

9. If the paper is approved by the Cabinet, and if a statement is thereafter issued on the proposed lines, the way would be open for us to give suitable publicity to Sir Harold MacMichael's mission either before or after he leaves this country.[10] It could be stated simply that Sir Harold will be visiting Malaya in order to help in the arrangements necessary to implement the new policy. Sir Harold indicated last night that he would welcome something on these lines before he leaves the U.K.

---

[9] Not printed, but the final version of this paper see 56.

[10] To this point Bourdillon added the following manuscript marginalia: 'We shd. also, of course, have to forewarn the recipients of the "Statement of Problems", and Mr Dening, so that the full advantage of the S. of S's announcement could be secured.'

53 WO 203/5642, no 28/16/45 9 Sept 1945

'Initial relations with Malay sultans on the liberation of Malaya': instructions from Admiral Mountbatten to General Sir M Dempsey[1]

[Although the Japanese retained the Sultanates, they deposed Sultan Alam Shah of Selangor, replacing him with Tengku Musa-Eddin whom the British had barred from the succession in the 1930s. Elsewhere the deaths of rulers during the Japanese occupation had resulted in the accession of Raja Ali in Trengganu (1942), of Tengku Syed Hamzah in Perlis (1943), of Tengku Badlishah in Kedah (1943) and of Tengku Ibrahim in Kelantan (1944). A priority of the British on their return was to investigate the wartime records of the rulers (see 57) and they subsequently deposed Musa-Eddin, Raja Ali and Syed Hamzah.]

The initial attitude of the Military Administration and the British Forces generally to the Malay Sultans is one of paramount importance for reasons which are set out below.

2. In the first place it must be appreciated that the Sultans of the nine Malay States who had been previously recognised by H.M.G. and were in office at the date of the Japanese invasion are not all still officiating. It is believed that some Sultans have died and have been replaced by Japanese nominees who may or may not be persons of repute and worthy of our recognition; while other loyal Sultans may have been deposed by the Japanese and replaced by puppets of pro-Japanese sympathies and/or ill-repute.

3. It is, therefore, of vital importance that no course of action should be adopted by British Commanders in Malaya which might be construed as a formal recognition of any "Sultan" until the position has been carefully examined and H.M.G.'s directions have been received. Further, it should be noted that, for the general advancement of the peoples of Malaya as a whole, H.M.G. has in mind that certain constitutional changes may be desirable in the future government of the Malay Peninsula when the control of the territory reverts to the Colonial Office. These changes may considerably affect the post-war political authority of the Sultans and hence any officer who, by speech or conduct, leads any Sultan to believe that his status as ruler has received recognition from the Supreme Allied Commander and his Commanders, may prejudice the plans of H.M.G.

4. Orders should therefore be issued to all concerned that when contacts with the Sultans (or soi-disant Sultans) in liberated areas are made, the above considerations will be borne in mind, and Commanders concerned should as far as possible be guided by the advice of the C.A. staff. Steps must be taken to ensure that a senior C.A. officer who is qualified to give such advice and who has been adequately instructed is available whenever the necessity arises.

5. When contacts between the military authorities and Sultans are unavoidable, it should be laid down that they must be made only by a senior officer commanding the troops in the area, accompanied by a senior Civil Affairs Officer. Conversations should be strictly formal, courteous but non-committal; on no account should gifts be exchanged. Social interchanges will be prohibited and hospitality proferred by a

---

[1] Lt-General Sir Miles Dempsey succeeded Slim as commander of the 14th Army for the reoccupation of Singapore and Malaya and, in early 1946, as commander in chief ALFSEA; was commander in chief Middle East, 1946–1947.

Sultan will be politely refused on account of pressure of military activities. If any request or petition is presented to a Military Commander by a Sultan or one of his high officials it should merely be acknowledged and passed without delay through the normal command channels to the formation C.A. staff for action.

6. Special arrangements must be made for the D.C.C.A.O. or, failing him, a Senior Civil Affairs Officer selected for the purpose in each case, to make early formal approach to any "Sultan" who is located in territory occupied by our troops. Formations will be directed to issue clear instructions to all troops to report by signal and D.R., the location of any "Sultan" with the minimum of delay.

7. In carrying on discussions with "Sultans", once first contact has been made, the C.A. staff will handle the matter exclusively unless for special reasons it is considered desirable to act in conjunction with G.S.1(b).

8. The method of handling a "Sultan" will depend on the personality involved; special instructions may be issued in individual cases by the DCA(M) but for general guidance, the Sultans fall into three categories as follows:—

(i) Pre-invasion Sultans still in office.

(ii) Puppet Sultans known to be disloyal or otherwise unsuitable whom the Japanese have placed in office by deposing the legitimate Sultan.

(iii) Sultans who have assumed or been appointed to office during the Japanese regime on account of the death, resignation or ill-health etc. of the legitimate Sultan.

The method of dealing with these three categories is described in Appendices A, B and C.[2]

9. Prompt reports of initial contacts with Sultans will be telegraphed to HQ ALFSEA, with copies to HQ SACSEA, to be followed by a full written record transmitted in duplicate without delay.

10. In view of the intention of H.M.G. to send a plenipotentiary at an early date to interview each Malay Sultan (or the de facto Malay ruler or "rightful" successor in any State where the pre-invasion Sultan is no longer available) and arrange fresh agreements to govern their relations with H.M.G. the fullest information regarding certain matters must be obtained without delay by the C.A. Branch. Appendix D[3] contains a questionnaire which should be answered as soon as reliable information is available. The replies should be transmitted in duplicate to HQ ALFSEA and should be kept up-to-date by subsequent reports as more information is obtained. It cannot be overstressed that the reliability of these reports is fundamentally important to the Secretary of State for the Colonies in its bearing on H.M.G.'s policy.

11. It may be added that these instructions cover only the initial period of contact, and it is appreciated that considerable modifications may be necessary in the light of experience.

12. These instructions are issued in substitution of the instructions contained in memorandum No. 6/CA dated 21 July 1945 which is hereby cancelled.

---

[2] & [3] Not printed.

54   WO 203/5642, no 33/16/45   14 Sept 1945
[Japanese surrender ceremony in Singapore]: inward telegram no 484
from M E Dening to FO

[On 15 Aug, when Japan agreed to unconditional surrender, SEAC's responsibilities were
extended to include the Netherlands East Indies and Indo-China as far north as the 16th
degree parallel. Reoccupation was delayed, however, partly through want of resources and
partly because General MacArthur forbade any reoccupation until he had taken the formal
Japanese surrender in Tokyo Bay on 2 Sept, see 81. The surrender ceremony in Singapore
took place ten days later but SACSEA headquarters did not move from Kandy to
Singapore until Nov.]

I returned last night from Singapore where the surrender ceremony on Sept. 12th
left nothing to be desired. It gave intense satisfaction to the prisoners of war and
internees who witnessed it and will, I hope, have done much to obliterate the bad
odour of our expulsion in 1942. There was no doubt about the welcome of the
populace and the Chinese of Singapore were particularly vociferous.

2.   Though the auguries are good, it seemed to me that there is a great deal to be
done to get Singapore going and I hope that generous financial support will be
forthcoming where it is needed. I refer in particular to the restoration of earning
capacity which is likely to necessitate Government assistance and without which the
prosperity of Singapore is unlikely to be restored. I mention this problem because
there are already indications that it is arising elsewhere (e.g. Siam) and applies in
particular to British subjects in the Far East whose entire interests and earnings
were out here and who have no resources in the United Kingdom or elsewhere in the
Empire.

3.   The Sultan of Johore was allowed to attend the surrender ceremony in a
private capacity. I gather that he is for the present subdued and docile and very
anti-Japanese. I have already referred to the friendliness of the Chinese community
of Singapore. It seems to me that we should be wise to take very early advantage of
these favourable conditions. Otherwise we may find that disillusionment and distrust
of our intentions may take the place of the friendly sentiments which our return has
brought to the surface.

4.   The spirit of the prisoners of war and internees whom I met is beyond praise
and the condition of many was better than one would have expected. But there are all
too many ugly stories of atrocities and Japanese inhumanity, and I think that there
will be a strong demand to know what action is being taken to bring those
responsible to justice.

55   CO 825/42/2   14 Sept 1945
[Implementation of policy]: minute by H T Bourdillon of a CO
departmental discussion about the Malayan Union   [Extract]

[Bourdillon's minute records a discussion of Far Eastern policy on 14 Sept between Mr
Hall, Mr Creech Jones, Gater, Gent, Duncan and other officials. The greater part of the
meeting was devoted to the Malayan Union and revealed the urgency of finalizing the
explanatory memorandum for MacMichael to give the Sultans and the new treaties and of

securing the affirmation of either Cabinet or the prime minister that the government would stand by the policy 'in spite of possible obstacles'.]

... 5. The greater part of the discussion was devoted to the proposal for the Malayan Union Constitution (see paragraph f of my minute of 5/9/45, on file No. 50823/6/45 beneath.[1] The Secretary of State noted that it was proposed to allow the Sultans, with the help of the Advisory Malay Councils, to legislate on matters of Mohammedan religion and Malay custom. He wondered whether it would not be possible to define the field of Malay custom. He felt that the Sultans themselves, who in any case would be facing a great reduction in their power, would be likely to want such a definition as one of their few remaining safeguards. The extreme difficulty of defining "Malay custom" was explained. It was pointed out that no difficulty had arisen owing to the lack of definition in the past, and that the necessity of obtaining the Governor's assent to legislation on these subjects in the future would avoid confusion and conflicts. It was agreed that in the circumstances no further definition was possible. The Secretary of State, however, in pursuing his point about the proposed diminution in the status of the Sultans, requested that a comparative statement should be prepared, showing the position of the Sultans as it was before the Japanese invasion, and as it will be under the new Constitution. I attach the draft of such a Statement on 50823/6/45.[2]

6. The Secretary of State then had to leave the meeting, and Mr. Creech Jones took the chair. He expressed anxiety lest the proposed Legislative Council of the Malayan Union should become a mere "talking shop", divested of all sense of real responsibility. He has studied this question in relation to other colonies, and he feared that the creation of Legislative Councils in the past, with all real power and authority confined to its official members, had led to a conflict between officials and unofficials and a growth of *irresponsibility* on the part of the latter. In particular, he wanted to know whether the Governor would be encouraged to appoint members of Legislative Council to the unofficial seats on his Executive Council. Sir George Gater supported this point, but remarked that the latest tendency in the Colonial Empire (e.g. in Jamaica) has been in the right direction. It was agreed that there was nothing to prevent the Governor from selecting his unofficial members of Executive Council from the ranks of the Legislative Council, and that this practice should be encouraged.

7. Mr. Creech Jones was also anxious, in view of probable criticism in Parliament, in this country in general and in the United States, that we should be able to promise a future development towards a democratic system of election. It was agreed that such a development could with advantage be foreshadowed, but that in the very early stages an electoral system on full democratic lines would be premature.

8. Mr. Creech Jones then referred to the probable criticisms, on traditional and sentimental lines, of the proposed dismemberment of the Straits Settlements, and to the inevitable feeling amongst people intimately concerned with the life of the colony, that a drastic change had been made without consulting them. This led to a discussion of the inherent advantages and disadvantages in the policy of splitting the Straits Settlements and attaching Penang and Malacca to the Malayan Union.

---

[1] & [2] Not printed.

Colonel O'Connor[3] expressed the conviction that this policy would cause considerable local bitterness. Sir George Gater wondered whether the present Cabinet realised that, in approving our Malayan policy as a whole, they had approved this particular proposal with all its implications.[4] Mr. Gent pointed out that the present Prime Minister had been Chairman of the Ministerial Committee under the War Cabinet which had considered the whole matter in great detail, and had concluded in favour of the present policy. It was further pointed out that Sir Harold MacMichael, who was expected to leave the United Kingdom by air for the East in *10 days from now* (he was scheduled to leave London on Tuesday the 25th of September),[5] would have to take with him a Memorandum for the benefit of the Malay Rulers, in which the essential points of our policy, including the splitting up of the Straits Settlements, would be set out. This made it impossible to defer the question of the future of the Straits Settlements, or to treat it as less urgent than the rest of the policy. Sir H. Duncan also observed that a Bill to repeal the existing Straits Settlements Act of 1866 would have to be introduced into Parliament in the very near future. Mr. Creech Jones felt that if this part of our policy had been recommended by a Ministerial Committee, provisionally approved by the War Cabinet and now finally approved by the present Cabinet, there was no question but that it must go through. He was still very anxious, however, about the "Public Relations" aspect of the matter. What steps would be taken to explain our policy as regards the Straits Settlements, to disarm criticism and to enlist co-operation?

9. At this point, Sir George Gater mentioned the matter of publicity for our Malayan policy as a whole. He was at present considering a draft Cabinet Paper submitted by the Eastern Department, in which it was proposed that publicity should be in two phases. The first phase would consist of an almost immediate statement by the Secretary of State, outlining our future policy in general terms. The second phase would consist of a further statement by the Secretary of State, timed to coincide with the opening of Sir Harold MacMichael's work in Malaya, which would go into greater detail on all points and would disclose the intention to split up the Straits Settlements. He himself was not happy about the proposal to split publicity into two phases. He was afraid the first phase, partial as it was, would merely arouse questions and criticisms which would not be answered. He would be much in favour of a *single* statement by the Secretary of State, to be made in Parliament immediately after it re-assembled on October the 10th, which would go the whole way.[6] Mr. Gent said that if nothing was published immediately, it would be very hard to hold the position for the next month. The Chinese communists in Malaya had already declared their attitude. It coincided to a remarkable extent with our own policy, but unless there was a ready response, that attitude would harden. He felt that opportunities would be missed and difficulties created unless there was *some* immediate measure of publicity.

10. It was agreed that in any case publication of the details of our policy must not be allowed to wait until Sir Harold MacMichael had proceeded some way with his negotiations. He would be bound to reveal our intentions to the Sultans, and this

---

[3] Kenneth K O'Connor, member of the MPU; attorney general, Malaya 1946 and Kenya 1948; chief justice, Jamaica 1951 and Kenya 1954; president, Court of Appeal for East Africa, 1957–1962.

[4] See 50.   [5] In fact he left on 27 Sept.

[6] See written answer, *H of C Debs*, vol 414, cols 255–256, 10 Oct 1945.

would be bound to result in leakage. It would be most unfortunate if that leakage occurred before an authoratitive [sic] statement had been made by the Secretary of State himself.

11. In this connection, it was pointed out that the draft Cabinet paper to which Sir George Gater had referred did not merely contain the proposal for publicity. It also contained the proposal that the Cabinet should strengthen Sir Harold Mac-Michael's hand by now affirming their intention to carry through their policy for the future of Malaya, in spite of recalcitrance on the part of any or all of the Sultans. It was essential that Sir Harold should have this assurance "in his pocket" before he left the U.K.

12. Mr. Gent mentioned that apart from the immediate urgency of getting things ready before Sir Harold MacMichael started his task, we should be under increasing pressure from the Military Authorities, who would very naturally be anxious to terminate the Military period in Malaya at the earliest opportunity.

13. It was finally agreed that Sir Harold MacMichael's departure constituted the immediate "date" against which all our plans must be considered. I was instructed to draft a telegram to the Supreme Allied Commander, asking for a very early reply to the telegram already sent, in which we had asked him if the ground in Malaya would be ready if Sir Harold MacMichael left the U.K., as intended, on the 26th of September. Before I had time to draft, I was notified by the War Office of a telegram from the Supreme Allied Commander, saying that the ground would indeed be ready by that date, and urging that Sir Harold should leave without avoidable delay. . . .

56   CAB 129/2, CP(45)199   4 Oct 1945
'Policy in regard to Malaya': Cabinet memorandum by Mr Hall.
Annexes: I 'Memorandum on future constitution for Malaya', II 'Basis for publicity (phase 1)'

[Although the Cabinet gave their final approval to the new Malayan policy on 3 Sept (see 50), the approval did not in itself amount to a resolve on the part of government to proceed with the policy whatever obstacles might be encountered. In order to obtain such an affirmation, the secretary of state drafted a further Cabinet paper. In the event it was agreed that it would be simpler and quicker for Hall to settle the matter directly with Attlee and in advance of the Cabinet meeting. Accordingly the secretary of state saw the prime minister at 5.45 pm on 20 Sept, having first sent him a copy of the paper for his perusal. Attlee approved the lines of action on two conditions: firstly, that any questions of security arising from the proposals be cleared with the chiefs of staff, and, secondly, that Annex II be strengthened on the economic side. When the Malayan Union ran into vigorous Malay opposition after the publication of the White Paper on 22 Jan 1946, CO officials for a time comforted themselves with the thought of the categorical affirmations given the previous Sept (see CO 273/675/7 nos 5 and 6, and CO 537/1540, minute by H T Bourdillon, 4 Mar 1946).]

At their meeting on the 3rd September, 1945,[1] the Cabinet approved the policy in regard to Malaya outlined in C.P.(45)133.[2] In connection with the question of the extent, method and timing of publicity for this policy, and in consultation and

---

[1] See 50.   [2] See 48.

agreement with the Lord Privy Seal, as Chairman of the Colonial Affairs Committee, I represented to the Prime Minister the following views and proposals as being matters for very urgent decision in the current situation in Malaya.

2.   Publicity in any detail about our Malayan policy commits us to the fulfilment of that policy. This means that we cannot allow ourselves to be deterred by an obstinate attitude on the part of any or all of the Malay Rulers with whom Sir Harold MacMichael will have to deal in his forthcoming mission. I regard it, however, as very essential, quite apart from the matter of publicity, that His Majesty's Government should now affirm their intention to carry through, in spite of obstruction on the part of any particular Malay Ruler, the policy which they have approved. All our plans for the Malay States depend upon the success of Sir Harold MacMichael's efforts to secure jurisdiction in each and all of the States. It is essential that his hand should be strengthened by the firm assurance that he can, if necessary, make it clear to any recalcitrant Sultan that we intend to carry our policy through. I attach as an Annex to this paper an explanatory memorandum, which I propose that Sir Harold should hand to each Sultan on opening discussions. It will be seen that this Memorandum leaves no doubt of His Majesty's firm intention to carry their plans into effect. This, then, is the first point on which definite assurance needs to be given.

3.   I then envisage three phases of publicity. The first phase will be a statement in general terms, designed to create public interest in the direction of that unity and common citizenship in Malaya which our policy will entail. I shall require some discretion as to timing, but I would propose to inaugurate this phase by a public reference, during the next fortnight, to these two points of unity and common citizenship. I attach, as Annex II to this paper, a brief statement which I would use as a basis.

4.   The second phase must be expected to follow after possibly only a short interval. This phase will involve a more explicit statement of our intention to form a Malayan Union and of certain contingent proposals, such as the securing of jurisdiction from the Malay Rulers and the splitting up of the present colony of the Straits Settlements. It will also involve an explicit statement about the separate treatment of Singapore.

5.   It will be best if this second phase of publicity can synchronise with Sir Harold MacMichael's work. Information as to our detailed intentions will inevitably be disclosed in Malaya as soon as he opens discussions with any Sultan, since it is necessary for the success of these discussions that he should give each Sultan an outline of the future Malaya and of their own place in it. It would be a mistake from the point of view of this country and of the Straits Settlements to let our policy leak out from the first of the Malay Rulers with whom Sir Harold MacMichael establishes contact; and therefore an authoritative *exposé* of the second phase should be made by myself in London at or about the time when Sir Harold starts his work in Malaya. He is expected to do so during the first half of this month, and I therefore propose to make a statement in the House of Commons after it reassembles, in which I shall (a) outline the specific proposals referred to in paragraph 4 above, and (b) promise a full disclosure in the form of a White Paper as soon as circumstances permit.

6.   This White Paper would constitute the third phase. It could not, of course, be laid until preliminary steps, such as the negotiation of the new Agreements with the Sultans, had been completed.

7.   In proposing the early inception of a programme of publicity, I am influenced

by very recent information as to the present political state of affairs in Malaya. This information indicates that politically the most difficult body of Chinese in the Peninsula (the main group of the Resistance Movement and largely Chinese "Communists") have set before themselves a goal which corresponds in very many respects with our own policy. It is not too much to say that the whole of our relations with the Chinese population of Malaya may be fundamentally affected by a timely statement of our intentions.

8. To sum up, I recommended:—

(a) that we should affirm His Majesty's Government's intention to carry through the policy which they have approved, in spite of possible obstacles in the form of, for instance, recalcitrance by any or all of the Sultans.

(b) that there should be a phased programme of publicity commencing with a public statement by myself in general terms, continuing with a more detailed statement by myself in the House as soon as it reassembles on the 10th October, and concluding with a White Paper as soon as circumstances permit.

The Prime Minister approved my proposals subject to the Chiefs of Staff having no objection from the security angle. I have ascertained that they have no objection, and I am circulating this memorandum to my colleagues to keep them informed of the lines on which I am now proceeding in these Malayan affairs.

Annex I to 56

The Cabinet has finally confirmed the policy of creating a Malayan Union (as opposed to an extended Federation of Malay States) which will comprise all the Malay States in the Peninsula, together with the Settlements of Penang and Malacca. The Constitution of the Union will provide for a central authority (both Executive and Legislative) from which all other authorities in the Peninsula should derive their powers. (This postulate is inherent in the conception of a Union as opposed to that of a Federation.)

2. Subject to this basic conception the nine Malay States and the Settlements of Penang and Malacca will be retained as geographical units with their present boundaries to deal with such local affairs as may be devolved upon them by the central authority.

3. One of the most important matters to settle is the position of the Malay Rulers under the new Constitution. The idea that there should be an Upper Chamber of Sultans has been examined, but it is not felt that this would be appropriate. The possibility has been rejected partly because of the difficulty of devising satisfactory relations between the Lower and Upper Chambers, partly because the Sultans do not possess the necessary qualifications to perform the functions of a Second Chamber in any real and effective manner, partly because a Second Chamber of Malay Sultans would be an inappropriate organ in the Government of a country of which important areas will be parts of the present British Colony of the Straits Settlements, and partly because it would be out of keeping with the proposal that Malayan Union citizenship should comprise not only Malays but people of every race who have made Malaya their homeland.

It is proposed, instead, that the Sultans collectively should form an Advisory

Council to the Governor. The subjects with which this Council would be concerned would be principally questions of Mohammedan religion (in relation to which the special position of the Sultans has always been recognised), but other subjects would also be open for discussion in the Council either at the instance of the Governor or at the instance of any of the Sultans with the Governor's consent. The functions of the Council are further described in paragraph 8 beneath. It would meet regularly under the presidency of the Governor and would be regarded as a permanent body. Its meetings would be attended by all the ceremony necessary to maintain the personal dignity of the Sultans. It would not, however, impair the right of direct access between individual Sultans and the Governor. It is felt that the new position of the Sultans should be defined in the Constitution itself. When the time comes to negotiate the new Treaties this will be necessary to satisfy the Sultans, who will not be content to be told vaguely that "an appropriate position" will be allotted to them by the new Central Legislature.

4. Apart from the Governor, the three principal officers of Government will be the Chief Secretary, the Attorney-General and the Financial Secretary. The position of the British Residents or Advisers in each of the States should be modified. Before the war, the status of these officers was higher than that of any other officials save the High Commissioner, but with the establishment of the Union Government their importance will diminish and they should be made subordinate to the Chief Secretary of the Union Government. It is proposed that these officers, as well as the officers at the head of the two Settlements, should be uniformly styled "Resident Commissioners."

5. It is proposed that Executive and Legislative Councils for the Malayan Union should be created with the following constitution:—

The *Executive Council* should have 5 official and 5 unofficial members, in addition to the Governor. Of the official members the Chief Secretary, the Attorney-General and the Financial Secretary should be *ex-officio*, while the other 2 would be nominated by the Governor. The unofficial members would also be nominated by the Governor. A racial basis should not be prescribed for such nominations, but in the first instance it would be desirable that there should be one European, one Malay, one Chinese and one Indian unoffical member, the Governor being left to nominate the most suitable unofficial to fill the remaining vacancy regardless of race. Save with the consent of the Governor, unofficial membership of the Executive Council would be confined to Malayan Union Citizens.

The *Legislative Council* should have, besides the Governor, 21 official and 21 unofficial members. Fourteen of the latter should represent areas on a population basis, and the remainder should represent important interests throughout the Union; there has hitherto been no experience of any system of elections in Malaya, and for an initial phase at any rate it would be desirable that the unofficial members should be nominated by the Governor, who would be required to select suitable persons on the above representative basis as far as possible. Five of the official members would be the official members of the Executive Council and the remainder would be nominated by the Governor.

6. When Military Administration ceases and the new Civil Government is established in the Malay Peninsula, it is likely to be impracticable, even if it were desirable, to complete the formal instruments necessary to set up a Legislative Council immediately. To cover the interregnum between the end of the Military

Administration and the setting up of a Legislative Council, the new Constitution should specifically provide for the Governor alone to be responsible for legislation, and for the establishment of an Advisory Council to assist him in this task. The Governor would normally consult this Advisory Council before enacting Legislation, but would not be bound to accept the Council's advice. The instrument should not specify the precise number of official and unofficial members, but the Governor should be instructed to guide himself as far as possible, when making appointments by the intended composition of the Legislative Council as set out in paragraph 5 above.

7.   The next question to be considered is the future of the State and Settlement Councils. In the past, the Sultans were Presidents of the State Councils, but the Councils were largely composed of Malays, and made scant provision for any representation of non-Malay interests. In the new constitutional arrangements it would be inappropriate that a Malay Sultan should preside, and it will be desirable that the President of the State or Settlement Council of the future should be the Resident Commissioner. Exact membership cannot be defined in advance, but members should be appointed by the Governor after consulting the Resident Commissioner. As regards the nomination of unofficial Representatives, all practicable regard should be paid to the racial proportions of the settled population of each State and Settlement, but broader public interests should also govern selections.

The State and Settlement Councils should be empowered to legislate (a) on all matters which, in the opinion of the Governor in Council, are of a merely local or private nature in the State or Settlement, and (b) on all subjects in respect of which power is delegated to them by law by the Legislative Council of the Malayan Union.

8.   In each State side by side with the State Councils there should be established Advisory Malay Councils to the Sultans, which should be presided over by the Sultan and whose members, subject to the Governor's approval, should be appointed by the Sultan.

The main functions of these Advisory Malay Councils would be in relation to matters affecting Mohammedan religion, but they would also advise the Sultan on other matters at the request of the Resident Commissioner and with the approval of the Governor. On matters of Mohammedan religion (with the exception of anything connected with the collection of taxes or tithes, which must be left strictly within the control of the Central Legislature or the State Councils), it is proposed that the Sultans should have powers of legislating in their individual States. In doing so, they would use their Advisory Malay Councils, which for these purposes would be virtually legislative bodies. Legislation resulting from this system would not, however, automatically and immediately become law, but would require the Governor's assent. The Governor would in no case grant or refuse his assent without consulting his own Advisory Council of Malay Sultans, though he would not be bound to accept their advice. It is felt that this proposal to leave legislative power on matters of Mohammedan religion in the hands of the Sultans individually and collectively (subject to the necessary checks as indicated above) should go a long way towards reconciling the Sultans to their new position, in that it would maintain their special status amongst their own Malay people in a field in which it has hitherto been always recognised. It is also felt that the proposal to refer legislation within this field to the Governor's Advisory Council of Sultans would lend reality to the deliberations of that body, which might otherwise be little more than a façade.

9. It is proposed that the organisation of the Courts should be as follows: It is suggested that there should be a separate High Court of the Malayan Union with a Chief Justice at its head. In addition to the Chief Justice, there should be judges of the High Court stationed at various suitable centres throughout the Peninsula. In acordance with previous practice and the dictates of economy the Chief Justice and the Puisne Judges of the Supreme Court in Singapore should be declared *ex-officio* judges in the High Court of the Malayan Union and *vice versa*. In practice the Court of Appeal, whether sitting in the Union or in Singapore, would invariably be composed of the two Chief Justices and one Puisne Judge. There seems to be no reason for creating a separate Court of Appeal, which would involve the appointment of Appeal Judges. The new constitution should provide for Appeals to the Privy Council from the Court of Appeal of the Malayan Union.

10. In order that the future Malayan Union may become a reality, it is felt that, subject to the exceptions noted below, all State and Settlement properties should be transferred to the Union Government, which should assume full liability for State and Settlement debts. The Union would take over all revenues from the States and the Settlements, their cash, bank balances, securites, &c., all State land, mines and minerals and all railways, ports and harbours (with the exception of the port and harbour properties vested in the Penang Harbour Board). The exception to this wholesale transfer of property relates to the residences and estates of the Sultans themselves and any buildings and land which are used for purposes of Mohammedan religion, as well as property pertaining to the endowment of Mohammedan religious institutions. It is felt that the above properties should be excluded from transfer to Union ownership, on the grounds that they are closely bound up with the Sultans' personal prestige, and with the position (which it is proposed to preserve) of the individual Sultans as leaders of their Malay subjects in their States in matters of Mohammedan religion.

In making provision for the exemption of these properties from transfer to Union ownership, it is important to bear in mind that no commitment should be given to the Sultans which would prevent the Defence authorities from acquiring the necessary rights in property which they might require at any time for strategic purposes. Provided such commitments are not given, it is felt that this aspect of the matter need not be specifically mentioned in the new Constitution. The mere exemption from transfer to Union ownership does not place the property in question irrevocably beyond the control of the Service authorities. The new treaties with the individual Sultans will themselves give His Majesty the power to legislate in each State. It is important, in fact, to distinguish in this connection between exemption from transfer to Union ownership and exemption from His Majesty's jurisdiction. The latter is, of course, not proposed.

11. In order further to safeguard the personal position of the Sultans, it is felt that special provision should be made as regards their emoluments. These cannot actually be exempted from transfer to Union control (i.e., left to be provided out of State funds), since under the new Constitution the States will have only those revenues which they may receive or collect by the decision of the central Legislature of the Union. But it should nevertheless be ensured that the Sultans' personal allowances are continued from year to year on a scale appropriate to their dignity and position.

12. Finally, it is proposed that there should be express provision in the Constitution empowering the Courts to interpret it, and laying down that in case of

conflict. Ordinances of the Malayan Union must prevail over enactments of State and Settlement Councils.

Annex II to 56

The Japanese have now been evicted from Malaya, and the time has come to lay down the broad lines which our future policy must follow, if we are to fulfil our duty towards Malaya and its people. From now on we must think of Malaya as one country with one destiny, that of eventual self-government within the British Common-wealth, a destiny to which all the inhabitants of Malaya can contribute. The conditions under which this goal can be reached must be fostered in Malaya. The essential rights of the Malays must be safeguarded, but henceforth each of the races forming the population of Malaya must have the full opportunity of helping to build the country's future, of developing and enjoying on a basis of common effort and common opportunity the great material wealth of the Peninsula, and of reaping the benefit of their efforts, provided they in fact regard Malaya as an object of loyalty. They must be citizens of Malaya, with all the rights and obligations which that term implies. No one must rely upon past privilege, or regard Malaya simply as a source of material wealth. While it is to the advantage of all the world, and not only Malaya, that the production of her mineral and agricultural resources should be restored and developed by industry and research, it is right that the Malayan people should be assured of their share in the rewards of their industry and should be able to feel the country's wealth reflected in their own fuller standard of life.

57   CAB 101/69, CAB/HIST/B/4/7   7 Oct 1945
[Interviews with the Malay rulers]: report by Brigadier H C Willan

[Willan, DCCAO Malaya, toured the Malay states from 8 to 29 Sept. He interviewed each Malay ruler in order to assess their roles during the Japanese occupation, their allegiance to the British and the credentials of those who had ascended their thrones during the Japanese occupation. His report prepared the ground for MacMichael's mission to conclude new treaties.]

Interview with the Sultan of Johore
Present: H.H. The Sultan of Johore; Brigadier H.C. Willan, D.C.C.A.O., Malay Peninsula; Colonel M.C. Hay, S.C.A.O., Johore.

Date: 8th September, 1945.

1. In accordance with the instructions contained in SACSEA Secret No. 6/CA of the 21st July, 1945, I proceeded to Johore Bharu on the 8th September, 1945, for the purpose of interviewing the Sultan. Col. Hay accompanied me.

2. After informing Major-General Mansergh, commanding the 5th Indian Division,[1] of my intentions, and having obtained his approval and also that of the

---

[1] The 5th Indian Division under Major-General E C Mansergh was shortly to be despatched to Java arriving off Surabaya on 1 Nov 1945, a few days after Brigadier A W S Mallaby had been shot in confrontation with Indonesian forces. After fierce fighting with the nationalists, the British were in control of Surabaya by the end of the month.

C.C.A.O., I left Singapore at 1630 hours. I called on Brigadier Grimshaw, 161 Indian Infantry Brigade, on the way. He is in charge of the Johore Bharu Area.

3.   I arrived at Johore Bharu at 1725 hours. A Malay in the town informed me that the Sultan was in residence at Pasir Plangi Palace. (Note: The Sultan has three palaces in Johore Bharu—the Istana Besar in the town; Bukit Serene Palace about four miles out just off the main road North; Pasir Plangi Palace about three miles to the east of the town. The last named is the smallest).

Col. Hay directed me to what he thought was Pasir Plangi Palace. On arrival there we found the building empty with four Japanese soldiers and a Malay in the porch. The Malay told me that the Sultan was residing at Bukit Serene Palace.

I then proceeded to Bukit Serene Palace where I met Tungku Ahmed, the third son of the Sultan. Tungku Ahmed told me that the Sultan was at Pesir [sic] Plangi. Tungku Ahmed telephoned the Sultan and informed him that two British Officers wished to see him. He then guided me to Pasir Plangi Palace which was about a mile further than the first palace visited. On arrival the Sultan was on the steps to receive us.

4.   The Sultan showed Col. Hay and myself into the lounge where we were introduced to his Rumanian wife.[2] After I had greeted the Sultan in the name of the Supreme Allied Commander the conversation became general. Within a few minutes a servant appeared with whiskies and sodas already poured out, and placed them beside Col. Hay and myself. I at once asked the Sultan if Col. Hay and myself could have a private audience with him. He led us into another room and thus, regretfully, we were able to leave our whiskies and sodas behind untouched without giving any offence.

5.   First I encouraged the Sultan to talk about his treatment under the Japanese.

He was genuinely pleased to see us and not once throughout the interview even hinted that the British had let him down by losing Johore. He needed no prompting to talk, in fact we only had to sit and listen, prompting an odd enquiry now and then.

The following are the main matters he talked upon.

(I took no notes at the interview in order to keep it on a friendly and cordial level. This memorandum is compiled from notes made by me after the interview).

(A) He expressed his hatred of the Japanese. His description of them in Malay was "They are neither human beings nor animals—God knows what they are".

(B) The Japanese had taken away most of his European clothes and used the Istana Besar as a boarding house. They had made no attempt to look after its furniture and fittings and the inside was filthy.

(C) The Japanese had sealed up two of his wireless sets at Pasir Plangi but he had hidden one set and so was able to listen in to the B.B.C. and other Allied broadcasts.

(D) The Japanese had at first paid him no allowance. Later they paid him 8,000 Japanese dollars per month which they ultimately increased to 20,000 Japanese dollars, *"which is the same as the British Government paid me"*. The words in the italics were actually used by him and are worthy of special note because his monthly allowance was paid from Johore State funds. Pre-war he would never have

---

[2] Having been divorced from Mrs Helen Wilson in 1938, Ibrahim married Marcella Mendl while in London in 1940. She was styled Lady Marcella Ibrahim, Sultanah of Johore. Amongst Ibrahim's decorations was 1st Class Order of the Crown of Roumania.

said that his allowance was paid by the British Government.

(E) The Johore Civil Service Club had been used by the Japanese as their Gestapo H.Q. and a large number of people, mostly Chinese, had been beheaded there. Some of them were buried in the Club grounds.

(F) Both he and his wife had had considerable difficulty in obtaining food and when they were able to obtain it the prices had been exorbitant. E.G. fish 400 Japanese dollars per kati (one and one third pounds); chickens 400–500 Japanese dollars each; eggs 20 Japanese dollars each.

(G) A Japanese General had visited him and demand all his jewellery. The Sultan asked him why he required it. The General replied he wanted it for its platinum contents to use in Japanese aeroplanes. The Sultan replied that all his jewellery was deposited in safe custody in London and that as far as he knew the only place available to the Japanese for platinum was Russia.

(H) The Sultan went on to say that whatever speeches he had made during the Japanese occupation had been done on their orders. They always composed his speeches and he had merely been used as a mouthpiece as ordered by them. They were not his own words or sentiments and no speech was delivered voluntarily by him.

(I) All the Sultans had been forced by the Japanese to contribute 10,000 Japanese dollars to the Japanese cause and they had done so on orders, not voluntarily.

(J) Raja Musa-Addin, who had been installed as Sultan of Selangor by the Japanese, should be watched. He was living in the palace at Klang and the rightful Sultan was also living at Klang. The Japanese had placed a sword into the hand of Musa-Addin and ordered him to kill his brother, Alam-Shah—the rightful Sultan. The only good thing the Sultan of Johore knew about Musa-Addin was that he refused to do so.

6. I explained to the Sultan the terms and implications of Proclamation No. 1—i.e. The British Military Administration Proclamation. That is:—

(a) The Supreme Allied Commander, is Admiral Lord Louis Mountbatten. The Sultan said he was very pleased to hear this because he knew Lord Louis personally.

(b) That property, private rights, religious liberty and Malay customs would be strictly respected.

(c) That all Japanese laws would be rescinded at once.

I then explained that only a British Military Administration could bring help to the population because it was impossible to set up the Civil Government immediately. I added, however, that it was the policy of H.M.G. to revert to the Civil Government and to Colonial Office control as soon as possible.

I then told the Sultan that it would not be possible for himself and his State Council to function during the period of a British Military Administration.

The Sultan said he fully agreed to a British Military Administration. In fact, he welcomed it.

7. The next day, 9th September, 1945 he wrote a letter to Col. Hay, S.C.A.O., Johore, stating that he was prepared to serve *under* the British Military Administration. The [emphasis] is mine. I have done so because it is remarkable in my view, for the Sultan to say he will serve under anybody.

8.   The Sultan then said that he would like to go into Singapore occasionally and especially to see the parade of troops marking the formal Japanese surrender. He requested that he might be given a Union Jack to fly on his car. I informed him that I would bring his request to the notice of higher authorities, but meanwhile he should stay in Johore Bharu as we were responsible for his safety.

The Sultan then said that both he and his wife wished to proceed to England as soon as possible. I suggested that after such a long spell in Malaya under difficult conditions it might be inadvisable to go to England during the winter months. The Sultan replied that he was certain he could stand the English climate in winter. I said the transport position was serious and that we should have our hands full for a long time sending some internees and prisoners of war.

9.   I finally informed the Sultan that it would be one of the duties of the British Military Administration to enquire into the conduct of Government Servants and State notables during the Japanese occupation. Their continued employment would depend on whether they had collaborated with the Japanese. I explained that a policy of clemency would be adopted, but, at the same time, ringleaders of collaborationists would be brought to justice and punished.

The Sultan showed no signs of nervousness when I touched on this subject. He said that the only person he knew who had collaborated with the Japanese was Ungku Aziz, the Prime Minister of Johore, and that he had been 80% pro-Japanese.

10.   In concluding the interview I gathered the impression that if I had not said that I had urgent business in Singapore the Sultan would have liked to continue for a longer period.

11.   To sum up both Col. Hay and myself came away with the impression that the Sultan was delighted that the British had come back. That he dislikes the Japanese intensely. He appeared to have no guilty conscience when the question of collaboration with the Japanese was mentioned. He was undoubtedly satisfied with the setting up of British Military Administration.

12.   I would say that if the policy of the British Government is to proceed with the new constitution and the necessary new treaties, the sooner the Sultan of Johore is approached in his present state of mind the better.

13.   I concluded the interview by informing the Sultan that his second son, Tungku Abubakar,[3] is at present well and in Madras. He said that he never wanted to see Tungku Abubakar again; that he had run away, whereas his first and third sons had remained behind; that he would not allow Tungku Abubakar to enter Johore again.

14.   After taking our leave, when both the Sultan and his wife came out to the porch to see us off, we took Tungku Ahmed back to the Bukit Serene Palace. As soon as we arrived there the first son of the Sultan, Tungku Mahkota, came rushing out to greet us. He asked us in for a drink. We refused on the ground we were overdue in Singapore. He appeared to both Col. Hay and myself to be very nervous at seeing us. (Note: He is marked as "Black" on the "Black and Grey Lists").[4]

---

[3] Between 1942 and 1945 Tunku Abu Bakar served with British forces in India and in the reoccupation of Malaya. Father and son feuded bitterly and it was rumoured that Abu Bakar left Malaya for India as much to escape Ibrahim as the Japanese. After the war he brought a legal action against Ibrahim over the matter of some land.

[4] 'Black' and 'Grey' were security categories. 'Blacks' were irreconcilables and were security risks; 'Greys' were affected by enemy propaganda and could be security liabilities.

15. The interview took from 1805 to 1915 hours.

Interview with H H the Sultan of Selangor

Present: H.H. The Sultan of Selangor; Brigadier H.C. Willan, D.C.C.A.O.; Malay Peninsula; Colonel J. Shields, S.C.A.O., Selangor; Colonel H.B. Langworthy, Col. (Police) C.A.

(Note: The interview was conducted mostly in the Malay language and Col. Langworthy did the interpretation where necessary).

Date: 14th September, 1945.

1. In accordance with the instructions contained in SACSEA Secret No. 6/CA of the 21st July, 1945, I proceeded to Klang on the 14th September, 1945, for the purpose of interviewing the Sultan. Col. Shields and Col. Langworthy accompanied me.

2. I arrived at the Sultan's house at 12.55 pm and the Sultan came to the door to meet me. I had already sent word to him that I would arrive. I greeted him in the name of the Supreme Allied Commander.

He was overcome with joy at seeing me. He had tears in his eyes and could not express himself for a few moments.

3. I explained to the Sultan the terms and implications of Proclamation No. 1—i.e the British Military Administration Proclamation. That is:—

(a) The Supreme Allied Commander is Admiral Lord Louis Mountbatten.

(b) That property, private rights, religious liberty the Malay customs would be strictly respected. (The Sultan said he was particularly pleased about this).

(c) That all Japanese laws had been rescinded.

4. I then explained that only a British Military Administration could bring help to the population because it was impossible to set up a civil government immediately. I added, however, that it was the policy of H.M.G. to revert to civil government as soon as possible.

I told the Sultan that it would not be possible for himself and his State Council to function during the period of British Military Administration and he replied he was perfectly content with that state of affairs.

5. Having given time to the Sultan to regain his composure and get over his excitement at seeing three British Officers I encouraged him to talk of his experiences under the Japanese.

He said:—

About one week before the Japanese entered Kuala Lumpur he, Raja Uda, Dato Hamzah and the Sultans's [sic] family went to stay in the Government Rest House at Dusun Tua. On the way they stayed one night in a deserted rubber planter's bungalow at Puchong. After staying 2 to 3 weeks at Dusun Tua they all returned to Klang.

On my asking the whereabouts of Raja Uda the Sultan replied that he was on leave at Kuala Kangsar. He added that Raja Uda was a great friend of his.

He said that Dato Hamzah was formerly his secretary and when Tunku Musa-Addin was installed as Sultan by the Japanese, Dato Hamzah had gone to him as secretary. The Sultan saw nothing wrong in this because as Secretary to the Sultan Dato Hamzah should be with whoever was functioning as Sultan.

Last year the Sultan said he had been very ill with malaria and had been well looked after by Dr. Gabriel, who is a Eurasian Doctor in Klang. Apart from this he had not had any other illness.

Col. Fujiyama, the Japanese Governor of Selangor, called the Sultan to King's House, Kuala Lumpur on 15th January, 1942. Also Tunku Musa-Addin, Raja Uda, Dato Hamzah and important Malays, including members of the Sultan's family. Raja Kamalazaram [Kamaralzaman] of Perak was also there. On arrival the Sultan was kept waiting for two hours before he was seen by Major-General Minaki.

The Seating was as follows:—

Raja Uda	The Sultan
Musa Addin	Col. Fujiyama

General Minaki.

The Sultan said that Col. Fujiyama had a moustache like a tiger.

There were also present three other Japanese Officers, two Japanese Press Correspondents and a Japanese Interpreter.

Gen. Minaki asked him who he was and what he did. The Sultan replied that he was Tunku Alam Shah, the Sultan of Selangor.

Every Malay there was similarly questioned and Haji Osman, the Chief Kathi, said he was a Government pensioner. Minaki told him to go outside and get his pension from the King.

Minaki told the Sultan that because of his pronouncement in the press (Malay Mail) on 10th December, 1941, he was no longer Sultan because he was pro-British. The Sultan said that after his pronouncement in the press, Mr. Jarrett, then Resident of Selangor, had asked him to do a broadcast on the same lines. He had done so because he thought it would bind the Malays together to resist the Japanese.

Minaki then turned to Musa-Addin and said he would be Sultan. He told Sultan Alam Shah that he must remain in his own house.

The Japanese at the same meeting produced a list of Malays whom they were going to put into official posts. Each name was considered in turn and senior posts were filled there and then. Everyone was then offered Saki to toast success to the Japanese. Musa-Addin, Raja Uda and Dato Hamzah were probably frightened and sipped a little of the saki and raised their glasses in a toast to the Japanese. The Sultan refused to do so.

When the new Japanese Governor of Selangor went to Klang Musa-Addin asked the Sultan to go to his house to meet him. The Sultan went and this is the only occasion he has been to that house during the Japanese occupation. Otherwise he has only seen Musa-Addin in the mosque.

On 27th January, 1942, Raja Uda, Dato Hamzah and Dato Abdul Hamid went to the Sultan's house and Raja Uda said Musa-Addin wanted the State Regalia. The Sultan gave it to him because it is government property. The Sultan told Raja Uda that so long as the Japanese remained Musa-Addin could retain it, but as soon as the British returned he must have it back again.

The Japanese paid the Sultan no allowance. For a year they paid his 4 sons and 3 daughters 50 dollars per month each. After a year the Sultan refused to accept any more allowances for his family and thus they ceased to be paid.

In order to get money to keep himself and 40 other Malays dependent on him, he had sold jewellery to the Chinese worth 25,000 Straits Settlements dollars for 100,000 Japanese dollars.

The Japanese had taken away his wireless set and so he could not listen in to broadcasts.

The Sultan said that Musa-Addin had made many Malays and Chinese Datos and had also made one Indian a Dato.[5]

The Sultan produced a diary which he had kept in 1942. It is written in Jawi.[6] He instructed his Secretary, Tunku Nong, to prepare an English translation of his diary and to send it to me.

I showed the Sultan the new Straits Settlements currency notes and explained that the Japanese currency is now worthless. He was delighted to hear this and asked if he could have some money. I asked him what his allowance was per month and he replied eleven thousand two hundred and fifty dollars per month. I asked him how much he would require per month and he suggested ten thousand dollars. The Sultan went on to say he had no money and I said I would arrange to get him some within a week.

I informed the Sultan that as we are now responsible for his safety he should not travel about the country and advised him to remain in Klang as much as possible. He fully appreciated this.

I also told him that the British Military Administration would enquire into the conduct of Government officials and high State dignitaries during the Japanese occupation. He said he was glad to hear this would be done.

I informed the Sultan that I had already seen Musa-Addin and that he was being taken away from Klang. The Sultan kept quiet but appeared very relieved to hear that Musa-Addin was being taken away. I told the Sultan that I had brought back his Rolls-Royce car which I had found in the possession of Musa-Addin. He was delighted. The Sultan then said that the State Regalia was in the possession of Musa-Addin and should be got back at once. I agreed and said I would do this before returning to Kuala Lumpur.

Raja Nong, the Sultan's Secretary, said that he, Raja Uda and the Chief Kathi, Haji Osman were told by the Japanese that they were all three to be beheaded. Raja Nong promised to send me a written English version of this.

The interview ended at 2.30 p.m. and on departure the Sultan shook me by the hand for about a minute. He was obviously overcome with joy and relief that the British are back again. As I was leaving he asked if a guard could be provided for his house. I said one would be arranged at once. The O.C. Klang Detachment is arranging for a guard.

After leaving the Sultan I went back to Musa-Addin's house with the Sultan's Secretary, Raja Nong. There I enquired about the State Regalia. Dato Hamzah produced the two crowns—one for the Sultan and the other for the Sultana—and also a bejewelled pendant. Raja Nong examined them and expressed himself as satisfied these were all the State Regalia in the possession of Raja Musa. I then sent Raja Nong back to the Sultan with this regalia accompanied by Lt. Col. Girdler, O.C. Klang Detachment. I told Raja Nong that the Sultan would now be responsible for the safe-keeping of this State Regalia.

---

[5] A title of distinction.   [6] Arabic-based Malay script.

DETENTION OF TUNKU MUSA-ADDIN

1. On the 14th September, Col. Shields, Col. Langworthy and myself proceeded to Klang. There I met Lt. Col. Usman, a very fine type of Indian Officer, who was in charge of a guard consisting of two British Officers and twelve Indian other ranks, which had been pre-arranged the day previously.

2. I proceeded to the house of Musa-Addin with Col. Langworthy followed by Col. Shields and the guard. On arrival there Col. Langworthy entered first and found Musa-Addin in the lounge upstairs, which was also occupied by a number of Malays. He told Musa-Addin that I wished to see him alone and Musa-Addin ordered the other Malays out of the room. I then entered the room followed by Col. Shields.

3. I asked him if he was Musa-Addin and he replied he was. The interview was conducted in English, which he speaks fluently. I then informed him:

(a) That under the orders of the Supreme Allied Commander he was detained and would be taken back to Kuala Lumpur by me where he would remain under house arrest.

(b) In Kuala Lumpur he would not be allowed out of the precincts of the house nor would he be allowed to communicate with anyone outside.

(c) That he was to be sent out of Malaya as soon as possible and to that end he would be allowed to take with him an entourage consisting of not more than three Malays.

(d) He asked if he would be allowed to take with him his wife and family and I replied in the negative. (As he will leave Malaya by air this could not be arranged but I think that we will have to try and arrange for them to follow him to the Cocos Islands by sea).

(e) That he must be ready to go back with me to Kuala Lumpur in one and a half hours with bed linen, cooking utensils and some rice. That he could take two servants with him.

(f) I asked Musa-Addin if the Rolls-Royce car which I had just seen in front of his house belonged to the Sultan and he replied that it did. I said in that case I was taking it with me as I was on my way to have an audience with the Sultan and would hand it over to him.

No further conversation passed.

4. I proceeded to the house of the Sultan where I interviewed him—see separate account. Having finished my audience with the Sultan I went back to Musa-Addin's house to take him back to Kuala Lumpur. He sat with me in the back of the car. Raja Wahid and the driver sat in front. Raja Wahid is his nephew whom he asked me, when I got back to his house, if he could take with him to Kuala Lumpur. I agreed he could do so.

5. We proceeded to Kuala Lumpur preceded by Cols. Langworthy and Shields in the first jeep, the Guard Commander and one British Officer in the second jeep, with a 15cwt truck behind containing one British Officer, twelve IORs, Musa-Addin's two servants and his luggage, which consisted of two suit cases.

On arrival in Kuala Lumpur we went straight to the house of the Sultan of Selangor, which had already been got ready for him. It is fully furnished, down to mosquito nets.

I asked him how much rice he had brought with him and he said very little. I told him that he would be provided with meat, vegetables, fruit and cheese and that any reasonable request he had to make could be made to the British Officer in charge of the guard and would be implemented. He expressed himself as satisfied with the arrangements.

He then asked if he could send Raja Wahid back to Klang the next day to contact the three Malays he would like as his entourage when he was sent out of Malaya. I said this could be done and that transport would be arranged for Raja Wahid to go to Klang and back.

6. The whole proceedings went smoothly without any unpleasantness. There was no fuss. I gathered the impression that Musa-Addin was very nervous at the beginning of the interview and showed signs of relief when I explained what was to happen to him.

7. Before leaving him I arranged for the house telephone to be disconnected.[7]

Interview with the Regent of Kedah
Present: H.H. The Regent of Kedah; Brigadier H.C. Willan, D.C.C.A.O. (M.P.); Col. F.S. McFadzean, D.C.F.A. (M.P.); Major Hasler, Ag. S.C.A.O., Kedah & Perlis.

Date: 17th September, 1945.

1. Following the instructions contained in Secret S.A.C. 6/C.A. at 1630 hours on the 17th September 1945, I proceeded to the Palace at Alor Star, accompanied by Col. F.S. McFadzean and Major Hasler, Acting S.C.A.O., Kedah and Perlis.

I found the Regent, who had been informed of my visit, waiting to meet me on the front steps. I greeted him in the name of the Supreme Allied Commander. He appeared overjoyed to see me. With him were three Malay members of the State Council and after a general conversation for a few minutes with the Regent and those members of the State Council I requested a private audience with the Regent. This was granted immediately.

2. After expressing my condolences on the death of His Highness the Sultan of Kedah, which occured [sic] in 1943, I first encouraged the Regent to speak about his experiences under the Japanese and Siamese. He said that soon after the Japanese occupation he had to attend a ceremonial parade at which the Japanese Flag was lowered and the Siamese Flag hoisted in its place. The Siamese, when they took over Kedah, had allowed the Malay Government of Kedah to function as it did before the Japanese occupation and they interfered very little with the administration of the State. He was rather reticent about having been appointed Sultan during the Japanese occupation and so I did not press him on the matter.

3. The Regent said that he could not think of any cases in Kedah of real cruelty by the Siamese or Japanese and, on the whole, though the people of Kedah had suffered under the Japanese, they had been fortunate.

He said he could not understand the Japanese—Britishers, who are a Western race and Malays, who are an Eastern race, have never had any difficulty in understanding one another.

He went on to say that he grew very tired of the Japanese veneration for their

---

[7] Musa-Eddin was deported to the Cocos Islands; in May 1946 he was brought to Singapore where he stayed for a time with relatives in Kampong Glam.

Emperor, giving him divine qualities because they alleged he could trace his descent back to a contemporary of Adam.

He said there is a word "Jinn" in the Japanese language. He knew that in the Koran "Jinn" means a devil, which exactly describes the Japanese.

On being asked about the furniture and fittings etc, in the Palace he replied that they were safe except for a few articles of cutlery and crockery which the Japanese had borrowed and failed to return.

4. At first the Japanese ordered him to fly their flag at the Palace but later relented and allowed him to fly the Kedah flag.

5. The Japanese had not made him any allowance at the beginning. Later they had allowed him 5,000 Japanese dollars per month which they increased eventually to 10,000 Japanese dollars per month.

(Note: The Sultan of Kedah's allowance pre-war was $7,000 a month).

6. The State Council had sat during the Japanese occupation but the Regent said it had not enacted any new legislation. The Regent added that Japanese school teachers had tried to teach him and members of his State Council Japanese. Two had died in their fruitless efforts and the third had retired with a nervous breakdown.

7. The Regent constantly got back to the subject of how bad and evil the Japanese are and seemed puzzled to find words to accurately described their villainy.

8. After I had given the Regent time to settle down I explained to him that it was necessary to set up a British Military Administration with the Supreme Allied Commander at its head. I added that the Military Administration would be staffed as far as possible, though few are available, with officers with previous experience of Malaya.

I made it clear that all property, private rights, religious liberty and Malay customs would be strictly respected and that all Japanese laws no longer had any effect. I explained generally that a British Military Administration was necessary to restore law and order and that only the Army can obtain and bring into Malaya supplies necessary to rehabilitate the country.

I informed the Regent that as a result of the setting up of a British Military Administration neither he nor his State Council could function at present but the intention is to revert to civil government as soon as possible, at the same time I warned him that it would be some months before this could be done.

The Regent seemed a bit shaken by this. I reassured him that we would do all in our power to assist him in the rehabilitation of the State and provided the inhabitants remained law-abiding they had no reason to be afraid of the Military Administration. I added that we should require the co-operation of himself and his people and that on our part we would give him all the help and co-operation which lay within our power.

9. On the question of collaboration I informed the Regent that the policy would be one of leniency, except in cases where investigation proved conclusively that there had been active and serious collaboration with the Japanese to the detriment of the Allied cause. In such cases the leaders would be brought to justice.

10. As we were responsible for his personal safety I informed the Regent that we should be grateful if he would not travel about more than was really necessary.

11. I told the Regent that His Majesty's Government could not recognise him as Sultan because the present policy is not to recognise any Sultan who had been appointed during the period of the Japanese occupation. I went on to say that this

was an added reason why he could not perform any functions of a lawful Sultan. He seemed nervous and disturbed when I told him this. Finally I told him that it was the intention of the British Military Administration to pay him an allowance, that this allowance could not in any event be as much as that which had been paid to the legitimate Sultan before his death. I asked the Regent if he would suggest a sum. He hesitated. I suggested $5,000 per month (the Sultan's allowance pre-war was $7,000 per month). The Regent asked me for time to consider the matter and said he would give me his answer later. I agreed.

(Later the same evening the State Secretary Tuan Haji Sheriff told me that the Regent left the amount of the allowance to my discretion. I informed him that this was generous on the part of the Regent, and added that I would recommend $6,000 per month. Haji Sheriff said the Regent would be very pleased if I could make that recommendation).

12.   The interview ended at 1730 hours and the Regent still look worried. He had tea ready for us and during tea he recovered his composure and became more his normal self. When I left he came to the front to see me off and appeared much more cheerful.

13.   Later the same evening at 2130 hours the State Secretary Tuan Haji Sheriff telephoned Major Hasler and asked if he and other members of the State Council could come and see me. I told Major Hasler to inform them that I should be pleased to see them as individuals and not as members of the State Council (i.e. Tuan Haji Sheriff, State Secretary, Che Ismail Mericam, Legal Adviser, Che Kassim, State Treasurer, and Tungku Yacob, Principal Agricultural Officer). They arrived about 2200 hours and said that the Regent had told them of my interview with him and what I had said. They expressed considerable concern because they wondered that since the State Council could not function whether this meant that all Government offices must be closed down and the staff told to go home. They said they could not think that this was our intention. I replied that it was certainly not our intention; that we require all the Government offices to keep open and all the Government officers to report back to duty. I added that later we would investigate to see if any of the staff had been active collaborators and if so they would be dealt with.

Col. McFadzean who was present explained the financial policy with regard to the treatment and payment of all Government servants.

They were obviously very relieved at these statements by Col. McFadzean and myself and said that they now understood the position more clearly and were entirely satisfied with it. They said they would go back and inform the Regent.

They went away smiling and we parted on very friendly terms.

14.   It was a good thing Col. McFadzean and myself arrived in Alor Star on the 17th September. Major Hasler was very worried as to what was the position because he was afraid that when the Japanese, who were still in occupation of the State withdrew and before British troops could arrive, the Chinese guerillas, of whom there were many, would take charge and probably Alor Star would be looted. Major Hasler said that all the leading Malays were wondering when the British were coming back. Col. McFadzean and myself were the first British officers to arrive at Alor Star; we were followed by a Company of the Sussex Regiment who arrived about 4 hours later. On their arrival I contacted their Commanding Officer and requested that he should arrange for his troops to patrol the streets to maintain law and order. He said this would be done.

I might add that within an hour and a half of my arrival the Japanese Liaison Officer came to see me and asked what instructions I had for the surrender of the Japanese troops in Alor Star. I informed him that he would receive his full instructions when the Commanding Officer of the British Troops arrived in Alor Star.

Perlis

Whilst I was in Alor Star on the 17th September, 1945, I saw Major Burr of Force 136, who had come down from Kangar to meet me. I told him I had no knowledge of the political situation in Perlis. He told me that the Raja of Perlis Tungku Syed Alwi had died early in 1943 (subsequently in Kangar I obtained the exact date which is the 1st February 1943) and that Syed Hamzah, half-brother of the deceased Raja, had been installed as Raja by the Japanese. I subsequently discovered he was so installed as Raja on the 2nd February 1943, i.e. on the day after the death of the Raja.

There have been adverse reports about Syed Hamzah by successive British Advisers in Perlis.

2. Major Burr advised that it would be best for me to see Syed Hussein, younger brother of Syed Hamzah, who was officiating as State Secretary.

I asked Major Burr the whereabouts of Syed Putera, who in April 1938 was, on the proposal of the Raja, nominated as Bakel Raja i.e. heir or prospective successor of the Raja by the votes of all the members of the State Council, except Syed Hamzah who did not vote but pressed his own claims in opposition to those of Syed Putera. Major Burr informed me that Syed Putera was living in a small shack near the Railway Station at Arau. On my instructions Major Burr returned to Perlis on the 17th September, 1945, called for Syed Putera at Arau and took him on to Kangar where he arranged for him to be comfortably housed in Goverment quarters. At the same time he arranged that I should see Syed Hussein at 9 a.m. on the 18th September, 1945.

3. On the 18th September, 1945, I left Alor Star by car at 8 a.m. with Col. F.S. McFadzean, D.C.F.A., and arrived at Syed Hussein's house at Arau at 9 a.m. Syed Hussein speaks English and so there was no need for an interpreter.

He told me that prior to the Japanese occupation he had been Controller of Customs, Perlis, and that when Syed Hamzah had been appointed Raja by the Japanese on the 2nd February, 1943, he Syed Hussein, had been appointed State Secretary. I informed him that his appointment could not be recognised and he appeared to fully understand that.

I asked him who was occupying the Palace at Arau and he said Syed Hamzah was living there. I informed him that Syed Hamzah must move out at once.

Syed Hussein said Syed Hamzah would like to see me. I replied that I had no intention whatsoever of seeing him. Syed Hussein then said that Syed Hamzah wished to write a letter stating he had abdicated from the position of Raja. I replied that if Syed Hamzah wished to write a letter I would take it back with me but it must be understood that he did so of his own volition and not by any request or order of mine. I added that in my view Syed Hamzah could not in any case abdicate from a position he had never legitimately occupied.

Syed Hussein said he would go at once and inform Syed Hamzah of what I had said and that if Syed Hamzah still wished to write a letter he would bring it back with him. I informed him that if Syed Hamzah did write such a letter he must sign it and that Syed Hussein must also sign it as a witness.

4. I then proceeded to Kangar where I interviewed Syed Putera in the presence of Col. F.S. McFadzean.

Syed Putera speaks very good English. He is 25 years of age.

First I encouraged him to talk of his experiences during the Japanese occupation.

He said that in December 1941 he was Second Magistrate in the Criminal Court in Kuala Lumpur.

On the 9th December, 1941, he received a telegram from the British Adviser, Perlis, to remain in Kuala Lumpur. Copy of telegraph attached and marked (A).[8]

In January 1942, whilst he was still in Kuala Lumpur he received a letter signed by the Raja stating that he, Syed Putera, could no longer be recognised as Bakel Raja. This letter appears to have been written under the authority of the Japanese Military Authorities. Copy of the letter attached and marked (B).[9]

Syed Putera said that as regards the letter marked (B) it appeared to him that the Raja had signed the paper whilst blank and that the typing had been done later, probably at the instigation of Syed Hamzah.

Syed Putera added that he did not return to Perlis because of receiving the telegram marked (A).

5. When the Japanese forces came south and reached the outskirts of Kuala Lumpur Syed Putera went to Dusun Tua, near Kuala Lumpur, where he stayed in a Malay house for about a month.

(Note: Dusun Tua is also the place where the Sultan of Selangor stayed for a short time after the Japanese reached Kuala Lumpur).

After he had stayed at Dusun Tua for about a month Tengku Musa-Eddin (he was appointed Sultan of Selangor by the Japanese) sent his car to Dusun Tua and Syed Putera went to live in a house at Klang near to where Dato Hamzah (Private Secretary to the Sultan of Selangor) lived.

Syed Putera remained in Klang for 3 months and then received a letter from Perlis, brought by Haji Mat, Penghulu of Arau, asking him to return to Perlis. On the advice of Tengku Musa-Eddin, Syed Putera returned to Perlis to see what circumstances were like up there. On his way he stopped at Alor Star and saw the Japanese Military Authorities who appeared friendly towards him. He then went on to Arau where he saw the Raja who was very friendly. The Raja asked him to remain in Perlis

---

[8]Annexure (A) reads:—

From: Adviser, Alor Star.

To: ESSAR, Selangor, Kuala Lumpur.

Date: 9th December, 1941.

Following from adviser Perlis begins: tell Syed Putera to remain in Kuala Lumpur

[9] Annexure (B) reads:—

The Palace, Arau, Perlis.

25th Dzi'l-Hijjah 1360 A.H.   13 Jan. 1942. No. 2 in M.M.K. 51/60.

Under Command of the Japanese Military Authority

Seal and Signature.

To Tuan Syed Putera, son of the late Syed Hasan, at Arau, Perlis.

We hereby inform Tuan Syed Putera that (according to the decision taken) in the session of the State Council which was held at the Palace Arau on 23rd of Dzi'l-Hijjah 1360, we have deposed you, Tuan Syed Putera, from being the *Bakal Raja* (Heir or Prospective Successor to the Raja) of Perlis; and so you, Tuan Syed Putera, no longer has any claim in the matter of the Office of Bakal Raja.

The words in the seal are: "Alwi Safi Jamal' l-Lail, Raja of Perlis".

H.H. the Raja Perlis.

and promised to give him his former post with the same salary and allowances i.e.

Allowance	$400 p.m.
Salary Malay Officer Class II, Perlis	195 "
Motor car allowance	25 "
Total	$620 "

Syed Putera agreed to go back to Perlis and returned to Klang for his wife and family and also his belongings.

He, his wife and family went back by train from Klang to Perlis, where he at once saw the Raja who again promised to reinstate him in his former position. The Raja told Syed Hussein to arrange this.

Syed Putera was not reinstated in his former post. He was merely given an allowance of $90 per month and he told me he was certain that Syed Hamzah had prevented him from being reinstated to his former position.

He went on to say that when the Raja was ill he was prevented by Syed Hamzah from visiting him. Three days before the Raja died he was allowed to visit him and this was the only occasion after his return to Perlis that he did see the Raja.

Syed Putera continued to live at Arau but even his allowance of $90 per month ceased when the Raja died. In order to live, he and a few local Malays started trading in local produce. He said that but for the help of those local Malays he would not have been able to obtain a livelihood.

About 6 months ago, i.e. about April 1945, the Japanese ordered him to vacate his house at Arau and he went to live in a hut near the Railway Station at Arau. He lived there for about a month and then went to Kota Bharu, in Kelantan, together with his wife and family where he lived with his wife's father and mother. He remained there until the Japanese surrendered and returned to Arau on the 14th September, 1945, four days before I interviewed him.

6. At the beginning of my interview I had greeted him in the name of the Supreme Allied Commander and told him that I was pleased to see him looking so well after his difficult time.

I explained to him that there would be a British Military Administration which would continue until such time as the Civilian Government could take over. Under the British Military Administration full jurisdiction and powers were vested in the Military Authorities for the government of Malaya.

I also told him that property, private rights, religious liberty and Malay Customs would be strictly respected and that all Japanese laws had been rescinded.

Col. McFadzean then outlined in general terms the policy regarding currency and the payment of Government servants, and also measures which would be taken to bring relief to the civil population.

I informed Syed Putera that he could not officiate as Raja at present and also that the State Council of Perlis could not function.

I had already asked Major Burr to arrange to get a car for Syed Putera but I informed Syed Putera that as we are responsible for his personal safety I should be grateful if he would restrict his travelling.

On the question of collaboration I informed him that full investigation would be made and that any one, especially State dignitaries, who had actively collaborated with the Japanese would be dealt with by law. I added that the general policy on this subject was one of leniency but if any persons in responsible positions had been active collaborators then they must be dealt with. He expressed himself in agreement with this policy and showed no nervousness when I had described it to him. In fact the impression I got was that he welcomed it.

7. He informed me that the State Council of Perlis before the Japanese occupation consisted of:—

The Raja
British Adviser
Syed Hamzah, Vice President
Haji Ahmat, Chief Judge
Wan Ahmat, Co-operative Officer and A.D.C. to the Raja
Haji Mohamed Noor, Chief Kathi.

After the Japanese occupation the last three had ceased to function. Syed Putera said that he trusted these last three Malays implicitly.

Haji Ahmat, Chief Judge, was replaced by Che Mat, formerly Commissioner of Police. I saw Che Mat later and he appeared to me to be a very shifty individual.

Haji Mohamed Noor, Chief Kathi, was replaced by Haji Ismail.

8. I explained the system of Military Courts to Syed Putera and he expressed himself as satisfied with it. I added that the President of the Superior Court, who would be stationed in Alor Star, and who would have jurisdiction over Kedah and Perlis, must be a British Officer. Syed Putera agreed with this. He suggested that Haji Ahmat, Chief Judge and Che Wahab, formerly Magistrate, might be appointed as Presiding Officers in the District Courts. He said that neither of them had functioned during the Japanese occupation and they had his complete trust. I saw both Haji Ahmat and Che Wahab and was impressed by their demeanour.

9. Syed Putera said that the members of the State Council during the Japanese occupation had been, up till the death of the Raja:—

The Raja
Syed Hamzah,
Syed Hussein
Syed Alwi, formerly Clerk of State Council
Che Abdullah, formerly Commissioner of Lands.

10. On the question of an allowance for Syed Putera, he said he left it entirely to me. (The Raja's allowance was $3,200 per month). I did not tell Syed Putera what I would recommend but having considered the matter I have decided to recommend that he should be paid an allowance of $2,000 per month.

11. The interview was throughout conducted on a cordial and friendly level and there is no doubt that Syed Putera is very pleased to see the British back again. He thanked me profusely for going to see him. In my view he is an intelligent young man and also pro-British.

12. Before I left Kangar on my return Syed Hussein came to me and handed me a letter signed by Syed Hamzah, witnessed by Syed Hussein, in which the former renounced all claims to the office Raja of Perlis. Copy of letter attached and marked (C).[10]

---

[10] Annexure (C) reads:—
The Palace, Arau, Perlis. (continued overleaf)

Interview with the Sultan of Perak

Present: H.H. The Sultan of Perak; Brigadier H.C. Willan, D.C.C.A.O. (M.P.); Colonel F.S. McFadzean, D.C.F.A.; Colonel J.A. Harvey, S.C.A.O. Perak.

Date: 19th September, 1945.

On the 19th September, 1945, I arrived in Kuala Kangsar from Taiping at 6 p.m. I had already telephoned from Taiping to arrange an interview with the Sultan. I arrived at the Palace at 7 p.m. the same night.

2. The Sultan who is personally known to me, was obviously pleased to see me and from the beginning the interview was conducted on a most cordial and friendly level.

3. I commenced the interview by asking about his experiences under the Japanese.

He was ready to talk on this subject and said that in Kuala Kangsar he had been more or less left to himself by the Japanese. He could not think of any atrocities that had been committed by the Japanese in or around Kuala Kangsar.

He admitted he had attended several functions arranged by the Japanese and also that he had made speeches, but, like the Sultan of Johore, he said he had been instructed by the Japanese what he should say and had been merely a mouthpiece for them.

He went on to say that the Japanese did not really trust him and that towards the end they suspected that he had been in touch with the British General in Burma by wireless. As a result of this suspicion the Japanese had stationed a Japanese officer in the Palace, who had lived there for 4 months, for the sole purpose of spying on the Sultan.

Asked about general conditions in Perak the Sultan said that the matter he was most worried about was that of the Chinese Guerillas. He said that the one-star Chinese Guerillas were a law-abiding crowd but that the 3-star Chinese Guerillas were merely bandits.

The Japanese had not interfered with his Palace which had remained intact.

He said there had been no large numbers of Japanese forces in Kuala Kangsar but that the large Japanese Military Headquarters had been stationed in Taiping.

4. I have omitted to mention that when I first met the Sultan I greeted him in the name of the Supreme Allied Commander, Admiral Lord Louis Mountbatten, a relative of His Majesty the King.

After his account as set out above, I informed the Sultan that the S.A.C. had assumed full jurisdiction and powers over the whole of Malaya during the period of Military occupation. I explained that it was necessary to have a British Military Administration, because the Army is the only body which can restore law and order and get in relief supplies of various kinds for the civil population.

I went on to say that the British Military Administration would strictly respect all

---

To: H.E. General Officer, Commanding British Forces at Singapore.

On Tuesday 18th September, 1945, I, Syed Hamzah son of the late Syed Safi, do of my own free will and accord lay down the office of Raja of the State of Perlis, to which office I was raised by the Japanese Military Governor of Kedah on the 2nd of February 1943; and I shall not make any claim in connection with the Office of the Raja. That is all.

Signed: Hamzah bin Syed Safi.

Witness: Syed Hussin 18.9.45. He is State Secretary.

property, private rights, religious liberty and Malay Customs. The Sultan, who is a deeply religious person, expressed himself pleased with the statement especially as regards religious liberty and non-interference with Malay customs.

I informed the Sultan that the Military Administration would be terminated as early as possible but that its termination would depend on when the civil Government could be re-established.

The Sultan said that he appreciated the reasons for a Military Administration and agreed that it could be the only form of Government until the civil Government could be reinstated.

Col. McFadzean explained to him in general terms the currency and financial policy and what measures would be taken for the relief of the civil population. The Sultan stated that he was somewhat concerned about the relief of Malays living in the kampongs. I said I agreed it would be difficult in the first instance to bring relief to them and to get currency notes to them. I added however that it was the policy of the British Military Administration to purchase rubber from small holders at a price of 36 cents per pound (equals 48 cents per katty). I added that this would be started at once and that a Rubber Buying Unit was already in the country and would be followed as quickly as possible by stocks of coagulants and other accessories for rubber estates. The Sultan said that this would ease the difficult situation in the kampongs and would help to alleviate the distress amongst the Malays living there.

I then informed the Sultan that one result of the British Military Administration is that neither he nor his State Council can function at present. He at once saw the force of this and made no demur.

I then dealt with the question of the treatment of persons who had collaborated with the Japanese. I informed him that the general policy is one of leniency but that ringleaders who had been in responsible positions must and should be brought to justice. The Sultan showed no nervousness when I touched on this subject and agreed that it was the right policy.

I informed him that as we are now responsible for his personal safety I should be grateful if he would not travel about more than is necessary. He agreed to this.

On the question of his allowance he said that it was $12,500 per month. He said he had no money at present and would be pleased if his allowance could be paid at once. I said that as soon as I got back to Kuala Lumpur I would arrange for this to be done. Asked if the Japanese had paid him an allowance he said at first they had paid him nothing, then he was paid half his allowance i.e. 6,250 Japanese dollars per month which eventually they increased to his full allowance of $12,500 per month.

5. The interview terminated at 7.45 p.m. on the same cordial and friendly level as it had begun.

6. After the interview Col. McFadzean, Col. Harvey and myself had a cup of tea with the Sultan and I talked with several of his relatives and Palace officials. I remember many of them from the days I was stationed in Kuala Kangsar in 1925–26.

The Sultan told me that Raja Uda of Selangor was staying with him in Kuala Kangsar for a change because Raja Uda had been ill. I did not see Raja Uda, he did not appear.

7. I left the Palace at 8 p.m. and on leaving the Sultan asked me to sign his visitors' book. I did so.

There is no doubt that he was genuinely pleased to see me and welcomed the British back again. I myself was well satisfied with the interview because I came away under the impression that the Sultan has nothing to fear from us regarding his conduct during the Japanese occupation.

Interview with the Yam Tuan of Negri Sembilan
On the 23rd September, 1945, I went to Seremban from Kuala Lumpur for the purpose of interviewing the Yam Tuan of Negri Sembilan. I was accompanied by Col. Daniels, Chief Secretary, Malay Peninsula. We picked up Col. Calder, S.C.A.O., Negri Sembilan and Malacca, on our way and arrived at the Palace at Sri Menanti at 3.30 p.m. Col. Calder had already informed the Yam Tuan that we were arriving and he was ready to meet us.

2. Before describing my interview with him it is necessary to describe the preliminary interview which Col. Calder had with him at Sri Menanti on 14th September 1945 as soon as Col. Calder had arrived in Seremban.

The following is the account of that interview given to me by Col. Calder:—

(a) This preliminary interview lasted from 11 a.m. to 12 noon on the 14th September, 1945. The Yam Tuan was slightly reserved (this is normal for him) but was at his ease at the end of the interview. He informed Col. Calder that things had not been too pleasant for him during the Japanese occupation. They had turned him out of his Astana in Seremban and he had to live in another house there. After living for a few months in that house the Japanese had allowed him to return to his Palace at Sri Menanti. The Japanese took away all his cars except one, including a Daimler which was practically new before the war.

The Japanese had forced him to attend functions in Seremban and in attending those functions he had not been allowed to have his umbrella bearer with him. He admitted having made speeches in favour of the Japanese but claimed that he had done so under their orders and had no alternative except to appear to be friendly disposed to them. At all the functions he attended he had been put down to sit amongst the clerks and the Japanese seemed to take a delight in humiliating him. The Japanese had not allowed him to fly his flag.

(b) Col. Calder explained to him the general set up of the Military Administration and gave him copies of the first few Proclamations.

(c) He informed Col. Calder that he had practically no food in the Palace and Col. Calder sent out a week's supply of rice and I.O.R. rations the next day. On the 19th September, 1945, Col. Calder took out $3,000 to the Yam Tuan and handed it personally him. (The Yam Tuan's allowance is $6,250 a month).

(d) Col. Calder told the Yam Tuan that the British Military Administration would have to investigate the conduct of officials and State dignitaries and those whom it was found had actively collaborated with the Japanese would have to be dealt with. Col. Calder added that the Yam Tuan's Private Secretary Tungku Nasir and his A.D.C. Tungku Ahmat were under suspicion and also his son Tungku Jaffar. Col. Calder informed me that the impression he got when he told the Yam Tuan this was that the Yam Tuan knew all about it.

(e) Col. Calder told the Yam Tuan if he had any difficulties he should bring them to him. The Yam Tuan replied that he was pleased to see Col. Calder because he knew that he had had previous experience in Negri Sembilan. The Interview ended with the Yam Tuan expressing regret that the relations between the Chinese and the Malays were somewhat strained at present.

3. On the 23rd September, 1945, at 3.30 p.m. I interviewed the Yam Tuan in his Palace at Sri Menanti together with Col. Daniels, Chief Secretary and Col. Calder.

On my arrival I greeted him in the name of the Supreme Allied Commander and at that time there were present with the Yam Tuan the Tungku Besar (he is the uncle of the Yam Tuan and invariably referred to as the "Wicked uncle"), Tungku Laksamana, Tungku Suleiman, Tungku Nasir, Private Secretary, Tungku Ahmed, A.D.C., and the Tungku Muda.

4. I first explained the necessity for the British Military Administration by stressing that the Army is the only body which can get in supplies for the relief of the civilian population and that in the absence of the civil Government the only form of government which is possible at the moment is that of a Military Administration.

I continued by informing the Yam Tuan that the British Military Administration would strictly respect all property, private rights, religious liberty and Malay customs. The Yam Tuan was delighted to hear this because he is very religious and has always taken a keen interest in the Malay people in his State.

He appreciated the need for the British Military Administration and saw no objection to it and when I informed him that neither he nor his State Council could function he expressed no apprehension.

5. When I touched on the question of his experiences under the Japanese occupation he confirmed all that he had told Col. Calder, and which I have set out above, but to my mind he seemed more reserved on this subject and I was surprised he was not more forthcoming.

6. In order to obtain money during the Japanese occupation he had to sell two of his houses in Seremban, one for $80,000 and the other for $70,000, both of which were bought by Chinese. The Japanese Military Authorities had taken away all his cars except one, which he still has, and for his Daimler car, which as I have already stated above was practically new just before the war, the Japanese paid him $17,000.

7. I tried as much as possible to get further information out of him with regard to his experiences under the Japanese but he was so reserved on this subject that I dropped it.

8. I told him that I was pleased that Col. Calder had taken out $3,000 to him and also that he had supplied him with food. I informed him that his full allowance of $6,250 per month would be paid.

9. With regard to the subject of collaboration, I told him that the general policy is one of leniency but that ringleaders in responsible position[s] who had actively collaborated with the Japanese must be dealt with. He appeared to appreciate this to the full. The interview ended at a little after 4 o'clock and then Col. Daniels, Col. Calder and myself had tea with the Yam Tuan and the other Malays enumerated in para. 3 above. I noticed that the Yam Tuan did not sit Tungku Nasir, Private Secretary, or Tungku Ahmed, A.D.C., at the same table as myself and the main party but put them away at a side table. (On our way back from Sri Menanti to Seremban Col. Calder remarked on this and said this was undoubtedly due to the fact that he had already told the Yam Tuan at his preliminary interview that both these Malays are under suspicion).

10. I would have expected of the Yam Tuan whom I know personally (I served in Ipoh some years ago as Deputy Public Prosecutor in the Supreme Court when he was Deputy Registrar in the same Court) to have been more forthcoming but I understand from various sources that he has been very quiet during the Japanese

occupation. On considering this matter although I was disappointed at the time, I think that it will take him a little time before he loses his present reserve. As I have stated, even pre-war he was more reserved than other Sultans, but I certainly found him much more reserved than I have ever found him before. I left the Palace at 4.30 p.m. to return to Seremban and Kuala Lumpur.

11. I should add that when I arrived at the Palace, his flag was already flying and he seemed pleased when I informed him that Col. Calder would fly on his office at Seremban the Union Jack and the Negri Sembilan Flag with equal status.

Interview with the Sultan of Pahang

On the 28th September, 1945, I left Kuala Lumpur with Lt. Col. D. Ambler (Education Department at present in Force 136) for Kuantan. I reached Kuantan at 10 a.m. There I was met by Lt. Col. F.S. Chapman[11] of Force 136 who is carrying out the duties of Civil Affairs Officer, Kuantan, until relieved by the Civil Affairs Officers earmarked for Kuantan who are in Kuala Lumpur waiting for their transport.

2. I left Kuantan by car for Pekan, where the Sultan lives, at 11.30 a.m. Pekan is about 28 miles from Kuantan. The journey involves passing the Pahang River twice by ferry and consequently I did not reach the Astana Saadah, where the Sultan was, until 1.10 p.m.

(Note: The Sultan has three Astanas in Pekan of which Astana Saadah is the smallest).

3. I had been informed by Lt. Col. Chapman that although the Sultan can speak English he prefers to speak Malay. As my Malay is somewhat rusty after an absence of 8 years from Malaya, it was arranged that Tungku Mohamed, uncle of the Sultan, and also his Secretary, should be present at the interview as interpreter. Lt. Col. Chapman and Lt. Col. Ambler, both of whom know the Sultan personally, were also present.

4. Arriving at the Astana I found the Sultan on the front steps waiting to receive me. He looked very well. I greeted him in the name of the Supreme Allied Commander.

I reminded the Sultan that I had attended his wedding in Kuala Lumpur in 1926, when I was Assistant District Officer there. The Sultan replied that he remembered me quite well and was very pleased that a senior officer with Malayan experience had come to see him.

5. I kept the conversation general for a few minutes and told him of the plight of members of the Malayan Civil Service who had been in internment in Singapore. I then proceeded to the main object of my mission.

6. The Sultan, who has never been very talkative, seemed slightly nervous when I tried to encourage him to talk about his experiences during the Japanese occupation. I found it rather an up-hill task to carry on the conversation because he only appeared capable of answering direct questions.

7. The Sultan said he had kept aloof from the Japanese as much as he could and had only come into contact with them when he had received orders from them to attend their functions at Kuala Lipis and elsewhere. He said he could not refuse to obey their orders but admitted that the Japanese had not ill-treated him and had allowed him to attend their functions in ceremonial Malay dress.

---

[11] See 43, note.

He also admitted having made speeches in favour of the Japanese but said that he was forced to do so by them. These speeches had either been composed by the Japanese themselves with the Sultan merely as a mouth-piece or he had been told by the Japanese what he should say and he had no alternative but to obey their orders.

He had been forced by the Japanese to attend their functions in Kuala Lumpur and once he was taken to Singapore for a meeting which was attended by all the Sultans. Asked what this meeting in Singapore was about he seemed quite vague, except that the Japanese had suggested to each Sultan that it would be a good gesture on their part to contribute funds to the Japanese cause. He admitted having subscribed $2,000 on two occasions to the Japanese cause making a total of $4,000 in all.

8.   At first the Japanese had forced him to fly the Japanese Flag but later they allowed him to fly his own personal standard.

9.   On the question of allowances the Japanese had paid him $4,000 per month in the first instance raising it to $8,000 later. (Note: The allowance of the Sultan of Pahang is $8,000 per month).

10.   He said that the Japanese Governor of Pahang was very angry with him because he did not obtain information for the Japanese as to the whereabouts of a Pahang Dato who was supposed to be operating with the Malay Guerillas. The Japanese forced the Sultan to telegraph to see if he could get the Dato to appear before them but the Dato never did appear. The Japanese Governor considered that the Sultan was responsible for the non-appearance of the Dato and was very angry with him after questioning him closely on the matter. The Sultan made no allegation that the Japanese had slapped his face and in fact he inferred that they had not. I particularly questioned him about this because I had heard rumours that the Japanese had treated him in that undignified manner.

11.   He seemed very concerned about the Chinese Guerillas operating in the jungle in Pahang and said that they are terrorising the Malays in the kampongs.

12.   I explained the set up of the British Military Administration to the Sultan and also the reasons for a Military Administration. I also informed him that the Military Administration would strictly respect all property, private rights, religious liberty and Malay customs.

I then went on to say that one consequence of the British Military Administration is that neither he nor his State Council can function at present.

He replied that he quite understood the position and is fully content with it.

I added that it is the intention of the British Government that the Military Administration shall be as short as possible in order that the Civil Government can be re-established without undue delay.

I then touched on the question of collaboration and informed him that the general policy is one of leniency. At the same time I said that persons in responsible positions who had actively collaborated with the Japanese would be dealt with according to law and the Sultan said he quite agreed with that policy. He showed no nervousness at all when we discussed this question of collaboration. (From all reports which I heard from persons in Pahang it appears that the Sultan has in no way actively collaborated with the Japanese—in fact the members of Force 136 in Pahang all speak well of his conduct during the time they were in Pahang whilst the Japanese were still in occupation).

13.   I told the Sultan that since we are responsible for his personal safety I should be grateful if he would not travel about too much. He said he had only one small car

of his own and would be grateful if he could be supplied with another car. I said that a British car suitable for him would take a long time to obtain and he then said he would be content with any reasonable car which could be found in Malaya. He also gave me a list of cutlery, crockery, linen etc. which he requires for his Astana and also a list of the spare parts required for his electric light engine. These are attached and marked "A" and "B".[12]

14. I informed the Sultan that his full allowance of $8,000 a month would be paid with effect from the 1st. September, 1945 and instructed Lt. Col. Chapman to pay at once. The Sultan was delighted when he heard this.

15. I was well satisfied with the interview which was kept at a cordial level throughout. The Sultan pressed me to stay to lunch. I informed him I regretted I was unable to accept his kind invitation but I had to get back to Kuantan where I had a lot of work to do and I was proceeding on to Kuala Trengganu. The Sultan said he fully understood how busy I was and hoped that next time I paid a visit to Kuantan and Pekan I would have more time and would then be able to have lunch with him.

16. The Sultan has 8 children—5 daughters and 3 sons. The eldest child is a daughter and the second child a son, Tungku Ahmed, age 16. The Sultan's wife is a daughter of the late Sultan of Perak, Sultan Iskandar Shah.

17. There is no doubt whatsoever that the Sultan is genuinely pleased to see the British back and at present is 100% with us.

Trengganu

I left Kuantan by air on the 29th September, 1945 at 9.05 p.m. and arrived at Kuala Trengganu at 10.20 p.m. where I was met by Lt. Col. D. Headley [Headly], Senior Civil Affairs Officer at Kuala Trengganu. Col. Headley has previously had considerable experience in Trengganu, knows the State like a book and has the full confidence of the Malay population.

2. I ascertained that Sultan Suleiman, the legitimate Sultan of Trengganu, died on the 25th September, 1942, of blood poisoning and that his son Raja Ali was installed as Sultan during the Japanese occupation on the say day.

Sultan Suleiman had at least 3 sons:—

Raja Ali the eldest son age about 31 or 32 years.
Tungku Aziz about 23 years of age.
Tungku Abdul Rashid about 16 years of age.

I ascertained from Col. Headley that the Siamese took over the Government of Trengganu from the Japanese on the 18th October, 1943, and immediately allowed the Malay Government to function as it did prior to the war. Estimates have been prepared and passed each year just as they had been prepared and passed prior to the war.

3. Col. Headley told me that Raja Ali had married a daughter of the Sultan of Pahang. In addition he had married a Malay prostitute named Tuan [sic] Nik. She is said to be about 29 years of age and his official wife, the Sultan of Pahang's daughter about 18 years of age. He had a son by his official wife about 12 to 18 months ago and a daughter by the Malay prostitute about 6 months ago. Col. Headley told me that Raja Ali had given several parties in the Astana to Japanese officers and said he

---

[12] Not printed.

thought it would be a good thing if I had a talk with Dato Jaya, the Mentri Besar, who is absolutely reliable and very pro-British.

4. Col. Headley said that Dato Jaya told him that if the British had been in Trengganu and could have seen how Raja Ali behaved they would not have for one moment allowed him to be considered for the position of Sultan. In Trengganu it appears that the succession between the Sultanate goes from father to son. Thus if Ali were passed over Aziz would be the next claimant. Col. Headley said that Aziz appeared to have behaved well during the Japanese occupation and is not a bad fellow.

Col. Headley said the feeling of the people of Trengganu is that they would like Tungku Paduka the late Sultan's younger brother, who speaks English, to be Sultan. He is very much respected by everybody in Trengganu but of course if he were made Sultan it would not be in accordance with the "adat" [custom] and Col. Headley could not say what the reaction locally would be if Tungku Paduka were declared Sultan.

5. Col. Headley told me that Raja Ali is still living with his Malay prostitute in a house called "Telaga Panchor" in Kuala Trengganu. The information is that he only goes to his official palace occasionally to visit his official wife.

6. At Col. Headley's suggestion I first saw Dato Jaya, Mentri Besar, in whom Col. Headley has implicit trust and has always been regarded by us as entirely pro-British. I had an exploratory talk with him to find out the political atmosphere.

Dato Jaya does not speak English and so Col. Headley interpreted for me.

Dato Jaya began by saying how pleased he and the other Malays are that Col. Headley is back again in Trengganu because he knows Trengganu and its people intimately.

He went on to say that when Tungku Ali was installed as Sultan on the 25th September, 1942, he, the Dato Jaya, was ill.

The Japanese custom was that if a Sultan died his eldest son, where there was one, must succeed despite any disabilities.

After Tungku Ali was installed as Sultan the leading Malays sought Dato Jaya's advice as to what should be done. He advised that Tungku Ali should be given a trial. His advice was written out by one of the leading Malays and put before a representative assembly of Malay notables. They agreed with the Dato's advice.

According to Dato Jaya many of the younger Malays in Trengganu were opposed to the appointment of Tungku Ali as Sultan, they would have preferred to have seen Tungku Paduka as Sultan. Dato Jaya advised them to wait and see how Tungku Ali conducted himself.

As time went on the population became more and more disgusted with the conduct of Tungku Ali and his Malay mistress. His Malay mistress is the illegitimate child of a Chinese man and a Malay woman. Tungku Ali married her but subsequently owing to pressure brought to bear on him by the British Adviser he divorced her but still continued to keep her as his mistress. The divorce was properly registered in the office of the Religious Affairs Officer, Kuala Trengganu, and he confirmed the divorce.

Ali on several occasions asked some Japanese Military Officers for presents such as cigarettes and other comforts. This is against the "adat" that no Sultan should ever ask for presents. Tungku Ali was extremely friendly with the Japanese and invited several of the Japanese Military Police officers to banquets at the Astana where ronggengs [dances] were held.

Dato Jaya also stated that Tungku Ali had reported those Malay officials who were pro-British.

Tungku Ali is heavily in debt. He took possession of a piece of open ground in the town of Kuala Trengganu which he had fenced and then leased it out to a Chinese for $6,000 at first, later $10,000, per month as an amusement park. Heavy gambling took place there every night.

When the Japanese were themselves in control of Trengganu before it was handed over to the Siamese Tungku Ali's conduct disgusted every one. When the Siamese took over they allowed the Government of Trengganu to function as it was before. At first under the Siamese, Tungku Ali's conduct improved a little but later he reverted to his former habits and still continued to entertain any Japanese troops who remained in Kuala Trengganu. A certain number of new laws were enacted during the Siamese regime, they were all signed by Tungku Ali as also any Rules and Regulations made thereunder. Dato Jaya was appointed Tungku Ali's Secretary and he signed all State documents except Laws, Rules and Regulations. He signed them for President of the Council, which is the title the Siamese gave Tungku Ali.

The Japanese regarded Dato Jaya as British Spy No. 1 and often had guards placed around his house and also searched his house on several occasions.

(Note: I was very impressed by Dato Jaya. He is obviously a man of great character and undoubtedly very pro-British).

After I had seen Dato Jayo I saw Tungku Ali at 1.55 p.m. My interview with him was short and concluded at 2.10 p.m.

I told him that H.M.G. could not recognise him as Sultan and that he must at once take down the Sultan's personal flag which he was then flying at his house and also on his motor car.

I explained briefly to him the set up of the British Military Administration.

I also told him that the conduct of all Government servants would be inquired into to see if any of them had actively collaborated with the Japanese and that a similar investigation would be made into his own conduct and also that of the State dignitaries. He was very nervous when I told him this and became somewhat pale.

I told him that in no circumstances would he receive an allowance equivalent to that of a Sultan. He admitted having been paid an allowance of $6,000 a month by the Japanese.

I asked him what the position was in 1941 with regard to his allowances. He said he received a political pension of $270 a month and worked as a learner in the Court of Kuala Trengganu on a salary of $75 per month making $345 a month in all.

I told him he should continue to live in the house in which he is at present living and that we would allow him not more than 5 servants which would be paid by the Senior Civil Affairs Officer. His light and water would be supplied free and that his only expenses would be food and clothing. I said in my view an allowance of $450 a month was sufficient which is the $345 he was getting in 1941 plus an extra 33⅓% on it. I informed him that his allowance of $450 a month would be paid from the 1st September, 1945. He appeared to be considerably shaken when I told him this was the only allowance he would get.

7. After I had finished interviewing Tungku Ali I addressed all the Government clerks etc. at the Government Offices and received a warm welcome.

Individually I met:—

(a) Tungku Paduka, the younger brother of the late Sultan who impressed me very favourably.

(b) Che Hashim, a Perak Malay, now Commissioner of Lands, Trengganu, and formerly District Officer, Dungun.

(c) Che Yeop Osman, a Perek Malay, Assistant Commissioner of Police.

These three Malays according to Col. Headley, are extremely reliable and all of them are pro-British.

Kelantan

On the 29th September, 1945 I left Kuala Trengganu by air at 4.30 p.m. and arrived in Kota Bharu at 5.45 p.m. where I was met by Lt. Col. D. Somerville, S.C.A.O., Kelantan.

Having had a talk with Col. Somerville he advised me it would be a good thing if I met Tungku Hamzah, the State Secretary and Nik Ahmed Kamil bin Haji Nik Mahmood, the Deputy Prime Minister.

I saw both these Malays in the British Adviser's house and Col. Somerville was present at the interview.

They informed me that the late Sultan Sir Ismail died on the 20th June, 1944, of T.B. The Raja of Kelantan, Tungku Ibrahim, was installed as Sultan on the same date. According to them he was officially installed with the usual coronation ceremony. No approval from the Japanese was sought because it was not necessary. The Siamese agreed to Tungku Ibrahim becoming Sultan. The official papers were signed and kept in the usual way and these will be made available to Col. Somerville. These two Malays told me that from the time the Japanese came in on 8.12.1941 they continued to govern the country until October, 1943, when the Siamese took over. At first, government was by Japanese military authorities alone but on 31st December, 1941, they governed the country by means of Japanese civil affairs officers. The later Sultan was still officiating and the Japanese more or less let him alone.

In February, 1942, a Japanese military governor arrived and then the Japanese governed directly without any reference to the Sultan except on matters of Muhammadan religion and Malay custom.

In May, 1942, the Japanese re-organised the departments and Malay officers and clerks were changed about from department to department.

When the Siamese took over in October, 1943, they allowed the Kelantan Government to function as it did in pre-war days.

These two Malays told me that the Japanese did not like the Raja of Kelantan, Tungku Ibrahim, and they smashed up all the furniture in his house for no apparent reason whatsoever.

They told me that the late Sultan gave $10,000 to the Japanese cause because the Japanese told him it would be a good gesture and he did so.

Nik Ahmed Kamil at the end of the interview informed me that he was sent to Japan by the Japanese in August 1943 and remained there for about 5 or 6 weeks to learn propaganda. He said it was an absolute waste of time, he learned nothing, and it took him 45 days in a ship to return to Kelantan.

At first Japanese flags were flown on official buildings in Kelantan, and when the Siamese took over they flew their own flags in the place of the former Japanese flags. The Siamese did not allow Kelantan flags to be flown.

The Siamese handed the whole Government back to the legitimate Kelantan Government on the 25th August, 1945, and only then allowed the Kelantan flags to be flown.

Before they left they told me that the late Sultan's allowance was $6,000 a month and that Tunku Ibrahim, now 47 years of age got $1,500 a month as Raja of Kelantan and that he has a son aged 31 years who was installed as Raja Muda when the Raja of Kelantan was installed as Sultan.

I thanked them both for their information and said I was going to see the Raja of Kelantan the same night.

2. I arrived at the Raja of Kelantan's house, he is not living in the Astana, at 9.10 p.m. and interviewed him in the presence of Col. Somerville and the son of the Raja himself.

I first of all explained to him the set up of the British Military Administration and the reasons why a military administration is the only possible form of government at the present time. I told him that it is the policy of the British Government that Malaya should revert to civil government as soon as possible.

I said that the British Military Administration will respect all property, private rights, religion and Malay customs.

I then encouraged him to talk of his experience during the Japanese and Siamese occupation. He told me about the Japanese going into his house and smashing up all his furniture. He also told me that the local Japanese Gestapo took him to their headquarters where they questioned him for 5 hours sometimes at the point of the pistol because they said they suspected he had something to do with the looting of Chinese banks. He added that when the late Sultan was called down to Singapore by the Japanese for a meeting with all the other Malay Sultans, the Sultan was too ill to travel to Singapore and so he, Tungku Ibrahim, went there as his representative. On arrival at the Singapore Railway Station he was searched by the Japanese before leaving the Station.

There is no doubt that Tungku Ibrahim hates the Japanese and in my view he has avoided contact with them as far as he possibly could.

I told him that we could not recognise him as Sultan because we could not recognise anything done during the Japanese occupation. I said on that account I should be grateful if he would cease flying the Sultan's personal flag at his residence and on his motor car. I said there was no objection to him flying the Kelantan State flag and he readily agreed to my request.

3. I then explained to him the policy which will be adopted regarding collaborationists i.e. that the general policy is one of leniency but that responsible persons who had actively collaborated with the Japanese will be brought to justice. He said this was a fair policy and he entirely agreed with it.

4. I asked him not to travel about too much as we are responsible for his personal safety and that when he does travel about he should let the S.C.A.O., Col. Somerville, know where he is going. He said he would do so and added that he was very pleased to see Col. Somerville back again in Kelantan because he was well-known there and trusted by the local population.

5. I said that we could not allow him the full allowance of $6,000 a month which was the Sultan's allowance but we would make him an allowance of $4,000 per month. I said that Col. Somerville was authorised to pay him this from the 1st September and payment would be made the next day i.e. 30th September, 1945. He

cheered up a lot when I told him this.

6. I found this an easy interview, he was very friendly, genuinely pleased to see me and was agreeably surprised when I was able to carry on a certain part of the conversation in Malay. In my view he is very friendly to us and at the moment will take any advice we give him.

The interview ended at 10 p.m. when the Raja of Kelantan thanked me most profusely for coming to see him and said he hoped I would visit Kota Bharu again in the very near future.

Brigadier Willan's views after interviewing the Sultans

1. *Johore*
In view of the difficulties which the Sultan of Johore has caused to Government in the past[13] and also because of reports regarding his co-operation with the Japanese, I considered this would be the most difficult interview of all. In fact it turned out to be a very friendly and cordial one. I had never met the Sultan of Johore previously.

On arrival at his Istana I met his Rumanian wife, whom I summed up to be a very intelligent and attractive woman with pro-British sympathies. The Sultan seemed to be very fond of her and told me how grateful he was to her for standing by him during the period of the Japanese occupation.

The Sultan is undoubtedly much more pro-British than he ever was before as shown by his joy at the return of the British; his request to fly the Union Jack on his motor car; and his statement that he welcomed the British Military Administration and is prepared to serve *under* it.

He is certainly very much perturbed at the activities of the Chinese Guerillas in his State and in my view realizes that without British aid he cannot regain his former control over the State of Johore.

He has three sons:—

(a) Tungku Mahkota—elder son.
(b) Tungku Abubakar—second son.
(c) Tungku Ahmed—third son.

In my view it would be wise to approach the Sultan of Johore first with regard to the negotiations for the new treaties. I think in his present state of mind he will sign. He is a realist and is fully aware that he is dependent on H.M.G's support.

If he refuses to sign considerable care must be exercised as to which of his three sons should then be approached.

Tungku Mahkota should not be approached without first making full investigation as to his activities during the Japanese occupation. He is listed as "Black" on the "Black and Grey" lists. He certainly appeared very nervous when I met him for a few moments on the evening of the 8th September 1945, after I had interviewed the Sultan.

If Tungku Mahkota's proves to be "Black" then Tungku Abubakar is the son to approach first regarding negotiations of the new treaty. He is at present a Major in the B.M.A. carrying out the functions of Chairman, Sanitary Board, Kuala Lumpur.

---

[13] Sultan Ibrahim ibni Almarhum Sultan Abu Bakar (1873–1959); succeeded his father in 1895; accepted a British general adviser most unwillingly in 1914 and throughout the 1920s and 1930s had asserted Johore autonomy and points of personal prestige.

At my interview the Sultan was emphatic that he would not allow Tungku Abubakar to enter the State of Johore again because he had fled the State at the time of the Japanese occupation.

In my view Tungku Abubakar might well be willing to sign the new treaty which would put the prize of the Sultanate into his hands and thus allow him to return to the State of Johore. In such an event it would however be necessary to remove the present Sultan out of the State and also out of Malaya; it would be too dangerous to leave him there with Tungku Abubakar installed as Sultan. As regards the third son, Tungku Ahmed, he has not a sufficiently strong character to fit him for the office of Sultan.

2. *Selangor*

With the removal to the Cocos Islands of Tungku Musa-Addin, the first son of the late Sultan of Selangor, who was appointed Sultan by the Japanese when his brother Tungku Alam Shan, the legitimate Sultan, was removed by them, the way is now clear for direct negotiations with the legitimate Sultan.

He is a pleasant person with not a very strong character and at present is so overjoyed at the return of the British and re-recognition of himself as Sultan, that in my view, he will sign the new treaty. I suggest he be approached next after the Sultan of Johore. If he refuses to sign it is a matter for serious consideration whether it would be wise to negotiate with the late Sultan's second son, Tengku Panglima Besar, who was passed over by H.M.G. in favour of the third son, Tungku Alam Shah, the present legitimate Sultan.

There is no doubt that this action of H.M.G. was opposed by a large section of the Selangor Malays at that time, and the late Sultan resented H.M.G's action so much that he petitioned the Secretary of State for the Colonies and even went to England to interview him. His mission proved unsuccessful.

I must however mention that the second son Tengku Panglima Besar, has been largely under the influence of Tungku Musa-Addin and is somewhat stupid. In fact some people think that he is so stupid as to be incapable of directing the affairs of State. This opinion was expressed at a time before a new constitution was being considered and with the powers of Sultans considerably reduced under the new constitution this lack of intelligence is not such a material factor for the position of Sultan of Selangor.

If the legitimate Sultan does not sign—I think he will—Tengku Panglima Besar might well be persuaded to do so with the Sultanate as the prize. In such a case it would be essential to keep Musa-Addin permanently out of Malaya.

3. *Negri Sembilan*

In my view the Yam Tuan of Negri Sembilan should be approached next. In his present state of mind he is somewhat depressed and appears to me to be perplexed as to how his State can recover itself and would welcome directions rather than advice. Being a lawyer he will appreciate better than any other Sultan the reasons behind the new constitution and having done so I think he will sign the new treaty.

The constitution of Negri Sembilan is such that the approval of the Undang is necessary and not having talked to them I have no idea what their reaction will be to a new treaty.[14]

---

[14] Negri Sembilan was a confederation and, in addition to the agreement of the *Yam Tuan* (or ruler), that of the four *Undang* (or lawgivers) would also be required before any constitutional change could be made.

4. Pahang

If success is achieved with the Sultans of Johore and Selangor and also with the Yam Tuan of Negri Sembilan the Sultan of Pahang should be approached next.

He should not prove difficult if those three have signed. His eldest son Tungku Ahmed is only 16 years of age.

5. Perak

If all the above four mentioned have signed I do not see how the Sultan of Perak can refuse to sign.

After my interview with him which was most friendly and cordial—I know him personnaly [sic]—I came away with the impression in my mind that he might prove the most difficult of all. He is a deeply religious man and would weigh up more than any other Malay Ruler the effect the new treaty would have on the Perak Malays.

If he does not sign then the only course open is to deal in turn with the Raja Muda, a somewhat simple person, failing him with Raja Bendahara and finally with the Raja di-Hilir. This is the adat of Perak.[15]

6. Kedah

Once the Sultans of Johore, Selangor, Perak, Pahang and the Yam Tuan of Negri Sembilan have signed there will be no difficulty with the four northern States where there are no recognised Sultans due to all four having died during the Japanese occupation.

Tungku Badlishah, the Regent of Kedah would undoubtedly be swayed by the opinions of his State Council and he would be bound to consult it on account of a clause in the Kedah treaty. The most astute member of the State Council is Tuan Haji Sheriff, State Secretary, and once he has consented there should be no further difficulty. The Regent is a nervous and timid individual and left to himself would, in my view, readily sign. If Johore has signed Kedah will not hold out. He is the heir presumptive selected by the State Council in March, 1938, but on the British side the stipulation was made that His Majesty's acceptance must await the time of actual succession and that should Tungku Badlishah suffer or evince any disability or disqualification in the meantime, the choice would be [sic] in the interests of the people need to be referred back to the State Council for reconsideration.

Tungku Yacob is the most progressive of the Royal Family of Kedah but he was selected by the Japanese to go to Japan to learn their agricultural methods (he is Principal Agricultural Officer in Kedah) and was in Japan during the Japanese occupation of Malaya for a few weeks. I have not had the time to ascertain what the local reaction is to this.

7. Perlis

The heir apparent is Syed Putera who was chosen as such by the Perlis State Council in April, 1938. He is the son of Syed Hasan, half nephew of the late Raja. Syed Hasan died in 1935.

Syed Putera is only 25 years of age. He is of a pleasant disposition and very friendly disposed to the British. He has had a very hard time during the Japanese occupation

---

[15] The *adat* or custom of Perak was for the succession to rotate between three leading families. Raja Muda Yussof was the son of a former Sultan, Abdul Jalil, and came to the throne in 1948 on the death of Sultan Abdul Aziz. The Raja Bendahara and Raja di-Hilir were major chiefs.

and I have little doubt that he himself will sign a new treaty. As in the case of Kedah he is bound to refer the matter to the State Council. I met the loyal members of the State Council who had not been allowed to function during the Japanese occupation and they struck me as pleasant, easy persons who would not create difficulties.

8. *Trengganu*

In Trengganu the succession is from father to son. Sultan Suleiman died during the Japanese occupation leaving three sons:—

Raja Ali the eldest about 31 years.
Tungku Aziz about 25 years.
Tunku Abdul Rahman about 16 years.

On account of the conduct of Raja Ali during the Japanese occupation he cannot possibly become Sultan.

According to the adat the next in succession is the second son Tungku Aziz who appears to have behaved well during the Japanese occupation. There is no doubt however that many people in Trengganu would prefer to see Tungku Paduka, the late Sultan's younger brother, installed as Sultan. This would mean breaking the adat and before it is decided to do this the important local Malays would have to be consulted. To that end I advise that a preliminary discussion should take place with Dato Jaya who is very pro-British and much respected by the Trengganu Malays. If he agrees with the new constitution then I anticipate no difficulty in obtaining the signature of either Tungku Aziz or Tungku Paduka, whichever one is approached.

9. *Kelantan*

In Kelantan the next in succession to the Sultan, who died on the 20th June, 1944, is his brother Tungku Ibrahim, the Raja of Kelantan. He is a pleasant person with not much strength of character and should not prove difficult. I have little doubt he will sign. He is only too anxious to be properly confirmed as Sultan and to get his son confirmed as Raja Muda. They were both elevated to these respective positions after the death of the Sultan and in my view the Raja will sign anything to get both himself and his son firmly entrenched in those positions.

In Kelantan there is a school of younger Malays who are very progresssive in ideas and are pro-British. One of them is Tungku Mahyiddeen[16] who is a Major in Civil Affairs and is now stationed in Kota Baharu. He is the second son of the former Raja of Patani. In my view he would agree with the new constitution and would be a good propaganda agent in its favour if the Raja of Kelantan proved unexpectedly to be difficult.

10. I have been bold enough to hazard the above opinions because they may be of some assistance to Sir Harold MacMichael. I felt it is my duty to do so even though events may prove me to be 100% wrong. I await the result with great interest.

---

[16] Tengku Mahyiddeen, son of the last Raja of Patani (a Malay kingdom absorbed by Siam), had been director of education in Kelantan before the war. During the Japanese invasion he escaped to India and was engaged in propaganda work on behalf of the allies; in 1943 he wrote a memorandum favouring some kind of Malayan union and Malayan citizenship and British planners regarded him as 'an enlightened Malay'. He returned as a major in the BMA but was bitterly disappointed that the British did not take the opportunity of post-war reconstruction to wrest Patani from Thailand.

58   PREM 8/189   9 Oct 1945

'Political organisation in the South East Asia Command': memorandum by J C Sterndale Bennett

[Sterndale Bennett here takes up the problems of political and economic co-ordination which Dening had brought to the attention of Whitehall on the eve of the Japanese surrender (see 39–42).]

The difficulties which we are meeting in various parts of the South East Asia Command, e.g. Burma, Malaya, Siam, Indo China and the Netherlands East Indies raise once more the question whether South East Asia Command is at present adequately organised to deal with the various political and economic problems which are bound to arise in increasing degree now that fighting against the Japanese has ceased.

2.   Admiral Mountbatten is responsible for an immensely wide area. His Chief Political Adviser is a member of the Foreign Service, Mr. Dening. He is an expert on Japan and was primarily appointed to advise the Supreme Commander on questions arising out of the war against Japan. He had no authority to speak on behalf of other Government Departments such as the India Office, Burma Office or Colonial Office.

3.   No doubt Admiral Mountbatten now receives advice about individual British territories through the Civil Affairs Administration in these territories. The system of Foreign Office representation is also being extended by the attachment of Foreign Service officers to the Force Commanders in Siam, Indo-China and the Netherlands East Indies. Apart from Mr. Dening however Admiral Mountbatten has no civilian advisers for the area as a whole. Mr. Dening has created for himself a position of considerable influence and some independence. But though appointed by the Foreign Office and corresponding direct with the Foreign Office he is still technically a member of Admiral Mountbatten's staff and responsible to him.

4.   Mr. Dening himself when in this country in June last raised the question whether the situation in which he, as Chief Political Adviser, virtually served two masters should be allowed to continue.

5.   Just before the Japanese surrender the Foreign Office circulated Mr. Dening's memorandum to various Departments in London with two alternative suggestions:—

(a) to detach the office of Political Adviser from Admiral Mountbatten's staff, to make the Political Adviser responsible to London and to give him additional staff to enable him to advise the Supreme Commander not merely on questions of foreign affairs but on political, economic and financial matters generally.
(b) to appoint a Minister of State for South East Asia.

6.   I attach (a) a copy of Mr. Dening's memorandum, (b) a copy of the Foreign Office letter to the various Government Departments, and (c) a memorandum summarising the replies of the various Departments.[1] These replies show that, with the exception of the War Office who felt that action might be postponed until the situation was clearer and until it could be seen whether the various Departments in

---

[1] For (a) and (b) see 39 and 40; (c) is not printed.

London were in a position to resume direct control within their respective spheres, all the Departments favoured going at least as far as to make the Political Adviser directly responsible to London and not to Admiral Mountbatten.[2]

7. Apart from the various political questions now arising, Mr. Dening has separately drawn attention to the serious problems of supply which are going to arise in South East Asia Command and to the need of some better coordinating machinery.

8. There is a third point. Unless some action is taken soon the tendency will be for the various territories concerned to drop back into working in more or less water-tight compartments. The existence of South East Asia Command does provide an opportunity for working on a regional basis and perhaps for laying the foundation of some kind of regional organisation when the immediate military tasks of South East Asia Command are over.

9. It is not at all clear that the appointment of a Minister of State would be the ideal arrangement and it may be thought that such an appointment would be difficult to reconcile with the responsibilities of the Supreme Commander and of the Governments which will in due course take over from him the responsibility for the administration of the various territories.

10. But if the appointment of a Minister of State is either undesirable or not feasible it seems necessary to provide at South East Asia Command Headquarters a panel of experts on political, financial, economic and particularly supply questions who can coordinate the needs of the whole area. The relation of these various experts to the Supreme Allied Commander needs some consideration. It seems desirable that although nominally members of his staff they should have a responsibility towards their parent Departments in London and should be in direct correspondence with those Departments. It is perhaps desirable that there should be a Chief Adviser responsible to London.

11. It is suggested that this matter might be discussed generally in the first place by the Secretary of State with the Ministers concerned, namely the Secretary of State for the Colonies, the Secretary of State for Burma, the Secretary of State for India, the Secretary of State for the Dominions and the Secretary of State for War. It would then seem a suitable subject for full discussion at the Conference of Far Eastern Representatives which the Secretary of State [for foreign affairs] has in mind; and in the meantime Ministers may wish to refer it to the Far Eastern Offical Committee with the idea of working out some draft scheme for the consideration of the Conference.[3]

---

[2] For the CO response see 41 and 42.

[3] On 18 Oct a meeting of ministers, which was chaired by Attlee and attended by Morrison (lord president), Cripps (Board of Trade), Addison (Dominions), Pethick-Lawrence (India and Burma), Hall (Colonies), and officials (Sir E Bridges, Cabinet Office; Sir O Sargent, FO: J C Sterndale Bennett, FO; E A Armstrong, Cabinet Office), concluded that the appointment of an official of ambassadorial status directly responsible to the foreign secretary should be made a matter of 'the first urgency' for the co-ordination of both economic and political matters in the region. Sir H MacMichael was mentioned as 'a very suitable candidate' and Hall undertook to consider whether he could be released from his Malayan mission. By the end of Nov a draft directive on a 'Special Commissioner responsible to the foreign secretary in South East Asia' was approved; the final version was sent to Mountbatten in Feb (see 71) and Lord Killearn took up the appointment in Mar. See CAB 21/1954, GEN 97/1st meeting; PREM 8/189; and CO 273/677/3.

59   CO 273/675/19, no 1   22 Oct 1945

[MacMichael mission]: letter from Sir H MacMichael to Sir G Gater.
Enclosures: notes of interviews with His Highness the Sultan of Johore

[Following Willan's visits to the rulers (see 57), MacMichael, accompanied by Newboult
and Bourdillon, toured the Malay States, starting with Johore on 18 Oct and concluding
with Kelantan on 21 Dec. Only a selection of MacMichael's accounts of his meetings with
the rulers is printed here: Johore (59), Selangor (60) and Kedah (64). Ibrahim of Johore
was the senior sultan and one who had caused the British embarrassment in the past (see
57, note 13). It was felt, consequently, that once his agreement to a new treaty had been
secured, the other rulers would prove compliant. In his published account, MacMichael
admitted to running into a groundswell of Malay antagonism only in Negri Sembilan
(whose Yam Tuan belatedly tried to reopen the issue two weeks after signing, see CO
273/675/18) and Kedah (see 64).]

I am sending you herewith copies of the notes I made of the two interviews which I
had with the Sultan of Johore on 18th and 20th of October respectively. These notes
were made immediately on my return to Singapore from the Sultan's palace and, I
think, adequately reflect the uniformly friendly and frank atmosphere which
pervaded our conversations. I do not think they call for any further comment on my
part.

The Treaty was signed on 20th October at 4.25 p.m. in duplicate. One signed copy
is being locked up here pending your instructions: the other has been retained by the
Sultan.

The witnesses to the Sultan's signature were his third son Tungku Ahmed and his
Secretary Abdul Kadir. My own signature was witnessed by H.T. Bourdillon.

After the signature of the Treaty the Sultan produced a Memorandum enumerat-
ing various points to which he wished the attention of His Majesty's Government
particularly drawn. I have thought it right to send this Memorandum to you under
cover of a formal despatch because I gave the Sultan a formal promise that it should
be sent at once to the Secretary of State. I have sent a copy of it (and of the despatch)
to Hone as C.C.A.O. and he will no doubt furnish you with his detailed comments in
due course. Newboult is, in fact, preparing a note upon the various points raised and
sending it to Hone.

The dignity and courtesy with which the Sultan of Johore conducted our business
greatly impressed me: his "touch" was perfect and there was never a hitch (I may
mention that I have just written him a personal line of appreciation and thanks). I
only hope that the rest of the Rulers will prove equally amenable, but I am quite
prepared for some of them, perhaps lacking his experience and background, to be a
little tiresome.

I am not attempting to prepare any rigid programme of procedure for the future,
beyond having arranged to see the Sultan of Selangor at Klang tomorrow afternoon.
It seems to me that the essence of the stage-management (which is of considerable
importance to Sultans) is that I should feel my way along from day to day according
to varying circumstance and personality. For instance there is some trouble about
the Dato Mentri Jelebu in Negri Sembilan, which leads me to defer dealing with that
State until a later stage where otherwise I might have taken it sooner. Similarly there
is some doubt about the rightful successor in Trengganu, which may lead to delay. In
the other cases all appears at present to be reasonably plain sailing but I "touch
wood" as I write this.

Newboult and Bourdillon are living with me and in constant touch with me. Their assistance, in their different spheres, is being of the greatest value to me at every stage. Willan is also close at hand as a very valuable counsellor. Both SACSEA himself and General Dempsey have been most cooperative upon the few occasions when I have needed their assistance. General Dempsey moves up to Kuala Lumpur on 1st November and Hone (who is getting married on 25th October at Singapore) accompanies the party.

The most vivid impressions I have formed so far (apart from such points as the overwhelming greenery, the absence of wild-flowers, and the magnificience [sic] of the buildings and the roads) are the general atmosphere of toleration and amiability among the various "men in the street" of all races: they all seem to be bustling and meandering about together on their various businesses—though naturally there are some feuds and recriminations in the background which are apt upon occasion to come to the surface—and the overwhelming Chinese atmosphere of the townships through which one passes. So far I have been unable to bring myself to any understanding of why the present policy has not materialised long before now. Its rightness seems to me completely obvious, but I realise that I am hampered by ignorance of the conditions of the past. Anyhow, the way in which the new policy has been received seems to bear out the contention that there is nothing revolutionary in its concept. The numerous organs of the press have all given it a mention and had a leading article or two, but they are clearly more interested in the cost of living, the price of rubber, the merits and demerits of various groups of "collaborators", events in Java, etc. This is all very much to the advantage of my mission. The contrast to Palestine is quite remarkable!

With kindest regards to yourself and Gent.

Enclosure 1 to 59: note of first interview (4 pm, 18 Oct 1945)

As previously arranged through Colonel Hay, the Senior Civil Affairs Officer, I drove from Government House Singapore on the afternoon of the 18th of October, with an escort of Military Police provided by General Sir Miles Dempsey, General Officer Commanding in Chief Fourteenth Army, to see the Sultan of Johore at his palace at Pasir Pelangi. I was accompanied by Brigadier Newboult and Mr. Bourdillon.

His Highness and Lady Ibrahim, accompanied by Colonel Hay, met us on arrival and at once invited us to take tea with them. I was seated next to His Highness (who was obviously suffering from gout). The conversation, which was all in English, was animated and easy: for the most part it consisted of stories told by the Sultan of his experiences during the period of Japanese control, and it was quite evident that his rancour and detestation of these "sub-human creatures" was deep and had left a lasting mark on his mind.

The only approach to "shop" was an enquiry by the Sultan as to whether I had discussed business with the Rulers of Selangor and Negri Sembilan. I replied that I should not have thought of doing so until I had first conversed with himself.

After awile [sic] the Sultan asked me whether I should like to come and talk things over in the adjoining room. I welcomed the suggestion and Brigadier Newboult, Mr. Bourdillon and I moved with the Sultan from the drawing room to the dining room, where His Highness asked me to occupy the chair at the head of the table, himself sitting on my right.

I opened the proceedings at once by saying that His Highness might like me to recapitulate the general background and reasons for my visit to Malaya, although in fact these had been made very clear by the Secretary of State in his speech of 10th October.[1] In doing so, briefly, I took the opportunity to allude in passing to such points as that the policy represented the considered decision of His Majesty's Government, that it was directed to the welfare of the country, and that my own task was strictly limited to the congenial (and I hoped easy) task of obtaining the cooperation of the Rulers. I also explained quite frankly that, in order properly and efficiently to carry out the policy decided upon, His Majesty's Government needed powers of jurisdiction which at present they had not got, and that the Treaty, which was simply directed to the grant of that jurisdiction, would then be followed by the issue of an Order in Council ordaining such steps as His Majesty's Government deemed necessary for the purpose required.

His Highness said little at this stage and appeared to regard matters in general with a mixture of goodwill and philosophy, though he asked one or two questions to which he reverted later.

I then told him that I had got an explanatory note printed strictly for his personal and confidential information, which would acquaint him more fully and better with the details of the case, and asked if he would care to read it now. He agreed and Mr. Bourdillon handed him the document the text of which had been prepared for this purpose by the Colonial Office, together with the Malay translation of the same made in Kuala Lumpur. (I would add in parenthesis that these documents had been printed at very short notice and with really remarkable efficiency, together with the text of the Treaty all ready for signature, by the Government Printing Office at Kuala Lumpur before my departure for Singapore).

The Sultan then proceeded to read the English version—ignoring the Malay—slowly and with great care, and to ask periodic questions. His first remark, in fact before he had begun to read the documents, was an emphatic expression of opinion, surprising to those who knew him in pre-Japanese days, that the real essential requisite was that there should be a British official at the head of every department to ensure that it was properly conducted: he had, he stated, lost all faith in the Malay and only knew about five men in his State whom he could trust.

Other points to which he made early reference were:—

(a) the position as regards the earlier Treaties (I referred him to clause 2 of the new Treaty,[2] and explained its meaning);
(b) the question of the postage stamps to be used (I told him that as far as I knew nothing had been settled, but that I thought that the old distinction between State

---

[1] See written answer, *H of C Debs*, vol 414, cols 255–256, 10 Oct 1945.
[2] Each treaty MacMichael concluded with the rulers contained two key clauses. In Johore's case they read as follows: '(1) His Highness the Sultan agrees that his Majesty shall have full power and jurisdiction within the State and territory of Johore. (2) Save in so far as the subsisting agreements are inconsistent with this Agreement or with such future constitutional arrangements for Malaya as may be approved by His Majesty, the said agreements shall remain in full force and effect.' Ibrahim had signed a treaty with Britain in 1914 agreeing to the appointment of a general adviser; an exchange of letters at the same time had safeguarded certain features of Johore's 'special status'. MacMichael's *Report on a Mission to Malaya* contains the explanatory note issued to the rulers (appendix 1) and the text of each agreement (appendix 2). The explanatory note was a considerably revised version of 56, Annex I.

and State would be maintained in the designs with something added to denote unity);

(c) the question of police badges (I said that I could not answer this: it was a matter for discussion and decision at a later stage).

The Sultan the passed to the financial position of Johore under the new system, and expatiated in some detail upon the theme of its solvency and surpluses as compared with some of the other States. Was Johore expected to finance these less fortunate States? (I explained that it was essential to the whole conception now envisaged that the rich should assist the poor in a reasonable measure and that I did not think Johore would suffer to any serious extent having regard to the benefit accruing to the whole, but that this, and indeed most of the problems arising, would have to be the subject of full consideration by the Governor and his Councils after the return to Civil Administration).

The Sultan appeared to find a little difficulty in disentangling the various Councils proposed but his most pressing query related to the provision made for proper representation of Chinese and Indian opinion. He had, he said, always had an Executive Council of his own,[3] upon which these parties were fully represented, and it was not very clear to him in what form and by what means this healthy manifestation was to continue. He dilated at some length, in this connection, upon the nationalist aspirations of the Chinese and the farsighted and ambitious policy of their rulers in China in respect of Indonesia in general, and he referred to the need for a statesmanlike provision of means whereby there could be some outlet for any grievances they felt or views they wished to express. It seemed to me that his views on this matter were well-considered and genuine, but their expression may, presumably, have been to some extent influenced by a desire to find out to what extent non-Malays in Johore would continue to be subject to his control.

In conclusion His Highness said he would like to study the papers further, and enquired as to the next move to be taken. I said that I had ventured to hope that when he had had a day or two in which to study the documents, he would feel able to sign the Treaty giving His Majesty's Government jurisdiction. His Highness nodded and said that he would like to prepare a memorandum expressing his views on the various points raised. I welcomed this suggestion cordially but added that I sincerely trusted that he would not think it necessary to put those views in the form of conditions. He categorically disclaimed any such intention, using the words—which he applied equally, by a wave of the hand, to treaty and explanatory note alike—"these are all right by me".

It was finally agreed that we should come and have tea again with him on Saturday the 20th October, by which time he hoped to have completed his memorandum and be ready to sign the Treaty. I gave him full assurance that all the points he cared to raise would receive the fullest consideration from His Majesty's Government—to whom I would at once refer them—and we parted on very cordial terms after an interview which had been marked at every stage by great dignity, courtesy and reasonableness on the part of His Highness. I reported the result very briefly to Sir G. Gater by telegram on my return to Singapore (See telegram No. 117 of the 18th

---

[3] The Johore Constitution of 1895, promulgated by Ibrahim's father (Sultan Abu Bakar), provided for a Council of Ministers and a Council of State.

October from South East Asia Command.), repeating the telegram to the Supreme Allied Commander for his information at the same time.

Enclosure 2 to 59: note of second interview (4 pm, 20 Oct 1945)

As arranged at our first interview on the 18th October, Brigadier Newboult, Mr. Bourdillon and I, excorted [sic] as before, visited the Sultan at 4 p.m. on the 20th October at his palace at Pasir Pelangi. His Highness and Lady Ibrahim met us with great cordiality on the porch, and after introducing his third son Tungku Ahmad and explaining that his eldest son, Tungku Makhota, was ill, His Highness took us into the drawing room. His first question was whether we would like to clear off business first and then have tea, or vice versa. Lady Ibrahim pleaded for the latter, and I supported her contention.

After tea we adjourned, as before, to the dining room, where the Sultan produced the Secretary who, with his son, was to witness the documents, and the great seal of Johore, and Mr. Bourdillon produced the documents for signature. These formalities had been very satisfactorily settled beforehand with the Sultan by Brigadier Newboult, who called upon him for this purpose on the 19th October. There was no hitch or awkwardness at any stage and we signed forthwith without formality or discussion and with a running commentary of an almost convivial nature. At the close the Sultan heaved a sigh of relief and I said "praise God" in Arabic, to which His Highness replied in kind. I should add that I told the Sultan that I did not intend to mention that the Treaty had been signed until the Secretary of State had announced the fact, and hoped he would follow suit. He at once agreed.

It was only then that His Highness produced his promised Memorandum containing suggestions for the future dispensation of things in Johore.[4] He did so with an almost deprecatory air, remarking that I must take the Memorandum for what it was worth, and that if I saw fit I could throw it in the waste paper basket. I replied that I would not dream of such a thing; I would make it my personal care to forward the Memorandum to the Secretary of State with all speed.

I then expressed the fervent hope that we might meet in England, mentioning that General Hone had told me at lunch-time that he had wired the Supreme Allied Commander, South East Asia, urgently requesting provision of passages for His Highness and Lady Ibrahim. I also asked the Sultan to grant me the personal favour of a signed photograph. He was pleased at this and gave me three (two of himself in different uniforms and one of Lady Ibrahim): he also gave each of the other members of the party three other photographs. We then parted with many protestations of friendship—which were as sincere on my part as, I firmly believe, they were on that of His Highness.

I reported the result to the Secretary of State at once on my return to Government House Singapore by telegram No. 142 from South East Asia Command Headquarters Camp, copies of which have been transmitted to the Supreme Allied Commander and General Dempsey (General Officer Commanding in Chief, Fourteenth Army).

---

[4] Ibrahim's memorandum contained three categories of points: (1) those relating to the Sultan's personal prestige over which the CO was prepared to make concessions; (2) those reaffirming the pre-war position of Johore which the CO could not allow; and (3) miscellaneous matters which, in the CO view, did not require answers. See CO 717/148, no 52038 for 1945 and 1946.

60   CO 273/675/18, no 5A   25 Oct 1945

[MacMichael mission]: letter from Sir H MacMichael to Sir G Gater on his interview with the Sultan of Selangor

I send you herewith, in confirmation of my letter of 22nd October[1] forwarding the notes of my interviews with the Sultan of Johore, a similar set of notes regarding Selangor.[2] The Treaty with the Sultan was signed at 12.15 on 24th of October at Klang in an atmosphere of great friendliness.

The Sultan of Selangor, whose age is apparently in the early forties, struck me as a simple-minded little man with an excitable temperament. One might be tempted to dismiss him as a nonentity, but from this criticism I fancy he is saved by his very deep devotion to religion. I can imagine his becoming a religious recluse, or an ardent fanatic, but I do not see him consenting with cynical resignation to any measure which he regarded as derogatory to his faith. His fussy nervousness cannot commend itself to the philosophic dignity of the East, but his obvious sincerity would always carry some counterweight in the eyes of his people. I should not judge him acute or particularly able, but here again sincerity and common sense leave him in credit on the balance.

I am, of course, sending a copy of the notes of my interview to Hone. The Sultan's points appear to me very well taken and full of substance. It is worth remarking that he never once mentioned finance (except once, in passing reference to tithes), and neither he nor the Sultan of Johore raised any difficulty about the omission of "adat": in fact it is quite obvious that, as I anticipated, they regard it as covered by the phrase "matters relating to religion."[3]

---

[1] See 59.   [2] Not printed.

[3] Replying on 17 Nov, Gater wrote:—

'Once again I would like to express my very warm admiration of your skilful handling of the Sultan. It seems to me to have been a well-conceived operation carried out with perfect taste, and to have secured all our objectives.

I greatly enjoyed reading your fascinating description of the scene on both occasions. I am submitting the papers to the Secretary of State who, I know, will read them with great delight.

I send you all good wishes for equal successes in the remaining negotiations. While I do not want to hurry you, from our point of view here the sooner they can be completed the better' (CO 273/675/18).

61   CO 273/675/5, no 4   31 Oct 1945

[Post-war rehabilitation]: British Military Administration, Malaya, fortnightly report no 4, for the period ending 31 Oct   [Extract]

General.—The rate of progress in general rehabilitation is so accelerated that a great strain has been put on the available staff during this period. Though the machinery of the Administration has now settled down to efficient working, the volume of work and the variety of problems have made the tasks of the Administration very difficult.

The first excitement and relief consequent upon the surrender of the Japanese Forces having evaporated, the bulk of the people find that their lot has not yet materially improved as an immediate result of victory. Prices are high, foodstuffs (particularly rice) are scarce, wages have been re-established in terms of British dollars at pre-invasion levels, profiteering is occurring, there are few piece-goods and cigarettes, and unemployment exists on a considerable scale. Conditions of peace, a sympathetic Government and charitable relief alone do not satisfy the desires of the people which demand, on the economic side, an immediate return to pre-war prosperity. Stories of the sufferings of other countries, of the general world shortages of all essential commodities and of shipping and other difficulties provide very small consolation to five and a half million people who have already suffered enough under the Japanese. The man in the street most requires regular work, sufficient wages and enough to buy at reasonable prices. It is clear that these desiderata cannot be achieved over-night but there is bewilderment because of the apparently slow progress towards normal conditions. There is uncertainty, too, as to the future course of events. Is there going to be enough rice for the next month's ration; are wages going up or prices coming down?

This state of anxiety in the minds of the people provides a fertile field for the agitator and the extremist and they have not been slow to try to exploit their opportunity; they do this covertly but none the less with determination. Consequently there have been sporadic occurrences of labour stoppages, strikes, political meetings, demonstrations and minor disturbances during the past fortnight in various parts of the territory. All have petered out before assuming serious proportions but they are indicative of the general feeling of uncertainty and bewilderment which exists. Though the B.M.A. by press statements and other forms of publicity has endeavoured to counter this state of affairs, the fact must be faced that the population is involved in a tiresome struggle to return to normal times when the world is still in a state of upheaval even though it is now at peace.

Certain sections of Malays and Chinese have become, as a result of Japanese occupation, increasingly politically conscious and articulate, and now that they are permitted to organise themselves and to express their feelings freely, wild talk and over-statements, some of a seditious nature, are apt to be indulged in on the Chinese side. Many of the youths of the country have been imbued with Communist sentiments, though with very little knowledge of the exact tenets of Communism. These young Chinese were a thorn in the side of the Japanese particularly during the latter part of the enemy occupation of Malaya, either as party agitators or active guerillas. They organised themselves into local Committees and societies and many are still armed and most are arrogant. They resort to the intimidation of others (including those of their own race) and by a show of force and threats extort rice and money in local areas where police or troops are thin on the ground.

Despite these disturbing factors it is clear that the articulate agitators have no real following though many people are nervous of their activities. However it is clear for all to see that the country is making remarkable progress and the power of the Administration for good is rapidly making itself felt. Wherever the Administration is firmly established, lawlessness is speadily diminishing and the lot of the people improving. But it is against a background of considerable uncertainty and disquietude, due entirely to adverse economic factors, that the following report must be viewed. . . .

62   WO 203/5642, no 74/16/45   8 Nov 1945

'Heads of agreement between Colonial Office and War Office': CO note on the steps required to facilitate the transition from military to civil administration in Malaya, Borneo, and Hong Kong

1. The Colonial Office will endeavour as early as possible to resolve the constitutional problems in Malaya and Borneo.

2. It is recognized that the continuation of the military administration in any of these territories would have to be justified by circumstances in the territory which might necessitate its continuance.

3. The Colonial Office will appoint Civil Governors and have them briefed and ready for consultation in good time before the target dates mentioned in paragraph 10 below. It would be desirable that they should be available for consultation in London at least two months before these dates.

4. The War Office will endeavour to build up the Military Administration of the territories as envisaged by approved War Establishments as far as possible with personnel acceptable to the Colonial Office and suitable to continue serving under the Civil Administration when set up. It is agreed that the Colonial Office will endeavour to accelerate recruiting for all those territories on a civilian basis and should endeavour progressively to build up the civilian personnel as far as possible to the full complement required for the Civil Administration. The War Office agrees that all the personnel recruited by the Colonial Office for the eventual Civil Administration can be attached to and commence work under the Military Administration pending the transfer to Civil Administration.

5. The Colonial Office agrees to press on with the creation of the necessary machinery of civil government and to prepare the necessary legislation required to give effect to any constitutional changes which His Majesty's Government may decide to effect.

6. The War Office and Colonial Office agree to press on with detailed arrangements whereby suitable military officers serving with the Military Administration can be released or otherwise made available for service under the eventual Civil Administration: and whereby civil officers can be appointed to and absorbed in the Military Administration pending the transfer to Civil Administration.

7. The Colonial Office and War Office will do their utmost to carry out their existing undertakings in regard to the procurement and delivery of supplies. The War Office will also facilitate the introduction and distribution, during the military period, of supplies and stores beyond the "disease and unrest" standard.

8. *Borneo.* The War Office will initiate discussion with G.H.Q. for the handing over of the Australian Military Administration in Borneo by the B.B.C.A.U. (responsible to the Australian Commander) to a British Military Administration by No. 50 C.A.U. (responsible to His Majesty's Government through the War Office) keeping SACSEA and the Colonial Office informed.

9. *Meetings.* It is agreed that representatives of the War Office and Colonial Office will continue to meet every fortnight to report progress and consider outstanding difficulties.

10. *Target dates.* It is agreed that for the purposes of planning and without prejudice to the eventual transfer dates which must be subject to military require-

ments, the local situation and recommendation by Theatre Commanders and civil arrangements, the War Office and Colonial Office should endeavour to work to the following target dates for the transfer:—

Malaya	1st March, 1946[1]
Singapore	1st March, 1946
Borneo	1st March, 1946
Hong Kong	1st February, 1946

---

[1] The resumption of civil government was later postponed from 1 Mar to 1 Apr, see 70.

63   CO 273/675/7   16 Nov 1945

[Reactions of Rubber Growers' Association to British plans for Malaya]: minute by J J Paskin to Sir G Gater about a meeting with T B Barlow[1]

I had a visit on Wednesday from Mr. Barlow, the Chairman of the Rubber Growers' Association, to talk about the announcement about the new constitutional arrangements proposed for Malaya.

He said that Sir Frank Swettenham,[2] at a recent meeting of the R.G.A., had expressed great concern about these proposals and had urged that they should be fought not only on the grounds that they constituted a breach of faith with Malaya and were intrinsically bad, but also on the ground that, from the point of view of bodies like the R.G.A. they were "bad business" since they would be bound to give rise to unrest in the country, and that this would be bad for business. Mr. Barlow, speaking for himself and not merely echoing the views of Sir Frank Swettenham, thought that the proposals would be very unpalatable indeed to the Malays, that therefore the old friendly atmosphere in Malaya would be destroyed, and that on these grounds it would be very much more difficult than in the past to carry on such industries as rubber planting.

I assured Mr. Barlow that so far as our information went the proposals have *not* met with the adverse reception in Malaya which he feared. Mr. Barlow thought this might perhaps be the case amongst the "high" circles with which Sir Harold MacMichael had mixed, but what about the generality of the population? I replied that we had had reports not only from Sir Harold MacMichael but also from the Military Administration whose officers were in touch with the general population.

As regards the suggestion that, by displeasing the *Malays* we should be creating a bad atmosphere for the conduct of business in Malaya, I reminded Mr. Barlow that there were other races in Malaya and that the rubber industry in particular depended largely on Indian labour and that the attitude of the Government of India had been adverse to the recruitment of Indian labour unless Indians were given equality of political rights in Malaya, which would in fact be achieved under this statement of

---

[1] Thomas Bradwell Barlow, chairman of the Rubber Growers' Association in 1945–1946.
[2] Sir Frank Swettenham (1850–1946); served in Malaya 1870–1904; resident general Federated Malay States, 1896–1904; governor and high commissioner 1901–1904; during his retirement he joined the boards of a number of rubber companies.

policy. Mr. Barlow was not very much impressed by this. He thought if we could have brought ourselves to hold out a threat to the Government of India that, unless they were co-operative, Indian labour would be replaced by Javanese, they would have come to heel. I contented myself with saying that this problem was not quite so simple as that.

As regards the general idea underlying the statement of policy, I reminded Mr. Barlow that all the political parties are committed to the advancement of dependent territories, such as Malaya, towards self-government and that it seemed clear that this goal could never be reached by Malaya unless it could be unified and unless the people of that country, of all races, could be brought to a sense of common citizenship and loyalty to Malaya as a country. I gathered the impression that Mr. Barlow was not himself a devotee of the ideal of self-government for dependent peoples.

Mr. Barlow then reverted to the theme that, before coming out with a strong positive statement of policy H.M.G. should have set in motion machinery for ascertaining the wishes of the local inhabitants; and in this connection he again mentioned the old "pledges" which had been given in the past. As to these pledges I reminded him that times and circumstances have changed and that after full consideration of what had happened in the past, H.M.G. had come to the conclusion that the declared policy was not only an enlightened one and offered virtually the only means by which Malaya could achieve political progress, but also that it would be recognised to be so by the inhabitants of the country.

As regards the form of the announcement, Mr. Barlow said that he would have had less quarrel with it if it had started off by saying that Sir Harold MacMichael was to be sent out to explore the ground with a view to securing the agreement of the local populations to the declared policy. To this I replied that the whole matter had been most carefully considered and that the conclusion had been reached that a statement on the lines of that issued provided the best atmosphere for Sir Harold MacMichael's mission.

I do not think I am able to flatter myself that Mr. Barlow was convinced that we have set about this matter in the right way, but at least he was good enough to recognise that the matter had received the fullest consideration and that all conflicting points of view had been taken fully into account before the policy was decided upon.

64 CO 537/1541, no 18   30 Nov – 3 Dec 1945

[MacMichael mission]: notes by Sir H MacMichael on interviews with the regent (later sultan) of Kedah

[Having obtained the signatures of the rulers of Johore, Selangor, Pahang, Negri Sembilan and Perak, MacMichael turned to the four northern states where the incumbents, who had succeeded during the Japanese occupation, yet lacked British 'recognition'. After Kedah, he went to Perlis, Kelantan and Trengganu in turn. In his letter of 8 Dec accompanying these notes, MacMichael told how Kedah 'gave considerable difficulty' and that 'the Regent (now Sultan) was obviously moved to the very depths of his rather shallow being by what he seemed to regard as the surrender of proud independence to a state of ignominious subjection.' MacMichael described Badlishah as being 'of the small shy and retiring "failed B.A." type, unstable and inclined to be introspective and lonely. At times he presented rather a pathetic figure.' Be that as it may, on 29 Jan Badlishah despatched a cablegram of protest to the secretary of state and followed this up with a long letter on 11 Feb (see CO 537/1555, no 19). He also wrote to former Malayan civil servants in Britain such as Sir Richard Winstedt (see 73, note 1) and a letter of protest from the sultan was read out in the House of Commons by Leonard Gammans (see *ibid*) during the debate on 8 Mar, see *H of C Debs*, vol 420, col 659. On the death of Badlishah in July 1958, the then secretary of state (Lennox-Boyd), minuted: 'I think the Sultan of Kedah (for whom I had great respect as a hard working & honourable Ruler) was quite right in being wholly opposed to the MacMichael proposals. This makes me even more anxious to say I'm sorry he's dead.' See CO 1030/766.]

Note of first interview (4 pm, 29 November 1945)

It is only a few minutes' drive from the house where the Senior Civil Affairs Officer (Colonel Day) resides to the Regent's Palace outside Alor Star. My party arrived by appointment at 4 o'clock preceded by Colonel Day, who was on the steps with His Highness to greet me. (It had originally been intended and arranged that the Regent, still not having been recognised as Sultan, should come and see me at the Residency, but I altered the arrangement, with the full agreement of Brigadier Newboult and Colonel Day, by telephone before leaving Taiping, on the grounds that the cause of courtesy was better served by my calling on one whose status as Regent was accepted).

After introductions we went upstairs to a large, comfortable drawing room, where we had some preliminary conversation on general subjects.

The Regent is a small man, stockily built, and his figure hardly permits him any great natural dignity, but he impressed me as a man of sense and honesty, courteous and friendly, and possessed of considerable self-assurance. The conversation was mostly about the Mohammedan religion and the Arab world, and he discussed these subjects with lively interest and good judgement.

After some twenty minutes we went downstairs to tea, and thereafter, on the initiative of His Highness, returned to the drawing room for our discussion. I was accompanied, as usual, by Brigadier Newboult and Mr Bourdillon, and also by Colonel Day, whose long personal friendship with the Regent made his presence particularly valuable.

I began, with the Regent's concurrence, by explaining the reasons for my visit and by outlining the policy upon which His Majesty's Government had decided. My remarks followed the general lines which I had pursued on previous occasions in other States, save in two respects, in which the position in Kedah warranted some variation. First, I pointed out that in addition to my task of seeking his co-operation in the new policy (at this point I named in confidence the five Rulers who had already signed fresh Treaties), I had been granted discretion by His Majesty's Government in the matter of recognising him as Sultan of Kedah, his appointment to that office having taken place during the Japanese occupation. I expressed the hope that this would present no difficulty. Secondly, having been informed that opposition in Kedah, which in the past has prided itself on its separatist tendencies, might be directed against the proposal for Union rather than against that for common citizenship, I dealt with the latter point first and then devoted special emphasis to the former, making no bones of the fact that its implementation would of course call for a departure from the existing Treaty.

My explanations concluded, I handed the Regent a copy of the new Treaty and of the Explanatory Note.[1] He read both very carefully and without comment and I then said that I hoped he found nothing unpalatable in them. He replied that they were "very devastating", and subsequent discussion revealed his reasons for so describing them. The point which disquieted him most, and to which he constantly returned, was the surrender of power by the Rulers. The previous position, he said, was being suddenly reversed. Hitherto the British Advisers or Residents, under the authority of the High Commissioner, had advised the Rulers. Henceforward it would be the Rulers who would advise the Resident Commissioners and the Governor, who need not take their advice; and moreover, even with this diminished status, the scope of the Rulers would apparently be restricted to religious matters. I contested this interpretation, and pointed out that on the contrary the field of the Rulers' influence would be greatly increased by their membership of the Governor's Advisory Council, which would discuss many matters of pan-Malayan importance and would by no means confine itself to religious questions. It was true that the final executive power would pass into the hands of the Governor, but this was no more than a *de jure* recognition of an already existing state of affairs. It was idle to deny that the Governor had previously exercised the real power, in that the Rulers had been bound to accept the advice of the Residents (or Advisers) and it was only right that the power and the overt responsibility should be in the same hands. His Highness demurred to the suggestion that the Rulers had always been bound to accept the advice of the Residents and referred to the right of appeal, under the existing Treaty,[2] to the High Commissioner or the Secretary of State. I responded that in future not only would this right be preserved but contact with the Governor would be greatly strengthened through the medium of the Governor's Advisory Council of Rulers. I went on to say that, if I might presume to offer His Highness a word of advice, I thought he had a great opportunity which it would be very foolish to miss. It was fortunate that His Majesty's Government had not concluded—as would have been consonant with modern conceptions of democratic government—that the Sultanates were altogether out of date. They had not done so. They had realised that the Rulers were a loyal body of men whose service to the country, and particularly in support of their own comparatively backward Malays, could be invaluable; but were the policy to be modified, the change would not be in the direction of greater power for the Rulers.

In spite of all reasoning, it was evident that the Regent, naturally jealous of his personal prestige, could not readily accommodate himself to the surrender of nominal power. His line of thought, as was to be expected, was fortified by arguments about the independent status of the Unfederated Malay States in general and Kedah in particular. Thus he persisted in comparing the Governor's Advisory Council to the Durbars of the past, for which he evinced no particular affection and which, he said, had rarely been attended by the Rulers of the Unfederated States. He also drew a sharp distinction between these Rulers and those of the Federated States, saying that the former had not, like the latter, handed over their executive authority to the Residents. And when, at an early stage in the conversation, he remarked that Malaya would now be "just like a Colony", (to which I replied that he could surely not find fault with the forms of Colonial Administration, since the whole purpose of the

---

[1] See 59, note 2.   [2] ie clause 5 of Kedah's 1923 treaty with the British.

changes was to make Malaya fit for self-government) it was plain that he was picturing a loss of autonomy not for Malaya as a whole but for the State of Kedah.

Brigadier Newboult asked him what alternative he could envisage to a Malayan Union. Kedah could not progress—could not even survive—as an isolated enclave. I endorsed this view, remarking with a smile that His Highness was perhaps thinking of the alternative of returning to Siamese control.[3] Luckily, I added, Malaya was a rich country, with a great future if only she could unite. I went on to say that, had His Highness's qualms been well-founded, they would surely have been voiced by the Sultan of Johore. When the Regent objected that he was not bound to follow Johore's example, I answered that I had not intended to suggest such a thing. I had merely pointed out that if the degradation of the Rulers' status were in fact implied in the new policy, it was most unlikely that the Sultan of Johore should have failed to notice the fact and raise strong objections.

The above paragraphs summarise the main part of our discussion. There was one brief reference to citizenship, when His Highness expressed the usual fears about Chinese immigration. I said that future immigration would be controlled in accordance with the economic needs of the country, and added that the citizenship proposals would safeguard the effective Malay majority.

Finally, the Regent said that he would consult the members of his State Council (whose assent is necessary under the existing Treaty).[4] I welcomed this proposal, and suggested for his consideration that Colonel Day's assistance in explaining matters to the members of the Council might be of value to him. It was agreed that this point should be left over, as would the date and time of my next visit, for subsequent arrangement by telephone.

The friendly way in which His Highness, at the end of the proceedings, led me to an inner room and showed me the lavish wedding regalia of the Kedah Ruling House, indicated that he did not allow his feelings on the subject-matter of our conversation to affect his personal courtesy. But of the strength of his feelings there can be no doubt. Colonel Day remained behind for a few minutes after I had left, and the Regent again expressed to him the sense of shock which he had sustained, adding that although the manner was much more polite, the technique adopted by His Majesty's Government appeared to be not unlike the familiar Japanese technique of bullying.

Note of second interview (4.30 pm, 2 December 1945)

Foreword. The whole of November 30th, December 1st and most of December 2nd was devoted, so far as can be judged, by the State Council (and maybe the Regent) to an elaborate series of manoeuvres, intrigues and procrastinations. The dominant motive on the part of all alike was unquestionably a deep reluctance to agree to any course which would result in any diminution of the degree of independance [sic] exercised by Kedah in the past both under British rule before the Japanese conquest and under the purely nominal rule of Siam between 1942 [1943] and 1945. The difficulty, equally obvious to all, was to visualise any alternative to acceptance of the

---

[3] Kedah, having been transferrred from Siamese to British suzerainty in 1909, was handed back to Siam by the Japanese in Oct 1943. Thai occupation had not been a happy experience for the Kedah royal family.
[4] ie clause 3 of the 1923 treaty.

new policy short of a flat refusal of which one consequence would clearly be the non-recognition of the Regent as Sultan.

Efforts to evade the issue and assert self-importance almost to the point of discourtesy took many forms:—Friday (November 30th) was unsuited to the discussion of business; Saturday morning (justifiably in this case) necessitated the presence of some of the Council at the farewell ceremony in honour of the A.J.A. (Anti-Japanese Army); Saturday afternoon was devoted to preliminary discussions between the Regent and his Council, but no attempt was made to avail themselves of the services of Brigadier Newboult or Colonel Day though these were offered; telephonic enquiries as to progress addressed to Haji Sheriff, the State Secretary (who seems to have been the real protagonist of obstruction) elicited replies suggesting that though he, Haji Sheriff, was working hard for the cause of reason, the Regent felt very deeply on the whole subject; a visit by Colonel Day to the Regent left the impression that while His Highness was prepared to sign, the State Council felt grave difficulties; no fixed time could be given by which any meeting was likely to be over; all attempted arrangements were obscured by a cloud of hopes and probabilities unlighted by any ray of certainty about anything. The final effort at evasion (mid-day December 2nd), when Colonel Day again visited the Regent while his Council was with him, consisted in the production of doubts, juridical in basis, (a) as to whether the State Council could be said to be properly constituted when there was no British Adviser, (b) as to whether there could be a Regent when there was no Sultan. The latter point was not difficult to answer, and the first was adequately met by the terms of the Interpretations Proclamation (No. 4 of September 22nd, 1945) which makes it clear that a Senior Civil Affairs Officer is empowered to exercise the functions of an Adviser (among which is membership of the State Council). This last hurdle cleared and the Regent and Council having assured Colonel Day that they would sign since they saw no alternative open, I was prepared to go at once and clinch matters (1.30 p.m.), but was met by a suggestion, transmitted by Colonel Day on the telephone, that signature should be deferred till tomorrow. This, in the absence of any perceptible cause for delay, I declined on the ground of other engagements. By way of counter I was told His Highness had not yet eaten anything today and hoped I would not come before 4.30. To this I at once agreed on the understanding that there would be no further hitch in the proceedings.

At 4.30 I arrived with my party at the Palace. As before, Colonel Day had preceded me and was at the entrance with His Highness when I drove up. They were accompanied by Haji Mohamed Sheriff, Tunku Yaacob and Che Kassim, the members of the Kedah State Council, to whom I was introduced. Tunku Yaacob is the full brother of His Highness and the Principal Agricultural Officer of the State. Haji Sheriff holds the office of Secretary of Government, and Che Kassim that of Under-Secretary.

Thereupon we proceeded upstairs to the scene of our previous conversation, and seated ourselves at the round table. I began by outlining, as I saw it, the programme before us. I observed that under Clause 3 of the existing Treaty the written consent of the State Council was required before the new Treaty could be signed, and added that I had already caused a draft Council Minute to be prepared, which the members of the Council, if they concurred in its terms, could sign forthwith. (In fact the terms of the draft were already known to the Regent and the Council members, having been shown to them by Colonel Day the same morning).

The next step which I envisaged was my formal recognition of His Highness as Sultan (on his assurance that he was prepared to sign the Treaty), and thereafter the signature of the Treaty could take place.

No sooner had I finished than His Highness pointed out that the Adviser was a member of the State Council, and questioned the validity of a Council Minute to which the Adviser, not being in existence, could not subscribe. The re-emergence of this juridical objection, which had already once been settled, necessitated my actually showing His Highness a copy of the Interpretations Proclamation which confers on the Senior Civil Affairs Officer all the powers and functions of the Adviser. The text of the document satisfied the Regent, and Haji Sheriff remarked in extenuation that His Highness had not previously seen it.

Next it emerged that the Sultan of Kedah is President of the State Council, and it was represented that the recognition of His Highness must therefore take place before the State Council could be properly constituted and could conduct business. I replied that I saw no objection to this, and proceeded at once to ask the members of the Council whether they were ready to sign the Minute, and His Highness whether he was ready to sign the Treaty. To both questions the answer was in the affirmative, though Tunku Yaacob said that he gave his consent "because there was no alternative".

I then rose to my feet, the rest of the company following suit, and announced that I had much pleasure in formally recognising His Highness on behalf of His Majesty's Government as Sultan of the State of Kedah. I added my good wishes for himself and his State. His Highness bowed, and we sat down again. The question next arose whether the Sultan himself as President of the Council, should sign the Minute, but it was concluded that this was unnecessary, since his signature of the Treaty itself would constitute his written assent. The Minute was thereupon signed in duplicate by the other members of the Council, including Colonel Day. One signed copy has been retained by the Sultan and the other by myself, pending the Secretary of State's directions. A third copy is attached to this record as an Appendix.[5]

I now asked Mr Bourdillon to produce the Treaty itself for signature, but at this point the Sultan said he would like to say a few words. He then delivered, standing, a short speech which he had obviously prepared with the minutest care and memorised. He said that this was the most distressing and painful moment of his whole life. Henceforward he would lose the loyalty, the respect and the affection of his subjects, and he would be pursued with curses towards his grave by the ill-informed. He called upon Allah to witness his act and to protect him for the future. He would sign because no other course was open.

I felt that I could not let the proceedings terminate on this note, so as soon as the Sultan had sat down I rose to my feet for the second time and replied, beginning with an expression of my deep regret that he had felt bound to take so pessimistic a view. He had referred to the curses of the ill-informed. Surely he would be unwise to pay attention to these. Nobody could prevent fools from talking; they would do so until the end of the world. What was infinitely more important was that the well-informed, those who knew and understood the facts, would appreciate that what had been done

---

[5] Not printed.

was—as I myself was entirely convinced—for the benefit and prosperity not only of Kedah, but of Malaya as a whole. It was a thousand pities, I continued, that he had forced me to report the expression of his reluctance to the Secretary of State, as I must now do. His Majesty's Government had asked for His Highness's co-operation, and it would have been much better had he trusted their assurances that they would maintain his prestige and continue to protect his people. However, I appreciated his feelings and would faithfully report them, in accordance with my duty.

The Treaty was then signed at 5.10 p.m. (Tunku Yaacob and Haji Sheriff witnessing His Highness's signature and Mr Bourdillon my own), and after we had partaken of tea downstairs I took my departure. The one relieving feature of an unhappy episode was the fact that the Sultan, during tea, emerged from his gloom and spoke with cheerful animation, and without a vestige of personal rancour towards myself, of his experiences under the Japanese. Before leaving I again expressed to him my good wishes, and asked if I might call on him again before I left the neighbourhood to say farewell. He bowed in acknowledgement and said that in any case he hoped I would have a pleasant journey home.

65 WO 203/5302 3 Dec 1945
'Malaya's political climate', IV for 10–30 Nov: report by V W W S Purcell from Singapore [Extract]

. . . It cannot be disguised that the Forces in Malaya are at present very unpopular with the people. The latter welcomed them at the beginning but the early goodwill has largely passed and there is a growing resentment. This is reflected in the current rumours and comment, in allusions in the Press (e.g. a skit in which sailors go away without paying) and some of them are no less damaging because they are witty (Asiatic wit, of course, being understood). The criticism differs with the various classes of Asiatics, but in Singapore the rudeness and the high-handedness of some officers, the careless way in which vehicles are often driven, and the ill discipline of many troops are common subjects of conversation. Robbery by troops is alleged to be widespread, and according to talk up-country rape by Indian soldiers is far commoner than reported cases suggest. The impression is that the authorities are very lenient with the offenders and take no pains to trace them. The huge Black Market in stolen Service stores is the subject of marvel. Chinese merchants say that the ricketty economy of Malaya is threatened with dislocation by the surfeit of currency due to the presence of the Army. But perhaps more acute and bitter than any other resentment is that there are so many civilian buildings and houses occupied by the Services. In particular there is not a single Chinese girls' school open because their premises are occupied. They cannot receive grants-in-aid, the teachers are unemployed, the children roam the streets.

It is very hard for the newcomer to detect this attitude among a population who are masters of restraint—indeed of self-repression—until they explode in uncontrolled hysteria. They vent their grievances however to myself and my staff to whom they feel that they can speak without reprisal. (The eloquent invective of the Headmistress of the Nanyang Girls' School would blister the ear drums of the officer responsible for the continued occupation of her school, whoever he may be.)

Regulations, presumably framed in London, lay down that civilians serving with B.M.A. shall have the same status as officers for rations and amenities—unless they happen to be Asiatics. Thus the Managing Director of the Overseas Chinese Bank and Mr. H.S. Lee[1] who is doing such good service in Selangor cannot get rations, cigarettes or any other N.A.A.F.I. supplies. All the diplomacy and political skill in the world cannot avail against such crass stupidities.

The unpopularity of the Services extends to the B.M.A. It is disconcerting to an old Malayan temporarily in uniform to see an expression of stolid defensiveness dissolve into a smile when its owner realises that he is dealing with a friend who knows his language and not with the Army of Occupation.

It may seem ungrateful that the natives should feel in this way towards the Army that has liberated them. But they do not look at it like that. In their minds they make no distinction between the heroes of Burma and the parasites and camp followers. They judge people merely as they find them.

The Leftist Press intersperses the shrill vituperation of the crapulous street-walker with articles of surprising reasonableness. The steadier Nanyang Siang Pau[2] even dares to admonish the communists in a very excellent article (17.11.45). This is the first time a newspaper has had the guts to do it. . . .

---

[1] H S Lee (Lee Hau Shik) (?1899/1901–1988); a Malayan-born Chinese; educated at St John's College, Cambridge; possessed extensive interests in tin mining and rubber estates in Selangor; a staunch KMT supporter in Kuala Lumper; during the Japanese invasion Lee escaped to India and became a Liaison Officer in negotiations between the Chinese government and the British, with the rank of colonel in the Chinese army; was president of the Selangor Chinese Chamber of Commerce, 1946–1948, and later became a principal leader of the Malayan Chinese Association.

[2] *Nanyang Siang Pau*, Chinese-language newspaper based in Singapore, 1923–1981, and strongly influenced by the KMT after the war.

66   CO 273/675/18, no 20   31 Dec 1945
'Political position in Malaya with regard to the new policy proposals': memorandum by Brigadier A T Newboult

[By the turn of the year Newboult (in this document), Mountbatten (see 67), and Hone (see 68) were urging London to be flexible in the implementation of policy. In response Hall reassured SACSEA that flexibility and local consultation were built into the constitution (see Hall to Mountbatten, 4 Feb 1946, CO 537/1528, no 42).]

As the conclusion of my secondment to Sir Harold MacMichael there are certain impressions which stand out very clearly and I have written these notes and made some suggestions in order to assist the Colonial Office in the final stage of preparation before the Civil Government is restored in the Malay Peninsula. All our discussions were with the Rulers themselves and in some cases with some of the leading Malays who were called in for consultation by their Ruler. These Malays varied from the died-in-the-wool conservatives of the old school and the progressive and intelligent men of the younger generation. Not only amongst the Rulers but amongst the leading Malays is the wide range of mentality manifest.

2.   It would be fair to say that the most noticeable common ground was the trust reposed in the British Government. As the Sultan of Kelantan said 'You only give a

power of attorney to a person you trust'. The most difficult case was Kedah and for
some unknown reason we were kept at arms length and all our discussions were kept
on a strictly formal (and painful) level. Kedah has always prized what it has regarded
as a greater degree of independence, fostered by the clause in the former agreement
requiring the State Council's written consent to any form of merger with another
State. That this feeling of independence was a false one has not been admitted by
them and I think that they seriously consider themselves capable of setting up an
independent State subject only to assistance from the British Government in matters
concerning relations with States outside their borders. It is all the more remarkable
that this should be possible in a State which is in many respects more advanced than
any other. The local Government managed to keep its machinery in working order
very efficiently with practically no interference in detail by the occupying powers,
and nothing would have pleased them more than a substitution of the corrupt but
disinterested Siamese administration by the just and incorruptible British Government, as long as this Government did not interfere more than its predecessor in
purely local administrative routine. On our re-occupation, the new policy came as a
ruder shock than elsewhere because their hopes of independence suffered a greater
set-back. Kedah is parochialism 'in excelsis'. We must take some of the blame for
this, but we must make allowance for this feeling in our dealings in the future and
direct special efforts at correcting their misapprehensions and fears. With the
material available this should not be impossible.

3.   For the rest, the Union proposal met with very little criticism. In some cases it
received support: in others it was regarded as inevitable, but not accepted without
misgivings. No State has forgotten the excessive centralisation in the Federated
Malay States in the years up to 1930 and their misgivings are that Union spells
centralisation. It is most important that this point should be corrected in authoritative statements on policy. The States will wish to retain control in matters of local
administration and stress should be laid on the fact that there will be a delegation of
such powers from the central government "as can best be exercised" by local bodies.
The extent of this delegation can only be determined in actual practice, but a
moment's reflection will show that it will be physically impossible for the central
government to exercise powers of local detailed administration. There is a human,
and universal, tendency in any central authority to take unto itself too much work
and responsibility and this tendency will have to be combated. I am sure that States
will not remain silent if they consider that powers which should be exercised by them
are being usurped.

4.   On the formation of a Union there will be a mass of problems arising from local
variations which cannot be solved by a single stroke of the pen. This will all take time
and I have no fears that they cannot be solved as long as the urge for uniformity is
kept within reasonable bounds. In no instance will the existing variations be more
evident than in the personalities and capabilities of the people who will now be
thrown together on Union Councils and Boards. Every presiding officer will have to
exercise the greatest tact in encouraging the shyer and less intelligent members to
come foward in debate and not allow themselves to be submerged by their more
forceful brethren. This applies equally amongst Malays themselves as amongst
Malays and other races.

5.   This variation in personalities is very noticeable amongst the Rulers. The
range extends from the Sultan of Johore to the new Raja of Perlis. The success of the

Advisory Council of Rulers will depend largely on how far the newer and less forceful Rulers take their place in debate. The scope of the Council is at the Governor's discretion, but I am convinced that it will form not only a useful Council for advice on subjects of common interest but a valuable index of the progress of thought in the acceptance of the new policy. It is worthy of remark that the added weight which will inevitably be derived from the views of the Sultans in Advisory Council was not appreciated, though it was repeatedly stressed. I formed the idea that this Council was generally regarded as window dressing and the increased influence it would give Sultans on questions of common interest was not fully appreciated.

6. At the moment the Rulers have signed the new agreements in the knowledge that His Majesty's Government intends to put into effect the new policy. It cannot be claimed that the idea of a Union or Common Citizenship has been properly appreciated by the majority of people. So far discussions have taken place with the Rulers only and public comment on the proposals has been noticeable by its absence. As further details are announced and as the time for the return of the Civil Government gets closer there will be more and more discussion. We must not expect a universal acceptance of the proposals as they stand. Little thought has been given locally to th·· implications of the new policy. We are, in fact, far in advance of general public opinion. After all it has taken over three years of hard thinking by a number of people at home to arrive at the policy as announced. During that time the people of the country were cut off from all outside communications and few of them gave the future constitutional set-up a second thought. Sufficient unto the day was the end of the Japanese occupation. The result is that we are far ahead of the rest of the country and it is essential to give them a chance of catching up. This will require a proper publicity campaign and careful nursing. It also demands insistence at the moment only on essentials to the working of a Union. Other steps will follow automatically in due course and by common consent, whereas the use of force now would only cause resentment and arouse fears and suspicions. There is sufficient common sense in the country to warrant this hope. It must always be remembered that in addition to introducing a radical change in policy (and it is a radical change and should be admitted as such) we are trying to restore a country which has with difficulty survived three and a half years occupation by a ruthless enemy. At the moment the strongest propaganda weapon would be the import of food and consumer goods to the available absorptive capacity of the country. Promises of good things to come, of a bright political future do not mean so much to a hungry underfed man, dressed in rags and short of the necessities of home and trade. When these have been met he will be ready to think of future policy.

7. The Malayan Citizenship proposal has caused far more heartburning than that for Union. This is largely on the score that no one can hazard a guess as to the number of aliens who will be automatically admitted to citizenship, and there is no certainty whether aliens admitted under the 10 years residence qualification will in fact either make a permanent domicile here or put the interests of Malaya before those of their country of origin. In order to try and inculcate the ideal of common citizenship amongst all and to avoid placing any obstacle in its path, it may be necessary to admit people by a flat rule. But the argument on the Malay side is that, having granted the privilege of citizenship, it is too late to draw back when it is discovered that those who are admitted have not in fact adopted this country as their domicile. It is a gamble and on a matter of such importance to the future of Malays is

it right to gamble on such an uncertain factor? 'Let us go slow in the beginning'. A property qualification, however desirable, would exclude many it is desired to include. In one case it was suggested that all intending citizens, except Malays, should apply individually for admission. Here there is the difficulty over Javanese and Sumatrans who have no claim for easier facilities than Chinese or Indians and in any case it is most important not to include any definition by race. The qualifications must be made regardless of race. A scheme for universal application would be administratively out of the question. As a result of much consideration I have come to the conclusion that the right solution is to admit automatically all people born in Malaya, and to admit others on application, after scrutiny and an oath of allegiance. Why should those who qualify under the 10 years rule come in without making any profession of allegiance? That is the kernel of the matter—'real loyalty to Malaya' and a perfectly equitable basis on which to argue. If a man is prepared to be loyal to Malaya let him say so: after all it is those people whom we want as citizens. What guarantee have we that those with the ten years residence qualification are not really birds of passage? Those born in the country start with Malaya as a background and it is up to the country of their birth to foster a loyalty to Malaya as part of their education. A birth qualification will be easy to prove with the registers of births. The ten years qualification would involve enormous labour when proof was required. I therefore recommend that the citizenship qualification be amended to admit:—

(a) automatically, all those born in Malaya.
(b) by application, those with 5 years residence who wish to do so and after careful examination are considered suitable and take an oath of allegiance.

Under this scheme there is no denial of the privilege of citizenship but only a right and proper scrutiny of those to whom it is given. To this I can see no objection. I realise that it is an alteration in the proposal; it is no departure from the general policy. But we have all had time to think further, especially in the light of local reactions, and there would be no loss of respect if it is announced that after further reflection the alteration had commended itself to His Majesty's Government and had been so accepted. In fact there would be a great political advantage in strengthening the trust in His Majesty's Government and raising the hopes that in the future the people of the country will have a say in their development and government. His Majesty's Government was far sighted enough to announce its policy in advance of consulting the people: in the circumstances there was no alternative except protracted and acrimonious negotiations. I see every advantage in saying that after considering representations which have been made, a modification has been accepted.

67   CO 537/1528, no 40   4 Jan 1946
[Implementation of the Malayan Union]: letter from Admiral Mount-batten to Mr Hall on the need for local consultations

It has been my habit to write to your predecessor from time to time, and the successful completion of Sir Harold MacMichael's mission gives me an opportunity to write to you about Malaya.

I am grateful to Sir Harold for the important work he has done and equally for the way in which he has accomplished it without friction, retaining the good will of the Sultans, and I am naturally anxious that the introduction of the new policy for Malaya which has begun so auspiciously should proceed stage by stage with the same success.

An announcement will presumably be made in Parliament at an early date of the creation of the Malayan Union and of the institutions that will enable it to be administered. It is intended, I understand, that there shall be a Legislative Council for the Union with an official majority and unofficial members either nominated by the Governor or appointed by him on the election of certain public bodies.

If the announcement of the creation of the Legislative Council on these terms is made without an intimation that it is to be purely provisional, I fear that its reception by Malayan and world public opinion will be most unfavourable. I feel that a small unofficial majority with an over-riding authority of the Governor would not be likely to impair the functioning of the Council, and, if this is so, an announcement of an unofficial majority would have a mitigating effect on any unfavourable public reaction to H.M. Government's present proposals.

However, whether the majority is official or unofficial, I am satisfied that unless the detailed organisation of the new constitution is represented as a purely temporary expedient, it will be considered to be a constitution autocratically imposed from London without prior consultation with local opinion out here; and, as such, will be stigmatised as a return to the old type of Colonial government and a denial of democratic principles.

I realise that the need for an immediate constitution, as an interim measure, has made any prior consultation with local opinion impracticable. But I would urge that, simultaneously with the announcement of the creation of the Union, a statement should be made to the effect that it is the intention of H.M. Government to appoint a Royal Commission to come to Malaya within the current year.

This Commission (which would of course be bound by the terms of the explanatory memorandum handed to the Sultans by Sir Harold MacMichael) would ascertain the views of individuals and public bodies out here, so as to recommend a constitution both suitable to the Union and in keeping with the spirit of His Majesty's Government's long-term policy for Malaya.

I am convinced that it is only in this way that the Malayan Union proposals have a chance of being welcomed by Malaya, and the world in general, as a progressive measure.

68   CO 537/1528, no 41   7 Jan 1946
[Implementation of the Malayan Union]: letter from Major-General H R Hone to Sir G Gater on the need for local consultations

I have not had the chance to write to you sooner since my return from England for I have been extremely busy. I want to thank you again for all your help and kind consideration to me during my visit.

Since MacMichael completed his mission, Newboult and I have had many talks with him as regards the organisation and the details of the future constitution in the light of the discussions I had in London. I also had many talks with McKerron and others in the Administration. We have all found the greatest difficulty in fitting the projected Governor-General into the constitutional picture and gradually crystallise our ideas on the subject. I was unexpectedly summoned to Supreme Headquarters where Admiral Mountbatten recounted to me the talks he had with the C.I.G.S.[1] regarding the future military set up and the views which he held regarding the co-ordination of British diplomatic, financial and economic interests in the Far East. MacMichael was also brought into these discussions and as a result I sent you a telegram a few days ago urging that at least there should be some delay in reaching final conclusions regarding the appointment of a Governor-General. I was anxious to say in the telegram that I hoped that you would not think that I was exceeding my brief but the general consensus of opinion was that this was an important matter on which you would be glad to have my personal views in a personal telegram. Since the telegram was despatched, however, I have been feeling that you might well think that I had committed an impertinence and if this is so I trust you will accept my apologies. It seemed to me, however, in our conversations that you are not entirely satisfied with the original proposals and saw various difficulties which were also evident to me.

You may be sure that the arrival of the Supreme Commander in Singapore has caused him to interest himself much more directly in the affairs of the Administration; this has not proved an embarrassment but in relation to our very acute food problem his interest has been of considerable assistance. Despite all my representations at various levels regarding the slowness of essential imports, very little improvement has been effected but I hope that the Supreme Commander will appreciate more and more our urgent needs for supplies and transport and that his special influence will make the machine move more quickly. In the meantime we are going through a very anxious period indeed.

The Supreme Commander has just written a further letter to the Secretary of State.[2] I wish that it could have been expressed a little more clearly for although I persuaded him to make several alterations in the draft, I had to leave a great deal of it in the form in which he had prepared it himself. I do, however, fully agree with the fundamental point which he was trying to make and in this I have the support of Newboult, McKerron and Purcell. You will remember that in the very early drafts that were prepared for the Cabinet, it was suggested that after the Treaties had been signed, a Royal Commission should come to Malaya to advise on the framing of the new constitution. At that time I resisted this proposal since it meant either a temporary return to the pre-war constitutional arrangements or an undue prolongation of the Military Administration while the Royal Commission visited the country, made its report and the Secretary of State arrived at his conclusions. Such a delay would have been intolerable and in consequence all reference to a Royal Commission was omitted from the Cabinet papers.

You will have gathered from our various reports that the country is now far more politically conscious than ever before, particularly among the Chinese and the Malays. So far there has been a fairly general acceptance of the major policy of the Union on the Mainland and a segregation of Singapore under a separate Governor. But we do feel that there is a considerable air of expectancy as to what the next steps

[1] Lord Alanbrooke, GIGS, 1941–1946.　　[2] See 67.

are going to be. It is important that the detailed Constitution should not appear to be merely evolved in the Colonial Office and imposed upon the people willy-nilly. At the same time every one realised that with the resumption of Civil Government (which they all favour) some sort of temporary constitution must be framed. I think most people realise also that prior consultation with public bodies etc. would take too long and would delay the return of Civil Government with unfortunate results. The only point that the Supreme Commander is really anxious to make is that the new Constitution should not be issued with an implication of finality. I am sure that we all realise that experience will inevitably show the need for modifications at a fairly early date but unless we announce the new Constitution as being interim in its details and subject to revision and modification in the light of experience and in response to considered local opinion, the Supreme Commander feels very strongly (and I agree) that the inauguration of the new system may start in an era of suspicion and mistrust. No doubt you and the Colonial Office may have already determined that the Secretary of State should be advised in this sense and indeed I told the Supreme Commander that I felt that this must be so. He thought however that it was his duty to bring this point to the Secretary of State's notice and I saw no reason to advise him otherwise. The point which he made regarding an unofficial majority on the Legislative Council of the Union Government is of course far more controversial and certainly would be unwise at present.

I am most grateful for the action that has already been taken on a number of matters which I discussed during my visit. Above all I am delighted to think that the services of Willan and Newboult have been recognised and that their appointments together with that of McKerron have been approved.[3] They have all done first class work and Malaya has every reason to be grateful to them.

Again, thank you for your kindness to me.

---

[3] On the resumption of civil government on 1 Apr, Willan and Newboult became respectively chief justice and chief secretary of the Malayan Union, while McKerron was appointed colonial secretary in Singapore.

69   CAB 128/5, CM 4(46)3   10 Jan 1946
'Malaya: future constitution': Cabinet conclusions on the draft White Paper

[On 7 Jan 1946 Hall approached the Colonial Affairs Committee for its immediate sanction of the new policy and three days later Lord Addison (secretary of state for the dominions, 1945–1947, for Commonwealth relations, 1947) presented a draft White Paper to Cabinet (see also CAB 134/52, C(46)1; CAB 129/6, CP(46)9, 8 Jan 1946; CO 537/1528; PREM 8/459).]

The Cabinet had before them a memorandum (C.P.(46)9)[1] submitted by the Secretary of State for Dominion Affairs acting Chairman of the Colonial Affairs Committee, covering a draft White Paper containing a statement of policy regarding the future constitution of the Malayan Union and the Colony of Singapore.

It was proposed that the White Paper should be presented as soon as Parliament

---

[1] Not printed.

reassembled so as to be available when the Straits Settlements (Repeal) Bill[2] was taken. The draft White Paper amplified a statement already made in the House of Commons on the 10th October, 1945.[3]

In discussion, *the Prime Minister* suggested that the reference to a Governor-General in the final paragraph of the White Paper should be either elaborated, so as to give some indication of his duties and responsibilities, or omitted altogether.

The Cabinet:—

(1) Invited the Secretary of State for the Colonies to amplify paragraph 13 of the draft White Paper on the lines suggested and to settle the terms of the revised paragraph in consultation with the Prime Minister.

(2) Subject to this amendment, approved the terms of the draft White Paper annexed to C.P. (46)9 and authorised the Secretary of State for the Colonies to present it to Parliament at the earliest opportunity.[4]

---

[2] This was the only piece of legislation necessitated by the new policy.   [3] See 59, note 2.
[4] On 22 Jan the White Paper was published simultaneously with the first reading of the Bill as *Malayan Union and Singapore: Statement of Policy on Future Constitution* (Cmd 6724, 1946).

70   CO 537/1528, no 39   4 Feb 1946
[Resumption of civil government in Malaya]: letter from Sir G Gater to Sir E Speed[1]

As you may be aware, Lord Addison has recently introduced into the House of Lords, on behalf of our Secretary of State, a Bill to repeal the Straits Settlements Act of 1866. The new Bill is necessary to enable us to split up the Colony of the Straits Settlements and to attach Penang and Malacca to the new Malayan Union, and is thus fundamental to the whole of our present Malayan policy.

The second reading of the Bill in the House of Lords took place on Tuesday, the 29th of January, and this was made the occasion for a Debate not only on the immediate implications of the Bill but on the policy in general. The tone of the Debate was favourable, but the Leader of the Opposition made one very strong demand which it has been found impossible to resist. He pointed out that the proposals were at present only known to Parliament through Lord Addison's own opening statement at the Debate, and through the White Paper (Cmd. 6724) which had been issued a week previously. He said that both these exposés, though clear and satisfactory, gave no more than the outline of the policy, and insisted that Parliament should be allowed to examine and comment on the Orders in Council in which the proposals would be set out in full detail.

This request, if acceded to in full, might have meant that the Orders would have to be laid before Parliament for the space of forty days, and this would involve very long delay. In conversation since the Debate, however, Lord Cranborne has made it clear that he requires nothing as drastic as this, and that he will be satisfied if a White Paper is laid before Parliament, summarising in some detail the contents of each of the Orders which it is proposed to issue.

---

[1] Sir Eric Speed, permanent under-secretary at the War Office, 1942–1948.

We have known for some time that we would be faced with the general problem of a demand from Parliament to examine Colonial Orders in Council, but we hoped to avoid the difficulty in this particular case. In the event there has been no alternative but to accede to Lord Cranborne's request in its modified form. But even in this form it will involve much time and effort. There might even be a demand for a further debate. It is therefore now quite clear, I am afraid, that we shall be unable to complete our plans by March the 1st.

There are to be three Orders in Council, the first introducing the Malayan Union, the second creating the Colony of Singapore and the third inaugurating Malayan Union citizenship. The drafting of these Orders is a very big job, and is not yet complete. The preparation of a White Paper—which cannot be laid before the drafting of the Orders is finished—will mean extra time spent and in addition the Bill still has to run its full course in the House of Commons. On top of that, we shall have to make all the arrangements with the Privy Council for the actual issue of the Orders.

The request to which I am leading up is obvious. It is that the termination of military administration and the return of civil Government both in the Malayan mainland and in Singapore should be delayed until the 1st of April.[2] I should have greatly preferred not to have had to make this request, but the reasons for it, as I know you will appreciate, are as much beyond our control as they are imperative. There is the additional very important point that those officers of the future Malayan administrations who are still with us in the Colonial Office are working overtime on these very problems, and will undoubtedly still be doing so on the 1st of March. I feel we cannot ask them to take up their new and arduous duties in the Far East without a short rest.

We shall have many arrangements affecting personnel to make and I shall be grateful therefore if you can let me have a very early reply to this letter.

P.S. Since this letter was drafted I have seen a telegram from Admiral Mountbatten (SEACOS 631 of the 31st January) strongly recommending that midnight 31st March–1st April should be taken as the date for the resumption of Civil Government in both Singapore and the Malayan Union.

---

[2] See 62.

71 CAB 21/1954   13 Feb 1946

[Appointment of special commissioner in SE Asia]: outward telegram no 656 from the Cabinet Office to Admiral Mountbatten

[According to the terms outlined in this document, Lord Killearn was appointed special commissioner in South-East Asia in March 1946 when Dening ceased to be chief political adviser to SACSEA. For Dening's report to Bevin on regional developments before Killearn's arrival, see 81. After three months in post Killearn sent London a survey of regional co-ordination, see 95.]

Personal for Admiral Mountbatten.

Following is sent to you at request of Foreign Office as a summary of considerations governing the appointment of a Special Commissioner to South East Asia to co-ordinate civil and political affairs. Draft directive to Special Commissioner is contained in our immediately following telegram.

2. Problem is still under consideration between Foreign and Colonial Office but your comments are requested as quickly as possible for discussion before final decisions are taken.

Begins

Before the war South East Asia was a comparatively unimportant and little known area. The war has demonstrated its political, economic and strategic importance. At present the existence of South East Asia Command provides a link between the various territories which did not previously exist. But the functions of South East Asia Command are dwindling as the various civil governments prepare to take over.

2. The tendency will be for the individual territories, each occupied with its own problems of rehabilitation and reconstruction, to pursue their individual courses without much regard to, or knowledge of, each others [sic] problems.

3. Yet there will be many problems of common concern to some if not all of the territories in the area, and consideration has therefore been given to the desirability of some representative of His Majesty's Government who can look at the problems of the area as a whole and who can promote the co-ordination of the views and needs of the British territories involved and relate them with developments in the non-British territories in the area.

4. The first project considered was the appointment of a Minister Resident or Minister of State. It was felt, however, that the appointment of a Cabinet Minister with executive powers would be difficult to reconcile with the responsibilities of the Governors of British territories and might encourage suspicion as to our intentions in relation to foreign dependent territories within the area. The more appropriate course has seemed to be to appoint someone of ambassadorial status who would promote co-ordination by maintaining close liaison with the Governors of British territories and British Service Commanders and with the administrations of foreign dependent territories without infringing the prerogatives and independent responsibilities of any of them.

5. It is in the sphere of foreign affairs that the need for treating the area as a whole is most obvious. Nationalist movements throughout the area will react one upon the other and there will be advantage in having someone who from the point of view of foreign affairs can keep track of racial questions throughout the area (e.g. Chinese penetration) and watch the tendencies of the Nationalist movements which the war with Japan has let loose. There is need also of someone who will survey the area as a whole from an economic point of view and will report on regional economic developments which may affect the conduct of foreign affairs as well as the economies of the individual British territories in the area. These will be the main functions of the Special Commissioner in South East Asia. He will be responsible to the Secretary of State for Foreign Affairs. He will build up the closest contacts with the Governors of British territories in the area and with the administrations in French Indo-China and the Netherlands East Indies. He will direct the activities of Foreign Service Officers in these territories. He will be available to give advice on foreign political questions to SACSEA or to any inter-Service headquarters which may succeed SEAC headquarters at Singapore, and will keep in touch with the Governor-General of India, with the Commander-in-Chief or Governor of Hong

Kong, with any representatives of the Dominions, India or Burma in Singapore, with the United Kingdom High Commissioners in Australia and New Zealand and with His Majesty's diplomatic representatives in China and Siam.

6. The terms of reference of the Special Commissioner are still under discussion, but a draft provisionally agreed upon towards the end of December follows. It will require slight verbal modifications to take account of the subsequent appointments of a Governor-General of Malaya and a Minister to Siam.

7. A question still under consideration is whether the Special Commissioner shall have any economic functions apart from the collection of information on economic developments in South East Asia. SEAC headquarters is at present concerned with a good many matters of economic administration arising out of military government or the care of prisoners and internees. It is particularly concerned, for instance, with the procurement and distribution throughout the area of rice and coal. It is not yet clear to what extent there will be a continued need of some organisation for dealing with such problems as and when civil government becomes established in the individual territories and as private trading revives. The present proposal is that the Special Commissioner shall be invited (not in his formal directive but in a supplementary letter or even orally) to make recommendations on the following points:—

(1) Whether the existing machinery in South East Asia is sufficient to deal with economic questions arising within the area at the moment; and
(2) what arrangements if any should be made for the period immediately after the military authorities have handed over control to the civil governments.

8. A third point on which discussion is still proceeding is whether he should be asked to make recommendations relating to long term international regional co-operation. The Colonial Office have urged delay on this point, since it involves many difficult questions of general policy, more particularly in regard to the relationship of any regional machinery with the United Nations Organisation, which the Colonial Office are still considering with a view to submission to Ministers. The Foreign Office, on the other hand, consider that there is a good case for having the problem investigated by the Special Commissioner, whose recommendations might afford a concrete and up-to-date basis for inter-Departmental discussion.

9. Questions of staff and accommodation have still to be decided. *Ends*

72   CO 537/1581   23 Feb 1946
[Local reactions to the White Paper]: HQ Malaya Command weekly intelligence review, no 17   [Extract]

[The publication of the White Paper on 22 Jan provided a focal point for what had been hitherto diffuse Malay political activity. On 24 Jan a call from Dato Onn for a Pan-Malayan Malay Congress was printed in the Malay-language newspaper, *Majlis*. After some discussion over choice of site—some favoured Malacca for historic reasons, others Kuala Lumpur for its better facilities—a committee of Selangor Malays (chaired by the Malay literary figure Za'ba or Zainal Abidin bin Ahmad) prepared to play host to representatives from many Malay associations which were kept informed of arrangements by announcements in the press.]

. . . 4. Reactions to the Malay[an] Union

This week the interest of all politically minded Malays has again been centred around the Government's proposed Malay[an] Union White Paper. On the whole reaction has been unfavourable and criticisms have been more outspoken. This criticism has been particularly noticeable in JOHORE and KELANTAN, and has been along the lines which were outlined in last weeks' [sic] Summary.

A very large number of Malay political parties have been springing up all over the country recently, and it is now intended to co-ordinate all these bodies, decide on a common policy, and unite all Malays into one powerful unified party. The White Paper on the Malay[an] Union is probably the chief item to be considered, but the Malays must also formulate some policy towards the Chinese, with whom they have got to live peacefully in this country, whether they like it or not.

With these ends in view an all Malayan Conference is planned for the 1 – 4 March. However, it is still not certain where it is to be held; reception committees are preparing for the Conference at both KUALA LUMPUR and MALACCA, and there seems a general lack of organisation about the whole affair. Moreover, there is certain to be a clash of personalities, for many of the prominent men hold widely differing views, and they are mostly leaders of newly raised parties in their own states.

Among those attending are probably Dato Onn himself, who is a moderate; Haji Wan Ahmad, leader of the Malay Association in KELANTAN, where there has recently been much outspoken criticism, coupled with some-what violent religious agitation; Raja Muda, son of the Sultan of KELANTAN, who has very definite and strong anti White Paper views; Dato Abdul Rahman who in a recent meeting expressed strong disapproval of the Sultan of JOHORE's action in originally signing the White Paper;[1] and Tengku Abdul Rahman son of the Sultan of KEDAH.

Latest reports indicate that the more liberal views of Dato Onn's JOHORE Malay Association are being widely supported in opposition to the others' more violent tendencies. He is alleged to have a following, in JOHORE State alone, of some 100,000 people as well as very wide support in KELANTAN, SELANGOR, MALACCA and NEGRI SEMBILAN.

A disturbing feature of the agitation is the strong religious theme which is being brought into the question. Again the main centre of this trouble appears to be in KOTA BAHRU where a certain Hyde Bin Khatib has been delivering speeches against the Malay[an] Union using militant passages from the Koran and stressing the religious aspect.

The MCP has shown little interest so far in the agitation but it will almost certainly try to use the political unrest and criticism of the Government to further its own ends. In only one place, again KOTA BAHRU, has any definite connection been established between the Malay Association and the Communist Party. Chin Yew the local MCP organiser has proclaimed that he has made contacts with Malay

---

[1] Ibrahim signed the MacMichael treaty, not the White Paper, see 59. Dato Abdul Rahman bin Mohd Yasin, pre-war state treasurer and member of Johore's executive council and council of ministers, was president of the Persatuan Melayu Johore (Johore Malay Association) which organised a meeting at the Abu Bakar Mosque, Johore Bahru, on 2 Feb 1946 protesting that Sultan Ibrahim had signed the MacMichael treaty in contravention of the Johore constitution of 1895. Dato Abdul Rahman's sons, Ismail and Suleiman, were later federal ministers in Tunku Abdul Rahman's cabinet, and Ismail rose to deputy prime minister of Malaysia.

Association, with the object of actively assisting in the agitation against the Government White Paper. Whether this is his own local policy or whether he is acting in accordance with central instructions remains to be seen. Chin Yew, himself is not interested in the Malay[an] Union agitation, except as a means of making difficulties for the Administration and increasing the prestige of his party. As already mentioned the Communist Party have also held a meeting in JOHORE to discuss the Malay[an] Union, but it does not appear that any firm Party policy has been decided on as yet.

In general then, the agitation against the Malay[an] Union plan has gathered strength in the last week and, although it is evident that while a large proportion of uneducated Malays still have little interest or knowledge of the subject, they are liable to be affected by propaganda of a religious nature, and can easily be swayed by the leaders and elders of this community. But the educated classes and political parties are genuinely perturbed and are trying to form the Malays into a firm party to oppose not only the White Paper, but also the Chinese and Communist infiltration of which they are very much afraid.

The results of the conference next week should do much to clarify the situation, and on its results much of the future of the Malay community may depend. . . .

73 CO 537/1528, no 44   23 Feb 1946
[Malay reactions to the White Paper]: minute by H T Bourdillon
[Extract]

[In this assessment of Malay reactions Bourdillon refers to specific communications from Malaya; these have not been reproduced here].

The urgent matter, as I see it, is to put up an objective appreciation, on the documents before us, of the importance and tenour of all these re-actions taken in the aggregate. When and if the S. of S. sees the "prominent ex-Malayans" who have been provisionally invited for Tuesday afternoon, it is certain that some of them will come armed with their own (highly coloured) accounts. We already know that Sir George Maxwell more or less regards the whole of Malaya as on the point of bursting into flames, and we also know that a rather inflammatory letter has been sent by the Sultan of Kedah to Sir R. Winstedt, who is fruitful soil for such letters.[1] It seems essential that the S. of S. should be in a position to meet these accounts with the nearest possible approach to the truth.

No. 3 on this file finishes with the following assessment by Brig. Newboult:—

"abundantly clear that active and intelligent propaganda required in Malay peninsula to put White Paper before all communities affected. Much pressure being put on the Sultans by their own subjects".

---

[1] Prominent former members of the MCS campaigned against the Malayan Union by writing letters to the national press and lobbying the CO. Hall invited leading 'old Malayans' to a meeting on 22 Feb, later postponed to 26 Feb, which was attended *inter alia* by Sir George Maxwell (chief secretary FMS, 1920–1926), L D Gammans MP (MCS, 1920–1934), Sir Frank Swettenham (see 63, note 2), Sir Cecil Clementi (governor and high commissioner, 1929–1934), Sir Richard Winstedt (MCS, 1902–1935, general adviser Johore, 1931–1935) and A S Haynes (MCS, 1901–1934). See CO 273/676/4.

Coming from Brig. Newboult, I think this can dispel from our minds any idea that the various reactions need not be taken seriously, or that they are merely the work of certain Sultans and their entourage with a pretence of popular support. On the contrary, we are told that the Sultans are the object of popular pressure. It is clear, then, that the White Paper made a direct impact on the more reflective Malays, whose responding protests were perfectly genuine though they varied in size and intensity from State to State. Nowhere do we find the universal conflagration seen from afar by Sir George Maxwell. On the other hand, the Selangor Malay Association, which is reported to be a considerable body and to reflect Malay opinion in Selangor generally (see Nos. 8 and 17) protested vigorously and spontaneously—we have had no word from the Sultan of Selangor—against the White Paper and in particular the citizenship proposals. The "Perlis Malays" also protested spontaneously, and were only supported after the event by the Raja[.] The "Trengganu Malay Association" (No. 9) did the same, as did the "Pahang Malay Association" (No. 16). The latter, it must be said, is reported to include "mainly Government servants and literary persons" and not to have a large membership. We have heard nothing either from the Sultan of Pahang or from the Sultan of Trengganu.

The local reaction in Johore (No. 22A) has been reported not to be very substantial, but there is a new telegram from Johore which I have now attached as No. 25. I have also attached, as No. 24, an ALFSEA situation report which speaks of Dato Onn, reported as a restraining influence in Johore, as a centre of resistance (albeit moderate resistance) to the White Paper in Malay[a] generally. The same telegram, incidentally, says that Malay feeling against the Union is increasing in Trengganu, though apparently without anti-British feeling, and that in Kedah "all Malays except the Malay Nationalist party are writing under Dato Onn to oppose the White Paper."

So far, I have tried to cover popular reactions as opposed to those of the Sultans. There is little very recent news about the latter, except the important telegram at 23. This is most encouraging about the Sultan of Perak, who should, I think, be very largely satisfied by the latest proposed concessions on the religious question. It is less encouraging about the Sultan of Kedah, who is sending us a letter which we are advised to await.

To sum up, I think we must admit a genuine and fairly widespread Malay revulsion against the White Paper. I have no doubt the White Paper has been misunderstood, but that does not make the revulsion any less real. In almost all the reactions from popular bodies, as opposed to Sultans, it is *citizenship* which is attacked. The only concrete reference in the Selangor, Pahang and Trengganu messages is to the citizenship proposals. At No. 4 on the Kelantan sub-file (50823/34/9 beneath) is a despatch from the C.C.A.O. forwarding a petition from "some Malays in Kelantan". The despatch contains the following interesting passage:—

> "I learnt afterwards that the petition is thought to have been inspired principally by Government servants who feared that the new policy of citizenship would result in nearly all the Government appointments being filled either by Europeans or Chinese".

This passage reinforces my impression that *popular* reaction amongst Malays is based almost entirely on fears, exaggerated but real, of the citizenship proposals.

The only other "bone of contention" (apart from the religious question, which has now, I hope, been cleared) is the loss of prestige and power by the Sultans. I cannot find anything like the same popular feeling on this score. If this were the only grievance, I could well believe that the trouble had no popular roots. It is a very real grievance in the mind of the Sultan of Kedah, but I doubt if even his own Kedah Malays would follow him far. When I was in Alor Star in December, Malay posters were already appearing on the walls saying "Support Malayan Union; reject common citizenship".

I would judge, then, from the documents on this and the attached files, that the surrender of jurisdiction by the Sultans and the creation of the Malayan Union are not the subject of deep Malay protest. Indeed, I know that many intelligent Malays, e.g. in Kelantan, would support the latter. On the other hand the citizenship proposals are regarded with genuine fear and dislike. . . .

74   CO 537/1528, no 43   23 Feb 1946
[Local reactions to Malayan Union citizenship]: inward telegram no 08009 from Major-General H R Hone to War Office

[By the Order in Council on Malayan Union Citizenship two categories of people would automatically be eligible for citizenship: (1) those born in the territory of the Union or of the colony of Singapore, and (2) those ordinarily resident in those territories for 10 out of the preceding 15 years (excluding the period of the Japanese occupation). In addition, provision would be made to enable a person to acquire citizenship through naturalization on application after 5 years' residence. It was also laid down that British subjects who acquired Malayan Union citizenship would not thereby lose their British nationality. Although Singapore was not part of the Malayan Union it was included in the qualification area for Malayan Union citizenship.]

Pass following to Colonial Office from Hone.

One. Present estimate of local reactions to proposals for creation of Malayan Union citizenship is as follows. Chinese and Indians appear generally indifferent neither applauding nor criticising them. Malay circles strongly oppose as they distrust future repercussions. Better informed Malay opinion probably does not dispute that full political rights should be conferred on all who are truly domiciled in Malaya but this section feels most strongly that proposed qualifications for citizenship throw net far too wide.

Two. While Newboult and I do not repeat not suggest that citizenship proposal should be dropped, we do strongly feel that it is neither necessary nor desirable to issue citizenship order in council on eve of resumption of civil government if this should be your intention; we consider Malay criticisms are substantial and that new Governors [of Malayan Union and Singapore] should take time to devise formulae to meet them. We feel that we stand to lose much good will of Malaya by being too precipitate.

75   CO 537/1528   25 Feb 1946
[Malay reactions to the White Paper]: minute by H T Bourdillon of a CO departmental meeting   [Extract]

[Officials considered their response to the growing Malay opposition to the Malayan Union, and especially its citizenship provisions, at a meeting in Gater's room on the morning of 25 Feb.]

. . . It was agreed without hesitation that there can be no question of retracting from the fundamental policy as outlined in the White Paper. Subject to this all-important proviso, however, it was felt that two alternative courses must now be considered:—

(a) The Secretary of State might refuse to let the Malay reactions to the White Paper affect his actions in any way, and might proceed as if nothing had happened, notwithstanding the contrary advice in the second paragraph of No.43.[1] In support of this, Sir Edward Gent argued that any deviation from the policy, or any delay over its implementation (particularly in the matter of common citizenship) would be likely to arouse far more dangerous antagonism from the Chinese, and to a lesser extent the Indians, than the antagonism which we were now meeting from the Malays. In this connection, Sir Edward doubted the accuracy of the statement in the first paragraph of No.43, that the Chinese and Indians "appear generally indifferent to the citizenship proposals, neither applauding nor criticising them". He said that, on the contrary, there was much recent evidence to show that the Chinese and Indians had taken a considerable, and favourable, interest in the proposals.

(b) The Secretary of State might hold up for the time being the implementation of the citizenship proposals, at the same time proceeding with all other aspects of the policy in the manner already planned. This would mean that work would immediately be completed on the Malayan Union Order in Council and on the Singapore Order in Council, but that the Malayan Union Citizenship Order in Council should be held back for the time being. We should still aim at a debate in the House of Commons next week,[2] and should still issue in advance of the debate a White Paper summarising the two Orders,[3] but the Secretary of State should announce during the debate his intention of withholding the introduction of the citizenship Order pending further local consultations. It was agreed, I think, that a commission as requested in No.42(a) would be neither necessary nor advisable, and that the consultations in question should be carried out by the Governor (or rather by the two Governors, for Singapore is also concerned). It was also felt that it must be made abundantly clear from the outset that there is no intention of abandoning the principle of common citizenship. On the contrary, the Secretary of State should be invited to say that he regards this principle as one of the essential foundations of the whole policy. He would add, however, that he had

---

[1] See 74.

[2] The Commons debate actually took place on 8 Mar on the occasion of the second reading of the Straits Settlements (Repeal) Bill (see *H of C Debs*, vol 420, cols 639–729).

[3] *Malayan Union and Singapore: Summary of Proposed Constitutional Arrangements* (Cmd 6749, 4 Mar 1946).

received a number of representations which led him to believe that the policy in this respect was not fully understood in Malaya, that he appreciated that the problem of citizenship was of vital concern to the whole people of the country, and that he had therefore decided to postpone the introduction of the citizenship proposals for some six months. During this period, the two Governors would be instructed first to ensure that the proposals were fully understood in Malaya, and secondly to consult local opinion on the exact provisions which would best achieve the fundamental objective.

I do not think that opinion on the respective merits of these two courses was unanimous. Sir Edward Gent, in favour of the former alternative, stressed the argument which I have already described. On the other hand Mr. Lloyd and Mr. Paskin felt that we could not disregard the advice in paragraph 2 of No.43, and argued that there were other points on which it had already been decided to withhold a decision pending local consultations by the Governors. The matter was not resolved at the meeting, and I was instructed to prepare a draft Cabinet Paper setting out the two alternatives, but omitting the final paragraph which would contain the Secretary of State's recommendation. . . .[4]

---

[4] As a result of discussion with Creech Jones and Gater, Bourdillon's draft was revised and a recommendation was added favouring the first alternative outlined in this minute, ie immediate implementation of the whole policy, see 76.

76   CAB 129/7, CP(46)81   26 Feb 1946
'Malayan policy': Cabinet memorandum by Mr Hall

I would invite the attention of my colleagues to Command Paper No. 6724, entitled "Malayan Union and Singapore", which was issued in January of this year, and which summarises the policy of His Majesty's Government towards these territories.

2. It will no doubt be recollected that the main features of the policy are:—

(a) The creation of a Malayan Union (to exclude Singapore in the first instance, but to include the Settlements of Penang and Malacca).

(b) The establishment of a Malayan Union citizenship, with the purpose of granting full political rights in the Malayan Union to all those, of whatever race, who regard Malaya as their true home and as the object of their loyalty.

3. This Command Paper was the sequel to the conclusion by Sir Harold MacMichael of new agreements with the Rulers of the nine Malay States, whereby the latter agreed to cede full power and jurisdiction in their States to His Majesty, thus enabling His Majesty's Government to bring the new policy into effect. The contents of the Command Paper have, of course, been made known in Malaya, and I am bound to inform my colleagues that I have received a number of representations and protests from Malay organisations and individual Malays in various parts of the Peninsula. Some of these protests come from the Rulers themselves, notwithstanding their signature of the new Agreements and their full knowledge, at the time of signature, of the intentions of His Majesty's Government. Thus I have received protests or expressions of anxiety from the Sultan of Perak, the Sultan of Kedah, the Sultan of Kelantan, the Sultan of Johore and the Rajah of Perlis, and I have now

received a request, addressed to me jointly by the Rulers of Perak, Kedah, Pahang, Selangor and Negri Sembilan, that an independent commission should visit Malaya to consult the Sultans and people before any decision is taken on the Malayan Union proposals.

5. I attach less importance, however, to these representations from the Rulers, some of whom are no doubt animated largely by considerations of their own prerogatives, than to the fact that the publication of the Command Paper appears to have caused a wide-spread and spontaneous reaction amongst the more reflective sections of the Malay population itself. I have received direct representations from at least one Malay Association in the majority of the States, and there is evidence of feeling in all. This evidence tends to show that antagonism amongst the Malay people (as opposed to the Malay Rulers and their immediate circle) is not directed against the conception of a Malayan Union, which many intelligent Malays, according to my information, would support, but against the citizenship proposals in particular. These have caused apprehension amongst the Malays on the ground that they open the door to a Chinese and to a lesser extent Indian predominance in the political field (there has long been a Chinese predominance in the commercial field).

5. I am confident that these anxieties on the part of the Malay population are based on a misunderstanding of the proposals, whose intention is certainly not the submergence of the Malays in their own country: but the anxieties are none the less real, and deserve consideration, I am convinced that the main policy, which has been the object of such careful consideration over so long a period by His Majesty's Government and which, in my view, is as necessary as it is just, must go through. Subject, however, to this all-important proviso, two courses appear open:—

(a) The first course is to refuse to let the Malay reaction to the Command Paper deter us in any way from the immediate implementation of the whole policy which we have judged to be right and fair as an essential foundation for political progress in Malaya. We must not forget that in Malaya Chinese and Indians between them outnumber the Malays, and that any step which the members of these races could regard as a withdrawal of the political rights already held out to them in the White Paper could be expected to evoke from them an antagonism as strong or stronger than that which we are now facing from the Malays.

(b) The second alternative is to proceed, as already planned, with all other aspects of the policy, but to defer the implementation of the citizenship proposals for a few months. If this latter course were adopted, it would have to be made clear from the outset that His Majesty's Government have no intention of abandoning the *principle* of common citizenship, which they regard as an essential feature of the whole policy. It would be stated, however, that His Majesty's Government realise the vital importance of this particular proposal to all the inhabitants of Malaya, and have therefore decided to suspend action in this regard for some few months, during which period steps will be taken first to ensure that the proposal is fully understood in Malaya, secondly to consult local opinion as regards the exact provisions best designed to achieve the fundamental objective. The adoption of this second course would correspond with the advice given me by the Chief Civil Affairs Officer, Malaya, who feels strongly that it is neither necessary nor desirable to issue the Citizenship Order in Council immediately upon the resumption of civil government, who considers that the Malay criticisms are substantial, and who represents that we stand to lose much goodwill in Malaya by being too precipitate on this matter.

6. If we are to be ready for the restoration of civil government in Malaya on the 1st April, it is necessary for the second reading of the Straits Settlements (Repeal) Bill to be taken in the House of Commons at a very early date, with a view to the issue thereafter of Orders in Council establishing the Malayan Union and the Colony of Singapore. I therefore submit this question to my colleagues as a matter of great urgency. My own recommendation, after considering the matter carefully from all angles, is that the first of the two courses outlined in the preceding paragraph should be adopted. We have announced our intentions clearly and firmly in the White Paper, and it would be most inadvisable for us now to appear uncertain of our policy in the judgement of world opinion. Moreover, Civil Government, when restored in Malaya, will in any event be faced with an extremely difficult task, and it appears to me that the difficulties will be increased by local doubts or uncertainty regarding the exact intentions of His Majesty's Government on the all-important question of citizenship. In this above all matters, I think we must start on a firm foundation and build on that foundation as best we may. I have nevertheless thought it necessary to bring the issue to the attention of my colleagues, in view of the substantial reactions which the White Paper have caused amongst the Malays—a reaction which is by now well-known to certain members of both Houses of Parliament.[1]

---

[1] On 28 Feb the Cabinet, having considered Hall's memorandum, decided that 'any such opposition which might develop in Parliament should be resisted' and that the policy outlined in the White Paper should be maintained 'in spite of the opposition which had since developed in Malaya'. In the week that followed, however, events moved so fast that, with the agreement of Attlee and Arthur Greenwood (lord privy seal and chairman of the Colonial Affairs Committee), Creech Jones adopted a more cautious approach and deferred citizenship pending consultations in Malaya. See 80; also CAB 128/5, CM 19(46)7 and CO 537/1529.

77 CO 537/1528, no 46   1 Mar 1946

[Malayan Union citizenship]: outward telegram (reply) no 99586 from War Office to Major-General H R Hone

Following from Colonial Office. *Begins.*
Your 08009 cipher 23rd Feb.[1]
ONE. Your recommendation for postponement of Citizenship Order in Council has been considered here at highest level, but it has been decided to maintain programme as previously planned. Matter will be debated in House of Commons on Friday 8 Mar, and decision cannot of course be regarded as final while proposals are still before Parliament.
TWO. Present view taken here is that, whilst strength of Malay reaction to citizenship proposals as set out in White Paper must be admitted, we stand to lose more than we would gain by postponement. Even if in reply to my 99153 cipher C.A.1 of 26 Feb you should advise that there is little or no likelihood of immediate adverse reactions by Chinese and Indians to deferment of citizenship Order it is felt

---

[1] See 74.

that period of some six months during which opposing points of view would be canvassed up and down Malaya might cause racial discord rather than avoid it.

THREE. Nevertheless recent intensification of Malay opposition, especially to citizenship proposals, increases necessity for effective local publicity which will explain the true purpose and effect of citizenship proposals, with a view to convincing the Malays in particular (e.g. Kelantan Government employees who imagine that they will henceforward be swamped by Europeans or Chinese) that their fears are groundless. In this connection further White Paper[2] which summarises contents of the three Orders in Council is to be published here early next week in readiness for debate on Mar 8. You will be informed of exact time as soon as possible, and meanwhile copies are being sent to you by fast air mail in proof form. White Paper should help you in preparing publicity, since it gives more detail about citizenship and other proposals than previous White Paper. For instance, it may not hitherto have been understood by Malays that acquisition of citizenship by five year's [sic] residence is based on U.K,. naturalisation practice and is thus limited to individual cases, each of which will be carefully scrutinised, Governor retaining discretion in all cases. Misunderstanding of this point may well have led to exaggerated Malay fears, and I trust you will do everything in your power, with help of new White Paper, to convince them that true purpose of citizenship proposals, is not (repeat not) to submerge the Malays but to associate all those with real loyalty towards Malaya in building the future of the Union.

FOUR. New White Paper also shows that further concessions have been made regarding ultimate control in Muhammadan religious matters (see your telegram 04809 cipher 23 Feb) and that there is now no question of Governor's assent to religious Bills being even formally required. Furthermore, appointments by Rulers to Malay Advisory Councils are not now to be subject to Governor's approval. Should be grateful if you would stress these points also in publicity henceforward.

FIVE. In general, force of Newboult's opinion that active and intelligent propaganda is required to put issues correctly before all communities affected (see last paragraph of your 04958 cipher 7 Feb) is fully appreciated here. We must at all costs avoid following two dangers:—

(a) that of encouraging e.g. Malays to unite in antagonism towards Chinese, thereby causing racial discord,
(b) that of rendering Government suspect by too obvious direct propaganda.

When Bourdillon was in Malaya, Newboult spoke to representative Malays in Ipoh and again in Kelantan on lines which avoided both these dangers and which should be admirably suited towards present needs. Main points which Newboult made were:—

(a) Malays must think for themselves, and in their own interests must not rely indefinitely on British protection to maintain them in a position of privilege.
(b) Malays must realise that the world has changed fundamentally during the war and that as isolated communities Malay States have no hope in the future.
(c) Malays must accept as their fellow countrymen all those who have established their claims to the rights and duties of citizenship.

---

[2] See 75, note 3.

Throughout, Newboult stressed necessity of Malays thinking out their own problems. Should be grateful if you would inform me as soon as possible whether you consider that publicity can be usefully pursued on these lines (bearing in mind dangers noted above), and if so, what actual measures you propose to take.

SIX. As soon as you receive proof copies of new White Paper, please inform all Rulers of latest religious concessions. In doing so should be grateful if you would:—

(a) inform Rulers of Perak, Kedah, Selangor, Negri Sembilan and Pahang that Secretary of State has carefully considered their request for an independent commission to visit Malaya, but does not feel that this would be advisable in present circumstances

(b) acknowledge in suitable terms telegrams received by the Secretary of State from the Sultan of Kelantan see your 04974 cipher 11 Feb and the Rajah of Perlis, (a brief telegram of protest sent through commercial channels on Feb 16th) and the letter now received from the Sultan of Kedah. Letter is dated 11 Feb and a fuller reply will be sent to it as soon as possible.

In communicating with all Rulers, please assure them that the Secretary of State is convinced that policy is necessary for Malaya's future, and adduce further concession on religious point as indication of his continued respect for their views. [*Ends*]

78   CO 537/1548, no 31   5 Mar 1946
[Pan-Malayan Malay Congress]: inward telegram no 08312 from HQ, British Military Administration (Malaya) to War Office

[This telegram came hard on the heels of telegram 08392 of same date (CO 537/1548, no 30). No 30 contained the text of the resolutions passed at the Pan-Malayan Malay Congress; no 31 provided an appreciation of their significance. Bourdillon assessed the first as 'a very important new development' and the second as 'a very important document' confirming 'the depth and breadth of feeling amongst the Malays and the fact that *citizenship* (sic) is their main grievance'. It was, he minuted, 'most important that Mr Creech Jones should know of this development' in advance of the Commons debate on 8 Mar (see CO 537/1548, minute by Bourdillon, 6 March 1946). Standing in for Hall who was indisposed, Creech Jones won the agreement of Attlee and Greenwood to postponing the introduction of the citizenship Order in Council until local consultations had taken place. Later more detailed reports became available on the Pan-Malayan Malay Congress held in Kuala Lumpur on 1–4 Mar, eg CO 537/1581, HQ Malaya Command weekly intelligence review, no 19.]

Pass following to Colonial Office. Reference our telegram 08392 dated 5th March. Following are our comments on resolution passed by Malay Congress.

1. Congress was composed by Representatives from all over Malaya. It had been much advertised and was fully attended. Proceedings have been widely criticised. Resolution passed far more hostile to new policy than anticipated. This due to depth of feeling among those present. Those who favour Union will not support it wholeheartedly until they know what they are committing themselves to. Those who oppose union do (? so solely) from fear of implications of new policy which they do not understand, and from way they were faced with fait accompli before they had opportunity for discussion. Given time and patience, bulk of opposition could probably be won over.

2. Citizenship proposals are chief bone of contention and very unpopular. Opposition is not so much to conception of common citizenship as to qualifications for admission. They consider it has been drawn too wide.

3. Rulers signed new agreements ceding jurisdiction which we are convinced they mean to stand by. MacMichael consistently emphasised that they were not being asked to sign explanatory note, but to show willingness to co-operate with H.M.G. They had objections to some of the specific proposals which they registered in writing, honestly believing that these would be subject of further consultation with responsible authority. They now strongly feel that this opportunity for discussion had not been granted. They find themselves in difficult position as their subjects are questioning their action in signing.

4. Majority of Government servants, including Police, are Malays and we are very dependent upon retention of their goodwill.

5. We can only implement new policy successfully with co-operation of Malays, which we have not (repeat not) at present got, but can get given further time for discussion with new Governors.

79　CO 537/1669　　　　　　　　　　　　　　8 Mar 1946
[Local reactions to the Malayan Union]: minute by W S Morgan[1]

[This minute, and particularly the last paragraph emphasizing the public relations opportunity provided by the imminent resumption of civil government, was brought to the attention of Gent who was due to be installed as governor of the Malayan Union on 1 Apr.]

Mr. Bourdillon yesterday drew Mr. Creech Jones' attention to these ALFSEA intelligence telegrams for February, as they related to Malay reactions to the White Paper policy.

Altogether these telegrams give a disturbing picture of continuing political and economic troubles in Malaya. The picture is complicated and difficult to appreciate since the reports are localised in detail and do not attempt an over-all survey. The following are the salient points to which attention should be drawn.

(a) The various movements – Malay, Chinese, and Indian – appear to be unrelated and to pursue their activities quite separately, but altogether they show that the Malayan scene is seething with political activity, though how far the mass of the population are interested or responsive it is hard to say.

(b) The issue of the White Paper has led to considerable opposition amongst the Malays, as is well known. From the telegrams the main centres appear to be Kelantan, Trengganu, Kedah and Johore, and the prime mover in organising the recent All Malay Congress at Kuala Lumpur was Dato Onn, the able and well-known Johore Malay, who is said however to be moderate in his views and is probably the progressive type that likes the idea of the Union but wishes it to be predominantly Malay. There is evidence (see L and J)[2] that religion is being used to

---

[1] W S Morgan entered the Malayan Education Service, 1931; fought in the Malaya campaign, 1941–1942; was appointed principal in the CO, 1947.

[2] The papers with the literal references F – L have not been printed with this document.

rouse opposition to the policy.

What is so striking about these telegrams is that there is no indication that the policy has provoked any reaction whatsoever amongst the non-Malays.

(c) The Malayan Communist Party and its close relation, the General Labour Union, continue to be openly opposed to the Military Administration and to foster strikes in widespread localities, including Singapore, Pensang, Kelantan, Ipoh and Province Wellesley. Their efforts have not been very successful, and the B.M.A., in taking a firm line, appear to be gaining public approval (see K).

It is significant, for instance, that in Penang (L), the G.L.U. were kept out of strike negotiations and that in Singapore Indian workers were forming a separate union outside the Chinese dominated G.L.U. (H).

(d) The telegrams at F and G point to Indonesian attempts to organise propaganda in Malaya.

(e) There have been a number of violent incidents, the most serious being at Batu Talam in Pahang, where Malays attacked Chinese in a clash which led to over 50 casualties, including 27 killed.

It may be wrong to be alarmist but it cannot be disguised that Malaya has not settled down under the Military Administration and the new policy has added a complication to an already confused scene. It is the heterogenity of Malaya's political activity which is, in my view, the most dangerous aspect because it can only lead to chaos. Some strong effort should be made to rally the moderate and responsible leaders to the support of the new administration. The success or failure of the Malayan Union should be the issue on which attention should be focussed, not communism, or China, or India, or Indonesia, and I should suggest that the installation of the Governors should not pass off as a piece of formal ceremonial but should be the occasion of speeches, eloquently and warmly phrased, explaining the new policy, stressing the hopes and aspirations of the civil government, and calling to the people to sink their divergencies and to unite to make a success of the Union (and the Colony of Singapore). This event will mark the passing of the not very popular Military Administration and the resumption of a much anticipated civil government. Hopes will run high for at least some message of hope, promise, and reassurance, and if it is not forthcoming there will be great disappointment and the Governors may have lost a useful and rare opportunity for winning support for the new regime. I do feel this suggestion is worthy of serious consideration.

80   PREM 8/459   15 Mar 1946
[Postponement of citizenship]: minute by Mr Creech Jones to Mr Attlee

[Encountering strong opposition during the second reading of the Straits Settlements (Repeal) Bill on 8 Mar (*H of C Debs*, vol 420, cols 637–727), Creech Jones agreed to postpone the implementation of the citizenship Order in Council to allow local consultation. Probably not least because the prime minister was being lobbied by 'old Malayan' representatives, such as Lords Elibank and Marchwood, the CO was anxious to reassure itself of Attlee's continuing support for the essence of the Malayan policy and the way it was being handled.]

Prime Minister

In the debate on Malayan policy in the House of Commons on March 8th, I maintained the essential basis of Government policy regarding Union and Common Citizenship and undertook to postpone for a few months the Order in Council on the latter principle so as to allow further local consultation. I agreed that the Government would consider certain points of detail. This was in harmony with your instructions and the advice of Lord Addison. The Opposition, I gather, is still not satisfied that our action is sufficiently conciliatory to The Sultans. But to go further is to jeopardise the whole policy. Some concessions on minor points can, of course, be made but the Opposition demand that the principal Order in Council setting out the framework of the Constitution be omitted. That must I feel be resisted. Besides the question of citizenship many other matters will be left for further consultation between the Governors and all sections of local opinion, particularly the question of the composition of the Legislative Council and Local Councils and the degree of authority delegated to the Local Councils. It is unreasonable of the Opposition to demand more. I attach a list[1] of the few minor modifications we can concede, and I shall be glad to know that you agree with this line of action. On that assumption, I have discussed with the Lord Privy Seal the statement for the Committee Stage on Monday next.[2]

---

[1] Not printed.

[2] Attlee agreed with this course on 17 Mar. During the third reading on 18 Mar, Creech Jones reaffirmed the concession on citizenship and, in addition, announced three concessions: the Council of Rulers would be allowed to discuss secular issues without the Governor's prior consent; the Malay Advisory Councils would be empowered to advise Rulers on secular issues; and a nominee of the Sultan should sit on the State Council. Although he agreed to hold in reserve details of the composition of various councils until local consultations had taken place, Creech Jones refused the demand for their excision from the Orders in Council. The Bill was then passed without a division (see *H of C Debs*, vol 420, cols 1540–1565) and the Orders-in-Council were made on 27 Mar. The postponement of citizenship was not, however, sufficient to conciliate the sultans. On 29 Mar Hall informed Attlee that they had asked John Foster MP (a lawyer who had been retained by the Malay rulers) for advice as to the legal action they could take to prevent the Malayan Union coming into existence on 1 Apr, 'it being their intention to secure an interval for further consideration in the hope that His Majesty's Government would agree to a policy of *federation* (which would not involve the cession of jurisdiction to His Majesty) instead of a policy of Union' (CO 537/1548, no 63, emphasis in original).

---

81 CAB 21/1954, F 5093/87/61   25 Mar 1946

'Review of political events in South-East Asia 1945 to March 1946': despatch from M E Dening to Mr Bevin.[1] *Enclosure*

On the 2nd March, 1945, I forwarded to the Foreign Office a review of political events as they affected the South-East Asia Command from its inception to the end of 1944.

2. With the appointment of a special commissioner in South-East Asia my functions as chief political adviser to the Supreme Commander have come to an end. It seems appropriate, therefore, to forward a further report covering events during 1945 and up to the present day, which I hope may also be of some use to Lord Killearn.

---

[1] Secretary of state for foreign affairs, 1945–1951.

3. The report is, I fear, rather long in these days when there is too much to be read. But a great deal has happened in the period. While the war continued political events were subsidiary to the main conduct of the battle. When the war ended it was the political situation which influenced military events.

4. Long though the report is, I have done no more than to give the general trend of events, except where, as in the case of Java, the picture had become so distorted as to require some correction of detail.

5. In the summary of my previous report I concluded with the words: "But the conclusion of hostilities will give rise to a host of intricate problems." That has proved to be true.

6. This report was shown in draft to the Supreme Allied Commander, who has received a copy, though I would in no way wish to suggest thereby that he assumes responsibility for any views I have expressed. Copies have also been sent to the Viceroy of India, the Governor of Burma, His Majesty's Ambassadors at Washington, Paris, Chungking and The Hague, to the Special Ambassador at Batavia, to His Majesty's Minister at Bangkok and to His Majesty's Consul General at Saigon.

Enclosure to 81

This review covers the year 1945 and the period up to the abolition of the office of chief political adviser to the Supreme Allied Commander, South-East Asia on the 15th March, 1946.

2. Up to the collapse of Japan in August the year 1945 was one of steady defeat for Japanese arms in South-East Asia as elsewhere. The greater part of Burma, including Rangoon, was captured the hard way, with heavy loss of life and material to the enemy, and when Japan surrendered a major assault on Malaya was about to take place.

3. As the year wore on, the campaign in South-East Asia became more and more a purely British-Indian affair. Towards the end of 1944 the decision had been made by the Sino-American command in China to withdraw two Chinese divisions from Burma to avert the possibility of an apparently imminent collapse. This was followed early in 1945 by a decision to transfer the remainder of the Chinese forces from Burma, and later the whole of the United States air forces operating with the South-Asia Command. The sole American brigade which had operated in S.E.A.C. in conjunction with the Chinese forces in Northern Burma was also transferred to China.

4. American strategy, in so far as the Asiatic mainland was concerned, was, in fact, concentrating upon China to the exclusion of South-East Asia, whereas the strategy of S.E.A.C. was directed towards opening the Malacca Straits and gaining access to the South China Sea. In so far as the diversion of Sino-American forces to China created gaps in the S.E.A.C. order of battle, the operations of the latter were hampered. The subsequent decision to provide a British Commonwealth force to take part in the main American assault on Japan would have placed further restrictions upon the S.E.A.C. effort.

5. Militarily there can be no doubt that the Pacific strategy as a means of bringing the war with Japan to an early end was sound. Whether the China strategy, which was also an American concept, was equally sound is more doubtful. Historians may

well argue that a combined, instead of a divided, effort might have led to an earlier opening of the Malacca Straits and thus greatly have facilitated redeployment at the close of the European war, whereas it was very doubtful whether the state of China would have admitted of any effective campaign through Chinese territory.

6. These military considerations are mentioned because they were not without their political cause and effect. The United States had come to regard the Japanese war as something peculiarly their own, just as they came to regard China as their particular protégé. Though commanders might or might not see eye to eye with their British counterparts (and on the mainland, on the whole, they did not), it is doubtful whether, in American eyes, there was any fundamental conception of a joint Anglo-American effort in the war against Japan, whatever might be declaimed from public platforms. In part there was resentment at the alleged unwillingness of Britain to do her share. But far more there was the feeling this was an all-American show in which American arms both could and would demonstrate both their superiority and their authority over all others.

7. In this American conception of the Far Eastern war, which was little realised in Europe, S.E.A.C. was always a poor relation. It was the unnecessary front, and as such could always be deprived of resources or have them withheld. The slow progress of its operations, which was due in part to the withholding of resources, and, in part, to American insistence on securing the air route through North Burma to China, was always regarded as a legitimate target for criticism.

8. In spite therefore of the fact that S.E.A.C. was an integrated Anglo-American command, and in spite of the cordial relations between the integrated staffs, it cannot be said on balance that the campaign in South-East Asia resulted in a better understanding between Great Britain and America. Nor was the existence of the American "India-Burma Theatre" within the command conducive to good understanding. On the contrary, though through no fault of ours, S.E.A.C. was a constant potential source of friction. At the root of the matter lay the fact that America always suspected British Far Eastern policy, and that, in her new-found strength, she was satisfied that her own policy was not only the right one, but also the more disinterested. Whether it was so right or so disinterested remains to be seen.

9. However that may be, the end of the war with Japan found the British forces of S.E.A.C. and the Sino-American forces of China apart from one another and faced with entirely different sets of problems.

10. From those problems which now confront S.E.A.C., America has remained aloof. At the same time she has maintained through O.S.S. (now transformed into S.S.U.) detachments in various places, posts of observation which not improbably combine the task of economic penetration, while in Siam she has a strong foothold, including an air staging post, which is no doubt intended to be the forerunner of a commercial air line. For the rest, she retains and exercises the right to continue to suspect us and to criticise us. Individual relations, however, remain cordial.

11. As regards China, the not unexpected troubles ensuing from the presence of her forces in Northern Burma continue. With the resumption of civil government over the greater part of Burma from the 1st October, 1945, and over the whole from the 1st January, 1946, the problem of the Chinese in Burma has become the responsibility of the Burma Government. In the rest of South-East Asia the large Chinese populations present a series of varying problems which, however, have not up to date become acute. In Siam there is a prospect of the early establishment of

diplomatic relations between that country and China, which heretofore had not existed. In Malaya at the moment the chief problem is that of the Malayan Communist party, of Chinese origin, but independent of the so-called Chinese Communist party in China proper. In the Netherlands Indies the Dutch are at present inclined to view the Chinese with favour as a counter-balance to the Indonesian independence movement, and the chief concern of the Chinese Consul-General is for the safety of the large Chinese communities and their property in the present state of turmoil.

12. With the exception of Burma, it may therefore be said that in general there are not, at any rate as yet, any major Chinese problems in South-East Asia to complicate relations with the Chinese Government, which itself is obviously much preoccupied with events in China proper and in Manchuria.

13. Before proceeding to review the problems of South-East Asia by countries in their intricate detail, it is well to consider the position of S.E.A.C. when hostilities ceased. The end of the war with Japan found the Command militarily readier than any other to take immediate action. But General MacArthur,[2] who had to take the initial occupation of Japan with comparatively slender forces, and who had by then been appointed Supreme Commander for the Allied Powers, was anxious lest any incidents in outlying areas might render his task more difficult. He therefore forbade any reoccupation until he had taken the formal Japanese surrender in Tokyo Bay, an event which did not take place until the 2nd September, 1945. A delay was therefore imposed upon S.E.A.C., which had important consequences, particularly in Indonesia.

14. On the very day that Japan agreed to unconditional surrender, namely, on the 15th August, 1945, Admiral Mountbatten became the unwilling inheritor of a large portion of the former South-West Pacific Command, including Java—unwilling because he was given no additional resources to meet his largely increased commitment. Indo-China as far as the 16°N. parallel was also placed finally in his Command. He had thus an area of 1,500,000 square miles, with a population of 128 million to deal with, in addition to some 750,000 Japanese. As for the forces under his command, the additional formations and shipping from Europe which he had been led to expect were no longer forthcoming now that the war was at the end, while there was a steady depletion of the ranks of trained and experienced officers and men by the inexorable demands of release and repatriation.

15. It is important to remember these military facts, because they were largely responsible for the situation which subsequently arose and which has given rise to widespread misunderstanding as well as to widespread criticism. Admiral Mountbatten was not, in fact, given the tools to finish the job. It is not suggested that there were not good reasons for this. But the results were inescapable.

16. One of the liveliest targets for criticism has been the continued employment, months after the Japanese surrender, of Japanese troops for the purpose of maintaining law and order. There could hardly be anything more repugnant to the world at large or to the populations which, after years of Japanese occupation, are still compelled to obey Japanese orders (even though they be delivered in a somewhat different voice).

---

[2] General Douglas MacArthur, c-in-c, Allied Forces, South-West Pacific, 1942; c-in-c, US Forces, Far East Command, until 1951; supreme commander, Allied Forces in Japan, until 1951; c-in-c, US Forces in Korea, until 1951.

17. But there was never any likelihood that the forces available to the Supreme Allied Commander could stretch to every hole and corner of the vast area allotted to him. Except in Siam, there was no Government exercising administration, while the organised police forces which existed in South-East Asia before the war had disintegrated under Japanese rule. The best that could be hoped for was that stable administrations could be set up at an early date in the areas to be occupied, and that the Japanese could thereafter immediately be disarmed and concentrated for ultimate repatriation. In the event, things turned out quite differently.

18. It was not only the absence of police forces which enlarged the task of the South-East Asia Command. Throughout the area there were already large quantities of arms in the hands of unauthorised persons. In addition, vast ammunition dumps and stores of arms and military equipment had to be guarded until they could be disposed of. There was thus plenty of material to put in the hands of an enormous population which, in the years of Japanese occupation, proved in the event to have suffered a serious decline in public morals.

19. The causes of this decline are not far to seek. Prior to 1941 the peoples of South-East Asia had lived in conditions of security and comparative plenty. Whatever the critics of colonial government may be pleased to say to-day, it is a fact that in South-East Asia the age between the wars was one of security, of comparative stability and of gradual development.

20. With little or no warning to the average person, his world was rudely shattered and his erstwhile governors and protectors ignominiously dispersed. All that he had looked up to had vanished without any immediate prospect of return, and in its place he was confronted with the harsh and inconsiderate rule of the Japanese, who, while they did nothing to improve the lot of the population, were indefatigable in their efforts to humiliate the white man and to prove that not only was his rule at an end, but that his return was something to fight against. These efforts were by no means entirely successful, but to a varying degree they left behind an unwelcome legacy which added to the already heavy burden of the S.E.A.C.

21. While the Japanese did their utmost to destroy what had been, they put nothing in its place and there grew up amongst native populations a spirit of resistance which manifested itself in covert attempts to evade Japanese regulations and to outwit them in devious ways. This spirit indeed formed the kernel of the resistance movements which were encouraged by our clandestine organisations, and which, in Burma and Malaya, rendered active assistance to the Allied cause.

22. But by its very nature this spirit of resistance encouraged a law breaking as opposed to a law-abiding temperament, and what was born of duress has to some extent become a habit difficult to eradicate with the disappearance of that duress. In particular this applies to the youth of the areas concerned, and even in Malaya, which compares very favourably with any other part of South-East Asia in its progress towards rehabilitation, juvenile delinquency is at a premium. Youth was neglected during the occupation except where it was deliberately cultivated to evil ends by the Japanese, as in the case of Java. There will be no complete cure until youth has found, or been given, a new orientation.

23. The tasks allotted to S.E.A.C. were to disarm and concentrate the Japanese forces and to succour Allied prisoners of war and internees. Together with these tasks there was the somewhat ill-defined responsibility for maintaining law and order, which, however, with the strictly limited forces available, could for practical

purposes not extend beyond the areas of actual physical occupation. The preceding paragraphs have shown to what extent the vast quantities of arms and ammunition, the generally prevailing atmosphere of unrest and lawlessness and the absence of organised police forces added to the difficulties of the tasks which were set to the Command. These difficulties were general and not entirely unforeseen. The difficulties likely to be encountered in Indo-China were also not unforeseen. But it was the situation in Java, which was only included in the Command on the day of Japan's collapse, which upset all previous calculations.

24. It was the necessity to divert much larger forces to Java to cope with a politico-military situation which had not been foreseen which delayed the concentration and disarmament of the Japanese and made it obligatory, in the absence of any stable administration, to continue to employ them on guard duties and even on occasion to use them in a defensive operational rôle.

25. The conditions described in the preceding paragraphs were general to the situation as a whole. From the date of the Japanese surrender it was the political situation in the various areas which influenced the military situation and to a much greater extent the situation in non-British than in British territories. The following paragraphs deal with developments in Siam, French Indo-China and the Netherlands East Indies. . . .[3]

Economic factors

147. The sudden end of the war with Japan brought S.E.A.C. face to face with economic conditions which, though they were not entirely unforeseen, yet demanded measures which the command was not equipped to undertake. Whereas in Europe elaborate planning had preceded the collapse of Germany, in the case of Japan planning was, almost up to the moment when the last shot was fired, based on the premise that the war would end in November 1946. The results of this unpreparedness, for which S.E.A.C. was in no way responsible, were unhappy. In the circumstances it is surprising that things have gone as well as they have.

148. The conduct of the war in South-East Asia had demanded the setting up of civil affairs organisations and of planning against the day of reoccupation. But while hostilities were in progress reoccupation envisaged no more, at any rate in the initial stages, than the prevention of disease and unrest amongst the population, and rehabilitation and reconstruction only to the degree that they facilitated the conduct of military operations. With the end of the war, however, rehabilitation and reconstruction are no longer of secondary, but of primary importance, and special machinery is required to bring conditions back to normal with as little delay as possible.

149. In the case of S.E.A.C. the sudden end of the war meant that there were only the war staffs to deal with the host of economic problems which were to descend upon them. Not only were the military staffs not reinforced; they became more and more depleted as time went on with the demands of retrenchment and demobilisation. The civil requirements of tens of millions of civil population had to be screened by the Principal Administrative Officer's staff. The military administrations, known somewhat misleadingly as civil affairs, which had always been starved of man-power, were called upon to perform superhuman feats, while the Economic Intelligence

---

[3] Paras 26–147 on Siam, Indo-China and Netherlands East Indies, omitted.

Section of the Directorate of Intelligence, originally created for a totally different purpose, was saddled in the early stages with the task of collecting the data without which future requirements could not be estimated. Great credit reflects on those who, with little or no warning, readily undertook new and in many cases unaccustomed labours.

150. But with the best will in the world the military command, with its operational commitments and the responsibility for the welfare of large military forces could do no more than devote part-time attention to what is unquestionably a whole-time job. The lesson to be learned from this is that it is as necessary to plan for the end of the war as it is for the beginning and for the conduct of it. Once again S.E.A.C. had not been given the tools.

151. The main economic problems confronting the command did not differ from those prevailing in other war-stricken areas. They were, and still are, shortage [sic] of food, of transportation and of inducement goods. In addition, Burma has been shattered by war; Siam is in the throes of a fearful inflation, while the political situation in Indo-China and the Netherlands Indies has prevented the movement of goods and the restoration of economic life, though in the latter area certain islands (such as Celebes) have made greater progress than others. Only in Malaya has there been steady progress towards recovery, though much remains to be done.

152. Rice being the staple diet of South-East Asia, the shortage of it is likely to have most serious consequences. Burma, the largest surplus producer of all, has been able to furnish a negligible quantity. In Siam, where there is known to be a considerable surplus, the political situation, inflation and general inefficiency have together conspired to prevent more than a trickle from flowing to deficit areas. In Indo-China, the arbitrary division of the country for military purposes, and the general unrest make it impossible to estimate at present whether any surplus will be available for export. Java, which was at one time self-supporting, has now become a deficiency area. The prospect is not an encouraging one.

153. Two immediate problems present themselves. The first is to extract and distribute available stocks. The second is to ensure maximum planting in the coming season. It is in connexion with this second problem that we come up against the question of inducement goods. The result of the introduction of Japanese currency and the debasement of existing currencies by the Japanese has been to destroy the faith of the peasant in money. That faith can only be restored if he is able to buy for the money which he receives in payment for his products the goods which he requires. Until he can do this he is unconvinced of the value of paper and will tend to grow only for his own requirements. The need, therefore, to provide goods, and in particular textiles, which will induce the farmer to grow a maximum crop, is an urgent one.

154. As was to be expected, the end of the war found South-East Asia in financial chaos. In Burma and Malaya it was found possible to ban Japanese currency with the entry of our troops. This somewhat drastic step cannot have failed to cause some temporary hardship, but it was effective. It has, however, had a curious after-effect in contributing to the lack of faith in paper money which still prevails amongst the ignorant, who reason that if one currency can become valueless overnight, what is to prevent the same thing happening to any other paper currency.

155. In Siam the note issue is eight times that of pre-war days, and Herculean steps will have to be taken to provide a remedy. Whether the Siamese are capable of

Herculean steps remains to be seen.

156.   In Indo-China the French maintained the value of the piastre. But in view of the division of the country is is likely to be some time before the financial picture becomes clear.

157.   In the Netherlands Indies the Dutch successfully introduced a new N.E.I. guilder issue in many of the outer islands. But in Java and Sumatra the Indonesians murdered anyone found in possession of Dutch notes, and as our position was for many months so insecure even in the areas nominally under control, the Japanese guilder continued to circulate, without any foreign exchange value at all. Only in March 1946 was it found possible to introduce the N.E.I. guilder within a limited area, while the Japanese guilder was given a temporary exchange value of 3 Dutch cents until it could be withdrawn. It is as yet too early to estimate the effect of this measure. The exchange rate of 2s. 7½d. to the new N.E.I. guilder is considered by a British financial expert to be too high, since that in Holland is understood to be only 1s. 10½d.

The Japanese

158.   Even to those who knew the Japanese before (if anyone knows a Japanese), it could only be a matter of conjecture in August 1945 how they would behave in defeat, since they had never been defeated before in living memory. It was, therefore, with mingled sentiments of curiosity, suspicion and doubt that a party set out with Admiral Mountbatten's Chief of Staff in August to meet Field-Marshal Count Terauchi's Chief of Staff, who had been summoned to Rangoon to discuss the implementation of the surrender terms.

159.   In the event the Japanese were correct, if ill at ease. Though as an act of courtesy they were allowed to retain their swords (since the formal surrender was not to take place until the 12th September in Singapore), for which they rendered formal thanks, their escorts and their close surveillance can have left them in no doubt of their defeat.

160.   From the outset—though on our part suspicion naturally died slowly—it became evident that the Japanese, having been ordered by their Emperor to surrender, intended to obey that order to the letter. Indeed, except for isolated instances and more particularly in Java, the Japanese have carried out their obligations.

161.   From the first they pleaded that they should carry out the surrender voluntarily themselves. That is to say, having received the orders of the Supreme Allied Commander, the Japanese High Command would then convey these orders to subordinate commands and accept responsibility for their execution. They also asked that all orders given by the Allies should be in the name of the Supreme Allied Commander. Both these requests were granted, and in practice, with only few exceptions, the procedure has worked very well.

162.   It has already been explained in this report why it was necessary to continue to use armed Japanese for defensive and guard purposes in certain areas. At times they became involved in hostilities and on occasion displayed as much gallantry and devotion to duty at the behest of the British as they had in the days of their own arrogant domination.

163.   Elsewhere the Japanese were employed as labour, and here, too, they performed the tasks assigned to them without question and with an efficiency which

often compared favourably with the performance of local native labour.

164.   The effect of all this has been vaguely disturbing. The Japanese have, in fact, been carrying out their "defeat drill" with the same discipline and determination which characterised their aggression. It is a mistake to assume that the spirit which animates them is not the same. But their general behaviour has been such as to give rise to a sneaking sense of almost admiration amongst the citizen-soldiers of a nation which notoriously cannot hate for long.

165.   Fraternisation with Japanese is fortunately not in question, for the customs and habits of our two nations are so different as to render anything of the sort distasteful. But the orderly behaviour of the Japanese in the midst of disorder; their efficiency, which is without doubt incomparably greater than that of most of the indigenous inhabitants of this part of the world, and their ready acquiescence are liable to give rise, even if only sub-consciously, to the thought that "they are not so bad after all."

166.   Nor would they be, if they were animated by a different spirit. But there is no convincing evidence that the Japanese in South-East Asia are changed in spirit. At any rate at first they did not even admit defeat. The vast majority of them had not been in Japan for a long time and had not witnessed its destruction. Their view was that they were undefeated, and that they were merely obeying the orders of their Emperor, who, in order to avoid further bloodshed in the world, had told them to lay down their arms.

167.   To-day most Japanese in this area are probably conscious of their defeat and to this the efforts of our former political warfare organisation have without doubt largely contributed. But what next? It is not difficult to change the words which issue from the lips of a Japanese—one could occasionally accomplish that even in the bad old days—but it is quite a different thing to change his way of thought. And it is far from being an advantage to have him under one's control far from his own country, since it is only in Japan that his regeneration can take place—if at all. However excellent our propagandists, they are too few in number even to begin to know what three-quarters of a million Japanese scattered over a wide area are thinking.

168.   The Japanese in South-East Asia have, in the main, not been defeated in battle (except those who were in Burma). They may be convinced of their defeat, but they may equally well be determined to do it again when opportunity offers. Segregation in remote areas will do nothing to convince them to the contrary. They will be outcasts in an alien land with much time for thought, which may well breed a spirit of revenge.

169.   There is another danger and that is that present discipline may break down. This may, in non-British territories, lead to reprisals, or it may, particularly in the case of Siam, lead to a restoration of Japanese confidence as a result of their ability to defy authority.

170.   Everything, therefore, points the same way, namely, that the Japanese should be repatriated to Japan as soon as possible. But S.E.A.C. has not the resources and the Supreme Commander for the Allied Powers has so far not proved helpful. At the present rate, repatriation will take several years, with consequences which can only be bad. The problem is an extremely serious one, which must be tackled resolutely—and soon.

82   CO 537/1548, no 66   **1 Apr 1946**
[Boycott of governor's installation]: inward telegram no 1 from Sir E
Gent to Mr Hall

[This telegram, which was despatched in the early hours of the morning of 1 Apr local
time and received in the CO at 9.30 am, refers to events that took place on the previous
day. Gent arrived in Kuala Lumpur on 31 Mar. The rulers had foregathered at the Station
Hotel, but an emergency meeting of the PMMC on 31 Mar passed resolutions calling upon
Malays to boycott the Malayan Union and inviting Dato Onn to request the rulers to
absent themselves from the inauguration ceremony.]

On the arrival of Gent this afternoon, all Sultans requested interview with him with
reference to their decision not (repeat not) to attend the swearing in ceremony. See
Sultan of Perak's telegram to the Secretary of State of 30th March. Gent endeavoured
to convince them that the decision could only give the impression of discourtesy to
H.M. Government and His Majesty's representative and that, while H.M. Government
had decided on policy of Union, nevertheless the whole detailed scheme of the
structure of the new Union Constitution was deliberately left for full consultation in
Malaya. At the interview, the Chief spokesman was the Sultan of Perak, who insisted
that, while H.M. Government had satisfactorily met the requirements regarding
religious affairs, the position and prestige of the Sultans required also that their
[secular] state of affairs was not removed as Union policy necessarily involves. He
gave particular assurances that no mark of disrespect to His Majesty or H.M.
Government or the Governor was intended. After adjourning for discussion amongst
themselves, the Sultans returned at 11.30 pm. for further interview with Gent to
report that they were unable to vary their decision not to attend tomorrow's
ceremony and repeated their assurance of no disrespect. On this occasion, the Sultan
of Kedah acted as spokesman and referred to telegram which had been sent to the
Secretary of State a few days ago stating that the Sultans would accept Federation
but not Union. Sultans are objecting to attending the formal meeting of the Council
of Sultans arranged for 2nd April, but it is hoped that they will consent to attend at
the same time and date if the meeting takes the form of informal meeting with the
Governor personally. Gent recommends that reply be telegraphed for communication to the Sultan of Perak in the following sense.

  First. Secretary of State greatly regrets their decision regarding the swearing in
ceremony.

  Second. Policy of the Union has been decided by H.M. Government with the
approval of Parliament and has been implemented by Order in Council.

  Third. Within that policy, the Sultans will have the fullest opportunity to advise on
details of constitutional provisions which, in their view, will best serve Malay
interests no less than those of Malaya as a whole.[1]

---

[1] The secretary of state replied accordingly, outward telegram no 4, 1 Apr 1946.

83   CO 537/1548, no 69   2 Apr 1946
[Boycott of governor's installation]: inward telegram no 13 from Sir E Gent to Mr Hall

Your telegram No. 4.[1]

Sultans.

1.   I am writing to each Sultan as directed and I note your instructions regarding publication. So far, the text of the telegram of 30th March from the Sultan of Perak has not (repeat not) been published.

2.   Sultans declined to attend even the informal meeting on 2nd April mentioned in my telegram No. 1, but yesterday evening asked to come to King's House[2] to say goodbye before leaving Kuala Lumpur (with the exception of the Sultan of Selangor who has private residence here). I welcomed this gesture and saw each of them separately for few minutes personal talk. All extended to me cordial personal invitation to visit them in their States and the rulers of Perak and Negri Sembilan gave me the impression that, as soon as your reply was received definitely disposing of the question of Union versus Federation, we might hope to make headway with matters as to constitutional provisions necessary to satisfy their feelings and (? ensure) their position.

3.   Probable basis of the Sultans embarrassment and difficulty is that they have put themselves in the position of responsiveness to the new political Malay organisation known as Malay Congress, of which Dato Onn of Johore is the President, and the attitude of this organisation is not at all promising at present.

---

[1] See 82, note 1.

[2] King's House was the governor's residence; Carcosa, which had been built for Swettenham as first resident general of the FMS, was the chief secretary's house. Since the Malay states had been sovereign territories until the war, the residence of the high commissioner in Kuala Lumpur had been named King's House not Government House. When, in the pre-war period, the high commissioner of the Malay states switched roles to function as governor of the colony of the Straits Settlements he had occupied Government House in Singapore.

84   CO 537/1548   8 Apr 1946
[The Pan-Malayan Malay Congress]: minute by Mr Creech Jones

The development among the Malays of some Malay organisation was to be expected and the prospect of a movement throughout the peninsula need not be bad if it is handled now with understanding & discretion. The agitation over here by the ex-Governors & the Conservative M.P.s in an area not remote from "Indonesia" has encouraged it just as the Sultans under similar influences have renounced their earlier stand and gone into opposition. Now, the Sultans are aware that their people are sceptical of them and are turning from them to the Malay Congress. So the Sultans, to curry the popular favour they are in danger of losing, are demonstrating an obstinacy to Britain in the hope that leadership of the Malays shall not pass to the Congress. At the same time the Malays through Congress are evolving a new leadership & Dato Onn will exploit his opportunity. He will undoubtedly be joined by the discontents, impatient youth & the ambitious but they will not find political satisfaction either by backing the Sultans or by demanding Federation. An outlet for the Congress then might be found through the new political institutions where the Malays are likely in most to be dominant. The Malays need to know that they are "lost" in a measurable time unless British policy is broadly accepted.

85   CO 537/1528   25–26 Apr 1946

[Malay opposition to Malayan Union]: minutes by H T Bourdillon, J J Paskin and Sir G Gater

. . . During the past few weeks, the attitude both of the Malay Sultans and of leading Malays, as represented by Dato Onn's organisation, has steadily hardened. As regards the former, we may take up the story from the point at which they telegraphed the Secretary of State, announcing that they could not recognise the MacMichael Agreements as effective. The telegram is registered at (64) on 50823/34/46. It goes on to say that the Rulers require further time for consultation with their State Councils and people, and that they are axious to re-open negotiations regarding the future of Malaya, on the basis of a Malayan Federation in place of a Malayan Union. The telegram was sent on the 30th of March, and since that date the Sultans have adopted a perfectly firm and clear attitude. They have been at pains to deny any intention of personal discourtesy towards the Governor, or of disrespect towards His Majesty or His Majesty's Government (see No. 66.)[1] They have behaved cordially towards the Governor in private, but have refused to meet him publicly or to attend his swearing in ceremony, on the grounds that this would imply an acknowledgment of the existence of the Malayan Union, which they do not recognise. They had assembled at Kuala Lumpur at the time of the Governor's arrival, but they left soon afterwards (No. 69)[2] and since then their actions have been in keeping with the position they had already adopted. They have acted throughout as a united body, and have maintained contact with the Sultan of Johore in this country. On the 15th of April, they held a meeting at Kuala Kangsar (the Headquarters of the Sultan of Perak—(see No. (85) on this file) as a result of which they wrote to the Governor (No. (88) on this file), expressing their desire to proceed to England at the earliest opportunity, in order to lay personally before the King their request that Federation might be substituted for Union. In the meanwhile they had received, through the Governor, the Secretary of State's reply to their "repudiation telegram", and in their letter they expressed great regret at the terms of this reply, which had evidently failed to move them from their attitude. It will be recollected that the Secretary of State had told them (No. (67) on 50823/34/46) that he was aware of no circumstances attending the signing of the Agreement with Sir Harold MacMichael which would justify the Sultans in refusing to recognise these agreements as effective, and that he could not admit the right of one party to withdraw from engagements solemnly entered into.

That, then, is the present position as regards the Sultans. In response to his own suggestion, Sir Edward Gent has been asked (see Nos. (89) and (90) on this file) to keep them in play for the time being by seeking to elicit their ideas on the distinction between Federation and Union, and on the form of machinery which they have in

---

[1] See 82.   [2] See 83.

mind for the former. He is due to proceed to Perak today, and we shall probably hear further in the near future. In the meanwhile, though we have no detailed indication of what happened at the Sultans Conference at Kuala Kangsar, it is plain that the result of the Conference has been to strengthen their resolve and to confirm their unity of purpose. There is some indication (see No. (90) on 50823/34/46) that they used the occasion to elaborate a federal scheme for Malaya.

As regards Dato Onn and his organisation (the Malay Congress) alternatively known as the U.M.N.O., (which presumably stands for United Malay Nationalist Organisation),[3] there is less direct evidence of recent activities, though it is clear that the Congress has indeed been active and has exercised a powerful influence. As I reported in my minute of 5/4/46 on 50823/34/46, our earlier impressions of the extreme moderation of the Organisation were dispelled some time ago. No. (69) on that file (see also No. (65) as regards Dato Onn's personal attitude) speaks of the position adopted by the Congress as "not at all promising" and indicates that the Sultans are to a considerable extent under its influence. This influence is also, without doubt, to be detected in the last minute failure of the Malay members to attend the first meeting of the Governor's Advisory Council. The hardening of attitude on the part of Dato Onn himself is said to have been due to the second White Paper, whose contents he apparently regards as "tantamount to annexation".

There is one further development which must be recorded though its importance cannot be gauged at present. According to information received from Dato Onn at the end of March a strong youth movement with Indonesian sympathies has been gaining ground among Kampong Malays.

It is clear from the above, first that the Sultans are now more than ever united in an attitude of polite but catagorical [sic] non-cooperation, and secondly that there is a large measure of unanimity, in the same sense (though possibly not so polite?) amongst the more thinking Malays. The former of these developments cannot be entirely regarded as due to the influence of prominent ex-Malayans here and the advice received from Mr. John Foster,[4] though these factors have undoubtedly played a large part in influencing the Sultans' attitude. It must be emphasised that the Malays themselves are uniting as they have never united in the past, and are uniting against the present policy of H.M.G. We had hoped that Malay opposition would be won round by the modifications of the policy on religious and other matters, and particularly by the deferment of the citizenship Order in Council. But this has not proved to be the case.

In the present deadlock, which means that Sir Edward Gent can expect no cooperation either from the Rulers or from the Malays in his task of elaborating and establishing the machinery of the Union, two alternatives seem to present themselves. The first is to proceed on the lines at present laid down, and to do without this cooperation until and unless the Sultans and the Malays see that it is useless to resist further. It can be held that Sir Edward Gent has been at pains to offer full opportunities for cooperation, and that if these opportunities are rejected, the dissenters have themselves to blame for any disadvantages which the Malays may thereby suffer in the future. If this line is adopted, we shall presumably inform Sir Edward Gent accordingly. The Sultans will then reiterate their demand to come to

---

[3] The United Malays National Organisation was formally inaugurated at the Pan-Malayan Malay Congress in Johore Bahru, 11–13 May 1946, see 90.   [4] See 80, note 2.

this country in a body, and it is difficult to see how this demand can be refused indefinitely.

The second alternative is to see whether we cannot, without in any way undermining the conception of the Malayan Union or the efficacy of the central legislature, take certain steps to grant the Sultans a strictly constitutional place in the Union system. Enclosed in No. (84) is a memorandum by Mr. Hone, in which he has embodied the outcome of his reflections on this subject during the last few months. Mr. Hone has, of course, had an unrivalled opportunity to study the situation as it has developed, and he suggests that it is not only possible but desirable to bring the Sultans right into the picture, on a strictly constitutional basis, rather than leaving them right out of it (except on strictly religious questions) as has been the doctrine hitherto. The emphasis, of course, is on the word "strictly constitution-al" and the pre-requisite of any action on the lines suggested would be that the Sultans would undertake in all cases to accept the advice tendered to them. The most important individual suggestions made by Mr. Hone are as follows:

(a) That the Sultans, as well as the Governor, should assent to *State Council* enactments, and that, as a corollary to this re-introduction of the Sultans into the constitutional affairs of their States, they should be in constant contact with the Resident Commissioners and should be very active in making themselves known through the State and in visiting hospitals, schools, etc.

(b) That the Sultans as well as the Governor should assent to Ordinances passed by the Central Legislature (with present facilities for communication, Mr. Hone doubts whether this would involve very much waste of time, and suggests that draft Ordinances might in certain cases be circulated in advance).

(c) That the Sultans should be mentioned in sanctions, approvals, issues of orders etc. under some such formula as "His Excellency the Governor and their Highnesses the Rulers have been pleased to etc." Mr. Hone considers that this would be a substantial improvement on the practice previously followed in the Federated Malay States, where it was made abundantly plain that the Heads of the local Governments were the Residents, and the [sic] where the formula "the British Resident has been pleased to etc." was all too familiar.

It will be observed that in his telegram No. 136 ((87) on this file) Sir Edward Gent has a suggestion on the same lines, but he only covers part of the ground. One point about Sir Edward Gent's proposal is that we cannot tell how much this would mean in practice (if anything), since the whole relationship of the State Councils with the Central Legislature remains to be decided. Until local consultation has been completed and Sir John Maude[5] has come home, we cannot say whether the State Councils will be granted *any* substantial legislative powers. In any event, it seems important not to tackle this problem piece meal. Either we must stand pat or we must frame comprehensive proposals for bringing the Sultans within the constitution on a purely constitutional basis. The first part of Mr. Hone's memorandum (the second part deals with citizenship) is a reasoned plea for the latter course.

If this course is favoured, at least as a possibility worthy of exploration, the first step would be for the Department to elaborate a definite scheme which could be put

---

[5] Sir John Maude, lawyer, KC 1943; Conservative MP 1945–1951; appears to have been observing the procedure in Malaya by which consultation with respect to citizenship was being conducted.

to Sir Edward Gent for his views. If his reactions were favourable, the scheme could be put to the Sultans forthwith; and according to our advice (see for instance paragraph 3 of No. (86)) there is reasonable hope that the cooperation of the Sultans and of moderate Malay opinion could be secured. Certainly the present emphasis of the Sultans themselves on federation as opposed to Union is dictated by their prospective disappearance, under the latter, from a *formal* position in the organisation.

Since everything we have heard hitherto has been from the Malay side, the above appreciation does not mention Chinese or Indians. It might be held that any departure from the lines at present laid down would merely antagonise the other sections of the community and create a stronger opposition than that which we have experienced hitherto. It should be noted, however, that action under the second alternative outlined above would in no way prejudice or affect the status of these communities under the new policy. And it is noteworthy that Sir Edward Gent, who has always been very much alive to these considerations, is in favour of some further move in the direction suggested.

H.T.B.
25.4.46

I agree generally with Mr Bourdillon's appreciation of the position as it has developed in Malaya since Sir E. Gent's arrival there. The present position, as he points out, is one of deadlock: & the question for decision is whether, in order to secure the cooperation of the Malays (N.B. not only the Sultans), there shd. be any modification of the constitution as promulgated in the O-in-C. I have no doubt that it would be possible to devise some means of giving the Sultans some formal & strictly constitutional place in the structure, without detracting from the effective authority of the Gov. & the central legislature of the Union (& without changing the Union to a Federation), which would save the face of the Rulers & secure the cooperation of the Malays.

What formal changes wd. be required to produce this effect would require careful [consideration], & wd. probably differ in form from those suggested by Mr Hone.

If we *are* to make an attempt to placate the Malays in this way, it wd. certainly be best for a coherent scheme to be prepared in the C.O. rather than to proceed piecemeal as Sir E. Gent seems disposed to do.

On one point I would differ substantially from the suggestion made both by Sir E. Gent & Mr Hone, i.e. as regards the State Councils. I think it wd. be a great mistake to "boost" their legislative functions by associating the Sultans directly with them.

I imagine that the S. of S. will wish to discuss the present position & the line now to be taken on it.

J.J.P.
25.4.46

Secretary of State

Mr. Bourdillon has at my request prepared in his minute of 25/4/46 an appreciation of the present position in Malaya in regard to the new Constitution. I have nothing to add to what he and Mr. Paskin have said except that I should like to stress two points. The first is, that I think it is essential to take a decision now between the two alternatives set out by Mr. Bourdillon, as it is most important that Sir Edward Gent should be in no doubt of the attitude taken here. A decision between these two alternatives must obviously govern the attitude of Sir Edward Gent in dealing with the Sultans and with the Malay Congress. The second point is that I strongly endorse Mr. Paskin's observation that if any concessions are to be made, they should be made comprehensively and not piecemeal.

I am sending this direct to you to save time but when you have read the papers perhaps Mr. Rogers[6] could send the file to Mr. Creech Jones. Is it possible for you to discuss the matter with the Department on Monday afternoon?[7]

G.H.G.
26.4.46

---

[6] Philip Rogers was private secretary to the secretary of state.
[7] Despite Gater's advice that a decision should be taken immediately. Hall concluded on 29 Apr, after further discussions with Creech Jones, Gater, Lloyd, Paskin and Bourdillon, that he must await further developments before even considering any modification of the sultans' position in the new constitution.

86   CO 537/1528, no 95A   4 May 1946
[Sultans' constitutional proposals]: inward telegram no 222 from Sir E Gent to Mr Hall recommending conciliation

My telegram No. 216 of 3rd May.

1. My immediately following telegram contains text of proposals for Federal system which the Sultans brought to me this afternoon.

Sultan of Perak was their spokesman and explained that, if His Majesty's Government would agree in principle with the constitutional system on these lines, all details could then be matters for further discussion, including the citizenship issue which though important was secondary to agreement on the independent status of the States under His Majesty's protection and consequent Federal system.

2. There is general consensus of opinion strongly held by unofficial as well as official opinion (?independently) in touch with Malay feeling in towns and villages that it is essential to satisfy Malay feelings (accurately reflected by the Sultans in this matter) which have certainly been widely stirred and (corrupt group),[1] but so far earnestly seeking the restoration of happy relations with His Majesty's Government, which was expressed by the Sultan of Perak today in words to the effect that Malays had only been under British help and care for 60 or 70 years and had no other great power to rely upon in the difficult years ahead to ensure their preservation and development as Malay States and peoples.

3. Officer in charge of Security Services Malayan Union,[2] who has long and extensive experience of Malaya, discussed the position and prospects with me this afternoon with his (?this intended) conclusion:—

(1) Malayan opposition (not only the Sultans but generally) must be satisfied if we are to avoid very serious likelihood of organised and widespread non

---

[1] ie phrase garbled in transmission.
[2] Lt Col J D Dalley, director, Malayan Security Service, 1946–1948.

co-operation and disorder on the part of Malay people, which would (?actively) assist (corrupt group):—

(a) Malayan Communist Party
(b) Indonesian political organisations.

(2) At present, both (a) and (b) are resented and rejected in Malay political circles.
(3) We shall have such opposition to any course as M.C.P. are able to muster, but their influence is not at present substantial.
(4) Local Chinese and Indian feeling would not become antagonistic if Federation replaced Union and if fairly stringent qualifications were decided for Malayan citizenship.

4. Advice on these lines is almost universal here and, even in circles in which the principle of Union is favoured, it is (?impressed) on me that:—

(1) Value in practice depends upon agreement with Malays.
(2) Essential and progressive advantages of Union can be equally obtained by Federal system covering the whole territory.

5. In the light of this advice and my own intensive study of public opinion which is in accord generally, I do advise you that the main principles of the Sultans' proposals deserve to be most sympathetically received by His Majesty's Government, with a view to our essential long term purpose being attained as stated by His Majesty's Government in the House of Commons on 8th March, *viz.* "Co-operation and unity of purpose so that self-government can become reality". We shall have achieved surprisingly early and with Malay consent that unity which was the ultimate object of democratic policy.

The political interest and cohesion exhibited by all ranks of Malays is surprising but real, and extends to rural as well as urban districts. Administration and revenue would be effective (corrupt group) increasing Malay non co-operation, which is to be expected from any policy which does not meet substantially these conclusions, which the Malay rulers have put forward with the unquestionable support of popular Malay opinion. You will observe that radical Malay opinion has been accommodated by provision for unofficial majority in the Council.

6. His Majesty's Government's own policy for constitutional unity in all important (?fields) can, in my opinion, be essentially fulfilled under the Federal system to which Malay opinion has come to attach the greatest importance. I believe that if His Majesty's Government were to make favourable response with expression of confidence and goodwill to Malay opinion, there would be ample room to secure agreement here on many points in present proposals which need revision, e.g. financial arrangements and scope of Federal authority.

7. You will notice that on two matters of procedure:—

(1) MacMichael agreement
(2) Journey to London to petition His Majesty,[3]

---

[3] The rulers first asked Gent for facilities to travel to London on 13 Apr. Three days later they formally withdrew from the MacMichael treaties and resolved to send a delegation. On 28 Apr Sultan Ibrahim of Johore (who had arrived in London in Jan) made the first of several requests for an audience with the King all of which were courteously refused. See CO 717/148, no 52048/46.

the Sultans' proposals now deal with the first in more reasonable manner than "repudiation", and as regards the second are willing to await His Majesty's Government's response to the Federation proposals.

8. Propsals are under close study here. I shall telegraph comments on certain particulars as soon as possible.

87　CO 537/1529, no 98　　　　　　　　　　　　　　8 May 1946

[Sultans' constitutional proposals]: outward telegram no 366 from Mr Hall to Sir E Gent requesting a detailed appreciation of the local political situation

[This telegram was drafted by Bourdillon and sent after consultation with Creech Jones and Hall.]

Your telegram Nos. 222,[1] 223 and 225. Sultans' Constitutional proposals.

I appreciate that you have submitted your latest recommendations in the light of evidence of local feeling which has forcibly impressed you, but I confess that your sudden and fundamental change of attitude has come as a great shock to me. I find it hard to believe that it has been possible for you to reach a complete assessment of public opinion in so short a time. Moreover, as recently as 19th of April (see your telegram No. 136) you advocated a solution to our present difficulties on the lines of certain purely formal concessions to prestige of Rulers within (repeat within) framework of Union. Your present recommendations, if I understand them aright, not only cannot fall within that framework but will involve the abandonment of the basic principles upon which we had always thought the political progress of Malaya must depend.

2. As you know, H.M.G. made a thorough examination of Malayan political problems after the fall of Singapore to the Japanese, and were forced to the conclusion that no (repeat no) solution was possible on the basis of the existing Treaties. The possibility of adjustments within the framework of those Treaties was considered and abandoned. It was felt that, as the prerequisite of any real political development in Malaya, new Agreements must be negotiated under which His Majesty would acquire full jurisdiction in each of the Malay States. Only by this means would H.M.G. be able to act on vital matters affecting the whole of Malaya in time of emergency, or to initiate progressive measures in the future without having to negotiate a new Agreement with each Malay Ruler on each occasion. Furthermore, it was decided that this jurisdiction, once acquired by His Majesty, must be used to bring into force a full constitutional Union, which would provide for a strong central authority with powers to delegate to local bodies on a local government basis matters of purely local concern, and which would enable other racial communities side by side with the Malays to take their full share in the political rights of the country.

3. This policy was elaborated and approved for planning purposes by Coalition Government. As soon as present Government came into Office, proposals were submitted to the Cabinet and received their final approval. On October the 10th last I

---

[1] See 86.

outlined the new policy in Parliament. Since that date, policy of Union has been fully debated in both Houses, and has been approved without a division in either House after long discussions in the course of which even the strongest critics of the Government hardly hinted at changes so radical as those which you now advocate. Lastly, Order-in-Council has been passed by His Majesty giving effect to Malayan Union Constitution.

4. In these circumstances, it would be very wrong if I were to conceal from you that I feel quite unable, at present to contemplate any course which would involve abandonment of fundamental principles of Union. I should like to have from you a much more detailed appreciation of the local political situation and a reasoned presentation of the arguments by which, in your view, so complete a change of front could be justified to the Cabinet and in Parliament. In particular, your political appreciation

(a) should state clearly the nature and reliability of any evidence that the Malays generally, as represented by e.g. Dato Onn's organisation, are firmly behind the Sultans,

(b) should show what proportion of Malays are, on best possible estimate, still favourable to Union, provided that minor modifications are made within existing framework, and

(c) should include comprehensive account of attitude of Chinese and Indian communities which have hitherto received only a bare mention in paragraph 3 of your telegram No. 222,

(d) should include a more detailed appreciation of the significance in the life of Malaya of (1) the Malayan Communist party (2) the Indonesian political organisations.

5. Possibility of further formal modifications within (repeat within) framework of Union, with object of satisfying Malay opinion, is of course an entirely different matter. Proposals as put forward in original White Paper have already been considerably modified in this sense, and I would not rule out reasoned suggestions from you along these lines.

6. I am most anxious to discuss Malayan policy with Governor-General[2] before he leaves, and his departure is being postponed for a few days for this purpose. I will address you separately regarding his movements, but in order that I may acquaint him fully with my views before he leaves, I should be grateful if you would furnish me, by most immediate telegram to reach me not later than Monday, May the 13th with such comments as you feel able to provide on this telegram in the short time available.

---

[2] In Apr MacDonald returned to London from Canada, where he had been high commissioner since 1941, to prepare for his new appointment as governor-general, British territories in South-East Asia. He arrived in Singapore on 21 May. For the record of a discussion between Hall and MacDonald on 16 May, see 91, minute.

88 CO 537/1529, no 100 **11 May 1946**
[Sultans' constitutional proposals]: inward telegram no 267 from Sir E Gent to Mr Hall on the strength of the Malay opposition to the Malayan Union

[This telegram and the one that followed (see 89) were received simultaneously in the CO at 7.15 am on 12 May.]

Personal for the S. of S.
My secret telegram No.268.[1]
2. I want to assure you of my personal regret that I have had to form the conclusion that almost universal Malay political opinion here gives no basis for expecting effective operation of constitution on Union basis of present Orders-in-Council. Strength and organisation of Malay opinion and their free criticism of their own Rulers has surprised all who have experienced Malaya, including especially the Rulers themselves. There is no doubt of its depth and extent and there are signs of its beginning to apply itself in practical ways, such as police rank and file resignations on very small scale at present. Security sources as well as Senior Administrative Officers expect growing scale of Malay non-co-operation and former apprehend that substantial Indonesian elements in West coast states may develop acts of violence against non-Malay communities. Main point is general agreement that Malay leaders and people will not come to accept "Union" and the situation will deteriorate with consequent frustration in every essential object of unity and political progress. But advice I have felt it my duty to convey to you is based on equal general expectation that, if the Governor would go so far as to meet Malay request in principle to substitute federal system, we should have Malay goodwill and co-operation, without alienating non-Malay opinion, and should achieve our two essential objects in practice by a different road acceptable to Malayan opinion. There are many matters in the Sultans' present proposals which must, of course, be modified in consultation, and we must especially secure satisfactory form of Malayan citizenship.

---

[1] See 89.

89 CO 537/1529, no 101 **11 May 1946**
[Sultans' constitutional proposals]: inward telegram (reply) no 268 from Sir E Gent to Mr Hall advocating a federal system as a means to achieve closer unity

Your telegram No. 366.[1]
Constitutional proposals.
1. I do not fail to appreciate the present feeling, which you expressed in paragraph 4, of the inability to contemplate any course involving abandonment of the fundamental principles of Union. I agree that my recommendations would

---

[1] See 87.

involve abandoning "Union" in return for securing basically unified system on federal principles. Briefly, my reason is that I am now convinced that insistence on Union as essential principle of progress of constitution on all-Malayan basis will not (repeat not) result in achieving the object of H.M. Government in the face of Malay resistance whereas "co-operation and unity so that self-Government can become a reality" can be expected under the alternative form of a federal system covering all territories in the existing Union, I appreciate that a federal system was considered before the Union was decided upon and I still have no doubt that the latter would be more direct and satisfactory if it had been possible to secure agreement of the major local leaders and people.

2.   I have most carefully reviewed the information from my expert advisers on the general and particular questions mentioned in your paragraph 4, supplemented by my own observations in the six intensive weeks following my arrival in circumstances which could not fail to impress me forcibly. I offer my appreciation on each point severally.

(a) Without exception, reports of each Resident Commissioner have shown that general Malay opinion in every State is firmly behind Ruler's resistance to Union and various groups of Malay associations (?we hope to) combine in U.M.N.O.,[2] which uncompromisingly supports the Sultans in this matter and has, in fact, directed them. Only Malay Party which still gives lukewarm support to the contemplated Union is M.N.P., whose chief influence now depends upon Indonesian and Communist elements and is not to be compared with representative character of U.M.N.O. as concerning Malays. I wish to stress that the force of Malay opinion is not due to personal views of the Rulers, but is expression of Malay popular feeling and that it is considered that Rulers are, in fact, now playing moderating part. Above information is confirmed by secret sources of security and police organisations throughout the Country, as well as articles and reports in Malay press.

(b) With negligible individual exceptions, Malay opinion throughout the States is generally favourable to federation of all Malay States but is solidly against "Union", and minor modifications would not change their feelings. "Union" is (corrupt ?believed) by them to be tantamount to act of annexation, destructive of independent status of Malay Rulers and states.

(c) Neither Chinese nor Indians have displayed interest or preference in respect of Union as against federation. They are specially interested in questions of citizenship and popular representation in the councils, and, with the exception of a small group of Straits-born Chinese, both communities are concerned to retain their Chinese and Indian national status along with Malay[an] citizenship.

(d) (1) M.C.P. has, for many years, constituted problem in Malaya. Its influence normally ebbs and flows with economic conditions here and with consequent opportunities at any time to disturb the peace. Its object has always been the achievement of communist revolution and the overthrow of the British Government in Malaya. Its methods are intimidation, violence and extortion; and it is at all times feared by the mass of the Chinese population. It was prominent and

---

[2] The United Malays National Organisation was formally inaugurated at the meeting of the PMMC in Johore Bahru on 11–13 May, ie at the time this telegram was despatched. See 90.

powerful in the days following the Japanese surrender but soon antagonised the public, which supported the strong policy B.M.A. were forced to take. This restored confidence and influence of moderate K.M.T. who still maintain their predominant position in the Chinese community, while the power of M.C.P. is at present declining. One of the M.C.P. weapons against the Government and public order is General Labour Union and it looks for other weapons by infiltration into any Malay Indonesian groups or organizations.

(2) Indonesian political organisation is in two rival camps divided by issue of indiscriminate infiltration. They are both considerable and well organised groups and their influence, which is strongly Malay-Indonesian Nationalist, lies chiefly on the West coast. Their future local significance is likely to depend on Netherlands East Indies political developments and, if the British can be credited with sympathy for Indonesian aims there, we may look for favourable attitude in Malaya, provided that Malay opinion is sufficiently met in our own political problem in Malaya.

3. Reasoned presentation of arguments for which you ask in paragragh 4 of your telegram, might, I suggest, take the following line.

(a) Purpose of H.M. Government was to create in post-war Malaya unified political system at centre with provision of subsidiary local legislative and administrative bodies. This policy of unified centre was designed to be both practical and economical and to provide necessary basis for future political progress based on the exercise of citizenship rights.

(b) Two courses were considered:—

(1) Union
(2) Federation, and of these, Union was considered more direct and effective and required agreements with each ruler to secure jurisdiction for His Majesty.

(c) such agreements were duly obtained with some reluctance from some rulers, but they have been subjected to increasing and now intense criticism by Malay political groups as to (corrupt group)[3] as they came to (corrupt group) them. Basis of criticism is ostensibly annexation and loss of political status of rulers and states.

(d) But conception of closer unity of Malayan territories nevertheless generally acceptable to Malay political opinion provided that it is done by federal road.

(e) This acceptance of All Malaya Federation is in itself remarkable development of Malay opinion away from open separationist ideas and is one which H.M. Government welcome as having similar objective to their own policy. But Malay co-operation essential for the purpose of developing unity and political progress. If this can be secured by federal, rather than by Union road, and (corrupt group) central system with representative political institutions can be ensured them, H.M. Government can well afford to allow local views to influence their decision on which road to go forward, as earnest of their policy of developing local self governing institutions.

---

[3] ie phrase garbled in transmission.

90   CO 537/1581, no 11   16 May 1946
'The inaugural conference of UMNO': HQ Malaya Command weekly
intelligence review, no 28   [Extract]

. . .

5. *The inaugural conference of UMNO*
The conference was held in JOHORE BAHRU and was opened on 11 May by H.H. the
Regent of JOHORE,[1] continuing on the 12 and 13 May. The proceedings passed off
much as had been expected, and it can be stated that it was an unqualified success in
that it obtained complete unity and that it is now able to show a united Malay front.
All 41 Malay Associations who had been invited attended the conference and agreed
to owe alleigence [sic] to UMNO while retaining their individual names. Dato Onn
was unanimously elected Chairman of the conference and it opened with the
approval and ratification of the Charter of incorporation. The next item on the
agenda was selecting a title, and it was officially decided that the association would in
the future be called the United Malay[s] National Organisation (UMNO). Zainal
Abidin suggested that Pan Malay League would be a more suitable title, but this
proposal was not agreed upon.
   Having agreed upon the name, the conference then met in the official capacity of
UMNO and proceeded to elect Dato Onn as president and Abdul Wahad [sic] alias Dato
Panglima Bukit Gantang, President of Malay League of PERAK, as Chairman of the
organisation. JOHORE BAHRU is to be its HQ, and the following departments would
be inaugurated: Secretariat, Finance, Public Relations, Education and Religion,
Anti-Malayan Union, and Commerce and Industry.
   The most important decision taken was to despatch to LONDON a delegation
representing the people and submitting their objection to the Malayan Union to H.M.
the King. Dato Onn, Tengku Abdul Rahman, and Abdul Wahad, it was agreed, would
comprise this delegation and proceed with the Sultans: $100,000 were allotted to the
delegation to defray the costs. It is not, however, clear whether this delegation is
going in an advisory capacity to the Sultans or whether it will present an individual
case to the British Government. It has been suggested that the Sultans may now wish
to modify their connections with UMNO as they feel that if they are always guided by
UMNO's decisions that may prejudice their position. If this is the case, then it is
likely that UMNO and the Sultans will submit separate cases, though in actual fact
the cases will probably be essentially similar. The powers and views of the UMNO
delegation to be expressed in ENGLAND were discussed in a secret session, but the
views of UMNO and the Malays have been so frequently expressed that they are not
likely to deviate from their previous policy, although they have recently agreed to
support, in principal [sic], a Federation of the Malay States as opposed to the Malayan
Union.
   It was further decided that in tune with the current policy of non-cooperation and
passive resistance that they should boycott the arrival in MALAYA of the Governor
General, Mr Malcolm MacDonald. This shows, if further proof is necessary, that the

---

[1] Sultan Ibrahim spent much of his time in London until early 1948. During his absence the Tunku
Mahkota (crown prince) Ismail acted as regent of Johore.

Malays are adamant in their opposition and propose to carry out their programme against the Malayan Union. As regards the forthcoming visit of Capt Gammans and Lt Col Rhys [sic] Williams,[2] who are expected on 19 May, it was agreed that UMNO would be responsible for organising receptions throughout the country. Processions and displays with banners would be arranged to show the Malays [sic] disfavour of the Union. KUALA KANGSAR was to be the meeting place for the discussion between the two MPs, the Sultans and UMNO, and the latter elected a Select Committee of 26 members, under the Chairmanship of Dato Onn, to express their views.

The MNP[3] have again been in difficulties as regards their policy towards the Malayan Union, UMNO and the Sultans. Previously it was reported that the MNP were no longer "persona grata" with UMNO as they were not supporting the continued opposition to the Malayan Union. However inspite of this Dr Burhannudin and Zulkifly Owney attended the conference and have now decided that they will support UMNO and the anti Malayan Union policy whilst retaining the right to be the left wing opposition faction.

The results of the conference are certainly considerable and have again proved that the Malays have united under the able leadership of Dato Onn. UMNO has become a definite power in Malayan politics and is likely to play a big part in the months to come during which the opposition to the Union will come to a head in the two LONDON-bound delegations. . . .

---

[2] L D Gammans (Conservative MP) and D R Rees-Williams (Labour MP) were sent to Sarawak by the British government to sound local opinion on its cession to the Crown. They broke their return journey in Malaya where they witnessed Malay demonstrations against the Malayan Union.
[3] The Malay Nationalist Party, a radical nationalist party with aspirations for union with Indonesia, held its inaugural conference in Ipoh (Perak) in Nov 1945 and moved its headquarters to KL the following Feb. In 1946 Dr Burhanuddin al-Helmy succeeded Mokhtaruddin Lasso (the first president) and Zulkifli Ownie took over as secretary from Dahari Ali. Ambivalent in its response both to the Malayan Union and UMNO, the MNP finally withdrew from UMNO in June 1946, ostensibly over the proposed design of UMNO's flag.

91   CO 537/1529, no 104   16 May 1946
[Sultan's constitutional proposals]: outward telegram (reply) no 442 from Mr Hall to Sir E Gent. *Minute* by H T Bourdillon of a discussion between Mr Hall and Mr M J MacDonald

Your telegram No. 268.[1]
Sultans' Constitutional proposals.

Am grateful for full and useful information which you have been able to provide at such short notice. I have now discussed whole subject with Governor General and have fully acquainted him with my views. I think it is important that you should likewise know clearly my present attitude.

2.   There are two points which I regard as fundamental. The first point concerns the question of jurisdiction. The proposals by the Sultans appear to imply the surrender of jurisdiction by His Majesty and a reversion to the previous treaties. I cannot (repeat cannot) see how such a reversion can be contemplated. The Sultans

---

[1] See 89.

signed the new Agreements without coercion[2] and in full knowledge of the facts, and I have already informed them that I cannot admit the right of one party to withdraw from engagements solemnly entered into. Moreover, my preliminary legal advice is that the surrender of jurisdiction by His Majesty might involve legislation by Parliament. As I see it, this would place His Majesty's Government in an indefensible position.

3. Second point which I regard as fundamental is maintenance of strong central authority in Malaya, with control over all matters of importance to the country as a whole. The basic purpose of His Majesty's Government's policy, as reflected in the Order-in-Council, is unity; that is to say, a real coherence which will make possible progressive political development in Malaya without the constant drag of powerful parochial interests. In my view, the Sultans [sic] proposals are very far from achieving this unity. Under these proposals, the State organisations would be strengthened as never before, and these organisations would only remit to the Central authority a very few subjects, further remissions depending on the unanimous approval of all Rulers. I note from paragraph 2 (iii) of your telegram No. 225 that you have appreciated inadequacy of Sultans [sic] proposals in this respect and that you are studying the matter with Maude's[3] help. I am very ready that you should pursue these consultations with Maude. You will recall that intention has always been, as was made clear in Parliamentary Debate, to leave over for later decision, in the light of local consultations, the exact division of functions as between Central and local authorities.

4. Subject to these two fundamental points, I have already indicated (see paragraph 5 of my telegram No. 366)[4] that I would not rule out adjustments with the object of satisfying Malay opinion. It remains to be seen, of course, whether the attitude at present adopted by the Sultans and the Malays generally would permit of any solution within this essential framework. I am very anxious that the Governor General should form his impressions on the issues involved, and I should be grateful if, as soon as possible after his arrival, you would discuss the whole matter with him.

Minute with 91

See my minute of 18/5. The file has now come back to me to record the discussion with the Secretary of State and the Governor-General last Thursday afternoon (May 16th).

The Secretary of State began by making clear to Mr. MacDonald his views on Malayan policy, as set out in the draft telegram which was despatched after the meeting (see No.104). Mr. MacDonald expressed his full personal agreement with these views, and said he hoped a solution would be possible within the framework which the Secretary of State regarded as essential. He himself would do all in his power to work for this. He asked whether the Secretary of State would be prepared to indicate any modifications in the policy which he would regard as permissible within

---

[2] The issue of duress – whether it had been contemplated and whether it had been authorized – was being examined within the CO at about this time. Officials concluded that it would be legitimate to deny the allegations that the sultans' signatures were obtained under the threat of deposition. See CO 537/1553, minutes by P Rogers, Bourdillon, Paskin, Lloyd, Gater, and Lloyd, 18–24 May.
[3] See 85, note 5.   [4] See 87.

the framework, or whether he would prefer a scheme to be worked out locally and submitted to the Colonial Office. The Secretary of State said that he favoured the latter course, since it was difficult to assess from this end the relative importance which would be attached in Malaya to any modifications which might be considered.
. . .

While reaffirming his agreement with the Secretary of State's views, Mr. MacDonald said he hoped he would be at liberty to be quite frank if, after a thorough study of the situation on the spot, he was forced to the conclusion that no solution could be achieved within the framework laid down. The Secretary of State said that this could be taken for granted, but added that he hoped there would be no disappointment if his own communications were equally frank. He recalled that the Malayan Union scheme had been blessed by the Coalition Government as well as by the present Labour Government, and has been approved in both Houses of Parliament without a division in either House. In these circumstances, he would require a great deal of persuasion before considering any variations in the essential framework of the policy. He also asked Mr. MacDonald to bear in mind that the present unsatisfactory economic conditions in Malaya had the effect of magnifying political difficulties, and that a solution to these difficulties might become easier with the passage of time.

The Governor-General's programme for handling these questions after his arrival in Malaya was also discussed. Mr. MacDonald emphasised that he was most anxious to avoid any appearance of supplanting Sir Edward Gent, who, as Governor of the Malayan Union, must continue to play the principal part in these affairs. Mr. Hone made the point that the Sultans were not acting on their own, but were under pressure from probably quite a small group of influential Malays who were afraid of losing their present influential position under the new system. Any programme for future discussion in Malaya must take full account of these people, who must be persuaded that their opportunities for service and advancement would in future be increased rather than diminished. The importance of this point was agreed. It was concluded that the Governor-General could not map out an exact programme until he had talked to Sir Edward Gent, who would meet him on his arrival in Singapore. Perhaps the best plan would be for Sir Edward Gent and himself to hold further consultations with the Sultans in the first instance, and then to widen their discussions so as to include influential Malays. This might lead ultimately to a public announcement, which would be very necessary at some stage in order to explain His Majesty's Government's policy and dispel prevalent misunderstandings.

During the discussion, the question of amendments to the Malayan Union Order-in-Council was raised, and the Secretary of State laid great emphasis on preserving the basis of the present Order. Mr. Roberts-Wray[5] said that the Legal Advisers had made a rapid preliminary survey of this particular matter, from which his tentative conclusion was that nothing more drastic would be needed than a supplementary Order of some 8 to 10 clauses, even if all the policy modifications which had been suggested from time to time were to be put into effect. At the Secretary of State's request he gave examples, from which it became clear that the importance lay in the nature of any particular concession in itself, rather than in its effect on the text of the Order-in-Council. The essential thing was that the basis of

---

[5] Legal adviser, CO.

the policy, and consequently the basis of the Order embodying the policy, should remain untouched.

Mr. Creech Jones, who had joined the discussion after its inception, then made two points:—

(a) *Publicity*. This had already been mentioned in connection with the possibility of a public announcement in Malaya, but Mr. Creech Jones emphasised in general terms that insufficient attention appeared to have been given to the problem of "putting over" H.M.G.'s policy in Malaya, with the result that the wildest misconceptions, which never should have gained credence, were now rife amongst Malays and were greatly increasing our difficulties. He suggested that Mr. MacDonald should look into this on his arrival in Malaya. The Secretary of State agreed with this, and mentioned the possibility of sending out a special officer to be in charge of Malayan publicity, should Mr. MacDonald so recommend. At the same time, he pointed out that this was an administrative matter, in which the Governor-General must take care not to play too prominent a part.

(b) *Social and economic policy*. Mr. Creech Jones stressed that in our pre-occupation with constitutional problems in the Malayan Union, we must not forget the economic and social side. Mr. MacDonald undertook to bear this in mind, though here again the questions involved were mainly administrative.

Finally, the Secretary of State spoke in very appreciative terms of Sir Edward Gent, and asked Mr. MacDonald to convey to Sir Edward a special personal message from himself. Mr. MacDonald undertook to do this, and the meeting terminated.

I do not think any further action is required at this end for the time being. We must await reports of further developments from Malaya.

? put by.

H.T.B.
23.5.46

92   CO 537/1529, no 110   25 May 1946
[Proposed concessions to Malays]: inward telegram no 6 from Mr M J MacDonald to Mr Hall

[MacDonald arrived in Singapore on 21 May; the next day Malays boycotted his installation as governor-general. After intense dicsussions he submitted the following proposals (from Penang) for the modification of Britain's Malayan policy.]

I have had long and thorough discussions with Gent, Gimson and their principal Advisers, including Sir John Maude, as to the next steps to be taken in the constitutional problem of the Union. Gent has given me a most careful and, I am sure, penetrating analysis of the situation. He and I have also had several talks with Rees Williams and Gammans,[1] who are in personal touch with important sections of Malayan opinion, e.g. Dato Onn and other leaders of U.M.N.O., and both of whom are being co-operative at the moment. I have also discussed the matter informally with experienced unofficial Europeans from whom I have the impression of full and

---

[1] See 90, note 2.

remarkable sympathy with the general sense of Malay claims. Whilst indicating firmness on the principle of Union I have not, of course, given either the Members of Parliament or other unofficials any indication of our more detailed official views. I am all the more impressed, therefore, by the fact that they have independently and unanimously reached the same general conclusions on the problem as Gent, Gimson and I. In particular, both Members of Parliament are so impressed with the need for some modification in our original plan to meet Malay Rulers and people that they would be prepared to go further in the direction of meeting the Sultans on Federation than Gent's and my recommendations contained in my immediately following telegram.[2]

2. I believe that there are certain definite factors to be taken into account in deciding what our policy should be. It may be helpful to you if I recapitulate those factors which seem to me of most importance.

3. The Sultans are by no means free agents. When contact has been established with them, either individually or collectively, they make no statements but merely a reply that they must consider or consult. Any reply comes after an interval of time and in carefully phrased language. There is no doubt that the Sultans are in every case being instructed as to their attitude by U.M.N.O., headed by Dato Onn. Locally Onn has established himself firmly with the Sultans. Rees Williams, who has little use for the Sultans, is particularly insistent that we are in fact dealing with the leaders of progressive Malayan opinion. Sultans, for their part, maintain constant contact with the Sultan of Johore, who is advised by (?London Lawyers). The opposition is, therefore, widely representative, well organised and ably directed.

4. We must face the fact that Malayan[3] opinion is, in effect, solid. At the same time, Malayan opinion is friendly to Britain and H.M.G. and wishes for complete restoration of understanding and good will. We can secure that 100% if we reach early settlement of the dispute, but shall try it too hard and lose it by any considerable delay or, of course, by failure to reach agreement. Though Malays would deplore this, they honestly and determinedly believe that the policy they are adopting is the only one that will preserve their independence and prevent the complete political and economic submergence of Malay by other races in the territory.

5. Both conservative and progressive Malayan opinion charge the Sultans with having completely surrendered their position as Malayan leaders by the MacMichael agreement, by which "Full power and jurisdiction is vested in His Majesty". U.M.N.O. assert that the Order in Council proves their case up to the hilt. They complain that all public lands are vested in the British Crown: that all oaths of allegiance are to the King: and that virtually all legislative and executive powers are vested in Governors and Resident Commissioners. From this, they argue that whatever legal phraseology of MacMichael Agreement and Order in Council, practical effect is deposition of the Sultans in all temporal affairs and annexation of States. They regard this as a breach of our past undertakings and, on this ground, bitterness against H.M.G. is beginning to develop.

---

[2] This telegram, which is not printed here, outlined a 'Malaya Federal Union' which would retain the key principles of British policy (ie a strong central authority, the maintenance of British jurisdiction as secured by the MacMichael treaties, the establishment of institutions to facilitate political development, and a common citizenship) and could be established by means of a short supplementary Order in Council. See CO 537/1529, no 111, 26 May 1946.

[3] MacDonald means 'Malay' since the term 'Malayan' includes all communities residing in Malaya.

6. Some of this is due to lack of publicity and explanations here at the time and following publication of the White Paper.[4] Nevertheless, it is agreed here that no range in explanations or arguments will substantially alter Malay opposition. Gent feels strongly that confidence in our good faith can only be (?group omitted) and by substantially adapting our line of approach to objectives of H.M.G.'s policy so as to meet reasonable Malay feeling without thwarting legitimate share of non-Malay citizenship in future political institutions. Those objectives are largely approved by Malay opinion which, however, insists that they can and should be achieved without such injury to individuality of state institutions as "Union" involve. These ?prevalent opinions are universally shared by those Europeans and others here who can claim knowledge of Malays and I believe that a wholly rigid attitude by H.M.G. would lose the support of our other friends besides Malays.

7. As happens in these situations, position has steadily deteriorated since publication of the White Paper, and is capable of further deterioration. It is now three weeks since the Sultans submitted their Federation proposals to you and they (and Malay political leaders generally) are beginning to become restive and dissatisfied that no answer is yet forthcoming. It will not, of course, be reasonable for them to expect H.M.G. to be rushed over their conclusions on these most important issues and now that I have myself arrived here, I hope that advice I am now sending you may help you to reach conclusion.

Gent apprehends that the Sultans may not be prepared to meet him and me unless and until we can assure them that he has a definite and constructive reply from H.M.G. to make to the Sultans [sic] proposals. In any case, the longer this is delayed, the more difficult will it be to reach satisfactory solution of present impasse.

8. At the same time, I believe there is good chance of reaching agreement by making variations in our proposals which are reconcilable with you and our desire to preserve principle of unity and common citizenship. Malayan Union will accept strong central Government and common citizenship for all who fully recognise Malaya as their permanent home.

9. I have only been short time here. If I thought delay did not matter I would refrain from offering you advice until I had been here longer, but I am convinced that time is of the essence in this matter. Moreover, all this week I have given consideration to the problem in the light of talks with advisers in whom I feel great confidence. I am particularly interested by Gent's modification of view since he arrived here. Far from feeling this change too great or too hasty, it increases my respect for his courage, honesty, and capacity as one of your servants and I fully agree with his present view. In (?group omitted ?general) situation is one of major political importance, involving good relations between H.M.G. on one side and Malays in particular and Malayans in general on the other. If we can get agreement now, we can retain full trust in British leadership in this region which is the main base of the British position in the Far East.

If we do not, we shall begin to lose acceptance of our leadership by local peoples and process of our being at each stage bit behind local political opinions (such as has been so unfortunate in the history of the Indian problem) will start. We must, of course, keep in mind that there are powerful political groupings in Asia which are ready to exploit any weakening of our position i.e. Indian nationalists and Imperial-

---

[4] ie *Malayan Union and Singapore: Statement of Policy on Future Constitution* (Cmd 6724, Jan 1946).

ism, Chinese Imperialism and especially Pan Malayan Movement led by Indonesians.

10. My next following telegram sketches the lines on which Gent and I believe reply to Sultans should be framed. We believe, if our proposals can be approved as a whole, there is reasonable chance of early agreement. If they are only accepted in part, our chances will be by that much reduced. We feel assured that such a plan will have no unfavourable reactions on Chinese or Indian sections of the population. Indeed, local Chinese's main interest is in restoration of peaceful conditions for their business and they are positively interested that agreement between us and Malays should be quickly achieved.

93   PREM 8/459   31 May 1946

[Fundamental principles of Malayan policy and proposed concessions to Malays]: minutes by Mr Hall and T L Rowan[1] to Mr Attlee

[Given the pace of events in Malaya and the fact that Gent and MacDonald were due to meet the rulers for lunch on 1 June, an immediate reply to MacDonald (see 92) was necessary. Having consulted Arthur Greenwood (chairman of the Cabinet Colonial Affairs Committee) on 30 May, Hall despatched on the same day a telegram in which he went through the points detailed by MacDonald in 92, making a number of minor concessions but insisting on the retention of a strong central authority and the MacMichael treaties which underpinned it. Hall prudently kept the prime minister informed of developments (see CAB 118/29; CAB 128/5, CM 54(46)5; and CO 537/1529 and 1549).]

Prime Minister

As you know, since the restoration of civil government in Malaya on April 1st, we have had our troubles with the Malay Sultans and with Malay Organisations. The Governor of the Malayan Union has kept me fully apprised of the situation as it has developed, and I had a long discussion with Mr. MacDonald before he left this country to take up his duties as Governor-General.[2] Our difficulties with the Malays over the form of the Malayan Union Constitution have led to a mass of suggestions and counter-proposals, and it seemed to me from the outset that we could only achieve a solution if we were first quite clear in our own minds on those points which are really fundamental to the policy of His Majesty's Government. Apart from the question of common citizenship (which is the subject of separate local consultations), I concluded that there were two essential points on which we must stand firm if the policy is to remain intact. The first is the retention by His Majesty of the jurisdiction in the Malay States acquired under the MacMichael Agreements, and the second is the preservation in Malaya of a strong central authority, having control over all matters of importance to the welfare and progress of the country as a whole. I gave a clear indication of my views on these points both to the Governor and to Mr. MacDonald, and I asked the latter to devote as much of his time as possible, after his arrival in Malaya, to the task of working out, in consultation with the Governor, the

---

[1] T Leslie Rowan, assistant and later principal private secretary to prime minister (Churchill, 1941–1945, and Attlee, 1945–1947); permanent secretary, Office of Minister for Economic Affairs, 1947; second secretary, Treasury, 1947–1949; economic minister, Washington Embassy, 1949–1951; second secretary, Treasury, 1951–1958; KCB, 1959.

[2] See 91.

basis for an early approach to the Sultans as nearly as possible within the framework of the Malayan Union Order in Council.

Mr. MacDonald wasted no time after his arrival and sent me on the 26th of May a detailed appreciation and a list of recommendations,[3] based on exhaustive discussions with the Governor and others concerned. The main points in his appreciation are that the Malay people, who have not yet lost their feeling of friendship for Great Britain, have none the less been deeply and genuinely stirred, and that the prospects of a happy solution depend upon speed in reaching a settlement. The only points in his recommendations with which I need bother you are those directly concerned with the two matters of retention of jurisdiction and the maintenance of strong central authority. As regards the latter, I am satisfied that the position is thoroughly understood both by the Governor and by Mr. MacDonald, and the only problem is the practical one of working out the best division of functions between the Central Legislature and the various State Councils. The recommendation as regards jurisdiction is that the MacMichael Agreements should be retained, but that there should be, in addition, a new agreement with the Sultans, in which His Majesty's Government would bind themselves to obtain the Sultans' consent before making any further changes in the constitution. I do not see how we could contemplate any arrangements which would thus make all future progress in Malaya dependent upon the caprice of the Sultans and of the Sultans alone, but I think we might devise a different procedure, which would keep us clear of any new Agreements, but would include an unilateral statement by His Majesty's Government to the effect that they would not of course envisage further changes without *consulting* the Sultans and without giving full opportunity for the free expression of local opinion.

I felt it was most important to discuss the matter with the Lord Privy Seal,[4] in view of his special interest as Chairman of the Colonial Affairs Committee. I had a talk with him yesterday afternoon, and have since, with his agreement, sent Mr. MacDonald a telegram which contains my views on the two major questions, as well as on the minor points (mostly matters of pure form which will help towards a solution but will in no way affect our policy) which were included in the recommendations sent to me.

I learn that Mr. MacDonald and the Governor will be meeting the Sultans at an informal lunch party to-morrow, and that they hope to embark on further discussions on Monday. I was most anxious, therefore, not to delay my reply to the recommendations, but I have made it quite clear that I shall have to submit the whole problem to my colleagues at a later stage.

During the course of our exchanges of telegrams, I have ascertained from Mr. MacDonald that he and the Governor do not propose to confine their discussions to the Sultans, but have in mind a full programme for consultations with all representative sections of opinion in Malaya.

The purpose of the present minute (of which I am sending a copy to the Lord Privy Seal) is to keep you fully abreast of developments. As I have just said, I propose to submit the matter to my colleagues later on.

G.H.H.
31.5.46

---

[3] See 92, note 2.   [4] Mr Greenwood.

Prime Minister
I do not know all the intricacies of the Malayan question, but it is clear from the public reaction, from Questions in Parliament and indeed from the attached minute from the Colonial Secretary, that this matter is of the greatest importance to our position in the Far East. It has already aroused considerable controversy, and although the line which the Colonial Secretary is taking may be the right one, I feel that it would be wise for it to be considered by the Cabinet before matters go too far. Admittedly, he says that he has made it clear to the Governor-General that he will have to submit the whole problem to his colleagues at a later stage, but the impression I get is that at the later stage it may be found that things have gone too far for changes to be made. At the very least I should have thought that the telegrams about this matter should be given Cabinet distribution, and this, so far as I know, has not been done. You may possibly like to speak to the Colonial Secretary on these lines.[5]

T.L.R.
31.5.46

---

[5] On reading these minutes, Attlee instructed Hall to explain the position to Cabinet on 3 June when it was decided to stand firm on the MacMichael Treaties.

94 CO 537/1581, nos 14, 15 and 16   31 May – 22 June 1946
[Communal violence and political militancy]: HQ Malaya Command weekly intelligence reviews, nos 30–32   [Extract]

[Communal fighting occurred throughout the peninsula and particularly in west Johore and along the Perak river during the closing months of the Japanese occupation and throughout the interregnum, though there is no real evidence that the Japanese instigated the clashes. Conflict also flared up in the BMA period, and, as Malay opposition to the Malayan Union mounted, there were fears of a recurrence of communal fighting. Sufi *Kiyai*, combining Islamic authority with occult powers, played a major part organizing the Malay struggle against the MPAJA and Chinese in west Johore. The leading figure here was Kiyai Salleh of Batu Pahat. Salleh was believed to have been a gang leader before the war and had been detained for a time, but the British did not imprison him after their return in 1945 largely because of his significance for Malays and his connections with Dato Onn. On the Japanese surrender Sultan Ibrahim had appointed Onn as district officer of Batu Pahat where he won a reputation for bravery and as a peacemaker; thereafter Salleh was Onn's faithful follower.]

No 30 (to 31 May 1946): Views of a Malay on the Sino-Malay differences
From the Malay point of view, the quarrel between Malays and Chinese which originated in the Japanese time was brought about by the following items in the programme of the Communists when fostering their anti-Japanese activities:—

(a) Compulsory subscriptions.
(b) Taxing of Malay produce.
(c) Demanding mosques to be made their meeting places.
(d) Demanding Malay girls to work for them in the jungles.
(e) Abducting and killing Malays and destroying their houses and property.

(a) and (b) were not minded by the Malays very much, but (c), (d) and (e) were too much for them; they were absolutely contrary to the Malay custom, honour, principle and religion. Consequently, the friendly relations were severed, the Malays began organising and planning retaliation and were resolved to die fighting to uphold their belief, rather than give way and see their religion desecrated, their women molested, their relations killed and kidnapped and their houses burnt. Aggravating the situation and fostering the Malay courage was, of course, the 'invulnerability Cult' and hence clashes broke out.

At present, the communal situation is not smooth and there is still the feeling of fear and distrust between the communities. The condition now seems to be that in areas where there has been fighting, the Chinese fear the Malays, and in areas where there has been no fighting, the Malays fear the Chinese. That is why the Malays at PARIT SULONG are always distrusted by the Chinese.

This mutual distrust is being encouraged by some, especially by those people who did a great deal of mischief during the Japanese occupation. The Chinese who took a great part in troubling the Malays do not feel safe now. Their guilty conscience makes them fear the Malays foremost for they know that these people when they have trouble are there and might take their revenge. It is these guilty Chinese, who seek to create tension in the feelings of the Chinese against the Malays so that they might get support in case the Malays were to take their revenge.

On the other hand, these Malays who are guilty, fear the same thing from the Chinese. So they, in order to gain support and protection incite the Malays to fight the Chinese. Thus, the presence of this element in both the communities, though small in proportion is a standing influence endangering the peaceful Sino-Malay relationship.

Another element which is aggravating the strained relations comes from the labourers in kampongs who do not have a steady income. These people, both Malays and Chinese included, now find that it is more profitable to tap rubber illegally, in plantations whose owners are absent, rather than to earn an honest livelihood. So, they use the Sino-Malay differences as a means to prevent the owners from knowing what is happening to their lands, and organising work systematically.

The Malay labourers would speak bad of the Chinese, and the Chinese would in turn speak bad of the Malays. Consequently idle rumours spread, the owners are frightened to return to their lands and the authors of these rumours are happy, daily becoming rich by their undisturbed illegal work.

Business people, both Chinese and Malays, who are already established in the villages are using the same tactics. When competition is encountered the established traders spread idle rumours concerning communal activities of their oponents.

Though only seeking to protect their businesses, they overlook the final consequences of their deeds.

Still another element is the armed robber, the robbers threatening all honest and peace loving people. They do not feel as safe as the people living in the towns, who enjoy the protection of the police and military forces. So to protect themselves and ensure their safety, they have to stand together with their own communities. Thus outwardly it appears the communities are severing their relations.

Malays and Chinese who possess a high spirit of nationalism are working against one another. The Malays who claim MALAYA for Malays are enlarging minor incidents and are always speaking ill of the Chinese and propagating the Chinese desire to make MALAYA a part of her empire. Such talk often puts fear in the minds of the Malays, especially amongst the literate and semi-literate classes. On the other hand, the Chinese condemn the Malays, exaggerating whatever is unpleasant to the Malays with the idea of showing and proving that all Malays are bad.

Thus people who have lost their houses, property and relatives help to maintain the tension. They wish for revenge, are irreconcilable and will never learn to forgive and forget.

So, summarising the whole situation, it seems that the unsettled relations are due to genuine fear in certain sections of the communities, and for other sections, it is purposely kept as a medium to benefit their own ends. Thus it is the working of all these various elements spreading and enlarging minor incidents which result in stirring the communities to strife. . . .

No 31 (to 11 June 1946): Che Salleh and the "Red Band"

During the Japanese Occupation JOHORE was the scene of some of the worst Sino-Malay troubles of this century. Various reasons may be assigned for this, not the least of which was the Japanese application of the policy of "Divide & Rule". Unfortunately, that was not the only reason, and recent reports indicate how incorrect it would be to assume that with the removal of the Japanese the situation would become entirely peaceful. Initiative in the present instance has been taken by the Malays, and the Golden Needle Invulnerability cult has now spread almost throughout the State from the centre of BATU PAHAT. About the turn of the year this cult was mentioned in this review, and was blamed for instigating trouble as far away as PAHANG; since then a vast amount of information has been received about it from which the following picture of the situation as it stands today has been compiled.

The leader (and he can scarcely be so unwillingly) would seem to be Che Mohamed Salleh bin Abdul Karim, the Penghulu of Mukim 4[1] in the District of BATU PAHAT. This man, of mixed Malay and Indian parentage, has had a varied life which includes three spells in gaol for theft. He was chosen for Pneghulu [sic] by Dato Onn bin Jaffar (of UMNO), but during the past two months the latter has been made fully aware of Salleh's tacit admission to complicity in the Cult. Whilst admitting in principle that Salleh ought to be removed, the Dato has stated his preference that he should be allowed to continue in office – provided he refrains from further trouble-making – in order to avoid antagonising his appreciably large following, which would produce a split in the unity the Malays have so lately won.

Che Salleh has spread his own deep-seated mistrust of the Chinese by appeals to the fanatical and superstitious side of the kampong Malays. Working in the main through the Imams, the religious teachers of the Muhammadan community, he has apparently established "cells" not only in every Parit [? Parish] in his own Mukim, but as far away as MERSING and KOTA TINGGI. Che Salleh has gone a step further than most traditional preachers of Holy Wars who merely promised Paradise to those who died killing the infidel, and has appealed to the pre-Muslim animist background of the Malays with the promise of invulnerability. The Malays' faith in charms and ritual magic (which, though theoretically irreconcilable with orthodox Muhamma-danism, he has in fact reconciled with his Faith even as, in Eastern EUROPE, the

---

[1] *Mukim* is an administrative subdivision of a district; *penghulu* is a headman of a mukim or group of mukims.

Christian peasant has found his religion in no way incompatible with many a pagan ritual) is a known characteristic of his race, and the magic employed in the present instance follows the traditional forms. Being pierced with the Golden Needle achieves for one Invulnerability; so does the drinking of a potion previously blessed by the Imam; or the wearing of the Red Band from which Che Salleh's organisation takes its name. In every case the pagan form is coupled with the use of warlike texts from Al-Koran, and the power of the latter alone to arouse unthinking fanaticism is already famous wherever a Muhammadan community exists.

It will not be out of place to review the powers Che Salleh's supernatural gifts are reputed to confer upon him, and which he can delegate to his followers, because only by an understanding of these can one appreciate the power which a fanatical belief in their possession can engender. Nor should it be imagined that defeat and the death of numerous Invulnerables would immediately shake belief, because the failure could always be attributed to the unworthiness of the individual, in that the Power is conferred only on those who are without pride, who do not loot in war, who rob not the dead, and who never look back when fighting. Che Salleh himself – it is popularly claimed – cannot be killed by bullets; he can walk dryshod across rivers; he can burst any bonds that are put upon him; his voice can paralyse his assailants, making them drop their weapons; and were the Chinese to take him and set him in a cauldron of boiling water he would emerge alive and unharmed. These powers he has delegated to two principal assistants, known as Haji Fadil and Haji Adnan, of PASIR PLANGI, who, together with himself, have the ability to confer Invulnerability upon devotees who faithfully observe a certain ritual. The Power, however, lasts only as long as the Faith of the Initiate in his own Safety is firm. Initiates are known in battle by the band of red cloth they may wear on their arm, and leaders bear a wider band across their chests.

Amongst his disciples Che Salleh also numbers one Endar, known to the Faithful as "Selamat" (which comes from the Arabic, and means "peace, security or safety") who has been to SEGAMAT, to LENGGENG and as far afield as to MANTIN in NEGRI SEMBILAN recruiting followers. He is thought to be of British North BORNEO birth. Another is Haji Salihon, who visited SINGAPORE, and assembled a large Malay meeting to hear Che Salleh speak, but when the appointed time came, Haji Salihon himself addressed the crowd in his place. Although the connection between these men and Che Salleh has never been conclusively proved, it is scarcely likely that he is unaware of what is being done in his name, and when he was interviewed recently in the presence of Dato Onn he tacitly owned to all that was said of him. In practice, anti-Chinese activity has so far been confined to boycotts in the estates, but a feeling of alarm is spreading amongst the Chinese, many of whom began to drift away from the kampongs in the MINYAK BEDU area, some twenty miles SW of KLUANG, in the middle of May. When interrogated these refugees gave as the causes of their evacuation the movement by night of armed parties of Malays and pressure by Malays who had leased estates to the Chinese for the winding-up of these leases before their expiry. Although the Chinese are prone to exaggerate, these stories undoubtedly have some foundation, and the Chinese were so convinced of their danger that they were firmly intending to send away their families, leaving only the menfolk to work the estates. It is possible that the inability of the Japanese to protect them from massacre during the occupation has left them uncertain of the effectiveness of the protection where the British can offer. . . .

No 32 (to 22 June 1946): The Malay "Youth Corps for Justice" (API)

A reliable and interesting, indeed intriguing, report has recently been received regarding the Ankatan Pemuda Insaf (API). This was previously mentioned in this review as a Youth Movement then in the process of formation under the control of the Malay Nationalist Party (MNP). Literally, the full name means "Youth Corps for Justice"; what is possibly more to the point, and is certainly easier to mouth, is the word "API" formed by its initials, which means "Fire" or "Flame", and may be presumed to describe the ardent nationalism its organisers hope to inspire in their recruits. So far, API is still in its infancy. The report referred to states that, when fully developed, it will work on the lines of the terrorist organisations now operating in INDONESIA. Its aims would then be to coerce the Malay community into supporting the MNP to a greater degree that [than] its unrepresentative character would justify in a democratic country. If UMNO's proposals for the amendment of the Malayan Union proposals are not accepted, API might well come under the indirect control of this organization by means of the affiliation of the MNP to it; if, on the other hand, UMNO achieves a satisfactory settlement, API may be still-born. Its plan is reported to envisage three phases, all dependant upon the establishment of the MNP, its parent body, as a force to be counted with in Malay politics. This has, in view of its organisers, already been achieved, and API has entered on its first phase, the formative stage, during which the preliminary underground organisation is to be set up. The second phase is to be affiliation [affiliated] with the GLUs, thus tightening the bond between the MNP and the MCP, and providing a useful variety of elimination squads for their joint use. Lastly, the Youth Militant will launch "AROBA" (Asia Raja Oentok Bangsa Asia, which means ASIA for the Asiatics). This phase will presumably involve a "Quit MALAYA" campaign against the British administration and a demand for self-government within the Indonesian Federation.

The HQ of API is to form part of the central HQ of the MNP. Its present leader is reported to be Ahmad Bestamam [sic],[2] of KUALA LUMPUR. He will probably be the organiser of the API congress which has already been twice postponed but is said to be planned for the near future. The choice of site for this congress has fallen on MALACCA, both because this city is the traditional "capital" of Malay fanaticism and because it is the headquarters of the "Holy War" movement. Many of API's members will probably take advantage of the occasion to don invulnerability, and it is of interest that they too are to be known by a red armband (the sign of Che Salleh's "Invulnerables"), but with the letters A.P.I. inscribed on it. The relationship between API and MNP on the one hand and PIM (Pembantoe Indonesia Merdeka – the Indonesian Freedom movement) on the other is uncertain, but is at present thought to be merely one of "mutual sympathy" and cooperation. API's formal aims are to unite nationally-conscious youth in order that it may play its full part in the struggle for the freedom of the Race and Country. Membership is restricted to members of the MNP or its affiliated bodies between the ages of 18 and 35, and recruits must be sound in mind and body and willing utterly to subordinate themselves to the orders of their higher commanders.

API is to have a central committee of nine members, with State committees under

---

[2] Ahmad Boestamam recorded his memories of his days with API in *Merintis Jalan Ke Punchak* (Kuala Lumpur, 1972) translated by William R Roff as *Carving the path to the summit* (Athens, Ohio University Press, 1979). See 116.

this to organise and integrate all activities within their respective States, and the whole organisation is designed to enforce a strict almost fascist discipline, based on the four precepts:

Respect your Seniors
Obey your Orders
Always be Prepared
Abide by all decisions of the MNP.

After the sensationalism of the above report, it may be worth while to observe here that the activities of the API have up to date been almost nil. A few meetings have been held. A few branches have been established. But the whole organisation is still nebulous, and will doubtless remain so until the first Congress has met and the Committees have been formally established. Nevertheless API is a movement to be watched with close interest, and the possibility of its developing into an armed body of extremists is by no means remote. One need only remember the close kinship between the Malays of MALAYA and the Malayan peoples of the rest of INDONESIA. What the latter can do, can be done equally well by the Malays of this Peninsula. . . .

95 CAB 21/1954   17 June 1946
'Survey of co-ordination within the territories of South-East Asia': inward savingram no 12 from Lord Killearn to FO

[After three months as special commissioner, Killearn urged that steps be taken to improve the co-ordination of British activities in the region. Though despatched on 17 June this savingram was not received in the FO until 1 July. Writing to Sir Norman Brook on 12 July, E A Armstrong pointed out that it was the FO's view that adequate co-ordinating machinery already existed in the Far East (Official) Committee. For Killearn's annual report to Bevin, see 'South-East Asia: work of the Special Commission during 1946', 12 Apr, CAB 21/1955, F 6151/6151/61 (see also 119).]

The area
1. At the end of the war the Supreme Allied Commander, South East Asia, was, broadly speaking, responsible for the area comprising Ceylon, Burma, Siam, Southern Indo-China, Malaya, Borneo, and the Netherlands East Indies.
2. This area will continue to be a bastion of vital political, strategic and economic importance to the British Commonwealth.
3. In addition to the Kingdom of Siam, the Governments of France and Holland have a territorial stake in the area. Australia, New Zealand, and India are interested neighbours. China and the United States are intimately concerned. The Soviet Union might become active within the area in the future.

Possible threats to the area
4. There are a number of contingencies which, to a greater or lesser degree, would imply a threat to British interests in the area as a whole. Among these are:—

(a) The collapse of law and order in any given area.
(b) An increased revival of trouble in the Netherlands East Indies.
(c) Difficulties with Nationalists [sic] movements.

(d) Trouble with the inhabitants of the South East area of Chinese race. (If the general relations of His Majesty's Government with China become bad, and still more, if (however remote the prospect) China and the Soviet Union were working together against us, the threat might become extremely serious).

There are many other sources of possible concern to the interests of His Majesty's Government in the area as a whole.

5. Even if none of these contingencies should arise, the positive advantages, in terms of commerce and of the prosperity and political development of the Commonwealth as a whole, and of the United Nations concerned, of a co-ordinated approach to the problems of the area are very great.

Departments of His Majesty's Government concerned

6. The Departments of His Majesty's Government in the United Kingdom which are primarily concerned with the area include the Foreign Office, the Dominions Office, Colonial Office, India Office, the Burma Office, the Services Departments, the Treasury, the Board of Trade, the Ministry of Transport, the Ministry of Food, the Ministry of Supply, the Ministry of Civil Aviation, and the Post Office.

The problem

7. The political (both foreign and internal), strategic and economic interests of the Commonwealth in the area are interlocking and ought to be treated as such. What happens in one part of the area is of interest to all other parts of the area. A reversion to the pre-war system of handling these problems in water-tight compartments and penny packets would be a fatal step. Recent years and the war have taught us lessons which, if we benefit from them, cannot fail to ensure that the Commonwealth, both administratively, economically, and strategically, is on a far surer footing than it has been in the past.

Co-ordinating machinery

8. Until recently the Supreme Allied Commander was the only co-ordinating authority in all matters but with the resumption of civil authority on a peace-time basis in the various countries of the area, the Supreme Allied Commander is progressively and as quickly as possible, passing his responsibilities in regard to civil matters to other authorities. Under present arrangements, the machinery available for co-ordination is centred in:—

(a) The Governor-General, Malaya (and prospectively Borneo).
(b) The Special Commissioner.
(c) The Supreme Allied Commander.

It is important that there should be the closest co-operation between these three authorities and that, through them, effective co-ordination should be achieved within the area. The staffs of these authorities will work as a team in intelligence and planning and in directing executive action in all matters of common interest; to this end, the staffs concerned will be located in Singapore and, if possible, in the same building. There will be constant personal contact and mutual consultation at the staff level between the Chief of Staff and Principal Administrative Officer, S.A.C.S.E.A., Deputy Special Commissioner, and the Secretary General to the

Governor General. These officers will comprise a standing committee to be known as the Co-ordination Committee.

Defence committee
9. A Defence Committee is to be set up immediately comprising the following members:—

Governor-General, Malaya. (Chairman).
The Special Commissioner.
The Supreme Allied Commander.

The Governors of British territories and Service Chiefs will attend as required and Dominion and Foreign authorities will be called into consultation as occasion arises.

Functions of governor-general
10. *Sphere of Authority.* At present the sphere of authority of the Governor-General is restricted to the Malayan Union and the Colony of Singapore, but very shortly British North Borneo, Brunei and Sarawak will be added. Hong Kong is at present outside his sphere but arrangements will be made for him to represent the interests of that Colony in matters coming within the purview of the Defence Committee.

Co-ordination of policy and administration
11. The main purpose of the Governor-General's appointment is to ensure co-ordination of policy and administration throughout all the territories within his sphere, with particular regard to political, economic and social questions. Planning is to be directed to the co-ordinated development of sea and air communications and to ensure that the more backward parts of the territories share equally in programmes for social and economic advancement and the organisation of many forms of research. On the political side it will aim at progressive and closer political co-ordination and the development of self-governing institutions among the peoples concerned.

Co-operation with other colonial powers
12. In matters of Colonial Administration co-operation should be encouraged between Great Britain and other Colonial Powers in the Far East, and, for this purpose, the Governor-General will, by arrangements with and through the Special Commissioner, keep in touch, with the principal administrative authorities in the foreign territories concerned.

Co-operation with foreign territories in all matters of common interest
13. In these wider matters the Governor-General will maintain close contact with the Special Commissioner who is primarily responsible for advising His Majesty's Government on these aspects of co-operation. The Supreme Commander will be consulted on all matters of defence in relation to foreign territories.

Contact with governments of the dominions etc
14. The Governor-General will maintain close contacts with any representative who may be established within his sphere of authority by the Governments of any of

the Dominions, India, Burma, or Ceylon. He will also keep in touch with the Viceroy
of India, the Governors of Burma and Ceylon, and United Kingdom High Commissioners in Australia and New Zealand, through whom contacts with the Governments
of those countries may also be made as occasion arises.

Authority of Governor-General

15. The Governor-General will have power to give any Governor or British
Representative in charge of any territory within the Governor-General's sphere, such
directions as may be necessary, either in discharge of his responsibility for
co-ordinating policy, or in order to give effect to the policy of His Majesty's
Government in any matter. He will not, however, exercise direct administrative
functions in any territory and will invariably address his directions or advice to the
Governor or British representative himself. The Governor-General will have power at
any time to convene and preside over Conferences of British Governors and
representatives in his sphere of authority for any purpose that he may consider
necessary. He will also have power to convene any other Conferences deemed
necessary in the exercise of his responsibilities. He will further have authority to act
as arbiter in any disagreements between Governments within the sphere of his
authority on matters of policy or administration and if disagreements persist he may
decide any such matter, unless any Governor concerned asks for it to be referred to
the Secretary of State for the Colonies or the Defence Committee at home if Defence
and other interests clash.

Functions of the Special Commissioner

16. *Foreign affairs*. The Special Commissioner is charged with the duty of
advising His Majesty's Government in the United Kingdom on problems affecting
foreign affairs which may arise in the area comprising Ceylon, Burma, Siam,
Indo-China, Malaya, Borneo, and the Netherlands East Indies. (The situation as
regards Hong Kong remains to be clarified). He is to give guidance to the Supreme
Commander, South East Asia Command, on matters relating to Foreign Affairs, and
in particular on non-military matters arising in foreign territories within the South
East Asia Command. In respect of foreign affairs he is to maintain contact and will
confer personally as required with the Viceroy of India, the Governor-General of
Malaya, the Governors of Burma, Ceylon, and Hong Kong, and His Majesty's Minister
in Siam, and will arrange for interchange of information with them. He will maintain
close contact with the Governments of Australia, New Zealand, India and Burma as
may be required, whether by personal visits, by correspondence with the United
Kingdom High Commissioners in any of the Dominions concerned, or by the close
co-operation which he will, in any case, maintain with any representatives which
these Governments may establish in Singapore. He is to direct the activities of
Foreign Service Officers within the area, (otherwise than in Siam), and when civil
administration has been restored in the foreign territories at present in South East
Asia Command, he will maintain contact with the foreign administrations in those
territories in such manner as may appear most suitable from time to time.

17. *Food*. The Special Commissioner has been given by the Cabinet special
authority and responsibility in regard to food and related matters in respect of
Ceylon, Burma, Siam, Indo-China, Malaya, Borneo, the Netherlands East Indies and
Hong Kong. In respect of food he is to maintain close contact with the Government

of India and to take India's needs into account. He is also to maintain close contact with Dominion representatives at Singapore and with United Kingdom High Commissioners in Australia and New Zealand. His responsibility will be without prejudice to, and will in no way affect, the position or the individual responsibilities of the Governors of British territories, His Majesty's Minister in Siam, and the British Service Commanders within the area. He is to endeavour to secure agreement between all authorities concerned, both British and Foreign, on the adoption of measures designed to alleviate the food crisis and in particular to ensure that the availability of foodstuffs, especially rice, is phased according to the productive capacity and harvests of the various territories. A Special Committee, the Official Committee on South East Asia (Food Supplies) has been set up to co-ordinate action by United Kingdom Departments on Communications with the Special Commissioner which are concerned with food problems and related economic questions in South East Asia.

18. *Publicity.* The Special Commissioner is considering separately whether any problems of publicity require consultation between the Governor-General and the various other British authorities in the area, whether in British or in foreign territory.

19. *Economic questions.* The Special Commissioner was instructed to consider, in consultation with the Governor-General, the Supreme Allied Commander, and other authorities concerned, whether:—

(a) the existing machinery in South East Asia is sufficient to deal with economic questions arising within the area at present, and

(b) what arrangements, if any, should be made for the period immediately after the military authorities have handed over control to the civil governments, and to make recommendations on these points.

Action has already been taken on some of these points. Further consultation is required on others.

Immediate recommendations

20. *Meetings.* Periodical meetings should be held under the chairmanship of the Governor-General or the Special Commissioner, as may be appropriate in each case, to discuss problems of concern to all British representatives in the area. These may, as action warrants, be attended by the representatives of British territories only, or in addition, either by British representatives in foreign territories, or by representatives of foreign territories, or by both. It should be borne in mind that if the status of Burma and Ceylon changes, whether into that of a Dominion or otherwise, attendance at such meetings may become inappropriate. In that event either Cabinet Ministers from these areas or the United Kingdom High Commissioner (if such appointments are made), or both, might participate.

21. *Visits.* It is desirable that the Governor-General and the Special Commissioner and the Supreme Allied Commander and their staffs should keep in personal touch with London by periodic visits, and that there should be frequent interchange of visits within the area.

Note: If these visits are paid, suitable accommodation and locomotion would have to be provided.

Communications

22. Co-ordination within the area cannot be achieved without efficient methods of communication. It is essential that:—

(a) all British authorities in the area should possess both a cypher and a code in which they can communicate with each other. The Foreign Office are now issuing a special cypher for communication between British representatives in South East Asia.

(b) British representatives should be able to travel within the area, to neighbouring countries, and to London by air as, and when required, without delay. The Supreme Allied Commander is enquiring into the means necessary to ensure this.

(c) British representatives in the area must be able to communicate with each other and with London by frequent and quick bag service. The Special Commissioner is examining this question which is, of course, linked with (b).

Co-ordination in London

23. Most of the measures of co-ordination outlined above can be achieved by action on the part of British authorities within the area on their own initiative. But co-ordination in London is also desirable. It may be that such co-ordination can be effected by the existing machinery. Alternatively, it might be effected either by enlarging the scope of the Nathan Committee[1] or by setting up some other machinery. In any case, the advantages of some body in London which would co-ordinate the work of the various Government Departments in dealing with all questions affecting South East Asia, and which would have direct access to the Cabinet, are obvious.

Future development

24. Only experience will show whether the basis outlined above for co-ordination in the area is the right one, and if so the full measure of what can be built upon it. Fully successful co-ordination can only grow in the light of events. But the need is there. If one solution fails another must be tried.

Summing up

25. To sum up. The problems of South East Asia are inter-related and there is vital need to treat them as such. This requires closer co-ordination both within the area and in London. The necessary machinery has now been set up in respect of the Defence Committee, of Foreign Affairs, and of food. Publicity, economic, and social welfare questions are to be examined. Periodical meetings should be held within the area to discuss problems of concern to the various British authorities. These may, on occasion, be attended by appropriate foreign representatives. There should be frequent interchange of visits within the area, and the Governor-General, the Special Commissioner, and their staffs should be in constant personal touch with London. There must be adequate cypher and bag arrangements for communication within the area and with London, and arrangements for rapid air travel within the area and to

---

[1] Lord Nathan, parliamentary under-secretary for War, 1945–1946, chaired the Official Committee on Food Supplies for SE Asia; Nathan was succeeded first by Lord Pakenham in Oct 1946 and later by M E Dening, see CAB 21/1714.

and from London. Further development and adaptation must be sought in the light of experience.

Co-ordination with Australia, New Zealand and India

26. No attempt is made in the above Survey to cover the question of co-ordination with Australia, New Zealand and India. This requires further consideration. Meanwhile it may be noted that the closest relations have been established with [the] Australian Commissioner in Singapore who attends all important meetings convened by the Supreme Commander, or the Special Commissioner. In addition, an Australian representative has been appointed in Singapore who is combining the functions of political adviser to the Australian Commissioner and of Special Liaison Officer with the Special Commissioner.

96   CO 537/1529, nos 149–152   21–22 June 1946
[MacMichael Treaties and conciliation of Malay opposition]: inward telegram no 57 from Mr M J MacDonald to Mr Hall

> [The goverment's intransigence over the MacMichael treaties hardened the rulers' resolve to go to London. Anxious to prevent this, MacDonald despatched in four parts the following telegram urging Hall to reconsider his position on the treaties.]

Part 1
Governor Malayan Union's telegram No. 431 containing text of reply from Rulers.

Gent and I regret that our warning in paragraph 11 of my telegram G.G. No. (?) and in paragraph 5 of telegram M.U. No. 380, in spite of the long way which your last proposals went to meet Malay opinion, the MacMichael Agreements might prove serious stumbling block to successful negotiations on Federal Government has been justified. This telegram and my two immediately following telegrams contain our considered comments and advice on the situation. We fully realise you may find great difficulty in accepting the proposals which we make about the MacMichael Agreements. We are sorry we have to bother [you], but know you wish us to give you our honest appreciation of the position and whatever advice we consider necessary on the merits of the case for your consideration. We do not however suggest (unless you are prepared to do so) that you should now commit yourself to accepting our proposal on this matter. Our suggestion is as follows:—

As you know, Gent and I are meeting Dato Onn and some of his colleagues in Penang next Wednesday 26th June. Would you be willing that we should try out on them in general terms and without committing ourselves, let alone you, the gist of the suggestions in my immediately following telegrams? We would then try to discover whether U.M.N.O. leaders (who have great influence over the Rulers) would regard this as acceptable basis for agreement. We would report to you our findings after the meeting and you could then decide whether or not you would authorise us to put forward these proposals formally and on your behalf.

Part 2
Having now been here for a month with many opportunities to gauge Malay opinion, I can confirm everything that Gent and I have said in previous telegrams about its

strength and unity. Malay opinion is roused as never before. By itself, this is not a bad thing, for it is highly desirable that Malays become politically conscious so as to prepare themselves to play appropriate part in developing self-Governing institutions. But it will be extremely unfortunate if this awakened political consciousness and interest gets rail-waded [sic: rail-roaded] into extremist and anti-British channels. If we can restore Malay confidence in Britain as a result of the present negotiations and secure in possession of agreement we can prevent this. Then Malay nationalist movement is likely to be friendly with the administration here and to cooperate with us in political affairs instead of being swept into Indonesian anti-European currents. If, on the other hand, we do not succeed in this, we shall miss great chance. We should then face probability of widespread non-cooperation and begin to tread the (?) full road of local opposition and bitterness which has led to such damaging situations elsewhere.

Gent and I have considered carefully whether publication of your last proposals now would counteract the present opposition to gain effective popular support for your proposals and thus enable (?) us to hold the position. If we thought it would help, we would advocate this course. But at the present stage, such action would not be helpful. Strong feeling against MacMichael agreements does not spring so much from rulers as from U.M.N.O. and Malay opinion generally. If we published proposals which left in the air the question of replacement of MacMichael Agreements, on which Malay opinion is especially vigilant, form of criticism would concentrate on that [and] the effect of your proposals would be spoiled, and their advantages be forgotten amidst agitation against MacMichael Agreements. We should get no thanks for your proposals and opinion would harden in undesirable directions.

I have been more and more forcibly impressed with the fact that the core of opposition is to the MacMichael Agreements as such, and that unless we satisfy opinion on this, we shall lose the opportunity to heal the breach between Malays and us. Gent and I are certain that in a better atmosphere, your last proposals would be appreciated and form basis of firm agreement. But they will not be considered in the proper light if the shadow of the MacMichael Agreements is thrown across them. We believe Rees Williams, Gammans, Sir John Maude and Sir Theodore Adams[1] will all agree with this. We must therefore consider most seriously opposition to MacMichael Agreements.

Part 3

In this case neither Gent nor I feel any sympathy whatever with the Rulers, except to some extent with one or two like the Sultan of Kedah who, as MacMichael stated frankly in his report, signed in effect under protest.[2] Other Rulers signed voluntarily although not anticipating strength of Malayan[3] reactions. Subsequent attitude results from that latter mistake, which has landed them in personal prevarication for which we can have little respect. On the other hand, we feel impelled to state frankly

---

[1] Sir Theodore Adams (1885–1961). As British resident of Selangor, 1932–1936, he had advised the British to bar Musa-Edin from the succession and prefer Alam Shah in his place (see 57). Adams was in Malaya from mid May to mid June and acted as adviser to the rulers in their informal negotiations with the Malayan Union government.

[2] See 64 and also Colonial Office, *Report on a Mission to Malaya by Sir Harold MacMichael, GCMG, DSO (October 1945 – January 1946)*, Col 194, paras 13 and 20.

[3] He means, of course, 'Malay' since 'Malayan' includes Chinese and Indian residents.

that we have considerable sympathy with U.M.N.O. in their opposition to the MacMichael Agreements. Their opposition is what has really provoked the Rulers into eagerness to repudiate the agreements. When Malayan Congress feelings found support amongst retired Malayan officials in Britain, their views became all the firmer and crystallised in U.M.N.O. Conduct of retired Malayan officials in publicly attacking H.M.G.'s policy and aggravating the difficulties is indefensible.[4] But we shall only prevent ourselves from seeing the issue in its proper perspective if we become rigid on the point because of righteous indignation at the conduct of the Rulers and retired Malayan officials. The central fact is that the opposition to MacMichael Agreements comes strongly from Malayan democratic opinion as a whole. That is what we have to reckon with. It is a case of the will of the people expressing itself. This was born out in Gent's talk with Dato Onn and colleagues the other day,[5] on which he has reported in his telegram to me No. 423 repeated to you.

Our sympathy with democratic Malayan opinion is based on consideration that Agreements were signed by most Rulers without anything like adequate consultation with their peoples. Whether this was strictly constitutional or not, it is morally and politically of doubtful rectitude. It flouted all the rules of democratic Government and of Government on satisfactory lines we confirmed, and has caused deep resentment in Malaya.

Part 4

Although Malayans highly prize His Majesty's protection, and although they are in favour of strong central Government of the kind proposed by you, they are at the same time proud of their States and desire to preserve their sovereign status. They are convinced that the terms of MacMichael Agreements transferring "full powers and jurisdiction" to His Majesty deprive them of this status. We are advised by legal authorities that their conviction may well be justified and courts would interpret the Agreements as having wholly transferred soveriegnty [sic] from State Rulers. Sir John Maude has discussed this aspect of the matter with us and I am sure will be helpful to you in consideration of the point.

At the same time, we recognise the impossibility of agreeing that MacMichael Agreements should be revoked forthwith. Weighing all these various considerations together, we venture to offer the advice contained in my two immediately following telegrams.[6]

With regard to the Rulers' request that they and their advisers should now be enabled [to] travel [to] London for negotiations, we trust that you will reject this. Proper place for negotiations is here. Gent and I have been fully authorised by you [to] conduct discussions on your behalf and have started to do this in our talks with the Rulers and other representatives. Transference of discussions to London now would undermine Gent's and my authority in Malaya, even if it were possible both of us to go to London to help you in negotiations. Our leaving Malaya at the present would cause serious interruption to our other talks here. Moreover, if the Rulers go to London, they will fall into the hands of retired Malayan officials and lawyers with

---

[4] See 73, note 1.   [5] MacDonald is referring to Gent's talk with Onn on 19 June.
[6] In these telegrams (not printed here) MacDonald argued that the revocation of the MacMichael treaties should not take place until the government were satisfied that the fundamental principles of their policy were guaranteed and that their revocation would enhance Britain's reputation.

consequent increase in the difficulties of reaching agreement.

Gent will, of course, tell the Rulers that he is transmitting to you their request that they should be enabled to go to London. This will keep them in play for a while. Subject to what transpires at our meeting with Dato Onn and Company, we strongly hope however that you will later feel able to reply to them on the lines of suggestions in my immediately following telegrams. *Ends.*

97   CO 537/1529, nos 169–171   5 July 1946
[MacMichael treaties and conciliation of Malay opposition]: outward telegram no 848 from Mr Hall to Sir E Gent

[MacDonald and Gent were heartened by informal talks with Onn and other Malay leaders at MacDonald's temporary quarters in Penang on 26 June (for a record of this meeting see CO 537/1529, no 208), and, recognizing the need to strengthen UMNO against the radical MNP, again urged Hall to make concessions on the MacMichael treaties. In his reply on 5 July Hall appears to be shifting his position from principles to tactics.]

My telegram No.813 of 29th June (addressed to Governor-General as No.61): Malayan Constitution.

I have now considered the whole position as carefully and rapidly as my other preoccupations, particularly with Palestine, have permitted. I fully appreciate from paragraph 2 of Governor-General's telegram No.59 and from paragraph 3(c) of his telegram No.73, that the assurance which I am now recommended to give regarding the eventual replacements of the MacMichael Agreements would be dependent upon the reaching of a solution satisfactory to H.M.G. I welcome the fact that Dato Onn and his associates appear to have adopted in this regard a less intransigeant attitude than might have been feared. Nevertheless, I confess that I see great difficulty in the proposed course of action for the following reasons. It is suggested that I should forthwith not only give the assurance but announce in Parliament that I have done so, without any concrete knowledge of the attitude taken on the Malay side either as regards the definite constitutional proposals put forward in my telegram[s] 581, 582 and 586, or as regards the form of agreement which they propose in substitution for the MacMichael Agreements. This I am not inclined to do, for if I now give the assurance on the basis of such vague premises, I foresee that this may involve great difficulties later on not only for H.M.G. in London but for the Governor-General and yourself. We cannot blink the possibility that the Malay negotiators, after the assurance has been given, may prove not (repeat not) to be amenable either as regards constitutional proposals as such or as regards the form of a new agreement or as regards both. In that event, H.M.G. will be placed in the unenviable position either of having to accept a solution which they do not approve or of appearing to be entirely responsible for subsequent breakdown in negotiations. In short, I am still afraid that H.M.G. may be forced to concede point after point without receiving anything tangible in return.

2. In any case such soundings as I have been able to take show that even if I myself were convinced that the present recommendations are sound, the above point of view would undoubtedly be taken by my colleagues. If I now place before them your recommendation that the assurance should be given as proposed, they are

bound to ask me what concrete suggestions or offers have been put forward as an alternative; and I shall have nothing to say.

3. My present position is that I have made constructive constitutional proposals which deserve to be considered. I have also indicated that I shall be prepared to limit future use of jurisdiction acquired by His Majesty, by binding H.M.G. to consult leaders of Malayan opinion to fullest extent before initiating further constitutional changes. If Sultans or Malay leaders are not satisfied as apparently they are not, then the least they should be willing to do is to work out with Governor-General and yourself a position [sic] alternative.

4. I am encouraged by the friendly tone of your conversation with Dato Onn and his associates into believing that they can be brought to see the matter in a reasonable light, and to work out with the Governor-General and yourself practical proposals which I can with confidence put before my colleagues. What I am suggesting is that, in an endeavour to bring about a resumption of discussions, you should put forward the proposal that they should be recommended on the basis that:—

(a) we for our part fully recognise the objection which the Malays see to the MacMichael Agreements, but the question whether those agreements should be replaced should be put on one side without prejudice to its later consideration;

(b) if and when a sufficient measure of agreement has been reached on all other matters, the question of some amended or new agreement could be considered, and I should be agreeable to proposals being formulated on the clear understanding that willingness of H.M.G. to accept such amended or new agreement would depend entirely on the nature of that new document.

5. The above must of course be considered together with the proposals made by Adams on which I have consulted you in my telegram No.842 and I shall be grateful for frank views of Governor General and yourself on both telegrams.

98 CO 537/1598, ff 24–27   20–21 Aug 1946

[Closer association of Malaya and Singapore]: item 7 of minutes of governor-general's conference in Penang, 20–21 Aug

[A significant constitutional problem, though one that was less pressing in 1946 than was the crisis over the Malayan Union, concerned regional consolidation. The White Paper of Jan 1946 had announced the government's commitment to the closer association of the Malayan Union and Singapore in the longer term. Yet two separate governments, each under a different governor, threatened to pull in different directions. MacDonald, one of whose functions was to facilitate liaison between the territories, took up the matter of merger when the committee, which Sir F Gimson had appointed to examine the reconstitution of Singapore's legislative council, made recommendations likely to enlarge the gulf between island and peninsula.]

*Future constitutional arrangements: Malayan Union and Singapore (Reference)**
The Governor-General said that he had caused this item to be placed on the Agenda to enable him

* (Ref: Report of the Committee appointed by H.E. the Governor of Singapore to make recommendations for the reconstitution of the Legislative Council of the Colony.)

(1) to get further information as to what the Governors had in mind about constitutional developments in their respective territories in the early future, and (2) to consider the situation in relation to the possibility of the Malayan Union and Singapore being more closely associated constitutionally at a not too distant date.

With regard to the first point, the paper before the Conference was a report of the Committee appointed to consider the scope and nature of the future Legislative Council of the Colony of Singapore. He considered that the proposals were sound and progressive and that, by themselves, they were generally to be welcomed. However, with regard to the second point, if the proposals were accepted and a Legislative Council with an unofficial majority were established in the near future in Singapore, a step might have been taken which would be prejudicial to the ultimate objective of a closer union between the Malayan Union and Singapore. It had been stated in the White Paper that the formation of the Malayan Union would not prejudice closer constitutional arrangements at a later date between the two territories. When he left London he felt that this was a problem which could be considered in a serious but more or less leisurely fashion by the authorities concerned over, say, the next two years, with a view to policy being settled after that in the light of experience in the meantime. Since reaching Malaya he had altered this view. Practical problems of administration and policy indicated that there was some danger of the two territories drifting apart. He now felt that an early examination of the problem was desirable, with a view to the Governors and himself making up their minds, even if only tentatively, what was ultimately desirable in the way of a closer constitutional tie-up. Then they would be able to ensure that policies were not pursued in either territory which would ultimately prejudice the possibility of realising their long term objective. He knew that no actual constitutional change should take place before, say, eighteen months. It would be a mistake to suggest anything of the kind before the new constitution on the Peninsula had been not only agreed but also put into effective and steady working. But, without giving publicity to what they had authorised, he thought that they should appoint an informal sub-committee of their principal advisers to start an examination of the matter.

The Governor, Malayan Union, said that economically it was not desirable that the Malayan Union should be dominated by the commercial consideration of Singapore. He considered that there was every reason why the Malayan Union should remain a single Government and that its needs and activities should be regarded independently and not in the light of Singapore aspirations. He felt that there would be very strong opposition from the Malayan Union to the inclusion of Singapore and that unless public opinion in the Malayan Union as well as in Singapore was favourable to the change, it could not be contemplated. He felt that any immediate change is out of the question.

The Governor-General stated that he was not advocating an immediate change. He felt that the immediate urgency was to consider the problem especially in view of the proposals for an unofficial majority in the Legislative Council of Singapore.

The Governor, Singapore, said that there was a very strong feeling in unofficial circles in Singapore that the severance of the two territories was a mistake and that Singapore should be linked constitutionally and administratively with the Government of the Peninsula. In various ways the commercial community did not consider the present arrangements were working satisfactorily.

The Governor, Malayan Union, said that the opinion of the commercial people of Singapore should not be a deciding factor. It was one thing for Singapore to want to come into the Malayan Union but the crucial question was whether the people of the Malayan Union would accept the inclusion of Singapore. The economies of Singapore and the Malayan Union were entirely different and they should each develop on their own lines. Penang, for example, as a free port was most important to the Malayan Union and it was desirable that more and more ships should go there.

The Colonial Secretary, Singapore,[1] said he felt that in many ways the economies of the two countries were complementary. There was a great deal of work that the commercial community of Singapore could and should do for the Malayan Union. Singapore provided, for example, a large and adequate port which was quite competent to deal with the trade of the whole territory. Singapore was the natural port of Malaya and it was only an accident of nature which divided it from the Peninsula.

The Governor, Malayan Union, said that having regard to the size of the territory and the value and importance of its produce, he would not regard the existence of three major ports as excessive. It would not therefore be satisfactory for the Malayan Union to rely on Singapore alone, in fact before the war only 20% of the import and export trade of Singapore derived from Malaya. Singapore lived on the entrepot trade which admittedly may be threatened by the Dutch. The task of Singapore is to hold that trade and endeavour to expand it.

The Colonial Secretary, Singapore, said that in addition to imports and exports, Singapore provided for the Malayan Union a number of 'invisible' services the extent and nature of which it is very difficult to estimate but he considered that they were of great importance.

The Governor, Malayan Union, presumed the Colonial Secretary was referring to the services such as Banking, Insurance, Shipping, etc. As to this is was possible that there might be some shifting of the balance to the Union but it was a matter for business interests to consider for themselves.

The Governor-General felt that Kuala Lumpur could never replace Singapore in its political capacity as the principal city of the South East Asia area.

The Chief Secretary, Malayan Union,[2] said the discussion so far had dealt with the economic aspects. He felt that there was a very important political consideration to be borne in mind. Their Highnesses, the Rulers, in the recent political discussions had directed their minds to a federation of the Malay States and showed some reluctance to the inclusion of Penang and Malacca. He felt that if it became known that any consideration was being given at present to the inclusion of Singapore in a wider federation, some of the present negotiations would break down and a charge of 'bad faith' might again be made.

The Governor-General said that it was most important that any further exploration of the problem should be strictly confidential but that he felt it might be wise to appoint a sub-Committee of the Secretary-General,[3] Colonial Secretary, Singapore, and the Chief Secretary, Malayan Union, to consider the matter in more detail and report later.

---

[1] P A B McKerron, colonial secretary of Singapore, 1946–1950.

[2] A T Newboult, chief secretary of Malayan Union, 1946–1948.

[3] Sir Ralph Hone, secretary-general to governor-general, 1946–1948.

The Governor, Malayan Union, drew attention to the references made to Malayan Union citizenship in the report regarding the proposed Legislative Council for Singapore.

The Colonial Secretary, Singapore, said that they were included to show that they had not been overlooked but pointed out that until status &c. of a Malayan Union citizen had been defined, the Committee felt unable to say any more on the subject.

The Governor, Malayan Union, enquired if any Malayan Union representative was consulted by the Committee on this point.

The Colonial Secretary, Singapore, said no such consultation had taken place and as the subject was still under discussion he did not feel that any useful purpose would have been served by referring the point to the Government of the Malayan Union.

The Governor, Malayan Union, said that if the report was to be published he would ask that references to the Malayan Union on citizenship should be excised.

The Governor, Singapore, said that he had asked the Secretary of State for permission to publish the report and, if this was received, he and the Colonial Secretary would arrange for the references to be omitted.

The Governor-General, enquired whether the Government of the Malayan Union had any other observations to make on the report or whether they felt that it might serve as a useful guide to certain of the future representative bodies in the Malayan Union.

The Governor, Malayan Union, said that he thought it was a notable report and that he hoped to adopt a similar principle in regard to the more advanced political bodies in the Malayan Union. In regard to the future constitutional relations of Singapore with the Malayan Union, he stressed that it was important that the wishes of the people of the Malayan Union should be ascertained and given their full weight.

After further discussion it was agreed that (a) if the Secretary of State approved the publication of the proposals for Singapore Legislative Council, references to Malayan Union citizenship should be excised, and (b) that a sub-Committee comprising the Secretary-General, the Chief Secretary, Malayan Union, and the Colonial Secretary, Singapore, should examine the wider problem further.

99 CO 537/1530, no 245 29 Aug 1946
'Developments in Malayan constitutional discussions': note by H T Bourdillon on deliberations of the Anglo-Malay working committee

[On 18 June MacDonald and Gent met the rulers and UMNO leaders together for the first time. Despite their continuing mistrust of the British over the treaties, which the secretary of state was most reluctant to abrogate, the Malays signalled their willingness to enter formal talks. On 24 July the rulers and UMNO representatives submitted draft proposals for fresh constitutional arrangements and an Anglo-Malay working committee was set up the following day (coinciding with a Commons debate which, contrary to the fears of some, did not upset the delicately poised negotiations). The members of the working committee were: (for the government) A T Newboult, K K O'Connor, W D Godshall, W Linehan, A Williams, with D C Watherston as secretary; (for the rulers) Dato Hamzah b Abdullah (Selangor), Hj Mohamed Sheriff (Kedah), Raja Kamaralzaman b Raja Mansur (Perak) and Dato Nik Ahmed Kamil (Kelantan); (UMNO) Dato Onn (Johore) and Dato Abdul Rahman b Mohd Yasin (Johore). Its sessions were also attended by Hone (for MacDonald), Adams (for the rulers) and Roland Braddell (for UMNO). The working committee met over four periods: 6–16 Aug, 6–28 Sept, 11 Oct–1 Nov and 11–18 Nov. Bourdillon's note assesses its deliberations until it adjourned on 16 Aug.]

Before the Secretary of State went away, we had heard that discussions with the Sultans and Malay Leaders on Constitutional questions had been successfully resumed, and that a Joint Working Committee, consisting of five Government representatives plus Sir R. Hone as an observer and five Malay Representatives plus Sir T. Adams, had been set up to study details.

2. The Working Committee assembled on August the 6th. It held meetings from that date until August the 16th, when it adjourned, for Mohammedan religious reasons, until the 6th of September.

3. In his telegram No.784, Sir Edward Gent has given us an account of progress made up to the date of adjournment. In certain respects this progress has been remarkable, though in others much ground remains to be covered. The main points may be tabulated as follows:—

(a) *Establishment of strong central government in Malaya.* The Working Commiteee spent the first week of its life in drawing up a list of subjects which are to be under the control of the Central Legislature. The results have been very satisfactory. In his telegram referred to above, Sir Edward Gent tells us that the list as finally agreed is very comprehensive, and this can be verified by reference to the list itself, which he has sent home under cover of a letter to Mr. Paskin. The list includes *all* the subjects which the Secretary of State, at an earlier stage, laid down as being essentially "central", besides a number of others. At first sight, in fact, there seemed to be no important subjects of any kind which are not placed under central control, though the Malays have stipulated in a number of cases that a measure of executive authority shall be entrusted to the State Councils. We have always ourselves envisaged this. Sir Edward Gent tells us that having gone thus far (and they have gone a very long way), the Malays are likely to insist on the "unallocated residue" of subjects being left under State control. We have hitherto resisted this, but it is open to question whether we need continue to do so – should the Malays maintain their present attitude – seeing that we have secured such a comprehensive list of central subjects.

(b) *Common citizenship.* The Malays were at first unwilling to admit Chinese as Malayan Union citizens at all, but it seems that they are likely to modify this attitude if they can be assured that Chinese in Malaya already have the status of British Protected Persons (i.e. that Chinese will not for the first time acquire that status by virtue of their status as Malayan Union citizens). The reasons for this stipulation are not entirely clear, but Chinese born in the Malay States have always been treated as British Protected Persons in the past, and this is still the case. We are in consultation with the F.O. with a view (if the S.of S. approves) to Sir Edward Gent being authorised to inform the Malays accordingly, and it is to be hoped that a solution will be reached on these lines. But we shall know nothing further until the meetings of the Working Committee are resumed.

(c) *His Majesty's jurisdiction in the Malay states.* This question, and the connected question of the modification or replacement of the MacMichael Agreements, have not hitherto been discussed by the Working Committee. This is in accordance with the Secretary of State's wish that the question of any new Agreements to replace the MacMichael Agreements should be reserved for a later stage in the discussion. We know from the record of the renewed meetings with the Sultans which preceded the establishment of the Working Committee, that the Sultans at that time were still adopting a rigid attitude on this question, which will undoubtedly prove the most difficult to solve.

4.   The three points enumerated above are those which the Secretary of State has always regarded as representing the essential basis of our Malayan policy. It will be seen that very good progress has been made on the first of the three points, that progress now appears to be possible on the second, and that the third remains to be tackled. On the whole, there seem to be grounds for cautious satisfaction with the results hitherto achieved; but Sir Edward Gent warns us that a point conceded by the Malay side of the Working Committee is not necessarily a point conceded by the Sultans and Malay Leaders themselves. In the last paragraph of his telegram No.784, he sums up the position as follows:

"Much will depend on the attitude of Malay Members when the Working Committee re-assembles, and on the extent to which they have been able to carry Rulers and U.M.N.O. with them in conclusions so far reached in Committee's discussions. It has been continually evident that Malay members of the Committee have themselves felt that, in compromising with our views on many important matters, too much has had to be conceded by their side".

100   CO 537/1542, no 94   14 Sept 1946
'Citizenship': inward telegram no 855 from Sir E Gent to Mr Hall

[The Working Committee reassembled on 6 Sept and Gent reported 'encouraging' progress despite 'extreme sensitiveness' to what members called 'dictatory' British attitudes (inward telegram no 854, CO 537/1542 no 93). It began by considering the categories of people qualified for citizenship, summarized by Gent in this telegram.]

My immediately preceding telegram No. 854.
    Citizenship.
    (1) Proposed categories are:—

(a) British subjects and subjects of Rulers born and permanently resident in the country.
(b) Any person applying for citizenship who satisfies High Commissioner as to:—

(i)   birth in country and local residence for 10 out of 15 years preceding application;
(ii) good character;
(iii) adequate knowledge of Malay or English language.
(c) Any applicant not included in (a) or (b) who satisfies High Commissioner as to

(i)   residence for 15 out of 20 years preceding application;
(ii) good character;
(iii) adequate knowledge of Malay or English language.

2.   Categories (b) and (c) would be required to make declaration of permanent settlement and take oath of citizenship.

101   CO 537/1530   17–24 Sept 1946
[Developments in Anglo-Malay constitutional discussions]: minutes by H T Bourdillon, T I K Lloyd and Mr Creech Jones

I understand that the Secretary of State has asked for an appreciation of the state of constitutional negotiations in Malaya, as affected by the two latest telegrams from Sir E. Gent (247 and 248).[1]

I have flagged No. 245 on the file,[2] which is an earlier appreciation submitted to the Secretary of State at the end of last month. It will be seen that I then dealt with the subject under three heads (paragraph 3 of No. 245), and it would perhaps be best if I now proceed in the same way, since these heads represent the principles which the Secretary of State has always regarded as fundamental to our Malayan policy:—

(a) *Establishment of strong central government in Malaya.* In my previous appreciation I reported good progress under this head, though I pointed out that the progress hitherto made was only progress in the *Working Committee*, and that it could not be taken for granted that the Sultans and Malay leaders would accept all the Working Committee's conclusions. It seems clear from the latest telegrams (see in particular paragraphs 2 to 8 of No. 247) that progress has been maintained and consolidated. Discussion has centred round the problem of finance, and it might well be expected that this would bring into the open any latent difficulties in the allocation of powers between the Central Legislatures [sic] and the State Councils. In the last resort, whoever has the money has the power; so the Malays would undoubtedly have shown fight on the financial issues if they were going to show fight on this particular question at all. Sir E. Gent says that there have indeed been difficulties, but I think we may regard the conclusions as definitely satisfactory. First and foremost, the Working Committee appears to have agreed to a general pooling of existing State assets and liabilities. This, I think, is a big point gained. It is true that in taking this step, the Malay members of the Working Committee have tried to impose certain conditions, and that these conditions may prove difficult (paragraph 2 of No. 247). If pushed to its logical extreme, the stipulation desired by the Malay members would mean that assistance granted from Federal funds to the individual States for rehabilitation purposes would go in the main to the richest States. This, of course, would militate against one of the main objects of the pooling of resources, which is to enable the poorer and more backward States to benefit from the common exchequer. But I do not feel that this need be taken too seriously. The words "due consideration" in paragraph 2 of No. 247 allow of much latitude, and it is natural that the States which will contribute most towards the Central pool should ask for some recognition of that fact. The main point seems to be that the Malay negotiators have crossed the Rubicon by accepting the conception of the common pool.

The examination of the Working Committee's conclusions regarding the allocation of future revenues and expenditure (paragraphs 3 and 6 of No. 247) confirms, I think, that the main battle has been won. So far as revenue is concerned, it is proposed that the division between Central and States revenues

---

[1] 248 is a copy of inward tel no 855, see 100.

[2] See 99.

should follow the F.M.S. practice immediately before the Japanese invasion, with certain important modifications in favour of the Central authority. We are referred to the relevant statement in the 1941 F.M.S. Estimates, which shows that out of a total revenue of $87,000,000, the "Federal" figure amounted to over $58,500,000. This means that the Federal revenues in 1941, which included all revenues from Customs and Excise, amounted to more than twice the revenues of all the States put together. Bearing in mind that the important revenues from motor licenses, electrical installations and posts and telecommunications are now to be added to the Central list, I think we have a clear indication that, generally speaking, the finances of the country will be firmly under Central control. This is further borne out by the proposed allocation of responsibility for expenditure, which involves the transfer to the Central authority of some of the most important items previously under the control of the States.

Paragraph 8 of No. 247 shows that the Malay negotiators object strongly to any title for the new system which will include the word "Union". In this they are apparently supported by Sir Theodore Adams, who told us before he left this country that the Malay translation of the word "Union" conveys something much more uncompromisingly centralized than its English equivalent. The Secretary of State has not hitherto indicated that he would be prepared to go further than the title "Federal Union", but Sir Theodore Adams warned us in one of our last conversations with him that this, when translated into Malay, amounts to a contradiction in terms. If satisfactory agreement can be reached on the substance of Central control, I would personally hope that we do not remain too adamant over the title.

(b) *Citizenship*. In my previous appreciation, I indicated that the Malay nego-tiators had been at first unwilling to admit Chinese as Malayan Union Citizens at all, but that they were showing signs of modifying this attitude. The latest telegrams (see paragraph 1 of No. 247 and the whole of No. 248) at least confirm that the Malays are no longer talking about rejecting the idea of Malayan Citizenship altogether. But given this amount of progress, I do not think we can regard the latest position as either very clear or very satisfactory. The present proposals of the Working Committee would appear to make it necessary for any Chinese in Malaya (apart from Chinese British subjects), whether or not he was born in the country, to reside there for a long period in addition and then to make individual application to the High Commissioner before being admitted to Citizenship. But the proposals as regards Citizenship are far from clear. They are at present being studied in the Department on the Citizenship file [ie CO 537/1542], and this file will be submitted as soon as possible.

I do not think, in fact, that we can regard the passages in these telegrams which deal with Citizenship as definite proposals at all. For one thing, they are far too short and leave far too many gaps. They seem to be rather in the nature of an interim report, with definite proposals to come. Nevertheless, they do seem to demand comment from us, and are being studied with this end in view.

(c) *His Majesty's jurisdiction in the Malay States*. This subject has still not been touched upon. This is in accordance with the Secretary of State's wish that the whole question of the future of the MacMichael Agreements, or of any new agreements to take their place, should be reserved for a later stages [sic] in the discussions.

When I last reported on the position, it was doubtful to what extent concessions made by the Malay negotiators would be accepted by their own "principals". The fact that the Malays, after the resumption of the Working Committee, have not attempted to retreat from any of their previous concessions, indicates, I think, that the progress made in the past can now be regarded as reasonably firm. In particular, I feel fairly confident that one of the three main battles (that of the strong Central Legislature) has been won, though the same can by no means be said of the other two.

This minute is merely an attempt at a preliminary appreciation of the latest telegrams. The telegrams are now being studied in detail, and will be submitted as quickly as possible with recommendations for action.

H.T.B.
17.9.46

I sent forward on Saturday the draft of a telegram replying to the Governor's latest report (No.248) about citizenship. That draft criticised freely the "categories" as set out by Sir E. Gent in No.248 and the fact that we have had to dissent from so much of what has been agreed in local discussions on citizenship makes it the more necessary, in the hope of avoiding deadlock, to accept as much as possible of what has been agreed on central government and finance.

I share the view that on finance the proposals in No.247 are on the whole very satisfactory. But they are clearly based, as is the legislative list enclosed in No.246, upon the conception not of a union but of a federation. That point is made equally clear by paragraph 8 of No.247 where we are told that only some such title as "Federation of Malaya" would be tolerable to Malay opinion.

While we should not ourselves use language which implied that the Secretary of State has accepted the idea of federation (and for that reason I have made some verbal changes in Mr. Williams' draft), I hope that it will not be regarded as necessary now to challenge that conception or to ask the Governor to remind the Malay Rulers and U.M.N.O. that the Secretary of State has not yet gone further than to agree that, if all other matters are satisfactorily settled, some such title as "Federal Union" might be adopted.

If in fact we can get a central government with the legislative powers and the financial rights now proposed, we shall have made really substantial progress. Not only will the four [five] unfederated Malay States have thus become aligned with the five [four] States formerly federated but the new Federal Government will have considerably wider powers and rights in relation to the whole of the nine States than it previously had in relation to the five that were federated.

On those subjects of importance (e.g. elementary education, agriculture, health) where the State Governments are, under the latest local plan, to have responsibility for expenditure, the Central or Federal Government is at least (under the list enclosed in No.246) to have the legislative powers necessary to ensure a common policy and a common system of administration. That should give a measure of control good enough for all practical purposes.

Draft telegram submitted.

T.I.K.L.
23.9.46

These negotiations are obviously difficult but we seem to be reaching agreement for a strong and comprehensive Central Authority (legislating for the whole of Malaya), and the states with certain limited powers & claims on revenue & expenditure. But on most important subjects there will be common legislation. . . . The difficulties in regard to common citizenship have still to be cleared.

The scheme which is emerging *does* assure a measure of local government though not altogether on the English pattern. The draft telegram does not raise the question of title. I don't like the "Federation of Malaya" because it is inaccurate & suggests a retreat by the British Gov. from union, whereas it is the substance of union which has been achieved & in any case the MacMichael agreements have formalised the transfer of authority. The Malays don't like the implications of "Union" & dislike the word & undoubtedly want a "face-saving" title. "Federated Union" is not good & in any case appears unacceptable. In these circumstances, can't we ask the local people for their suggestions?

A.C.J.
24.9.46

102   CO 537/1542, nos 95/96   24 Sept 1946
[Citizenship]: outward telegram (reply) no 1327 from Mr Hall to Sir E Gent

[Following the government's concession to defer the implementation of Malayan Union citizenship until local consultations had taken place (see 80, note), a committee chaired by W Linehan met between mid May and late June to consider citizenship qualifications. Its report, which was submitted on 2 July, recommended some tightening up of the original proposals and was broadly acceptable to the CO. This committee was, however, boycotted by Malays while its proposals were overshadowed by those of the Constitutional Working Committee. The latter deviated significantly from Malayan Union principles in providing for differential treatment in the automatic qualification for 'first generation' citizens as between Malays, British subjects and others (ie Chinese who were not British subjects).]

Your telegrams Nos. 854 and 855.[1]

Constitutional Working Committee.

I am grateful for these further reports, and am glad to see that earlier progress towards agreement on the need for a strong Central Legislature appears to have been continued and consolidated. I am studying further those passages in your telegram which deal with this problem, and I will send you my comments, if any, as soon as possible.

2. Subject of the present telegram is citizenship (your telegram 855 and paragraph 1 of your telegram 854). It seems clear that your account of the latest position in this respect, which is extremely summarized in character and which omits many important points, is not intended as a submission of definite proposals but rather as a progress report on a subject still under discussion. In these circumstances, detailed comment by me seems neither necessary nor desirable at the present stage. Nevertheless I think you will welcome general guidance, and indeed I feel bound to express my views forthwith, since I cannot pretend to regard the present position, if I have understood your telegrams aright, as at all satisfactory.

---

[1] See 100.

3. I am glad that Malays have overcome their earlier disinclination to discuss citizenship at all, but they seem still to be far short of anything which I could regard as conforming to the principle of "common citizenship" as affirmed throughout by His Majesty's Government. Crux of the whole matter is category (a) as stated in your telegram No. 855. I have been willing to consider changes in His Majesty's Government's original proposals, such as the exclusion of Singapore and the "tightening up" of the residence qualification (see my telegram No. 1034), since I appreciate that original proposals might have admitted to citizenship a number of people with no real stake in the country, and might thus have tended to weaken rather than strengthen the basic conception of common loyalty. I might even be prepared to consider further modifications on these lines, if it can be shown that they are in accordance with the principle which we aim to establish. Category (a) in your telegram No. 855 appears, however, to resort to an overt discrimination between races and thus to cut right across this principle. I fear that I should find it impossible to defend in Parliament any such fundamental reversal of policy. Moreover, I have watched with interest the recent emergence of a real interest in this problem amongst the Chinese community in Malaya, under the leadership of Mr. Tan Cheng Look and others. It seems to me that if any proposal on the lines of category (a) were to be introduced into the wider consultations which are to follow your present discussions, it would certainly give rise to an outcry from the Chinese, who would justifiably regard His Majesty's Government of [sic] having abandoned their promises, and to an access of racial bitterness which it is our first object to avoid.

4. There also appear to be the following fatal practical objections to category (a) which I assume is intended to operate in the future as well as at the date of coming into force of Order

(a) It is confined to persons from within Malaya and makes no provision for persons equally belonging to the country (even the children of Malays) who happen to have been born outside.

(b) It would involve a definition of the phrase "subjects of Rulers", which has always been found to present insuperable difficulties in the past. Rulers themselves have refused to regard as their subject anyone who is not "of Malay race and Mohammedan religion", but any attempt to define this status would only bring to light the anomalous position whereby immigrants from the Netherlands East Indies have been automatically regarded by the Rulers as their subjects immediately upon entry, whereas immigrants from China have never been so regarded however long they have resided in Malaya.

(c) Chinese born in Penang or Malacca would qualify for citizenship under category (a), whereas Chinese in the Malay States, though equally belonging to the country in every real sense, would not so qualify. Such a situation would obviously be impossible to maintain.

(d) The words "permanently resident" cannot be applied to children at birth. Even in regard to persons residing in Malaya at the time of the Order it cannot be said that a person is permanently resident unless he furnishes proof of the fact, and this would mean that category (a) would cease to be automatic and would become a matter of individual applications in the same way as categories (b) and (c).

5. Acceptance of the above arguments would mean that there would be no room for category (b). As regards your category (c) I assume that this is intended to be a

variation of the "10 years residence" qualification (see paragraph 5 (c) of my telegram No.1034), and is not intended to cover naturalization, by whatever name that may be described (see paragraph 2 of my telegram 110). I will, however, refrain from detailed comment on this and other points until I receive a fuller report from you. In the meanwhile my views remain as stated in my telegram No. 1034, and in particular, as I have said above, I cannot regard any radical alteration of the birth qualification on the lines of your category (a) as acceptable. I greatly hope you will be able to persuade Malays in further discussion to adopt a less restrictive attitude. In doing so, you may find it helpful to emphasize the practical arguments, and particularly the argument in paragraph 4 (c) (repeat 4 (c)) above.

---

[1] See 100.

103   CO 537/1542, no 97   28 Sept 1946
[Citizenship]: inward telegram (reply) no 919 from Sir E Gent to Mr Hall

Your telegram No.1327.[1]

Citizenship.

Very grateful for the guidance you have given me on this most delicate question and I at once confirm your assumption that my telegrams Nos.854 and 855[2] were intended as progress reports and not submission of definite proposals. You will appreciate that the present Working Committee is engaged in search for definition of practical arrangements to which Malayan representatives could be brought subject to later review by their own principals.

2. In view of conclusion you have (?formed) regarding category (a) in my telegram No.855, I regret that within the compass of that telegram I did not include the following fuller explanation on certain points.

3. Category (a) is qualified by birth and permanent residence in the country. Permanent residence is defined as follows. *Begins.*

"(a) A person shall be deemed to be permanently resident in the Federation who has completed a period of fifteen years residence therein, whether such period be completed before or after entry into force of this agreement;

(b) In computing any period of residence, there shall be included

(i) any period or periods of absence from the Federation for the purpose of education; and

(ii) temporary absence from the Federation not inconsistent with essential continuity of residence therein". *Ends.*

4. In all their discussions, the Committee has been guided by two principles of H.M. Government's declared policy.

(1) That Malayan citizens are to be people who regard Malaya as their real home and the object of their loyalty.

(2) That the special position of Malays must be safeguarded.

---

[1] See 102.   [2] See 100.

5. Category (a) of my telegram No.855 includes British subjects and subjects of Rulers born and permanently resident (as above) in the country. Mere birth qualification has been deliberately rejected, because it would admit large numbers of persons who do not in any sense regard Malaya as their real home and object of loyalty, and because Malay members insist that Malays should not be swamped by persons who have no real stake or interest in the country.

6. In reply to your paragraph 4, I venture to offer the following explanation:—

(a) Category (a) of my telegram No.855 deals with citizenship rights which cannot be exercised before completion of the stipulated period of minimum residence by the particular individual concerned. This limitation was insisted upon by representatives of the Rulers, who were strongly averse to automatic acquisition of citizenship by Indonesians and certain Indians. With this view U.M.N.O. representatives agreed. Persons not born in Malaya are admittedly not covered by my category (a) but, if they belong to the country, are eligible under my category (c) whether children of Malays or not.

(b) It has been agreed that there must be a definition of "subjects of Rulers", but immigrants from the Netherlands East Indies, even if included in this definition, will not acquire citizenship upon entry. Caterogy [sic] (a) applies to persons born (repeat born) and permanently resident (as above defined).

(c) Category (a), which is automatic category, includes only respective subjects of parties agreeing to constitute the proposed Federation, namely His Majesty and the Malaya [sic] Rulers. I cannot be too emphatic that conception of consensus of these parties forms whole basis of proposed agreement. With all respect, I suggest that an unquestioned assumption of loyalty by their subjects born and permanently resident in the country (? is justifiable). Provision is made under my category (b) for others born in (? Malay States) if belonging to the country in a real sense to acquire citizenship.

7. Chinese British subjects (of whom Tan Cheng Loch [Lock] is example) have been accustomed to regard themselves as having a special status, which will be recognised by the Committee's proposals. We have constantly in mind the importance of securing from Malay representatives proposals at least sufficient to justify the expectation that local non Malay community could not reasonably reject them.

8. In the light of the above explanation, I trust that you will not feel it necessary, at any rate at this stage, to reach adverse decision on Working Committee's proposals on this most crucial and difficult part of their work.

104   CO 537/1542, no 98   11 Oct 1946
[Citizenship]: outward telegram (reply) no 1446 from Mr Hall to Sir E
Gent   [Extract]

Your telegram No. 919.[1]

Citizenship.

I am grateful for this further explanation of proposals in your telegram No. 855.[2] I regret, however, that I must adhere to my view that in certain respects these proposals are unsatisfactory in principle. You will appreciate that the following comments are confined to matters which I regard as of fundamental importance, and that I am reserving any more detailed observations for a later stage.

2. As stated in paragraph 3 of my telegram No. 1327,[3] present proposals involve an overt discrimination between races and therefore conflict with principle of common citizenship as formulated and re-affirmed by H.M.G. Since there appears to be some misunderstanding of this principle, and of its relationship to assurances by H.M.G. that special position of Malays will be safeguarded, further elucidation appears necessary. Paragraph 11 of the explanatory memorandum handed to the Malay Rulers by Sir Harold MacMichael states that "it will be the policy to safeguard the rights of the Malay people in matters of land reservation and in their facilities for education and progress". Paragraph 7 of the January statement of policy on future constitution of the Malayan Union and Singapore (Cmd.6724) confirms that the Malay Land Reservation Policy, in particular, will be maintained. Special measures overtly designed to safeguard the Malay race have thus always been envisaged as operating in relation to specific matters, amongst which citizenship has not (repeat not) been included. The policy regarding citizenship is clearly laid down in paragraph 10 of Cmd.6724, where it is stated that citizenship "will include, without discrimination of race or creed, all who can establish a claim, by reason of birth or a suitable period of residence, to belong to the country". It was this policy which I categorically reaffirmed in Parliament on March the 18th, when I said that "the Government cannot abandon the basic principle of common citizenship, that is to say, the basic principle which demands that political rights in the Malayan Union should be extended to all those who regard Malaya as their real home, and as the object of their loyalty".

3. This statement of mine was intended to be, and should in practice be, as full a safeguard as the Malays can reasonably expect seeing that while the great bulk of them have no other object of loyalty than Malaya, this is only true of a limited proportion (who alone would acquire citizenship) within other racial communities. I regard it as most important, for the following reasons, that we should adhere to this defensible and relatively simple criterion, and should not have recourse to measures which can and will be attacked on grounds of racial discrimination:

(a) Clear undertakings have been given, and these are known to the Chinese community in Malaya. In these circumstances, I cannot see how the present proposals "could not reasonably be rejected by the local non-Malay community" (your paragraph 7).

---

[1] See 103.   [2] See 100.   [3] See 102.

(b) These same undertakings have been given in Parliament, and I could not defend my position in Parliament if I were to abandon them.

(c) As you are aware, we have throughout regarded the institution of common citizenship as the surest line of defence, in the interest of the Malays, against future pressure from outside (e.g. China) for the indiscriminate extension of political rights in Malaya to non-Malays. We can maintain this line of defence so long and only so long as we can show that we have offered political rights to all those, irrespective of racial origin, who accept the attendant responsibilities.

4. Nevertheless, I appreciate that this whole question is extremely delicate, and that measure of progress recorded in your telegram represents a considerable achievement. I am most anxious not to make your task unnecessarily difficult, and I wonder whether we could not work towards a more satisfactory solution by using the present proposals as a basis, and by merely effecting certain modifications in these proposals which would bring them into line with the fundamental principle discussed above, but which could nonetheless be presented to the Malays as in no way endangering their essential position. With this end in view, I have the following comments.

5. I assume that your categories (a) and (b) are not (repeat not) merely intended to apply to first generation of citizens, and that these proposals mean that a person born in the country in the future, whether or not the child of Malayan citizens, will not possess citizenship until after fifteen (ten according to your telegram No. 855) years residence. It is our aim, however, to encourage Malayans of the future to unite from childhood onwards in a real sense of common loyalty, and it seems to me that this cannot be achieved unless citizenship comes to be regarded as a birthright and not merely as something to be acquired after a long period. I feel strongly, therefore, that children born in the country of Malayan Union citizens should themselves be citizens by birth. It appears to me that this change could be urged on the Malay members of the Working Committee as being advantageous from their point of view, since it would do much to encourage a sense of patriotism towards a united country in future generations of the Malays themselves. Citizenship by birth would of course apply equally to non-Malay (repeat non-Malay) children born in the country of parents who are Malayan Union citizens, but I do not think the Malay negotiators, if they are brought to consider the matter carefully, need regard this with concern. Such non-Malay children will in any case be descended from persons who have given proofs of loyalty necessary for acquisition of citizenship, and the presumption therefore is that the children themselves will make Malaya their permanent home. But in cases where this is not so (i.e. in cases where non-Malay citizens by birth decide to sever their ties with the country), no problem will arise, since such persons, being absent from Malaya, will not be able to exercise their right of citizenship to the detriment of the Malays. If it is feared that such persons, while owing no real allegiance to the country, might nonetheless return after a protracted period of absence and immediately claim full citizenship rights, this contingency could be circumvented by laying it down that citizenship should be forfeited after, say, ten years absence. . . .

105 CO 537/1530, no 303   5 Nov 1946

[Anglo-Malay constitutional negotiations]: letter from Sir E Gent to Sir G Gater. *Enclosure*: extract of a letter from R Braddell to A T Newboult, 1 Nov 1946. *Minute* by H T Bourdillon

[On 1 Nov the Constitutional Working Committee adjourned for a third time on the occasion of the Hari Raya holiday marking the end of Ramadan.]

Thank you for your telegram No. 1550. I very much hope that our answer has been able to set your apprehensions at rest and that you will be able to advise the Secretary of State that the proposals which will emanate from here on H.M.'s jurisdiction and other points are not unacceptable.

There has been a noticeable increase of nervous tension, not only on the part of the Malay representatives on the Working Committee, but also in Malay political opinion generally here. The two advisers, Roland Braddell and Theodore Adams, have themselves very definitely come to feel the delicacy of their own position and both are in a fairly advanced condition of strain. But the recess these few days will, I hope, help to give things a chance of cooling off until the final round next week.

Braddell has gone off to Singapore for his few days holiday, from where he has sent to Newboult a longish letter of which I attach the substantial part. The information we are getting from secret sources tends to agree that the Malays in the Rulers' and UMNO camp have come as far as they dare towards our point of view, and they are very conscious of the fact (which is also borne out by our intelligence) that there are considerable Malay elements gunning for them for having gone so far – to wit, the Nationalist Party[1] and the diehards. These will be only too happy if the local proposals are rejected on any substantial point which will give the Malays generally an opportunity of backing out and definitely non-cooperating. The position will then pass into the hands of the Indonesian forces of the M.N.P., supported for so long as it suits them by the Malayan Communist Party.

And, of course, as is generally the case in such a situation, a quick settlement with UMNO and the Rulers is necessary, if there is to be a settlement.

Although one makes as few predictions as possible in the circumstances, it can still be expected, in our view, that the Indians and Chinese are likely to accept the local proposals, if they are accepted by H.M.G.

I feel sure you and the Secretary of State will appreciate that the position here is a critical one and may be calamitous if things go wrong (the tension is, of course, greatly increased by the continuing severe food shortage) but we all hope that it should not be necessary for that contingency to be allowed to arise.

Pyke[2] turned up in good fettle and seems to have done extremely useful series of works at home and in Washington. I am sure you found what he had to tell you of our affairs interesting.

Enclosure to 105

It is a strange coincidence that almost all that I said on Wed. morning with respect to

---

[1] ie Malay Nationalist Party (MNP).   [2] C J Pyke, see 49, note 2.

O'Connor's fears has been corroborated in *The Straits Times* of Thursday and today. I attach the clippings.

If only the S. of S. would understand that

(1) the Chinese are apathetic generally
(2) the Straits Chinese and Indian Malaya-borns resent the immigrants
(3) the Malays are adamant,

he would accept the present section on citizenship as we left it on Wednesday morning.

I am (and my record proves it) an optimist and not an alarmist but I place myself on record with you that the "Malay" situation at the moment is loaded with dynamite which will not need much to touch it off. Our friends are the Peninsular Malays. With them behind us we can handle the Merdeka[3] movement. The present proposals are those of the Peninsular Malays. Accept them and we have a solid backing which will include the Straits Chinese and the Indian Malaya-borns and Eurasians. Reject these proposals and you will have a state of affairs very quickly that will mean much bloodshed and an anti-British spirit which will never be quelled or quellable. We have our very last chance in this Committee and the Plenary Meeting which is to follow it.

I also want to say that any idea of building up a Malayan Empire as a fulcrum for British influence in the Far East will go too, for the reason that not only the Malay movement but, alas, the Merdeka movement is very strong in Sarawak and probably in B.N.B.[4] though my information as to the last is not very good.

I want you to be kind enough to pass this private letter on to Sir Edward and to Mr. MacDonald in justice to myself. I feel very deeply the responsibility I accepted when I agreed to be the legal adviser to U.M.N.O. and I only accepted it because I felt that I might be able to help not only them but my own fellow-countrymen. It disturbs me deeply to think that, if the present conciliation fails, the safety of British people in Malaya is certain to be endangered and the good name of our country and ourselves dragged in the mud. And all for what? The sake of immigrants who do not, never have and never will, either regard Malaya as their real home or show it any loyalty. The utter unfitness of the Chinese for any form of citizenship has surely been proved by their behaviour these past 4 months, to put it no further back. They have shown a total want of public spirit, a desire to gauge out every singe cent of profit, regardless of ethical or legal restrictions. And it must surely be obvious that behind all that is going on there must be powerful influences who cannot have the excuse of not knowing any better.

In the Straits-born Chinese we have a fine mass of citizens. So too have we in the third and even second generations of the Malaya-settled Chinese. They are protected in our proposals.

These remarks apply to the Indians tho' in a less degree because Indians are so politically minded where the politics of India are concerned.

I am positive that none of these people would regard it as anything but natural and proper that all Malay subjects of the Rulers should come in by reason of their birth-right. . . .

---

[3] *Merdeka* means independence. It would appear that Braddell is referring to the radical movement campaigning for Greater Indonesia.
[4] British North Borneo (later Sabah).

Minute on 105

... Sir George Gater has handed me the attached extremely important letter from Sir Edward Gent, together with its equally important enclosure (a copy of a letter from Mr. Roland Braddell, Legal Adviser to U.M.N.O., to Mr. Newboult). Mr. Braddell has been for very many years one of the foremost lawyers in Malaya, and his opinion, if not entirely unbiased, is entitled to great respect. We know from past telegrams that his influence has been very useful in controlling and guiding the Malay side of the Working Committee, and it is evident from his own letter that he accepted the post of Legal Adviser to U.M.N.O. as much out of a sense of responsibility to Great Britain as to the Malays.

I need not recapitulate the extremely clear, if disturbing account given in both letters of the complex and dangerous situation which exists in Malaya not only as between the races, but within the individual racial communities. Mr. Braddell openly expresses the fear that failure to handle this situation promptly will spell ruin for the whole British position in South East Asia. Sir Edward Gent does not endorse this opinion in so many words, but he does not contradict it, and the last sentence of his third paragraph points pretty clearly in the same direction.

The moral to be drawn from both these letters, if we accept in the main the picture which they present (even leaving out of account Mr. Braddell's extreme views about the Chinese), is that a quick settlement is necessary on the general basis of the Working Committee's proposals. It is common ground that we want to solve our Malayan constitutional problems as quickly as possible, but we must face the difficulties. Mr. Braddell says:—

"We have our very last chance in this Committee and the Plenary Meeting which is to follow it."

This suggests that His Majesty's Government must be ready with at least a provisional approval of the Working Committee proposals in time for the Plenary Conference,[5] but such a course is obviously out of the question. H.M.G. must see the final proposals as they emerge *from* the Plenary Conference, and must discuss the resulting position with the Governor-General and Mr. Newboult, before they can reach even the most tentative conclusions. This position has always been clearly understood. It was reiterated in the most explicit terms in paragraph 4 of our telegram No. 1595 (No.298), and it is obvious from No.302 that Sir Edward Gent fully understands and endorses the Secretary of State's attitude in this matter. Paragraph 5 of his own letter, however, reveals a possible source of further misunderstanding. He says:—

"Although one makes as few predictions as possible in the circumstances, it can still be expected, in our view, that the Indians and Chinese are likely to accept the local proposals, *if they are accepted by H.M.G.*" (My [emphasis]).

This leaves no doubt that in Sir Edward Gent's view, H.M.G., admittedly after seeing the Malay proposals in their final form and discussing the matter with the Governor-General, must give a pretty clear indication of their approval of these

---

[5] The Constitutional Working Committee reconvened on 11 Nov and submitted its report to the plenary session of officials, rulers and UMNO representatives on 20 Nov.

proposals before the other communities are consulted. It has always been our conception, on the other hand, that H.M.G. would refrain from any positive pronouncement until all the communities concerned had expressed their views. It is true that in paragraph 2 of his telegram No.963 of the 5th of October (No.258), on which we did not comment at the time, Sir Edward Gent spoke of the Malay proposals being submitted to H.M.G. for "conditional approval" before the wider discussions took place, and in paragraph 3 of the same telegram he said that the Malay proposals would be forwarded to the Secretary of State for the latter to decide "whether any part of the proposals would be unacceptable to H.M.G." We have always taken this, however, as meaning no more than that H.M.G. should approve the proposals as the basis for further discussion, having first ensured that there were no obviously unsatisfactory features. It looks as though Sir Edward Gent is now going a good deal further than this, and the point seems to need clearing up.

There is, however, a further and more fundamental difficulty. Whatever form the "conditional approval" of H.M.G. for the Malay proposals were to take, Sir Edward Gent is pleading for an early settlement on the basis of these proposals. Fully as we may sympathise with these reasons, we cannot get over the fact that (unless a miracle happens between now and the end of the Plenary Conference) certain aspects of the proposals are definitely unsatisfactory. The Secretary of State's views on the two points which he at present regards as unacceptable are set out in No.298. First, there is the provision for future changes in the constitution, over which the Sultans would have a complete power of veto. Secondly, there is the whole question of citizenship. On this, Sir Edward Gent has himself told us in his telegram No.1072 (on the citizenship file) that he recognises the unsatisfactory nature of the proposals and is fully reserving his position.

Against the background of these hard facts, we have to take into account the imperative need, as shown in Sir Edward Gent's present letter, for an early solution.
. . .[6]

H.T.B.
13.11.46

---

[6] Bourdillon concluded his minute by suggesting that it might be tactically wise to separate citizenship from the rest of the constitutional proposals, making the latter the basis of further consultation with Chinese and Indians while deferring further consideration of the former. This proposal was not taken up.

106   CO 537/1543, no 106   [Nov 1946]
'Malayan citizenship': note by H T Bourdillon   [Extract]

[When the Constitutional Working Committee reconvened on 11 Nov it made what Gent reported to be a 'substantial advance' on citizenship. The CO was now faced with what Bourdillon called 'the fundamental and comparatively simple question', namely: could HMG accept any scheme which entailed different racial categories for the automatic acquisition of 'first generation' citizenship? This issue was addressed by Bourdillon's note and the departmental discussion on 22 Nov (see 107).]

Part I. Federal exposition
. . .

4. Next we come to the *Malay* ideas on the subject, as evolved in the

Constitutional Working Committee which has just completed its labours. At first the Malays refused to consider citizenship at all, but they were later persuaded to discuss it on the basis of the Citizenship Committee's report and the Secretary of State's comments thereon. Subsequent history has shown many vicissitudes, with the Malays alternately freezing into rigidity and thawing to the persuasions of the British side of the Working Committee. There was an unexpected thaw at the final session (see tels. Nos. 1140 and 1141 from the Malayan Union), and the resultant position, as extracted from these telegrams and the earlier telegrams Nos. 1072 and 1073, may be summarised as follows:—

I.   Qualification by birth in the Malayan Union.*

(a) Malays to have automatic qualification by birth alone.
(b) British subjects born in either of the Settlements to qualify automatically if they have ordinarily resided in the Union for fifteen years.
(c) British subjects born anywhere in the Union to qualify automatically if their fathers were either born in the Union or have ordinarily resided there for fifteen years.
(d) Others born in the Union to qualify automatically if *both* their parents were born in *and* have ordinarily resided in the Union for fifteen years.

II.   Qualification by descent. Any person whose father is a citizen at the time of that person's birth to qualify automatically (whether born in the Union or not).
III.   Qualification by application.

(a) Any person naturalised as a subject of a Ruler, under any law for the time being in force, to qualify, by virtue of such naturalisation, for citizenship.
(b) The High Commissioner to have discretion to confer citizenship on any applicant (and on his minor children) who satisfies him

(i)   either that he was born in the Union and has resided there for 10 out of the last 15 years *or* that he has resided there for 15 out of the last 20 years,
(ii)   that he is of good character,
(iii)   that he has an adequate knowledge of Malay or English, and who makes a declaration of permanent settlement and takes the oath of citizenship.

5.   These proposals are very different in form from those which emerged from the Citizenship Committee. The following remarks may assist in making a true comparison. His Majesty's Government's original proposals, both before and after they had been through the Citizenship Committee, envisaged a distinction between initial entrants and subsequent entrants. Thus the "ten years' residence" qualification was to apply only to those who had completed their ten years' residence before the date when the Order came into force, and was designed purely to create, as it were, a body of "foundation members". Subsequent entry was to be either by birth or naturalisation. Under the Malay proposals this distinction has disappeared, but in its place two other distinctions have sprung into prominence. First, there is the distinction between "first generation" and "second generation" citizens (children of citizen fathers would automatically be citizens); and secondly, there is the distinction within the "first generation" group, between the qualifications required for

---

* This name is used throughout for convenience, though the Malays, of course, do not admit the title.

Malays, those required for British subjects (these are again sub-divided), and those required for "others".

Part II. Tentative comments
In considering the Malay proposals, it would not seem profitable to judge them too closely in strict relation to the original detailed scheme of His Majesty's Government, as set out in the draft Citizenship Order in Council and as summarised in the Appendix[1] to this note. In deferring that scheme for further consideration in the light of consultations with local opinion, His Majesty's Government showed that they had taken into account the criticisms which had been made in Parliament against the scheme as it then stood. There had been widespread acceptance in both Houses of the principle of common citizenship, but there had also been widespread anxiety (by no means confined to the Opposition), lest the actual scheme, by casting the net too wide, would admit to citizenship many people without any ties of loyalty to Malaya. His Majesty's Government, then, recognised the force of these criticisms, and in so doing recognised that the scheme as finally brought into force might be substantially different from the scheme set out in the draft Order. But at the same time they reiterated the fundamental principle that political rights in Malaya should be extended "to all those who regard Malaya as their real home and as the object of their loyalty". It is against this principle, therefore, that the present Malay proposals must be judged.

2. At first sight, the feature in these proposals which seems clearly to conflict with the principle is the provision for differential treatment in the automatic qualification for "first generation" citizens as between Malays, British subjects and others (i.e. Chinese who are not British subjects). This feature was adversely commented upon by the Secretary of State in his telegrams 1327[2] and 1446[3] to the Malayan Union, on the grounds that it constituted an element of overt racial discrimination. At that time, however, differential treatment was proposed not only for "first generation" citizens but for their descendents *ad infinitum*, since there was no provision for automatic acquisition of citizenship by children of citizen fathers. Such a provision has now been added, and this means that there will grow up in the course of years a body of people, Chinese and Indians as well as Malays, who will have citizenship as a birth-right. In the long run this will clearly do much to promote a common bond of loyalty which will ignore racial barriers, so the position is undeniably much more satisfactory than it was. But for "first generation" citizens the differential treatment remains. Is this incompatible with the fundamental principle referred to at the end of paragraph 1 above? If so, it cannot be contemplated. If not—if it is in accordance with the principle and can be shown to be in accordance with it—then it may be expected (a) that Parliament, which has always endorsed the *principle* as such, would not only accept but applaud a scheme based on the present proposal, and (b) that such a scheme would be in the interests of Malaya itself, since it is clear that the imposition of any form of citizenship which would include large numbers of people with no loyalty to the country can only promote racial discord.

3. It is proposed that Malays shall qualify automatically for citizenship by birth alone. Can it be said, by and large, that any Malay born in the Union regards the

---

country as his real home and the objective of his loyalty? The answer seems to be in the affirmative. Even those Malays who are descended from recent immigrants from Indonesia have settled on the land and have come to regard Malaya as their only home. This very probably cannot be said of all Malays or Javanese who have entered the country in the present generation, but such people are excluded.

It is proposed that British subjects born in the Settlements shall qualify automatically for citizenship subject to the additional qualification of 15 years' residence. Is this proposal, and in particular the stipulation regarding 15 years' residence in accordance with the fundamental principle? Here again, the answer would seem to be in the affirmative. Mere birth, in the case of British subjects born in the Settlements, might well be considered to open the doors too wide, since it would admit *anybody* who happened to have been born in either of the Settlements. The fifteen years' residence qualification would exclude transitory elements, but on the other hand it would not exclude the established population. In particular, it would admit all those Chinese families, having their roots in the Settlements, who form much the most stable and "Malayan-minded" element in the whole Chinese population of the Union.

Thirdly, it is proposed that British subjects born anywhere in the Union shall qualify automatically for citizenship subject to the addition[al] that their fathers were born in the Union or have resided there for fifteen years. This gives British subjects born in the Settlements a measure of preference over British subjects born in the Malay States. The Malays apparently refused to be budged from this position, and presumably they had in mind the large Indian population, mainly consisting of Tamil workers on the rubber estates. The stipulations of (a) birth and (b) fifteen years' residence should, however, be sufficient to exclude the transitory elements within the Indian community, and it therefore seems hard to justify this distinction.

Finally, it is proposed that "others" born in the Union (this, in effect, means Chinese born in the Malay States) shall automatically qualify for citizenship subject to the additional qualification that both their parents were born in the Union *and* have resided there for fifteen years. If mere birth, in the case of British subjects born in the Settlements, would open the doors too wide, then the same is true, *a fortiori*, of Chinese born in the Malay States. It could also be reasonably argued that birth plus fifteen years residence, in the case of the latter, is not a sufficient stipulation, since many Chinese, even after long periods of residence in Malaya, revert to China. It is another question, however, whether this argument can be used to justify the stipulation that both parents must have been born in the Union *and* have resided there for fifteen years.

4. The preceding paragraph would appear to indicate that *some* distinction between racial categories in the automatic qualifications for "first generation" citizens is compatible with the fundamental principle of His Majesty's Government. If this can be accepted (and it should be borne in mind that acceptance at present merely means acceptance subject to the views of the non-Malay communities), then at least the present Malay proposals need not be rejected out of hand. This is not to say, of course, that they can be accepted in every detail. They would have to be carefully scrutinized, and one of the most important matters demanding scrutiny would be the provisions for acquisition of citizenship by *application*. It will be noted that two methods are proposed: first, direct application for citizenship, and secondly, application for naturalisation as a subject of a Ruler. If the second class of application

is to be based on the existing F.M.S. laws, this would permit of citizenship via naturalisation after five years' residence, whereas direct application for citizenship would require a much longer period of residence. This position seems anomalous.

107 CO 537/1543 22 Nov 1946
[Citizenship]: minute by H T Bourdillon of a CO departmental meeting [Extract]

... This morning's discussion confirmed the view tentatively put forward in paragraph[s] 3 and 4 of the *second* part of the Memorandum[1]—namely, that *some* distinction between racial categories in the automatic qualification for "first generation" citizens is demonstrably compatible with the fundamental principle of His Majesty's Government, and is in fact both reasonable and just. In particular, it was felt that it would be very hard to find fault with the proposal that all Malays born in the country should automatically be citizens; and it was considered that this proposal would be readily understood and accepted by the other communities in Malaya. It was also felt that there are good grounds for the proposal that, amongst the non-Malay population, British subjects should receive special treatment as regards automatic qualifications for "first generation" citizenship, especially in view of the large number of Chinese British subjects living in the Settlements of Penang and Malacca, whose families have been settled in the Settlements for many generations.

Given this general feeling, however, it was considered that there are two points in the Malay proposals as they at present stand which require further explanation, and which, in view of their considerable importance, might well be raised by the Secretary of State with Mr. MacDonald. These points are as follows:

(a) It will be seen from paragraph 4 in the first part of the Memorandum opposite that a distinction is proposed, in the automatic qualifications for "first generation" citizenship, as between British subjects born in the Settlements and British subjects born in the Malay States. The former would automatically acquire citizenship *either* if they themselves had resided in the Union for fifteen years *or* if their fathers had either been born there or had resided there for fifteen years, whereas the latter (i.e. British subjects born in the Malay States) would only have the benefit of the second of these alternatives. Now the great majority of British subjects born in the Malay States are Indians, and it was presumably in view of this fact that the Malays insisted on the above distinction within the category of British subjects. Even granted, however, that it is necessary to exclude from citizenship the large transitory element in the Indian population, are there sufficient grounds for any such distinction, particularly having regard to the possibility that it may bring complaints from the Indian Government?

(b) It will also be seen from paragraph 4 in Part I of the Memorandum that under the present proposals, *applicants* for citizenship can either apply to become citizens *tout court*, or can apply to become naturalised as subjects of one of the

---

[1] See 106.

Rulers, which status will carry with it the status of citizenship. Applicants by the former method must either have been born in the Union and resided there for ten out of the last fifteen years or must have resided there for fifteen out of the last twenty years, whereas applicants by the latter method, assuming that the law would be based on the existing F.M.S. Ordinance, need only have resided in the Union for five years. Are there any good grounds for this marked discrepancy between the two methods of application? Indeed, given that the only people who are likely to apply for naturalisation as subjects of the Rulers or to be accepted as such are immigrants of Malay race from Indonesia, would not any such discrepancy be positively objectionable, on the grounds that it would place Malay immigrants of the present generation (and very recent arrivals at that) in a more favourable position not only than other *applicants* for citizenship but even, in certain cases, than British subjects born in the Union?

108   CO 537/1531, no 320   22 Nov 1946
[Anglo-Malay constitutional proposals]: letter from Sir E Gent to T I K Lloyd

[The Constitutional Working Committee presented its report to the plenary session of officials, rulers and UMNO representatives on 20 Nov; on 22 Nov MacDonald and his party departed for constitutional talks with the CO.]

MacDonald, Newboult, O'Connor and the rest of our party will be accompanied in their rapid aircraft by the papers emanating from the Malay Working Party and Plenary Conference with all Their Highnesses etc. regarding the constitutional proposals. I have rapidly put together a covering despatch in the interval of continuous visits from British and Malay personages of one sort and another (including Lord Killearn who pops in and out while his wife is in the hospital here and a candidate for a minor operation).

I want to urge the importance of two things:—

(1) a broad acceptance of the scheme as a whole at this stage, without permitting any "clever" points to be made either of a legal or political nature—real cleverness will lie in avoiding any disturbance of the better relations we have succeeded in restoring. We can correct at leisure in the next year or two any inconsistencies and so on in the constitutional scheme;

(2) the importance of a *quick* response from H.M.G. giving a provisional favourable reaction to the scheme.

I may be asking a lot but a lot is at stake with China, India and Indonesia as very strong forces pulling us apart here.

I can ill-spare Newboult and O'Connor but I told MacDonald that I should feel happier if both went to London at this stage. Please let nothing interfere with a very early return of O'Connor at any rate; but if there is a Debate before Christmas in Parliament I think you should keep Newboult for it.

They will tell you all the local news and as the bag and the aircraft are just to go I will finish up.

With all good wishes to yourself and the Eastern Department.

109   CO 537/1543, no 109   29 Nov 1946

'Malayan policy': memorandum by Mr Creech Jones for Cabinet Colonial Affairs Committee (C(46)6)

[MacDonald's party arrived in London on 24 Nov and began discussions at the CO the next day. By 29 Nov the CO completed this policy paper which went to the Cabinet Colonial Affairs Committee on 2 Dec (see 110). Papers of the Colonial Affairs Committee are also at CAB 134/52.]

On 31st May, 1944, the War Cabinet, taking as their basis the recommendations of a Ministerial Committee[1] under the chairmanship of the present Prime Minister, gave their provisional approval, for planning purposes, to a new policy for Malaya whose fundamental objectives were the creation in that territory of a real and effective constitutional unity, and the establishment of a common citizenship which would grant political rights to all those who genuinely regard Malaya as their home and as the object of their loyalty. On 3rd September, 1945,[2] my predecessor sought and obtained the Cabinet's final authorisation of this policy, and their agreement to the proposal that Sir Harold MacMichael should visit Malaya in order to conclude new agreements with the nine Malay Sultans, whereby the latter would grant jurisdiction in their States to His Majesty.

2.   Sir Harold MacMichael had completed his task by the end of last year. In due course, the policy was approved by both Houses of Parliament, and the Order in Council setting up the Malayan Union was then issued, in time for the Governor of the Union to take up his functions at the termination of military administration on 1st April last.

[3.] On 3rd June,[3] my predecessor gave the Cabinet an oral account of developments since 1st April. An organised Malay nationalist movement extending over the whole Peninsula had emerged, and it will be recollected that certain features of the new constitution had met with vigorous and united resistance from the Malays, who did not consider that they had been sufficiently consulted before the new system had been brought into force, and who expressed their objections in a refusal to co-operate in the activities of Government. This situation threatened at one time to become extremely dangerous, with the prospect of the Malays, united as never before, pursuing a policy of wholesale non-co-operation which might at any moment have degenerated into actual violence. Although the constitution provided for the fullest consultation between the central authority and the local State Councils proposed as to powers, representation and structure, and for consultation on the terms of citizenship, it was evident that the enforcement of the proposals against the will of the largest section of the community in Malaya would only defeat the very objectives of His Majesty's Government as stated in paragraph 1 above. Accordingly, with my predecessor's approval, the Governor of the Malayan Union and later the Governor-General entered into discussions with Malay representatives for the purpose of arriving at an agreed solution within the essential framework of His Majesty's Government's policy. I am happy to say that, notwithstanding initial hesitations, the Sultans and the Malay leaders responded to this approach in a statesmanlike manner, and from the beginning of August until the middle of November a Working

---

[1] See 25.   [2] See 50.   [3] See 93, note and note 5.

Committee, consisting of representatives of the Sultans and the principal Malay political party on the one hand and Government representatives on the other, was busy elaborating the details of a revised constitution. At a subsequent plenary conference, the Sultans and the representatives of the political party mentioned above indicated to the Governor-General and the Governor of the Malayan Union that they were satisfied with the scheme. The proposals were thereupon submitted to me for my provisional scrutiny. It must be understood that these proposals represent a considerable effort at accommodation by the Malays, and a basis which they agree can be offered for further consultation with the other communities in Malaya.

4. I have now had time to study the whole scheme with the assistance of the Governor-General and of certain officers of the Malayan Union Government who have flown with him to this country. One of the most encouraging features of the Working Committee's deliberations has been the manner in which the whole Committee, Malays and Government representatives alike, accepted the essential purposes of His Majesty's Government as described above, as the basis of their deliberations, and I am happy to record my own convictions, after examining the documents in detail, that the resultant proposals, in their main provisions, are calculated to achieve these purposes in an effective manner.

5. First, I am satisfied that the proposals will achieve the object of establishing in Malaya a strong central Government, with control over all matters of importance to the welfare and progress of the country as a whole. There has been drawn up a list of subjects upon which the right of legislation has been reserved for the Central Legislature alone, and this list, which embraces 144 items (see Appendix for list of important examples)[4] is extremely comprehensive. It ensures that so far as can be foreseen all legislation of any considerable importance will in fact be in the hands of the Central Legislature, which will also maintain effective control in the all-important sphere of finance. On the other hand, it is proposed that executive authority, under central legislation, will be entrusted in a number of fields of local administration to the authorities in the individual States and in the settlements of Penang and Malacca. I do not regard this as materially detracting from the authority of the centre, but rather as ensuring healthy and constructive local activity within a limited sphere.

6. The organisations of Government which are envisaged as carrying out the functions described above are as follows. First, in place of the Governor there will be a High Commissioner with an Executive Council. Secondly, there will be a central Legislative Council, consisting of the High Commissioner as President, three *ex-officio* members, eleven other official members and thirty-four unofficial members, of whom eleven will be representatives of the State and Settlement Councils. Thirdly, there will be a Legislative body in each State, with the title of "Council of State", and similar legislative bodies in each of the two British Settlements. Fourthly, it is proposed that there should be established in each State a body with the title of "State Executive Council", which will carry out the executive functions provided for under Central or State Legislation. Fifthly, there will be a central Conference of Rulers, whose functions will be almost entirely formal and consultative (see paragraph 9 below). I have been in some doubt regarding the necessity for State Executive Councils and it may be that in course of time some "streamlining" of

---

[4] Not printed.

State Government machinery may be found advisable. I am advised, however, that the Malays attach great importance to the establishment of the State Executive Councils, on the grounds that the Sultans, who are envisaged as presiding over the State Executive Councils but not over the Councils of State, should henceforth be treated as strictly constitutional princes and not as absolute Rulers. I am further advised that adequate provision has been made to prevent the possibility of deadlock between the Legislature and the Executive in the States.

7.   I also consider (subject, of course, to the views of the non-Malay communities, a point of fundamental importance to which I shall revert later) that the proposals regarding citizenship are designed to give reality to His Majesty's Government's essential objective of granting political rights to all those who regard Malaya as their real home and as the object of their loyalty. This matter is one of peculiar delicacy (a fact which His Majesty's Government recognised when they agreed, in the House of Commons on 18th March, to defer the implementation of citizenship proposals pending local consultations), and the task of the Working Committee has according-ly not been easy. A most important feature of the present proposals is the provision that children of citizens will themselves automatically be citizens. This will encourage the growth, in course of time, of an increasing body of men and women, irrespective of race or creed, who will regard citizenship as a birth-right, and an effective bond of common loyalty will thus be created. As regards the provisions for the initial creation of a body of citizens, it is proposed, in effect, that a Malay should qualify automatically for citizenship if he is born in the country (or if he is the child of a father who is a subject of one of the Rulers), that a British subject born anywhere in the territory should automatically qualify if his father was either born there or has resided there for fifteen years, that a British subject born in either of the Settlements should alternatively qualify automatically if he himself has resided there for fifteen years, and that all others born anywhere in the territory should automatically qualify if both their parents were born there and have resided there for fifteen years. My provisional view is that these stipulations are reasonable. The special provision for Malays is justified on the grounds that Malays born in the country, whether or not they are descended from comparatively recent immigrant stock, regard Malaya as their only home and the only object of their loyalty. The special provision for British subjects born in the Settlements, as against British subjects born elsewhere in the territory, is justified on the grounds that the two Settlements include a large body of Indians and Chinese who are truly "Malayan" in spirit, who are intensely proud of their status as British subjects and who, incidentally, would be the first to resent any indiscriminate "opening of the flood-gates" to Indians and Chinese whose loyalties lie elsewhere than in Malaya. In general, the proposals are designed to exclude the large transitory element in the population, but to include all those who are ready to accept the duties as well as the rights of citizenship. Finally, it is proposed that the High Commissioner should be empowered, subject to his entire discretion, to grant citizenship on application to persons who fulfil certain residence and language qualifications and who are ready to make affirmations of loyalty and continued residence in the country.

8.   One matter which has given rise to special difficulties in the deliberations of the Working Committee has been the question of His Majesty's jurisdiction, in the Malay States (his jurisdiction in the Settlements, of course, remains complete). Under the MacMichael Agreements the Sultans conferred full jurisdiction in their

States on His Majesty, and this is one of the principal points to which the Malays have objected. His Majesty's Government, however, have never regarded jurisdiction as an end in itself, but merely as a means of ensuring the future progress of Malaya towards self-government. Subject to one exception to which I shall refer later, I regard the present proposals, judged from this point of view, as satisfactory. It is proposed that the revised constitution should be embodied in a new agreement, but it has been agreed that legal force in the Malay States should be given to the new agreement by His Majesty's Order in Council under the Foreign Jurisdiction Act. There would also be separate agreements with the individual Rulers superseding previous agreements (including those negotiated by Sir Harold MacMichael). All these agreements would be ratified by enactments of the various Councils of State. Thus a firm legal foundation is provided for the *establishment* of the revised system. Thereafter it is proposed that His Majesty should have jurisdiction in all matters relating to external affairs and defence. This would include the necessary internal jurisdiction in relation to such matters, the advantages of which, particularly in times of crisis, are obvious. It is further proposed that His Majesty should have jurisdiction for the purpose of appeals to the Privy Council, that His Majesty should in effect have the power to disallow laws, and that there should be the usual provision for the reservation of bills for His Majesty's pleasure. Lastly, it is proposed that in all matters of Government, excepting (a) amendments to the constitution and (b) matters relating to Moslem religion and the custom of the Malays, the High Commissioner, and the British Adviser in each of the States, should have the power of tendering advice to the Ruler, which the latter would be bound to accept. In this whole connection it will, of course, be appreciated that under the scheme great powers have been surrendered by the States to the Central authority, and that the Sultans have delegated powers over an immense field to the High Commissioner.

9. The one feature of the proposals regarding jurisdiction which I regard as unsatisfactory is the provision that future amendments to the constitution would require the consent of the Sultans, a provision which would in theory enable any one Sultan to block future constitutional progress. I am advised that the recent emergence of political awareness amongst the Malays is such that it is most unlikely that any Sultan would be able to follow his personal will in such matters in future, but the provision remains unsatisfactory in principle. The present proposals (as stated in paragraph 6 above) include the establishment of a Conference of Rulers—a body with certain purely consultative and formal functions—and I have it in mind, subject to my colleagues' consent, to stipulate that future constitutional changes should require the agreement of this body (that is, in effect, of a *majority* of Sultans) and not of each Sultan individually.

10. It is proposed that the revised constitutional system should be described as the "Federation of Malaya". I would have preferred some title which would have included the word "Union", as being more indicative of the closely-knit system which is in fact envisaged, but I am advised that this is a point on which the Malays have proved adamant, and in these circumstances I consider that it would be most unwise to press the point further.

11. It cannot be too strongly emphasised that there is no question of His Majesty's Government giving their final approval to any of these proposals until the other communities in Malaya, besides the Malays themselves, have been fully and freely consulted. The Malays themselves have clearly recognised this, but at the same

time they have pressed that if there are any points in the present proposals which His Majesty's Government consider definitely unacceptable, these shall be referred back to them for further consideration before the wider discussions commence. In this connection the Governor-General and the Governor of the Malayan Union have emphasised two points. First, they have told me that while the political situation in Malaya has greatly improved during the past few months, there is a danger amounting to certainty that the improvement will vanish unless His Majesty's Government now act with all reasonable speed. Secondly, they have urged that at the time when the wider discussions are opened, His Majesty's Government should indicate in definite terms their provisional acceptance of the general scheme, subject always to the views of the non-Malay communities. It is emphasised that such an indication by His Majesty's Government will carry a stage further the process of recovering the good will and confidence of the Malays, will prevent the projected wider discussions from becoming extravagant and irresponsible, and will greatly help to achieve that speedy solution which is so essential.

12. I see great force in these views, and I accordingly submit the following programme of action for approval of my colleagues. First, I would ask the Governor to take up with the Malays, with the least possible delay, the following points which I still cannot regard as entirely satisfactory or as entirely clear:—

(a) The agreement to be signified to future constitutional changes should be that of the Conference of Rulers and not of the Sultans individually.

(b) The Constitution, and in particular the exact conposition [sic] of the Councils of State, in the various States has not yet been determined. It is of great importance that the State legislatures should be of a truly democratic character, and I would propose to say that His Majesty's Government must reserve all judgment on this matter until they see detailed proposals.

(c) It is proposed that the Central Legislative Council should have twenty-three unofficial members besides the representatives of the States and Settlement Councils. It is further proposed that steps should be taken to institute an electoral system as soon as possible, but this is not considered feasible as an immediate measure. In the meanwhile it is proposed that the High Commissioner should nominate these twenty-three members, of whom nine would be Malays and the remainder would be chosen as representing important interests such as labour, mining and planting—a device which was primarily intended to ensure adequate representation for the Chinese and Indians. I regard such specific representation by interests as liable to produce an unduly sectional point of view in the members of the Council, and I would propose to say that, subject to the selection of nine Malays (which I regard as reasonable) the High Commissioner should have discretion in nominating the remainder, though he should bear in mind the importance of securing a chamber broadly representative of all important economic, social and communal interests in the Peninsula.

(d) There is one point in relation to citizenship which must be clarified. It is proposed that persons naturalised as subjects of any of the Rulers should acquire citizenship by virtue of such naturalisation. There is room for discrepancy here between the qualifications required for naturalisation as a subject of a Ruler and those required for direct application for citizenship, and it must be ensured that there is in fact no such discrepancy.

13. Subject to the above points being satisfactorily resolved, I would propose to inform the Governor of the Malayan Union that the proposals have the conditional approval of His Majesty's Government, and may forthwith be used for discussions with the non-Malay communities. I also think it would be very desirable that before the Christmas recess I should make a statement in Parliament, outlining the present position. After making it clear that there were still some matters both of substance and important detail to be discussed with the Malays, I should propose to conclude such a statement with words to the following effect:—

> "I am happy to say that the present proposals, which represent the outcome of much patient and devoted work and of much constructive good will on both sides, appear to His Majesty's Government to be calculated to achieve those fundamental objectives in Malaya for which His Majesty's Government have always striven. There can be no question, however, of His Majesty's Government reaching any final decision on any of the matters involved until all interested communities in Malaya have had full and free opportunity of expressing their views. I am glad to say that the necessity of consulting to the fullest extent the other interest[ed] communities has been clearly appreciated by the Malay representatives themselves. It is now intended, therefore, that the proposals should, with the minimum of delay, form the subject of wider discussions in Malaya. His Majesty's Government will again consider the matter in the light of the results of these discussions, and at that stage the House will be given the opportunity of commenting on the proposals as a whole. Meanwhile, copies of the proposals as published in Malaya will be placed in the Library of the House as soon as they are received."[5]

[5] See Creech Jones's written answer, *H of C Debs*, vol 431, cols 228–229, 11 Dec 1946.

110   CO 537/1543, no 110   3 Dec 1946[1]
'Malayan policy': Cabinet Colonial Affairs Committee minutes (C 3(46))

The Committee considered a memorandum by the Secretary of State for the Colonies (C.(46) 6)[2] regarding future policy in Malaya.

The Secretary of State for the Colonies recalled that at the beginning of the year His Majesty's Government had announced a policy whereby an effective constitutional union would be created in Malaya, backed by a common citizenship open to all, whether Malays, Indians, Chinese or others, so long as they had adopted Malaya as their true home. The policy entailed the grant of jurisdiction by the Sultans to His Majesty; this had already been covered by agreements with the Sultans which had been negotiated by Sir Harold MacMichael.

On the announcement of this policy there had been very strong resistance to it from the Malays, who considered that they had not been sufficiently consulted in the preparation of it: it had then been decided that negotiations should take place with Malay representatives with the object of working out a revised policy which would be

[1] The meeting was held on 2 Dec 1946; the minutes are dated 3 Dec.   [2] See 109.

agreeable to them. These negotiations had now been completed and the results were set out in the memorandum now before the Committee.

While, as indicated in the memorandum, he had comments on certain points, the *Secretary of State* said that he was satisfied that the new proposals preserved the principles of the policy which the Cabinet had approved and he now asked his colleagues to agree that, subject to these points, they should be used for the purpose of discussion with the other communities in Malaya. While there was no intention of final approval being given until these discussions had taken place, it was desirable to indicate in those discussions that the proposals had the conditional approval of His Majesty's Government. The precise course of action which he proposed was indicated in paragraphs 12 and 13 of his memorandum.

The following points were raised in discussion.

(a) There was no one body representative of all the Chinese or Indian interests in Malaya and it would therefore be necessary to consult various bodies. Between them, however, these should give an adequate indication of Chinese and Indian opinion. There was reason to suppose that these communities as a whole, and in particular the more stable elements would accept proposals on the lines of those now put forward.

(b) The provision for separate Executive Councils for the individual States was cumbrous, but were a concession to Malay feeling. They would have executive authority only in a limited number of fields of local administration.

(c) The proposals regarding citizenship would permit practically all Malays and a considerable number of Chinese and Indians to acquire Malayan citizenship. There were in Malaya, in round figures, $2\frac{1}{4}$ million Malays, $1\frac{1}{2}$ million Chinese, and 750,000 Indians. British subjects would be able to obtain Malayan citizenship rather more easily than others except Malays. A considerable number of Indians and Chinese in Malaya were British subjects.

(d) While the jurisdiction of His Majesty would not be so comprehensive as under the agreements negotiated with Sir Harold MacMichael, the provisions on this subject in the new proposals appeared adequate.

(e) Under the proposals all courts would be set up by federal legislation. The Supreme Court would have jurisdiction throughout the federation and provisions would be made for appeal to the Privy Council.

There was general agreement that proposals had been evolved which besides satisfying Malay feeling, preserved the fundamental objectives of His Majesty's Government.

The Committee:—

Invited the Chairman to submit a memorandum to the Cabinet seeking their approval of the action proposed in paragraphs 12 and 13 of C(46) 6).[3]

---

[3] The memorandum was submitted to the Cabinet by the committee's chairman (Lord Addison, secretary of state for the Dominions) and considered on 5 Dec. Cabinet approved the proposals subject to clarification in Malaya of a number of issues listed in paragraph 12, and Creech Jones cabled this conditional approval to Gent the same day. On 11 Dec the secretary of state supplied Squadron Leader Donner MP with a written answer on the revised constitution. The necessary amendments went through the Plenary Conference in Kuala Lumpur on 20 Dec, and, on Christmas Eve the constitutional proposals were published. The same day the Consultative Committee, chaired by H R Cheeseman, was appointed to sound local opinion on the constitutional proposals. See CAB 134/52; CAB 129/15, CP(46)439, 3 Dec 1946;

CAB 128/6, CM103(46)5, 5 Dec 1946; *H of C Debs*, vol 431, cols 228–229, 11 Dec 1946; *Constitutional Proposals for Malaya: Report of the Working Committee Appointed by a Conference of His Excellency the Governor of the Malayan Union, Their Highnesses the Rulers of the Malay States and Representatives of the United Malays National Organisation* (Kuala Lumpur, 1946).

111   CO 537/2165, ff 19–21   19 Jan 1947
'Federation proposals': minute 7 of the 5th governor-general's conference in Penang about the consultative process

The Governor-General asked the Governor of Malayan Union to explain the local course of events in regard to the Federation Proposals since the Governor-General had left for London.

The Governor of Malayan Union gave a detailed account of political events since the 23rd November, 1946.

The Governor-General said that he appreciated that the Council of Joint Action[1] could not be considered to be representative of the masses in any sense. At the same time, he wondered whether it would not be wise for the Governor to see them.

The Governor of Malayan Union said that he had already communicated to the Council the Secretary of State's reply to their telegram. He had said that they were open to communicate their views to the Governor who would pass them to the Consultative Committee. He had also said that he was prepared to see representatives of any of the Organisations represented on the Council in order that they might clarify their position. He was in fact arranging to have a talk with Mr. Thivy[2] of the Malayan Indian Congress informally on his return to Kuala Lumpur.

The Governor-General said that he felt that if some means could be found by which the Council of Joint Action could state their objections to the Committee, many of their arguments could be knocked down with considerable ease.

The Governor of Malayan Union said it was a question of procedure; the Consultative Committee had been set up in order that all communities could ventilate their views. The Council of Joint Action had categorically refused to accept the machinery of a Consultative Committee.

The Governor-General said that if they stuck to that and gathered considerable support in the country it would seem to him that the Malayan Union Government would have to eat its words and establish contact with the Council of Joint Action, as had been necessary previously in regard to U.M.N.O.

The Governor of Malayan Union said that if it should be necessary to do so later, he would be prepared to eat his words but he was not willing at present to do anything which would weaken the position of the Consultative Committee. It was also necessary to have regard to the position of the Malays. Their confidence in the Government had been largely restored and U.M.N.O. had now consolidated their position in support of the Federation plan. To bypass the Consultative Committee at the present stage might result in resignations from that Committee; and from the Advisory Council itself, and this would be a most undesirable result.

---

[1] See 113, note.

[2] John Thivy, born in south India; trained as a lawyer in London and practised in Malaya until 1942; joined Subhas Chandra Bose's Indian Independence League; interned by the BMA until Apr 1946; founded the Malayan Indian Congress in Aug 1946 and was a key figure in the Council of Joint Action.

The Governor-General felt that the claims of the Council of Joint Action were so bad that if contact could be established early, their arguments could be largely discredited.

The Governor of Malayan Union said that, apart from a few individuals, the Council of Joint Action comprised 17 associations of little account. The Malayan Nationalist Party had disassociated itself from the Council. The 17 associations referred to were nearly all associated with the General Labour Union, a Communist group, whose only purpose was to make trouble for the government and to prevent the successful organisation of registration of genuine Trade Unions. It had no constructive policy and in the Malayan Union it had not achieved the large scale influence it was understood to have gained in Singapore. His present view was that it would be dangerous for him to agree to see the Council of Joint Action collectively.

The Governor-General trusted that the Governor of Malayan Union would do nothing finally to close the door to seeing the Council of Joint Action collectively; he agreed that, at present, they did not represent very much but if they were mishandled there might be a swing of popular opinion in their favour.

The Governor of Malayan Union took the view that, if he were to see the Council of Joint Action collectively at the present stage, he would immediately enhance their position, and appear to indicate a lack of confidence in the Consultative Committee. The Governor of Malayan Union referred to the recent action of Mr. Chettur, the Representative of the Government of India in Malaya, who appeared to have been circularising all Indian Associations in the Malayan Union asking for views in regard to the Federation proposals.

The Governor-General said that he had interviewed, Mr. Chettur the previous day. Mr. Chettur hoped to go to India to report to his Government and had felt it desirable that he should be informed by the various Indian Associations in Malaya as to their reaction to the Federation proposals. So far he had received no reports, except from Ipoh. The Governor-General did not think that there was any harm in this. He had, however, asked Mr. Chettur as to his own views on the proposals. In reply, Mr. Chettur had mentioned only three points, as follows:—

(a) He felt strongly that the proposal to insist on a written as well as a conversational knowledge of English or Malay from intending citizens, after two years from the inauguration of the new Federation, was too limiting.

(b) He did not like the implications of the Report which suggested that the Malays should have the final control in the fixing of the future immigration policy.

(c) He was not clear that the whole plan was open for discussion.

The Governor-General stated that he had impressed upon Mr. Chettur that the Consultative Committee had been established to enable anyone to make his representations for the amendment of the plan in regard to any of the matters in it. He had also informed Mr. Chettur that, if the Government of India wished to make any official representation in regard to any aspects of the plan which affected India, the proper procedure would be for the Government of India to address their remarks to the India Office which would transmit them to the Colonial Office, and thence to the local Government.

It was agreed that the situation required careful watching; that while not closing the door to approaches from the Council of Joint Action, nothing should be done which would be likely to weaken the position of the Consultative Committee, or to

give rise to apprehensions on the part of the Malays—particularly the Rulers and
U.M.N.O., that the individual bodies represented on the Council of Joint Action
should be encouraged if possible to convey their views to the Governor who would
transmit them to the Consultative Committee, and that if possible a start should be
made with the Malayan Indian Congress.

112   CO 537/2165, ff 22–25   19 Jan 1947
'Singapore constitution': minute 8 of the 5th governor-general's conference in Penang about closer association

The Governor-General said in relation to the discussion which had just taken place[1]
there was the question of the possibility of Singapore coming into the Federation at a
later date. He had discussed this aspect with the Secretary of State who was ready
that it should be achieved if both Governors agreed. He wondered whether the
appropriate time had not come for some announcement on policy on this matter to
be made. It was clear that Singapore could not come into the Federation until the
new constitution of the Mainland had been promulgated and had got into working
order, but it might be most politic to state now that as soon as the constitution of the
Mainland was settled, a Working Committee would be established of representatives
of both territories to consider and plan for the inclusion of Singapore in the
Federation.

The Governor of Malayan Union said that he felt that this was a matter not to be
rushed, and that if any statement of policy was to be made it should be made by
H.M.G. and not locally. He did not disagree with the view that the inclusion of
Singapore in the Federation should be considered and put into effect at the
appropriate time, but he felt that popular opinion in the Mainland at any rate might
say that this matter could not be adequately considered until the stage had been
reached in the Malayan Federation when Elections were held, so that those who
joined in the consultations could claim to have the status of really representative
people.

The Governor of Singapore then said that there was a very strong feeling indeed in
Singapore that the Island should be included in the Federation. If the problem were
to be delayed until Elections were held in the Malayan Union an impression might be
created that the project would be held up indefinitely.

The Governor General said he felt that on a short term view, it would be most
politic, if the Governors agreed, to make an early announcement of their intention to
set up machinery at a fairly early date to consider the inclusion of Singapore in the
Federation. This would take a great deal of sting out of the present agitation of the
Council of Joint Action. One of their fundamental points was that Singapore was not
included in the new proposals and in this they undoubtedly had the support of a large
number of people, particularly in Singapore. This point undermined, by a pronouncement from H.M.G, there would be comparatively little of real substance left in
the criticisms of the Council of Joint Action and such other opposition to the plan as
had already emerged. There were criticisms with regard to the position of the

---

[1] See 111.

Sultans, with regard to the details of citizenship and the fact that Elections were not going to be held immediately. But they could all be met, or satisfactorily adjusted by the Government. The inclusion of Singapore was a big point. He, therefore, proposed, if the Governors agreed, that a statement should now be drafted and submitted to the Secretary of State for consideration.

The Governor of Malayan Union said that, in his view, the statement should come from H.M.G. and he saw no reason at all to object to that.

The Governor of Singapore said the feeling on this point in Singapore was strong; he had not invited the local communities to address him on the subject and they had not done so, but there was no doubt as to the local wishes.

It was decided that the Governor-General should prepare a draft telegram on the subject of the inclusion of Singapore as from himself and the two Governors, and that this should be circulated for consideration as soon as convenient.

The Governor-General said that the question they had been discussing was linked up with the proposals that had already been made by the Governor of Singapore for the constitution of a new Legislative Council for the Colony.[2] The Secretary of State had discussed with him (the Governor-General), Sir Franklin Gimson's recommendations and a Colonial Office despatch would be sent shortly on the subject. In general, the Secretary of State agrees to all the proposals that have been made except that he feels that the age limit for voters should be reduced from 25 to 21, and that the number of members to be nominated by the Governor should be three or four instead of two.

The Governor of Singapore said that the recommendation for two was based on the existing Order in Council.

The Governor-General said that the Secretary of State's feeling was that a greater number of nominations might be desirable after Elections are instituted in order to redress an overwhelming preponderance of any one community among the elected members.

The Governor of Malayan Union said that popular opinion is becoming increasingly averse to the system of nomination by the Governor.

The Governor-General said that this point could be reconsidered when the despatch was received; the general desire of the Secretary of State was to proceed with the inauguration of the new Legislature at the earliest possible moment.

The Governor of Singapore said that a Committee was already working on the preparation of the legislation and machinery for conducting elections, and that once approval is received from the Secretary of State, the new Legislature could not be set up too quickly.

The Governor-General pointed out that the inauguration of a full and more advanced constitution for Singapore at an early date might postpone the entry of Singapore into the wider Federation; in fact, it might hold up this step indefinitely, as the new Legislature might not be prepared to make the concessions necessary to enable Singapore to enter the wider Federation. It could be argued that it might be politic to withhold the new constitution pending the setting-up of the new Joint Working Party which had been mentioned earlier in the discussions.

The Governor of Singapore said that he did not think that the present arrange-

---

[2] See 98. On 20 Mar 1948 a minority of six members were elected to Singapore's first Legislative Council which was sworn in on 1 April 1948.

ments of governing Singapore through an Advisory Council could be allowed to continue indefinitely and that a more satisfactory Legislature must be substituted for it.

The Governor of Malayan Union said that if the new constitution of Singapore were held up indefinitely, an unfortunate effect might be produced in the Malayan Union. It might be argued that H.M.G. was being deliberately slow in implementing its promises regarding constitutional advancement.

The Governor-General enquired if there was any public agitation in Singapore for the adoption of a new constitution on the basis of the report which had been published.

The Governor of Singapore said that there was no such agitation; this was perhaps due to the fact that the Advisory Council hitherto had not been called upon to deal with any highly controversial legislation.

The Governor of Malayan Union said that, at his Advisory Council on the previous day, the T.U. member had already pressed for the setting up of a Committee to explore the future electoral system in the territory in the first instance for local Government purposes. In this connection, he mentioned that he had just received the report of a Committee established to advise on the constitution of the Municipality of Kuala Lumpur. He hoped to adopt the report and to recommend the constitution of the Municipality of Kuala Lumpur with effect from 1st Jan, 1948.

The Governor-General enquired whether Sir Edward Gent had in mind any programme regarding the final setting up of the new constitutional arrangements for the Malayan Union.

The Governor of Malayan Union said that it was thought that the Consultative Committee would probably take six weeks to hear the views of the local communities and individuals. They were starting their sessions on the 28th January. They should, therefore, be able to report in eight weeks; about one month would be required for consideration of their Report and the necessary debate in the Advisory Council. It should be possible, therefore, for him to refer the Report, with his conclusions, to the Secretary of State, by the beginning of May.[3]

The Governor General enquired when the new constitution could be put into force, presuming that the reply of the Secretary of State and the decisions of H.M.G. were not unduly delayed.

The Governor of Malayan Union said that he did not think it would be possible to inaugurate the new constitution until the 1st January, 1948, at the earliest.

The Governor-General then enquired when the new constitution in Singapore and the holding of elections could be put into force, assuming that the Secretary of State's despatch was received in the course of the next few weeks.

The Governor of Singapore thought that this would not be possible until the 1st January, 1948.

The Governor-General said that this would probably be the time when the inclusion of Singapore became a practical issue and it might be better to introduce the new constitution in Singapore, with the necessary modifications, to enable

[3] The report of the Consultative Committee was submitted to Gent on 21 March 1947. It was later published as *Constitutional Proposals for Malaya: Report of the Consultative Committee Together with Proceedings of Six Public Meetings, a Summary of Representations Made and Letters and Memoranda Considered by the Committee* (Kuala Lumpur, 1947).

Singapore to enter the Federation by the middle or end of 1948, since it will be necessary to get the Federation working properly before this further step was taken. It was to be presumed that the machinery for elections in Singapore will be required in any case. The shape of the Island Council would probably be very much on the lines of the recommendations already made. Only the legislative powers of the Singapore Council in regard to certain subjects would be curtailed in favour of the Federal Legislative Council.

The Governor of Malayan Union said that it would be unwise to hurry unduly this development; there would be some hard bargaining between the two territories to be done and those negotiations must not be hurried.

The Governor-General said that it looked as though Singapore could not be brought into the Federation earlier than 18 months, or two years, from the present time—even if all went well.

113   CO 537/2174, no 1   27 Jan 1947
[UMNO]: despatch no 92/47 from Sir E Gent to Mr Creech Jones.
Annex: report on UMNO general assembly, 10–12 Jan 1947   [Extract]

[Agreement having been reached between the British and Malay leaders, opposition to the constitutional proposals arose from two quarters. The Pan-Malayan Council of Joint Action, comprising some 17 political groups and with Tan Cheng Lock playing an important role, was formed on 22 Dec 1946. Its object was to achieve the political unification of Malaya and Singapore, liberal citizenship and staged advance to self-government. The PMCJA was later renamed the All Malayan Council of Joint Action and opposed the constitutional proposals in partnership with a separate front of radical Malays known as PUTERA. Meanwhile, Malay negotiators were criticised from within UMNO. When UMNO's general assembly came to debate the constitutional proposals, the press were ejected and it continued in camera. While many specific amendments were made, the assembly eventually accepted the essence of the proposals.]

The Governor of the Malayan Union presents his compliments to the Right Honourable the Secretary of State for the Colonies and submits for information the attached copy of a secret report on the proceedings of the General Assembly of the United Malays National Organisation held at Alor Star, Kedah, on the 10–12th January, 1947.

Annex to 113

UMNO held a general assembly at Alor Star, Kedah, from the 10th – 12th Jan. 1947. Anti-UMNO propaganda was in evidence as early as the 5th Jan., when cyclostyled Jawi[1] pamphlets were distributed in the streets. The pamphlet declared that "Dato Onn has sold the Sultans and the Raayat[2] like slaves. We must liberate ourselves. Do not accept the Federation proposals. Our Sultans must be treated as true Sultans with prerogatives to command our respect, and should be able to govern us on democratic principles. The Council of Joint Action demands Independence for the Sultans and the Raayats, and unity with our friends. We can achieve greater success

---

[1] *Jawi* is the Arabic-based Malay script.   [2] *Raayat* means 'the people'.

and victory than Dato Onn who has become a British satellite. Oppose the Federation proposals! Support the Council of Joint Action!"

2. The Conference opened at 9.45 a.m. on the 10th instant when Dato Onn and H.H. the Sultan of Kedah, [sic] each was received by a guard of honour of youths of the Kesatuan Pemuda Melayu,[3] Sebrang Perak, wearing white uniform.

3. H.H. gave a speech of welcome of no great importance, and he left the assembly immediately afterwards.

4. In his opening address Dato Onn stressed that the Malay people are not ready for Independence. He ridiculed those Malays who demand immediate Independence, pointing out that there is no Malay fitted to be a Minister, or a representative to UNO or an Ambassador, and that Malaya could not expect practical aid from Indonesia. In conclusion he said: "Who was ruling the country immediately after the Japanese surrender?—the Chinese. We have been greatly endangered by the Three Stars[4] and by the MNP. We do not care for these people. We must rise united to defend our birth-right; the 2,500,000 Malays in Malaya must be united, and once unity is achieved we will have no fear of foreigners."

5. Inche Mohd Tahir bin Stia Raja was unanimously elected vice-Chairman.

6. The whole of the Congress was completely dominated by the personality of Dato Onn. The principal opponents to Dato Onn and his ideology were: (1) Dr. Hamzah[5] of the Kesatuan Melayu, Muar, who recently has attended the Council of Joint Action, (2) Che Gu Senu[6] of Soberkas [sic], Kedah, (3) Sa'adon Zubir[7] of the Kesatuan Melayu, Singapore. Dr. Hamzah suggested that Dato Onn should confine his activities to the office of the Mentri Besar of Johore, and that the Presidency of UMNO should be filled by some other person. This proposal was not accepted. Dato Onn made a counter attack on Dr. Hamzah by stating pointedly that someone has disclosed the "secret" of UMNO to Mr. Tan Cheng Lock at the recent Conference of the Council of Joint Action.

7. Che Gu Senu was prominent during the discussions of the Constitutional Proposals. At the outset, he asked for postponement of the debate to the 2nd day; this motion was seconded by Dr. Hamzah. But Dato Onn ruled out this request, declaring that the delegates had already had ample time to study the Proposals. Che Gu Senu, referring to page 8 of the Proposals, pointed out that the partnership in the Federation Agreement between H.M. the King and H.H. the Rulers was not on a proportionate basis; he went on to declaim the desire for Independence. He was seconded by Sa'adon Zubir and Dr. Hamzah. Dato Onn ruled that UMNO did not claim Independence but the abrogation of the MacMichael Treaty. Che Gu Senu finally did declare that Soberkas agrees with the wishes of UMNO. . . .

---

[3] Or 'Association of Young Malays'.   [4] A reference to the Malayan Peoples' Anti-Japanese Army.

[5] Dr. Hamzah, enraged by the thought of Anglo-Malay compromise, stormed out of the assembly. He attempted to re-open the issue at assemblies in Mar and May, and in May 1947 withdrew from UMNO altogether.

[6] Senu b Abdul Rahman, secretary-general of Saberkas (a radical Malay association in Kedah); in the USA and Britain, 1947–55; became secretary-general of UMNO and joint secretary of the Alliance in 1955.

[7] Sardon bin Haji Jubir attended the inaugural conference of the MNP in Nov 1945; president of Kesatuan Melayu Singapore 1947–1951; elected to the first Legislative Council, Singapore, 1948–1951; president of UMNO Youth, 1951; federal minister, 1956–1972.

114   CO 537/2174, no 2   17 Feb 1947

[UMNO's reactions to federation proposals]: letter from Dato Onn bin Jaafar to Sir E Gent

As promised I enclose herewith two copies of the amendments to the Draft Federation Agreement passed by the General Assembly of the U.M.N.O. at its Alor Star Meeting in January.[1]

You have kindly agreed to meet my Committee on the 23rd and I trust you can let me know the time most suitable to you in order to discuss the amendments with you.

Regarding the Federation Proposals, Malay opinion is getting extremely restive and highly suspicious of the motives and sincerity of the British Government. I do not blame them either.

As I said the British Government must choose *now* between Malay support and co-operation or sacrificing them to political expediency.

You will remember asking me whether there was any possibility of the U.M.N.O. and the M.N.P. getting together. My reply was not at the moment but the future trend of Malay action will depend entirely on the outcome of the Proposals which U.M.N.O. has accepted in principle.

Undue pandering to elements who do not conform to the conception of Federal citizens or to any attempts to further minimise the legitimate rights and the special position of the Malays will have disastrous repercussions.

I cannot conceal from you that the Malays will undoubtedly swing wide into a coalition with parties definitely anti-British if only because of frustration and despair at British hypocrisy.

I shall speak frankly and freely when we meet on the 23rd.

---

[1] See 113.

115   CO 537/2141, no 28   22 Feb 1947

[Constitutional proposals]: report by Mr Thomas on his visit to Malaya, 9–16 Feb 1947   [Extract]

Minute by H T Bourdillon

[Ivor Bulmer-Thomas, who was first a Labour MP, 1942–1948, and then a Conservative MP, 1949–1950, was briefly parliamentary under-secretary for the colonies, succeeding Creech Jones in Oct 1946 and being succeeded by Rees-Williams later in 1947. Thomas visited Malaya on his way back from the South Seas Conference in Canberra.]

. . .

6. *Constitutional proposals.* There is great interest in the constitutional question, and it would be perilous to underestimate the immense advance in political consciousness which has taken place in Malaya since the outbreak of war. The Malays are, of course far behind the other communities in their political training, but even the Malays are being swept by big changes; the small Communist-ridden Malay Nationalist Party is the only section which openly proclaims its solidarity with the events in Dutch Indonesia, but the more representative U.M.N.O. is also influenced,

both directly and because it cannot afford to see the M.N.P. steal its thunder. It is particularly significant that a women's section of U.M.N.O. is being encouraged, and we may expect to see the Malays move rapidly towards the full form of western democracy. But they have not got there yet, and it must be admitted that to attempt to give Malays full self-government within the next five years would probably mean the rule of the Malays by the Chinese. The Chinese are exceedingly industrious, prolific and able, but in few cases do they acknowledge Malaya as their "permanent home and the object of their loyalty". It is disturbing to see the Chinese flag flying over Chinese schools and a portrait of Sun Yat-sen[1] as the principal object of veneration within them. For a long time to come the Chinese will undoubtedly have this dual loyalty—if indeed they feel any loyalty to Malaya. A friend who was born in China and has lived for twenty years in Malaya writes to me: "I am absolutely sure that the Chinese Government and the Triad Group (which has been and usually can be considered as anti-Chinese Government) both wish and intend the rich land of Malaya to leave the British Commonwealth and to be available for them to squeeze dry. If Malaya does become part of China we will have betrayed the Malays who trusted us. The Chinese—all—in their hearts of hearts believe that they are the only civilized people and the rest of the people of the world are barbarians. Some Chinese have settled here and become real Malayans. They have attended our schools, but they are a small minority. We have subsidized and permitted the Chinese schools teaching Chinese language and the Chinese ideas that China is the only civilised land. The Chinese who have settled here amongst the other inhabitants are not resented, but the Chinese who have formed tight Chinese colonies where no-one dare report any illegality to our police are very dangerous and are rightly and strongly resented and hated by the Malays." The Indians, like the Chinese, have this loyalty to a land outside Malaya. Mr. John Thivy spoke most reasonably to Mr. MacDonald and myself about the possibilities of co-operation with the Malays, but Malayan leaders, such as Dato Onn, distrust him and consider that his change of tactics is on recent instructions from [the Indian National] Congress. If the Indians achieve a unitary Government it is likely to be one which will make the protection of its oversea Indians a primary concern, and where more naturally than in Malaya? Nevertheless, it is impossible not to be gratified at the extent to which the different communities in Malaya get on with each other. There is no immediate likelihood of communal disturbances such as mar the peace of India itself, though with growing political consciousness this cannot be ruled out. The Eurasians would like to align themselves politically with the Europeans, and it would be good tactics to encourage them to regard themselves as Europeans; the only noteworthy exception is Mr. John Eber,[2] secretary of the Pan-Malayan Council of Joint Action, but his political views are disowned by the other members of the community.

7. Full self-government being not immediately practicable, the field is held at the present time by the proposals of the Working Committee on which the Consultative

---

[1] Sun Yat-sen (1866–1925) Chinese revolutionary politician and founder of the Kuomintang.

[2] John Eber, a Eurasian lawyer who was interned during the Japanese occupation, campaigned vigorously for the social democratic objects of the Singapore-based Malayan Democratic Union and the PMCJA. In 1951 he was detained under Emergency Regulations and after his release went to England where he helped edit *Malayan Monitor*, which claimed to be the organ of the PUTERA-AMCJA (Malayan People's United Front) and regularly published MCP documents. He later became general-secretary of Fenner Brockway's 'Movement for Colonial Freedom'.

Committee is now prepared to hear expressions of opinion. There has been some tendency to boycott the Consultative Committee, but the tendency is breaking down, and evidence is beginning to be offered. Dato Onn told me that the Working Committee's proposals were the limit to which the U.M.N.O. was prepared to go; Mr. Thivy told us that the Indians were not prepared to accept them without modifications, more particularly with regard to the length of residence and the language tests of citizenship. These may appear to be irreconcilable standpoints, but it became clear to me that we shall never win support from all the communities to any set of proposals. The best we can hope for is that when we put forward our proposals we shall secure sufficient acquiescence to carry them, and I believe we could probably get this acquiescence on the basis of the Working Committee's proposals. I used all my endeavours to persuade the various communities not to be too precise about details, but to accept any proposals which gave Malaya a reasonably satisfactory constitution, knowing that modifications could be made later; I found a [sic] acceptance for this point of view, although there was some scepticism about the possibility of later modifications.

8. Nevertheless, I am persuaded myself that on merits two big changes should be made in the Working Committee's proposals.

(a) *Singapore*. The separation of Singapore from Malaya was strongly denounced by many with whom I spoke and it was admitted by all that eventually it must be included in the Federation. I presumed at first that there must be a military reason for the separation, but this does not appear to have been suggested. The argument that it is the different character of Singapore's trade convinces one, and in any case the trade of Singapore is not fundamentally different from that of Penang. The real reason is presumably the predominantly Chinese character of the population of Singapore; but I am bound to record that in my talks with Malays no-one suggested that Singapore must be excluded. This is not conclusive evidence, as I did not raise the subject myself, not wishing to put ideas into the heads of the Malays, but if there had been any real hostility to the inclusion of Singapore I should have expected to have heard of it. As it is inevitable that some day Singapore must be brought into the Federation, I suggest it should be done at once. Otherwise the exclusion of Singapore will be a source of controversy until it is brought in. The exclusion of Singapore from the Working Committee's proposals may, however, turn out to be advantageous, as it will probably be necessary to make some concessions to the Chinese, and the inclusion of Singapore is the least harmful concession. To resort to metaphor, I regard Singapore as a card up our sleeve. If it is brought into the Federation it should, of course, have its own Settlement Council like Penang, and it might be advantageous for this Council to assume also the local government work now done by the Municipal Commissioners and the Rural Board. It would be a by-product of these proposals that the present plethora of the apparatus of government in Malaya would be reduced. Malaya is acknowledged by all, including the Governors, to be much over-governed at present. The presence of a Governor-General and two Governors, not to mention a Special Commissioner, though all are personally esteemed, is puzzling to the public and inevitably leads to administrative delays when pan-Malayan action is required. I do not, of course, imply any criticism of the Governor-General, the Governors and their staffs, for whose work I formed the highest admiration, and I believe they would themselves endorse what I have said.

(b) *Elections.* I found much criticism that the Working Committee's proposals make no provision for elections. "What advance is this on what we had before the war?", I was asked, and it is not a satisfactory answer to say that the elections would now be over a wider area. It has always been the weakness of British policy to do the right thing too late, and I am certain that we shall fail to do justice to the immense political advancement in Malaya if we do not make provision for elections both to the Federal Legislature and to the State Councils. It may prove to be impracticable to get a satisfactory register by the time the new Constitution is brought into force, but if this is the case the constitutional proposals should lay down a date not very far distant when elections will take place; Article 69 of the Draft Federation Agreement is not nearly precise enough to meet the point.

I am convinced that it is necessary to bring the new Constitution into effect at an early date as the uncertainty is hindering many developments.

I therefore recommend that definite constitutional proposals should be formulated by His Majesty's Government this summer and should be based on the Working Committee's report but should make provision for the incorporation of Singapore in the Federation with a Settlement Council and should make provision for elections both to the Federal Legislature and to the State Councils before a definite date within the next few years. . . .

Minute on 115

. . . Mr. Thomas has made two recommendations. First, he has proposed that there should be a much more definite statement about the early introduction of elections, both in the Central Legislature and in the Councils of State, than is contained in the Federation proposals. This seems to me to be a very important suggestion, particularly since Mr. Thomas has found considerable local feeling on the subject, but for the moment we can only bear it in mind. Secondly, he has pleaded for the very early inclusion of Singapore in the Federation. I think this recommendation demands further consideration at once. The point is, of course, not a new one. It was first put to us by the Governor-General in a letter to Sir G. Gater dated 13th September last (13 on 50823/40/46). At that time Mr. MacDonald was very worried by the lack of administrative co-ordination between the Governments of Singapore and the Malayan Union. He felt that proper co-ordination was unattainable so long as the two Governments remained separate, and therefore expressed the view that fusion would prove necessary at a much earlier date than had previously been envisaged. The immediate context was the establishment of the Singapore Legislative Council. Mr. MacDonald feared that the setting up of a separate Legislature for Singapore, on however sound and progressive lines, would be likely to render fusion more difficult. Our feeling here was that we could not interfere with this particular development, though at the same time we were impressed by the arguments in favour of early amalgamation. The Governor-General was informed accordingly in No. 14 on 50823/40/46. The matter was carried further with him during his visit to the U.K. at the beginning of this year, by which time the Pan-Malayan Council of Joint Action had already come forward with "fusion" as one of the principal planks in its platform. It was agreed on the one hand that the establishment of the Singapore Legislative

Council and the introduction of the revised Constitution for the Malayan Union must be allowed to go through; but on the other hand it was also agreed that as soon as these events had taken place, there would be great advantage in H.M.G. making it clear that they were sympathetic towards, and in earnest about the fusion of the two territories as soon as possible thereafter. Mr. MacDonald's actual suggestion was that a joint "Working Committee" consisting of representatives of both territories, might be set up at an early date to study the problem, and that a public announcement to this effect might accompany H.M.G.'s final approval of the revised Malayan Union Constitution. It was left that we might expect a telegram with firm proposals to this end after MacDonald's return to Malaya, but hitherto no such telegram has arrived. We know from Item 8 of the Governor-General's Conference at Penang on January 19th (1 on 52738/1/47)[3] that he indeed discussed the matter with the two Governors on his return, that both Governors were sympathetic (Sir E. Gent, I think, unexpectedly so), and that a telegram was to be drafted. But there have been no further developments.

Mr. Ivor Thomas appears to envisage the incorporation of Singapore in the Malayan Federation from the outset. I still feel that we must first allow the present constitutional developments in the two territories to reach finality, since by disturbing them we stand to lose more than we should gain, but I think that Mr. Thomas's remarks strongly emphasise the desirability of the procedure outlined in the previous paragraph. The arguments in favour of the early inclusion of Singapore in the Federation are as follows:—

(a) *Political.* This has been one of the fundamental and common features of all the local criticisms of the Federation proposals. See for instance No. 17 on 52243/2/47, which denounces the separation of Singapore in the strongest terms. To judge from Mr. Ivor Thomas's experience while in Malaya, from Sir E. Gent's attitude at the Governor-General's Conference and from the fact that Mr. Roland Braddell, Legal Adviser to U.M.N.O., is also a supporter of "fusion", it does *not* appear, after all, that the Malays are *acharnés*[4] on the subject. Here, then, we are surely presented with an opportunity of showing, without antagonising Malay opinion, that H.M.G. have paid heed to criticisms of the present Constitutional scheme.

(b) *Administrative.* I can find no evidence that administrative co-ordination between the two Governments is markedly better than it was. On the contrary, we have had two very recent instances of the Governments pulling apart on vital matters—Societies Legislation and policy towards the General Labour Union. If, as I am convinced, we cannot lay the blame for this on either of the two Governors, we can only lay it on the system itself. I know from personal conversation that Sir R. Hone feels strongly that the system does not and cannot work. With two territories as intimately connected as these, the somewhat vague "co-ordinating" powers of the Governor-General are not enough. The Governor-General usually only gets to hear of the trouble (I am quoting Sir R. Hone) when it has already been clogging the wheels for several months.

(c) *Financial.* It is hard to be specific on this point, but it has been said on good authority that Singapore cannot stand financially on its own feet. At the very least, the maintenance of two actively separate machines of Government is a waste of money.

---

[3] See 112.   [4] ie furious.

For all these reasons, then, but principally for the first, I think we need to consider the inclusion of Singapore in the Federation very seriously at the same time as we consider Sir E. Gent's recommendations on the Federation proposals.[5] We have none too much time, and I suggest we might send a brief personal telegram from Sir T. Lloyd to the Governor-General on the lines of the second draft submitted herewith.[6]

H.T.B.
8.3.47

---

[5] While in favour of fusion, Bourdillon's seniors stressed that timing and local advice were all important. When Creech Jones raised the matter with the prime minister he agreed that the priority was to clear up the Malayan problem before embarking on merger. CO 537/2141, minute by Creech Jones, 18 Mar 1947.
[6] Not printed.

116   CO 537/2151, no 1   24 Feb 1947
[Malay extremism and API]: despatch no 1 from Sir E Gent to Mr Creech Jones

[The government's concern about Malay extremism and its connections with the Indonesian revolution focused upon Ahmad Boestamam's API. Boestamam's *Testament Politik API* led to his conviction on a charge of sedition in April 1947. Having paid the fine he resumed the leadership of API which was proscribed on 17 July 1947 (see also 94, note 2).]

I have the honour to forward for your information a list of the resolutions passed at the first congress of the Angkatan Pemuda Insaaf (API) held on the 22nd, 23rd and 24th December, 1946, at Malacca and attended by 70 delegates from all States in Malaya.

1. The API demands a democratic government of the people and an open declaration of the sovereignty of the Malay people.
2. The API demands that the Malay Regiment should replace the present British and Indian soldiers in Malaya.
2. The API demands that the open door policy in Malaya should be abolished.
4. The API demands the quitting of all Dutch forces in Malaya.
5. Japanese prisoners of war should be repatriated.
6. The API supports the Indonesian struggle for independence.
7. The API will contact the Federation of Democratic Youth.

2.   The Angkatan Pemuda Insaaf, an organisation confined to Malays, first came to notice in February, 1946, when the SUARA RAYAT (Voice of the People) of Ipoh announced its information and appealed for members. The announcement stated that at a meeting at the Malay Nationalist Party Headquarters it had been decided to inaugurate an "entirely new movement", and published the following particulars:—

Name. Angkatan Pemuda Insaaf. Literally, the name means "Youth Movement for Justice". What is possibly more to the point and is certainly easier to mouth, is that "API", formed by its initials, means in the Malay language "Fire" or "Flame" and may be presumed to describe the ardent nationalism which its organisers hope to inspire in their recruits.

Establishment. A branch of the Malay Nationalist Party.

Policy. Nationalisation based on self-determination.

Objects. (i)   To organise patriotic youth in a united front.

(ii) To promote and develop patriotism.

(iii) To give training in politics, culture and religion.

(iv) To rebuild and develop Malaya in line with the true democratic principles on the basis of the People's Right. Membership to be open to youths between the ages of 18 and 35, preference being given to members of the Malay Nationalist Party and those with previous military training.

The financial resources of the organisation are believed to be considerable and to have been contributed in part by ex-members of the Indian National Army, including Sikhs, and by extreme leftist sections of the Chinese Communist Party.

3. The present policy of A.P.I. as set out in a brochure entitled "A.P.I's POLITICAL TESTAMENT" distributed by the API congress at Malacca on the 22nd-24th December 1946 is said to be as follows:—

(a) To unite and organise all awakened youths.

(b) To strengthen the fighting front of the nation and motherland.

(c) To give training, political, physical and spiritual, to its youths in order that they may be prepared to lead whenever required.

(d) To build Malaya on democratic lines.

(e) To obtain the right of representation in the Malayan Government.

In the same pamphlet it is declared that API will struggle for the achievement of national independence by all available means—gently if possible but by force if necessary. In this connection it is interesting to note that in addition to the objects quoted above a sixth has also been clearly stated, namely, the training of men to assist the Indonesians in their struggle for independence in order to obtain help from Indonesia to secure independence in this country at a later date. This is in keeping with API's "Asia for the Asiatics" objective inherited from the Japanese. API sees two ways open to it:—

(1) revolution

(2) evolution

API has confidence only in the first way. The ideology of API is set forth under three headings:—

(1) *Political.* API is directed towards the founding of an independent state based on true democracy.

(2) *Economic.* API wants a planned economy not for the benefit of one or two sections of the people but for the masses. "A planned economy cannot possibly be set up in a state where imperialism is still predominant or when the governing power is not in our hands."

(3) *Social.* API wants social justice in which there shall be complete absence of social discrimination between one section of the people and another. At present a disorganised society is responsible for the existence of at least two prominent classes of people, namely the capitalists and proletariat.

API's preparations for the achievement of independence are divided into two, internal and external. Internal training to fit youths for the responsibilities of leadership when the present leaders have gone includes the development of patriotism, political science and economics, and training in gymnastics, drill, sports and warfare. In fact, API's most obvious and disturbing public activity is reported to be the holding of public parades at which drilling in military formation is practised. External training is directed towards the formation of relationships with similar organisations outside the country. API declares that it will affiliate with the World Federation of Democratic Youth. In keeping with the military nature of API's internal training was the proposal put forward at API's Malacca congress that "every member of API must maintain in a condition of readiness weapons such as sharpened bamboos, parangs and krises", and a report from Malacca states that 30 youths, seen going to the training area, were armed with sharpened bamboo poles.

4. The present President of the Organisation is AHMAD BOESTAMEN, an Indonesian whose real name is ABDULLA SANI bin RAJA KECHIL. He was born in Perak but is of Sumatran origin. He is well educated in Malay and English and has had journalistic experience. During the Japanese campaign in Malaya he was arrested as a suspected Fifth Columnist but was released when the Japanese entered Singapore. During the Japanese occupation he attended the school founded for the training of Malay officers in military propaganda. In fact, most of the leading figures in API, as in the Malay Nationalist Party, were notably pro-Japanese during the occupation.

5. At the celebration of the first anniversary of the Malay Nationalist Party at Kuala Lumpur on the 17th October, 1946, Ahmad Boestamen announced that API had been in existence for 8 months and that its members were prepared to sacrifice their lives and liberty in the cause of freedom. API believed that independence could not be gained without bloodshed but the day for this had not yet arrived. Imperialism would not be tolerated and independence was possible only through revolution. Our national cry is 'merdeka' (independence), the API cry is 'darah' (blood)". API in fact is primarily an Indonesian sponsored organisation, with Malay Nationalist Party and Malayan Communist Party backing, and strong affiliations with the Indonesian Youth Movements in Java and Sumatra. The present strength of the organisation is said to be some 2,500 men, most of whom appear to belong to Perak, Malacca and Pahang. The latest information indicates that API is strong in all States except Perlis, Trengganu and Johore but the type of follower it succeeds in attracting is more frequently than not the unemployed loafer between the ages of 18 and 30. Boestamen has emphasised that a huge membership is not required and claims that 5,000 persons were enough to make the revolution in Ireland a success. Similarly, it is stated, Lenin had only about 6,000 members of the Communist Party to support him in revolution against the Czar of Russia. In "API's Political Testament" it is stated that API intends to support the Representative Assembly of All Asiatic Races proposed recently by Pandit Nehru, which is taken to be an allusion to the Inter-Asian Congress to be held at Delhi in March, 1947.

6. An assessment of API would not be complete without reference to the support it received from the parallel women's organisation known as Angkatan Wanita Sedar (Women's Progressive Corps) whose membership is said to number some 600 Malay women and whose aims are reported to be as follows:—

(1) To unite all Malay women for Malaya's independence.
(2) The abolition of conservative customs regarding the social position of Malay women.
(3) The abolition of forced marriage.
(4) The support of API.
(5) The formation of Red Cross Units.

There can be no doubt that extremism amongst the young men of API is encouraged by such speeches as that made by the leader of the AWS when she declared that youths "should not die in their beds but must die in the battle for Malaya's freedom". The joint purpose of the Angkatan Wanita Sedar and API has been symbolised recently by a marriage between their respective leaders.

7. Another disturbing feature of API's activities that has just come to light is the penetration of its propaganda into the schools. Reports from Malacca and Johore indicate that some Malay school teachers are spreading the gospel of API amongst their pupils, and school children who succumb to the influence of API are known as "semut api" or "fire ants." In Perak, the symbol is preserved by the designation "bara" which means "hot cinders". It is noteworthy that the influence exerted by API on Malay vernacular school teachers has been facilitated by the wide following amongst them commanded by the Malay Nationalist Party. I am considering the proper form of deterrent action that should be taken to restrain such extra-curricular activities on the part of school teachers paid by Government.

8. There is reason to believe that Boestamen and his extremist policy is proving an embarrassment to the more moderate Malay Nationalist Party leaders and this belief is strengthened by the decision that API should hold a separate congress, at which a member of the Malay Nationalist Party pointed out that API is no longer under the control of MNP. Boestamen also declared that API would watch the course of the MNP closely and break away completely "if necessary". By the words "if necessary" Boestamen clearly means if MNP is too moderate. This breach between API and its parent body is in keeping with recent suggestions that UMNO, which represents moderate Malay opinion, and MNP are coming closer together. Apart from political differences, however, a consideration which is likely to weigh heavily with MNP is that, in the event of a rapproachement with UMNO, the Party would lose the financial support which it is said to be receiving at present from certain sections of the Chinese.

9. While API undoubtedly owes much of what vitality it has to the legacy of the Japanese occupation and to infection with the political ferment in the Netherlands East Indies, it is fortunately true that until now it has been more remarkable for the fire-eating, and at times allegedly subversive, speeches of its leader Boestamen than for any positive political activities, but as there are features of its avowed programme which suggest that it contains an element which in certain circumstances might be provocative to other communities and prejudicial to the well-being and security of society, I am considering what measures, such as the banning of political uniforms, might properly be taken to discourage its more irresponsible tendencies.

10. I am sending copies of this despatch to the Governor-General and the Governor of Singapore.

117   CO 537/2166, ff 8–12   11 Mar 1947

'The labour problem': minute 3 of the 6th governor-general's conference in Singapore on 11 March   [Extract]

[The MCP fomented labour unrest through the General Labour Union. There had been a twenty-four-hour general strike at the end of Jan 1946. A second general strike set for 15 Feb 1946, the anniversary of the British surrender to the Japanese, had been thwarted by a show of force. From Feb 1947 violence, intimidation and lawlessness was increasingly reported in mines, on estates and in labour relations elsewhere; riots in Kedah were a notable instance.]

At this stage of the meeting, Mr. J.A. Brazier,[1] Trades Union Adviser, and Mr. R.P. Bingham,[2] Commissioner for Labour were present.

The Governor-General said this was a most important question and it was necessary to keep the position constantly under review. A situation had now arisen in regard to the action required in relation to strikes. The Governor of Singapore had sent a telegram to the Secretary of State in which:—

1. he said the F.T.U. would not be registered in Singapore;
2. he asked for freedom of action in the use of the Banishment Ordinance in cases where he considered it necessary;
3. he proposed in the case of banishment to publish simultaneously a general statement on the Government's labour policy with a view to gaining the support of the public.

The Governor of the Malayan Union, on the other hand, had sent a telegram to the Secretary of State in which he had stated:—

1. that action had not been taken in the Malayan Union to refuse registration to the F.T.U. nor was it intended to do so;
2. he did not consider banishment by itself a complete answer to the problem. It might exacerbate the situation.

The Governor of the Malayan Union said that if it were made impossible for the F.T.U. to register as a lawful body, we thereby forced them into the position of becoming a lawless body and subject to banishment.

The Governor-General then suggested that the discussion should be split into three component parts:—

(a) The question of banishment.
(b) The question of F.T.U. registration.
(c) Other necessary action to deal with the situation.

He considered the best way to start would be to examine the Governor of Singapore's proposal to the Secretary of State that he should be given authority to banish without further reference to the Secretary of State, rather than detain intended banishees while awaiting confirmation from the Secretary of State.

---

[1] J A Brazier, trade union adviser, Malaya, 1946–1956.
[2] R P Bingham, entered MCS, 1926; interned, 1942–1945; commissioner for labour, Singapore, 1946–1951; secretary for Chinese affairs, Malaya, 1951–1952; resident commissioner, Penang, 1952–1958.

The Governor of Singapore said that banishment was a common feature of the administration before the war and the public were unable to understand why it had now been discontinued. The particular persons concerned were nearly all non-British subjects whose loyalties lie elsewhere and they were preventing the growth of healthy trade unionism. They were also suspected to be members of a Branch of the Communist Party and therefore opposed to democratic policy of Government.

The Governor-General said he had an open mind regarding the registration of the F.T.U. but considered that Singapore's proposals regarding banishment were absolutely essential in Singapore even if not in the Malayan Union. The Governor might not have to act but if action was taken it must be immediate without any reference to London. It was necessary to try to persuade the Secretary of State to let Singapore have that authority, whether it was used or not. Everything that he had heard lately confirmed this view.

The Governor of Singapore said that if this is not approved it might lead to the wholesale resignation of his Advisory Council.

The Governor-General said that as an interesting side-light on this matter, he had had a talk with United Kingdom and American pressmen a week ago, and they were quite unable to understand why the weapon of banishment was not used. The "News Chronicle" correspondent and Tiltman of the "Daily Herald"—both very Leftist papers—said exactly the same thing and the latter had warned his paper privately that a very dangerous position was arising here. He said that he was convinced that without banishment we could not get to the root of the trouble.

The Governor of the Malayan Union said that the terms of the Singapore telegram were that G.L.U. leaders as such should be liable to banishment. He said the Malayan Union already had powers to banish criminals, such as extortioners, intimidators etc., but he did not agree with the request for the Secretary of State's approval that G.L.U. leaders as such should be liable to banishment for organizing strikes. Banishment was a very serious penalty and one which was outside any appeal to the Courts, and mere membership of the G.L.U. or participation in strikes was no justification.

The Governor-General replied that it would be made clear that intimidation was involved.

The Chief Secretary, Malayan Union, said that powers were already given to banish criminal intimidators.

The Governor-General asked if all the intended banishees in Singapore fell within that qualification. He said it was not necessary to say with which Society they were associated, but merely that they were associated with an intimidating section within a Society.

The Governor of the Malayan Union said that when we have a show-down we must be sure that we deal with the chief figures and have a cast iron case. It might well cause a general strike and questions in Parliament. A statement would have to be given as to the grounds on which the man is banished and which gang he belonged to etc.

The Governor-General said he would have thought it would suffice to say that inside some trade union organizations in Singapore there were some sections going in for a policy of intimidation, and that Government was satisfied that the men concerned were members of these sections.

The Governor of the Malayan Union thought that we should have an enquiry on the responsibility of the particular individuals and not a general allegation against a large and powerful labour organization.

The Governor-General said he would not mind that if action had already been taken. Although there would be questions and some uneasiness in the House of Commons, the Secretary of State would have the large support of the evidence of a number of press correspondents who had been in this part of the world and from whom news was infiltrating to newspapers of all shades of political opinion in London. In Singapore, the public were so ready to back this action that we should have an overwhelming body of opinion, including labour opinion, supporting the Government. The public here were not so ready to question things as they were in Britain, and the risk of awkward questions in London was far less than the risk of a disastrous state of affairs here. He asked whether he was right in supposing that all the intended banishees were known to be associated with the intimidation school of thought.

The Colonial Secretary said there was evidence that the people concerned were responsible for intimidation. If they could be picked up they could be banished. If the body could be proved to be responsible for initimidating labour then the leaders could be banished as being actively concerned and responsible for the intimidation going on now.

The Governor-General then asked Mr. Brazier for his opinion.

Mr. Brazier said it was the policy of His Majesty's Government to assist in the development of democratic Trade Unionism in Malaya. He said he had been directed to give certain ideas to the members themselves. He was not concerned whether an individual was anti-government or not. He had tried to build up the idea of Trade Unionism on a democratic basis, he had concentrated on compulsory registration and there had never been any complaints about this. Mr. Brazier went on to say that if he was to give his advice now, he must first give a little of the background and history of his work during the past sixteen months as Trade Union Adviser. Up till the February, 1946, incident, in which Mr. Brazier said he was actively concerned, undoubtedly labour was being organized by the Communist Party as a political weapon. He saw nothing wrong with that, and was not surprised, but he did wish to know what was the purpose behind it. If there was any restriction on the right of free association in this country, it was from Communist controlled associations in this country. He said he had expected it but in Singapore during the first six or seven months, he had carried out his policy with a degree of success.

His policy had been to insulate certain key industries and employees of Public Services, but the G.L.U's next step was infiltration and this was quite cleverly done. The position in Singapore now was worse then in February 1946, as everything now was under the control of the G.L.U. That was not the case in the Malayan Union since the G.L.U. infiltrated there only in July 1946. In the Malayan Union he had carried out the same policy as in Singapore concentrating on large Unions such as the Railways etc., since the country was too large for him to tackle small units. The time had now come when the Trade Unions were asking for protection from the G.L.U. who were block voting at their meetings and generally interfering. The positions in Singapore and Malayan Union were not yet comparable, though it is the policy of the Communist Party to control directly or indirectly all labour in this country in order to embarrass Government. He said it was clear to him now that in Singapore the ground was impossible even for him to work on. His problem now was to stop things happening in the Malayan Union as they had in Singapore. He knew of the list of 21 'bad hats' and what they were working for. Singapore labour is controlled by the Communist Party and firm action was required since it would be unwise to under-estimate the Communist organization. These particular men on the list are the small-fry and it would be very difficult to get the big ones. They know now that Government is going to get tough. In the last six weeks there have been deliberate attempts to resist arbitration etc., Most of these 21 men have anticipated banishment and were probably now in the Malayan Union.

Mr. Brazier went on to say that he had inside information that the Singapore F.T.U. was going out of existence as they now have full control anyhow and the organization was going to be run in the future from Kuala Lumpur. The P.M.F.T.U. office was now in K.L. He was already getting complaints from Trade Unions in the Malayan Union, such as the Electrical Union and the Railway Union, both good Unions, which are being rapidly undermined by the Selangor F.T.U. The problem now was what could be done apart from banishment. The first period had been one of experiment, registration was now over and we should soon know how many Unions wanted to be registered. The policy agreed in the Malayan Union and in principle in Singapore was that we must have an effective inspectorate to see that the provisions of the Trade Union Legislation are complied with. Obviously the G.L.U. would not agree that Mr. Brazier himself was a proper person to advise on the democratic forms of Trade Unionism, but all these Trade Unions have got to be trained in the provisions of the Trade Union Legislation and how to comply with their own rules and regulations. He felt sure that there were a number of Trade Union officials who would attend week-end schools, but he would require one or two extra officers to help him. Sooner or later, the Trade Unions would develop and it was essential to avoid the mistakes made in Ceylon and the West Indian Colonies which had tried to keep the Trade Unions working in a political vacuum. The Trade Unions required our protection and he said that he would be quite ruthless in regard to banishment of dangerous and subversive elements from Singapore, but in the Malayan Union he considered that he would be able to stop the rot.

In the Malayan Union it was considered that by bringing in a Gazette Notification as to how much can be subscribed by way of affiliation fees and by restricting unlawful expenditure, we should be able to exercise control. These affiliation fees should be limited and should not come out of T.U. Provident funds. The F.T.U. must also be compelled to register or take the consequences. It was too late to do this in Singapore, where in any case he thought the F.T.U. would shortly be out of existence. The Singapore F.T.U. got a lot of their money from levies on shop-keepers apart from affiliation fees.

Mr. Brazier stressed that the problems of Singapore and the Malayan Union should be treated separately. . . .

118 CAB 21/1955, F 6151/6151/61 (enclosure) 12 Apr 1947

'South-East Asia: work of the Special Commission during 1946': despatch no 119 from Lord Killearn to Mr Bevin

[Killearn's despatch, received on 6 May, was later printed by the FO for 'secret' circulation.]

Establishment of the Special Commission

I arrived in Singapore on 16th March, 1946, to take up the newly created post of Special Commissioner in South-East Asia. Mr. Scott[1] and Mr. Empson[2] accompanied me as political and economic advisers. Mr. Wright[3] joined me as my deputy on 13th April.

2. Among the reasons which led to the appointment of the mission were the following. Before the war no adequate regional machinery existed for co-ordination between British service and civilian authorities in South-East Asia or for local consideration of British interests throughout the area as a whole. The appointment of Viscount Mountbatten as Supreme Allied Commander, South-East Asia, more than filled this deficiency so long as his command remained in existence. But the South-East Asia Command was already preparing for its termination at the end of 1946. Some alternative was necessary unless there was to be merely a return to the pre-war system of watertight compartments, which had proved inadequate to meet the strain of war. At the same time South-East Asia was threatened with imminent famine owing to the scarcity of supplies of food, in particular of rice, and of the difficulty of re-establishing methods of distribution. For this reason also co-ordinating machinery was required. A further task laid upon the mission was the furnishing of political advice to the Supreme Allied Commander during the last phase of his work.

3. Simultaneously it was decided to appoint a Governor-General, who would be concerned with the general supervision and co-ordination of policy in Malaya and the British Borneo territories.

Directives of the special commissioner

4. The directives of the Special Commissioner were in general terms to advise His Majesty's Government and the local colonial Governments on problems concerned with Foreign Affairs in South-East Asia; to take all possible steps for the alleviation of the food crisis by the increase of food production in producing areas, and the final distribution to deficit areas of the food produced; and to examine the co-ordination of economic machinery in the area.

5. For this purpose the term "South-East Asia" was defined as comprising Burma, Ceylon, Malaya, Borneo, French Indo-China, Siam, Netherlands East Indies and Hong Kong; with close liaison with the Government of India, and the maintenance of close contact with Dominion representatives at Singapore and with the United

---

[1] Released from internment, Robert H Scott served on Killearn's staff until 1948 when he was transferred to the FO.

[2] Charles Empson, minister (economic) Special Commission in SE Asia, 1946–1947; previously commercial counsellor, Cairo, 1939–1946.

[3] Michael Wright, Special Commission SE Asia, 1946–1947; previously served in Cairo, 1940–1943, and Washington, 1943–1946.

Kingdom High Commissioners in Australia and New Zealand.

6. The Special Commissioner was, therefore, entrusted with wide responsibilities, but with no executive authority.

Co-operation with the governor-general and with the services

7. In my despatch No. 32 of 25th January, 1947, I tried to express something of my appreciation and gratitude for the help and encouragement given to the mission by Viscount Mountbatten and his staff. During the period of military administration in South-East Asia the political and economic reconstruction of the area had been started under his direction. Without the knowledge and experience of himself and of his staff, and without their unfailing and generous assistance, the problems encountered by the mission at the outset would have proved insurmountable.

8. I wish here to express my equally warm appreciation and gratitude to the Governor-General. Progress inevitably depends upon day-to-day collaboration between the Governor-General, the services and the Special Commissioner. Mr. MacDonald's support has been unstinting.

9. It was obvious that the necessary degree of co-operation could only be achieved if the offices of the respective authorities concerned and of their staffs were adjoining. Adjacent floors of the Cathay Building were accordingly secured for this purpose. So long as the Supreme Allied Command remained in being a system of joint and interlocking committees was devised, and the integration of the work of the Supreme Allied Command and of the Special Commissioner's Offices was developed to a high pitch. It was recognised that virtually every problem in South-East Asia had both a service and a civilian aspect, and they were treated accordingly.

10. The Supreme Allied Commander, the Governor-General and the Special Commissioner all represented to London in the strongest terms the desirability of maintaining a Supreme Allied Commander in peace-time. This combined recommendation was not, however, accepted. After the termination of the Supreme Allied Command the British Defence Committee in South-East Asia included the commanders-in-chief of the three services in addition to the Governor-General and the Special Commissioner. Under this main committee an attempt has been made to set up machinery which will minimise the formidable difficulties of maintaining co-ordination between the services and the civilian authorities, and of obtaining joint recommendations and decisions, after the reversion to the system of three separate and independent service commanders. A Joint Inter-Service Secretariat has been established which works side by side with the offices of the Governor-General and the Special Commissioner, and parallel machinery for the co-ordination of service and civilian intelligence has been established in the same building. The Joint Intelligence Committee, Far East, for which the Special Commissioner provides the chairman, meets once a fortnight.

11. A Political Committee was also created, consisting of the Governor-General and the Special Commissioner, to consider all matters of common concern to both, and this committee has an economic sub-committee consisting of the Economic Adviser to the Governor-General and the Economic Counsellor to the Special Commissioner.

Food

12. I reported fully in my despatch No. 32 of 24th August, 1946, on the activities

of this mission as regards the food situation and the various measures taken to alleviate it up to the end of July 1946. The following paragraphs contain a recapitulation of the work accomplished during that period and a brief account of the main developments on the food front for the remainder of the year, on which I have reported separately in my despatches Nos. 53, 82 and 115 of 1946, and No. 35 of 1947.

13. On arrival in Singapore I found that I was expected to take over from the Supreme Commander the co-ordination of all economic functions hitherto exercised by him (distribution of food, transportation, coal supplies, economic intelligence, &c.), which he could not pass to any one individual Governor. Thanks to his co-operation and assistance we were able to do this without any major dislocation occurring, although staffing difficulties and accommodation problems hampered us in our work in the beginning stages.

Short term

14. My first preoccupation was to get to grips with the food situation in South-East Asia and to help in the fair distribution of rice supplies in this area in accordance with the allocations made by the Combined Food Board (later superseded by the International Emergency Food Council) in Washington. After three and a half years of enemy occupation and the dislocation caused to the food supplies of the whole area first by Japanese depredations and then finally by the suddenness of the enemy surrender, rice deficit territories in South-East Asia were on the brink of starvation.

15. Of the rice exporting countries Burma had been fought over and ravaged for two years and the acreage under food cultivation had accordingly suffered very severely. French Indo-China was in a state of political upheaval strongly prejudicial to the production of rice. Siam alone had preserved her territory almost unscathed throughout the war; yet even in her case the peace terms imposed upon the Siamese Government, the cupidity of the Chinese rice merchants and other internal factors had an adverse effect on the procurement of rice.

16. Thus from a pre-war combined total of rice available for export from Burma, Siam and French Indo-China of 6 million tons a year the prospects of the exportable surplus from these three countries for 1946 had sunk to less than 2 million tons. After deducting the shares allocated by the International Board to India, China and other claimants outside South-East Asia, there was very little left on which to keep the peoples of Borneo, Ceylon, Hong Kong, Malaya and the Allied controlled areas in the Netherlands East Indies fed above starvation level. Before the war India alone imported on an average about $1\frac{1}{2}$ million tons of rice a year and China half a million or more. Malaya and Ceylon, too, imported on an average over half a million tons each. Moreover, the populations of India and China, if not of the other territories in the Far East, were increasing at an alarming rate so that there was the constant problem to be faced of more mouths to feed that before the war with far less food available to do it.

17. There was, therefore, a compelling urgency to tackle the problem at its roots and to devise ways and means of averting widespread starvation and malnutrition through the deficit territories of South-East Asia. My first task was to call two food conferences in Singapore: the first in March at a technical level, and the second in April, a high level conference which was attended by the Governors of all the British

territories concerned, and the Supreme Allied Commander in person. At these conferences plans were made for concerted action in regard to increased production and controlled consumption of foodstuffs. I also flew personally to Bangkok on 29th April, as His Majesty's Minister at Bangkok had been unable to attend the main Food Conference of Governors, and conferred with the Siamese Prime Minister, who expressed his determination to see that the maximum quantity of rice was shipped from Siam.

18.   To follow up the lines of action laid down at the main food conferences it was decided that I should call monthly meetings in Singapore of representatives of all the territories with which I was concerned, British and foreign, who would act generally as "liaison officers" with this mission. These meetings have since been held regularly under the chairmanship of Mr. Empson. I think I may say that they have not only proved successful in their primary duty, namely, fair distribution of the available rice supplies of South-East Asia in accordance with the international allocations, but have also provided a valuable forum for the solution of food and connected problems confronting the various territories in the area.

19.   A Special Food Drive Committee for Malaya met at the end of May and made a number of practical recommendations for increasing food production and regulating food consumption in Malaya. Many of the committee's recommendations have since been acted upon in the Malayan Union and Singapore.

20.   *Nutrition Conference.*—Closely allied with the provision of food was the problem of safeguarding the peoples' health in South-East Asia through adequate and scientifically balanced diets. A Nutrition Conference was therefore convened between 13th–16th May at which delegates were present from Australia, Burma, British Borneo, Ceylon, French Indo-China, Hong Kong, India and Malaya to discuss methods of warding off malnutrition and educating the public generally to supplement their meagre cereal rations with wholesome substitute food-stuffs which would bring the calorie content of their diet to a level sufficient to keep them in good health. In this way the foundations were laid for immediate action in the event of a threat of localised or widespread malnutrition or famine due to failure of or further serious decline in staple food supplies. At the conference various far-reaching recommendations were made many of which have borne fruit.

I.E.F.C. Sub-Committee

21.   In October the arrangements for distribution of South-East Asia rice operated by this mission were brought within the direct orbit of the I.E.F.C. with the appointment of an I.E.F.C. sub-committee on rice in Singapore, consisting initially of delegates from China, French Indo-China, India, Netherlands East Indies, Philippines, the United Kingdom and the United States and later in the year of a delegate from Burma who was granted full voting rights. At the first meeting on 22nd October, Mr. Empson was elected chairman of the sub-committee for a year and at the request of the sub-committee the organisation for rice distribution already operated by me was put at their disposal. Mrs. Russell, Cereals and Rice Assistant to this mission, was appointed acting secretary. Meetings of the sub-committee were by common consent arranged to take place immediately after the monthly liaison officers' meetings so that the programme for rice shipments prepared at these meetings might conveniently be reviewed by the sub-committee and approved or amended as necessary.

22. Throughout the year we had to suffer many bitter disappointments in the fight against famine. On many occasions with the availabilities of rice at our disposal for distribution it was touch and go whether even the pitifully small rations could be maintained on which the population were then existing. In October, for instance, we touched our lowest depth when we were only able to arrange a supply programme on a basis of 55 per cent. of the I.E.F.C. allocation. In December the situation was temporarily restored and improved supplies from Burma and Siam made it possible for us to raise the entitlement for the second half of 1946 to 83 per cent, of the I.E.F.C. allocations. No territory in South-East Asia, however, was able to increase its total average cereal ration beyond 9 oz. per head per day or 5 oz. of rice during the second half of the year and some territories (e.g., Malaya and North Borneo) went well below that for their rationed populations. An average cereal ration of 12 oz. is generally speaking considered just sufficient to keep the population in reasonable health, so that during the year the gap between theory and practice remained all too great.

Long term
23. It was reasonably clear from the outset that the dislocation caused by the war to rice production in South-East Asia would be of lengthy duration and that even a return to normal pre-war production, when it eventually came, would not solve the problem of feeding a constantly increasing population. Apart therefore from the principal exporting territories, Burma, Siam and French Indo-China, which are doing everything possible to return and even expand normal production, importing territories were also asked to consider with every sense of urgency the question of long-term food production and whether they could increase the land under cultivation with a view to relying less on outside imports of food. I repeatedly stressed to governors the importance of increased internal food yields and drew their attention to the various factors contributing to the critical food situation in 1946 and, as I saw it, in the years to come. There was, indeed, a general awareness of what lay ahead and a readiness to take all possible measures to deal with the problem. That there were large additional tracts of land in South-East Asia which might be brought under cultivation was never questioned, and it was only shortage of equipment, man-power and financial and technical resources that prevented any appreciable expansion of cultivation in 1946. There are, however, prospects of increased cultivation in importing territories in 1947–50, particularly in Malaya and Borneo, although labour shortage will continue to present serious difficulties.

Advisers
24. When I left Cairo I had with me Dr. Clyde as principal adviser on food matters and Major-General Russell joined me in India to advise on all matters connected with transport. I also acquired from headquarters, S.A.C.S.E.A., in April the services of a technical coal adviser, Lieutenant-Colonel Day. Later Mr. F.W. South joined the mission as agricultural adviser and Dr. Lucius Nicholls as nutrition adviser. In September Dr. and Mrs. Bentley and Mr. Gracie, disinfestation advisers, arrived to look into the very serious question of the destruction and deterioration of padi and also of rice and flour stocks in South-East Asia territories caused by rats and insect pests. And in October a statistical expert, Miss E. Tanburn, was appointed.
25. The personal help and advice of these advisers have at all time been freely and unreservedly at the disposal of all territories concerned.

Economic Intelligence Section

26. In May I took over from the Supreme Allied Commander the functions of co-ordinating economic intelligence throughout the area and established in my mission an Economic Intelligence Section headed by Lieutenant-Colonel Kerr, who had been performing the same duties at headquarters, S.A.C.S.E.A. Among the various other duties carried out by this section (such as the general dissemination of economic intelligence) was the production of a monthly *Economic Bulletin*, the first issue of which was published in September and which was designed primarily to keep local territories informed of each other's economic position and to give a comprehensive picture of the economic activities of the area. The *Bulletin* proved to be a success and was much appreciated by the recipients in South-East Asia for the information and statistical tables which it contained. Delegates to the Liaison Officers' Conference were asked at each meeting for contributions and for any ideas they might have with a view to improving it.

South-East Asia Freight Movement Committee

27. A further commitment which I took over from the Supreme Commander soon after my arrival as the result of the general reversion to civil administration in South-East Asia was the Freight Movement Committee set up in accordance with a Cabinet Office instruction to ensure the most economic use of shipping in this area and to establish priorities for all types of cargoes, according to availabilities of shipping space, being carried between United Kingdom, Indian, Middle East and South-East Asia ports. In course of time relaxation of control of ports became possible as their loading and unloading capacity increased (e.g., Rangoon and Hong Kong) and a number of foreign ports (i.e., Saigon, Bangkok and Batavia) reverted to their own Government control. During the last quarter of the year the committee was only controlling cargoes coming into and leaving the ports of Singapore, Port Swettenham and Penang. Although all types of cargo came under the jurisdiction of the committee, the setting up of ships to carry out the rice shipping programmes agreed by the liaison officers' meetings and later by the I.E.F.C. Sub-Committee covered a large part of its activities.

Transportation

28. The proper organisation of transport of all kinds, particularly rail and sea transport, and the rehabilitation of ports were of course essential to the smooth distribution and marshalling of food supplies and more generally to the economic reconstruction of the territories in South-East Asia. In addition to the activities of the South-East Asia Freight Movement Committee in all matters connected with sea transport the expert advice of my transport adviser, who had had great experience of this work as D.Q.M.G. (movements and transportation) in India, was constantly at the disposal of territories. Heavy-lift ships were in continuous use throughout the year bringing locomotives, rolling stock, tugs, &c., to Borneo, Burma, Malaya and Siam to assist in the rehabilitation of these countries and to expedite the assemblage and transportation of badly needed rice.

Coal

29. The distribution of coal supplies throughout the area was another commitment which I took over from the Supreme Commander. It was decided that such

distribution could best be discussed and agreed on by the delegates from the various territories at the monthly liaison officers' meetings.

30.   The part that coal, already in world short supply, was destined to play in the rehabilitation of South-East Asia and in the working of essential transport services made the continued planned control of available supplies a paramount necessity. This mission accordingly undertook to assemble demands for coal from Burma, Hong Kong, Malaya, and later the Netherlands East Indies. Long-term forecasts of requirements on a six months' basis were submitted to us by these territories, and after deducting quantities available to us within South-East Asia we tried to make good our deficiencies from India in the first place and the London Coal Committee, which dealt with supplies from Canada, South Africa and the United States, in the second place. Our provisional programmes of shipments were then tabled at the liaison officers' meetings.

31.   Throughout the year our supplies for all purposes were extremely thin, and on several occasions we had only one or two days' supply available for bunkering ships at our major ports. Fortunately, however, we managed to survive every threatened crisis, and no instance actually occurred of any ship being refused bunkers due to lack of coal. Strikes, both in the Malayan Union collieries and in the United States, added to our difficulties, however, and made an already precarious situation even more precarious. Meanwhile, in view of the acute world coal shortage, the possibilities of increasing indigenous coal supplies from resources within the area were being urgently explored, but lack of machinery prevented further exploitation and development of known resources. Prospects of increasing local production will, of course, improve as mining equipment and machinery become available from the United Kingdom.

Health Intelligence Section
32.   On 7th May 1946, I took over from the Supreme Allied Commander the Health Intelligence Section which had been set up within the Medical Section of his headquarters. This section was created to carry out work which before the war was undertaken by the Far Eastern Bureau of the League of Nations; and to meet an urgent need resulting from the large-scale movements of displaced persons and high incidence of infectious diseases throughout the area which were an aftermath of war. Its main function is the collection and dissemination of information regarding the major infectious diseases throughout the sea and air ports of the Far Eastern area. Reports of outbreaks of infectious diseases are received by weekly cables and by returns and quarantine notes; from these reports tables of epidemiological information are compiled and sent to the chief health authorities of the Far Eastern countries, London, Paris, Washington and Alexandria. In addition, in order to ensure early dissemination of vital information broadcast services have been arranged through the R.N. W/T Station, Krangi, over a network which included Labuan, Saigon, Shanghai, Hong Kong and Tokyo. It has been agreed that on 1st April, 1947, the Health Intelligence Section will be taken over by the newly formed World Health Organisation.

Visits
33.   On my way to Singapore in March I visited the Viceroy at Delhi and the Governor of Burma. In April I spent a few days at Bangkok as the guest of the

Siamese Government. In June I visited Nanking on the invitation of Dr. T.V. Soong, and Hong Kong at the invitation of the Governor. On 4th July I represented His Majesty's Government in Manila at the proclamation of Philippine Independence. I had accepted an invitation from the High Commissioner, Admiral D'Argenlieu, to visit Saigon in September. As I was prevented from leaving by an infected foot, Mr. Wright represented me. Mr. Wright also paid a visit to Bangkok and to Sumatra, and two visits to Rangoon. Other members of the staff have repeatedly visited neighbouring territories. Between September and the end of November I was almost continuously in Batavia with Mr. Wright for the political negotiations.

Political

34.   Up to the end of the year a large proportion of the work of the mission was concerned with advice to the Supreme Allied Commander on political aspects of the last phase of South-East Asia Command. These particularly affected the Netherlands East Indies, French Indo-China and Siam.

Netherlands East Indies

35.   When I arrived in Singapore in March, Lord Inverchapel was on the point of leaving South-East Asia for The Hague with the Dutch and Indonesian representatives to discuss the tentative proposals which had been worked out in Batavia for a political agreement between the Dutch and the Indonesians. Lord Inverchapel proceeded shortly afterwards to take up his appointment as His Majesty's Ambassador at Washington and I was instructed to take over his responsibilities as regards the Netherlands East Indies.

36.   No decision was reached at The Hague upon the March proposals and, with the disappointment of the hopes which had been aroused, tension between the Dutch and the Indonesians increased. Meanwhile the Supreme Allied Commander was proceeding with the task of disarming and repatriating Japanese surrendered personnel and rescuing Allied prisoners of war and internees. It had been anticipated that shipping to complete the former task would not be available until the end of 1947. But in April General MacArthur made available a sufficient number of liberty ships to enable the operation to be completed by the middle of 1946. An agreement was made with the Indonesian authorities for the progressive evacuation of Allied prisoners of war and internees, and it appeared possible that this second task might be completed by the end of the second or third quarter of 1946. The question, therefore, arose how much longer British forces should remain in Netherlands East Indies.

37.   The decision was eventually taken in August that the last British forces should leave Netherlands East Indies by 30th November, 1946, and the Dutch and the Indonesians were so informed. This decision had a most important bearing on political events, since it became increasingly obvious that unless a political agreement were reached by the time British forces withdrew it would be difficult to prevent the outbreak of general hostilities between the Dutch and the Indonesians.

38.   In May a new Government was formed at The Hague following the holding of general elections, and it was decided to send a Commission-General to Batavia for the resumption of political negotiations. At the end of August I went to Batavia with Mr. Wright and paid a visit of a few hours to Djogjakarta, where I met Mr. Sjahrir and his Cabinet. I urged upon them the importance of their showing themselves on their

side willing and prepared for negotiations with the Commission-General on their arrival, and added that, in my view, the conclusion of the truce was an almost essential prelude to successful talks. The Indonesian Cabinet agreed in principle on both points, and also undertook to proceed with arrangements for the evacuation of Allied prisoners of war and internees which had recently been interrupted.

39.   The Commission-General arrived in Batavia on 18th September, and I went back there again from Singapore on 21st September. The Indonesians at first raised objections (which in Djogjakarta they had agreed to waive) to proceeding with a truce unless the despatch of reinforcements from Holland were halted, and for some time difficult discussions over the truce and over political matters proceeded simultaneously. Both delegations invited me to preside at the first meeting of the political talks, but while the Indonesians desired a British representative to take part at subsequent meetings, the Dutch wished them to be bi-partite. A compromise was reached under which I should preside over periodic formal meetings of the Political Conference, but actual negotiations should take place direct between the two delegations in the intervals between the formal meetings.

40.   On 14th October a truce was signed by the Dutch and Indonesian leaders and myself, and by the Allied Commander-in-Chief.

41.   After many crises and disappointments the political talks were transferred to Linggadjati, near Cheribon, on 12th November (so as to permit of consultation with Dr. Soekarno), and the two delegations there reached agreement on a draft document which was initialled at Batavia on 15th November. It had been hoped to proceed with immediate signature, but the Commission-General found it necessary to return to Holland first. There the Linggadjati Agreement was approved by the Dutch Parliament, but an interpretation was given by Dr. Jonkman, the Minister of Overseas Territories, which the Dutch Government wished the Indonesians to accept. This led to further delays, and it was not until 25th March, 1947, that the agreement was finally signed at Batavia, on the basis that the Indonesians recognised that the Dutch placed the Jonkman interpretation on Linggadjati, but themselves were bound only by their signature of the agreement itself. Meanwhile the last British forces had left the Netherlands East Indies on 30th November.

42.   I wish here to record again my high appreciation of the assistance and support of the Allied Commander-in-Chief, Lieut.-General Mansergh, and of his Chief of Staff, Major-General Forman, during the period leading up to the departure of the last British forces on 30th November.

French Indo-China

43.   It is unnecessary to rehearse here the course of events in French Indo-China during the past year, since this mission was not called upon to participate directly.

44.   What happened in French Indo-China had, of course, a decided influence on what happened elsewhere in this region. Both the Dutch and the Indonesians watched the situation closely, and their respective policies and tactics could not but be affected accordingly. On the other hand, the position in French Indo-China, though superficially similar to that in the Netherlands East Indies, was in many ways quite dissimilar. In the Netherlands East Indies a Government of moderate character, which steadily increased its authority, represented a broad-based national- ist movement covering the whole of Java and Sumatra. In French Indo-China, on the other hand, although the general awakening of a desire for freedom amongst the

peoples of the East had not by-passed the country, there were many factors which weakened the translation of this desire into united and forceful expression; there was the opposition to the Annamites, with their Republican system and the strong Communist leanings of their principal leaders, on the part of the racially different populations of Cambodia and Laos, with their monarchical systems and their irredentist claims against Siam, both of which tended to cause them to look to France for support; there was the fact that the French had, until March 1945, been in a position to maintain their suppressive measures against nationalist movements, which had resulted in the formation of a large number of small and local parties which subsequently had difficulty in combining forces; and there was the artificial division of French Indo-China into two parts, the northern, controlled by the Chinese occupation forces, and the southern, by the British and French. The problem of dealing with nationalist opposition in Indo-China, therefore (although it still remains), constituted an entirely different problem to that in the Netherlands East Indies.

45. Moreover, from the British point of view, our relations with the colonial Power in French Indo-China were not strained, as they were in the Netherlands East Indies by the prolongation of our military responsibility for the occupation, the main body of British occupation forces having been withdrawn from French Indo-China at the beginning of 1946.

46. The attitude of the French authorities in Indo-China has been coloured by their appreciation of the part played by His Majesty's Government in the return of the French to Indo-China (General Gracie[4] [sic] is remembered with particular affection, and Mr. Meiklereid[5] has been most successful in cultivating friendly relations), and they have shown a desire to co-operate with us in all fields. While I have endeavoured to avoid giving the impression of wishing to back the French in a reactionary policy, I have done my best to reciprocate their goodwill with the aim of building up friendly contacts with the French, which it is to be hoped will in due course extend to co-operation with a new State in Indo-China involving some form of French-Asiatic partnership.

Relations with neighbouring foreign countries

47. The Supreme Allied Commander expressed the emphatic view that Malaya was untenable in the event of war with a major Power unless protected by an outer ring of airfields in neighbouring countries, and, indeed, without their active or passive co-operation. In peace-time it is no less necessary that there should be the closest co-operation between British and foreign territories. The view I formed at the outset, and which I still believe to be sound, is that the best method of achieving a solid and durable system of regional co-operation or association is to build up gradually step by step, starting with the practice of working together in technical and practical fields and encouraging more formal association as habit grows.

48. In the case of the Netherlands East Indies a political agreement between the Dutch and the Indonesians was necessary before much progress could be made, but now that Linggadjati has been signed we may hope to make some advance. The seeds have already been sown. In the case of Indo-China I have done my best during the

---

[4] General Douglas Gracey, commander Allied Land Forces, French Indo-China, 1945–1946.

[5] E W Meiklereid, consul-general, Saigon, 1945–1947.

past year to cultivate friendly contacts with the French. If, as there is now a prospect, political negotiations between the French and Indo-Chinese are to be resumed, further progress may become possible here also. In the case of Siam the outstanding progress made is, of course, entirely the reward of the work of His Majesty's Ambassador, Mr. Thompson, to which I should like to pay a special tribute.

49. Apart from individual contacts and exchanges of visits, the holding, firstly, of monthly food liaison conferences in Singapore, and, secondly, of nutrition and fisheries conferences, to be followed soon, I hope, by a social welfare conference, has proved a valuable method of putting our aims into practice. Representatives, European and Asiatic, of all territories concerned have begun to acquire the habit of a common approach to regional problems, and we should foster this development as opportunity offers. Equally valuable in its way is the work of the various special advisers in building up contacts, each in his own field, with the experts in neighbouring countries.

Australia, New Zealand and other regional contacts

50. It has been my warm desire from the outset that His Majesty's Governments in Australia and New Zealand should associate themselves fully with all activities in South-East Asia. The Australian Commissioner for Malaya in Singapore, Mr. Claude Massey, takes part in the work of all committees in Singapore, and his presence and advice have been invaluable. For a number of months a representative of the Department of External Affairs at Canberra, Mr. Henry Stokes, was specially appointed to Singapore for liaison with this mission, and his presence was much appreciated. In the case of the Defence Committee, Mr. Massey attends as an observer.

51. I may add that I am leaving Singapore on 14th April for a visit to Australia and New Zealand at the invitation of those Governments. I hope to be able to explore further while I am there the association of Australia and New Zealand with the problems of South-East Asia.

52. It is also desirable that the United States should be associated as closely as possible with activities in South-East Asia. The United States Consul-General in Singapore attends the monthly Food Liaison Conference as an observer, and close contacts are maintained with him in other matters. It has been represented to the United States Government that it would be of advantage if there were some United States officer in South-East Asia authorised to keep in touch with this mission on the affairs of South-East Asia as a whole, but the State Department have not so far gone beyond explaining the difficulties of arranging this in practice, and suggesting that the United States Ambassador at Bangkok might perhaps be given some special functions on these lines.

53. So long as South-East Asia Command remained in existence, American, Dutch and French service missions and liaison officers were attached to headquarters in Singapore. Following the termination of South-East Asia Command, it is now proposed that such officers, some of whom have a valuable function to perform in maintaining liaison on intelligence and other matters, should be attached to their respective consulates-general in Singapore.

Conclusion

54. I trust that this report has given a sufficiently clear account of the diverse

activities of the commission, of the problems which have arisen and the way in which they have been tackled. Perhaps I may end by quoting an apt sentence from the Secretary of State's speech at the signature of the Anglo-French Treaty at Dunkirk: "I would rather take longer, exercise patience, but design and build well, than I would be impatient and make a mistake."

119   CO 537/2203, no 2   23 Apr 1947
'Special commissioner in South-East Asia': memorandum by M E Dening on the future of the office

Lord Killearn was appointed as Special Commissioner in South East Asia in March 1946—provisionally for a period of two years, which would therefore terminate in March next year. His functions are:—firstly to advise the Secretary of State on problems affecting the conduct of foreign affairs in South East Asia; secondly to cope with food shortages "and related matters"; and thirdly to consider coordination and cooperation between the different territories particularly in economic and social welfare matters.

2. Lord Killearn's organisation is admitted to have been of considerable use and value. Despite the partial failure of sources of rice supplies to meet the allocations by the I.E.F.C., he has by his control of shipping and monthly consultations with representatives of the various territories, been able to ensure an agreed and equitable distribution of food, and of other scarce commodities. On political questions, his work in connexion with the Netherlands-Indonesian dispute contributed greatly to the agreement which was recently signed. So long therefore as the international control of food and conditions of economic scarcity exist, and so long as major political problems are liable to recur in South East Asia, it will remain important to have an organisation on the lines of the Special Commissioner's in Singapore; and some organisation of the kind to deal with economic coordination throughout the area will be of permanent value.

3. There are other important functions which the Special Commissioner's organisation does, or can, perform. It is a focal point for the radiation of British influence throughout South East Asia; and a vital link in the South East Asia Defence Organisation which necessarily raises a number of "foreign" problems. Then there are the plans for a South East Asia Regional Commission, to which impetus was recently given by Dr. Evatt.[1] Singapore has also been recommended as the regional centre for certain international bodies such as the International Health Bureau and the International Labour Office. Finally the Special Commissioner's organisation is a useful adjunct to the newly established Economic Commission for Asia and the Far East.[2]

4. There is clearly a case for the continuance of Lord Killearn's functions in respect of food supplies well into 1948, while some permanent arrangement for coordination in South East Asia is considered desirable. The question then arises

---

[1] Herbert Vere Evatt (1894–1965); attorney-general and minister of External Affairs in the governments of the Australian Labor Party, 1941–1949. On 26 Feb 1947 Evatt had called for a 'regional instrumentality'.
[2] The Economic Commission for Asia and the Far East (ECAFE) was set up by the United Nations on 18 Mar 1947.

whether these functions can be performed more economically than at present. Lord Killearn himself has suggested a number of reductions which will, however, still leave his organisation on the 1st July of this year as shown in the attached list.[3]

5. Further reductions in Lord Killearn's present organisation should be possible, and if the civilian element in Singapore can now live as ordinary citizens, it may be practicable to cut down the considerable administrative staff at present held on Lord Killearn's establishment.

6. There is, however, the possibility of a further economy being effected through the merger of the functions of Lord Killearn and of the Governor-General. Such a merger would depend to a considerable extent upon constitutional developments in Malaya, but it is understood from the Colonial Office that both the title and the functions of the Governor-General are likely to be altered. While there are objections to a British Governor-General exercising functions in respect of foreign territories, if Mr. Macdonald [sic] were to discard this title and assume that of Special Commissioner together with the functions of that office, he would then in fact be a coordinator for both British and foreign territories. In such an event it should be possible, in consultation with the Colonial Office, to effect a considerable economy in staff.

---

[3] Not printed.

---

120   CO 537/2203, no 7   24 Apr 1947

[Special commissioner in South-East Asia]: Treasury note of an inter-departmental meeting with FO and CO

The meeting[1] had before it a note by the Foreign Office, describing the functions and organisation of the Special Commissioner, and drawing attention to the possibility of effecting economies in the latter by merging the Office of Special Commissioner with that of the Governor-General, Malaya (Mr. Malcolm MacDonald). It was agreed that the duties performed by the Special Commissioner were of the highest importance and should on no account be discontinued. On the other hand, Sir Edward Bridges said that even the reduced establishment proposed for July, 1947, (as set out in the Foreign Office note) was unjustifiably large. He therefore saw every advantage in the proposed "merger" and the meeting agreed.

2. The following points emerged in discussion:—

(a) The Foreign Office representatives pointed out that Lord Killearn had been appointed in March, 1946, provisionally for two years. The appointment would not therefore terminate, in any case, until March, 1948. It was agreed that, though the actual merger could not perhaps take place until that date, all possible cutting down of the Special Commissioner's staff and preliminary merging of the two *organisations* should be undertaken in the meanwhile. It was pointed out that the Secretary of State for Foreign Affairs would wish to be assured that the merger would not involve any abandonment of the policy of co-ordinating economic,

---

[1] Present: Sir E Bridges, Sir W Eady and Sir L N Helsby (Treasury); Sir O Sargent and M E Dening (FO); and G F Seel and H T Bourdillon (CO). The FO note referred to is not printed.

political and cultural affairs throughout South-East Asia and other matters at present being undertaken by Lord Killearn, to which he attached great import-ance. It was agreed that these functions would continue in spite of the merger.

(b) It was agreed to recommend that Mr. Malcolm MacDonald should be offered the new combined post. His present appointment extended only until May, 1949, and he would therefore have to be offered a new appointment extending beyond that date. Terms could be agreed between the Foreign Office and the Colonial Office. In his new capacity, Mr. MacDonald would doubtless function with a small "colonial" staff, and a small "diplomatic" staff, working side by side.

(c) The Colonial Office representatives pointed out the relevance of present constitutional developments in Malaya. It was likely that the new Federation of Malaya, replacing the Malayan Union, would come into being in a matter of months. Singapore might be expected to join the Federation later, though possibly not for a year or two. In that event, the Governor-General's duties (which at present consisted largely of co-ordinating policy as between Singapore and the Malayan Union) would become less onerous in that they would only involve co-ordination as between Malaya as a whole on the one hand, and British territories in Borneo on the other. This would make it easier for Mr. MacDonald to take on additional functions, as was now proposed.

(d) The Foreign Office representatives said that there would be political objec-tions to an officer with the title of "Governor-General" exercising the present functions of the Special Commissioner. It was agreed that the title "Special Commissioner", to cover the duties of the combined post, would probably be most suitable (the title "High Commissioner" was ruled out, since this would involve confusion with the High Commissioner for the Federation of Malaya.)

(e) It was agreed that the appointment, in due course, of a successor to Mr. MacDonald should be a matter for consultation and agreement between the Secretary of State for Foreign Affairs and the Secretary of State for the Colonies.

(f) The Colonial Office representatives said that the merger would, incidentally, solve Mr. MacDonald's present accommodation problem. He was now perforce living in Singapore, but if the merger took place he would doubtless be able to take over the residence in Johore Bahru now occupied by Lord Killearn, and this would have the great advantage that he would not be residing in the same place as any of the Governors within his sphere of authority.[2]

(g) It was agreed that Sir E. Bridges would circulate a minute to be agreed with the Foreign Office and the Colonial Office. This would then be submitted to Ministers, and ultimately to the Prime Minister. If the Prime Minister concurred, he thought that Lord Killearn and Mr. Malcolm MacDonald should be informed of the decision as having been reached by H.M.G. When the decision was final an inspector should be sent out to Singapore to examine the position and steps should be taken at once to bring about the merger, which should be completed by March, 1948.[3]

---

[2] Shortage of accommodation for high officials had provoked considerable sparring between them and also with the Sultan of Johore. MacDonald eventually moved into Bukit Serene, one of Ibrahim's palaces.

[3] On 31 May 1947 Attlee agreed to a joint minute from Bevin and Creech Jones proposing the amalgamation of the functions of the two offices under MacDonald when Killearn's term ended in Mar 1948, see CO 537/2203, PM/47/89, 28 May 1947.

121   CO 537/2142, no 97   28 Apr 1947

[Closer association of Malaya and Singapore]: inward telegram no 123 from Mr M J MacDonald to Mr Creech Jones

[The Cheeseman Consultative Committee reported to the governor, Malayan Union, in late Mar and, as regards the possible inclusion of Singapore, recommended no action until such time as Singapore should ask for admission. Document 121 follows up a telegram from MacDonald in which he had reported that the hardening of Malay opinion prevented an early announcement about merger (see CO 537/2141, no 64, 9 Apr 1947). Consequently, on 18 June the secretary of state made a non-committal comment on the issue in reply to a parliamentary question while the White Paper published the next month more or less reiterated the brief statement of intent regarding closer association contained in the White Paper of Jan 1946. See *Federation of Malaya: Summary of Revised Constitutional Proposals* (Cmd 7171, July 1947).]

1. My telegram No. 102.

Governors and I have now considered what you might say in Parliament about the possibility of Singapore joining the Federation of Malaya. Position is as follows:—

2. We believe it desirable that Singapore should be included sooner or later, by mutual agreement, in the Federation. In Gimson's view the sooner this happens the better, and I agree with him, subject to, of course, what is said in paragraph 5 below. There are however difficulties mostly political and economic, which make it necessary that the problem should be handled carefully. In Singapore opinion is freely held that Singapore and the Peninsula cannot properly be administered separately. Propaganda in the Colony in favour of inclusion of Singapore is already considerable and will, no doubt, increase. Singapore leaders in all communities regard the present division as having been imposed on the Colony without its consent and they are becoming increasingly impatient at what they feel to be difficulties contributable to the division. From this point of view the sooner a Government statement is made, proposing means by which the matter can be examined on its merits, the better.

3. On the other hand, general opinion in Malayan Union, on both political and economic grounds, is not attuned to any reversion to the pre-war predominant influence of Singapore in Malayan policy and business, and in Gent's view would require full safeguards against this contingency as condition of agreement to inclusion of Singapore in the Federation. This would, no doubt, mean that Singapore should be federated as one settlement in group of twelve units, but would have as far as concerns local self Government for local settlement of affairs, such constitution as Singapore may desire within the limits of Federal constitution. Gimson reserves his position on this aspect of the problem feeling that Singapore's prestige and outstanding economic importance in South East Asia can be used to great advantage of the Federation, if it is the political capital of the Federation. This is, of course, a matter which can be left for discussion and settlement if and when negotiations take place.

4. The most important political consideration in the Union is the view of the Malays. As you know they look at everything from the point of view of preventing their future position in the government of the Peninsula being swamped by or subordinated to non Malays, particularly the Chinese, either politically or economically and they are nervous at the prospect of the large Chinese population of

Singapore having an increased influence in the Government of their native land. It would be fatal to force this issue against their wishes. However, Malay opinion is not necessarily fixed in the matter. Some sections of non-Malay opinion in the Union are favourable to Singapore joining the Federation on conditions outlined in paragraph 3 above.

5. Our approach to the question needs, therefore, to be cautious and conciliatory. Your statement should be sufficiently encouraging to make such public opinion as is favourable to the inclusion of Singapore in the Federation feel that the Government is ready to have the matter considered on its merits at a reasonably early date. At the same time, it should make it clear that there is no question of forcing a solution on an unwilling Federation. In any case, it would be a mistake for any practical steps to be taken to have the matter actively considered on formal basis before the inauguration of the new Federal constitution and the inauguration of the new constitution in Singapore at the beginning of next year.

6. Cheeseman Committee considered the matter. It was not strictly within their terms of reference, but they received various representations for and against Singapore's inclusion, many of them from Chinese organisations or individuals in the Union favourable to the proposal. They dealt with the matter briefly in their report and in effect made the following suggestions:—

(a) The matter should not be considered unless and until Singapore applies for inclusion in the Federation.

(b) The Federal Council in Kuala Lumpur should then consider this application.

7. (a) above would appear to make Singapore a suppliant. It would seem wiser to propose that either Government can take the initiative in the matter. (b) is open to the criticism that it might mean that the Federal Council could turn down Singapore's supplication out of hand. If proposal for inclusion of Singapore put forward by either party were dismissed without adequate consultation between them friction between the two territories would increase and the prospects of cooperation, let alone of Singapore joining the Federation would be seriously prejudiced. No doubt, in practice, full consultation and negotiation between them would be arranged before any final views were recorded, and this should be expressly assumed in any statement you may make. It will (?group omitted) to be borne in mind that present draft Federation Agreement (Clause 3) requires agreement of the Rulers to admission of additional territories into the Federation.

8. In the light of these considerations, we suggest the following points for statement by you:—

(a) As expressly stated in the White Paper[1] and in Parliament with reference to Union constitution, it is recognised that there were and will be close ties between Singapore and the mainland and it is no part of the policy of His Majesty's Government to preclude or prejudice in any way the fusion of Singapore and Malayan Union in a wider Union at a later date, should it be considered that such a course were desirable.

(b) During the next few months new constitutions are being prepared both for Federation and the States and Settlements of Penang and Malacca and for the

---

[1] *Malayan Union and Singapore: Statement of Policy on Future Constitution* (Cmd 6742, Jan 1946).

Colony of Singapore. It would be mistake for inauguration of any of these to be postponed pending consideration of this other question. The introduction of these constitutions will, nevertheless, be without prejudice to the possibility of the Federation being extended to include Singapore later on.

(c) If at any time after these constitutions have been started either the Federal Government or the Governments of any States or Settlements in the Federation, or the Singapore Government, wishes to propose that Singapore joins the Federation they are free to make such proposals and to request its formal consideration.

(d) It would be a matter for the Governments concerned then to agree upon the appropriate means of examining the proposal. No doubt joint consultation machinery would be devised for necessary negotiations.

(e) We strongly advise that in your statement you should make it clear that the inclusion of Singapore in the Federation would not be decided without the consent of both the Federation and Singapore.

9. If you agree to these general lines we shall prepare a draft statement for your consideration should you desire this. Alternatively, we shall gladly consider any draft that you like to send us.

122   CO 537/2171   5–6 May 1947
[Labour policies in the Malayan Union and Singapore]: minutes by O H Morris and H T Bourdillon

[One aspect of the divergence between the governments of the Malayan Union and Singapore, which had not been resolved at the governor-general's conference on 11 Mar (see 117), was their differing approaches to growing labour unrest. On 10 May, after these minutes by Morris and Bourdillon had been submitted to Creech Jones, a telegram was despatched to MacDonald requesting 'with least possible delay, a report on the co-ordinated policy which it is proposed to pursue in the Malayan Union and Singapore regarding problems of labour unrest in general and the so-called Federation of Trade Unions in particular'. MacDonald replied on 22 May (see 125).]

Mr. Bourdillon
In this minute I attempt to set out some factors in the present labour situation in the Malayan Union and Singapore. I have placed on the files copies of two recent telegrams (Nos. 72 and 73) which are registered on 52754/2—Unrest among Estate Labour, now in urgent circulation, and, at 72a, a group of press cuttings which, with a copy of this minute, should be transferred when convenient to that file.

1. Labour unrest on estates
   (a) *The South Kedah disturbances.* Last autumn there were strikes on a number of rubber estates in Kedah. From 28th February to 3rd March there was an outbreak of violence—in which one Indian labourer was killed—on two estates in South Kedah. The Governor's report—a summary of which has been placed in the Library of the House—is at (20) on 52754/2. Now the Governor reports that on 28th April a crowd of some 300 Chinese and Indian labourers on the Dublin Estate in South Kedah attacked 30 Police who had unsuccessfully tried to restore the position after labourers had intervened to prevent a constable from arresting an agitator—a visitor

not employed on the estate—who was making an inflammatory speech. Seven shots were fired, one labourer was killed and five injured: three Chinese and seven Indians were arrested the following day on a charge of rioting: the situation that morning (29th) was reported quiet, with the labour force at work. Enquiries will be held. The Governor does not connect this incident with the February–March disturbances in Kedah.

(b) *A threatened new strike.* At 72A are three press cuttings which refer to a threatened strike.

(i)   on 240 estates in Selangor, (cutting A)
(ii)   on 250 estates in Perak (cutting C)

The men's leaders in Selangor, at any event, threaten to strike on *10th May* if six demands (including a 100% wage increase) are not met: these were recently rejected by the Estate managers, and the "Central Committee of the Unions concerned" is apparently negotiating now with the United Planting Association of Malaya (A). The Perak leaders are said (C) to have put forward similar demands.

While these reports are not to be neglected, the fact that the Governor has so far given no information on this development suggests that they may be somewhat exaggerated. It is worth adding however that a Representative of the Malayan Indian Congress at Singapore has announced the party's intention to take greater interest in labour disputes in order to convince Trade Unions of its sincere desire to further the cause of Indian workers. (SEALF ISUM No. 261 – (36) on 55217/8/1), while Mr. Chettur[1] is reported as saying after a recent tour of Pahang that Labour unrest was due to the lack of a living wage for Indian workers. There are also some signs of greater cohesion among the planting interests. The implications of a major and prolonged strike in the rubber estates are manifold. There would be great scope for unscrupulous agitators, and risk of incidents such as those in Kedah at the end of February. The Governor is now better equipped to deal with such troubles by:—

(1) the Public Order Ordinance—by which he can take action against drilling and wearing of uniforms.
(2) The Criminal Procedure (Amendment) Ordinance—offence of criminal intimidation made *non-bailable*.
(3) The Societies Ordinance—under which societies may be required to register.
(4) The Trade Unions Ordinance—discussed below.

2. *The Perak hydro-electric strike.*

I have noted briefly the progress of this strike in minutes of 14/4 and 22/4 above. One fifth of the workers were reported back at work on 29th April (SEALF ISUM 261). It is only worth remarking here that any interruption of power transmission (now maintained by Government and Army technicians) to the tin mines would further impede the slow rehabilitation of the industry. (The strike at Batu Arang earlier this year of course affected the supply of coal to tin undertakings dependent on coal.)

3. *Registration of societies, and registration of trade unions.*

With some misgivings, the Governors have been allowed to follow divergent paths in this matter.

---

[1] Representative in Malaya of the government of India.

(a) While the Malayan Union Government enacted a "liberal" measure which:—

(a) allowed Societies to register but did not require them to do so,
(b) empowered Government to require Societies thought to be of an undesirable nature to register,

Singapore has brought back into use the old Societies Ordinance, enacted in 1909, which *requires* Societies to register and prescribes penalties against Societies which do not. Accordingly in Singapore all societies which are still in existence and which were registered or exempted under the Ordinance before 30th April 1941 have to notify the Registrar not later than 15th May of their continued existence: and similarly societies which have changed their names must inform the Registrar. Societies formed since 1st May 1941 have to apply for registration or exemption by 15th May. The question of *societies* registration is not as intimately connected with labour developments as that of *Trade Union* registration. Nevertheless, it is worth noting that something very like a trial of strength seems to be taking place on this issue in Singapore: Mr. Chang Ming Ching, a representative of the Malayan Communist Party, declared recently that "the M.C.P. will not apply for registration unless the Government abolishes the existing Banishment and Sedition Laws" but he added that the M.C.P. would apply for recognition as a legal political organisation (9 on 52241 at p. 3). (The H.Q. of the M.C.P. moved to Kuala Lumpur before Christmas last.)

(b) Distinct from these measures are those requiring *Trade Unions* to register:—

Straits Settlements (now in force in Singapore)	Trade Unions Ordinance, 1940 (No. 3 of 1940)
F.M.S./Malayan Union	Trade Unions Enactment, 1940 (No. 11 of 1940) Trade Unions Ordinance, 1946 (No. 12 of 1946)

These provide for the registration of all Unions by a date to be appointed. Owing to the war, this date was not fixed, until, after the liberation, 1st April and 1st May were appointed in the Malayan Union and Singapore respectively. Unfortunately, on the question of the registration of a *Federation* of Trades Unions, the policies of the two territories again diverge. We learn from the most recent S.E.A.L.F. Intelligence Summary that in "Malaya" (presumably the Malayan Union is meant)

> "Registration of the Federation of Trades Unions (is) to be accepted provided that all Unions represented by the Federation are themselves registered."

The Federation is of course the old G.L.U., now the Pan Malayan Federation of Trades Unions (PMFTU). The history of the registration questions is as follows. On 2nd March the Governor of Singapore reported in a telegram (38 on 52754) of great importance that registration of the Singapore F.T.U. (= G.L.U.) was being refused. The main issue in that telegram was banishment: the Governor of Singapore makes it clear that in his opinion the F.T.U. in Singapore was a subversive body, and a menace to public order. Three days later the Governor of the Malayan Union, who had received a copy of No. 38, joined issue with Sir F. Gimson not only on the subject of banishment, but on registration of the F.T.U. (in its "Pan-Malayan" manifestation) as well (44 on 52754). "[I]t appears to have been decided", he says, "that the F.T.U. cannot be registered as a Trade Union in Singapore, in spite of similar provisions in the F.M.S. and S.S. T.U. Legislation (noted above) enabling the federation of 2 or more Unions to register itself as a Trade Union. Application of the Federation in the Malayan Union is under active discussion by the Registrar of Trades Unions with the Unions concerned, and no similar decision of rejection has been taken in the Malayan Union".

It was hoped (and so the Governors were told, 46 on 52754) that the Governor General's Conference on 11th March would result in some uniform policy: but, as on banishment, no agreement was forthcoming on registration of the Federation. Both Sir E. Gent and Mr. Brazier were of the view that things had not gone so far in the Malayan Union as they had in Singapore, and that much might be achieved by guiding the F.T.U. into legal channels. It seems to be hoped that a careful surveillance over the F.T.U.'s accounts, and over the contributions of member unions—not to exceed 10% of their monthly income per month—would have a salutary effect. It should be interposed here that there are reports, in the press and elsewhere, of one instance at least of sound and co-operative union activity in the case of the State Federations, components of the F.T.U. In the Governor's Conference (the discussion on F.T.U. registration is sidelined on pp. 9, 12 and 13 of the minutes on 52738/2) the divergence is shown as one of legal interpretation, and the Governor General then urged that the respective legal advisers should "get together and see if they could offer combined advice", but it seems clear that the difference is at bottom a fundamental difference of policy.

After the conference, in acceding to Sir F. Gimson's request for powers of banishment without prior reference to the Secretary of State, the Secretary of State asked again (tel. to the Governor General, 54–6 on 52754) "for an early indication of the co-ordinated policy which it is proposed to pursue in the two territories regarding problems of Labour unrest in general and the so-called F.T.U. in particular. I can readily understand that exactly similar procedure in the Malayan Union and in Singapore is neither necessary nor desirable, but I regard it as essential that there should be no fundamental divergence of policy"—and the telegram went on to refer to the paragraph of Sir E. Gent's telegram of 5th March which I have quoted above (44 on 52754).

However, the Governor of Singapore declared at a press conference on 15th March ("Straits Budget" 20th March p. 13): "Government is determined to take firm action against any organisation which has not brought itself within the law"—by 1st May: and presumably in Singapore the F.T.U. will now be illegal, while in the peninsula— the P.M.F.T.U. H.Q. moved to Kuala Lumpur early this year—it will be registered and legal. The danger is, of course, that the G.L.U. will now operate "underground" in Singapore from its Kuala Lumpur H.Q.

Thus in 3 cases, all more or less closely connected with labour unrest, policies in Singapore and the Malayan Union diverge: banishment, societies registration, and Trade Union registration. In every case Sir F. Gimson and Sir E. Gent have pointed to reasons, undoubtedly valid, which call for differing treatment in the two territories, and the point has been conceded by the Secretary of State that uniformity, though desirable, is not absolutely essential. Advantage was taken of a despatch to the Governor General (71), in reply to a petition from a group of European employers of estate labour, to call a third time for

"an indication of the co-ordinated policy regarding labour unrest which it is
intended to pursue in the Malayan Union and Singapore".

but it may be that the position is serious enough to send yet another reminder. What
we should want to know is, firstly, whether there is any prospect of a satisfactory
wages policy: this will depend largely on the success of the attempts now being made
to settle the salaries of government employees, whether European or Asiatic, and
involves (probably) as a corollary a satisfactory cost of living index. (It is of course
true that stable wages and prices are difficult to achieve in a country so dependent on
imported food and consumer goods.) Again, the progress which has been made in
setting up and operating a Joint Advisory Board for Labour should be known: in
Singapore, there are press reports of a vigorous start to their Advisory Board, which
is to tackle the outstanding tasks of revising the Labour Code and preparing a
Factories Ordinance. Lastly, we should, I think, wish to know whether the
development of sound Unionism in Singapore can proceed with the G.L.U., under
whatever name, established in Kuala Lumpur but "underground" in the Colony. I
submit a draft telegram[2] which should, I think, go to the Governor-General, and not
(as we thought on first impression) to Sir E. Gent.

O.H.M.
5.5.47

I have already stated, in submitting the file about labour unrest in Kedah, that Mr.
Morris was undertaking a general review of the labour situation in the Malayan
Union and Singapore. The result is to be seen in the immediately preceding minute,
which seems to me to be a particularly useful piece of work.

I do not think we can be entirely satisfied with the position as revealed. As Mr.
Morris has recalled, the Secretary of State has acquiesced in the pursuit of different
policies in the two territories both as regards Societies Legislation and as regards
recourse to banishment. It now appears (though we cannot say for certain) that we
are faced with a similar divergence in a third related matter—the registration of the
so-called "Federation of Trade Unions" (alias the General Labour Union) as a Trade
Union. There is no reason why the policies of the two Governments should in all
respects be identical, and it is quite possible, *provided* the whole thing has been
thoroughly thrashed out and co-ordinated, that variations in the treatment of the
"Federation of Trade Unions", as between the two territories, are justified and even
demanded. Unfortunately, we are not in a position to say whether this co-ordination
has taken place. When the Secretary of State asked the Governor General (in No. 54
on this file) for an early indication of the co-ordinated policy to be pursued in the two
territories, he had in mind this particular question of the treatment of the Federation
of Trade Unions. There has been no reply to that telegram, which was sent six weeks
ago, and we have been left to glean such information as we can from information
summaries and minutes of conferences.

There is another feature in the present situation which I find very obscure. During
March, the Governor of Singapore sent us, with the Governor-General's support and
with every indication of extreme urgency, a request that he should be allowed to use
his powers of banishment more freely. The representations were very strong, and

---

[2] Not printed.

were promptly acceded to by the Secretary of State (in the telegram at No. 54 on the file, to which I have already referred). Thereupon, the governor sent us (in No. 61) the draft of a long statement which he proposed to make whenever he decided to take banishment action in accordance with the permission now granted him. Our comments on this draft statement were sent over a month ago (see No. 62), but since then we have heard nothing. We have not been told that banishment action has been taken, but on the other hand we have not been told that the situation has improved. In view of the almost sensational urgency of the Governor's original requests (see Nos. 38 and 52), I find this silence a little mystifying.

I do not think we can allow this matter to rest. The labour situation both in the Malayan Union and in Singapore is explosive. There was a fresh incident on a Kedah estate at the end of last month (see No. 72 and 73), and there has been press reports (No. 72A) of threatened rubber strikes on a very wide scale. The "Federation of Trade Unions" lurks, or is reported to lurk, at the back of all these troubles, and the Secretary of State therefore has every right to assure himself that a co-ordinated policy is being pursued, and to know what that policy is. It is true that one reminder has already been sent (in the last paragraph of No. 71), but that reminder was in very general terms and was at the end of a despatch on different, though related matters. I hope it will be found possible to telegraph to the Governor-General on the lines of the attached draft.

H.T.B.
6.5.47

123   CO 537/2142, no 103   11 May 1947
[Federation proposals]: despatch no 119 from Sir E Gent to Mr Creech Jones

[The first seven paragraphs provide background to the Cheeseman Consultative Committee, whose report was published on 31 Mar and discussed by various Anglo-Malay bodies in Apr. On 11 May, having spent 'my days and nights' on preparing the material for London, Gent completed two despatches: a long confidential one (reproduced here) containing detailed constitutional proposals, and a shorter secret one providing a gloss on aspects of the other (124). In a covering letter to Bourdillon dated 10 May, he stressed that 'if H.M.G. can bring themselves to agree with the recommendations I am putting in, we may build a solid British core surrounded by an anti-British China, India and Indonesia, with a tolerably free trade for the Indians, Chinese and Americans to make their money here (and we shall take some of it from them in the process) and I have little doubt that it will accrue to British influence and British trade if we keep the friendship of the Malays.' Gent's two despatches were followed up on 29 May by a telegram from MacDonald (126) and answered by the secretary of state on 11 June (127).]

I have the honour to submit to you my report on the outcome of the discussions on the Constitutional Proposals which were contained in the draft Federation of Malaya Agreement and the model State Agreement.

2. The report of the Constitutional Working Committee in December 1946 which contained those proposed forms of Agreement was published in Malaya on the 24th December, 1946 under cover of a Note in the following terms:—

"Today there is published for the consideration of all interested people in

Malaya a report containing fresh constitutional proposals for the territories in the Malayan Union.

These proposals have been submitted for scrutiny by His Majesty's Government with the result that the Secretary of State has stated that their essential features appear to His Majesty's Government to be calculated to achieve those fundamental objectives in Malaya for which His Majesty's Government have always striven, namely, the establishment of a strong central government with control over all matters of importance to the progress and welfare of the country as a whole and the creation of a form of citizenship which will be extended to all those who regard Malaya as their real home and the object of their loyalty.

But His Majesty's Government have declared that there can be no question of their reaching any final decisions on any matters involved until all the interested communities in Malaya have had full and free opportunity of expressing their views. The conditional approval expressed by His Majesty's Government has reference only to the present proposals as such—that is, the draft Federation Agreement with its schedules and the model State Agreement and is not to be regarded as extending to all the recommendations in the Working Committee's report, many of which are of a long-term character and will require detailed consideration at the appropriate time.

His Majesty's Government must also reserve all judgment on State Constitutions until detailed proposals are available for their consideration."

3. In order to implement the intention of His Majesty's Government that all interested communities in Malaya should have full and free opportunity of expressing their views before His Majesty's Government reached any final decisions, I appointed a Consultative Committee with the following terms of reference:—

"To invite the opinion of all interested individuals, communities and groups in Malaya on the Constitutional Proposals which have been published as a result of consultation between the Government and Malay representatives; to hold such public or private sessions as may be necessary to give the fullest opportunity of expressing their views, whether orally or in writing, in accordance with the undertaking given by His Majesty's Government: and to collate the views so expressed and to report their substance to the Governor of the Malayan Union for consideration in the Advisory Council with such comments and recommendations as the Committee may see fit."

4. The Committee was comprised of 4 representative Members of the Advisory Council and 4 other gentlemen chosen from the principal non-Malay communities who were not themselves Members of the Advisory Council, and I nominated also Mr. H.A.R. Cheeseman, C.M.G., Director of Education, whom the Committee then proceeded to appoint as their Chairman.

5. The report of this Committee was published on the 31st March, 1947, and laid on the table of the Advisory Council on that date. On the 10th April the Advisory Council debated the report on the following resolution:—

"That this Council records its appreciation of the work of the Consultative Committee on the Constitutional Proposals for Malaya and, being of opinion that the pledge of His Majesty's Government that all interested communities in Malaya should have a full and free opportunity of expressing their views has thus been fulfilled,

RESOLVES that the Report of the Consultative Committee be transmitted to the Secretary of State and to Their Highnesses the Malay Rulers for their consideration."

The resolution received the unanimous approval of the Council.

6. Since the original draft Agreements had resulted from discussions between representatives of the Government, of the United Malays National Organisation, and Their Highnesses the Rulers, and Their Highnesses would be signatories to the Agreements in the terms to be finally settled, a further meeting of the Constitutional Working Committee and of the Plenary Conference, in the latter of which Their Highnesses themselves and the Governor-General took part, was convened to consider proposed amendments of the draft Federation Agreement and the model State Agreement. The Constitutional Working Committee accordingly reassembled on the 17th of April and presented its report to the Plenary Conference on the 24th of April. A copy of the report is annexed to this despatch.[1]

7. It is recommended that certain modifications should be made in the draft Agreements, and the full list of these is appended to the Annex to this despatch. Some of these amendments are more important than others and I propose in the following paragraphs of this despatch to discuss seriatim those which are of substantial importance.

References in this despatch to the clauses of the draft Federation Agreement are references to the clauses as numbered in the printed Report of the Working Committee of December, 1946.

8. *Additional recital in the federation agreement*

The Plenary Conference recommended that to the opening recitals in the draft Federation Agreement there should be added a further recital which should set out the intentions of His Majesty the King and Their Highnesses the Rulers to provide for eventual self-government of the Federation of Malaya and that, as a first step to that end, they had agreed that, as soon as circumstances and local conditions permitted, legislation should be introduced for the election of members to the several legislatures to be established in pursuance of the Federation Agreement. This expressed declaration is designed to meet certain sections of opinion which have criticised the proposed constitutional arrangements on the ground that the draft Agreement contains no sufficient expression of purpose to promote democratic development towards self-government on the lines of election of representatives to the legislatures.

9. *Federal Executive Council*

An increase of Unofficial membership from 5 to 7 as recommended by the Consultative Committee was acceptable to the Plenary Conference, but they recommend that the numbers should be expressed as not less than 5 or more than 7, and they consider that, if in fact more than 5 Unofficial Members are appointed to the Executive Council, there should be an increase in the Malay Unofficial membership to not less than 3. This condition follows upon the proposal in the December report of the Working Committee that, in a Council comprising 5 Unofficial Members, not

---

[1] Annexes not printed.

less than 2 should be Malays. If, as I recommend, the present amended provision for Unofficial membership is adopted by His Majesty's Government, it would be reasonable that there should be not less than 3 Malay Unofficial Members.

10. *Legislative Council*

The changes in the Federation Agreement in the matter of the composition of the Legislative Council, which have been proposed by the Consultative Committee and in the main adopted by the Plenary Conference, raise issues of the first importance to all communities in Malaya and to none more than the Malays themselves. The social, economic and political life of Malaya is unquestionably based in the present phase on racial alignments, and in this phase any scheme of composition of the Legislative Council, which could claim to have a representative character, in whatever degree, must necessarily reflect this racial consciousness. To the Malays who comprise much the largest racial group of those who can claim Malaya as their motherland, the picture presents itself principally as one in which they are faced with the risk of being outnumbered in their own country by immigrant peoples and thus eventually ousted from political control in the internal affairs of the country and falling into impoverishment in the face of economic competition from the ever increasing numbers of the immigrant races with their greater resources, more highly developed organisatiion, and higher standard of technical skill.

11. In the inauguration, therefore, of democratic institutions in Malaya on a pan-Malayan basis, it is natural that the Malays should insist that their undoubted position as the largest group of people in Malaya whose homes and loyalties are, and can be nowhere else than, in this country should be reflected in the composition of the Legislative Council. Many political and economic questions of first-rate importance which will face the legislature from the beginning, such as immigration policy and the enactment of an electoral law, serve to stress in the Malay view the vital importance to them of agreeing only to a constitutional scheme for Federation which will accord to them security against the risk of being outvoted in the legislature, apart from the *ex-officio* and Official vote.

12. It is to be hoped that in years to come the course of social and economic developments in Malaya may tend to weaken and lower the racial barriers which are so apparent in the present phase, and it is right to search for any supplementary system of representation which can be encouraged as a factor, already existing to some extent and likely to grow in the future, and serving to qualify a purely racial system of representation. In the December report of the Constitutional Working Committee and also in the report of the Consultative Committee and now in the current recommendations of the Plenary Conference, such a supplementary system is shown to exist on a functional or occupational basis, but in the recommendations which I make for the consideration of His Majesty's Government in this vital matter, I must explain that in this phase the composition of the Council will in fact be judged by the racial representation which it provides and that any adjustments of functional representation will necessarily be judged from the point of view of any racial redistribution which such adjustments entail.

13. The Malay claim in respect of their representation in the Legislative Council is justified on the ground of their considerable numerical superiority in the domiciled population of Malaya. The estimated population figures of 1941 were as follows for the whole country excluding Singapore:—

Malays	2,199,931
Chinese	1,781,333
Indians	684,364
Europeans	16,181
Eurasians	11,009
Others	48,909
Total	4,741,727

Some dislocation has taken place during the war but it has not been possible to frame any useful estimate of the immediate post-war population figures. A census, as you are aware, is to be held this year but it is unlikely that even preliminary figures sufficiently precise will be available before decisions have to be reached on the present constitutional proposals. It is unlikely, however, that there has been any such considerable change in the population ratios as to affect materially the immediate pre-war picture. But the above figures relate to the total resident population and it will be borne in mind that an element, and probably a considerable element, of the non-Malay communities are not domiciled in the country and could not reasonably claim to qualify for Citizenship. So far as it has been possible to form any opinion of the extent to which the immigrant communities will qualify for, or desire, Malayan Citizenship, it appears likely that a very considerable percentage would not so qualify, and it is also thought likely that a considerable number of Chinese, Indians, and Ceylonese will choose not to risk any form of disqualification in the country of their, or their parents', origin by committing themselves to a declaration of permanent settlement in Malaya. It is safe, therefore, to assume that the Malays' claim to a substantial majority position in Malaya is justified.

It is significant that in the last complete census in 1931 the Malays born and resident in the territories now forming the Malayan Union outnumbered the combined Chinese and Indians locally born and resident by more than 3 to 1.

14. Before considering in any detail the composition of the Legislative Council it is desirable to deal with the position of the 11 State and Settlement representatives for whom provision was included in the December report of the Constitutional Working Committee and accepted by the Consultative Committee. The latter Committee, however, met the criticism that this group could not properly be deemed an Unofficial group in the ordinary sense by transferring the 9 State representatives to the category of Official Members. This classification however is also incorrect since in fact it has always been expressly intended that these Members should have the freedom of Unofficial Members in the proceedings of the Legislative Council. The Constitutional Working Committee have accordingly recommended the solution that the whole group of 11 should be classified in a new category as State and Settlement representatives who would be expected in practice to take up a middle position independent both of the Official and Unofficial blocs. The Council would then consist of 4 categories of members viz. ex officio, State and Settlement representatives, Official and Unofficial Members.

15. The Consultative Committee recommended a considerable increase in the number of Unofficial Members of the Legislative Council as compared with the membership recommended in the December report of the Working Committee. This increase is in principle acceptable to the Plenary Conference but with the important qualification that the membership should be so adjusted as to ensure that the Malays should not be in a minority amongst the members other than ex officio and Official.

The Plenary Conference considered a proposal that this should be achieved by increasing the 50 Unofficial Members recommended by the Consultative Committee by additional Malay membership under the occupational category of "Agriculture" as defined in the April report of the Working Committee. At that stage of their work and before they came to consider the vital issue of Immigration policy, it appeared that the Malay representatives in the Conference would accept a position of equality in the Unofficial (including State and Settlement representatives) voting strength, but, as explained in paragraph 23 of this despatch, later consideration of the subject of Immigration showed that they could not be content with anything less than an assured majority, unless a special constitutional provision were conceded by His Majesty's Government which would secure the acceptance of Malay views in the matter of Immigration.

16. It is unlikely that on every important issue the Malays will find themselves faced with a solid opposition vote from the non-Malay Unofficial Members, nor would they themselves ordinarily expect any such situation, but they insist that insofar as it is possible on issues vital to their community they must be free from dependence on the chance support of one or more representatives of other communities. My own opinion is that the Malay apprehensions are exaggerated in this matter, but, nevertheless, I cannot fail to appreciate that, in the interests of the majority of the people of the country whom they represent they do not feel justified in agreeing to accept any risk whatever in that matter. There are leaders in the Malay and non-Malay communities who are not backward in appreciating the importance of compromise and the promotion of a patriotic feeling of an all-Malaya character, as essential if political and social progress is to be well based in this country, and I do not myself fear that to concede a Malay majority of the Unofficial voting strength in the Legislative Council will mean that the power will be misused. But in the absence of such an assured position I can only foresee the likelihood of a very rigid attitude on the part of the Malay members in policies and problems which would not ordinarily be regarded as involving issues vital to the Malay community.

17. On a balance of all the factors, therefore, my recommendation is that the numbers and distribution of seats in the Legislative Council recommended in the April report of the Working Committee and endorsed by the Plenary Conference should be adopted with the modification that two additional Malay members should be appointed under the category of "Agriculture and Husbandry".

18. Before leaving the question of representation, I should refer to a specific plea made in the Advisory Council on the 10th of April by the Honourable Dr. (Miss) Soo Kim Lan in which she commented on the absence of adequate provision for women to play their role in the proposed Federal Legislative Council. She asked that women should be allocated at least 8 seats in the proposed Council, namely, 2 as Official and 6 as Unofficial Members. It is certainly my hope that the scheme of representation will leave the High Commissioner free to nominate suitably representative women to the Council, but I do not believe that it would contribute to a solution of this sufficiently difficult problem if special reservation of seats were made for women members; rather should it be left to the High Commissioner to use his discretion to select women equally with men where they could be suitably representative of important interests.

19. *Immigration*

Of all the policy problems facing the Government in Malaya immigration is probably the one which raises in the most acute form a difference of opinion, each in respect of the interests of their own community, between the Malays on the one hand, and the Chinese, and to a lesser degree the Indians, on the other hand. It is also a problem in which employers of immigrant labour are seriously concerned. For some years before the war there was, as you are aware, a quota system governing the immigration of Chinese unskilled labour into Malaya; and in respect of Indians the Government of India itself immediately before the war had placed an embargo on the immigration of Indian labour to Malaya. Since the end of the war, in the case of Indians the Government of India's policy has been maintained: and in the case of Chinese no immigration has been authorised save for a few individuals joining relatives already resident in Malaya. In the period between the two wars a very considerable flow of immigration had taken place with results which caused increasing apprehension to the Malays. Provision was made in the draft Federation Agreement (Clause 75 (3)) to the effect that the Immigration policy of the Federal Government, and particularly any proposal for a major change in such policy, should be matters in regard to which a particular duty was laid on the High Commissioner to consult the Conference of Rulers and that, in the event of disagreement between the majority of the Rulers and the High Commissioner, the difference should be referred to the Secretary of State for his decision.

20. The Consultative Committee have stated (Section B(3) of their report) that fears had been expressed to them that this provision might mean that major changes in the Immigration policy of the Federal Government might be made without reference to the Federal Legislative Council, and the Consultative Committee have recommended that the Federal Legislative Council should be consulted before any major change is introduced.

21. The Chinese community's interest in the question is a very obvious one, and the strong objection expressed, for instance, in the memorandum of the Selangor Chinese Chamber of Commerce, which is annexed to the Consultative Committee's report, may be taken as commonly shared by Chinese opinion in Malaya. The strength, however, of the Malay case for an assurance that Malay opinion should be a determining factor in Immigration policy rests on the position that they have no other homeland but Malaya, and that they are in danger of being outnumbered and outmatched in this homeland of theirs by immigrant peoples unless they are in an unquestionable position to control the volume and nature of such immigration.

22. Since the issue of the December report of the Constitutional Working Committee there has been a hardening of Malay opinion in respect of the completeness of the assurance they seek in this matter, and this is attributable in part to their acceptance of a scheme of Citizenship which would give political rights in Malaya to numbers of non-Malay people who have become well established in the country and who have transferred their homes and loyalties to it, and partly to the far wider claims which have been publicly expressed both to the Consultative Committee and elsewhere by Chinese and Indian residents in this country. Recent strengthening of Malay opinion showed itself in the April report of the Working Committee which, while responding to the criticism that the Legislative Council should have a voice in Immigration policy, nevertheless was no longer content that the Secretary of State should have the final decision in the event of any local disagreement with the Malay view, as expressed by the majority of the Conference of Rulers, on any Immigration issue. At the Plenary Conference it was very clearly explained on behalf of the Malays

that they regarded the power to control immigration as a matter of life and death to the Malay people and that no solution could be acceptable to them which did not exclude the possibility of decisions being taken on Immigration policy which were contrary to the Malay views. It was proposed on their behalf that if any disagreement with the Conference of Rulers were to be remitted to the Secretary of State for his decision it should be only on an express assurance from the Secretary of State that he would take no decision which would require the adoption or continuance of an immigration policy to which the Malays objected.

23. An alternative proposal introduced into the discussion at the Working Committee was that the decision should be left to the High Commissioner and the Conference of Rulers provided that there should be no exercise of the power of "Advice" to the Rulers should they not be willing to accept the policy advocated by the High Commissioner.

24. Failing either of these two lines of solution, a third suggestion was that the determining factor in decisions on Immigration policy should be the vote of the Legislative Council excluding ex official and Official Members. On that basis the Malays would not be content with anything less than an assured majority of such voting members of the Legislative Council.

25. I and my advisers have carefully considered this difficult and important issue and we advise that the intense Malay concern in it should receive due recognition.

26. It is highly inadvisable that Their Highnesses the Rulers should themselves be involved in the dust of the arena in such a first-class political contest as this subject may on any occasion involve. It also is inadvisable, in our view, that if provision were made in the Constitution for a reference to the Secretary of State for his decision, he should have been previously bound to give a decision in a particular sense, and especially so if that sense proved to be contrary to the opinion of the Legislative Council.

27. It is also, in our view, inadvisable that the power of "Advice" to Their Highnesses should be qualified in any particular matter other than in respect of matters relating to the Muslim religion or the custom of the Malays.

28. It is, therefore, our recommendation that the reasonable claim of the Malays should be met by agreeing to their having an assured majority in the Legislative Council (apart from *ex-officio* and Official Members) which, as explained in paragraph 13, is justified by their numerical predominance in the list of future Federal Citizens, and equally by their vital concern to control the flow of future immigration into Malaya. It appears to us that not only is the Legislative Council the rightful representative body in which all policies of domestic importance should be debated and determined, but that it would be appropriate in such a highly controversial matter as Immigration policy that the determining factor as far as the Council is concerned should exclude the ex officio and Official votes. At the same time, the power of His Majesty or the High Commissioner to implement any particular policy, involving Immigration, which might be necessitated by His Majesty's responsibility for Defence and External Affairs would need to be safeguarded. If this recommendation is accepted by His Majesty's Government, it will be a consequence that further provision should be made for two Malay members to be nominated by the High Commissioner to the Legislative Council (see paragraph 17 of this despatch), and the necessary amendment of Clause 75(3) of the draft Federation Agreement should be in the following terms:—

"75 (3) It shall be the particular duty of the High Commissioner to consult the Conference of Rulers from time to time upon the Immigration policy of the Federal Government and, in particular, when any major change in policy is contemplated. If such policy or major change in policy is objected to by a majority of Their Highnesses the Rulers, the point of difference shall be determined by resolution of the Legislative Council. Upon any such resolution the ex officio and Official Members of the Council may speak, but shall not vote."

29. *Electoral law*

There has been some criticism expressed locally as to a genuine early intention to introduce a system of elections to the Federal Legislative Council, but with the present provision in Clauses 69 and 113 of the draft Federation Agreement and the addition to the Recital Clause proposed in paragraph 8 of this despatch (which will equally apply to the Settlements of Penang and Malacca), this criticism should be satisfied and it will rest with the future Legislative Council of the Federation to proceed as soon as it is ready to do so with the preparation of an appropriate Federal electoral law.

30. *Citizenship*

In the conclusion provisionally reached in December by His Majesty's Government on the draft Federation Agreement, the Citizenship proposals there contained were an essential feature which appeared to His Majesty's Government to be calculated to achieve the fundamental objective of the creation of a form of Citizenship which would be extended to all those who regard Malaya as their real home and the object of their loyalty. Further, in a reply to Mr. Rees-Williams in the House of Commons on 29th January you stated that the Constitutional Proposals contained revised provisions for Federal Citizenship which had been framed in an endeavour to open the doors of Citizenship to those, and only those, who genuinely regard Malaya as their home and as the object of their loyalty—a definition which of course included, besides the Malays, the very considerable number of Chinese, Indians and others who were firmly rooted in the country.

31.   This part of the draft Federation Agreement naturally figured with prominence amongst the comments and criticisms received by the Consultative Committee. The subject divides itself into two sections:

(a) acquisition of Federal Citizenship by operation of law;
(b) acquisition of Federal Citizenship by application.

The Consultative Committee recorded their conclusions in paragraphs 12 and 13 of Part III.A. of their report.

32. As regards acquisition of Citizenship by operation of law, two Chinese members of the Committee recommended that the provisions should be widened so as to enable Citizenship to be acquired by operation of law by any British subject or Protected Person born in either of the Settlements or any of the Malay States or any other British territories whether before on or after the appointed day who is permanently resident in the Settlements or any of the Malay States. The conclusion of the other 7 members of the Committee, after prolonged consideration and discussion of the representations received, was, however, in favour of accepting the provisions of the draft Federation Agreement (Clause 128).

The Constitutional Working Committee discussed at length the question of widening the provisions in the draft Federation Agreement and their conclusion was that they could not recommend the adoption of the considerable extension advocated by the 2 Chinese members of the Consultative Committee. In view, however, of the fact that a number of British subjects born in the Settlements of Penang and Malacca having become permanently resident not in the Settlements but in a Malay State, provision should be made for them to acquire Citizenship by operation of law and the necessary amendment should be made to Clause 128(1)(b) of the draft Federation Agreement which would thus give Federal Citizenship by operation of law to "any British subject born in either of the Settlements whether before, on or after the appointed day who is permanently resident in the territories now to be comprised in the Federation." This amendment was acceptable to the Plenary Conference and a consequential amendment will be needed in Clause 128(3)(c) of the draft Federation Agreement. I recommend this modification to His Majesty's Government for their approval.

33. As regards acquisition of Federal Citizenship by application, the Consultative Committee endorsed the provisions in the draft Federation Agreement, except that they considered the qualifying period under Clause 129(1) (a) to be over-long, and they recommended that an application for Federal Citizenship should be able to be considered if the applicant had been born in any of the territories of the Federation and had been resident for 5 out of the 10 years preceding his application (instead of 10 out of 15 years), and that in the case of an applicant who had not been born in the Federation it should be sufficient that he had been resident for 8 out of the 15 years preceding his application (instead of 15 out of 20 years).

On the recommendation of the Working Committee, the Plenary Conference was not willing to cut the residence qualification so far, but they agreed to reduce to 8 out of 12 years the qualifying period necessary for applicants born in the Federation. This modification in favour of those who were born in the Federal territory seems to myself and my advisers a fair and reasonable one and we agree also that in the case of those born elsewhere, 15 out of 20 years is not an undue period of residence for testing the genuine nature of claims that homes and loyalties have been permanently transferred to Malaya.

34. Two further points affecting the Citizenship proposals were discussed at the Plenary Conference, and are recommended for His Majesty's Government's acceptance, namely

(1) that provision should be made for applicants to be not less than 18 years of age at the time of their application; and
(2) that the provision, recommended in the Consultative Committee's report, that applicants of not less than 45 years of age, who have had 20 years residence in Malaya and who apply within 2 years of the inauguration of the new Constitution, should be exempted from the language qualification.

35. *Official languages*

There is a keen and growing desire on the part of Their Highnesses and the Malay representatives that the Malay language should be recognised as having an equal status with English in a Federal Constitution. This feeling was fully appreciated both in the Working Committee and in the Plenary Conference itself, but it was also recognised that considerable administrative inconvenience and delay would be caused if every Council document had to be printed in two languages. It was therefore considered that both in the case of the Federal Executive Council (Clause 35 of the draft Federation Agreement) and the Legislative Council (Clause 66) the present provision should be altered to read that the official languages should be English and Malay provided that anything which is required to be printed or reduced into writing should be expressed in the English language. At the same time the Working Committee drew attention to Clause 60 under which the Council would have power to regulate its own proceedings, and it was agreed that this clause could be invoked for the purpose of making regulations regarding the use of either language in the Legislative Council and for the translation of documents. I recommend that these amendments of Clauses 35 and 66 should be accepted.

36. *District judges*

The reorganisation of the Courts system which has been effected since the liberation of Malaya included the institution of District Courts, with limited jurisdiction, as part of the judicial system of the Malayan Union and the District Judges were required to have professional legal qualifications. At the same time the pre-war system of First Class and Second Class Magistrates (without legal qualifications) was discontinued in favour of a single class of magistrates with jurisdiction more limited than that of District Judges and with powers

(a) in civil cases corresponding to those of First Class Magistrates
(b) in criminal cases less than the pre-war First Class but more than the pre-war Second Class Magistrates.

37. This decision has been much criticised on the Malay part on the ground that few Malays in the present phase had been able to acquire full legal qualifications and, secondly, that the restriction of the sphere of the magistrates has had a directly adverse effect on the eligibility of Malays for higher judicial appointments, since the First Class magistracies have been discontinued and the District Judgeships require full legal qualifications. Further, they point out that the magistrates were before the war State Officers appointed by the Ruler of the State, whereas District Judges are part of the central Judiciary and appointed by the Governor, so that, in addition to the complaint of lack of opportunity for Malays for higher judicial appointments, the change has raised a political question of importance as affecting the Ruler's authority as the fount of justice in his own State. These views were exhaustively considered by the Constitutional Working Committee without however their being able to agree on any satisfactory solution; but in the Plenary Conference further analysis of the position revealed a possible solution on the lines of making a marked distinction between what are now known as District Judges on the one hand and the Magistrates on the other. A solution on these lines would involve a reconstruction of the present judicial system in the following respects.

38. There would be First and Second Class Magistrates with the pre-war powers provided under the Courts Enactment of the Federated Malay States, and such Magistrates would be appointed by the Ruler of the State and would not need to possess legal qualifications. The Federal Judiciary would consist of Judges of the Supreme Court with powers of punishment limited by law only, and another class of Judges, who for the sake of clarity may for this purpose be referred to as "Sessions Judges", with jurisdiction up to 7 years and powers of punishment up to 3 years. The "Sessions Judges" would be appointed by the High Commissioner and together with

the Chief Justice and Supreme Court Judges would form the Federal Judiciary. The "Sessions Judges", if this solution were to meet the present Malayan objections, would need to carry out their functions separately from the State magisterial system and to sit elsewhere than in the Magistrates' Court and to be provided with their own necessary subordinate staffs.

39. I have discussed these proposals with the Chief Justice who is prepared to accept them with certain modifications. In the light of these proposals the judicial system recommended by the Chief Justice is briefly as follows:—

(A) A Federal Judicial Department consisting of the Supreme Court, District Courts (in the Federation to be known as "State Courts" in the Malay States and as "Settlement Courts" in the Settlement of Penang and Malacca), and First Class Magistrates' Courts.

The Judges of the Supreme Court, District Judges (in the Federation to be called "Presidents of State or Settlement Courts", as the case may be) and First Class Magistrates to be under the control of the Chief Justice as head of the Judiciary.

Supreme Court Judges and Presidents of State or Settlement Courts to be appointed by the High Commissioner; full-time First Class Magistrates to be appointed by the High Commissioner on the advice of the Chief Justice in the Settlements and by the Ruler on the advice of the Chief Justice in each Malay State.

This would have the advantage that, full-time First Class Magistrates would partake fully of the independence of the judiciary by reason of the authority which the Chief Justice would exercise in respect of their functions.

In addition to the full-time First Class Magistrates, all District Officers shall be ex-officio First Class Magistrates but they will not form part of the Judicial Department.

(B) The jurisdiction of State and Settlement Courts to be:—

(a) *Civil*:—Not exceeding 1,000 dollars as at present.
(b) *Criminal*:—Power to try offences where the maximum imprisonment does not exceed 7 years or which are punishable with fine only, as opposed to the present jurisdiction to try offences where the maximum imprisonment does not exceed 4 years or which are punishable with fine only. Powers of punishment, as regards imprisonment to be increased from 2 years, as at present, to 3 years.

(C) The jurisdiction of First Class Magistrates' Courts to be:—

(a) *Civil*:—Not exceeding 500 dollars.
(b) *Criminal*:—Power to try offences where the maximum imprisonment does not exceed 3 years or which are punishable with fine only, as opposed to the present jurisdiction of Magistrates to try offences where the maximum imprisonment does not exceed 1 year or which are punishable with fine only. Powers of punishment, as regards imprisonment, to be increased from 6 months, as at present, to 12 months.

Note:—This jurisdiction accords with the pre-war jurisdiction of First Class Magistrates in the Federated Malay States.

(D) The jurisdiction of Second Class Magistrates' Courts to be:—

    (a) *Civil*:—Not exceeding 250 dollars.

    (b) *Criminal*:—Power to try offences where the maximum imprisonment does not exceed 12 months or which are punishable with fine only, which is the present jurisdiction of Magistrates. Powers of punishment, as regards imprisonment, to be reduced from 6 months, the present powers of the Magistrates, to 3 months.

Note:—This jurisdiction accords with the pre-war jurisdiction of Second Class Magistrates in the Federated Malay States.

I agree with the scheme outlined by the Chief Justice and recommend its acceptance. I attach considerable importance to full-time First Class Magistrates coming under his control and thus being independent of the Executive. Moreover this scheme presents the special advantage that it would provide clear opportunities for Malay officers with a bent for law to qualify for promotion in the ladder of full-time judicial appointments up to the Supreme Court Bench itself.

Accordingly I seek permission to place this scheme before Their Highnesses the Rulers for their acceptance.

I might add that it is a matter of agreement between Their Highnesses and the Malay leaders and this Government, and a view shared by the Chief Justice, that means should be devised to facilitate legal studies by promising Malay officers, so that they may acquire in increasing numbers those full professional qualifications which are necessary to preside in Courts of more extensive jurisdiction.

40. *Interpretation of the federation agreement*

Local criticisms have been expressed that the Interpretation Tribunal to be set up under Clause 158 of the draft Federation Agreement might consist of two laymen under the chairmanship of the Chief Justice (or presiding Judge). As the decision was to be by majority, it would, therefore, be possible for the Chief Justice (or presiding Judge) to be outvoted by laymen on a point of law. It was also objected that there was no appeal from decisions of the Tribunal. It was suggested by one of the Bar Associations that the members of the Tribunal should be Judges of the Supreme Court and that there should be provision for appeals.

41. The Working Committee considered these objections and maintained its previous view that to provide for appeals from the decisions of the Interpretation Tribunal would not be desirable as tending to uncertainty and delay. With regard to the other objection, the Working Committee considered that there were occasions when laymen might usefully be appointed to the Tribunal and that to confine the membership in all cases to Judges of the Supreme Court would be unduly restrictive, besides involving serious inroads upon judicial time. The Working Committee had little doubt that lay members would, in practice, take their law from the Chief Justice or presiding Judge. After discussion the Working Committee decided to recommend, by way of compromise, that the Tribunal to decide any question of interpretation of the Constitution arising in Court proceedings and referred to the Tribunal under sub-clause (3) of the clause, should consist of the Chief Justice (or a Judge of the Supreme Court to be appointed by him) as Chairman and two members who should either be Judges of the Supreme Court or possess the qualifications required by law to be possessed by a Judge of the Supreme Court, and that in other respects the clause should remain as drawn.

This solution was endorsed by the Plenary Conference and has my support.

42. *Powers reserved to His Majesty and sovereignty and jurisdiction of Their Highnesses the Rulers*

Clause 159 of the Federation Agreement reads as follows:—

> "Power reserved   159. Nothing in this Agreement shall affect the power of
> to His Majesty   His Majesty or the Imperial Parliament to make laws
>   from time to time relating to the defence or external
>   affairs of the Federation or shall affect His Majesty's
>   sovereignty and jurisdiction in and over the Settle-
>   ments."

In the discussions in the Working Committee the Malay representatives proposed that this clause be amended by adding the words:—

> "and nothing in this Agreement shall prejudice the sovereignty and independ-
> ence of the Rulers of the Malay States."

Their view was that the clause as it stood was one-sided in that it preserved His Majesty's powers, but not those of the Rulers: if His Majesty had powers, so had the Rulers and they also should be mentioned.

It was pointed out by the legal members of the Committee that the powers of His Majesty as the Protecting Power and of the Imperial Parliament to make laws relating to the defence and external affairs of the Federation were admitted, and that the object of saving His Majesty's sovereignty and jurisdiction in and over the Settlements was to enable His Majesty to continue to legislate for the Settlements by Order in Council, notwithstanding any delegation which might have been, or might be, made in setting up Constitutional arrangements in the Settlements. As regards the powers of the Rulers, the amendment as put forward was unacceptable, because the Federation Agreement would, in fact, necessarily affect the sovereignty and independence of the Rulers of the Malay States.

After considerable discussion, it was agreed to leave Clause 159 of the Federation Agreement as drawn and, subject to the reservation mentioned below, to insert a new Clause 160 in the following terms:—

> "Sovereignty and juris-   160. Save as expressed herein, nothing in this
> diction of Their High-   Agreement shall affect the sovereignty and juris-
> nesses the Rulers.   diction of Their Highnesses the Rulers in their
>   several States."

The position of the Government representatives with regard to this amendment was reserved and it was expressly stated that, as important questions of constitutional law and practice were involved, the suggested amendment would require to be considered by yourself and your Legal Adviser in London.

43. *Appointment of high commissioner*

As drawn, the draft Federation Agreement (Clause 7) provides for the appointment of the High Commissioner to be made by Commission under His Majesty's Sign Manual and Signet. The Malay representatives asked that an amendment be made by adding the words "with the concurrence of Their Highnesses the Rulers". The reason advanced for the suggestion was that, as the proposed Federation would be a partnership between His Majesty and Their Highnesses the Rulers and as each would delegate powers to the High Commissioner who was, therefore, the representative of all, each should concur in appointment the joint representative. In reply it was pointed out that it was universal practice throughout His Majesty's dominions, Protectorates and Protected States to leave His Majesty's prerogative in the appointment of His representative unfettered, that this was a matter which affected His Majesty's prerogative as the Protecting Power and that the proposal could not be adopted without affecting His Majesty's prerogative which was everywhere unimpaired: the difficulty was that the person of the High Commissioner could not be split and it was difficult to see how so considerable a constitutional innovation could be accepted by His Majesty's Government.

I am advised that having regard to the constitutional significance of this matter I can do no more than transmit the proposal for your consideration.

44. On the revenue and financial aspects of the draft Federation Agreement there has been no local expression of criticism, but an amendment to the second schedule of that Agreement (matters with respect to which the Federal Legislative Council has power to pass laws) was reviewed in the Constitutional Working Committee and is recommended for adoption viz. that Item 137 in that schedule should be expanded to read:—

"Exchange control; control of capital issues; taxes on remittances abroad."

The intention in thus expanding this item was simply to define the authority which would be empowered, if it were at any time necessary after the Federation had come into operation, to legislate in the field of those matters, for instance, in an emergency for the defence of sterling; the amendment is not to be taken as itself indicating a present intention to adopt any particular fresh policies.

45. An amendment of the third schedule of the draft Federation Agreement (sources of revenue of States and Settlements) is considered to be necessary in respect of Item 7. The revenues of Municipalities established under the Municipal Ordinance in Penang and Malacca accrue to the Municipal Commissioners and not to Government and it is not intended that this system should be altered. Accordingly Item 7 in that schedule should be amended to read:—

"Revenues of Town Boards, Rural Boards and similar local authorities, other than Municipalities established under any Municipal Ordinance."

46. Provision is made in the Federation Agreement whereby State and Settlement Constitutions shall be framed in conformity with that Agreement. The main details of the State Constitutions are in process of being considered with a view to formulation in full as soon as His Majesty's Government decide to approve the Federation scheme as now recommended. Proposals for constitutional arrangements for the Settlements of Penang and Malacca are also under consideration; to a large extent these arrangements would be based on Part VII of the Malayan Union Order in Council, 1946, adapted to conform with the Federation scheme.

47. It remains for me to express my sense of indebtedness to those who have given their skill and overtime and patience to the delicate task of working out these constitutional proposals in circumstances of strain and dislocated conditions in this country. A spirit of compromise and political reality has animated the discussions of the Constitutional Working Committee and of the Consultative Committee, and it is not a mean feat that general agreement has been reached over so wide an area of the

Federation scheme in the findings of those two committees. There has become more and more apparent in these last few months an appreciation amongst all communities that the most important need is that decisions should be taken and a substantive Constitution established with the least possible delay, so that Malaya could pass on from the present transitional phase of constitutional arrangements. I may, for instance, refer to the resolution of the Penang Settlement Advisory Council on the 17th April, 1947, following upon their consideration of the report of the Consultative Committee on the Constitutional Proposals for Malaya. The Council's resolution was in the following terms:—

> "That this Council is unanimously in favour of accepting the Constitutional Proposals in order to facilitate the early establishment of a stable Government."

It is generally recognised that the Constitution will need amendment from time to time in the future to meet the developing conditions of a progressive society, and that it must fall to the Federal, State and Settlement authorities to show themselves responsive to the will of the people as those developments require. The wide field of operation of the Federal Legislature under the scheme now proposed will ensure the strong central authority which is one of the fundamental objectives of His Majesty's Government and is no less appreciated to be necessary by Their Highnesses the Rulers and the leaders of all sections of the people in Malaya. The considerable part which Unofficial Members will take in the Federal Legislature should ensure that lively and progressive policies will be followed.

124 CO 537/2142, no 104   11 May 1947
[Federation proposals]: despatch no 11 from Sir E Gent to Mr Creech Jones

With reference to my Confidential despatch of even date[1] in which I have submitted to you my report on the outcome of the discussions on the Constitutional Proposals for a Federation of Malaya, I have the honour to inform you that I have drafted that despatch with the possibility in mind that you may in due course decide that it should be published at some time. Accordingly I think it as well to transmit also to you along with it this Secret despatch in which I may throw light on certain features of the Confidential despatch and of the proposed Constitutional scheme in general.

2. First, I annex a copy of the record of the Plenary Conference at King's House on the 24th of April.[2] That Plenary Conference, attended by His Excellency the Governor-General, Their Highnesses the Malay Rulers, their advisers and the members of the Constitutional Working Committee, received and considered the April report of the Constitutional Working Committee, a copy of which is annexed to my Confidential despatch of even date, and in the main the Conference endorsed those recommendations and discussed certain additional points which arose in the course of the examination of the Working Committee's report.

3. In my Confidential despatch I have explained how basic is the racial factor of

---

[1] See 123.   [2] Annexes not printed.

the present social and political organisation of Malaya, and it is regrettably the case in present conditions that both on the side of the Malay and non-Malay communities the whole stress is in fact on community representation. In the hope that it will be possible to weaken this feeling and convert it into channels more beneficial to the future development of the country I have recommended that His Majesty's Government should admit the conception of occupational representation which will tend to deflect the attention of all communities from a straight system of racial representation.

4. In the case of the Malays the racial feeling is particularly sensitive in respect of Chinese, and to a slightly lesser extent Indians; their feeling is not so strong vis-à-vis Europeans and Eurasians, but, nevertheless, it is clear that they will place no reliance on a European or Eurasian vote in a future Legislative Council in matters which they regard as of vital interest to them such as Immigration and a future electoral system. It will be necessary, therefore, to bear in mind that any adjustment of the non-Malay figures in the proposed composition of the Legislative Council would be closely scrutinised by them from the point of view of racial representation and, for instance, an increase of Chinese or Indian membership at the expense of European or Eurasian would not find acceptance as far as the Malays are concerned.

5. The Malay majority amongst the Unofficial membership of the Council which I have brought myself to recommend is designed to include not less than 2 Malay Labour Members who, it is generally supposed, would be sought in the ranks of the Malay Nationalist Party. That Party, as you will be aware, has an uncertain association with Indonesian Nationalist and Chinese extreme left-wing groups in Malaya and is not regarded by the majority of Malays as reliably supporting true Malay interests, and the Malay representatives of the Working Committee and the Plenary Conference have therefore pressed for a clear majority in the Council which would not include the 2 members if selected from Malay Nationalist Party circles to represent Malay labour. Nevertheless, I and my advisers feel that sufficient weight will have been given to Malay claims if a simple Malay majority is provided and that the Malay Nationalist Party Wing of Malay opinion, small and possibly extreme as it may be at present, cannot reasonably be accounted otherwise than as part of the Malay representation; and indeed it is not improbable, or wholly undesirable, that that section of Malay opinion may acquire increased support in the months and years to come amongst the Malay peoples.

6. The Consultative Committee in Section A (iii), paragraph 16, of their Report made a recommendation in respect of the equal eligibility of Federal Citizens for employment in the services of the Federal Government. This is, of course, a subject of great delicacy and the recommendation was not unskilfully evaded in the April report of the Working Committee (paragraph 29). It is possible to adopt the line which the Working Committee recommended and which in effect would mean to defer the question for the consideration in relation to the various branches of the Service; and in all the circumstances this solution would indeed avoid some at least of the difficulties which are raised by the general issue. At present it is a fact that in some Departments, and particularly the professional and technical Departments, there is a majority of non-Malay officers; but on the other hand, if the Malays had any reason to suppose that in the Administrative Service, in particular, there was likely to be any considerable admission of Federal Citizens of Chinese or Indian race, it would be likely to compromise seriously the prospect of their accepting the present

proposals. I therefore strongly advise that the matter should be left by His Majesty's Government as recommended by the Working Committee, and that no comprehensive promise should be given that all Federal Citizens would be equally eligible for admission to all Public Services of the Federation.

7. In paragraph 39 of my confidential despatch I referred to the issue of the District Judge system and to certain modifications of the proposals made at the Plenary Conference which I have recommended in agreement with the Chief Justice and my advisers. I attach to this despatch a memorandum by the Chief Justice setting out the recommended scheme in greater detail and the arguments in support of it. I include this memorandum in this Secret despatch, rather than in my Confidential despatch, as it would in certain respects be inadvisable to make it public should a decision be taken to publish the latter.

8. In your telegram 1719 of the 28th November, 1946, you referred to the present Naturalisation Enactment of the Federated Malay States and its relation to the Citizenship scheme for the proposed Federation of Malaya. The distinction between national status and Citizenship has been maintained throughout the discussions on the Federation proposals. The act of obtaining naturalisation as the subject of a Ruler would under the present Constitutional proposals carry with it the status of Citizenship. This facility is, of course, under the Enactment open to persons of any racial origin, and it may be considered not unreasonable that a person complying with the provisions of the Enactment, including the taking of an oath of allegiance to the State Ruler, should thus qualify for Citizenship after a shorter period of residence than one who has not chosen to acquire such national status in the country. The distinction between a person naturalised as the subject of a Malay Ruler and a person naturalised in one of the Settlements as a British subject is in my view justified by the fact that the latter is not thereby committing himself, as is the former, to a national status particularly related to, and confined to, Malaya, but to the wider concept of British nationality. Subject to your instructions, therefore, I do not propose that the provisions of the Naturalisation Enactment should be specially amended in connection with the Citizenship proposals.

9. The question of the eventual incorporation of Singapore in the proposed Federation has been the subject of telegraphic communication between yourself and His Excellency the Governor-General—see your telegram to him repeated to me as No. 596. The policy agreed upon for recommendation to you in respect of the method and timing of investigating the question was set out in the Governor-General's telegram to you No. G.G. 123 of 28th April;[3] I feel that at this juncture I cannot usefully add to the views expressed in that telegram, and I note that you will consider the matter further in the light of the Constitutional arrangements for the proposed Federation which I am now submitting to you.

10. The question referred to in paragraph 41 of my despatch led to a consequent issue being raised in the Working Committee and later in the Plenary Conference, namely, the question of expressly restoring the prerogatives of each Ruler in his State. I am advised that at any rate it will be desirable, and perhaps essential, expressly to restore sufficient prerogative to each Ruler to enable him to promulgate the Constitution of his State; and it will probably be desirable expressly to restore to each Ruler the prerogatives, power and jurisdiction which the Ruler of the State

---

[3] See 121.

possessed on, say, the 1st of December, 1941 *viz.* before the Japanese occupation and the MacMichael Agreements. This could probably best be effected by inserting a Clause in the Model State Agreement on the following lines:—

"Sovereignty of the Ruler.	2. The prerogatives, power and jurisdiction of His Highness within the State of . . . shall be those which he (*or* his predecessor where there has been a change) possessed on the first day of December, 1941, subject nevertheless to the provisions of this Agreement and of the Federation Agreement."

11. Finally, I would refer to the important matter of the order of procedure in which these Constitutional Proposals would be put into effect if they are found to be acceptable by His Majesty's Government. In paragraph 24 of the December report of the Constitutional Working Committee and paragraph 24 of the Legal Report by the Attorney-General of the 14th November, 1946 (see my secret despatch 162 of the 14th November, 1946), the order of events proposed was there set out, and I am advised that there is nothing in the revision of the proposals which would require that order to be modified.

125 CO 537/2171, no 85   22 May 1947
[Labour policies in the Malayan Union and Singapore]: inward savingram no 6 from Mr M J MacDonald to Mr Creech Jones[1]

Reference your secret telegram 230 on the subject of Labour Policy, following is the report promised in para. 1 of my secret telegram 154 of the 21st. May:—

1. Subsequent to Governor-General's Conference of 11th. March action was taken on the Governor-General's instructions (see Page 13 of conference minutes) to endeavour to reconcile the conflicting views of the legal officers of the two administrations as to the eligibility of Federations of Trade Unions to be registered themselves as Trade Unions. The result of these discussions is summarized in attached copy of a minute by Attorney-General, Singapore.[2]

2. The Singapore Government accepted the advice of the Attorney-General and the way then became clear for federations to be registered in the Colony in the same way as they were already being accepted for registration in the Malayan Union. Uniformity of legal interpretation in this important matter was thereby secured.

3. At the same time the two Governments agreed to follow a uniform policy in administering the law in so far as it related to the registration of federations by agreeing to insist that before federations can qualify for registration the Registrar must be satisfied that the Unions wishing to federate are themselves already registered Unions and have passed resolutions recording their decision to form a federation or affiliate with an existing federation. A copy of the official statement of the Singapore Government's policy in this matter is attached. This statement was issued on 23rd. April. Incidentally an order has now been issued whereby Trade Unions can legally contribute to a Federation.

---

[1] cf 122; also 117.   [2] Annexes not printed.

4.   In the Malayan Union the Registrar of Trade Unions informed all Trade Unions between the 24th. of January and the 15th. of February that it would be necessary for him to be satisfied that individual registered Trade Unions had resolved to join a Federation by the majority ballot vote and that their rules permitted a contribution to be made to such a Federation. Pending such action by individual Trade Unions, the applications made by 11 State Federation of Trade Unions for Registration were allowed to stand on the Registrar's books. The draft rules and regulations of the Pan-Malayan Federation of Trade Unions provided for a Federation of State Federations none of which have yet completed the formalities required for registration.

5.   In Singapore representatives of the Singapore Federation of Trade Unions (whose application for registration in its existing form has been rejected, pending its reorganisation to enable it to comply with the conditions stated above) are now discussing with the Registrar ways and means of effecting this reorganisation. They are being given a reasonable time to put their house in order and negotiations with the Registrar are at present proceeding in a friendly spirit.

6.   Provided that a certain amount of "face" can be saved there is no reason at the moment to suppose that they will not comply with the conditions imposed which will result in the formation of a normal federation consisting entirely of legally registered Trade Unions.

7.   If on the other hand the present negotiations were to break down or if the present Singapore Federation of Trade Unions were to interfere actively in any trade dispute in defiance of Section 18 of the Trade Unions Ordinance, then a serious situation would arise in that it might be necessary to prosecute the organisation as an illegal Trade Union.

8.   The question of "saving face" does not arise in the Malayan Union as Federations were never left in doubt of the fact that they themselves would have to register as soon as Trade Unions wishing to federate to them had themselves registered.

9.   After the incidents in Kedah and, on a minor scale, incidents in Selangor, the firm action by the Police resulted in an increase in public confidence which was shown by the number of idividuals who came forward and laid information leading to prosecution for intimdation. The Federation of Trade Unions are taking all possible measures to complete their registration and the present calm may be attributed to this fact. The possibility, however, of a recrudescence of strikes in the future is not to be overlooked.

126   CO 537/2142, no 110   29 May 1947

[Federation proposals]: inward telegram no 160 from Mr M J MacDonald to Mr Creech Jones

1.   I have been in touch with Sir Edward Gent throughout the discussions of the last few months on constitutional proposals and, as you know, attended the Plenary Conference with Malay Rulers and leaders on 26th April. I discussed with Gent the general terms of his confidential despatch No. 119[1] and secret despatch of 11th May[2]

---

[1] See 123.   [2] See 124.

before these were drafted. I agree with his recommendations with the solitary exception of that concerning numerical representation of the various communities in the Legislative Council. On that I should like to put forward a slightly different alternative suggestion. This is referred to in paragraph 4 below.

2. I would also like to make comments on two other points. First, it is desirable that, following the long discussions which have taken place, final decisions should now be taken as early as possible. I need not labour the point, for the desirability of it is obvious and most members of all communities here are anxious for the matter to be settled and action to be taken very soon to put the new constitution into effect. In the Plenary Conference, Dato Onn expressed some apprehension on this point, fearing His Majesty's Government and Parliament might not take the decisions before Parliament rises for the summer recess. You will see from the minutes that Gent and I assured him that Parliamentary debate was likely to take place well before that.

3. Second point concerns Malay request that, before a High Commissioner is appointed, the Rulers should concur in his appointment. I agree that this is a matter touching the King's Prerogative, on which we should not and cannot formally meet them. But they feel the point strongly and I think there is some (?group omitted) in their contention that, as the new proposals envisage a partnership in some respects between His Majesty and their Highnesses, and as the High Commissioner is to be the Rulers' representative in many matters and is to have powers delegated to him by the Rulers, they should have something, somehow to do with his appointment. I venture to suggest that we might go some way to show recognition of all this by assuring them, in whatever is the appropriate way, that before a High Commission-er's name is submitted to the King for appointment, it shall be communicated informally to the Rulers, so as to make sure that they have no positive objection to the man. I believe that some such practice is followed when a new United Kingdom Ambassador is about to be appointed to a foreign state. This presumably does not involve any infringement of the King's Prerogative in appointing his Ambassador. I realise that the cases are not parallel, but cannot as a layman in these matters detect any practical objection to the proposal. Rulers and U.M.N.O. leaders will not be wholly satisfied with it, but it will to some extent please them.

4. Point on which I should like to suggest a possible alternative to Gent's recommendations is the following. He recommends in paragraph 17 of his confiden-tial despatch that "The number and distribution of the seats in the Legislative Council recommended in the April Report of the Working Committee and endorsed by the Plenary Conference should be adopted with the modification that two additional Malay members should be appointed under the categories of agriculture and husbandry". I suggest that only one additional Malay member should be appointed and that the number of unofficial Europeans should be reduced by one. This would reduce the European representation to the number recommended by the Cheeseman Committee.

5. My reasons for this suggestion are as follows:—

(a) We shall be criticised by our critics in some of the domiciled communities, especially the Chinese, for our proposals about the distribution of seats amongst the various communities in the Legislative Council. The closer we stick to the Cheeseman recommendations, the less effective criticism will be. I maintain that we shall open ourselves to rather unfortunate criticism if our deviation from the Cheeseman recommendations consists of bumping up the Malay representation by two and the European by one whilst reducing the Chinese. Critics will claim that this is indeed an unholy alliance of British and Malays against the other communities. They will add that it is a British trick to maintain British Imperialist domination in Malaya. I do not wish to exaggerate the importance of this, for we shall get that sort of criticism from extremists in any case. But I fear that the proposal under reference will give them ammunition on this point which they can shoot off quite effectively.

(b) In any case, I think that the European representation is too high. We should remember that, in addition to unofficial Europeans, there will be a considerable representation of *ex-officio* and official European members.

(c) My suggestion, like Gent's retains a situation in which Malay representatives have a clear majority over all other members excluding *ex-officio* and official representatives. I firmly support Gent's arguments and recommendations concerning this.

6. There is much to be said for the figures suggested by Gent. In particular, it should be pointed out that it was the Malays, not ourselves, who suggested the additional European members. But on balance, I personally favour the figures suggested in paragraph 4 above. I have shown this telegram to Gent, who concurs in my sending it for your consideration and who fully agrees with the points made in paragraphs 2 and 3 above. But he does not agree with my proposal in paragraph 4, although he appreciates my supporting reasons. In particular, he feels that European unofficial interests are of sufficient importance to warrant what he has recommended, and are or should be in no way represented particularly by official or *ex-officio* members. He agrees with me as to the likely criticism on the part of the Chinese and Indians, but feels that my proposed reduction of Malay and European representation will not appease that criticism to the extent that it will provoke Malay and European criticism also.

Gent and I are meeting in ten days time. In the meantime, we are preparing a telegram giving our appreciation of the likely effect on public opinion in Malaya of the revised constitutional proposals, if they are adopted. We are sending you this as soon as we have completed it, probably on 9th June.

127 CO 537/2142, nos 111–112 11 June 1947
[Federation proposals]: outward telegram no 738 from Mr Creech Jones to Sir E Gent

Your despatch No. 119 Confidential, and your despatch No. 11 Secret. See also Governor-General's telegram addressed to me as No. 160.[1]

Constitutional proposals.

I am most grateful for the full and clear manner in which you have set out the results of your latest consultations with the Malay Rulers and representatives, and I wish to congratulate you and all those associated with you on the manner in which

---

[1] See 123, 124, 126.

you have reconciled the need for some demonstrable advance as a result of the Cheeseman Committee's activities with a not always easy and sometimes intransigent Malay attitude. Naturally I cannot say in advance what the views of my colleagues will be, but I see no reason to suppose that they will react unfavourably to a scheme on the lines which you now recommend, and I would propose to submit the proposals to them with the least possible delay. Before I do so, however, I should be grateful for your observations on the following points of major importance:—

(a) *Appointment of high commissioner.* See paragraph 43 of your despatch No. 119 Confidential, and paragraph 5 of Record of Plenary Conference enclosed in your despatch No. 11 Secret. It appears to me that Malay representatives, in maintaining in spite of your explanation their insistence that Conference of Rulers should be consulted about appointment of High Commissioner, have not fully understood the position, and that if they had done so they would readily appreciate impossibility of their request. In the first place, High Commissioner will be His Majesty's representative not only in the Malay States but in the British Settlements of Penang and Malacca, and it is inconceivable that His Majesty should be bound to consult any third party in appointing his representative in territories within his own dominions. In the second place, while it is no doubt true that the High Commissioner will in some measure exercise powers delegated by both His Majesty and the Rulers he will nonetheless remain, in a fundamental sense, in relation to the Malay States the representative of His Majesty and His Majesty alone—namely, for the purpose of carrying out His Majesty's obligation to protect those States. This is an obligation undertaken at the request of the Malays themselves. There is thus no question of "dictation", as contended by Dato Onn at Plenary Conference. The Malays cannot on the one hand ask His Majesty to continue to protect their country while denying him, on the other hand, the power to choose, at his own discretion, the representative to whom he will entrust this task. I hope that you will be able to inform me that the Malays, in the light of these further explanations, have dropped their request.

I have noted Governor-General's suggestion in paragraph 3 of his telegram No. 160, which may have to be considered in the last resort if the Malays remain obdurate. I should be most reluctant, however, to grant any concession at all in this matter.

(b) *Immigration.* I note from paragraph 19 to 28 of your despatch No. 119 Confidential that the Malay attitude on this subject has hardened, and that the Malay representatives now regard power to control immigration as a matter of life and death to the Malay people. I have considerable sympathy with the Malay apprehensions on this subject, but the recommendations in paragraph 28 of your Confidential despatch require elucidation. In the first place I assume intention is to grant the Malays a simple power of veto, to be exercised through a majority in the Legislative Council only in the last resort, over proposed changes in immigration policy, and not repeat not a power of *initiating* changes unhampered by the normal safeguards (e.g. High Commissioner's assent, High Commissioner's Reserved Power, His Majesty's Power of disallowance). If this is indeed the intention, wording of proposed amendment to Clause 75(3) of draft Federation Agreement would have to be clarified so as to prevent Conference of Rulers from putting forward positive proposals under the guise of "objecting" to Government policy, and then claiming that future of these proposals must be determined by unofficial members of Legislative Council. Also unofficial members of Legislative Council would have to be prevented from injecting positive proposals into their resolutions. Moreover, I am not clear how suggested machinery would work in the various categories of cases which might arise. Any proposed changes in immigration policy will fall into two classes:—

(a) those involving administrative action,
(b) those involving legislation.

In cases where the Conference of Rulers agrees to the proposed change, presumably no difficulty will arise in relation to either of these classes. Administrative action or legislation, as the case may be, will proceed in the normal manner. Similarly, procedure seems fairly clear as regards proposed changes in class (a) above to which Conference of Rulers has objected. Resolution of unofficial members of Legislative Council will either confirm objection of Conference of Rulers (in which case proposals will be dropped), or uphold the High Commission (in which case administrative action will proceed). But what about proposals involving legislation, to which Conference of Rulers have objected? I assume it is not contemplated that legislation would nonetheless be introduced into Legislative Council, unofficial members alone voting upon it, and that their vote without any of usual safeguards would finally determine what this law was to be. This would surely be open to grave objections. Proposal is, I take it, that the unofficial members would first pass a simple resolution in effect approving or disapproving the introduction of a Bill to implement the High Commissioner's policy, and that the High Commissioner, if upheld, would thereafter introduce legislation, in the normal way and with all the normal safeguards maintained.

In the second place, while you state that the power of His Majesty or the High Commissioner to implement any particular policy involving immigration which might be necessitated by His Majesty's responsibility for defence and external affairs would need to be safeguarded, you appear to make no actual suggestion how this essential point should be met. I should welcome your views on this.

(c) *Composition of Legislative Council.* I see great force in the suggestion made by the Governor-General in his telegram No. 160 that the number of European unofficials should be reduced by one, and that only one additional Malay member should be added to the number recommended in the April Report of the Working Committee. I note that you have hitherto disagreed with this suggestion, but I should be grateful if you would consider it further and hope that on reflection you will feel able to accept it.

(d) *Citizenship by naturalisation as a subject of a ruler.* See paragraph 8 of your despatch No. 11 Secret. Although, as you say, it is technically open to persons of any racial origin to become naturalised as subjects of a Malay Ruler, it cannot in fact be expected of Chinese, if only on account of religious scruples, that they should take this step. Nor can it be assumed that their application would be readily granted. Practical effects of continuance of present position would therefore be that Chinese, unless born in Malaya, must reside in the country for 15 years before they can hope to acquire citizenship, whereas certain others (e.g. immigrants from Indonesia) could acquire citizenship after 5 years' residence only. When Newboult and O'Connor were here last Christmas, I was given to understand that there should be little difficulty in securing agreement of Rulers to necessary extension of qualifying period under F.M.S. naturalisation law, and I still regard it as important that this should be done. I think this will actually be in the interests of the Malays. There is bound in any case to be criticism to the effect that the Federation scheme unduly favours the Malays at the expense of the other communities. By and large such criticism has no (repeat no) justificiation, but failure to remove irritants of this kind will surely excite anti-Malay feeling and breed racial discord.

(e) *Status of British protected persons.* This is not mentioned in your despatches, but I mention since it figured in conversation with Colonel Lee when he was recently in this country. As you know, it was the past practice of Malayan Government to treat all Chinese born in the Malay States as British Protected Persons for the purpose of granting passports. It is understood that this privilege was highly prized by Chinese, who would now be correspondingly alarmed if it were decided that privilege in question could only be granted to those possessing the much more rigorous qualifications required for Malayan citizenship. I should be glad if you would confirm or otherwise from your own knowledge Colonel Lee's impression that this factor will weigh largely with stable elements of Chinese population in accepting or rejecting citizenship proposals and indeed Federation scheme as a whole.

2.   My Legal Advisers are still considering memorandum by Chief Justice enclosed in your despatch No. 11 Secret, and comments will be sent as soon as possible. There are also a number of drafting points, of varying importance, which arise on proposals in their latest form, and on which I shall address you separately. In the meanwhile, I should be grateful for earliest possible comments on the five major points discussed above.

128   CAB 129/19, CP(47)187   28 June 1947
'Malayan policy': Cabinet memorandum by Mr Creech Jones. *Annex*: citizenship proposals

On 5th December, 1946, my colleagues gave their provisional approval (C.M. (46) 103rd Conclusions), to certain revised proposals (C.P. (46) 439)[1] for a new Malayan Constitution, on "Federal" lines, which had resulted from the discussions of a local Working Committee representing the Malayan Union Government, the Malay Rulers and the principal Malay Political group (the United Malays National Organisation).

2.   In conveying this provisional approval to the Governor of the Malayan Union, I made it clear that there was no question of His Majesty's Government giving their *final* approval to any proposals along these lines until all interested communities in the peninsula had been given full and free opportunity to express their views. Accordingly, in December 1946, the Governor appointed a Consultative Committee

---

[1] cf 109 and 110.

composed mainly of influential representatives of the non-Malay communities, which was instructed to hold meetings throughout the peninsula, to receive oral and written representations, to collate the evidence submitted to it, and to report the substance of this evidence to him with such comments and recommendations as they should think fit.

3. After a series of meetings in various centres, the Consultative Committee presented its report to the Governor at the end of March 1947. It was not to be expected that the Federation proposals would escape all criticism, and in fact there sprang up from the outset a small but vocal section of opinion which rejected the proposals outright and which refused even to lay its views before the Consultative Committee. I am satisfied, however, that these elements, in spite of their extravagant claims, never represented more than a noisy minority amongst the population, and that the Consultative Committee, in recommending that the basis of the Federation proposals should be maintained (though with substantial modifications), spoke for the great bulk of the people, whose firm desire is to see the early establishment of a stable system of Government. It is noteworthy that the Governor's Advisory Council, in resolving early in April that the Consultative Committee's Report should be submitted for the consideration of the Malay Rulers and His Majesty's Government, expressed the unanimous view that the Committee had fulfilled His Majesty's Government's pledge of full and free consultation with all interested parties.

4. The final stage in the local consultations—the consideration of the Consultative Committee's Report by the Malay Rulers and Representatives—duly took place in the latter part of April, and the Governor's comprehensive recommendations were submitted to me in May. Before describing briefly the main features of these recommendations, I should say a word about the political background against which the Governor has had to work. There has been no doubt that the Malay attitude, partly owing to the mere fact of enforced inactivity while the other communities were being consulted and partly owing to the more extreme Chinese and Indian points of view which were expressed during that consultation, hardened considerably during the early months of this year; and I therefore regard it as all the more remarkable that the Governor and those who have assisted him should have been able, by dint of patient persuasion, not only to hold their ground but to secure the agreement of the Malays to several notable advances on the earlier proposals.

5. These earlier proposals, as my colleagues will recall, provided for a "Federation of Malaya" with a strong Central Government, having control over all matters of importance to the progress and welfare of the country as a whole, and for a form of common citizenship whose object was to afford political rights to all those, of whatever race or colour, who might fairly be held to regard Malaya as their true home and as the object of their loyalty. There has been no departure from these two fundamental principles of constitutional cohesion and common citizenship (which have throughout, of course, represented the basic objectives of His Majesty's Government in their whole Malayan policy), and this fact alone should, I think, influence us greatly in favour of accepting the scheme in its latest form. Having emphasised this general point, I have the following comments on matters of greater detail:—

(a) *Introduction of an electoral system.*—The original Federation proposals did not provide for the immediate introduction of elections, either in the Central Legislature or in the Legislatures of the individual States and Settlements. I accepted this position in view of the practical difficulties in the way of the immediate establishment of an electoral system; but whereas the original proposals merely spoke in non-committal terms of the introduction of elections at a later date, there is now to be a firm undertaking that, as soon as circumstances and local conditions will permit, legislation should be introduced for the election of members both to the Central Legislature and to the State and Settlement Councils. I regard this as a welcome advance.

(b) *Citizenship.*—The Consultative Committee recommended no fundamental change in the Citizenship provisions as set out in the original Federation proposals and as provisionally approved by my colleagues last December, but suggested that certain comparatively minor modifications should be effected, and in particular that the terms of application for citizenship, as opposed to automatic acquisition, should be made less onerous. The Malays have now gone some way, though not the whole way, towards meeting the Consultative Committee's suggestion. As the matter is inevitably somewhat complicated, I attach a brief tabular summary as an Annex to this memorandum. I regard it as particularly satisfactory that the Governor should have secured some modification, however slight, in the Malay attitude on this matter which they consider to be absolutely fundamental to their interests, and I am confident that the citizenship provisions, in the form in which they now stand, are designed to achieve the essential objective of common citizenship in Malaya as throughout upheld by His Majesty's Government.

(c) *Composition of central legislature.*—The original "Federation" proposals envisaged a Central Legislature of forty-eight members, with an unofficial majority. On the unofficial side, the seats were to be so arranged that the Malay Representatives (including the nine Malay Chief Ministers from the individual States, who would attend in virtue of their official State position but would nonetheless rank, at least for some purposes, as unofficials on the Central Legislature) would outnumber all other representatives by a small margin. The Consultative Committee recommended a large increase in the size of the Council and in the preponderance of unofficial over official members, coupled with a slight readjustment in the balance of Malay and non-Malay representatives which would deprive the former of their base majority on the unofficial side of the Council. The Malays have now accepted the conception of a larger Council (numbering nearly eighty members) and a large unofficial majority, but have again insisted that the Malay representatives amongst the unofficial members should slightly outnumber all the rest. The Governor has recommended the acceptance of the Malay point of view in this matter, and I support his recommendation. The increase in the unofficial majority is an undoubted advance, and as regards the balance between Malay and non-Malay representatives, I do not consider that the Malays are asking more than is justified by their essential position in the country. In the absence of recent census figures, it cannot be said whether the Malays form an absolute majority of the population in the territories now comprising the Malayan Union; but there is no doubt that they form an absolute majority amongst those who really belong to the country, who will qualify for citizenship, and who are justified in demanding a stake in the country's future.

My support for the Governor's recommendations is very closely linked, however, with the proposals for the early introduction of elections. In formulating his latest proposals for the basis of nomination of unofficial members of the Central Legislature, the Governor has been able to steer away from an overtly racial system.

That is to say, members will not be nominated as representing Malays, Chinese or Indians, but as representing certain functions or interests. The fact remains, however, that these functions and interests have been chosen with the avowed object of producing certain fixed proportions as between races, and I can only accept this system, which is obviously far from ideal, provided it begins to give place in the near future to a system of elections whereby representation is demonstrably based upon the will of the people. I do not think the Malays have anything to fear from the introduction of elections, and I propose, with my colleagues' approval, to make clear to the Governor my views on this point.

(d) *Immigration policy.*—It is in this connection that the recent hardening of the Malay attitude has been most apparent. At the time when the original "Federation" proposals were formulated, the Malays were content with a provision which laid it down that the High Commissioner should consult the Conference of Rulers about immigration policy and that differences of opinion between himself and the Conference should be referred to the Secretary of State for a decision. Now, however, they will be content with nothing less than a provision which enables the Malays, in the last resort, effectively to block any immigration policy which they regard as inimical to their own interests. I must say at once that I have some sympathy with the Malay point of view on this matter, though it must be confessed that the degree of economic prosperity depended in large part on the immigration into Malaya of other races. Their present precarious numerical position in their own country is mainly due to immigration policy in the past, over which they had no control, and I think it would be both wrong and fruitless to try to deny them the substance of their claim. The Governor's recommendation, however, is based on a proposal that in matters of immigration policy the final decision should rest with the unofficial members of the Central Legislature (on which, as we have seen, there is to be an absolute Malay majority); and it appeared to me that this proposal, as it originally reached me, might enable the Malays not merely, in the last resort, to block changes in immigration policy which they did not like, but also to *introduce* innovations in such policy which would not be subject to the normal checks and safeguards. I pointed this out to the Governor, who has now submitted a revised recommendation which in my view obviates the danger. Put briefly, the recommendation is that the High Commissioner shall discuss with the Conference of Rulers any important changes in immigration policy which he proposes to introduce, and that if the Conference cannot be brought to agree any particular change, the matter shall become the subject of a resolution by the unofficial members of the Legislative Council. If this resolution sustains the objections of the Conference of Rulers, no further action will be taken (whether by legislation or administrative action), unless the High Commissioner can certify that such action is essential in connection with the external affairs or defence of the "Federation"—matters on which His Majesty will continue to exercise jurisdiction. The Governor points out, however, that this revised recommendation has not been put to the Malays and that their reaction to it cannot be guaranteed.[2]

6. Such, then, is the essence of the Malayan constitutional proposals in their latest form. I consider that the governor has achieved a remarkable measure of

---

[2] When it considered this proposal on 3 July, Cabinet called for modifications to the provisions on immigration.

success in evolving proposals so satisfactory, in the face of a difficult and sometimes intransigent Malay attitude, and I am satisfied that the scheme, as a starting point, meets the real needs of the country and its various communities. The Governor-General, Mr. Malcolm MacDonald, has throughout been closely associated with the discussions and gives his full support to the Governor's recommendations, being convinced that the essential need is the early establishment of a staple [sic] form of Government. Before proceeding to my recommendations, however, I wish to draw attention to the following further points:—

(a) the Malays have pressed that the Malay Rulers should in future have the right of concurrence in the appointment of successive High Commissioners. Besides constituting a most dangerous precedent, this is a point touching on His Majesty's prerogative, and I have fully explained to the Governor the reasons why the Malay demand cannot be granted. He has advised me, however, that it would be unwise to re-open this individual point with the Malays in advance of the settlement on the whole range of the proposals. He recommends, in fact, that His Majesty's Government's negative decision on this point should be conveyed together with their acceptance of the proposals as a whole. I propose to act accordingly.[3]

(b) It is proposed that, at the outset, the "Federation of Malaya" should consist, as does the present Malayan Union, of the nine Malay States and the British Settlements of Penang and Malacca, and should exclude Singapore. The immediate Union of Singapore with the rest of Malaya has been one of the demands most loudly reiterated by that section of local opinion which has flatly opposed the Federation proposals, and there is no doubt that there are many links between the mainland and Singapore which may render desirable the early inclusion of Singapore in the "Federation." But after fully considering this problem in consultation with the two Governors, the Governor-General has recommended to me that any reorganisation on these lines should only be further considered *after* the "Federation" has been safely established. I agree with the Governor-General, and I would now propose, with the approval of my colleagues, to inform the Governor of the Malayan Union that His Majesty's Government have decided in this sense.

(c) As I have indicated above, the Governor's latest proposal regarding immigration policy has not yet been put to the Malays. In propose now to invite him to do so, and to urge him to advise them most strongly to accept the proposal, on the grounds that it meets their essential point of view and that it is coupled with the general acceptance of a scheme which is largely of their own making.

7. I now recommend that my colleagues should authorise me to inform the Governor, subject to points (a), (b) and (c) paragraph 6 above, and subject to the necessary emphasis being placed on the early introduction of an electoral system (see paragraph 5 (c) above), that the proposals are approved by His Majesty's Government.

---

[3] At the same meeting, Cabinet refused the request that the rulers should have the right of concurrence in the appointment of the high commissioner. Consequently, the rulers' views were not taken into account at the time of Gurney's appointment in 1948, but, in response to their protests and after the matter had been taken to the prime minister and Buckingham Palace, the principle of informal consultation was conceded, see part II of this volume, 165 and CO 537/3760. Lyttelton, the Conservative colonial secretary, was punctilious in keeping them abreast of prospective changes at the top during his visit to Malaya in Dec 1951.

If, as I greatly hope, the Governor is able to tell me in the near future that he has secured Malay agreement on all outstanding points. I would propose to take an early opportunity of announcing His Majesty's Government's decision in Parliament and of publishing a summary of the proposals in their final shape, in the form of a Command Paper. Thereafter, an Order in Council would have to be made providing for the establishment of the Federation of Malaya in place of the Malayan Union, and the necessary new agreements would have to be signed with the Malay Rulers. With these formalities completed, it is hoped that it will be possible to establish the "Federation" early next year.[4]

Annex to 128

Original "Federation" Proposals (Working Committee, December 1946)	Amendments, etc., Proposed by the Consultative Committee (January–March 1947)	Governor's Present Recommendations, May, 1947
Citizenship. (Principle of a common citizenship established to include those who make Malaya their home and the object of their loyalty.)	(In both cases, general policy maintained and principle of a common citizenship accepted.)	
1. AUTOMATIC ACQUISITION		
A. Qualification by birth in the "Federation"—	No change; but the two Chinese members wished to substitute for (b), (c) and (d) simply that any person who is a British subject, or any person born in any of the States, who is permanently resident anywhere in the "Federation," would become a citizen automatically	As proposed in December, but in the case of (b) the submission of the Chinese members of the Consultative Committee is so far followed as to permit British Subjects born in either of the Settlements to acquire citizenship by operation of law if they are permanently resident anywhere in the "Federation."
(a) Malays to have automatic qualification by birth alone (b) British subjects born in either of the Settlements, to qualify automatically if they are permanently resident *in the Settlements* (c) British subjects born anywhere in the "Federation" whose fathers were either born in the "Federation" or resident for a continuous period of 15 years (d) Others born in the "Federation" *both* of whose parents were born in and have been resident on the "Federation" for a continuous period of 15 years.		
B. Qualification by descent—	No change	No change.
Any person whose father is a citizen at the date of that person's birth		

---

[4] In presenting this paper to the Cabinet on 3 July, Creech Jones referred to its earlier approval of revised constitutional proposals (see 110, note 2) and stressed: 'It had not been necessary to suggest any departure from the basic aim of creating a strong central government with a common citizenship open to all who had adopted Malaya as their home'. Cabinet authorised the substance of the recommendations (though see notes 2 and 3 above). The proposals were then referred back to the rulers and UMNO before being published on 21 July in London and on 24 July in Kuala Lumpur. Creech Jones informed parliament during the debate on colonial estimates on 29 July. See CAB 128/10, CM 59(47)3, 3 July 1947; *Federation of Malaya: Summary of Revised Constitutional Proposals* (Cmd 7171, July 1947); *Federation of Malaya: Summary of Revised Constitutional Proposals Accepted by His Majesty's Government, 24 July 1947* (Kuala Lumpur, 1947); *H of C Debs*, vol 441, col 269, 29 July 1947.

Original "Federation" Proposals (Working Committee, December 1946)	Amendments, etc., Proposed by the Consultative Committee (January–March 1947)	Governor's Present Recommendations, May, 1947
2. ACQUISITION BY APPLICATION		
(a) Any person naturalized as the subject of a Ruler becomes also a citizen of the "Federation"	No change	No change.
(b) The High Commissioner to have discretion to confer citizenship on any applicant, and his minor children, who satisfied him that *either*:—		
(i) He was *born* in the "Federation" and has resided there for 10 out of 15 years preceding his application	Resident for 5 years out of the last 10 years	Resident for 8 out of 12 years.
or		
(ii) he has resided in the "Federation" for 15 out of the preceding 20 years;	Resident for 8 out of the preceding 15	Follows December propsals— 15 out of 20.
and		
(i) he is of good character	No change	No change.
(ii) has an adequate knowledge of Malay or English	In the case of a person over the age of 45, and resident in the "Federation" for 20 years, and applies within 2 years for citizenship, the language qualification should be waived	Consultative Committee's proposal accepted.
(iii) makes a declaration of permanent settlement	No change	
(iv) takes the citizenship oath	No change	In addition an applicant for citizenship is to be of the age of 18 or over.

129 CO 537/2208, no 16   30 Sept 1947

[Serious crime and the governor's powers of banishment]: despatch no 19 from Sir E Gent to Mr Creech Jones. *Minute* by H T Bourdillon

I have the honour to refer to your secret telegram No. 139 dated the 3rd of February, 1947, in which you conveyed your approval of my proceeding under Banishment legislation against ceretain classes of aliens. These powers have been used sparingly and, in the case of persons falling in the second category in paragraph 2 of my secret telegram No. 57 of the 17th January, 1947, only on the production at the banishment enquiry of evidence of guilt which the person concerned is unable to rebut. Since the receipt of your telegram I have approved a total of 47 Orders of Banishment in all.

2. The incidence of serious crime continues to be very high and the necessity for retaining banishment as one of the most important weapons in the armoury of the Government for maintaining law and order is at least as great as it was at the beginning of the year. The most serious obstacle to the administration of justice in Malaya today is the extent to which sections of the public have been intimidated by gangs of one kind or another. These gangs fall into two categories:—(a) gangs composed of Chinese who are, for the most part, successors to the resistance movement organised originally against the Japanese and who now continue activities such as banditry, abduction, armed robbery and extortion from a profit motive; and (b) semi-disciplined organisations of Indian estate labourers, such as the "Thondar

Padai" or Youth Corps in Kedah mentioned in the report sent under cover of my secret despatch No. 8 of 8th April, 1947.

3. The Chinese gangs falling within category (a) are well armed with firearms, including Sten guns and grenades. The "Thondar Padai" are not armed with firearms; but, as a semi-disciplined force, have succeeded from time to time in intimidating very completely the easily frightened Indian labourers on estates.

4. Administration of justice by the Courts is crippled if witnesses are too frightened to give evidence or if the public are afraid to inform the police of the actions and whereabouts of criminals. As an example of the fate which befell one informer I enclose a portion of a record of a recent banishment enquiry.[1] The informer's house was burnt down, he himself was dangerously stabbed, but escaped. His brother, his brother's wife and two nephews were stabbed while his wife, child, mother, father and niece were killed and their bodies burned and charred. In face of such reprisals, the reluctance of witnesses to give evidence in open court is understandable, and banishment is the only weapon available to deliver sections of the public from the terror caused by these gangs. There is a strong and insistent public opinion, manifest amongst Asiatics no less than Europeans, in favour of a freer use of the banishment weapon for the purpose of ridding the country of criminals and undesirables against whom the ordinary processes of justice cannot, for the reasons given, be invoked.

5. In the special circumstances which obtain at present in this territory I propose the following modifications of the categories mentioned in paragraph 2 of my telegram No. 57, *viz.*:—

(a) deletion from category One of any limitation as to period of residence. It is shown to be necessary to have the power to expel an alien convicted of violent crime notwithstanding a long period of residence in Malaya. It is also found to be necessary to have the power to expel aliens who are convicted of possession or carrying of firearms or grenades, or who are habitual criminals, if the crimes are of a serious nature. Inclusion of such persons in this category is recommended.

(b) inclusion in category Two of persons who engage in violent crime.

I should be grateful for your approval of these proposals.

6. As regards organisations such as "Thondar Padai" their activities have been considerably curtailed by the enactment of the Public Order Ordinance, 1947 and by police action; but intimidation among estate labourers is still a most serious problem and a substantial impediment to the rapid rehabilitation of the country. The intimidation is usually organised by Communist or other agitators who are not actuated by concern for the welfare of the labourers. In many cases the ring-leaders are Indian British subjects.

7. It is not, at present, the policy to banish British subjects; but experience has shown that it is highly desirable that the pre-war system under which British subjects were not immune from banishment from the Malay States should again be invoked, and I recommend this course. As you are aware, the banishment Enactments of the Federated and Unfederated Malay States do not, as does the Banishment Ordinance of the Straits Settlements, contain an exception in favour of British subjects and it has been expressly held by the Supreme Court of the Federated Malay

---

[1] Not printed.

States that a British subject is not immune from banishment (*Yap Hon Chin* v *Parry* (1911) 2 F.M.S.L.R.(P.C.) 70). It does not appear that the scope of the existing Banishment Enactments were necessarily curtailed by the creation of the Malayan Union.

8. The encouragement and support given by the Japanese during the occupation to such organisations as the Indian National Army and the Indian Independence League,[2] and to their anti-British tenets, has left as its legacy a substantial number of Indians in this country who engage in such activities as intimidation, extortion, blackmail and other serious forms of crime, including murder.

9. As an instance of the type of case for which banishment would provide the only possible remedy, I would refer you to that of that of the person named in paragraph 4 of my telegram No. 256 of the 6th March, 1947, in connection with the riots in Kedah earlier this year. Shortly after those riots this person disappeared. He has now reappeared and is steadily reinstating himself in his former influential position. There is evidence that he was one of the ring-leaders of a gang of estate labourers who, as the Japanese were approaching in December, 1941, beat to death and buried, probably while still alive, the senior conductor on the estate and had the body thrown into a river the next day; and that in 1946, he was, with the help of his "Thondar Padai" concerned in two cases of criminal intimidation, one of which might have resulted in the suicide of an intimidated girl. In none of these cases is there any likelihood of persuading the witnesses to give evidence in open court owing to their fears of the consequences. The report on the disturbances in Kedah, which was forwarded under cover of my secret despatch No. 8 of the 8th April, 1947, provides abundant evidence of the extent to which intimidation is practised amongst Indians and of the necessity for having powers of banishment of Indian British subjects available as the only remedy which can have any hope of being enforced.

10. A difficulty which at once suggests itself is that the Government of India or of Pakistan, as the case may be, may not always agree to accept Indians whom this Government proposes to banish from Malaya. In the case of the Government of India at least, any application made by this Government would undoubtedly be referred for advice to the Representative of the Government of India in Malaya and the close connections of the present Representative, Mr. Thivy, with the I.N.A., and more especially the Indian Independence League during the occupation, might lead him to recommend his Government to refuse the application. I am of the opinion, however, that, provided satisfactory evidence was forthcoming that the person whom it was proposed to banish was born in India or Pakistan, it should not be essential to obtain in advance the concurrence of the Government concerned. The categories of British subjects, which I recommend should be eligible for banishment, would be identical with those for aliens.

11. I am also considering the enactment of legislation on the lines of the Aliens Order, 1920, of the United Kingdom. The present Enactments dealing with aliens are unsatisfactory in various respects and it would be much better to supersede them by legislation on the lines of the Aliens Order, 1920. A provision corresponding to Article 12 of that Order would be of the utmost assistance in present circumstances.

---

[2] The Indian Independence League was formed by Rash Behari Bose, under Japanese auspices, to muster support amongst overseas Indians for the liberation of India from Britain; the Indian National Army was a parallel military force led by Subhas Chandra Bose.

Proceedings for deportation could be taken under it in many cases which now have to be dealt with under the banishment enactments. Similar safeguards as in the case of banishment, e.g., enquiries by a responsible officer, would be observed, but deportation under an Aliens Ordinance would have the advantage of disarming criticism in England, because it would not be termed "banishment" and it would be effected under powers which have their counterpart in the United Kingdom and have been in force there for twenty-seven years. The proposed Ordinance would not apply to British subjects or British Protected Persons in which latter category would be included every person born in any of the Malay States. The legislation could be made renewable annually, if desired. I should be grateful for approval of this proposal.

12. I should appreciate a very early reply to this despatch by telegram. The recommendations made have the strongest possible support of the Attorney-General[3] and the Commissioner of Police[4] and their acceptance would undoubtedly be welcomed by all law-abiding sections of the public. The procedure by which banishment orders will only be made after most careful enquiries by competent officers would be continued.

Minute on 129

During the past month there have been repeated and very serious cases of violent crime—armed robbery, savage reprisals against informers and the like—in the Malay States, particularly in Johore. We have been told that the situation in Singapore, on the other hand, has recently shown a remarkable improvement, and Mr. Pierpoint (a planter who came and saw me recently about the Johore troubles) expressed the view that a number of ringleaders had crossed into the mainland. Be that as it may, the recent outbreaks in the Malayan Union have been extremely alarming, and as soon as we saw reports of them in the Press, we asked Sir Edward Gent for a report (see No. 12). The reply to this enquiry is in the telegram at No. 21, and it will be seen that the information given is to a certain extent reassuring. Seen in perspective against the whole of 1947 and the whole of the Malayan Union, the trouble is apparently not so serious as might have been feared. The police are doing their work well and are gaining control. There has indeed been a recrudescence of lawlessness, but it has occurred in outlying areas where the police are thin on the ground. In the big centres, the menace has already been largely defeated.

Nevertheless, Sir Edward Gent does not minimise the danger, and in his despatch at No. 16 (sent before the telegram at 21) he proposes certain remedies, all of them connected with the freer use of his powers under the Banishment Legislation. Before I proceed to discuss these proposed remedies, I should remark that paragraphs 2, 3 and 4 of the despatch give further sensational evidence of the horrible nature of the crimes being committed, as well as describing the origins of the two principal classes of criminals. The instance, given in paragraph 4, of the reprisals against the family of one informer is by itself enough to explain the outburst of public indignation (and criticism of Government) which has apparently taken place in the Malayan Union. I do not think it is an exaggeration to describe in these terms the local interest which the whole matter appears to have aroused. In paragraph 4 of the despatch, Sir

---

[3] K K O'Connor. [4] H B Langworthy.

Edward Gent refers to the "strong and insistent public opinion, manifest amongst Asiatics no less than Europeans, in favour of a freer use of the "banishment weapon", and the press cuttings sent to Mr. Rees-Williams by the Straits Times Press (see No. 22) leave no doubt about the tone of local comment. It is very ugly indeed. Sir Edward Gent is bitterly accused of not having used the banishment weapon with enough resolution in the past, and the accusation is freely extended to the Colonial Office and to the Secretary of State himself. Indeed, it is suggested that the Secretary of State is the real cause of the whole trouble.

Sir Edward Gent's proposed remedies are given in paragraphs 5, 7 and 11 of his despatch. The two latter proposals (banishment, in certain circumstances, of British subjects and the enactment of legislation on the lines of the United Kingdom Aliens Order) obviously require close consideration, and the former in particular may give rise to grave difficulties. These suggestions, however, are not of first rate urgency, and the file can be recirculated for their further consideration. The matter demanding instant attention is Sir Edward Gent's main recommendation, in paragraph 5 of his despatch, in which he asks for immediate authority to extend in certain respects the use of the banishment weapon against criminal aliens. I attempt to show, in the top draft opposite,[5] the line which I think should be taken in reply to this recommendation. The draft, as will be seen, does not give Sir Edward Gent the authority for which he asks. It goes further. It tells him that he already has this authority and more. I go into a certain amount of historical detail on this point, because I think, it is important that Sir Edward Gent should know, beyond a shadow of doubt, that we are firmly behind him in any action which he deems necessary against criminal gangsters. I need not repeat here the recapitulation given in the draft, but I have long felt uneasy lest Sir Edward Gent might be staying his hand, perhaps to a degree which justifies some of the local criticisms, in the belief that we at this end were far more nervous about the use of the banishment weapon than is in fact the case. See for instance my minute of 23/1/47, in which I commented on his previous request of this type. There has in fact never been any suggestion from this end (except as regards *political* agitators) that the Secretary of State wished to impose restrictions on the Governor's discretion in the use of the banishment weapon. It has merely been stipulated, for obvious reasons, that the whole matter shall be reviewed after a certain period. This stipulation is repeated in the draft opposite, and Sir Edward Gent is also requested to give us full, up-to-date and accurate information on action taken. . . .

I spoke earlier in this minute of a visit from a Mr. Pierpoint. He is the President of the Johore Branch of the United Planters Association, and he has a good knowledge of this part of the country—including, incidentally, a considerable insight into Johore politics and a close personal acquaintance with Dato Onn. He expressed to me the extreme concern of the Johore planters at the recent outbreaks of lawlessness (there has been one example of a European clubbed to death and robbed before the eyes of his wife), and he has just rung me up to acquaint me with the terms of a resolution by his Association. It is couched in the strongest possible terms, and calls for the immediate replacement of the Governor. This particular manifestation need not perhaps be taken tragically, but in my view there is no doubt whatever that the menace is really grave and that local opinion, Asiatic and European, is really stirred.

---

[5] Not printed but the final version is at 130.

This is not a case of the Governor or the Secretary of State imposing repressive measures against the will of the people. It is a case of popular demand. I feel sure that we must go as far as is proposed in the draft telegram, and that we must act without delay.

H.T.B.

15.10.47

130   CO 537/2208, no 24   18 Oct 1947

[Violence and the governor's powers of banishment]: outward telegram (reply) no 1305 from Mr Creech Jones to Sir Edward Gent

Your despatch No. 19 Secret.[1] Banishment.

I fully share your anxiety over continued prevalence of violent crime as described in your paragraph 2, 3, and 4, and you may rest assured that your efforts to control the situation will not be needlessly obstructed from this end. In this connection, I think it is essential that I should begin by making clear my whole attitude regarding banishment from Malaya of criminals of the "gangster" type. In your paragraph 4 you speak of a strong and insistent public opinion in favour of a freer use of the banishment weapon. The existence of this public opinion, particularly since the latest outrages in Johore, has been forcibly brought to my notice from more than one quarter, and I am disturbed to see that there is apparently a widespread belief that an over-cautious policy is being imposed, possibly against the wishes of your Government from Whitehall. There are, of course, no grounds for such a belief, but I feel it is important that I should remove any possibility of misunderstanding between us.

2.   In my telegram No. 1545 of 1946, I approved your proposal to banish certain leading members of the Ang Bin Hoey Society.[2] In doing so, I drew your attention to a distinction which had been made in the case of Singapore between criminal gangsterdom pure and simple and certain activities of a political nature, and I invited you (as I had already invited the Governor of Singapore) to consult me before taking banishment action in cases falling within the latter (repeat latter) category. It was not my intention, either then or later, to circumscribe in any way your freedom of action, subject only to the limitations imposed by the law itself and by your own discretion in applying it, in proceeding against undesirable aliens whose activities were not (repeat not) of a political character. Even as regards political ringleaders I have always been, as you know, ready to reconsider the position in the light of changing local circumstances. In my telegram of the 27th March last addressed to the Governor-General as No. 156 and repeated to you as No. 407, I gave authority to the Governor of Singapore, in response to his urgent representations, to use powers of banishment against political agitators without prior reference to me. Similar authority was not conveyed to yourself because you had stated that you did not require it. I naturally do not wish to force upon you a freedom of action which you do not require, and the position as regards political agitators in the Malayan Union therefore remains the same as before. That is to say, you should continue (pending my consideration of any representations from yourself on the lines already made by

---

[1] See 129.   [2] Ang Bin Hoey was a pro-KMT Triad society.

Singapore) to consult me in each individual case before taking banishment action against persons in this category. As stated above, however, there is no (repeat no) restriction imposed from here on your use of banishment powers against violent criminals pure and simple. In cases of persons who have been resident in Malaya for a considerable period, however, you should use these powers with the utmost circumspection and only where you are convinced that action is necessary for the good of the country. I would ask you to provide me periodically (say at monthly intervals) with up-to-date information on action taken, and that you would send me prompt and full answers to any enquiries which I may make on specific cases. You will appreciate that this whole subject is liable to excite Parliamentary interest and that I must be fortified with the full facts.

3.　The above recapitulation clearly affects the recommendations in paragraph 5 of your despatch. As I see it, you are still proposing to limit, though not to the same extent as hitherto, the categories of persons within the "gangster" class to whom action under the banishment legislation would be applicable. If you wish to impose such limits yourself, and if you are convinced that the menace can be effectively checked by action within these limits, I would naturally have no objection, but so far as I am concerned you have full authority, as described above, for action against undesirable aliens other than political agitators. The position, however, should be reviewed in a year from now. In my telegram No. 139 I requested that a review should be taken a year after that date, but in view of your latest information I am content to extend the period.

4.　Your further suggestions regarding the possible banishment of British subjects and the enactment of legislation on the lines of the United Kingdom Aliens' Order are still being considered here. I see much to commend the latter suggestion, but the former may raise difficulties. Further telegram will be sent as soon as possible, and in the meanwhile I trust that the explanations given above will help you in your present difficulties, in which you have my full sympathy.

5.　Please send Governor Singapore and Governor-General copies of your despatch under reference, unless you have already done so.[3]

---

[3] Replying to the secretary of state on 22 Nov 1947, Gent commented: 'I have had no reason to consider the banishment of any alien for political activities and I note your instructions in such circumstances should I have occasion to consider banishment in the future.' See CO 537/2208, no 34.

131　CO 537/2144, no 264　　　8 Nov 1947

[Chinese demand for constitutional review]: inward telegram no 367 from Mr M J MacDonald to Mr Creech Jones

[After the publication of the revised constitutional proposals in July 1947, the Associated Chinese Chambers of Commerce joined the AMCJA-PUTERA coalition in staging a countrywide 'hartal' (or work stoppage) on 20 Oct. While MacDonald appeared to sympathize with the Chinese demand for a Royal Commission, Gent, who was pushing hard to inaugurate the Federation on 1 Jan 1948, would not entertain any suggestion that threatened to stand in the way of immediate implementation of the new constitution (see 132).]

Following personal for Secretary of State from Governor-General. *Begins.*

1. You will have seen letter dated 26th October sent to you by Lee Kong Chian[1] on behalf of Associated Chinese Chambers of Commerce in Malaya. This telegram gives part of the background to it and touches upon the question of your reply.

2. Some leading members of Chinese Chambers of Commerce, including Lee, made informal approaches to me arising out of my two broadcast speeches and following hartal of 20th October. I have had conversations with several of them (corrupt group)[2] they sought any indication that I could give them that the hartal might lead the Government to modify its policy in relation to the Constitutions for the Federation and Singapore. They said that my speeches had had considerable influence for good on Chinese opinion, but that the community in general are still seriously critical of certain aspects of the Constitutions.

3. I made it clear that the hartal could and would have no influence. I said that no change whatever would be made in the Constitutions and that they would be introduced in their present form early next year. I added that they would be amended in due course, but that they must be given fair trial first to see where they needed improvement and when further constitutional advances could wisely be made. Lee Kong Chian and his moderate colleagues now fully understand this position and I believe that they are prepared to conciliate it. On the other hand the more extreme Chinese element, led by Tan Cheng Lock, are seeking to create further immediate difficulties. They are pressing Lee and Associated Chinese Chambers of Commerce to continue the controversy and put new pressure on the Government for changes in the Constitution of the Federation. They have allies in this cause in the Council of Joint Action and associated bodies. Lee and his moderate friends are endeavouring to check the spread of rival influence amongst the Chinese. They are pursuing delaying tactics. Amongst other things they are using Lee's letter to you as a factor in these tactics. In response to pressure from the more extreme elements, Lee has written this letter on behalf of the Associated Chambers and they must await your reply. He tells me that he does not expect reply for three or four weeks

4. I understand that he and a group of his moderate colleagues drafted the letter carefully after their talks with me. They did not tell me at the time that they proposed writing to you and I had no knowledge of what action they intended to take. But Lee has since told me that the terms of the letter were influenced by our conversations. You will note the following points in it:—

(1) It does not ask for any early or specific change in either the Constitution of the Federation or the Constitution of Singapore.
(2) It merely suggests that a Royal Commission should review the Constitutional (?group omitted).[3]
(3) It is indefinite as to when this review should be made and does not suggest that it should take place before the Constitutions are inaugurated.

5. This is deliberate. Lee states that there is good chance that he and his friends could persuade all moderate Chinese opinion to accept the position if you indicate in your reply that Constitution will be impartially reviewed in a few years' time. In conversations Lee suggested in three years' time. I discouraged any idea that the Government would make a commitment about any particular period of years and he

---

[1] Lee Kong Chian, a pre-war supporter of the KMT, was president of the Singapore Chinese Chamber of Commerce.   [2 & 3] ie phrase garbled in transmission.

and his friends accept this. They are anxious for an "impartial enquiry". Their strongest remaining fears arising out of the present Constitutions are that:—

(1) the power which Malay Rulers have to veto changes in Federal Constitution will prevent the process of constitutional evolution which I described in my broadcasts, and that Constitution will therefore remain fixed indefinitely in its present form;

(2) the Malays will use their power to control immigration policy in a way which will be unfair to Chinese and will prevent the economic development of Malaya.

I have done my best to reassure them on these points, but they remain sceptical. Therefore, they do not wish the revision of the Constitution to rest wholly with His Majesty's Government on one side, and Malay Rulers and Malay Unofficial majority in the Legislature on the other. That is why they urge a Royal Commission. Lee tells me that an answer from you, promising a Royal Commission in a few years' time, would remove the apprehensions of a great majority of those Chinese who feel strongly on this matter and he and others of his friends have told me that this would enable them to accept for some time to come the present constitutional proposals and to detach a great deal of Chinese support from Tan Cheng Lock.

6. I have expressed to Lee informally the following general opinions on this matter:—

(1) We must abide by the provisions of the Agreements with the Malay Rulers giving them certain powers in connection with revisions of the Constitution.

(2) I do not think that Rulers will be rigid. They will be greatly influenced by opinions of their Malay subjects and of His Majesty's Government and to a minor extent by non-Malay public opinion in Malaya. Constitutional (?stagnation) is unthinkable and Malay Rulers could not be allowed to secure this. The Chinese can influence them by closer co-operation with Malay leaders and by convincing these Malay leaders of any injustices to the Chinese community or any obstacles to Malayan development which may exist. If such things do turn out to exist, His Majesty's Government will use its influence to help them.

(3) I personally would not rule out the possibility of need for commission assisting His Majesty's Government, the Malay Rulers and Malay peoples to work out a revision of the Constitution when the time for that comes some years hence. This would not necessarily be a Royal Commission. For example, it might be a commission of Members of Parliament. On the other hand a commission may not (repeat not) be necessary. The best solution will be if the Malay and Chinese leaders in Malaya can in due course agree with the local Administration on desirable changes. Therefore it would be unwise at the present time to commit ourselves positively to a commission. Moreover, if we were to do so now, that would be the best guarantee that no such commission could ever function in Malaya. An announcement that such a commission would come to Malaya later on to consider constitutional changes might well arouse suspicion and hostility of Malays, ensuring that they would oppose any such plan.

(4) Nevertheless I agree that we should make clear that the Constitutions could not be (?could be intended) reviewed in due course, so that constitutional advance is wisely planned. I am prepared to consider the possibility of our announcing that, if it seems desirable at the time when a review takes place, a Parliamentary or

other commission from the U.K. might visit Malaya to help the Rulers and peoples of Malaya, as well as Parliament, to decide what changes should take place.

7. Lee seems ready to accept the arguments in 6 (2) and (3) above. He nurses the hope that your answer to his letter of 25th October will take the line in 6 (4).

8. My appreciation of the position is that great mass of the Chinese in the Country are not (repeat not) interested in this issue. Nevertheless, the section of educated Chinese opinion which has become politically conscious about the constitutional problem almost wholly shares the dissatisfaction and apprehension of Lee and his Chamber of Commerce colleagues about Federal Constitution. This is as true, for example, of moderate professional and commercial Chinese in Penang and Singapore as of the irresponsible ones in Malacca. They are the Chinese who count most in these matters, and, though they are a small minority, they are the leaders of the community as a whole and exert widespread influence. If they are seriously dissatisfied they can not only embarrass the Administration quite a lot, but they will also feel less disposed to seek a reconciliation and accept compromises with Malays. Moreover, the moderate Chinese in that case would be inclined to suppose that they have no alternative but to associate themselves with Tan Cheng Lock and some of the more extreme political factions in the Country. In my opinion it is important that we should do anything that we properly can to conciliate the moderate Chinese now. If we can, for example, meet them sufficiently on the issue raised in Lee's letter to you we shall probably greatly weaken Tan Cheng Lock's and the Council of Joint Action's appeal to the Chinese.

9. There are indications that the Council of Joint Action's and P.U.T.E.R.A.'s policy may be not only to boycott the Singapore elections[4] but also attempt to induce representatives of the Chinese and other domiciled communities to refuse nomination to the Federal Legislature in Kuala Lumpur. It would be serious if the Associated Chinese Chambers of Commerce adopted this line. I believe they will not (repeat not) do so if we can satisfy them sufficiently on the present issue. Lee Kong Chian tells me that apart from the question of separation of Singapore from the Federation, the Chinese have no quarrel at all with the Singapore Constitution. The Singapore Chinese Chamber of Commerce has done its best to encourage registration of voters, and will do all that it can to get those who have registered to cast votes next year. I believe that he and like-minded Chinese throughout Malaya will also be ready to co-operate in working the Constitution for the Federation. But whether they will do so depends to a considerable extent, I think, on the terms of your answer to Lee Kong Chian's letter.

10. In all this it is, of course, extremely important that we should do nothing to alienate the Malays. I shall consult Gent and Gimson immediately on this matter, with the purpose of sending for your consideration a draft reply to Lee Kong Chian's letter.
Ends.

---

[4] In Mar 1948 elections were held returning a minority of six members to Singapore's new Legislative Council.

132 CO 537/2144, no 267   8 Nov 1947

[Chinese demand for constitutional review]: inward telegram no 1185
from Sir E Gent to Sir T Lloyd   [Extract]

Following personal for Lloyd from Gent.
Begins.

1. I have received from the Governor-General copy of his personal telegram to
the Secretary of State No. 367,[1] and I expect that the Governor-General had not
received copy of my savingram to the Secretary of State No. 46 before he sent his
personal telegram.

2. I feel it absolutely necessary to send you my advice without delay that the
whole issue of the successful conclusion of the Federation Agreement would be
jeopardised at this juncture, if the Malays received any impression from action by His
Majesty's Government that the intention of the latter was to revise Federal
Constitution in the next few years by means of decision to send out Commission or
otherwise in order to conciliate present local Chinese opposition.

3. Core of present Chinese opposition is concerned substantially with separation
of Singapore and is centred in Singapore. This basic attitude is less strong in Penang
and much less strong amongst Chinese in the Malay States. As soon as they are
convinced that His Majesty's Government's determination to implement the Federation proposals, finally and inflexibility, I do not expect influential Chinese opinion in
general in Malayan Union (apart from the extreme Left Wing) to indulge in
non-co-operation on any serious scale, if at all. As long as they are not convinced of
this by reasons of waiting on the debate in Parliament, or if they receive qualified
answer from the Secretary of State to the letter of (?25th October) from the
Associated Chinese Chambers of Commerce, they will continue to stage public
opposition and gravely exacerbate Malay relations with both Chinese and the
Government. . . .

---

[1] See 131.

133 CO 537/2144, no 271   12 Nov 1947

[Chinese demand for constitutional review]: outward telegram (reply)
no 652 from Mr Creech Jones to Mr M J MacDonald

Your telegram G.G. No. 367.[1]

I am most grateful for this full and lucid exposition, and for your patient and
statesman-like attempts to work upon moderate Chinese opinion.

2. I have now seen letter from Lee Kong Chian to which you refer, and also Gent's
savingram No. 47. Before I reach a final view on this matter, I must await result of
your consultations with Gent and Gimson. Nevertheless, it may help if I give you at
once my preliminary reactions to your telegram.

3. I appreciate that opposition amongst Chinese in Malaya appears to have

---

[1] See 131.

become more widespread and deep-seated than we had previously hoped, and that this, in spite of all your efforts, may cause considerable embarrassment in the future. Nevertheless, I should have thought that any statement by myself or His Majesty's Government at the present juncture, to the effect that the Constitution so recently decided upon will be specifically reviewed a few years hence either by a Commission or by any other method, would at once exacerbate all that suspicion and irritation amongst the Malays which we have tried so long and patiently to allay, but which the recent hartal has evidently, in some measure, aroused again. In this connection, please see my telegram No. 1406 to the Malayan Union, repeated to you as No. 651. I still feel, subject to your views and those of Gent, that arranged Parliamentary Question and Answer on lines I have proposed may be very necessary. It might, however, go some way to meet the situation described in your telegram under reference if I were to add to the Parliamentary reply something to the effect that it has always been agreed that the new Constitution is merely a beginning, that the conception is dynamic and not static, and that the whole purpose of His Majesty's Government is to allow all those who belong to Malaya, of whatever race, to guide the Constitution in future development on lines of democracy and toleration.

My reply to Lee Kong Chian's letter might be on the same lines, if it is to be fuller than Gent suggests in his savingram No. 46.

4. You will doubtless take the above into consideration in your consultations with Gent and Gimson. I feel sure that anything which would risk alienating Malays at the present moment would be absolutely fatal. I have just seen Gent's telegram No. 1185,[2] which further confirms this view.

---

[2] See 132.

134   CO 537/2144, no 317   12 Dec 1947
[Chinese demand for constitutional review]: inward savingram no 28 from Mr M J MacDonald to Mr Creech Jones

Following for Secretary of State from Governor-General.

My telegram No. 422. I handed to Mr. Lee about 10 days ago your letter in reply to communication from Associated Chinese Chambers of Commerce. When he read it through he said that he wished to express to you his thanks for the friendly and courteous tone of the note. This, he felt sure, would impress his colleagues, who had been disappointed at the tone of your earlier letter to them. He added, however, that beyond that the reply would give no satisfaction to the Chinese. It amounted to a complete rejection of the substance of their representations and request to you. He said that in their letter they had deliberately avoided making any proposals for changes in the constitution of the Federation and had only sought an assurance that at some time in the future an impartial enquiry into the working of the Constitution would be held. He said that even a general reference to the possibility of something in the nature of a Royal Commission would meet the needs of the moderate Chinese in their effort to keep the Chinese disappointment about the Federal Constitution within reasonable bounds.

2. I told him that it was impossible to include any such reference in your letter. I

emphasised that the letter indicated that Constitutional development in Malaya would be evolutionary, and agreed that the Chinese could influence that evolution through the proper Constitutional channels. I thought it wise to tell him also that 2 or 3 days later you would make a statement in Parliament that the new Federal Constitution in its present form would be inaugurated on January 1st or as soon as possible after that. I did not want him or his colleagues to be taken by surprise by that statement.

3. He said that he fully understood that the Constitution would come into operation at an early date, and emphasised that the Chinese would be willing to co-operate in working the Constitution if they felt assured that any defects or injustices embodied in it would come under review by some impartial body in due course. Without such an assurance he was apprehensive that the Chinese might not feel able to co-operate. We discussed this matter at some length. I urged that the Chinese should (a) now accept the present position, and (b) agree to the High Commissioner's nomination of Chinese representatives to sit on the Legislative Council, where those representatives could raise any questions on which the Chinese community felt dissatisfied. At the end of our talk he assured me that he personally would do his best to persuade his colleagues that this was the wise course for them to take. He told me that he would circulate the text of your reply immediately to the Chinese Chambers of Commerce, so that its contents were known to them before your Parliamentary answer appeared in the Press. They would all meet to discuss the situation a few days later.

4. Two or three days after that Mr. Lee telephoned to ask me whether I would be willing to receive him and 4 or 5 of his friends to discuss the matter. He told me that it would be helpful if I would urge on them the policy which I had urged on him. I said that I would be delighted to receive them. When he brought the party on Sunday, December 7th, it turned out to consist of ten leading representatives of the Chinese Chambers of Commerce in Singapore and various places in the Malayan Union. Colonel H.S. Lee was amongst them, and Mr. Tan Cheng Lock was also there. They represented to me strongly their dissatisfaction with various points in the Federal Constitution. I replied to their points one by one. They then expressed their dissatisfaction with your letter on the grounds that it did not promise an impartial review of the Constitution after it had been working for a few years. I replied to them also on this point. They then asked whether I would give you a personal account when I visited London of their strong feelings in the matter. I promised to inform you on the subject faithfully and objectively. They then indicated that they would consider later what further action they should take to impress the Government with the strength of their views. I urged that the proper course was for them to co-operate in working the Constitution. It provided means by which a considerable number of Chinese representatives could present their feelings on any matter in the Legislative Council. I used all the obvious arguments in favour of their doing this and against their standing aside from the Legislative Council. I stressed in particular the vital importance of their not repeat not alienating the Malays, but working in a co-operative spirit with them. They listened carefully to what I said, but did not make any comments beyond agreeing in general with the principle of inter-racial co-operation.

5. I understand that they spent the rest of the day trying to decide what their policy should be. At the moment of dictating this savingram in Hong Kong I do not

know what their final decision will be. Before I left Singapore one of my Chinese friends told me that Mr. Lee Kiang Chen [Lee Kong Chian] proposed to send a personal letter to all the Chinese Chambers of Commerce urging that they should co-operate with the Government in the nomination of Chinese representatives for the Legislative Council. His letter will suggest that when they do this they should take the opportunity to make one more formal protest against the Constitution. My informant told me that opinion amongst the leading members of the Chinese Chambers of Commerce is divided on this matter, and that neither Mr. Lee nor anyone else yet knows what the response to his letter will be. There may have been further developments in Malaya since I left Singapore four days ago.

135   CO 537/2144, no 318   17 Dec 1947
[Dato Onn]: inward savingram no 52 from Sir E Gent to Mr Creech Jones

1. My telegram 1305. Following appreciation of Dato Onn's present general attitude may be of interest to you.

2. Dato Onn has throughout held political leadership amongst Malays, and UMNO was his original creation to organise and maintain Malay political hostility to Union constitution and MacMichael Treaties. He has never flagged in his efforts to remove as completely as possible any surviving relics of Malayan Union in new Federal constitution, and to restore Johore Constitution as completely as existence of Federation Agreement permits.

3. He is not pure Malay but mother was Circassian and his character, thought and speech are of keener and more restless nature than customary to Malays. Good demagogic speaker, apt to speak and write rudely and thoughtlessly, and is inherently distrustful and suspicious.

3. As final stage of Federation negotiations is reached his temperamental qualities are subject to exceptional strain in face of increased Chinese propaganda against Federation scheme and their more and more overt claim to political predominance. At the same time within Malay ranks there is a natural movement on one hand to exact up to the last moment highest possible terms for Malay general interest and for each State interests. There is also in Malay ranks sign of a development in direction of a more liberal policy in UMNO which involves a resistance to full control hitherto by right wing Malay leaders many of whom will now become Mentri Besars and State Secretaries. This also adds to Dato Onn's problems and his personal aggressive qualities do not naturally serve to attract friendship or spirit of comradeship even amongst Malays. In Kedah particularly Sultan and his leading Malay advisers are increasingly resentful of Onn's methods and manners and his interference in internal State affairs of Kedah.

4. Finally Sultan of Johore's return has to some extent created a complication for Dato Onn in his immediate Johore position in which he has needed to go more warily.[1]

---

[1] Dato Onn swung in and out of royal favour. An adopted son of the Sultan who had been educated with Johore princes in England, in the 1930s he had written critical press articles that incurred Ibrahim's displeasure. Nonetheless, he played an important part in defusing the so-called 'conspiracy' to dethrone

Ibrahim in early 1946 and was appointed *mentri besar* (chief minister) of Johore later that year. Towards the end of 1947 Ibrahim returned from London for the final stage of the federal negotiations and, while *mentri besar* and Sultan combined in their defence of Johore rights, their relationship soon suffered. Onn increasingly questioned the role of the rulers in modern Malaya while Ibrahim claimed that Onn's political activities interfered with his obligations as chief minister. After many rumours and threats, Onn resigned as mentri *besar* on 1 Oct 1949. See CO 537/4790.

136   CO 537/3671, no 28   22 Jan 1948
[Signing the State and Federation Agreements]: letter from Sir E Gent to H T Bourdillon

[The inauguration of the Federation was postponed from 1 Jan 1948 because of Malay opposition—especially from Dato Onn and Sultan Ibrahim—to provisions for Britain's power of advice in the states and her control over their external affairs and defence. Although regarded as crucial, even more important than these matters to the British was an end to constitutional negotiations and they decided not to hold things up any longer. At the Plenary Conference on 20–21 Jan Gent (for the King) and their Highnesses signed the nine State Agreements, revoking the MacMichael treaties, and the Federal Agreement which were to come into effect on 1 Feb. An Order-in-Council gave the agreements legal force from the side of the Crown while state enactments confirmed them from the side of the rulers.]

We had tremendous fun and games here yesterday with the signing of the State and Federation Agreements—no less than about 50 signatures required—and it took about two hours with everyone dressed up to the nines and the Malays looking most magnificent and myself a picture of purity in my white uniform. The whole show was accompanied by a Hollywood atmosphere of brilliant lights and movie-cameras. I expect our Information Department will be sending a set of the pictures. The Sultan of Johore's gout, which prevented him from being in the party, was not, as one would expect, diplomatic. I got a doctor's certificate (a Government doctor) to certify that he was immobilised. We had to hurry the signing of all these documents on in order to get Linehan and Dato Onn off by air in daylight to Johore with the signed documents for completion by his signature and all that was duly organised with numbers of the Secretariat people in charge of various sets of documents to see that they were pushed along to the next person without undue delay.

The temperature in the room here at King's House finally was about 150 degrees, what with the filming lights and the natural atmosphere in this part of the world in the afternoon. The previous day, when we had our last Plenary Conference in order to clear up all the dozens of little drafting points, we all had our fingers crossed in case Dato Onn, who had not been at the final meeting of the Working Committee, should turn sour on any particular point which might have made the signing impossible on the following day. However, it went with a swing and before he had time to raise his usual series of grouses, we closed the formal meeting and despatched the drafts for the all-night working of the Printing Department and then we were able to listen to him in an informal gathering. It is quite surprising how he maintains a barracking on every conceivable action of this Government, mostly fruitless and childish, but he is very alert for any possible ground for offence.

We deeply appreciate the Secretary of State's message of appreciation which reached me on the morning of the signing day and I made full use of it in my harangue on that occasion. I hope he will agree to send us a message for the opening meeting of the new Legislative Council in the middle of February and I have been so bold as to ask for a message from His Majesty for the first meeting of the Conference of Rulers, a few days earlier.

Last night we had an enormous dinner party before all the Rulers and their entourages dispersed, which both have now done. There was a slight restlessness on the part of the Sultan of Perak that we did not have the signing in the morning. The straight answer to that was that we could not have possibly got the documents printed by that time. But it subsequently occurred to me that his real trouble was that he had a horse running at Kuala Lumpur in the 5.30 and rightly guessed that he would not be free to go and see it lose by that hour. The hardest worked man, these last few months, has been O'Connor and he is about at the end of his tether. He insists, however, on carrying on at the same tempo until early February when he will consider having a week's holiday at Fraser's Hill.

I am immensely indebted to you and Seel and Roberts-Wray and Lloyd and Secretary of State for giving me a final discretion on any points which might threaten to come up and wreck the whole procedure. In fact there were none but it was a great relief to know that I had a bit of room to spare in case of necessity.

My grateful thanks and good wishes.

137   CO 537/2177   23 Jan 1948

[Indonesian influences in Malaya]: minute by H T Bourdillon recording the views of Mr M J MacDonald

[In Jan 1948 MacDonald returned to Britain on leave. One of the subjects he discussed at the CO was the extent of Indonesian influences in Malaya against which the Malayan Security Service under J D Dalley was ever vigilant. In June 1947 Dalley produced a paper on 'Indonesian Influences in Malaya', which was issued as a supplement to the fortnightly Political Intelligence Journal, MSS/PIJ no 10/47, 30 June 1947. In June the following year supplement 5, issued with MSS/PIJ no 11/48, 15 June 1948, dealt with 'Malay and Indonesian Communists' (see CO 537/3752 and CO 537/3753).]

This is the file dealing with attempts by Indonesian influences to gain a foothold in the Malay Peninsula, and with the repercussions in Malaya of the troubles between the Indonesians and the Dutch. As shown in Sir Thomas Lloyd's letter to the Governor-General of 18th November last (No. 6 on the file), this is a subject which in our view requires constant watching. It therefore figures prominently in the Agenda of our departmental discussions with Mr. MacDonald, and has in fact been fully discussed with him since his arrival.

Our reasons for keeping the question under review have been rather to guard against an inflammable situation in the future than to deal with one now. Indeed, it has always seemed to us that hitherto, in spite of the geographical propinquity of the two territories and the racial connections between them, Indonesian affairs have had remarkably little effect in Malaya. We asked Mr. MacDonald whether this impression was correct, and whether the underlying reason was to be found, as we have supposed, in the fact that the Malays of the Peninsula tend to regard themselves as a cut above the Indonesians and to resent attempts to drag them into Indonesian politics. Mr. MacDonald confirmed all this, but told us a great deal more which is of immense value in completing the picture. He gave us, in particular, a most interesting account of relevant developments in Malaya since the Dutch "police action".[1] When that event took place, we at this end were anxious lest the existing quiescence in Malaya *vis-à-vis* the Indonesian problem might now be replaced by a strong and emotional partisan feeling, accompanied by greater bitterness against the Dutch in which it would be difficult for the British not to become involved. This anxiety was evidently shared in Singapore, and when the Indonesians began to make broadcast appeals for help in sending Red Cross supplies, the Governor-General, after urgently consulting H.M.G., had been quick to respond. He and Mrs. MacDonald had headed the list of subscribers, and their names had been followed by those of the two Governors. And there the matter stopped, no more subscriptions being forthcoming! The whole thing, in fact, fell as flat as a pancake, and the interest which was so signally lacking then has been equally lacking ever since. Mr. MacDonald attributes this partly to the reasons which we ourselves have imagined, partly to the fact that news of Indonesian atrocities aginst [sic] Chinese nationals quickly alienated any sympathy which the *Chinese* in Malaya might otherwise have felt, and partly to the simple fact that the Indonesians, from the beginning of the Dutch police action, made such a very poor showing. Mr. MacDonald has said that he himself was surprised at this. He expected and in many ways hoped that the Indonesians would do better. But in the event they did conspicuously badly. The Dutch had no difficulty in quickly achieving the objectives they had set for themselves, and the much heralded guerilla activity against them was a serious flop. Moreover, they succeeded in winning over not only a number of puppet leaders whose support meant nothing but a few highly respected Indonesian figures whose support, in public estimation throughout Indonesia, meant a great deal. As against this, the Indonesian resisters were manifestly in very imperfect control of their own side and were incapable of effective cohesion. In short, it was obvious that there was "something wrong with the Republic of Indonesia", and this was not lost upon the Malays of the Peninsula, who tended to thank their stars that they were under British (as opposed to Dutch) protection and thus safely out of the way.

Not that Mr. MacDonald is out of sympathy with the Indonesians. On the contrary, he made it clear to us that he definitely favours the aspirations of the more moderate and responsible Indonesian leaders. This fact is apparently recognised and appreciated by the Indonesian leaders themselves, who understand on the one hand that we cannot take sides with them against the Dutch but regard Lord Killearn and Mr. MacDonald himself, on the other hand, as "their best friends in Asia". What the Governor-General told us about the attitude of Mr. Shahrir[2] is particularly important. Mr. Shahrir does *not* want to involve Malaya in the Indonesian struggle.[3] Indeed, his attitude is quite the contrary. He has met Dato Onn a number of times under Mr. MacDonald's roof, and his advice to Dato Onn has always been to remain in friendship with the British and to "build up his own show".

---

[1] The Linggajati Agreement (Nov 1946) between Indonesian republicans and the Dutch collapsed in June 1947 and the Dutch launched their first 'police action' in which some 150,000 troops were deployed. In Jan 1948 another conference culminated in the Renville Agreement which was similarly shortlived being followed by the second 'police action' in Dec 1948.

[2] Sutan Sjahrir was prime minister of the republic from Nov 1945 to July 1947.

[3] At this point in his minute Bourdillon added the following comment in the margin: 'There are, of course, many Indonesian extremists who do, but that is another matter.'

(On his side, Dato Onn apparently thinks of a future "Federation" of Malaya and British Borneo under British protection, which can develop in contra-distinction though not in opposition to Indonesia and would only merge with the latter, if at all, in the distant future.)

Mr. MacDonald went on from this point to make some more general remarks. He thought it was very important that H.M.G., and above all the local representatives of H.M.G. should be sympathetic towards the moderate nationalist movements in Asia. He said that there was much promising material in these movements, and he felt that the whole future of Britain in Asia might depend on the attitude we adopted towards them. At the moment we were not at all regarded as the reactionary Imperialist power, bent on maintaining European domination in the East at all costs. On the contrary, our reputation, as a result of the developments in India, Ceylon and Burma, stood very high, and it was most important that this position should be maintained. Whilst, therefore, we must obviously maintain a friendly attitude towards the French and the Dutch in the Far East, and whilst Mr. MacDonald was in favour of much day-to-day contact with French and Dutch officials at technical levels,[4] he was insistent that we must not lay ourselves open to the charge of "ganging up" with the other European powers in the Far East at the expense of "native aspirations". (It seems very important that we should bear all this in mind in considering the developments, within our spehere, of the new Western European policy announced by Mr. Bevin yesterday.)[5]

Mr. MacDonald said he thought it was very important from the Indonesian point of view that they should now come to terms with the Dutch. He also said that, in the long term, this was very important from the Dutch point of view. He was afraid the Dutch were now in an ugly mood. Vindictiveness, however, would not suit their real interests. The Indonesians might fail this time, but next time they would succeed.

I have noted this subject for further discussion with Ministers at the meeting which is to take place at 10.30 next Tuesday morning. I now send the papers forward urgently in advance of the meeting.

(The original of No. 9 hereon is the I.R.D. papers. Mr. Galsworthy is putting up a draft reply on those papers.)

P.S. I should perhaps add as a postscript (it is not relevant on this file) that Mr. MacDonald told us that events in *Indo-China* have had no effect in Malaya whatever.

---

[4] Sir T Lloyd underlined the words 'at technical levels' and commented in the margin that they were 'the all important limiting factors'.

[5] In the Commons foreign affairs debate on 22 Jan, Bevin proposed a 'Western Union' which, with 'the closest possible collaboration with the Commonwealth and with oversea territories', would aid economic recovery and hamper Soviet expansionism.

138   CO 537/3671, no 29   18 Feb 1948
[Inauguration of the Federation of Malaya]: letter from H T Bourdillon to Sir E Gent

Very many thanks for your letter of the 22nd of January,[1] in which you describe the

---

[1] See 136.

ceremony of the signature of the Federation and State Agreements at Kuala Lumpur on the previous day. We have since received a series of photographs of the event, and we can imagine what a colourful and animated spectacle it must have been. We in the Office, unfortunately, could provide nothing comparable on the great day!

We all feel that the successful conclusion of these negotiations, in so cordial an atmosphere, is a great triumph for yourself and your advisers. The inauguration of the Federation on the 1st February, with so few dissident voices, and the emergence of Ceylon as a Dominion[2] are two very significant manifestations of the solidarity of the British family of nations which it is good for the world in general to see in these troubled times.

We are very impressed by the cordiality of the final stages of the settlement, in spite of the occasional acerbities from Dato Onn. This is the more remarkable in view of the severe shaking which Malay confidence had both in the debacle of 1941/2 and after MacMichael, and in comparison with the bitterness and distrust which had marked the negotiations in Indonesia it is very reassuring. We shall try to emphasise this cordiality, which of course says much for British administration, past and present, and I am writing to Sabben-Clare[3] at Washington to draw his attention to it and to suggest to him that it could be unobtrusively pointed out to the more responsible of American writers on political subjects. We should also like to show some evidence—press cuttings, speeches by Malays, etc. in favour of the Federation—to demonstrate the welcome given to the new Constitution by the Malay population: "hartals" get into the papers, but Malay rejoicings don't!

---

[2] Ceylon achieved independence within the Commonwealth on 4 Feb 1948.

[3] E E Sabben-Clare, colonial attaché to the British embassy in Washington, 1947–1950.

Index of Main Subjects and Persons: Parts I–III

This is a consolidated index for all three parts of the volume. It is not a comprehensive index, but a simplified and straightforward index to document numbers, together with page references to the Introduction in part I, the latter being given at the beginning of the entry in lower case roman numerals. The index is designed to be used in conjunction with the summary lists of the preliminary pages to each part of the volume. A preceding asterisk indicates inclusion in the Biographical Notes at the end of Part III. Where necessary (eg particularly in long documents), and if possible, paragraph or section numbers are given inside round brackets. In the case of a British official or minister (such as Lennox-Boyd, Malcolm MacDonald and Templer), who appears prominently in the volume, the index indicates the first and last documents of his period of office. Further references to his contribution can be identified from the summary lists.

The following abbreviations are used:

A – appendix or annex (thus 257 A I = first appendix to document 257)

E – enclosure

N – editor's link note (before main text of document)

n – footnote.

Documents are divided between the three parts of the volume as follows:

nos   1–138   part I

nos 139–303 part II

nos 304–467 part III.